URBAN SOCIETY

Fifth Edition

Editor

Jeffrey M. Elliot
North Carolina Central University

Jeffrey M. Elliot is professor of political science at North Carolina Central University. He received his Bachelor of Arts degree in 1969, his Master of Arts in 1970 from the University of Southern California, and his Doctor of Arts from the Claremont Graduate School in 1978. In 1985 he was awarded an honorary Doctor of Humane Letters degree from Shaw University, and in 1986 California State University, San Bernardino, established The Jeffrey M. Elliot Collection, a permanent archive of his published work. He is the author of 62 books and over 500 articles, reviews, and interviews. His work has appeared in more than 250 publications, both in the United States and abroad, and has been nominated for numerous literary awards. Recent book titles include: *Voices of Zaire: Rhetoric or Reality?* (The Washington Institute, 1990); *Third World* (Dushkin Publishing Group, 1990); *The Arms Control, Disarmament, and Military Security Dictionary* (ABC-Clio, 1989); *Conversations with Maya Angelou* (University Press of Mississippi, 1989); *The State and Local Government Political Dictionary* (ABC-Clio, 1987); *Fidel Castro: Nothing Can Stop the Course of History* (Pathfinder Press, 1986); *Black Voices in American Politics* (Harcourt Brace Jovanovich, 1985); *The Presidential-Congressional Political Dictionary* (ABC-Clio, 1984); and *Tempest in a Teapot: The Falkland Islands War* (Borgo Press, 1983). A free-lance journalist, he has conducted over 350 interviews, among them: President Jimmy Carter, Nobel Prize-winner Bishop Desmond Tutu, Cuban president Fidel Castro, Zairian president Mobutu Sese Seko, UNITA president Jonas Savimbi, PLO chairman Yasir Arafat, Contra leader Adolfo Calero, and Jamaican prime minister Michael Manley. In addition to his academic duties, he serves as Distinguished Advisor on Foreign Affairs to Congressman Mervyn M. Dymally (D-Calif.), editor or contributing editor to six journals, chairperson of the Durham County Youth Services Advisory Board, vice president and a member of the board of directors of the Academic Help Center, and a member of the Durham Housing Authority Crime Prevention Board. He is the subject of a book-length study, *The Work of Jeffrey M. Elliot: An Annotated Bibliography and Guide* (Borgo Press, 1986).

Cover illustration by Mike Eagle

A Library of Information from the Public Press

The Dushkin Publishing Group, Inc.
Sluice Dock, Guilford, Connecticut 06437

The Annual Editions Series

Annual Editions is a series of over fifty volumes designed to provide the reader with convenient, low-cost access to a wide range of current, carefully selected articles from some of the most important magazines, newspapers, and journals published today. Annual Editions are updated on an annual basis through a continuous monitoring of over 200 periodical sources. All Annual Editions have a number of features designed to make them particularly useful, including topic guides, annotated tables of contents, unit overviews, and indexes. For the teacher using Annual Editions in the classroom, an Instructor's Resource Guide with test questions is available for each volume.

VOLUMES AVAILABLE

Africa
Aging
American Government
American History, Pre-Civil War
American History, Post-Civil War
Anthropology
Biology
Business and Management
Business Ethics
Canadian Politics
China
Comparative Politics
Computers in Education
Computers in Business
Computers in Society
Criminal Justice
Drugs, Society, and Behavior
Early Childhood Education
Economics
Educating Exceptional Children
Education
Educational Psychology
Environment
Geography
Global Issues
Health
Human Development
Human Resources
Human Sexuality

Latin America
Macroeconomics
Management
Marketing
Marriage and Family
Microeconomics
Middle East and the Islamic World
Money and Banking
Nutrition
Personal Growth and Behavior
Psychology
Public Administration
Race and Ethnic Relations
Social Problems
Sociology
Soviet Union and Eastern Europe
State and Local Government
Third World
Urban Society
Violence and Terrorism
Western Civilization,
  Pre-Reformation
Western Civilization,
  Post-Reformation
Western Europe
World History, Pre-Modern
World History, Modern
World Politics

Library of Congress Cataloging in Publication Data
Main entry under title: Annual editions: Urban Society. 5/E.
        1. Sociology, Urban—Addresses, essays, lectures—Periodicals.   2. Urban policy—United States—Addresses, essays, lectures—Periodicals.   3. Metropolitan areas—United States—Addresses, essays, lectures—Periodicals.   I. Title: Urban Society.
301.34′05   ISBN 1-56134-039-1   82-646006

© 1991 by The Dushkin Publishing Group, Inc. Annual Editions is a Trade Mark of The Dushkin Publishing Group, Inc.

Copyright © 1991 by The Dushkin Publishing Group, Inc., Guilford, Connecticut 06437

Fifth Edition

Manufactured by The Banta Company, Harrisonburg, Virginia 22801

To the Reader

In publishing ANNUAL EDITIONS we recognize the enormous role played by the magazines, newspapers, and journals of the *public press* in providing current, first-rate educational information in a broad spectrum of interest areas. Within the articles, the best scientists, practitioners, researchers, and commentators draw issues into new perspective as accepted theories and viewpoints are called into account by new events, recent discoveries change old facts, and fresh debate breaks out over important controversies.

Many of the articles resulting from this enormous editorial effort are appropriate for students, researchers, and professionals seeking accurate, current material to help bridge the gap between principles and theories and the real world. These articles, however, become more useful for study when those of lasting value are carefully *collected, organized, indexed,* and *reproduced* in a *low-cost format*, which provides easy and permanent access when the material is needed. That is the role played by *Annual Editions*. Under the direction of each volume's *Editor*, who is an expert in the subject area, and with the guidance of an *Advisory Board*, we seek each year to provide in each *ANNUAL EDITION* a current, well-balanced, carefully selected collection of the best of the public press for your study and enjoyment. We think you'll find this volume useful, and we hope you'll take a moment to let us know what you think.

In 1972, Democratic presidential candidate George McGovern beckoned America with these words: "The challenge of our age is whether we shall seize the opportunity to decide what kind of life, what kind of environment, and what kind of opportunities we want for ourselves and for our children." It has been said that survival in today's world is a race between awareness and catastrophe. I believe this to be true. The task of formulating solutions to our present problems—both at home and abroad—is not only extraordinarily complex but extremely urgent. It involves discarding many of our old ideas and fashioning radical new ones. As Rollo May expresses it, "The old ideas are dying and the new ones have not yet been born."

This period of crisis, however, has two faces. The ancient Chinese were well aware of this duality, for their written character for "crisis" is made up of two characters: one means danger, the other opportunity. America's cities face a plethora of difficult and complex problems: a deteriorating infrastructure, high unemployment, a dwindling tax base, shrinking resources, decaying housing, congestion and noise pollution, inadequate transportation, crime and violence, racial strife, and faltering institutional support systems, among others. These problems defy simple solutions; they are the products of historical forces that have evolved over the past 200 years—forces that have both created and exacerbated the decline of urban America.

Still, it needs to be remembered that writers and critics since Thomas Jefferson have often projected a one-sided view of urban life, portraying it as a cold, impersonal, and brutal environment in which alienation, rootlessness, and helplessness predominate. On the other hand, the urban environment is far more than the sum of its problems. It is, in many ways, the center of innovation, excitement, and vitality—a place rich in social diversity, artistic expression, and economic opportunity. As political scientist Edward Banfield argues: "The plain fact is that the overwhelming majority of city dwellers live more comfortably and conveniently than ever before. They have more and better housing, more and better schools, more and better transportation, and so on. By any conceivable measure of material welfare the present generation of urban Americans is, on the whole, better off than other large groups of people have ever been anywhere."

Despite these problems, the crisis of America's cities is not unsolvable. Like the early jet pilots who hovered fearfully on their side of the sound barrier, engineers hover fearfully on this side of transforming cities into hospitable places in which to live and work. Like these pilots, planners must, with courage and daring, break the barrier, for the consequence of not doing so is continued decline. Clearly, if cities are to thrive and prosper, healthful conditions conducive to improved urban life must be established. The attainment of this ideal is dependent upon the ability to create conditions which will allow opportunity and progress to take root and grow. I use the phrase "take root and grow" advisedly, for opportunity and progress resemble a plant, in that they require a balanced environment to develop and mature.

This anthology represents but one step in the search for constructive solutions to the problems of America's cities. The selections reflect a broad approach to the study of urban society. The articles were chosen for their clarity and relevancy in addressing the issues surrounding urbanization, for their usefulness in the teaching/learning process, and for their ability to stimulate interest in students to pursue the study of urban life.

I think *Annual Editions: Urban Society* is one of the most informative, engaging, and current books available, but I would like to know what you think. Please offer your opinion by filling out the article rating form on the last page of this book. Any anthology can be improved. This one will continue to be, and your comments are important in this process.

Jeffrey M. Elliot
Editor

Contents

Unit 1

Urbanization

Eight selections review the urbanization process, the development of new patterns of living, and the dynamics of the urban "explosion."

The concepts in bold italics are developed in the article. For further expansion please refer to the Topic Guide and the Index.

Unit 2

Urban Experiences

Ten selections explore the social interactions that, in large measure, direct the urban experience.

The concepts in bold italics are developed in the article. For further expansion please refer to the Topic Guide and the Index.

Unit 3

Urban Problems

Thirteen selections examine the inherent problems of urban growth. Topics include urban transportation, drug abuse, poverty, homelessness, and urban health care.

The concepts in bold italics are developed in the article. For further expansion please refer to the Topic Guide and the Index.

The concepts in bold italics are developed in the article. For further expansion please refer to the Topic Guide and the Index.

Unit 4

Urban Policies

Ten selections discuss the effects of the current social policy process by which an urban center addresses its problems. Because of the complexity of these problems, many careful reassessments of urban planning and growth must be undertaken.

The concepts in bold italics are developed in the article. For further expansion please refer to the Topic Guide and the Index.

Unit 5

Urban Futures

Ten selections examine the implications of a rapidly rising urban population. What effects these changes will have on the entire world population must be taken into consideration and effective planning must be seriously instituted.

The concepts in bold italics are developed in the article. For further expansion please refer to the Topic Guide and the Index.

Topic Guide

This topic guide suggests how the selections in this book relate to topics of traditional concern to urban society students and professionals. It is very useful in locating articles that relate to each other for reading and research. The guide is arranged alphabetically according to topic. Articles may, of course, treat topics that do not appear in the topic guide. In turn, entries in the topic guide do not necessarily constitute a comprehensive listing of all the contents of each selection.

TOPIC AREA	TREATED IN:	TOPIC AREA	TREATED IN:
City (History/ Future)	1. How Man Invented Cities 2. Fear of the City 4. America's New City 42. Cities in the Year 2000 51. Cities Without Limits	Government: Federal, State, and Local (cont'd)	23. De-escalating the War 24. Youth and Drug Abuse 25. Down and Out in the City 27. Priced Out of House and Home 30. Invisible Jail 31. Crisis in AIDS Care 32. Memo to the New Manager 33. Hot Managers, Sizzling Cities 34. Neighborhood Politics 36. Have Asian Americans Arrived Politically? 40. Housing Program That Really Works 41. Cities Seek Alternatives to Bulldozer 50. Strategies for the Essential Community
Civic Leaders	11. Downtown Malls 17. Seattle 18. Creating Community 23. De-escalating the War 26. Making It 32. Memo to the New Manager 33. Hot Managers, Sizzling Cities 34. Neighborhood Politics 35. Volunteer Mentors 36. Have Asian Americans Arrived Politically? 39. Nonprofit Housing 50. Strategies for the Essential Community	Housing	15. Creative Alternatives to Urban Sprawl 27. Priced Out of House and Home 28. Us vs. Them 38. Rethinking Rental Housing 39. Nonprofit Housing 40. Housing Program That Really Works 41. Cities Seek Alternatives to Bulldozers
Congestion	8. Pace of Life 19. Out of the Car 20. Traffic Jams 21. Gridlock! 22. Supertrain	Immigration	7. Demographic Doomsayers
		Industrial Development	7. Demographic Doomsayers 43. Downtown 2040
Downtown	8. Pace of Life 11. Downtown Malls 16. Serv-Urbs, U.S.A. 17. Seattle 43. Downtown 2040	Landlords	27. Priced Out of House and Home 38. Rethinking Rental Housing 39. Nonprofit Housing 40. Housing Program That Really Works
Economic Issues	17. Seattle 22. Supertrain 28. Us vs. Them 29. Health and the City 30. Invisible Jail 32. Memo to the New Mayor 33. Hot Managers, Sizzling Cities 42. Cities in the Year 2000 49. Workless Society 50. Strategies for the Essential Community	Mass Transit	19. Out of the Car 20. Traffic Jams 21. Gridlock! 22. Supertrain
		Megastructures	4. America's New City 29. Health and the City
		Micropolitan Areas	5. Micropolitan America
Engineering Techniques	6. Radiant City's Dull Legacy 19. Out of the Car 20. Traffic Jams 21. Gridlock! 22. Supertrain 30. Invisible Jail 37. Recycling Our Most Prolific By-Product 41. Cities in the Year 2000 43. Downtown 2040 46. Small Space Is Beautiful 47. Urban Planning	Neighborhoods	9. Rootlessness Undermines Our Economy 13. New Suburbia 15. Creative Alternatives to Urban Sprawl 18. Creating Community 32. Memo to the New Manager
		New Federalism	33. Hot Managers, Sizzling Cities 34. Neighborhood Politics
Gentrification	6. Radiant City's Dull Legacy 11. Downtown Malls	Political Issues	10. Good-Bye, Good Hope 18. Creating Community 23. De-escalating the War 25. Down and Out in the City 26. Making It 32. Memo to the New Manager 33. Hot Managers, Sizzling Cities
Government: Federal, State, and Local	10. Good-Bye, Good Hope 11. Downtown Malls 17. Seattle		

Urbanization

Historically, the rapid growth of cities was largely a consequence of the developments of agricultural surpluses and factory systems. When farms produced surpluses, they needed a center for exchange. When factories were developed, the need for a concentrated labor supply and services was apparent. Thus, the city came into existence and became the center of both economic and cultural activity. While scholars agree that cities have existed for many centuries and in most parts of the world, only about 3 percent of the world's population lived in towns of more than 5,000 inhabitants before 1800. Even today, less than 30 percent of the world's population lives in cities larger than 20,000 people. Nevertheless, urbanization has profoundly influenced the course of global development.

Urbanization is a complex and continuous process. It involves the movement of people from rural to urban areas, the creation of new patterns of living, and the communication of these new patterns to both urban and rural populations. In the Western world, the emergence of cities as a dominant force in the lives of people has been so rapid, it has been characterized as an "explosion."

Social scientists have been fascinated with the process of urbanization. For the historian, the dynamics of urban growth illustrated the ways in which entire cultures and nations change over time. For the sociologist, the nature of urbanization became a way of explaining social arrangements and transforming social structures. The psychologist saw urbanization as a force in the ways individuals learned to cope with new threats to survival. Through the process of urbanization, the economist came to recognize cities, and more recently suburbs, as important units for generating wealth and for allocating resources. The political scientists, too, studied urbanization in order to gain a better understanding of the ways in which order and change were maintained in these dynamic units. The change was more gradual for the anthropologist but, nevertheless, urbanization proved to be a rich resource for observing and understanding the nature and importance of subcultural groups within the larger urban culture.

It is clear that urbanization has become a dominant force in the lives of people throughout the world—both those who live in cities and those who remain in rural areas. This examination of urbanization begins with John Pfeiffer's essay on the creation of cities. It is followed by an article by Alfred Kazin, which analyzes humankind's longstanding fear of cities in "Fear of the City, 1783 to 1983." Peter O. Muller then surveys the strengths and weaknesses of urban life. The next selection describes the emergence of a "new city"—one that is a marriage of technology and nature. That is followed by the rise of "micropolitan" areas, the changing face of America's cities, and analysis of the "demo-doom" scenario. Robert Levine concludes the section by assessing the relationship between a city's pace of life and its residents' physical health.

Looking Ahead: Challenge Questions

How and why did cities originate? What major functions do they serve?

What lessons have been learned regarding cities and their efforts to cope with and manage change?

What historical factors have contributed to humankind's fear of cities? Are these fears well-founded?

What are the main social features of the city? How does the process of urbanization affect social life today?

Has urbanization added to or detracted from the quality of human life? Is suburban life an answer to the problems of urban society?

What are the principal challenges facing the world's great cities? Is it likely that they will meet these challenges?

Why and how have many urban dwellers sought to revitalize urban America and exploit its diversity? How well have they succeeded?

In what ways, if any, does population affect urban life? Do current trends portend well for the future?

Why are "micropolitan" areas such a furtive market for business? What advantages does nonmetropolitan America boast?

Does the combination of hard work and a fast pace have to be lethal? In what ways, if any, can the two be life-threatening?

How Man Invented Cities

John Pfeiffer

The most striking mark of man's genius as a species, as the most adaptable of animals, has been his ability to live in cities. From the perspective of all we know about human evolution, nothing could be more unnatural. For over fifteen million years, from the period when members of the family of man first appeared on earth until relatively recent times, our ancestors were nomadic, small-group, wide-open-spaces creatures. They lived on the move among other moving animals in isolated little bands of a few families, roaming across wildernesses that extended like oceans to the horizon and beyond.

Considering that heritage, the wonder is not that man has trouble getting along in cities but that he can do it at all—that he can learn to live in the same place year round, enclosed in sharp-cornered and brightly-lit rectangular spaces, among noises, most of which are made by machines, within shouting distance of hundreds of other people, most of them strangers. Furthermore, such conditions arose so swiftly, practically overnight on the evolutionary time scale, that he has hardly had a

chance to get used to them. The transition from a world without cities to our present situation took a mere five or six millenniums.

It is precisely because we are so close to our origins that what happened in prehistory bears directly on current problems. In fact, the expectation is that new studies of pre-cities and early cities will contribute as significantly to an understanding of today's urban complexes as studies of infancy and early childhood have to an understanding of adolescence. Cities are signs, symptoms if you will, of an accelerating and intensive phase of human evolution, a process that we are only beginning to investigate scientifically.

The first stages of the process may be traced back some fifteen thousand years to a rather less hectic era. Homo sapiens, that new breed of restless and intelligent primate, had reached a high point in his career as a hunter-gatherer subsisting predominantly on wild plants and animals. He had developed special tools, special tactics and strategies, for dealing with a wide variety of environments, from savannas and semideserts to tundras and tropical rain forests and

mountain regions. Having learned to exploit practically every type of environment, he seemed at last to have found his natural place in the scheme of things—as a hunter living in balance with other species, and with all the world as his hunting ground.

But forces were already at work that would bring an end to this state of equilibrium and ultimately give rise to cities and the state of continuing instability that we are trying to cope with today. New theories, a harder look at the old theories, and an even harder look at our own tendencies to think small have radically changed our ideas about what happened and why.

We used to believe, in effect, that people abandoned hunting and gathering as soon as a reasonable alternative became available to them. It was hardly a safe or reliable way of life. Our ancestors faced sudden death and injury from predators and from prey that fought back, disease from exposure to the elements and from always being on the move, and hunger because the chances were excellent of coming back empty-

From *Horizon*, Vol. XIV, No. 4, Autumn 1972. Copyright © 1987 by John Pfeiffer.

handed from the hunt. Survival was a full-time struggle. Leisure came only after the invention of agriculture, which brought food surpluses, rising populations, and cities. Such was the accepted picture.

The fact of the matter, supported by studies of living hunter-gatherers as well as by the archaeological record, is that the traditional view is largely melodrama and science fiction. Our preagricultural ancestors were quite healthy, quite safe, and regularly obtained all the food they needed. And they did it with time to burn. As a rule, the job of collecting food, animal and vegetable, required no more than a three-hour day, or a twenty-one-hour week. During that time, collectors brought in enough food for the entire group, which included an appreciable proportion (perhaps 30 per cent or more) of dependents, old persons and children who did little or no work. Leisure is basically a phenomenon of hunting-gathering times, and people have been trying to recover it ever since.

Another assumption ripe for discarding is that civilization first arose in the valleys of the Tigris, Euphrates, and Nile rivers and spread from there to the rest of the world. Accumulating evidence fails to support this notion that civilization is an exclusive product of these regions. To be sure, agriculture and cities may have appeared first in the Near East, but there are powerful arguments for completely independent origins in at least two other widely separated regions, Mesoamerica and Southeast Asia.

In all cases, circumstances forced hunter-gatherers to evolve new ways of surviving. With the decline of the ancient life style, nomadism, problems began piling up. If only people had kept on moving about like sane and respectable primates, life would be a great deal simpler. Instead, they settled down in increasing numbers over wider areas, and society started changing with a vengeance. Although the causes of this settling down remain a mystery, the fact of independent origins calls for an explanation based on worldwide developments.

An important factor, emphasized recently by Lewis Binford of the University of New Mexico, may have been the

melting of mile-high glaciers, which was well under way fifteen thousand years ago, and which released enough water to raise the world's oceans 250 to 500 feet, to flood previously exposed coastal plains, and to create shallow bays and estuaries and marshlands. Vast numbers of fish and wild fowl made use of the new environments, and the extra resources permitted people to obtain food without migrating seasonally. In other words, people expended less energy, and life became that much easier, in the beginning anyway.

Yet this sensible and seemingly innocent change was to get mankind into all sorts of difficulties. According to a recent theory, it triggered a chain of events that made cities possible if not inevitable. Apparently, keeping on the move had always served as a natural birth-control mechanism, in part, perhaps, by causing a relatively high incidence of miscarriages. But the population brakes were off as soon as people began settling down.

One clue to what may have happened is provided by contemporary studies of a number of primitive tribes, such as the Bushmen of Africa's Kalahari Desert. Women living in nomadic bands, bands that pick up and move half a dozen or more times a year, have an average of one baby every four years or so, as compared with one baby every two and a half years for Bushman women living in settled communities—an increase of five to eight babies per mother during a twenty-year reproductive period.

The archaeological record suggests that in some places at least, a comparable phenomenon accompanied the melting of glaciers during the last ice age. People settled down and multiplied in the Les Eyzies region of southern France, one of the richest and most-studied centers of prehistory. Great limestone cliffs dominate the countryside, and at the foot of the cliffs are natural shelters, caves and rocky overhangs where people built fires, made tools out of flint and bone and ivory, and planned the next day's hunt. On special occasions artists equipped with torches went deep into certain caves like Lascaux and covered the walls

with magnificent images of the animals they hunted.

In some places the cliffs and the shelters extend for hundreds of yards; in other places there are good living sites close to one another on the opposite slopes of river valleys. People in the Les Eyzies region were living not in isolated bands but in full-fledged communities, and populations seem to have been on the rise. During the period from seven thousand to twelve thousand years ago, the total number of sites doubled, and an appreciable proportion of them probably represent year-round settlements located in small river valleys. An analysis of excavated animal remains reveals an increasing dietary reliance on migratory birds and fish (chiefly salmon).

People were also settling down at about the same time in the Near East for example, not far from the Mediterranean shoreline of Israel and on the border between the coastal plain and the hills to the east. Ofer Bar-Yosef, of the Institute of Archaeology of Hebrew University in Jerusalem, points out that since they were able to exploit both these areas, they did not have to wander widely in search of food. There were herds of deer and gazelle, wild boar, fish and wild fowl, wild cereals and other plants, and limestone caves and shelters like those in the Les Eyzies region. Somewhat later, however, a new land-use pattern emerged. Coastal villages continued to flourish, but in addition to them, new sites began appearing further inland— and in areas that were drier and less abundant.

Only under special pressure will men abandon a good thing, and in this case it was very likely the pressure of rising populations. The evidence suggests that the best coastal lands were supporting about all the hunter-gatherers they could support; and as living space decreased there was a "budding off," an overflow of surplus population into the second-best back country where game was scarcer. These people depended more and more on plants, particularly on wild cereals, as indicated by the larger numbers of flint sickle blades, mortars and pestles, and storage pits found at their sites (and also by an increased wear and pitting of teeth, presumably caused by chewing more coarse and gritty plant foods).

Another sign of the times was the appearance of stone buildings, often with impressively high and massive walls. The structures served a number of purposes. For one thing, they included storage bins where surplus grain could be kept in reserve for bad times, when there was a shortage of game and wild plants. They also imply danger abroad in the countryside, new kinds of violence, and a mounting need for defenses to protect stored goods from the raids of people who had not settled down.

Above all, the walls convey a feeling of increasing permanence, an increasing commitment to places. Although man was still mainly a hunter-gatherer living on wild species, some of the old options no longer existed for him. In the beginning, settling down may have involved a measure of choice, but now man was no longer quite so free to change locales when the land became less fruitful. Even in those days frontiers were vanishing. Man's problem was to develop new options, new ways of working the land more intensively so that it would provide the food that migration had always provided in more mobile times.

The all-important transition to agriculture came in small steps, establishing itself almost before anyone realized what was going on. Settlers in marginal lands took early measures to get more food out of less abundant environments—roughing up the soil a bit with scraping or digging sticks, sowing wheat and barley seeds, weeding, and generally doing their best to promote growth. To start with at least, it was simply a matter of supplementing regular diets of wild foods with some domesticated species, animals as well as plants, and people probably regarded themselves as hunter-gatherers working hard to maintain their way of life rather than as the revolutionaries they were. They were trying to preserve the old self-sufficiency, but it was a losing effort.

The wilderness way of life became more and more remote, more and more nearly irretrievable. Practically every advance in the technology of agriculture committed people to an increasing dependence on domesticated species and on the activities of other people living nearby. Kent Flannery of the University of Michigan emphasizes this point in a study of one part of Greater Mesopotamia, prehistoric Iran, during the period between twelve thousand and six thousand years ago. For the hunter-gatherer, an estimated one-third of the country's total land area was good territory, consisting of grassy plains and high mountain valleys where wild species were abundant; the rest of the land was desert and semidesert.

The coming of agriculture meant that people used a smaller proportion of the countryside. Early farming took advantage of naturally distributed water; the best terrain for that, namely terrain with a high water table and marshy areas, amounted to about a tenth of the land area. But only a tenth of that tenth was suitable for the next major development, irrigation. Meanwhile, food yields were soaring spectacularly, and so was the population of Iran, which increased more than fiftyfold; in other words, fifty times the original population was being supported by food produced on one-hundredth of the land.

A detailed picture of the steps involved in this massing of people is coming from studies of one part of southwest Iran, an 880-square-mile region between the Zagros Mountains and the Iraqi border. The Susiana Plain is mostly flat, sandy semidesert, the only notable features being man-made mounds that loom on the horizon like islands, places where people built in successively high levels on the ruins of their ancestors. During the past decade or so, hundreds of mounds have been mapped and dated (mainly through pottery styles) by Robert Adams of the University of Chicago, Jean Perrot of the French Archaeological Mission in Iran, and Henry Wright and Gregory Johnson of the University of Michigan. Their work provides a general idea of when the mounds were occupied, how they varied in size at different periods and how a city may be born.

Imagine a time-lapse motion picture of the early settling of the Susiana Plain, starting about 6500 B.C., each minute of film representing a century. At first the plain is empty, as it has been since the beginning of time. Then the pioneers arrive; half a dozen families move in and build a cluster of mud-brick homes near a river. Soon another cluster appears and another, until, after about five minutes (it is now 6000 B.C.), there are ten settlements, each covering an area of 1 to 3 hectares (1 hectare = 2.47 acres). Five minutes more (5500 B.C.) and we see the start of irrigation, on a small scale, as people dig little ditches to carry water from rivers and tributaries to lands along the banks. Crop yields increase and so do populations, and there are now thirty settlements, all about the same size as the original ten.

This is but a prelude to the main event. Things become really complicated during the next fifteen minutes or so (5500 to 4000 B.C.). Irrigation systems, constructed and maintained by family groups of varying sizes, become more complex. The number of settlements shows a modest increase, from thirty to forty, but a more significant change takes place—the appearance of a hierarchy. Instead of settlements all about the same size, there are now levels of settlements and a kind of ranking: one town (7 hectares), ten large villages (3 to 4 hectares), and twenty-nine smaller villages of less than 3 hectares. During this period large residential and ceremonial structures appear at Susa, a town on the western edge of the Susiana Plain.

Strange happenings can be observed not long after the middle of this period (about 4600 B.C.). For reasons unknown, the number of settlements decreases rapidly. It is not known whether the population of the area decreased simultaneously. Time passes, and the number of settlements increases to about the same level as before, but great changes have occurred. Three cities have appeared with monumental public buildings, elaborate residential architecture, large workshops, major storage and market facilities, and certainly with administrators and bureaucrats. The settlement hierarchy is more complex, and settlements are no longer located to take advantage solely of good agricultural opportunities. Their location is also influenced by the cities and the services and opportunities available there. By the end of our hypothetical time-lapse film, by the early part of the third millennium B.C., the largest settlement of all is the city of Susa, which covers some thirty hectares and will cover up to a square kilometer (100 hectares) of territory before it collapses in historical times.

All Mesopotamia underwent major transformations during this period. Another city was taking shape 150 miles northwest of Susa in the heartland of Sumer. Within a millennium the site of Uruk near the Euphrates River grew from village dimensions to a city enclosing within its defense walls more than thirty thousand people, four hundred hectares, and at the center a temple built on top of a huge brick platform. Archaeological surveys reveal that this period also saw a massive immigration into the region from places and for reasons as yet undetermined, resulting in a tenfold increase in settlements and in the formation of several new cities.

Similar surveys, requiring months and thousands of miles of walking, are completed or under way in many parts of the world. Little more than a millennium after the establishment of Uruk and Susa, cities began making an independent appearance in northern China not far from the conflux of the Wei and Yellow rivers, in an area that also saw the beginnings of agriculture. Still later, and also independently as far as we can tell, intensive settlement and land use developed in the New World.

The valley of Oaxaca in Mexico, where Flannery and his associates are working currently, provides another example of a city in the process of being formed. Around 500 B.C., or perhaps a bit earlier, buildings were erected for the first time on the tops of hills. Some of the hills were small, no more than twenty-five or thirty feet high, and the buildings were correspondingly small; they overlooked a few terraces and a river and probably a hamlet or two. Larger structures appeared on higher hills overlooking many villages. About 400 B.C. the most elaborate set-

tlement began to appear on the highest land, 1,500-foot Monte Albán, with a panoramic view of the valley's three arms; and within two centuries it had developed into an urban center including hundreds of terraces, an irrigation system, a great plaza, ceremonial buildings and residences, and an astronomical observatory.

At about the same time, the New World's largest city, Teotihuacán, was evolving some 225 miles to the northwest in the central highlands of Mexico. Starting as a scattering of villages and hamlets, it covered nearly eight square miles at its height (around A.D. 100 to 200) and probably contained some 125,000 people. Archaeologists are now reconstructing the life and times of this great urban center. William Sanders of Pennsylvania State University is concentrating on an analysis of settlement patterns in the area, while Rene Millon of the University of Rochester and his associates have prepared detailed section-by-section maps of the city as a step toward further extensive excavations. Set in a narrow valley among mountains and with its own man-made mountains, the Pyramid of the Sun and the Pyramid of the Moon, the city flourished on a grand scale. It housed local dignitaries and priests, delegations from other parts of Mesoamerica, and workshop neighborhoods where specialists in the manufacture of textiles, pottery, obsidian blades, and other products lived together in early-style apartments.

The biggest center in what is now the United States probably reached its peak about a millennium after Teotihuacán. But it has not been reconstructed, and archaeologists are just beginning to appreciate the scale of what happened there. Known as Cahokia and located east of the Mississippi near St. Louis, it consists of a cluster of some 125 mounds (including a central mound 100 feet high and covering 15 acres) as well as a line of mounds extending six miles to the west.

So surveys and excavations continue, furnishing the sort of data needed to disprove or prove our theories. Emerging patterns involving the specific locations of different kinds of communities and of buildings and other artifacts within communities can yield information about the

forces that shaped and are still shaping cities and the behavior of people in cities. But one trend stands out above all others: the world was becoming more and more stratified. Every development seemed to favor social distinctions, social classes and elites, and to work against the old hunter-gatherer ways.

Among hunter-gatherers all people are equal. Individuals are recognized as exceptional hunters, healers, or storytellers, and they all have the chance to shine upon appropriate occasions. But it would be unthinkable for one of them, for any one man, to take over as full-time leader. That ethic passed when the nomadic life passed. In fact, a literal explosion of differences accompanied the coming of communities where people lived close together in permanent dwellings and under conditions where moving away was not easy.

The change is reflected clearly in observed changes of settlement patterns. Hierarchies of settlements imply hierarchies of people. Emerging social levels are indicated by the appearance of villages and towns and cities where only villages had existed before, by different levels of complexity culminating in such centers as Susa and Monte Albán and Cahokia. Circumstances practically drove people to establish class societies. In Mesopotamia, for instance, increasingly sophisticated agricultural systems and intensive concentrations of populations brought about enormous and irreversible changes within a short period. People were clamped in a demographic vise, more and more of them living and depending on less and less land—an ideal setting for the rapid rise of status differences.

Large-scale irrigation was a highly effective centralizing force, calling for new duties and new regularities and new levels of discipline. People still depended on the seasons; but in addition, canals had to be dug and maintained, and periodic cleaning was required to prevent the artificial waterways from filling up with silt and assorted litter. Workers had to be brought together, assigned tasks, and fed, which meant schedules and storehouses and rationing stations and mass-produced pottery to serve as food containers. It took time to organize such activities efficiently. There were undoubtedly many false starts, many attempts by local people to work things out among themselves and their neighbors at a community or village level. Many small centers, budding institutions, were undoubtedly formed and many collapsed, and we may yet detect traces of them in future excavations and analyses of settlement patterns.

The ultimate outcome was inevitable. Survival demanded organization on a regional rather than a local basis. It also demanded high-level administrators and managers, and most of them had to be educated people, mainly because of the need to prepare detailed records of supplies and transactions. Record-keeping has a long prehistory, perhaps dating back to certain abstract designs engraved on cave walls and bone twenty-five thousand or more years ago. But in Mesopotamia after 4000 B.C. there was a spurt in the art of inventing and utilizing special marks and symbols.

The trend is shown in the stamp and cylinder seals used by officials to place their "signatures" on clay tags and tablets, man's first documents. At first the designs on the stamp seals were uncomplicated, consisting for the most part of single animals or simple geometric motifs. Later, however, there were bigger stamp seals with more elaborate scenes depicting several objects or people or animals. Finally the cylinder seals appeared, which could be rolled to repeat a complex design. These seals indicate the existence of more and more different signatures and more and more officials and record keepers. Similar trends are evident in potters' marks and other symbols. All these developments precede pictographic writing, which appears around 3200 B.C.

Wherever record keepers and populations were on the rise, in the Near East or Mexico or China, we can be reasonably sure that the need for a police force or the prehistoric equivalent thereof was on the increase, too. Conflict, including everything from fisticuffs to homicide, increases sharply with group size, and people have

known this for a long time. The Bushmen have a strong feeling about avoiding crowds: "We like to get together, but we fear fights." They are most comfortable in bands of about twenty-five persons and when they have to assemble in larger groups which happens for a total of only a few months a year, mainly to conduct initiations, arrange marriages, and be near the few permanent water holes during dry seasons they form separate small groups of about twenty-five, as if they were still living on their own.

Incidentally, twenty-five has been called a "magic number," because it hints at what may be a universal law of group behavior. There have been many counts of hunter-gatherer bands, not only in the Kalahari Desert, but also in such diverse places as the forests of Thailand, the Canadian Northwest, and northern India. Although individual bands may vary from fifteen to seventy-five members, the tendency is to cluster around twenty-five, and in all cases a major reason for keeping groups small is the desire to avoid violence. In other words, the association between large groups and conflict has deep roots and very likely presented law-and-order problems during the early days of cities and pre-cities, as it has ever since.

Along with managers and record keepers and keepers of the peace, there were also specialists in trade. A number of factors besides population growth and intensive land use were involved in the origin of cities, and local and long-distance trade was among the most important. Prehistoric centers in the process of becoming urban were almost always trade centers. They typically occupied favored places, strategic points in developing trade networks, along major waterways and caravan routes or close to supplies of critical raw materials.

Archaeologists are making a renewed attempt to learn more about such developments. Wright's current work in southwest Iran, for example, includes preliminary studies to detect and measure changes in the flow of trade. One site about sixty-five miles from Susa lies close to tar pits, which in prehistoric times served as a source of natural asphalt for fastening stone

blades to handles and waterproofing baskets and roofs. By saving all the waste bits of this important raw material preserved in different excavated levels, Wright was able to estimate fluctuations in its production over a period of time. In one level, for example, he found that the amounts of asphalt produced increased far beyond local requirements; in fact, a quantitative analysis indicates that asphalt exports doubled at this time. The material was probably being traded for such things as high-quality flint obtained from quarries more than one hundred miles away, since counts of material recovered at the site indicate that imports of the flint doubled during the same period.

In other words, the site was taking its place in an expanding trade network, and similar evidence from other sites can be used to indicate the extent and structure of that network. Then the problem will be to find out what other things were happening at the same time, such as significant changes in cylinder-seal designs and in agricultural and religious practices. This is the sort of evidence that may be expected to spell out just how the evolution of trade was related to the evolution of cities.

Another central problem is gaining a fresh understanding of the role of religion. Something connected with enormous concentrations of people, with population pressures and tensions of many kinds that started building up five thousand or more years ago, transformed religion from a matter of simple rituals carried out at village shrines to the great systems of temples and priesthoods invariably associated with early cities. Sacred as well as profane institutions arose to keep society from splitting apart.

Strong divisive tendencies had to be counteracted, and the reason may involve yet another magic number, another intriguing regularity that has been observed in hunter-gatherer societies in different parts of the world. The average size of a tribe, defined as a group of bands all speaking the same dialect, turns out to be about five hundred persons, a figure that depends to some extent on the limits of human memory. A tribe is a community of people who can identify closely with one another and engage in repeated face-to-face encounters and recognitions; and it happens that five hundred may represent about the number of persons a hunter-gatherer can remember well enough to approach on what would amount to a first-name basis in our society. Beyond that number the level of familiarity declines, and there is an increasing tendency to regard individuals as "they" rather than "we," which is when trouble usually starts. (Architects recommend that an elementary school should not exceed five hundred pupils if the principal is to maintain personal contact with all of them, and the headmaster of one prominent prep school recently used this argument to keep his student body at or below the five-hundred mark.)

Religion of the sort that evolved with the first cities may have helped to "beat" the magic number five hundred. Certainly there was an urgent need to establish feelings of solidarity among many thousands of persons rather than a few hundred. Creating allegiances wider than those provided by direct kinship and person-to-person ties became a most important problem, a task for full-time professionals. In this connection Paul Wheatley of the University of Chicago suggests that "specialized priests were among the first persons to be released from the daily round of subsistence labor." Their role was partly to exhort other workers concerned with the building of monuments and temples, workers who probably exerted greater efforts in the belief that they were doing it not for mere men but for the glory of individuals highborn and close to the gods.

The city evolved to meet the needs of societies under pressure. People were being swept up in a process that had been set in motion by their own activities and that they could never have predicted, for the simple reason that they had no insight into what they were doing in the first place. For example, they did not know, and had no way of knowing, that settling down could lead to population explosions.

There is nothing strange about this state of affairs, to be sure. It is the essence of the human condition and involves us just as intensely today. Then as now, people responded by the sheer instinct of survival to forces that they understood vaguely at best—and worked together as well as they could to organize themselves, to preserve order in the face of accelerating change and complexity and the threat of chaos. They could never know that they were creating what we, its beneficiaries and its victims, call civilization.

FEAR of the CITY
1783 to 1983

The city has been a lure for millions, but most of the great American minds have been appalled by its excesses. Here an eminent observer, who knows firsthand the city's threat, surveys the subject.

Alfred Kazin

Alfred Kazin is Distinguished Professor of English at the City University of New York Graduate Center. He is completing An American Procession, *a book about American writers from Emerson to T. S. Eliot.*

EVERY THURSDAY, when I leave my apartment in a vast housing complex on Columbus Avenue to conduct a university seminar on the American city, I reflect on a double life—mine. Most of the people I pass on my way to the subway look as imprisoned by the city as my parents and relatives used to look in the Brooklyn ghetto where I spent my first twenty years. Yet no matter where else I have traveled and taught, I always seem to return to streets and scenes like those on New York's Upper West Side.

Two blocks away on Broadway there is daily carnage. Drunks outside the single-room-occupancy hotel dazedly eye me, a professor laden with books and notes trudging past mounds of broken glass, hills of garbage. Even at eight in the morning a craps game is going on in front of the hydrant that now gives off only a trickle. It has been left open for so many weeks that even the cover has vanished. On the benches lining that poor polluted sliver of green that runs down the center of Broadway, each drunk has his and her bottle in the regulation brown paper bag. A woman on crutches, so battered looking that I can't understand how she stands up, is whooping it up—totally ignored by the cars, trucks, and bicycles impatiently waiting at the red light. None of the proper people absorbed in their schedules has time to give the vagrants more than a glance. Anyway, it's too dangerous. No eye contact is the current rule of the game.

I left all this many times, but the city has never left me. At many universities abroad—there was even one improbable afternoon lecturing in Moscow—I have found myself explaining the American city, tracing its history, reviewing its literature—and with a heavy heart, more and more having to defend it. The American city has a bad reputation now, though there was a time, as the violinist Yehudi Menuhin said during World War II, when one of the great war aims was to get to New York.

There is now general fear of the city. While sharing it, I resent it, for I have never ceased feeling myself to be one of the city's people, even as I have labored in libraries to seize the full background to my life in the city. But when in American history has there not been fear of the city—and especially on the part of those who did not have to live in it?

BEFORE THERE WERE American cities of any significance, the best American minds were either uninterested in cities or were suspicious of them. The Puritans thought of Boston as another Jerusalem, "a city upon a hill," but even their first and deepest impression was of the forest around it. This sense of unlimited space was bewitching until the end of the nineteenth century. In his first inaugural address in 1801, Thomas Jefferson pronounced, as if in a dream, that Americans possessed "a chosen country, with room enough for our descendants to the hundredth and thousandth generation." What was "chosen" was not just an endless frontier but the right people to go with it. This, as a matter of course to a great country squire like Jefferson, surveying the future from his mountaintop at Monticello, meant excluding the mobs he associated with European cities. Jefferson's attitude may have been influenced by the European Philosophes whom Louis XVI blamed for the French Revolution. Jefferson was a Philosophe himself; he would have agreed with a leader of the revolution, Saint-Just, that oppressed people "are a power on the earth." But he did not want to see any oppressed people here at all—they usually lived to become the kind of mob he detested and feared. "The mobs of great cities," he wrote in *Notes on Virginia*, "add just so much to the support of pure government, as sores do to the strength of the human body."

Jefferson knew what the city mob had done to break down ancient Rome as well as feudal France. America was a fresh start, "the world's best hope," and must therefore start without great cities. As a universal savant of sorts, as well as a classicist and scientist, Jefferson knew that Athens and Rome, Florence and Venice, Paris and London, had created the culture that was his proudest possession. And since he was an eighteenth-century skeptic, this cosmopolitan world culture was his religion. But anticipating the damage that "manufactures" could inflict on the individual, he insisted that on an unsettled continent only the proudly self-sustaining American "cultivator" could retain his dignity in the face of the Industrial Revolution.

It is not easy now to appreciate all Jefferson's claims for the rural life, and his ideas were not altogether popular with other great landowners and certainly not with such promoters of industry as Hamilton. Jefferson was a great traveler and world statesman who hardly limited himself to his country estate. Monticello, with its magnificent architecture, its great library, its array of inventions and musical and scientific instruments, more resembled a modern think tank (but imagine one this beautiful!) than the simple American farm he praised as a bastion of virtue.

But "virtue" was just what Jefferson sought for America. Whatever else they did, cities corrupted. The special virtue of rural folk rested on self-reliance, a quality unobtainable in "manufactures and handicraft arts" because these depended "on casualties and caprice of customers. Dependence begets subservience and venality, suffocates the germ of virtue, and prepares fit tools for the designs of ambition."

A few years later Emerson had a more complicated view of his society. The Sage of Concord was no farmer (Thoreau was his handyman) and did not particularly think the farmers in his neighborhood were the seat of all virtue. They were just of the earth, earthy. But believing in nothing so much as solitude, *his* right to solitude, his freedom only when alone to commune with Nature and his own soul ("Alone is wisdom. Alone is happiness."), Emerson found the slightest group to be an obstruction to the perfect life.

There is an unintentionally funny account in Emerson's journal for 1840 of just how irritating he found his fellow idealists. There was a gathering in some hotel—presumably in Boston, but one Emerson likened to New York's Astor House—to discuss the "new Social Plans" for the Brook Farm commune: "And not once could I be inflamed, but sat aloof and thoughtless; my voice faltered and fell. It was not the cave of persecution which is the palace of spiritual power, but only a room in the Astor House hired for the Transcendentalists. . . . To join this body would be to traverse all my long trumpeted theory, and the instinct which spoke from it, that one man is a counterpoise to a city—that a man is stronger than a city, that his solitude is more prevalent and beneficent than the concert of crowds."

Emerson finally agreed to help found Brook Farm but he could not have lived there. Hawthorne tried it for a while and turned his experiences into the wry novel *The Blithedale Romance*. Hawthorne was another Yankee grumpily insisting on his right to be alone but he did not take himself so seriously; he was a novelist and fascinated by the human comedy. A twentieth-century admirer of Emerson, John Jay Chapman, admitted that you can learn more from an Italian opera than from all the works of Emerson; in Italian opera there are always two sexes.

But Emerson is certainly impressive, bringing us back to the now forgotten meaning of "self-reliance" when he trumpets that "one man is a counterpoise to a city—that a man is stronger than a city. . . ." This was primary to many Americans in the nineteenth century and helped produce those great testaments to the individual spirit still found on the walls of American schoolrooms and libraries. Power is in the individual, not in numbers; in "soul," not in matter or material conglomeration. And "soul" is found not in organized religion, which is an obedience to the past, but in the self-sufficient individual whose "reliance" is on his inborn connection, through Nature, with any God it pleases him to find in himself.

CERTAINLY IT WAS easier then to avoid the "crowd." Thoreau, who went back many an evening to his family's boardinghouse for meals when he was at Walden Pond writing a book, said that the road back to Concord was so empty he could see a chicken crossing it half a mile off. Like Thoreau's superiority to sex and—most of the time—to politics, there is something truly awesome in the assurance with which he derogates such social facts as the city of New York: "I don't like the city better, the more I see it, but worse. I am ashamed of my eyes that behold it. It is a thousand times meaner than I could have imagined. . . . The pigs in the street are the most respectable part of the population. When will the world learn that a million men are of no importance compared with *one* man?"

To which Edgar Allan Poe, born in Boston and fated to die in Baltimore, could have replied that Thoreau had nothing to look at but his reflection in Walden Pond. Poe would have agreed with his European disciple Baudelaire on the cultural sacredness of great cities. He would have enjoyed Karl Marx's contempt for "rural idiocy." Poe was a great imagination and our greatest critic; as an inventor of the detective story and a storyteller, he was as dependent on the violence and scandal of New York in the 1840s as a police reporter. "The Mystery of Marie Roget," based on the actual murder of a New York shop assistant named Mary Rogers who was found dead in the Hudson after what is now believed to have been a botched abortion, was the first detective story in which an attempt was made to solve a real crime. Even the more than usual drunkenness that led to his death in Baltimore on Election Day of 1849 was typical of his connection with "low" urban life. He was found in a delirious condition near a saloon that had been used for a voting place. He seems to have been

1. URBANIZATION

To prevent immigrants from voting, squads of Know-Nothing party members rampaged through Baltimore on Election Day in 1856. The city had a nationwide reputation for political violence.

captured by a political gang that voted him around the town, after which he collapsed and died.

Yet just as Abraham Lincoln was proud of having a slow, careful countryman's mind, so Poe would have denied that *his* extraordinary mind owed anything to the cities in which he found his material. In the same spirit, John Adams from once rural Quincy, his gifted son John Quincy, and his even more gifted great-grandson Henry, all hated Boston and thought of the financial district on State Street as their antithesis. Herman Melville, born in New York, and forced to spend the last twenty-five years of his life as a customs inspector on the docks, hated New York as a symbol of his merchant father's bankruptcy and of his own worldly failure as an author. In a poem about the Civil War, when the worst insurrection in American history broke out in New York as a protest against the Draft Act, Melville imagined himself standing on the rooftop of his house on East Twenty-sixth Street listening to the roar of the mob and despising it:

. . . Balefully glares red Arson—there—-and there.
The Town is taken by its rats—ship-rats

And rats of the wharves. All civil charms
And priestly spells which late held hearts in awe—
Fear-bound, subjected to a better sway
Than sway of self; these like a dream dissolve,
And man rebounds whole aeons back in nature.

BEFORE THE Civil War there was just one exception among the great American writers to the general fear and resentment of the city. Whitman was to be prophetic of the importance of New York as a capital of many races and peoples and of the city as a prime subject in modern American writing. Whitman found himself as man and poet by identifying with New York. None of the gifted writers born and bred in New York—not Melville or Henry James or Edith Wharton—was to make of the city such an expression of personal liberation, such a glowing and extended fable of the possibilities released by democracy. "Old New York," as Edith Wharton called it (a patriciate that Melville could have belonged to among the Rhinelanders and Schuylers if his father had not failed in business), still speaks in Melville's rage against the largely Irish mob burning and looting in 1863. But Whitman, his exact contemporary, did not despair of the city's often lawless democracy when he helped put the first edition of *Leaves of Grass* into type in a shop off Brooklyn's Fulton Street.

Whitman found himself by finding the city to be the great human stage. Unlike earlier and later antagonists of the city, who feared the masses, Whitman saw them as a boundless human fellowship, a wonderful spectacle, *the* great school of ambition. The masses, already visible in New York's population of over a million, were the prime evidence Whitman needed to ground his gospel of American democracy as "comradeship." Formerly a schoolteacher, printer, carpenter, a failure at many occupations who was born into a family of failures and psychic cripples, Whitman felt that the big anonymous city crowd had made it possible for *him* to rise out of it.

One's self I sing, a simple separate person,
Yet utter the word Democratic, the word En-Masse.

Whitman found the model and form of *Leaves of Grass*, the one book he wrote all his life, in the flux and mass of the city—he even compared his book *to* a city. He never reached his countrymen during his lifetime, and the Gilded Age took the foam off his enthusiasm for democracy, but in decline he could still write, "I can hardly tell why, but feel very positively that if anything can justify my revolutionary attempts & utterances, it is such *ensemble*—like a great city to modern civilization & a whole combined clustering paradoxical unity, a man, a woman."

Whitman was that "paradoxical unity, a man, a woman." His powerful and many-sided sexuality gave him friends that only a great city can provide; his constant expectation of love from some stranger in the street, on the ferryboat, even his future reader—"I stop somewhere waiting for you"—made stray intimacies in the city as sweet to him as they were repellent to most Americans.

The trouble with the city, said Henry James, Henry Adams, and Edith Wharton, *is* democracy, the influx of ignorant masses, their lack of manners, their lack of standards. The trouble with the city, said the angry Populist farmers and their free-silver standard-bearer Bryan in 1896, is Wall Street, the "moneyed East," the concentration of capital, the banking system that keeps honest, simple farmers in debt. Before modern Los Angeles, before Dallas, Phoenix, and Houston, it was understood that "the terrible town," as Henry James called New York, could exist only in the crowded East. The West, "wild" or not, was land of heart's ease, nature itself. The East was the marketplace that corrupted Westerners who came East. There was corruption at the ballet box, behind the bank counter, in the "purlieus of vice." The city was ugly by definition because it lacked the elemental harmony of nature. It lacked stability and relentlessly wrecked every monument of the past. It was dirt, slums, gangsters, violence.

Above all it was "dark." The reporter and pioneer photographer Jacob Riis invaded the East Side for his book *How the Other Half Lives* (1890) because he was "bent on letting in the light where it was much needed."

Look at Riis's photograph "Bandit's Roost," 59½ Mulberry Street, taken February 12, 1888. "Bandit's Roost" did not get its name for nothing, and you can still feel threatened as your eye travels down the narrow alley paved with grimy, irregularly paved stone blocks that glisten with wet and dirt. Tough-looking characters in derbies and slouch hats are lining both sides of the alley, staring straight at you; one of them presses a stick at the ground, and his left knee is bent as if he were ready, with that stick, to go into action at a moment's notice. The women at the open windows are staring just as unhelpfully as the derbied young fellow in the right foreground, whose chin looks as aggressive as the long, stiff lines of his derby.

CONSIDER NEW YORK just a century ago: the rooftops above the business district downtown are thick with a confusion of the first telephone lines crossing the existing telegraph wires. The immigrant John Augustus Roebling has built a suspension bridge of unprecedented length over the East River, thanks to the wire rope he has invented. This wire makes for a rooted strength and airy elegance as Roebling ties his ropes across one another in great squares. Brooklyn Bridge will be considered stronger as well as infinitely more beautiful than the other bridges to be built across the East River. But a week after opening day in 1883, the crowd panics as vast numbers cross the bridge, crushing several people to death—and exposing a fear of numbers, of great bridges, of the city itself, that even city dwellers still feel. What they thought of New York in the prairie West and the cotton South may easily be imagined.

But here is Central Park, the first great public park in the New World, finally completed after decades of struggle to reclaim a horrid waste. Unlike the European parks that were once feudal estates, Central Park has been carved, landscaped, gardened, built, and ornamented from scratch and specifically for the people. And this by a Connecticut Yankee, Frederick Law Olmsted, the most far-seeing of democratic visionaries, who saw in the 1850s that New York would soon run out of places in which city dwellers could escape the city. Though he will never cease complaining that the width of his park is confined to the narrow space between Fifth Avenue and what is now Central Park West, he will create a wonderland of walks, "rambles," lakes, gardens, meadows. All this is designed not for sport, political demonstrations, concerts, the imperial Metropolitan Museum, but for the contemplative walker. As early as 1858, before he was chosen superintendent but after having submitted the winning design, "Greensward," in a competition, Olmsted wrote of his park: "The main object and justification is simply to produce a certain influence in the minds of the people and through this to make life in the city healthier and happier. The character of this influence is a poetic one, and it is to be produced by means of scenes, through observation of which the mind may be more or less lifted out of moods and habits in which it is, under the ordinary conditions of life in the city, likely to fall . . ."

Alas, Central Park is not enough to lift some of us out of the "moods and habits" into which we are likely to fall. Even Walt

Museum of the City of New York

"Bandit's Roost" on Mulberry Street by Jacob Riis (1888). Riis later found that five of nine children who lived in one of these houses were dead by the end of the year.

Whitman, who truly loved New York, acidly let it drop in *Democratic Vistas* (1871) that "the United States are destined either to surmount the gorgeous history of feudalism, or else prove the most tremendous failure of time." The "great experiment," as some English sardonically call the democratic Republic, may very well depend on the city into which nearly a million immigrants a year were to pour at the beginning of the next century. Whitman was not prepared to estimate the effect on America of the greatest volunteer migration recorded in history. It was the eclipse of virtue that surprised him at the end of the century. As if he were Jefferson, he wrote: "The great cities reek with respectable as much as nonrespectable robbery and scoundrelism. In fashionable life, flippancy, tepid amours, weak infidelism, small aims, or no aims at all, only to kill time. In business (this all-devouring modern word business), the one sole object is, by any means, pecuniary gain. The magician's serpent in the fable ate up all the other serpents; and money-making is our magician's serpent, remaining today sole master of the field."

ARE CITIES all that important as an index of American health and hope? The French sociologist Raymond Aron thinks that American intellectuals are too much preoccupied with cities. He neglects to say that most Americans now have no other life but the life in those cities. Paris has been the absolute center of France—intellectually, administratively, educationally—for many centuries. America has no center that so fuses government and intellect. Although Americans are more than ever an urban people, many Americans still think of the city as something it is necessary to escape from.

In the nineteenth century slums were the savage places Jacob Riis documented in his photographs, but on the whole the savagery was confined to the slums. The political scientist Andrew Hacker has shown that "there was actually little crime of the kind we know today and in hardly any cases were its victims middle class. The groups that had been violent—most notably the Irish—had by 1900 turned respectable. The next wave of immigrants, largely from Eastern Europe and southern Italy, were more passive to begin with and accepted the conditions they found on their arrival . . . they did not inflict their resentments on the rest of society . . ."

What has finally happened is that fear of the city on the part of those who live in it has caught up with the fear on the part of those who did not have to live in it.

American fear of the city may seem ungrateful, since so much of our social intelligence depends on it. But the tradition of fear persists, and added to it nowadays—since all concern with the city is concern with class—has been fear of the "underclass," of blacks, of the youth gangs that first emerged in the mid-fifties. Vast housing projects have become worse than the slums they replaced and regularly produce situations of extreme peril for the inhabitants themselves. To the hosts of the uprooted and disordered in the city, hypnotized by the images of violence increasingly favored by the media, the city is nothing but a state of war. There is mounting vandalism, blood lust, and indiscriminate aggressiveness.

The mind reels, is soon exhausted, and turns indifferent to the hourly report of still another killing. In Brooklyn's 77th precinct a minister is arrested for keeping a sawed-off shotgun under his pulpit. On Easter Sunday uniformed police officers are assigned to protect churchgoers from muggers and purse snatchers. In parts of Crown Heights and Bedford-Stuyvesant, the *Times* reports that "there, among the boarded-up tenements, the gaudy little stores and the residential neighborhoods of old brownstones and small row houses, 88 people were killed in one year—16 in one three-block area." A hundred thousand people live and work in this precinct, but a local minister intones that "Life has become a mean and frightening struggle." Gunshots are heard all the time.

I was born and brought up alongside that neighborhood; the tenement in which my parents lived for half a century does not exist and nothing has replaced it. The whole block is a mass of rubble; the neighborhood has seen so much arson that the tops of the remaining structures are streaked with black. Alongside them whole buildings are boarded up but have been broken into; they look worse than London did after the blitz.

Democracy has been wonderful to me and for me, and in the teeth of the police state creeping up elsewhere in the world, I welcome every kind of freedom that leaves others free in the city. The endless conflict of races, classes, sexes, is raucous but educational. No other society on earth tolerates so many interest groups, all on the stage at once and all clamoring for attention.

Still, the subway car I take every day to the city university definitely contains a threat. Is it the young black outstretched across the aisle? The misplaced hilarity proceeding from the drinking group beating time to the ya-ya-ya that thumps out of their ghetto blaster? The sweetish marijuana fumes when the train halts too long in this inky tunnel and that make me laugh when I think that once there was no more absolute commandment in the subway than NO SMOKING?

Definitely, there is a threat. Does it proceed from the unhelpful, unsmiling, unseeing strangers around me? The graffiti and aggressive smears of paint on which I have to sit, and which so thickly cover every partition, wall, and window that I cannot make out the stations? Can it be the New York *Post*—"Post-Mortem" as a friend calls it—every edition of which carries the news MOM KILLS SELF AND FIVE KIDS? The battle police of the transit force rushing through one car after another as the motorman in his booth sounds the wailing alarm that signifies trouble?

What a way to live! It is apartness that rules us here, and the apartness makes the threat. Still, there is no other place for me to work and live. Because sitting in the subway, holding the book on which I have to conduct a university seminar this afternoon, I have to laugh again. It is *Uncle Tom's Cabin, or Life Among the Lowly.*

ARE CITIES OBSOLETE?

The Fearful Symmetry of Post-Urban America

PETER O. MULLER

Peter O. Muller, professor and chairman of the geography department at the University of Miami, is the author of Contemporary Suburban America.

WHERE IS PENTHESILEA? So asks the traveler, Marco Polo, of the people he meets in Italo Calvino's book of imaginary places, *Invisible Cities*. Polo, who has been walking for hours through a vague landscape of low pale buildings and meandering streets, finds little guidance in the conflicting gestures of passersby. "I mean the city," he insists, to which, again, the residents reply with outstretched arms that may, or may not, indicate the very place where he stands, farther on, or back in the opposite direction. Before long, Polo's search for the thick vertical profile that he equates with urban existence gives way to an anguishing premonition: perhaps no matter how far he travels, he will pass only from one outskirt to another, unable to leave a city that, paradoxically, is both all around him and nowhere to be found.

After reading this tale, one cannot resist wondering what Calvino's itinerant might make of the urban geography of contemporary America. Today, the country's greatest expansion and development are taking place outside the big cities, along circumferential freeway corridors— the new main streets of the metropolises that bypass downtown and directly connect constellations of suburban cores. And this shift away from central-city development represents far more than a change in residential preferences; the new, postindustrial United States economy also is migrating to the suburbs. Almost overnight, such places as Tysons Corner, Virginia; Stamford, Connecticut; Schaumburg, Illinois; Costa Mesa, California; North Dallas, Texas; King of Prussia, Pennsylvania; and Dunwoody, Georgia, have become nationally recognized business centers—with their own worldwide ties—equal to, and virtually oblivious of their big-city neighbors (respectively, Washington, New York, Chicago, Los Angeles, Dallas, Philadelphia, and Atlanta).

Perhaps nothing so clearly signified this historic geographic event as did the itinerary of China's leader, Deng Xiaoping, when, in 1979, he visited the United States (in large part to learn how American-style technology could help propel his country into the ranks of the world's developed nations). After meetings with President Jimmy Carter, Deng traveled to Atlanta, Houston, and Seattle; in each case, though, his destination was not the central city itself but a major industrial facility in its suburban ring: a state-of-the-art automobile assembly plant in Hapeville, Georgia; NASA's Lyndon B. Johnson Space Center in Clear Lake City, Texas; and Boeing's massive manufacturing complex in Renton, Washington. Moreover, Deng could have visited any number of other high-technology complexes without setting foot outside suburban America— among them, Silicon Valley, pacesetter of the electronics and computer industries, located between San Francisco and San Jose; Antelope Valley, the booming new aerospace complex that stretches north from Los Angeles; and the research and development corridors along Routes 128 and I-495 outside Boston.

In short, the metropolis has been turned inside out. No longer bands of bedroom communities and no longer dependent on the old urban cores that spawned them, the suburbs are now home to every category of human activity. Although this profound transformation is partly rooted in the urban past and represents the fulfillment of a hundred-year-long process that has steadily dispersed people and activities from the hub of the metropolis to its burgeoning edges, it is largely an outgrowth of new forces that continues to reshape America. Today, residents of suburbia are turning inward, away from cosmopolitan cities, and suburbia is being subdivided into a more narrowly defined cultural mosaic. The climax of this revolu-

This article is reprinted by permission of *The Sciences* and is from the March/April 1986 issue, pp. 43-46. Individual subscriptions are $18.00 per year. Write to The Sciences, 2 East 63rd Street, New York, NY or call 1-800-THE-NYAS.

tion will be the creation of full-fledged "outer cities," where the promise (and many of the problems) of contemporary American urban life will come to reside.

I F BY *SUBURB* is meant an urban margin that grows more rapidly than its already developed interior, the process of suburbanization began during the emergence of the industrial city, in the second quarter of the nineteenth century. Before that period the city was a small, highly compact cluster in which people got about by foot and goods were conveyed by horse and cart. But the early factories, built in the 1830s and 1840s, were located along waterways and near railheads at the edges of cities, and housing was needed for the thousands of immigrants drawn by the prospect of employment. In time, the factories were surrounded by proliferating mill towns of tenements and row houses that abutted the older, main cities. As a defense against this encroachment, and to enlarge their tax bases, the cities appropriated their industrial neighbors. In 1854, for example, the city of Philadelphia annexed all of Philadelphia County (thereby growing from two to one hundred twenty-nine square miles in one fell swoop). Similar municipal maneuvers took place in Chicago, where most of the South Side was consolidated in 1889, and in New York, where, in 1898, Manhattan engineered a political amalgamation with the boroughs of Brooklyn, Queens, Richmond, and the Bronx. (Indeed, all of America's great cities achieved such status only by incorporating the communities along their borders.)

With the acceleration of industrial growth came acute urban crowding and accompanying social stress—conditions that began to approach disastrous proportions when, in 1888, the first commercially successful electric traction line was developed. Within a few years the horse-drawn trolleys were retired and electric streetcar networks crisscrossed and connected every major urban area, fostering a wave of suburbanization that transformed the compact industrial city into a dispersed metropolis. This first phase of mass-scale suburbanization was reinforced by the simultaneous emergence of the urban middle class, whose desires for homeownership in neighborhoods far from the aging inner city were satisfied by the developers of single-family housing tracts.

Residential balkanization of the suburbs became even more pervasive upon mass production of the automobile, after the First World War. The ever expanding middle class continued to spill from the cities in huge numbers during the prosperous 1920s, quickly occupying pockets between the densely populated commuter corridors. The automobile permitted lower population densities in these newly developed interstitial zones and allowed each socially uniform section of the suburban grid to separate itself from the others. The result was a splintered society of income-defined bedroom communities, an arrangement soon codified by zoning laws, which were widely adopted as a legal tool to preserve the socioeconomic character of local municipalities (through the imposition of ordinances that ensured that people whose incomes were below those of current residents could not afford housing).

Between the two world wars, the suburbs also underwent some nonresidential development. In fact, factories had begun to spring up in them before 1900, sown along railroad tracks beyond the city limits like so many seeds that grew into outlying mill towns. By 1920, the first sizable retail stores had appeared in the suburbs, and as early as 1922, Kansas City developer Jesse Clyde Nichols constructed his Country Club Plaza, the precursor of the modern regional shopping center. Other suburban retail centers followed in California, Texas, and elsewhere, as did the many large single-store facilities built by Sears, Roebuck & Company and Montgomery Ward & Company. But because urban downtown areas were still easy to reach and highway networks that connected the suburbs remained relatively inefficient, commercial suburban development proceeded sluggishly.

Hundreds of miles of urban expressways were constructed after the Second World War, however, and whatever residential and commercial advantages the old core cities once possessed were lost. Where the freeways went, the population, carting its social and cultural baggage, soon followed: between 1950 and 1980, the number of people living in suburbia swelled from thirty-seven million to just fewer than one hundred million, or from twenty-five to a commanding forty-four percent of the overall United States population (rural areas and central cities roughly divided the other fifty-six percent). Most significant, an increasingly large proportion of the population chose the suburbs not only as a place to live but a place to work as well.

B Y ELIMINATING the difference in cost between doing business in the central city and in the suburban ring, the construction of the metropolitan freeway system launched a second wave of suburbanization— a wave that apparently has not yet crested even though it has already wrought a reversal in the geography of American urban life. Since the postindustrial era dawned, in the 1970s, businesses have been free to locate where they pleased, and their choices have been governed by noneconomic factors: the presence of local environments in which work may be done in pleasant, stress-free surroundings; the ease of accessibility for a suburban-dwelling labor force (and management corps) that overwhelmingly prefers to commute by automobile; and, most important, the attractiveness of prestigious addresses, now concentrated in suburban centers.

In just a little more than ten years, these new factors have redrawn the economic map of metropolitan America. As early as 1973, suburbs nationwide surpassed the central cities in total employment, and that gap has widened steadily since. In certain places, such as the suburbs of Atlanta and Saint Louis, business complexes have grown so large that some already employ more people than work in the central business district of the old urban core. Examination of individual economic sectors shows the breadth of this change. In 1970, the suburbs of Philadelphia (an urban area that usually ranks close to national averages) accounted for forty-nine percent of the metropolitan area's total employment; by 1982, that share had jumped to sixty-three percent, and it is still climbing. Fifty-five percent of all manufacturing jobs were in the suburbs in 1970; in 1982, the number reached seventy percent. In wholesaling and retailing, the suburban shares in 1970 were forty and fifty-six percent, respectively; by

1982, those figures had soared to sixty-eight and seventy percent. And in the crucial office industry, the leading growth sector in America's postindustrial economy, the transformation was even more startling. In 1970, the aggregate finance-insurance–real estate, unskilled services, and business services sectors (which include such activities as computer maintenance) were heavily clustered in central-city Philadelphia; the suburban portions stood at only thirty-one, twenty-nine, and thirty-eight percent, respectively. But by 1982, the suburbs had become dominant, accounting, in turn, for fifty-one, fifty-five, and sixty-six percent of the metropolitan total. And suburban Philadelphia seems now to be experiencing its fastest employment growth yet.

And what has been good for suburban Philadelphia has been good for suburbs throughout the northern United States. For example, Washington, D.C., and Saint Louis each experienced a particularly rapid second wave of suburbanization during the 1970s; and even in the Greater New York area, where the presence of the national business community retards the deconcentration trend, suburban economic activity reached critical mass (holding a greater than fifty percent metropolitan-wide share) by 1982 in the categories of total employment (fifty-four percent), manufacturing (sixty-four percent), wholesale trade (fifty-seven percent), and retail trade (sixty-four percent). But perhaps one of the greatest Frostbelt growth booms is occurring in Megalopolis—the Boston–Washington corridor of the Northeast. A new study by the investment research department of Jones, Lang, Wootton reports that, in half of that region's thirty-six suburban counties, at least seven hundred fifty thousand square feet of new office construction was under way in late 1984, and seventeen of those counties planned to build at least an additional million square feet in 1985. In nonrecession years since 1978, most of the thirty-six counties showed annual employment growth rates of more than three percent (led by the financial and service sectors). And such suburban high-technology centers as Boston's Route 128 corridor; Philadelphia's Silicon Gulch, along Route 202; and New Jersey's Route 1 between New Brunswick and Princeton are spawning tertiary waves of office development to serve these research and fabrication complexes.

Similar economic expansion is beginning to affect the large metropolitan areas of the South and the West. Suburban New Orleans, in 1982, contained more than fifty percent of the metropolitan area's manufacturing, wholesaling, and retailing activities, and the outer city's total share of employment was more than forty-seven percent (up from only twenty-seven percent in 1970). By that same year, suburban Denver had already surpassed the central city in employment (fifty-three to forty-seven percent) and claimed more than half the manufacturing and retailing jobs. In other Sunbelt metropolises, central-city economies are still expanding but are being eclipsed by much faster growth in their suburban rings; Dallas, Houston, Phoenix, and San Diego are examples.

This staggering shift of economic activity from old urban centers to outer, suburban rings has been accompanied by the migration of every other kind of social and cultural enterprise, a movement of such momentum that it has already created a substantial disjunction between the worlds of urban and suburban residents. Signs of disengagement appeared early, as revealed in a *New York Times* poll conducted in 1978. Only one in five of the principal wage earners surveyed was working in New York City. Fifty-three percent visited the city on nonbusiness trips fewer than five times a year; twenty-five percent avoided it altogether; and a full three-quarters reported that their lives were largely unaffected by events occurring there. Most surprising, fifty-four percent were so detached from the central city that they no longer felt they belonged to the New York metropolitan area. To New Yorkers who still believe that Manhattan is the capital of the known universe, such sudden and final secession may come as a shock. But clearly, the days when the suburbs could be viewed as colonies subordinate to the will and ways of the inner city have passed for good. The band of bedroom communities has matured into a bustling zone of back-to-back minicities with self-sufficient financial, cultural, transportation, and communications facilities, most often anchored by a regional shopping mall.

IN ITS BROAD OUTLINES, the social makeup of the modern outer city is an outgrowth of the residential mosaic of earlier eras, but over the past few years the older tiles have been subdivided into an even more complex array of social and economic groupings. Clearly, this dramatic new episode of fragmentation is rooted in a nationwide movement toward intensified cultural pluralism, as witnessed in the explosive growth of such segregated residential arrangements as retirement communities, singles' condominiums, and inner-city gentrified neighborhoods. But it is in the suburbs that the new organizing principles of this mosaic culture—life-style and age—have yielded the most highly specialized communities, many of them defined by abrupt territorial boundaries—such as the walled compounds that dominate the landscape of single- and multiple-dwelling housing tracts built since 1975. Today, "living with one's own kind" means something considerably narrower than residing in an ethnically or racially prescribed neighborhood. And as the mosaic culture matures, it is not only likely these patterns will persist, but they may well accelerate throughout metropolitan America as well.

To the extent that suburban residents actively participate in a community beyond the physical borders of their chosen tile in the mosaic, it is a community of interest only, one whose geographically dispersed constituents are united by specific occupational, age, and life-style backgrounds, and by membership in exclusive residential settlements of similar character. The force and pervasiveness of this trend are abundantly evident in the real estate section of any metropolitan Sunday newspaper, replete with its aggressive advertisements for "total living packages" that promise to smoothly combine desirable life-style and residential features in a single, special community. And for those home seekers who want to eliminate the last shred of guesswork, the plainly thriving national real estate chains offer computerized systems that match the buyer with any number of socially and economically defined suburban neighborhoods throughout the country.

As might be expected, the success of this new phase of metropolitan growth has not been an entirely painless achievement. Saturated transportation systems pose the most urgent outer city problem, followed by the overburdening of public utilities and services, the inability of small independent suburban governments to resolve crises that involve entire regions, and by noise and visual pollution. But issues far more portentious than traffic snarls and overtaxed sewer systems attend intrametropolitan deconcentration and the ascendancy of the outer city. If, as Calvino has written, "cities, like dreams, are made of desires and fears," what does an urban civilization without large cities—a condition toward which we surely are advancing—reveal about itself? Always a place of strife, sometimes a field of frightening violence, the large city nonetheless has provided the only enduring common ground for the multitude of jostling cultures that make up America. In what crucible will future American societies be forged? When a weary and bewildered Marco Polo of the twenty-first century asks for directions to the American city, will we point to a continual mosaic of a thousand and one communities, equally self-reliant and, like so many provincial villages, equally incommunicative with one another?

AMERICA'S NEW CITY
MEGALOPOLIS UNBOUND

ROBERT FISHMAN

Mr. Fishman is professor of history at Rutgers University, Camden, New Jersey.

Jim and Delores Bach live in a redwood contemporary in West Nyack, N.Y., about 25 miles north of Manhattan. Twenty years ago, their cul de sac was an apple orchard, and today two gnarled old trees on the front lawn still hold up their fruit to the early autumn sun.

This morning, two of the Bach children will board buses to school and Delores will drive young Alex to a day-care center in nearby Nanuet. Then she will drive 20 minutes down the Garden State Parkway to her job at a medical laboratory in Montvale, N.J. Her husband, meanwhile, will be on the New York State Thruway, headed east over the Hudson River on the Tappan Zee Bridge to his job with IBM in Westchester County.

A decade ago, Delores Bach could not have imagined finding such a good job so close to home. She stayed home with the children and Jim commuted to midtown Manhattan. But since the 1970s, northern New Jersey and New York's Westchester County—the very county whose genteel "bedroom communities" the writer John Cheever lived in and wrote about for the *New Yorker*—have become carpeted with office complexes and stores. West Nyack and other towns in Rockland County have filled up with families who can't afford Westchester's stratospheric home prices. Others are moving even farther to the northwest, to Orange County. Now, the Tappan Zee, built as part of the interstate highway system 35 years ago to link New York City with Albany and other distant upstate areas, is jammed every rush hour. In fact, Jim Bach's trip will take about an hour, longer than his old 50-minute commute by express bus to Manhattan.

The Bachs still make it a point to get to Manhattan once every six months or so for a day at the museum with the kids or a night out at the theater. They still subscribe to the *New York Times*. But they have friends who have not been to "the City," as it is called, in 10 years. Why bother? They can get good jobs nearby, buy anything they could possibly desire at one of a dozen convenient malls, attend a college, get fine medical care or legal advice—virtually anything they could want is within a one-hour radius. All they have to do is get in the car and drive.

The Bachs are fictional, but West Nyack is a real place—one of literally hundreds of former suburbs around the nation which, without anybody quite realizing it, have detached themselves from the big city and coalesced into "new cities." They lack skyscrapers, subways, and other symbolic structures of the central city, but they have acquired almost all of its functions.

WRIGHT'S PROPHECY

"The big city," Frank Lloyd Wright announced prophetically in 1923, "is no longer modern." Although his forecast of a new age of urban decentralization was ignored by his contemporaries, we can now see that Wright and a few other thinkers of his day understood the fragility of the great behemoth—the centralized industrial metropolis—which then seemed to embody and define the modernity of the 20th century.

These capital cities of America's industrial revolution, with New York and Chicago at their head, were built to last. Their very form, as captured during the 1920s in the famous diagrams by Robert E. Park and Ernest W. Burgess of the Chicago School of sociology, seemed to possess a logic that was permanent. At the core was the "central business district," with its skyscraper symbols of local wealth, power, and sophistication; surrounding the core was the factory zone, the dense region of reinforced concrete factories and crowded workers' housing; and finally, a small ring of affluent middle-class suburbs occupied the out-

From *Current*, October 1990, pp. 10-18. Originally from "Megalopolis Unbound," by Robert Fishman, *The Wilson Quarterly,* Winter 1990, pp. 25-45. Copyright © 1990 by The Woodrow Wilson International Center for Scholars.

skirts. These were the triumphant American cities, electric with opportunity and excitement, and as late as the 1920s they were steadily draining the countryside of its population.

But modernism is a process of constant upheaval and self-destruction. Just when the centralized metropolis was at its zenith, powerful social and economic forces were combining to create an irresistible movement toward decentralization, tearing asunder the logic that had sustained the big city and distributing its prized functions over whole regions. The urban history of the last half-century is a record of this process.

MISLEADING NAME

Superficially, the process might be called "the rise of the suburb." The term "suburb," however, inevitably suggests the affluent and restricted "bedroom communities" that first took shape around the turn of the century in New York's Scarsdale, the North Shore of Chicago, and other locales on the edge of the 19th-century metropolis. These genteel retreats from urban life established the model of the single-family house on its own landscaped grounds as the ideal middle-class residence, just as they established the roles of commuter and housewife as social models for upper-middle-class men and women. But Scarsdale and its kind were limited zones of privilege that strictly banned almost all industry and commerce and excluded not only the working class but even the majority of the less-affluent middle class. The traditional suburb therefore remained an elite enclave, completely dependent on the central city for jobs and essential services.

Since 1945, however, the relationship between the urban core and the suburban periphery has undergone a startling transformation—especially during the past two decades. Where suburbia was once an exclusive refuge for a small elite, U.S. Census figures show that 45 percent of the American population is now "suburban," up from only 23 percent in 1950. Allowing for anomalies in the Census Bureau's methods, it is almost certain that a majority of Americans live in the suburbs. About one third remain in the central cities. Even more dramatic has been the exodus of commerce and industry from the cities. By 1980, 38 percent of the nation's workers commuted to their jobs from suburb-to-suburb, while only half as many made the stereotypical suburb-to-city trek.

Manufacturing has led the charge from the cities; the industrial park, as it is so bucolically dubbed, has displaced the old urban factory district as the headquarters of American manufacturing. Commerce has also joined the exodus. Where suburbanites once had little choice but to travel to downtown stores for most of their clothing and household goods, suburban shopping malls and stores now ring up the majority of the nation's retail sales.

During the last two decades, the urban peripheries have even outpaced the cores in that last bastion of downtown economic clout, office employment. More than 57 percent of the nation's office space is now located outside the central cities. And the landscaped office parks and research centers that dot the outlying highways and interstates have become the home of the most advanced high-technology laboratories and factories, the national centers of business creativity and growth. *Inc.* magazine, which tracks the nation's emerging industries, reported in a survey earlier this year that "growth is in the 'edge cities.'" Topping its list of "hot spots" were such unlikely locales as Manchester-Nashua, New Hampshire; West Palm Beach, Florida; and Raleigh-Durham, North Carolina.

The complex economy of the former suburbs has now reached a critical mass, as specialized service enterprises of every kind, from hospitals equipped with the latest CAT scanners to gourmet restaurants to corporate law firms, have established themselves on the fringes. In all of these ways, the peripheries have replaced the urban cores as the heartlands of our civilization. These multi-functional late-20th century "suburbs" can no longer be comprehended in the terms of the old bedroom communities. They have become a new kind of city.

THE FEATURES OF THE NEW CITY

Familiar as we all are with the features of the new city, most of us do not recognize how radically it departs from the cities of old. The most obvious difference is scale. The basic unit of the new city is not the street measured in blocks but the "growth corridor" stretching 50 to 100 miles. Where the leading metropolises of the early 20th century—New York, London, or Berlin—covered perhaps 100 square miles, the new city routinely encompasses two to three *thousand* square miles. Within such "urban regions," each element is correspondingly enlarged. "Planned unit developments" of cluster-housing are as large as townships; office parks are set amid hundreds of acres of landscaped grounds; and malls dwarf some of the downtowns they have replaced.

These massive units, moreover, are arrayed along the beltways and "growth corridors" in seemingly random order, without the strict distinctions between residential, commercial, and industrial zones that shaped the old city. A subdivision of $300,000 single-family houses outside Denver may sit next to a telecommunications research-and-production complex, and a new mall filled with boutiques once found only on the great shopping streets of Europe may—and indeed *does*—rise amid Midwestern corn fields.

The new city, furthermore, lacks what gave shape and meaning to every urban form of the past: a dominant single core and definable boundaries. At most, it contains a multitude of partial centers, or "edge cities," more-or-less unified clusters of malls, office developments, and entertainment complexes that rise where major highways cross or converge. As *Washington Post* writer Joel Garreau has observed, Tysons Corner, perhaps the largest American edge city, boasts more office space than downtown Miami, yet it remains only one of 13 edge cities—including Rockville-Gaithersburg, Maryland, and Rosslyn-Ballston, Virginia—in the Washington, D.C., region.

RAPID GROWTH

Even some old downtowns have been reduced to "first among equals" among the edge cities of their regions. Atlanta has one of the most rapidly growing downtowns in the country. Yet between 1978 and 1983—the years of its accelerated growth—the downtown's share of regional office space shrank from 34 percent to 26 percent. Midtown Manhattan is the greatest of all American downtowns, but northern New Jersey now has more office space.

If no one can find the center of the new city, its borders are even more elusive.

Low-density development tends to gain an inevitable momentum, as each extension of a region's housing and economy into previously rural areas becomes the base for further expansion. When one successful area begins to fill up, land values and taxes rise explosively, pushing the less affluent even farther out. During the past two decades, as Manhattan's "back offices" moved 30 miles west into northern New Jersey along interstates 78 and 80, new subdivisions and town-house communities began sprouting 40 miles farther west along these growth corridors in the Pocono Mountains of eastern Pennsylvania. "By the time we left [New Jersey]," one new resident of eastern Pennsylvania told the *New York Times*, "there were handyman specials for $150,000 you wouldn't put your dog in." Now such formerly depressed and relatively inexpensive areas as Pennsylvania's Lehigh Valley are gaining population, attracting high-tech industries and office employment, and thus stimulating further dispersion.

Baltimore and Washington, D.C., once separated by mile after mile of farms and forests, are now joined by an agglomeration of office parks, shopping strips, and housing. Census Bureau officials have given up attempting to draw a statistical boundary between the two metropolitan areas and have proposed combining them into a single consolidated region for statistical purposes. Indeed, as the automobile gives rise to a complex pattern of multi-directional travel that largely by-passes the old central cities, the very concept of "center" and "periphery" becomes obsolete.

Although a few prophets like Wright foresaw the downfall of the old city, no one imagined the form of the new. Instead, it was built up piecemeal, as a result of millions of uncoordinated decisions made by housing developers, shopping-mall operators, corporate executives, highway engineers and, not least, the millions of Americans who saved and sacrificed to buy single-family homes in the expanding suburbs. The new city's construction has been so rapid and so unforeseen that we lack even a commonly-accepted name for what we have created. Or, rather, we have too many names: exurb, spread city, urban village, megalopolis, outtown, sprawl, slurb, the burbs, nonplace urban field, polynucleated city, and (my own coinage) technoburb.

SPRAWL

Not urban, not rural, not suburban, but possessing elements of all three, the new city eludes all the conventional terminology of the urban planner and the historian. Yet it is too important to be left in conceptual limbo. The success or failure of the new city will affect the quality of life of the majority of Americans well into the 21st century. In a few scattered locales today, one can discern the promise of a decentralized city that fulfills its residents' basic hopes for comfortable homes in sylvan settings with easy access to good schools, good jobs, and recreational facilities of many kinds. More ambitiously, one might hope for a decentralized civilization that finally overcomes the old antithesis of city and countryside, that fulfills in daily life the profound cultural need for an environment that combines the machine and nature in a new unity.

But the dangers of the new city are perhaps more obvious than the promise. The immense speed and scale of development across the nation threaten to annihilate the natural environment of entire regions, leaving the tranquility and natural beauty that Americans seek in the new city perpetually retreating another 10 exits down the interstate. The movement of urban functions to an environment never designed for them has produced the anomaly of urban-style crowding and congestion in a decentralized setting. Through greed and ignorance we could destroy the very things that inspired the new city and build instead a degenerate urban form that is too congested to be efficient, too chaotic to be beautiful, and too dispersed to possess the diversity and vitality of a great city.

The new city is still under construction. Like all new urban types, its early form is necessarily raw and chaotic. The real test of the new city as a carrier of civilization will come when the first flush of hectic building slows down and efforts to redesign and reconstruct begin, as they have in the old downtowns today. But before we can improve the new urban world we are building we need to understand it.

In Europe, governments fearful of losing

precious farm land to the encroaching cities have severely restricted decentralization wherever they could. As early as 1938 the British government prohibited London and the other large British cities from expanding beyond their existing boundaries. A decade later it created permanent "greenbelts" of farm and park land around the cities, including an impressive five-mile wide Metropolitan Greenbelt which still rings London. (Paris, on the other hand, is ringed by a Red Belt, so called because its working-class residents consistently vote Communist. This reflects another unique quality of European development: The affluent middle-class generally prefers urban to suburban living.) In the United States, however, Washington, as well as state and local governments, indefatigably promoted expansion. Government "planning" was largely unconscious and unintended, but that did not lessen its effects. Between 1930 and 1960, state intervention in four different arenas profoundly affected the shape of the nation's cities:

• *Housing.* Although the American preference for single-family suburban houses was well-established by the 1920s, it took the New Deal's Federal Housing Administration (1934) to reform the nation's rickety system of mortgage finance and, ultimately, put the American dream house within reach of millions of citizens. As historian Kenneth Jackson has shown, FHA regulations also funneled mortgage money to newly built suburbs, considered good credit risks, while virtually starving the cities of residential construction loans.

• *Defense Industries.* During World War II, the new factories built to manufacture synthetics, alloys, aircraft, and other products under the auspices of the Defense Plants Corporation were rarely located in the central cities. For example, Nassau County, Long Island, future site of the archetypal postwar suburb of Levittown, became the East Coast's center for aircraft production during the war, as Grumman, Republic, and other manufacturers opened plants there. Unlike the old urban factories, they were built on a single level on great tracts of land, in accordance with new ideas of industrial efficiency. Almost overnight these new factories gave the metropolitan peripheries and decentralized sunbelt cities a substantial industrial base on which they could build during the postwar period.

• *Highway Construction.* From the beginning, highways were regarded as a public responsibility, entitled to subsidies with tax dollars, while the rail system was not. Rail freight (and often mass transit as well) remained under the control of private corporations. After 1920, the owners were increasingly unable or unwilling to improve their services to attract customers. Highway engineers presided over one of the most massive construction ef-

forts in history, culminating after 1958 in the 44,000 miles of the federal interstate highway system built at a cost of $108 billion. While these Main Streets of the emerging new cities flourished, the rail lines that served the downtowns stagnated or declined.

• *Local Government.* After the turn of the century, city after city failed to annex its suburbs because of suburban resistance. As a result, cities lost the tax base of the most prosperous and rapidly expanding areas of the region. And since zoning in the American system is essentially a matter of local control, the power to regulate new development passed to the hundreds of suburban governments, which had little interest in restraining growth to create a balanced metropolitan region. Developers learned they could play one small local planning board off another, escaping all control. As the developer Sam Lefrak observed, "There is no zoning: only deals."

Relieved of the task of delivering the full range of services required by a great city, suburbs could tailor public spending to the specific needs of their constituents. With surprising speed, suburban public school systems developed into formidable enterprises, soon rivaling and then surpassing the once-dominant big-city schools.

Without anybody intending for it to happen, all of these seemingly unrelated forces converged to generate enormous momentum behind the great tide of decentralization that washed over the American metropolis after 1945. The tide has continued relentlessly, through booms and recessions, under Democratic and Republican administrations, until the old industrial city became, if not an extinct species, at least a highly endangered one.

The first significant sign was a drop in population. Between 1950 and 1960, all of the large, established cities lost people. Boston, the worst case, shrank by 13 percent, while its suburbs gained 17 percent. New York and Chicago lost less than two percent each, but their suburbs gained over 70 percent. To these blows were added shrinkage of the industrial base. Between 1947 and 1967, the 16 largest and oldest central cities lost an average of 34,000 manufacturing jobs each, while their suburbs gained an average of 87,000. This trend continued through the 1970s, as the cities suffered the elimination of from 25 percent (Minneapolis) to 40 percent (Philadelphia) of the manufacturing jobs that remained.

ARE THESE "REAL" CITIES?

Building on their growing base of population and jobs, suburban entrepreneurs during the 1950s and 1960s began transforming the new city into a self-sufficient world. "We don't go downtown anymore," became the new city's motto. Shopping centers displaced downtown department stores; small merchants and repairmen deserted Main Street for stores "along the highway" or folded up shop under the competitive pressure of the growing national chain stores. Even cardiologists and corporate lawyers moved their offices closer to their customers.

By the 1970s and 1980s, the new city found itself at the top of a whole range of national and even international trends. The movement from snowbelt to sunbelt meant a shift toward urban areas that had been "born decentralized" and organized on new-city principles. The new city, moreover, moved quickly to dominance in the most rapidly expanding sections of the industrial economy—electronics, chemicals, pharmaceuticals, and aircraft —leaving the old city with such sunset industries as textiles, iron and steel, and automobiles.

Finally, during the 1970s, the new city successfully challenged the old downtowns in the last area of their supremacy, office employment. The "office park" became the locale of choice for many businesses, new and old. Jaded New Yorkers looked on in stunned disbelief as one major corporation after another pulled up stakes and departed for former commuter towns like Stamford, Connecticut, or more distant sunbelt locations. By the 1980s, even social scientists could not ignore the fact that the whole terminology of "suburb" and "central city," deriving from the era of the industrial metropolis, had become obsolete. As Mumford had predicted, the single center had lost its dominance.

But are the sprawling regions *cities*? Judged by the standards of the centralized metropolis, the answer is no. As I have suggested, this "city" lacks any definable borders, a center or a periphery, or a clear distinction between residential, industrial, and commercial zones. Instead, shopping malls, research and production facilities, and corporate headquarters all seem scattered amid a chaos of subdivisions, apartment complexes, and condominiums. It is easy to understand why urban planners and social scientists trained in the clear functional logic of the centralized metropolis can see only disorder in these "nonplace urban fields," or why ordinary people use the word "sprawl" to describe their own neighborhoods.

Nevertheless, I believe that the new city has a characteristic structure—one that departs radically not only from the old metropolis but from all cities of the past.

To grasp this structure we must return to the prophetic insights of Frank Lloyd Wright. From the 1920s until his death in 1959, Wright was preoccupied with his plan for an ideal decentralized American city which he called Broadacres. Although many elements of the plan were openly utopian—he wished, for example, to ensure that every American would have access to at least an acre of land so that all could reap the economic and psychological benefits that he associated with part-time farming—Wright also had a remarkable insight into the highway-based world that was developing around him. Above all he understood the consequences of a city based on a grid of highways rather than the hub-and-spokes of the older city. Instead of a single privileged center, there would be a multitude of crossings, no one of which could assume priority. And the grid would be boundless by its very nature, capable of unlimited extension in all directions.

Such a grid, as it indeed developed, did not allow for the emergence of an "imperial" metropolis to monopolize the life of a region. For Wright, this meant that the family home would be freed from its fealty to the city and allowed to emerge as the real center of American life. As he put it, "The true center, (the only centralization allowable) in Usonian democracy, is the individual Usonian house." (Usonia was Wright's name for the United States).

In the plans for Broadacres—a city he said would be "everywhere or nowhere"—Wright foresaw what I believe to be the essential element in the structure of the new city: a megalopolis based on *time* rather than space.

A CITY OF TIME INSTEAD OF SPACE

Even the largest of the old "big cities" had a firm identity in space. The big city had a center as its basic point of orientation—the Loop, Times Square—and also a boundary. Starting from the center, sooner or later one reached the edge of the city.

In the new city, however, there is no single center. Instead, as Wright suggested, each family home has become the central point for its members. Families create their own "cities" out of the destinations they can reach (usually travelling by car) in a reasonable length of time. Indeed, distance in the new cities is generally measured in terms of time rather than blocks or miles. The supermarket is 10 minutes away. The nearest shopping mall is 30 minutes in another direction, and one's job 40 minutes away by yet another route. *The pattern formed by these destinations represents "the city" for that particular family or individual.* The more varied one's destinations, the richer and more diverse is one's personal "city." The new city is a city *à la carte*.

It can be seen as composed of three overlapping networks, representing the three basic categories of destinations that define each person's city. These are the household network; the network of consumption; and the network of production.

NETWORKS The household network is composed of places that are part of family and personal life. For a typical household of two parents and two children, this network is necessarily oriented around childrearing—and it keeps parents scurrying frantically in station wagons and minivans from one place to another. Its set of destinations include the homes of the children's playmates (which may be down the street or scattered around a county), the daycare center, the schools, a church or synagogue, community centers, and the homes of the parents' friends. Although this network is generally more localized than the other two, it is almost always wider than the traditional urban neighborhood.

The two-parent family with children is the archetypical new-city household, but, especially since 1970, the new city has made a place for others. For single or divorced people, single parents, young childless couples or older "empty nest" couples, widows and widowers, the new city offers a measure of familiarity and security that many find lacking in the central city. Its housing is increasingly diverse. No longer confined to single-family homes, it now includes apartment towers, town homes and condominiums, and various kinds of retirement housing, from golf-oriented communities to nursing homes. There are more places to socialize. The same mall that caters essentially to families on weekends and evenings may also serve as an informal community center for older people in the morning, while its bars and restaurants play host to a lively singles scene after the stores close.

The network of consumption—Mallopolis, in economist James Millar's phrase—comprises essentially the shopping centers and malls which, as Wright predicted, have located themselves at the strategic crossroads of the highway system. It also includes movie theaters, restaurants, health clubs, playing fields and other recreational facilities, and perhaps a second home 30 to 100 miles away.

Although this network serves much the same function as the old downtown, it is scattered, and each consumer is free to work out his particular set of preferences from the vast menu of offerings presented by Mallopolis.

Finally, there is the network of production. It includes the place of employment of one or both spouses. It also includes the suppliers —from computer-chip manufacturers to janitorial services—which these enterprises rely upon. Information comes instantaneously from around the world while raw materials, spare parts, and other necessities are trucked in from the firms that cluster along nearby highways.

CONVENIENCE This network minimizes the traditional distinction between the white-collar world of administration and the blue-collar world of production. Both functions co-exist in virtually every "executive office park." Its most successful enterprises are those where research and development and specialized techniques of production are intimately intertwined: pharmaceuticals, for example, or electronics. Conversely, its most routinized labor can be found in the so-called "back-offices," data-processing centers that perform tasks once done at a downtown corporate headquarters.

Each of these networks has its own spatial logic. For example, primary schools are distributed around the region in response to the school-age population; shopping malls reflect population density, wealth, and the road system; large firms locate where their workers and their suppliers can easily reach them. But because the networks overlap, the pattern on the ground is one of juxtaposition and interpenetration. Instead of the logical division of functions of the old metropolis, one finds a postmodern, post-urban collage.

In some places, a particularly active locale like Tysons Corner, in Fairfax County, Virginia, may draw together elements from different networks—shopping malls and offices—to form an approximation of an old downtown. But the logic of the new city generally confounds that kind of concentration. Such areas immediately become points of especially bad traffic congestion, denying the ready access that is a hallmark of the new city. (It may be poetic justice that the leaders of the American Automobile Association, patron saint of the suburban motorist, have become so frustrated by the bumper-to-bumper traffic in the area around Tysons Corner that they have decided to move AAA headquarters to the relatively open roads of Orlando, Florida.) Tysons Corner is an exception. In general, the new city allows and requires each citizen to make connections among the three networks—to make a city —on his own. The new city has no center or boundary because it does not need them.

Women have been a not-so-hidden force behind the new city's economic success. Since 1957, the proportion of married women aged 27 to 54 with jobs has grown from 33 percent to 68 percent. More than half of all women with children aged three years or younger are now employed outside the home. Much of the economic life of the new city, especially with its concentration on retail trade and back-office data processing, would be impossible without these new workers. Indeed, the presence of *WOMEN* employment opportunities so close to home— convenient, with decent pay and flexible schedules—is surely responsible for part of the remarkable influx of married women into the work force (although the plentiful supply of workers could just as easily be said to have attracted employers). The outcome is more than a little ironic, considering the fact that the bedroom suburb had originally been designed to separate women from the corruptions of the world of work.

The new city thus decisively breaks with the older suburban pattern that restricted married middle-class women with children to a life of neighborhood-oriented domesticity. Women still work closer to home than men do, and they still bear most of the responsibility for childcare and housekeeping, but, in contrast to the old metropolis, the economic and spatial structure of the new city tends to equalize gender roles.

Indeed, one can argue that the new city has largely been built on the earnings of two-income families and thus reflects their needs more closely than did either the urban core or the traditional bedroom suburb. One large housing developer, Scarborough Corporation of Marlton, New Jersey, found that 72 percent of its customers during the mid-1980s were two-income couples, compared to less than 30 percent a decade earlier. Accordingly, the firm redesigned some of its houses, substituting a "study-office" for the "sewing room," scaling down the formal living room and enlarging the family room, providing more pantry space to cut down on trips to the supermarket, and selecting building materials to minimize maintenance.

In other ways, both trivial and important, the new city has responded to the changing character of families with more flexibility than critics of "the suburbs" are willing to admit. Encouraged by women's groups and planning boards, some developers have set aside space for day-care centers in new office complexes. There are extended school days for "latchkey" children and, during the summer, recreation programs. And only in the new city can one find the extensive array of Pizza Huts, Sizzler's, Denny's, and other inexpensive "family-style" restaurants which, though they may not delight Julia Child, are many a parent's salvation at the end of a hard day at the office.

THE CONDITION OF THE OLD CITY

When Frank Lloyd Wright envisioned Broadacre City, he failed to consider the role of the old centralized industrial cities in the new world of the future. He simply assumed that the old cities would disappear once the conditions that had created them were gone. The reality has not been so simple. Just as the industrial metropolis grew up around the older mercantile city, so the new city of our time has surrounded the old metropolis. What was once the sole center is now one point of concentration among many.

In general, the skyscraper cores of the central cities have adapted to this change and prospered. Even a decentralized region needs a "headquarters," a place of high status and high rents where the movers-and-shakers can rub shoulders and meet for power lunches. By contrast, the old factory zones have not found a function in the new environment. As a result, the central city has reverted to what it was before industrialization: a site for high-level administration and luxury consumption, where some of the wealthiest members of society live in close proximity to many of the poorest.

The recent boom in downtown office construction should not conceal the fact that downtown prosperity rests on a much narrower base than it did in its heyday during the 1920s. Most of the retail trade has fled to the malls; the grand old movie palaces and many of the nightspots are gone. Only the expansion of corporate headquarters, law firms, banks and investment houses, advertising agencies, and other corporate and governmental services has kept the downtown towers filled, and even in these fields there have been major leakages of back-office employment to the new city. Nevertheless, this employment base has enabled most core areas to retain an array of specialized shops, restaurants, and cultural activities unequalled in their region. This in turn encourages both the gentrification of surrounding residential neighborhoods and the "renaissance" of the core as a tourist and convention center.

Yet only blocks away from a thriving core like Baltimore's Inner Harbor one can usually find extensive poverty, decay, de-industrialization, and abandonment that stretches out to encompass the old factory zone. The factory zones have found no new role. Their working-class populations have largely followed the factories to the new city, leaving a supply of cheap, old housing which has attracted poor black, Hispanic, and other minority migrants with no other place to go. If the industrial city in its prime brought people together with jobs, cheap housing in the inner city now lures the jobless to those areas where employment prospects are dimmest. The old factory zone is thus doubly disadvantaged: The jobless have moved in, the jobs out.

Public transportation retains its traditional focus on the core, but the inner-city population generally lacks the education to compete for the high-level jobs that are available there. By contrast, the new city usually has an abundance of entry-level jobs, many of them already going begging as the supply of women and students seeking jobs diminishes. Unfortunately, residents of the new city have generally resisted attempts to build low-income housing in middle-class areas and have discouraged public transportation links. They want to keep

"RENAISSANCE"

the new city's expanding tax base for themselves and to avoid any direct fiscal responsibility for the urban poor. The new city has thus walled itself off from the problems of the inner city in a way that the Social Darwinists of the 19th century could only envy.

THE DRAWBACKS OF SUCCESS

If the majority of Americans have voted with their feet (or rather, with their cars) for the new city, we need not conclude that this new environment has been successful, whether judged by the standards of previous cities or even on its own terms.

Comparing the new city with the old metropolis, we can see that the new city has yet to evolve anything comparable to the balance of community and diversity that the metropolis achieved. The urban neighborhood at its best gave a sense of rooted identity that the dispersed "house-hold network" of the new city lacks. The downtowns provided a counterpoint of diversity, a neon-lit world where high and low culture met, all just a streetcar ride away. By comparison, even the most elaborate mall pales.

Of course, many residents of the new city were attracted there precisely because they were uncomfortable with both the community and diversity of the old. They wanted to escape from the neighborhood to a "community of limited liability," and they found the cultural and social mix of downtown more threatening than exciting. The new city represents the sum of these choices, but we should beware of accepting the architecture critic Ada Louise Huxtable's snooty judgment of the new city as "slurb" embodying "cliché conformity as far as the eye can see." The new city is rapidly becoming more diverse than the stereotypical suburb of old.

Beyond the inevitable distinctions between more and less affluent residential districts, the new city has begun to generate "communities of shared concerns" formed around areas of special historic, architectural, or environmental value. A neglected town bypassed by the malls and highways attracts homebuyers who want to restore the old houses and merchants who seek to revive its Main Street. An isolated area near a state park attracts those who are willing to sacrifice convenience for access to an unspoiled landscape.

CULTURE Inevitably, the central city will continue to shelter the dominant institutions of high culture—museums, concert halls, and theaters—but in our electronic age these institutions no longer monopolize that culture. As the French novelist and cultural critic André Malraux wrote in his *Voices of Silence* (1950), there exists a "museum without walls"—a world of high-quality prints, photographs, art books, and other images which are available outside the museums or the galleries. In the age of the compact disc and the VCR, we have concert halls, opera houses, theaters, and movie palaces without walls. The new city is still a cultural satellite of the old, but the electronic decentralization of high culture and the growing vitality of the new city could soon give it an independent cultural base to rival past civilizations.

The most fervent self-criticism coming from the new city has not, however, focused on the lack of art galleries or symphony orchestras. It comes from those who fear that the very success of the new city is destroying the freedom of movement and access to nature that were its original attraction. As new malls and subdivisions eat up acre after acre of land, and as highways clog with traffic, the danger arises that the three networks of communication that comprise the city may break down. Too often the new city seems to be an environment as out of control as the old metropolis. The machine of growth is yet again gaining the upper hand over any human purpose. The early residents of the new city worried little about regulating growth because there was still a seemingly endless supply of open land. Now that it is disappearing, the residents of the new city must finally face the consequences of get-and-grab development.

Once again we must turn for wisdom to the great prophets of decentralization, especially Frank Lloyd Wright. Wright believed that the guiding principle of the new city must be the harmonization of development with a respect for the land in the interest of creating a beautiful and civilized landscape. "Architecture and acreage will be seen together as landscape—as was the best antique architecture—and will become more essential to each other," he wrote. As his Broadacre City plans and drawings show, he largely ruled out large buildings or even high-rise structures. His plans show the same juxtapositions of housing, shopping, and industry that exist in the new city today. But they depict a world in which these are integrated into open space through the preservation of farmland, the creation of parks, and the extensive use of landscaping around buildings.

For Wright, an "organic" landscape meant more than creating beautiful vistas. It was the social effort to integrate the potentially disruptive effects of the machine in the service of a higher purpose. Wright, however, gave little practical thought to how this might be achieved. In one of his books he vaguely suggested that each county in Broadacres would have a "County Architect" with dictatorial powers to regulate the environment.

Lacking such a figure in reality, the new city must now undertake the difficult task of moving democratically from its virtually unplanned pell-mell growth to planning with a concern for balanced growth. In New Jersey, a public opinion poll taken in connection with the proposed "State Development and Redevelopment Plan" shows that, by a margin of five to one, the residents of the highly-developed Garden State prefer less growth even at the cost of less economic development. Half agreed that controls on development should be "extremely strict," and 25 percent more said regulation should be "very strict."

The ever-present threat of a veto by the state legislature as the plan develops into final form (scheduled for late 1990) shows that these sentiments are still far from determining policy. The New Jersey Plan, however, includes certain proposals that will have to figure into any effective landuse control program in the new city. Limited areas of the state are designated as growth corridors, while development is discouraged in still-rural areas. Scenic or historic sites that give identity to a region are strictly earmarked for preservation. Wherever possible, building is to be channeled back into Newark, Paterson, and other depressed cities. In a creative adaptation of the urban concept of saving historic buildings by selling the air rights to build above them, New Jersey's farmers are allowed to sell the "development rights" to their farms to entrepreneurs who can apply them as credits toward denser development in other areas where new construction is permitted. The farmers are thus allowed to tap the equity in their land without abandoning it to the bulldozer.

Preserving and enhancing the common landscape might become the issue on which the people of the new cities finally come together as communities. Not even Wright's County Architect could accomplish such a task unaided. It will be a slow effort of drafting regulations and making them stick; of patient upgrading of older construction to newer standards, and drawing together the privatized beauties of individual sites into a unified framework. Fifty years ago Lewis Mumford defined his ideal decentralized community as the "biotechnic city," the place where nature and the machine exist in harmony. He saw the coming age of decentralization as a great opportunity to embody the civilizing virtues of the great cities of the past in a new and democratic form. The last half century has not been kind to utopian expectations, but the promise of a new civilization in a new city need not be lost.

MICROPOLITAN
AMERICA

Fifteen million people live in "micropolitan" America, an area untapped by many businesses.

◆

G. Scott Thomas

G. Scott Thomas is a partner of Niagara Concepts in Tonawanda, New York.

ore than three-quarters of Americans—77 percent—live in metropolitan areas. The percentage has grown steadily for decades: 56 percent in 1950, 63 percent in 1960, 69 percent in 1970, and 75 percent in 1980. It seems likely that the figure will climb to 80 percent by 2000.

Americans are preoccupied with these population centers. Best-selling books rank metros by quality of life. The federal government ranks them by a variety of demographic characteristics. Businesses focus so intensely on these areas that many are saturated with retail out-

lets, and the resulting competition makes it harder to turn a profit.

There is an alternative. Nonmetropolitan America is much more than sparsely settled farmland. Smaller cities are as

influential in their regions as metropolitan areas are on a larger scale. There are 219 "micropolitan" areas—or small cities—that are under-served markets deserving of more business attention.*

---

* I have defined a "micropolitan area" as a single county with at least 40,000 residents, including the population of the core city, which must have at least 15,000 residents.

If a qualifying city has at least 40 percent of its population in each of two counties, the micro area includes both counties.

Any independent city with 15,000 or more residents can qualify for micropolitan sta-

tus. If the city is larger than 15 square miles, its boundaries become those of the micro area. If the city is smaller, it is joined with the adjacent county to form the area.

No micropolitan area may be a part of any officially designated metropolitan area (or a New England County Metropolitan Area in the New England states) based on 1987 metropolitan definitions.

More than 15 million people live in micropolitan America, 6 percent of the nation's population. Micropolitan areas are home to more than 10 percent of the residents of 20 states. Idaho has the largest proportion of micropolitan dwellers: 35 percent of its residents live in micropolitan areas. It is followed by New Mexico (32 percent), Maine (23), New Hampshire (22), and Montana (21). Ohio is the leader in numbers, with 1.1 million people living in its micropolitan areas. Four states (Hawaii, Massachusetts, New Jersey, and South Dakota) have no micropolitan communities.

Most micropolitan residents live less than a two-hour drive from a metropolitan area. Fully 121 of the 219 micropolitan areas are within 50 miles of the center of a metropolitan area. Only 29 are more than 100 miles from a metro. Despite this proximity, the residents of America's small cities are distinctly different from those of its larger ones. For starters, they are younger and whiter.

Among all micropolitan areas, 129 have a median age that is lower than the national figure. Many micropolitan areas are college towns, such as Mount Pleasant, Michigan (median age: 22.5), and Manhattan, Kansas (median age: 22.6). Others are the sites of military bases, such as Hinesville, Georgia (median age: 22.1), and Radcliff-Elizabethtown, Kentucky (median age: 23.0). Some of the older micros are retirement havens: Vero Beach, Florida (median age: 39.4), and Prescott, Arizona (median age: 39.0).

MICRO

AMONG THE NATION'S 219 MICROPOLITAN AREAS, THESE ARE

FASTEST GROWING

(micropolitan areas with the greatest percentage population growth, 1980–1986)

	percent growth
1 Rio Rancho, NM	48.6%
2 Bullhead City-Lake Havasu City, AZ	37.1
3 Vero Beach, FL	35.2
4 Hilton Head Island, SC	31.0
5 Huntsville, TX	29.4
6 Myrtle Beach, SC	28.8
7 San Luis Obispo-Atascadero, CA	26.5
8 Fairbanks, AK	25.3
9 Prescott, AZ	24.4
10 Palestine, TX	23.7
11 Madera, CA	23.4
12 Greenville, TX	21.4
13 Fredericksburg, VA	18.4
14 Hanford, CA	16.5
15 Gallup, NM	16.3
16 El Centro-Calexico-Brawley, CA	16.2
17 Hobbs, NM	15.9
18 Grants Pass, OR	15.8
19 Carrollton, GA	15.2
19 Carson City, NV	15.2
19 Gainesville, GA	15.2
22 Bowling Green, KY	14.8
22 Flagstaff, AZ	14.8
24 Key West, FL	14.7
25 Logan, UT	14.6

THE OLDEST

(micropolitan areas with the oldest median ages, 1980)

	median age
1 Vero Beach, FL	39.4
2 Prescott, AZ	39.0
3 Hot Springs, AR	37.2
4 Bullhead City-Lake Havasu City, AZ	37.0
5 Pottsville, PA	36.8
6 Key West, FL	35.5
7 McAlester, OK	35.0
8 Grants Pass, OR	33.5
8 Rogers, AR	33.5
10 Ponca City, OK	33.2
11 Paris, TX	33.1
11 Wenatchee, WA	33.1
13 Torrington, CT	33.0
14 Bartlesville, OK	32.9
15 Duncan, OK	32.7
15 New Castle, PA	32.7
15 Paducah, KY	32.7
18 Clarksburg, WV	32.6
18 Staunton-Waynesboro, VA	32.6
20 Gloversville, NY	32.5
21 Ardmore, OK	32.4
22 Carson City, NV	32.3
22 El Dorado, AR	32.3
22 Fairmont, WV	32.3
22 Okmulgee, OK	32.3

THE YOUNGEST

(micropolitan areas with the youngest median ages, 1980)

	median age
1 Gallup, NM	22.0
2 Hinesville, GA	22.1
3 Mount Pleasant, MI	22.5
4 Manhattan, KS	22.6
5 Radcliff-Elizabethtown, KY	23.0
6 Logan, UT	23.1
6 Ruston, LA	23.1
8 Flagstaff, AZ	23.2
8 Pullman, WA	23.2
10 Blacksburg, VA	23.3
11 Auburn-Opelika, AL	23.7
12 Stillwater, OK	23.8
13 Ames, IA	23.9
14 Farmington, NM	24.2
15 Carbondale, IL	24.4
15 De Kalb, IL	24.4
17 Athens, OH	24.5
17 Hilton Head Island, SC	24.5
17 Richmond, KY	24.5
20 Del Rio, TX	24.6
21 Bozeman, MT	25.1
22 Ithaca, NY	25.2
22 Morgan City, LA	25.2
24 Rock Springs, WY	25.3
25 Corvallis, OR	25.4
25 Greenwood, MS	25.4
25 Stevens Point, WI	25.4

Note: For definition of "micropolitan," see footnote, page 31.

MARKETS

THE TOP 25 IN GROWTH RATE, AGE, INCOME, EDUCATION, AND MINORITY SHARE.

HIGHEST INCOME

(micropolitan areas with the highest per capita money income, 1985)

per capita income

1 Torrington, CT $13,381
2 Fairbanks, AK 13,079
3 Bartlesville, OK 13,035
4 Key West, FL 12,319
5 Vero Beach, FL 12,155
6 Newport, RI 11,921
7 Concord, NH 11,313
8 Rock Springs, WY 11,241
9 Columbus, IN 11,209
10 Carson City, NV 10,937
11 Findlay, OH 10,903
12 Hilton Head
   Island, SC 10,771
13 Sandusky, OH 10,759
14 Muscatine, IA 10,695
15 Winchester, VA 10,675
16 Marshalltown, IA 10,658
17 Brunswick, GA 10,565
18 Kingston, NY 10,532
19 Frankfort, KY 10,529
20 Bay City, TX 10,523
21 Keene, NH 10,493
22 Jefferson City, MO 10,486
23 Fredericksburg, VA ... 10,479
24 Ponca City, OK 10,436
25 Laconia, NH 10,413

MOST EDUCATED

(micropolitan areas with the highest median years of school completed among people aged 25+, 1980)

years of school

1 Corvallis, OR 14.2
1 Pullman, WA 14.2
3 Bozeman, MT 13.6
4 Ames, IA 13.4
5 Ithaca, NY 13.2
5 Logan, UT 13.2
7 Manhattan, KS 13.0
8 Fairbanks, AK 12.9
8 Idaho Falls, ID 12.9
8 Missoula, MT 12.9
11 Eureka, CA 12.8
11 Flagstaff, AZ 12.8
11 Helena, MT 12.8
11 Pocatello, ID 12.8
11 San Luis Obispo-
   Atascadero, CA 12.8
11 Stillwater, OK 12.8

Fourteen micropolitan areas tie for 17th place with a median of 12.7 years of school completed:

Bartlesville, OK; Bend, OR; Carbondale, IL; Carson City, NV; Coeur d'Alene, ID; Concord, NH; De Kalb, IL; Grand Junction, CO; Hilton Head Island, SC; Mankato, MN; Minot, ND; Newport, RI; Traverse City, MI; Walla Walla, WA.

PERCENT BLACK

(micropolitan areas with the largest proportion of black residents, 1980)

percent black

1 Greenwood, MS 59.1%
2 Orangeburg, SC 56.0
3 Greenville, MS 55.6
4 Selma, AL 54.6
5 Roanoke Rapids, NC 47.1
6 Sumter, SC 44.2
7 Rocky Mount, NC 41.0
8 Kinston, NC 38.1
9 Opelousas, LA 38.0
10 Vicksburg, MS 37.4
11 Ruston, LA 36.7
12 Hinesville, GA 36.6
13 Wilson, NC 36.4
14 Greenville, NC 34.4
15 Columbus, MS 34.2
16 Hilton Head Island, SC .. 32.9
17 Goldsboro, NC 32.6
18 Minden, LA 31.9
19 Meridian, MS 31.4
20 La Grange, GA 31.3
21 Talladega, AL 30.8
22 Valdosta, GA 30.3
23 Bogalusa, LA 30.1
23 Hammond, LA 30.1
25 Greenwood, SC 28.9

PERCENT HISPANIC

(micropolitan areas with the largest proportion of Hispanic residents, 1980)

percent Hispanic

1 Alice, TX 67.2%
2 Del Rio, TX 62.9
3 El Centro-Calexico-
   Brawley, CA 55.8
4 Carlsbad, NM 30.7
5 Roswell, NM 30.6
6 Casa Grande-Apache
   Junction, AZ 29.4
6 Yuma, AZ 29.4
8 Rio Rancho, NM 27.5
9 Hanford, CA 26.9
10 Madera, CA 26.8
11 Sierra Vista, AZ 26.7
12 Alamogordo, NM 21.7
13 Hobbs, NM 21.3
14 Bay City, TX 21.1
15 Clovis, NM 19.5
16 Gallup, NM 13.5
17 Farmington, NM 11.8
18 Key West, FL 11.3
19 Flagstaff, AZ 9.8
20 Nampa-Caldwell, ID 9.7
21 San Luis Obispo-
   Atascadero, CA 9.5
22 Rock Springs, WY 7.8
23 Huntsville, TX 7.1
24 Grand Junction, CO 7.0
25 Sterling, IL 6.9

Source: Census Bureau

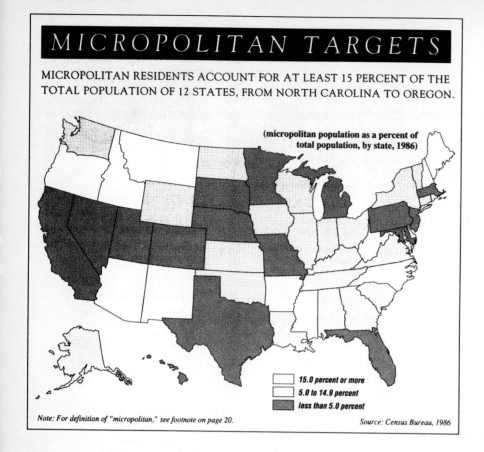

MICROPOLITAN TARGETS

MICROPOLITAN RESIDENTS ACCOUNT FOR AT LEAST 15 PERCENT OF THE TOTAL POPULATION OF 12 STATES, FROM NORTH CAROLINA TO OREGON.

(micropolitan population as a percent of total population, by state, 1986)

☐ 15.0 percent or more
☐ 5.0 to 14.9 percent
■ less than 5.0 percent

Note: For definition of "micropolitan," see footnote on page 20.

Source: Census Bureau, 1986

Micropolitan areas are not as racially diverse as metropolitan areas. Only 61 have a larger proportion of blacks than does the nation as a whole. Just 25 have a larger share of Hispanics than the national average. The 25 micros with the largest share of blacks are all in the South, led by Greenwood, Mississippi (59.1 percent). The top areas for Hispanics are in Arizona, California, Florida, New Mexico, and Texas. Alice, Texas, has the highest share of Hispanics, at 67.2 percent.

The residents of micropolitan areas are generally less educated than those of metropolitan areas. In fully 143 micropolitan areas, the median number of years of schooling of the residents falls below the national median of 12.5 years. In 23 areas—all in the South—the median educational level is less than a high school diploma. The college towns on the list are exceptions to this trend. The seven micros with a median educational level of 13 years or greater are the homes of major universities, with Corvallis, Oregon, and Pullman, Washington (each with a median of 14.2 years of schooling), at the top of the list.

Torrington, Connecticut, is the richest micropolitan area, with a per capita income of $13,381 in 1985. Incomes fall below the national average in most micropolitan areas, however: 208 had a per capita income below the national average of $10,797 in 1985. This relatively low income might be explained, in part, by the youthfulness of wage earners in many micros. The cost of living is lower in many micros as well. The per capita incomes in 23 areas fall below $7,500, with Gallup, New Mexico, at the bottom ($4,743).

MOVING UP

Given the continuing metropolitan boom, it might seem as though micropolitan areas are becoming an endangered species. This is not the case. Eighty-three micros (38 percent) grew faster than the nation as a whole between 1980 and 1986. Metropolitan areas did only marginally better, with 45 percent growing faster than the national average of 6.4 percent. But no metropolitan area could match the population surge in the Rio Rancho, New Mexico, micropolitan area. Rio Rancho grew by an astounding 49 percent over the six years, aided by its proximity to the burgeoning Albuquerque metropolitan area 11 miles down the road. Seven other micros gained at least 25 percent more people from 1980 to 1986. Six were Sunbelt cities. The seventh may be the frostiest micro of them all: Fairbanks, Alaska.

Slightly more than one-quarter of the nation's micropolitan areas lost population between 1980 and 1986. In comparison, 20 percent of metropolitan areas lost population during those years. Most of the losses occurred in the Northeast and the Midwest, which were home to 40 of the 56 declining micropolitan areas. All 15 micros in Indiana and Illinois lost population between 1980 and 1986.

Micropolitan areas, by definition, will always take a backseat to their metropolitan counterparts. But they may benefit from business competition in the 1990s as retailers look for untapped markets. Micropolitan areas may also become a haven for metropolitan residents seeking to escape the stresses of metropolitan life. The "other America" may become increasingly popular in the next decade.

Radiant City's Dull Legacy

RICHARD KOZAK / INSIGHT

Few care to visit L'Enfant Plaza, a vast expanse near the popular Smithsonian.

SUMMARY: To many critics, government-funded urban development projects have been an aesthetic, and ofttimes economic, disaster. Radiant City-style structures, unadorned and boxlike, were built over the ruins of dwellings and retail stores of a more human scale. With the razing of the buildings went much of a neighborhood's social fabric. But lately, it seems, some cities have switched gears, moving to recapture the diversity and vitality that made their locales livable.

Directly across Independence Avenue from the Victorian castle that is the headquarters of the Smithsonian Institution, whose museums are some of Washington's favorite tourist attractions, is a vacant concrete expanse called L'Enfant Plaza (designed by I. M. Pei, the man who put the glass pyramid in the Louvre courtyard), named after the French architect Pierre

Charles L'Enfant, who designed the District of Columbia's street grid. Surrounding the plaza is a cluster of concrete-and-glass government office buildings, architectural monuments of the Sixties. What a contrast: the fussy, turreted, fanciful Smithsonian with its tapestry of carpet-bedded flower gardens, abuzz with visitors and Washington residents alike, and the stark, gray, dull and empty plaza, visited by few.

L'Enfant Plaza is a product of an ambitious government-financed experiment in

changing the face of the urban landscape. It began in 1945 with a federal statute designed just for the District, then spread to almost every major city after Congress passed Title 1 of the 1949 Housing Act, promising to pay two-thirds the cost of every city's urban renewal program.

All the programs were similar: The government — or its authorized redevelopment authority — took over the land from private owners using its eminent domain powers, razed all existing structures, then sold the land to private developers at cut-rate, write-down prices in return for the developer's promise to rebuild in accordance with a master plan concocted by the local redevelopment agency and approved in Washington. The experiment petered out during the Sixties and formally ended in 1974, when Congress substituted a revenue sharing block grant program for community redevelopment. By then, the consensus was that large-scale urban renewal was out-of-date. It regularly proved to be a poor investment for cities, because it produced large tracts of land that would be off the tax rolls for decades between the bulldozing and the construction of anything new. Meanwhile, the municipality and its taxpayers had to eat the difference between the market price paid for acquiring the property and the write-down price it got from the developer.

Urban residents began complaining that their downtowns were being not so much renewed as ruined. They started to miss the buildings that had gone down: the Victorian houses deemed hopelessly old-fashioned by the master planners, the little neighborhood retail stores. Critics on both the left and the right had even less kind words for urban renewal, which typically involved bulldozing low-end housing to build property tax-generating upper-middle-class apartment and office buildings. "Socialism for the rich, laissez-faire for the poor," is the way Gideon Kanner, a real estate law professor at Loyola Marymount University in Los Angeles, expresses it. Over the years, Kanner has represented numerous small businesses that happened to be in the way when urban renewal came to their block. The renewers' message to small businesses: Drop dead.

Many of the developments failed to pay off in the form of the higher tax revenues their proponents had touted. But close — and, to many, objectionable — government intertwinement with the rebuilding of cities, in the form of federal block grants, tax-exempt bond financing, write-down sales of government-acquired property, tax abatements, zoning concessions and low-rent leasing deals, continues to this day, if on a reduced scale. The major difference: A few cities and city planners have lately learned how to do it better, to design projects with a little more respect for the human scale and the older fabric of the cities surrounding the brand-new architecture. There are fewer L'Enfant Plazas going up today, more developments with some kinship to the Smithsonian.

Washington's urban renewal experiment was one of the nation's most ambitious. It involved almost the entire Southwest quadrant of the city, from Independence Avenue along the Washington Mall, down along the Potomac waterfront to the juncture of the Potomac and Anacostia rivers. Large parts of Southwest are within walking distance of the U.S. Capitol. During the Forties, some 23,000 people lived in the quadrant. By the late Fifties, almost every one of them was gone, forcibly removed by government fiat (the typical method: a notice telling them their homes would be torn down to make way for "modern apartments and stores and playgrounds." By then, Southwest resembled a ghost town, in the words of one former Washington resident, a war zone, in the words of another former resident. Blocks of cleared, empty lots stretched as far as the eye could see, their occupants scattered elsewhere.

Before urban renewal, Southwest Washington was a very poor, 80 percent black district. Many of the 5,600 or so houses dated back to the 19th and even 18th centuries: small wooden buildings on tiny lots with stoops in front and back. More than 43 percent of the houses lacked indoor toilets and 70 percent lacked central heating. A large portion of the quadrant was a slum by any standard, but life was not all bad compared with today's underclass life. Of the families with children, two-thirds had both parents living at home. Incomes were low, but fewer than one-fourth of the households collected welfare payments. More than 60 percent of the residents had lived there for more than a decade. "A lot of people didn't realize the extent to which this slum was actually home to the people who lived there," says Daniel Thursz, president of the National Council on the Aging. In 1966, when Thursz was a professor of social work at the University of Maryland, he published a study of displaced South-

west residents called "Where Are They Now?" Says Thursz: "We say, 'My God! How could they stand living in a house with an outdoor privy?' But there was a very complicated, well-established social fabric in those neighborhoods."

Parts of Southwest were not a slum at all, but a tidy if run-down row house neighborhood, dotted with handsome redbrick Victorian churches. Journalist Ernie Pyle had lived there. Part of the area had once been a Jewish neighborhood where Al Jolson grew up. By 1950 most of the Jews had left, but there were still a number of small Jewish-owned stores. Down at the waterfront, a bar called Harrington's was a favorite with Washington's bohemian crowd, and several family-owned fish restaurants served family-style meals.

When the renewal plans were drawn up, almost everything was slated for demolition: wooden shacks, row houses, restaurants, bars, churches and businesses. Several of the stores sued the government to save themselves from the wrecking ball. Under the Fifth Amendment, the government can use its eminent domain powers to seize private property only if it is for a "public use." While slum clearance may indeed be a salutary public use, the stores argued, they were hardly slum buildings. The case went to the Supreme Court. In a unanimous 1954 ruling, the liberal Justice William O. Douglas said a public use was essentially whatever the legislature said it was. "If those who govern the District of Columbia decide that the national capital shall be beautiful as well as sanitary, there is nothing in the Fifth Amendment that stands in the way," he wrote.

That decision, Berman vs. Parker, was the great legal green light, not just for urban renewal but for every manner of government seizure of property that might seem to benefit private interests more than the public interest. In 1984, for example, the Supreme Court approved a land redistribution scheme in Hawaii that broke up large holdings and turned the plots over to tenants. The giant World Trade Center in New York is an urban renewal project, opened in 1970 by a joint New York-New Jersey agency that acquired the land for the office buildings by seizing going businesses in Lower Manhattan, all with court approval. The shopping malls in several California cities are 1970s urban renewal projects, the Glendale Galleria and Culver City's Fox Hills Mall to name two. "New shopping centers were being built in the suburbs back then on cheap land," explains Murray Kane, a lawyer who represented both cities in their redevelopment transactions. "There was a flight from the cities to the suburbs, so there had to be some incentive to make inner cities competitive."

The Fifth Amendment requires governments to pay "just compensation" to owners when they take property by eminent

domain. The rub is that the courts have interpreted just compensation to mean strictly the value of the real estate, not the goodwill that attaches to a going business at a particular location. To the owner of the hardware store, drugstore or luncheonette standing in the way of progress, that means not enough money to buy a new business elsewhere, and to an elderly owner, it means a penurious forced retirement. Property owners have started to fight back in recent years, learning how to use the courts to tie up development projects. Laws now usually require substantial relocation payments for evicted tenants.

The notion that the new, redeveloped Southwest Washington would be an improvement over the old stemmed from fashionable notions of what a city ought to look like. For more than a half-century before Douglas wrote his opinion, traditional notions of urban life — that it was by its very nature crowded, noisy, dense, variegated and seemingly disorderly — had been under attack among intellectuals. At the turn of the century flourished the Garden City movement, suggesting that the ideal city was a country village (minus the manor house and the parish church) carefully laid out in a large green park, with houses facing away from main streets and commercial uses carefully segregated from residential. Numerous U.S. and English suburbs and "new towns" consciously patterned themselves on the Garden City model, and it remains to this day the model for the tract house, town house, condominium and senior citizens developments that cover America's suburban landscape.

Next to come along was the vastly influential architect Le Corbusier, who adapted the Garden City model to more heavily populated urban areas. During the 1930s he devised the Radiant City, a utopian cluster of gleaming skyscrapers, some office buildings, some universities, hospitals, residences and administrative centers — all also sitting in a green park. Le Corbusier was a leading practitioner of the International style of architecture, the Bauhaus-inspired movement that favored unadorned boxlike buildings with ultraclean lines — in short, the dominant style of architecture for most of this century until the Postmodern movement of the Eighties.

Complementing the Garden City and Radiant City movements were the writings of the prolific (21 books) urban philosopher Lewis Mumford. Mumford hated most cities, and the city he hated most was New York, which struck him as vulgar, chaotic, overcrowded, full of "wasteful streets," as he called them, and lacking sufficient light and air. Mumford urged comprehensive urban planning as a cure for all of this — an analogue to the comprehensive economic planning of socialism that he and other intellectuals of the Thirties believed ought to replace the chaos of capitalism. The philosopher boldly urged cities to raze their "blighted" areas and start anew. "No urban community can afford the costly luxury of uncoordinated and insecure private enterprise," he wrote in his 1938 book, "The Culture of Cities." The kind of residential urban construction Mumford liked most was the high-rise, multibuilding, architecturally uniform housing project.

One cannot underestimate the influence of the architectural ideas of Le Corbusier and the philosophical ideas of Mumford; they still persist. To drive around Southwest Washington today, a melancholy journey, is to see the results of planning — when the planning, like the rest of the best-laid plans of mice and men, has gone agley.

L'Enfant Plaza, for example, was not meant to be quite so barren. Pei's original layout called for it to reflect L'Enfant's original design; it was to be a tree-lined promenade flanked by federal buildings in an area that would also contain numerous private office buildings and a street-level hotel. A series of compromises with Congress and the District of Columbia planted a large federal government office complex, the Forrestal Building, at the end of the promenade, and the trees never got planted. Plans are afoot at the National Capital Planning Commission to landscape and otherwise try to rehabilitate the plaza.

One of the aims of the renewal effort was to ease perceived overcrowding. The means in Southwest was deliberate depopulation by building only about half as many housing units. Another was to ensure architectural compatibility by permitting only a handful of architects to design the new quadrant. But it took years, in some cases as many as 20, before the last new developments were finished. The idle land went off the tax rolls, defeating another goal of urban renewal districts: raising the property tax base.

A large portion of the new Southwest is taken up by the blocklike office headquarters of Great Society government agencies (the biggest and ugliest building belongs, ironically, to the Department of Housing and Urban Development, designed by Bauhaus alumnus Marcel Breuer), whose workers chronically complain of a lack of cheap nearby restaurants. A shopping center designed to coordinate all the area's retail activity has never proved profitable. An office building is empty. On Fourth Street, where the little cluster of stores that unsuccessfully fought the bulldozers once stood, is a block-size, 10-story, late-Sixties apartment house of no particular architectural distinction. Another large apartment complex was turned into the Environmental Protection Agency's headquarters. There are some genuinely handsome town houses and multifamily buildings here and there, such as the Tiber Island complex on the Potomac waterfront.

The raffish Harrington's is gone, and the fish restaurants negotiated barnlike new structures for themselves along the waterfront that are today corporate-owned and considered strictly for tourists. Of all the Southwest churches, only one remains from the past: St. Dominic's, a rusticated stone Roman Catholic edifice whose green-shingled steeple rises bravely above the glass and concrete. The area's other churches were rebuilt in the airport-hangar style of Fifties religious buildings. One of the vaunted features of the development was supposed to be brand-new low-income housing, but relatively few units were built. Though constructed in the most enlightened mode of their era — row houses — the public housing went the way of most housing projects, turning into another slum within a few years.

A new elementary school was set up as one of the nation's first magnet schools, a model of integrated, high-quality education. A desegregation lawsuit ended its magnet status, and all families with school-age children who could afford to fled Southwest. Here and there are a few attractive features: a cluster of houseboats on the Potomac where some Washingtonians live year-round and a tatty open-air fish market that somehow escaped demolition and is now one of the city's liveliest spots.

"The waterfront was butchered; it's a horror, and the whole area is totally barren at night," says sculptor Theodore Fields, a longtime Washington resident. "The city had too much power, and it used it." The area contrasts dramatically with Capitol Hill, another run-down district of row houses, small stores and churches. Starting in the late Sixties, the area was gradually regentrified, entirely by private owners, and it is now one of Washington's most fashionable neighborhoods, all without losing a shred of its architectural integrity.

The Southwest debacle has parallels in many other areas. One was Los Angeles's Bunker Hill section. Unlike Southwest Washington, this downtown neighborhood of once-elegant Victorian houses could not have been called a slum; it was merely shabby. Here is how Raymond Chandler described it: "You could find anything there from down-at-the-heels ex-Greenwich-villagers to crooks on the lam, from ladies of anybody's evening to County Relief clients brawling with haggard landladies in grand old houses with scrolled porches, parquetry floors and immense sweeping bannisters of white oak, mahogany and Circassian walnut." The hill even had its own funicular railroad called the Angels' Flight. It is not hard to imagine that it would have been eventually regentrified by private owners, as has an adjacent turn-of-the-century neighborhood, Angeleno Heights.

Starting in the late Fifties, Bunker Hill was bulldozed with the help of Title 1 funds, to be replaced with residential high rises (none of which has been an economic success) and office and civic buildings. Boston's West End met the same fate, and the city's North End was supposed to be next to go, when city officials finally decided it would be wrong to tear down that colorful Italian neighborhood. Books like Thursz's appeared, delineating the grief and sense of dislocation poor people feel when wrenched from their neighborhoods.

During the Seventies, there was a good deal of retrenching and rethinking on urban redevelopment. Giant public housing projects, the kind Mumford liked, were abandoned when it became apparent that tenants felt stigmatized living there, and elevators, walkways and hallways became centers of crime. The 1972 demolition of the award-winning 1955 Pruitt-Igoe project in St. Louis was a milestone in this trend. The Department of Housing and Urban Development was marked by funding-corruption scandals — typically involving cozy relationships with builders — that prefigured this year's $2 billion contretemps.

The demise of bulldozer-style urban renewal did not mean the end of ways for governments to go on subsidizing land development projects that theoretically improved the appearance of cities. California pioneered a device called tax increment financing that has been widely copied. In such a system, the redevelopment agency has the authority to issue tax-exempt bonds to pay for a project — effectively, a low-interest loan to the developer. On the parcel in question, two tax valuations are calculated, one (called the frozen valuation) on what the property was worth before the development, the other at its current value.

The taxes on that difference go to pay off the bonds and other projects, such as low-income housing, that the redevelopment agency cares to fund. And because the bonds in California are not secured by general treasury revenues, they need no voter approval, putting the whole project outside voter scrutiny. The tax increment system has been criticized because of the likelihood that at least some of the increased value can be traced to other factors besides the redevelopment. Increment-financed projects tend to starve local tax rolls, meaning reduced revenues for other city services, critics say. Increment financing has gone to pay for industrial parks and for downtown shopping malls designed to compete with suburban malls — often with disastrous results for the life of the city. A blank-walled, fortresslike shopping center adds nothing to the vitality of a downtown, charge critics, and residents sometimes go to the suburbs for shopping anyway, leaving the inner-city mall to flounder.

The increment system, ensuring huge revenue increases for the redevelopment agencies whenever property values go up, is so popular that most localities now use federal block grants only for public buildings and other structures that cannot go onto the tax rolls. Government-subsidized projects keep alive a whole segment of the development industry. Atlanta architect John Portman's development firm is part of that industry. Many of the monumental "trademark" Seventies-era Portman hotels found in almost every major city that feature stadium-sized atria festooned with hanging philodendrons are there because a local government helped pay for them. The Rouse Co., famous for its festive port and downtown revitalization projects (Underground Atlanta, which reopened July 15, is the latest of these), is another company that lives mostly off the government.

Trying to compete with the suburban malls has been the kiss of death for many cities. A 1969 book by Bernard Rudofsky, "Streets for People," touted the narrow lanes, paseos and pedestrian-only plazas that give many European cities their charm. If ideas have consequences, poorly understood ideas have disastrous consequences. Many a U.S. city tried to turn its fading Main Street into Perugia by shutting it off to automobile traffic and installing dozens of oversize brass street lamps. Cities did not realize that pedestrian-only streets work well abroad because people live on them and they abound with sidewalk cafes and pushcart vendors. Blocked-off U.S. streets tended to kill what was left of downtown retail business because people missed the hum and honks of automobiles and they felt cut off from the rest of life.

The Le Corbusier-Mumford philosophic axis has also proved an urban bane. The loveliest product of the International style is the bronze-on-bronze Seagram building on New York's Park Avenue. Designed with Philip Johnson by Ludwig Mies van der Rohe in 1958 and sitting gracefully in the middle of a little plaza with a fountain in front whose ledge was ideal for sitting and people-watching, it draws the varie-

An Iconoclast from the Sixties Enters the Mainstream

It was 1961, the height of the bulldozer era of urban renewal, when every U.S. city scrambled to turn itself into Le Corbusier's Radiant City. The received wisdom among the most advanced minds in urban planning was this formula: Take an aging inner-city neighborhood, raze it and replace it with orderly rows of gleaming high rises in a neatly manicured green park. Jane Jacobs, then an instructor at New York's New School for Social Research and a mother raising three children in Greenwich Village, wrote "The Death and Life of Great American Cities."

The book was iconoclastic, to say the least. To Jacobs, those clean, symmetrical and spacious renewal projects so beloved of planners had "all the attributes of a well-kept, dignified cemetery." To her, the life of a city neighborhood was its density, diversity and human scale, its mix of new and old buildings, its hum and bustle of dozens of enterprises, its seemingly incompatible but actually quite orderly melange of residences, stores, churches, industries, restaurants and schools.

She called that the "fine-grained texture" of a city, where there is always something new to see and there are plenty of people for people-watching. Jacobs loved the crowded, busy streets in ethnic neighborhoods like Boston's North End and Chicago's Back of the Yards that planners regarded as archaic throwbacks to a dying and unhealthy way of life. No bank would then lend money to fix up the row houses of the North End, which were slated for demolition on Boston's master plan; since then, planning theories have changed and the North End has become chic and regentrified. The curse of cities, Jacobs wrote, was the "great blight of dullness."

To counter that, she favored a mixture of building heights, plenty of street-level activity, a variety of architectural styles, short city blocks over long ones, small parks over large ones and an intermixing of commercial and residential uses of property. On busy streets, no matter how poor the neighborhood, crime is always lower than on empty ones, she observed. "A city cannot be a work of art," she wrote. Jane Jacobs discovered a secret about people: that as long as they have enough personal privacy, they love living and working densely crowded together.

The centerpiece of the book was her rhapsodic description of her own neighborhood, Hudson Street in the West Village, where she, her architect-husband and their children lived over a defunct candy store. The Fifties were a golden age for Greenwich Village, then a lively mix of Italian families who had lived in the area's walk-ups for generations, Bohemians who liked the cheap rents and cafes and the upper-middle-class denizens of town houses dating from the Greenwich Village of Washington Irving and Henry James. Hudson Street, when Jane Jacobs lived there, bustled with taverns, restaurants, a bakery, a delicatessen, a locksmith, a drugstore, a cigar store, a butcher shop, a barbershop, a tailor shop, a fruit stand and a pizza stand. Longshoremen from the nearby docks ate lunch and drank beer on Hudson Street. It was filled with children from the neighborhood's public school and two parochial schools (one Roman Catholic, one Episcopal); they played on the sidewalks in the late afternoon. There was always something going on; Jacobs called it "the daily ballet of Hudson Street."

When the book appeared, its ideas were mostly ridiculed. Roger Starr, then head of New York's housing agency and now a member of The New York Times editorial board, wrote a widely circulated article, "Adventures in Mooritania," criticizing Jane Jacobs as a sentimentalist. The title was a reference to Grace Moore, an opera star of the Thirties who made a number of movie musicals. "There would always be a scene where she would arrive in some urban neighborhood and burst into song," says Starr. "Suddenly people would stick their heads out of the windows and start singing. A truck driver would come onto the scene and burst into song. It's sentimental nonsense, the ballet of the sidewalks and the truck drivers keeping an eye on the kids. It doesn't deal with the problem of people who can't afford to live in the Village. I like high density, but there's a limit."

For nearly two decades, urban planners ignored Jacobs. They continued to design and build high rises in parks for living quarters, high rises on pillars for offices and blank-walled monolithic complexes for shopping centers, even in the heart of cities. The great blight of dullness spread through the land. Jacobs had a huge readership among young people, however. It is likely that her book was at least partly responsible for the urban regentrification movement of the Seventies and Eighties, in which thousands of young professionals decided that old city centers were much more interesting places to live than new suburbs.

Lately, however, her ideas have come into their own. Two new books — William H. Whyte's "City: Rediscovering the Center" (Doubleday, 1988) and Roberta Brandes Gratz's "The Living City" (Simon & Schuster, 1989) — are explicitly in the Jacobs mold. Whyte urges developers to quit building blank walls at street level — a trend of the past three decades — and restore the vitality of city streets as places where people can stroll, schmooze, window-shop and sit. Gratz says governments ought to get out of urban redevelopment altogether and concentrate on helping inner-city residents bring their neighborhoods back to life through rehabilitation.

gated crowds that make urban life endlessly interesting. In 1961 New York revamped its 1916 zoning ordinance, a simple affair whose height and air limits were responsible for the city's many wedding-cake-shaped Art Deco apartment buildings and skinny skyscrapers like the Chrysler and Empire State buildings.

The new law allowed bulkier buildings, but it also offered what are called incentive bonuses that allowed developers to add more floors than the height limits permitted — in effect, a subsidy — in return for Seagram-like plazas. The result: Every new office building in New York came with a plaza. The problems: The oversize structures were not so nice as the Seagram building and they all looked alike. The worst

excess was the west side of Sixth Avenue, once an interesting row of little coffee shops, Irish bars and delicatessens. During the Sixties and Seventies, due to the bonuses, it turned into a monotonous row of hulking Mies-on-the-cheap high rises.

Nonetheless, Sixth Avenue is not such a bad place to be these days. The office buildings are just as homely, but the trees in many of the plazas have grown tall, and the ledges in front draw the sitters, the lunch-eaters and the people-watchers. Pushcarts, some legal, some not, hawking every sort of food from hot dogs to shish kebab, and street vendors of books, earrings, Islamic literature and incense dot the avenue. The 47th Street diamond district is nearby, mingling Hasidic Jews in black

coats with the shirt-and-tie crowd from several publishing houses along Sixth Avenue and ethnics of every variety. "It's the revenge of the streets," says urbanologist William H. Whyte, whose 1988 book, "City: Rediscovering the Center," hectors against blank walls at street level, big empty spaces, inward-facing buildings and other leftovers from Radiant City theory.

The heavy hand of the recent past, and even of the present, is hard to fight. For the past three decades, the chief nightmare of cities has been abandonment — that businesses, residents, retail customers and, worst of all, developers would just light out for the suburbs and beyond. This has made it easy for developers to "bribe" city officials via campaign contributions (a California court recently ruled that Los Angeles City Council members were not illegally influenced in a land use decision by contributions because every single member got a donation). But even more prevalent has been reverse bribery: subsidies and tax breaks of every sort for developers.

In 1982 New York again revamped its zoning law to cut back on wheeling-and-dealing, plaza-and-atrium trade-offs, downzone some areas such as the Upper East Side and set standards that allow developers to build without negotiating first as long as they are willing to stay within strict limits. But "land in New York is so heavily taxed that if you want to build something, you have to take the government as a senior partner; you have to make a deal," says urbanologist William Tucker.

Most current Washington redevelopment is at a discount, via tax abatements and write-downs on city land sales. One new Washington office and shopping complex was assessed no taxes last year even though it was open for business; a legal loophole regards a building as not completed if its roof is not finished.

Some cities will put anything a developer wants in their downtowns, just to get the new buildings and the business they are expected to bring. Big, self-contained megastructures such as the Portman-designed Detroit Renaissance Center have been favorites, although the urban fortresses have turned out to do nothing to bring life back to inner cities. In 1978, during New York's darkest financial hours, a desperate Mayor Edward I. Koch made a deal with Portman to build a hotel in Times Square in an effort to help clean up that porn-shop-afflicted area. The agreement included about $100 million worth of government sweeteners for Portman: a $21.5 million federal urban development action grant under a 1977 law that hands out money for projects involving some private investment; 10 years' worth of low-interest loans, a $33 million tax abatement, a $15 million sales tax exemption for construction products, and seven rent-free years on land acquired via eminent domain

Some architects now work to give their urban projects a dense and textured urban feel. New York's new Battery Park City development along the Hudson River works in many of Whyte's ideas, with a variety of building styles, street-level stores, urban-style street grids and numerous benches, miniparks and sidewalk cafes.

"You don't want to compete with the suburban malls," says Sanford Nelson, whose Washington firm, Cooper, Carry & Associates, designed the new Underground Atlanta, which retains some of the old existing commercial buildings, has street-level stores and a crowded, multilayered feel. Deliberately omitted is the "anchor store," the dominating department store branch that makes a mall a mall. In Boca Raton, Fla., Nelson's firm has designed a new open-air downtown for the city, replacing a hastily and poorly built enclosed shopping mall the city constructed in its heart when competition from a suburban center started to drain business away. The new downtown will have shops at street level, apartments and condominiums above, all in the style of the famous and flamboyant Palm Beach architect Addison Mizner. "It will all be designed so that it blends in with the rest of Boca Raton," says Nelson. "There is more of a sense now of how architecture can be the cultural glue that binds the generations together."

Jane Jacobs, now 73 and still writing (her most recent book, "Cities and the Wealth of Nations: Principles of Economic Life," appeared in 1984), lives in Toronto. It is the city that most architects and fans of urban life agree is the most civilized in North America — walkable, lively and architecturally interesting. Except for a few public housing projects that are "as awful as anywhere," says the writer, successful citizen resistance dissuaded the government from pursuing Radiant City-style re-

development projects. "There were a lot of disastrous ideas planned during the early Seventies when American cities were making their mistakes," she says. Other things that helped save Toronto: no federal highway project to carve up the city with expressways and no redlining of older neighborhoods by banks, she says.

Sad to say, a trip to New York's Hudson Street on a summer afternoon 28 years after Jacobs's book reveals a rather melancholy and diminished version of her ballet of the sidewalks, although Greenwich Village is still New York's most popular and crowded district. The street was declared blighted and slated for demolition in 1962, says Jacobs. This failed to happen, and rents began to rise steeply, due undoubtedly to the city's chronic housing shortage.

The neighborhood has lost quite a bit of its heterogeneity. The docks and longshoremen are, of course, a thing of the past, gone the way of all shipping on the Hudson River. Gone too are most of the small businesses her book describes. Of them, only the drugstore remains. Most of the commercial establishments are restaurants or antique shops (the former candy store in Jacobs's building is an antique store). The street is now too expensive for families, the children have vanished, except for one lone boy sitting on a stoop. The Episcopal school, St. Luke's, is still in business, although the Catholic school, St. Veronica's, is gone. Christopher Street, long the center of New York's homosexual community, bisects Hudson and turns it for a few blocks into a gay ghetto where a (heterosexual) female stroller feels out of place.

"That's what happens in a city where you have only a few viable neighborhoods," says Jacobs of the changes that have made Hudson Street more homogeneous, less interesting, less urban in the best sense of the word. "The supply is so small that some uses start to crowd out others."

Many people are starved for genuine urban life. Regentrification is likely to be the dominant development mode of the Nineties.

by the New York State Urban Development Corp., plus reduced rent after that.

Portman also got to pick the site he wanted, which also happened to be the site of four historic Broadway theaters, of which two, the Helen Hayes and the Morosco, were known for perfect acoustics and lush, classic theater design. Preservationists and an array of actors ranging from Charlton Heston on the political right to Susan Sarandon on the left battled for four years to save the theaters. Both won temporary landmark status from the U.S. Interior Department, but the presidentially appointed Advisory Council on Historic Preservation approved the demolition. In 1982 the theaters went down, and in 1985, Portman's 48-story Marriott Marquis Hotel opened. By this time, the Portman highrise atrium concept, which seemed fun in the early Seventies, looked tired and dated.

Landmark designation, like so many land use issues, is basically a political question. Two historic theaters could not be saved. Washington's concrete Convention Center is built over the ruins of Victorian residences whose landmark status was overruled by a mayoral decree that the center would serve the public interest. Yet neighbors recently secured provisional landmark status (since rescinded) as a "cultural institution" for a Los Angeles car wash from the 1950s. Observ-ers say the problem is few governments are willing to pay for historic designations or to give tax concessions to owners. Land use battles can turn conservatives into socialists, liberals into free market enthusiasts. "If private industry had just given itself the responsibility for dealing with Times Square redevelopment from the beginning, this wouldn't have happened," says Barbara Handman, a community board member for the area who helped spearhead the fight against the Portman project.

Fortunately, localities have learned a lot from 40 years of urban development mistakes. New York's new Battery Park City, built on publicly created landfill next to the Hudson River, is filled with architectural variety, street-level stores, a street grid that matches the rest of Lower Manhattan and genuine city-style sidewalks, sidewalk cafes, miniparks, benches, whimsical sculptures and a lengthy, popular esplanade with a breathtaking view of the Statue of Liberty, Staten Island and New Jersey. The condominium and apartment buildings started out Radiant City in design in the early Eighties but lately have moved toward real city. It is not perfect; it tends to be a "thirtysomething" age-and-income ghetto for Wall Street professionals, and too much of it is physically cut off from the rest of Lower Manhattan by an expressway. "It's like a suburb in a city," says a youthful female resident; sad to say, it is.

Rouse redevelopment projects, with their emphasis on small nonchain shops, some as tiny as pushcarts that rent for a couple of hundred dollars a month, and a bountiful variety of food and merchandise offerings (Boston's Quincy Market, New York's South Street Seaport and Baltimore's Harborplace), also have a pleasant, bustling flavor that draws crowds. A midweek visit to the brand-new Underground Atlanta reveals the place to be packed with people, in contrast to the rest of that city's sagging, underpopulated downtown.

Underground Atlanta, an indoor-outdoor revival of a below-the-railroad jazz district that succumbed to drug traffic and vacant storefronts during the early Eighties, is not perfect, either. Washington architect Sanford Nelson tried to bind a new multilevel mall with existing street-level retail structures, but with little else on the street outside, shop owners have already closed off their street-level doors to the public, making it mostly pure shopping center. There is not enough outdoor eating. In fact, not enough eating, period. A few too many chain stores: Oh, no, not another Ann Taylor, Eddie Bauer and Victoria's Secret. And Rouse projects themselves, for all their charm, are starting to look alike.

These are all faults that can be corrected, though. The burgeoning crowds reveal an Atlanta public that is starved for real urban life, and the Underground crowds are already starting to spill out onto this tired end of Peachtree Street. In fact, many people are starved for genuine urban life. Regentrification is likely to be the dominant development mode of the Nineties, with city after city coming back. "When a man is tired of London he is tired of life," said Samuel Johnson. The reign of the Radiant City may at last be over.

— *Charlotte Low Allen in Atlanta, New York and Washington*

DEMOGRAPHIC DOOMSAYERS
FIVE MYTHS ABOUT POPULATION

ROGER L. CONNER

Mr. Conner is a guest scholar at the Brookings Institution.

For the last five years a small but influential band of futurists have been wringing their hands in public about U.S. population trends. Made up primarily of writers, led by Ben Wattenberg, and economists, Julian Simon and Clark Reynolds among others, this group foresees an imminent—and threatening—decline in the size of the U.S. population. "There is a no-growth future ahead," Wattenberg warned in a recent column, "leading to a demographic deficit" that portends larger "budget deficits and future Social Security shortfalls," not to mention a collapse in America's "geopolitical and cultural influence."

Such high stakes call forth grand proposals. In the *Birth Dearth*, Wattenberg suggested that the federal government could avert these disasters by paying parents $2,000 a year for each child under age 16; the price tag would be $110 billion or so—unless the plan worked, in which case the bill would be higher still. Reynolds has called for a massive, European-style guest-worker program, even though every European country with such a program has canceled it after experiencing major problems. Simon's solution is to increase permanent legal immigration to a million a year, from its current level of about 625,000.

Ideas for major new spending programs do not get far in Washington these days, and the Wattenberg baby bonuses have been no exception. But immigration levels can be raised without an appropriation, and the fear of population decline is being used as a rationale for the largest increases in the history of U.S. immigration law. One bill passed in the Senate this summer, others are pending in the House. Combined with current law, these could push immigration to more than six million over the next five years alone.

While there are many sound arguments on both sides of the immigration debate, the demo-doom rhetoric is more fear than fact. Though new to American ears, it dates back to the 1870s, when French intellectuals called low birth rates "race suicide" and proclaimed *Finis Galliae*. By the 1930s demographers throughout the Western world had taken up the alarm, gloomily proclaiming that Western societies would soon disappear. Before policymakers buy the latest iteration of this demo-doom scenario, they would do well to consider five myths that frequently cloud clear thinking on population and America's future.

MYTH 1

The United States faces imminent population decline unless we increase immigration or births. Actually, the population of the United States is not shrinking; it is growing faster than any of the world's other developed countries. The National Center for Health Statistics reports 3.9 million births and 2.2 million deaths in 1988. Accepting the Census Bureau's very conservative estimate of 600,000 annual net immigrants (legal *and* illegal), the population is expanding by 2.3 million people a year.

Although the demo-doomsayers make it seem that decline is around the corner, when pressed they concede that what really concerns them is the size of the population 30 years and more from now. According to Wattenberg, under the "most likely" scenario the population will grow from its current level of 248 million to 300 million about 2020. It will stabilize at that level until 2050 and then return to 260 million or so by 2080. It is to avert the adverse consequences they associate with this scenario that moves the demo-doomsayers to insist that policymakers act now.

From *Current*, February 1990, pp. 21-25. From "Answering the Demo-Doomsayers," by Roger L. Conner, *The Brookings Review*, Fall 1989, pp. 35-39. Copyright © 1989 by The Brookings Review.

Even if government leaders were to assume that population stabilization or gradual decline would be bad, patience is called for. Long-range demographic projections have historically been off by huge margins. In 1944, for example, the Ben Wattenberg of his day, Dr. Frank Notestein, predicted that the combined population of the United States and Canada would be only 176 million in 1980 and called for government policies to promote larger families to avert a dismal future. Fortunately policymakers did not heed his warnings. Notestein was only off by 70 million or so. It is error of this magnitude, repeated over and over again, that makes trained demographers leery of treating long-range projections as certainties on which current policy should be based.

INACCURACY   Harvard's Dr. Nathan Keyfitz, one of the grand old men of American demography, recently compared past population projections with what actually happened. He found that "relatively short term forecasts, say up to ten to twenty years, do tell us something, but beyond a quarter century or so we simply do not know what the population will be."

Keyfitz argues that demographers are no better today than in the past at predicting the key variable in the population equation: how many children women will choose to have. Tiny errors in fertility assumptions are compounded over time, producing massive errors in projections that run beyond a decade or so. "We know virtually nothing about the population fifty years from now," Keyfitz concludes. "We could not risk better than two to one odds on any range narrower than 285 million to 380 million for the year 2030."

Recent experience suggests that it would be quite easy to expand immigration in 30 or 40 years if the demo-doomsayers' fears are realized. The reverse is not so simple. An immigrant stream inevitably creates a potent coalition of employers who want to keep a convenient labor supply coming, recent arrivals who want to bring friends and relatives, church leaders who identify with the aspirations of their new members, and civil libertarians who automatically assume that any restrictive law is motivated by ethnic or racial animus. And if today's level of illegal immigrants is any indication, once immigration flows are under way, more people, tempted by reports from friends of life in the United States, might ignore or evade any immigration restrictions that are imposed in the future.

Managing the possibility of future population decline with expanded immigration is like managing possible future recessions by creating entitlements, tempting in the short run and very difficult to reverse in the long run.

It follows that if the U.S. population does not decline as the demo-doomsayers expect,

the consequences they worry about are unlikely to occur either. Let us assume for the sake of argument, however, that their population forecasts are correct and go on to examine whether the anticipated consequences are as adverse as they fear.

MYTH 2

Immigration is needed to help "solve the Social Security problem." In one recent essay, Wattenberg predicted a shortfall in the Social Security fund if population growth stops after 2020. Increased immigration is the best solution, he argued, because the immigrants will be paying taxes "when the baby-boomers start retiring."

This is the wrong "solution" to the wrong "problem." Thanks to recent increases in tax rates, the Social Security trust fund is generating an annual surplus of $55 billion, which will grow to $150 billion a year by 1994 and continue for the foreseeable future.

What about 2020 and beyond? A recent Brookings study, *Can America Afford to Grow Old?*, argues persuasively that even if the demo-doom demographic projections turn out to be correct, fears that the retirement of the baby-boom generation will bankrupt the system are overblown. With only modest increases in productivity, the study found, Social Security revenues and benefits will be in balance, without increasing tax rates, well beyond the middle of the next century.

To put it another way, if the workers of the future are more productive and, perforce, more highly paid, they can comfortably generate the revenues needed to support an increasing number of retirees. Future productivity, in turn, will depend on increasing savings, decreasing government deficits, improving labor-management relations, and a host of other factors. There is no evidence that increased immigration will help resolve these central problems. Indeed, immigration has been at historic highs during the past 15 years, a period during which productivity growth has slumped and government deficits expanded.

Henry Aaron, co-author of the Brookings study, puts this all in perspective: "My wife and I do not decide on whether to adopt a child based on the possibility that my income will grow so slowly that I will need support from my children when I grow old. Rather I try to save enough so that I will accumulate enough to live on. That is my advice for funding future Social Security obligations. Then I can decide about whether to adopt a child for the important reason—do I want a larger family?"

The immigration "solution," in fact, could worsen any long-term problem with financing the system. Adults who immigrate today will retire while the baby boomers are still alive and drawing Social Security. How many more immigrants will be needed to finance their retirement?

In addition, the government's future liability to immigrants who are entitled to receive Social Security benefits after having made minimum payments should give pause to those who see them as a long-term asset to the system. Most immigrants work and pay Social Security taxes but for fewer years than natives. Some arrive in mid-career; up to 30 percent return home before retirement. But virtually all of them will receive benefits. In 1983 the General Accounting Office studied 194,000 non-citizen Social Security recipients. They had, on average, worked 10.5 years of Social Security-covered employment, compared with 20.5 for all recipients, and had four times as many dependents as the overall beneficiary population.

The demo-doomsayers are correct that immigrants paying into Social Security now will add to the retirement fund's surplus in the short term, but this contribution proves to be less than imagined. Families with taxable incomes below $19,000 receive an earned income credit. For families with income below $10,000, the credit exceeds their Social Security taxes; those with incomes between $10,000 and $19,000 receive a partial reimbursement. A Census Bureau study found that as of 1980, more than half of all immigrants who had arrived between 1970 and 1979 had incomes low enough to qualify for the tax credit.

Finally, even if there were a clear tax benefit at the federal level, there are offsetting costs at the state and local level that federal policymakers should take into account. Immigrants tend to concentrate in rapidly growing urban areas where the demand for publicly financed schools, health care, and housing exceeds supply. The Urban Institute, for example, found that in California, services for the average family of Mexican origin resulted in a net cost to state and local taxpayers of $2,245 a year. Even though few of these families received welfare, their incomes were too low to generate enough taxes to cover the cost of these services.

MYTH 3

A slowdown in population growth will harm the economy by creating a "customer shortage." The demo-doomsayers are also concerned that a slowdown in the rate of growth of the population will mean slackening in consumer demand, a "customer shortage." Here, they make the fundamental error of equating numbers with purchasing power. Switzerland, with a population of 6.2 million, and Norway, with 4.9 million people, are better markets than Nigeria, even though its population is 111.9 million.

They also make much of the anticipated rise in the median age of the population, which is now 33. It is true that a more mature population will buy a different mix of products; 40-year-olds will listen to more '60s releases and less hard rock. A more mature work force will also have proportionately fewer 20-year-olds and more experienced 45-year-olds in prime working years, with fewer dependent children as well as more dependent aged.

It is pessimistic in the extreme to fear that American companies cannot adjust to such changes in the marketplace. The median age rose more than twice as fast in the last 20 years as it will in the next 20, even accepting the worst demo-doom scenario. What does it matter to the economy if Johnson & Johnson features adults instead of babies in its commercials for shampoo and powder?

There is a special irony when such fears emanate from scholars associated with the Heritage Foundation (Simon) and the American Enterprise Institute (Wattenberg) and from *Forbes* magazine. These are the same places from which objections to government regulations are routinely issued on the grounds that the market can adapt, even when it comes to events—like international competition or leveraged buyouts—that hit with greater force and less warning than demographic changes.

MYTH 4

Population growth has no significant impact on pollution, natural resources, or the quality of life. For years ecologists have been preaching that a larger population would put dangerous pressure on natural resources. Demo-doom convert Malcolm S. Forbes, Jr., recently called for legal immigration of 1.5 million a year to avoid a slowdown in population growth. Forbes complained that "we have been overly influenced by nonsensical notions that more people mean more pollution." After all, he said, "man invents technology that can reduce pollution overall."

Forbes and his colleagues seem to have something approaching a mystical faith in the power of technology to bail us out of any environmental problems that arise from the increase in human numbers. A look at Los Angeles might begin to shake that faith. Despite the best pollution controls technology provides, the air in the Los Angeles region violates the clean air act's health standards more than 100 days a year. That is because reductions in the pollutants each car emits have been overwhelmed by the increased numbers of people driving.

The Environmental Protection Agency has concluded that the only way to provide safe air to the people in Los Angeles is to restrict people's right to drive and to invest heavily in mass transit and vehicles powered by alternative fuels. Contemplating such costs, most Los Angelenos probably agree with humorist Andy Rooney. "I haven't noticed that bigger is better anywhere but in basketball," Rooney recently admonished the demo-doomsayers. "Our little town has doubled since we moved here 35 years ago, and I still like it, but it isn't twice as good since it got twice as big, I can tell you."

Overcrowding and unrelenting traffic congestion are only the tip of the iceberg. Irreversible ecological changes brought on by the needs of an expanding population are far more serious. The exhaustion of groundwater supplies, destruction of agricultural land, erosion of topsoil, loss of wilderness and natural areas, filled-in wetlands, and diminished wildlife habitat are only part of the list. There are also costs that cannot be measured in dollars, as when regular, intimate contact with untamed nature is an experience reserved increasingly for the well-to-do.

Serious people see these losses as trade-offs to be weighed against other social values that immigration unarguably provides. The demo-doomsayers simply dismiss them as unworthy of concern.

MYTH 5

A decline in the population coupled with the aging of the population means a labor shortage that will harm the economy unless immigration is increased. There is no evidence of a general labor shortage in the United States today. More than six million workers are unemployed. As economist Robert Kuttner points out, this official figure takes no account of more than six million workers who are discouraged from seeking jobs, more than five million who are involuntarily working part-time, and more than one million who hold temporary jobs.

To be sure, there are spot shortages, particularly in areas with exceptionally high housing costs and in certain specialized skill categories, but immigration is a very blunt tool for meeting such needs. The majority of immigrants admitted to fill specific jobs go to work elsewhere within a short time, according to a study funded by the Labor Department. Some apparently exaggerate their qualifications and cannot do the job for which they were selected; some move to other jobs or locations. Talented immigrants obviously contribute to the country and to the economy just as talented natives do. But we should not expect to solve specific labor shortages through immigration unless we are willing to shackle immigrants to the bench or reinstate indentured servitude.

The demo-doomsayers are content to make a broader point. They argue that skills aside, unless immigration is increased, the labor market as a whole will continue to tighten over the next few years.

So what if it does tighten further? The market will respond. The real question is what the pattern of adjustment will look like. Who will win, and who will lose? Some employers will be forced to offer higher wages and improved working conditions, especially in those sectors where immigrants cluster. Other employers will change their attitude toward workers they now disdain because of age, sex, disability, or race. Managers and entrepreneurs will have an incentive to use this more expensive labor force more productively. Some of the sweatshops will move to Mexico or Jamaica, taking the jobs to the people instead of bringing the people to the jobs. *ADJUSTMENT*

It is this dynamic capacity for adjustment that explains why past predictions of labor shortages have not come to pass. It also explains why some employers are so enthusiastic about the demo-doom argument: population growth from increased immigration offers relief from market processes that would otherwise raise wages and working conditions.

To rephrase the earlier question, will a tighter labor market and consequent relative rise in the incomes of workers—especially the lower-skilled who compete with immigrants—be a good or bad policy outcome? Where you stand often depends on where you sit. Jay F. Rochlin, the director of the President's Committee on Employment of People with Disabilities, is cheered by the prospect of a tighter labor market. "Demographics have given us a 20-year window of opportunity" for millions of Americans with disabilities" he observes. Low-skilled workers would benefit, not only from higher wages but also from the improved schools, churches, and public services they could support. Immigrants who have been here only a short time would benefit most, as they compete most directly with newcomers. A tighter labor market would dismay business owners who have benefited from lower wages or cheaper immigrant labor in the past, though entrepreneurs in sectors or regions without access to this labor supply would see it differently.

Recent shifts in income distribution have consistently favored higher-skilled and professional workers over their fellow citizens who work at lower-skilled service and production jobs. It is well known that real per capita income was relatively flat in the United States between 1973 and 1986; it is less often realized that lower-skilled workers sustained a market decline in wages. Between 1973 and 1986, for example, 20- to 29-year-old males with high school degrees who did not attend college suffered a 25 percent decline in real income on average; for working male high school dropouts, it was 38 percent. This development provides a strong argument on grounds of equity that the government should not step in with immigration to interrupt market forces that might, for once, operate in favor of society's less advantaged.

In summary, it would be a mistake to change immigration policy now on the basis of a projection that the U.S. population will stabilize between 2020 and 2050, then decline very slightly over the next 30 years. Even if such projections turn out to be right, there is no reason for alarm.

It is, after all, a biological and physical fact that the population of the earth cannot grow indefinitely. By logical inference, every country in the world must ultimately pass through the transition that so frightens the demo-doomsayers—from growth to stabilization, with fluctuations thereafter. How ironic if the United States, which has spent the post–World War II era preaching the virtues of reduced population growth to the developing world, should react in panic at the prospect of stabilizing its own.

THE PACE OF
LIFE

Most cities where people walk, talk and work
the fastest also have the highest rates of heart disease.
But what do the exceptions tell us?

ROBERT LEVINE

Robert Levine, Ph.D., is a professor of psychology at California State University, Fresno.

" 'Will you walk a little faster?'
> said a whiting to a snail.
'There's a porpoise close behind us,
> and he's treading on my tail.' "

If you live in a city where people keep treading on you, are you more likely to have heart trouble? Our research says yes, generally speaking — though other factors of culture and personality play a big part in determining individual susceptibility to life in the fast lane.

Our research team — graduate students Karen Lynch, Kuni Miyake, Marty Lucia and six other volunteers — recently measured the tempo of life in 36 American cities of various sizes in all parts of the country to answer two questions: 1) How does the overall pace compare from one city and region to another? 2) Is there any relation between an area's pace of life and its residents' physical condition — specifically the prevalence of coronary heart disease (CHD)?

What makes these questions especially interesting right now is the continuing controversy between researchers who think that a strong sense of time urgency — the classic Type A struggle to make every second count — is an important element in CHD, and those who believe a combination of anger and hostility is the only Type A characteristic that really causes heart disease.

We studied three large (more than 1.8 million people), three medium-sized (850,000–1.5 million) and three smaller (350,000–550,000) cities in each of the four census-defined areas of the United States — Northeast, Midwest, South and West. In each, we looked at how fast people walked, talked and worked. (See "Measuring a City's Pace" for more details about the study.)

The Speedy Northeast
As the chart on page 47 indicates, the three fastest cities and seven of the fastest nine are in the Northeast. Northeasterners generally walk faster, give change faster, talk faster and are more likely to wear watches than people in other areas.

MEASURING A CITY'S PACE

To see if there is any relationship between a city's characteristic pace and its rate of CHD, we looked at four indicators.

Walking speed: We clocked how long it took pedestrians to move 60 feet along relatively uncrowded streets. To eliminate the effects of socializing, we timed only people walking alone. We also excluded children, pedestrians with large packages or obvious physical handicaps, and window shoppers.

Working speed: We timed how long bank clerks took either to give change, in set denominations, for two $20 bills or to give us two $20 bills in return for change.

Talking speed: In each city we tape-recorded how long it took postal clerks to explain the difference between regular mail, certified mail and insured mail. We then calculated their actual "articulation" rates by dividing the number of syllables in the response by the total time it took.

The watch factor: As a simple measure of concern with clock time, we counted the percentage of men and women who were wearing wristwatches.

Individually, each of these measures has its weaknesses: They all tap into special groups, not the city's general population; the second two are confounded by skill and efficiency; and the last is affected by fashion as well as concern with time. Taken together, though, they sample a wide range of people and activities and reflect many facets of a city's pace of life.

Finally, we created an index of the overall pace of life in each city by giving the four scores equal weight and adding them together. The chart below shows how the cities ranked, from 1st to 36th, in each category. —R.L.

Fast Cities, Slow Cities: How They Rank

	Overall Pace	Walking Speed	Bank Speed	Talking Speed	Watches Worn	CHD*
BOSTON, MA	1	2	6	6	2	10
BUFFALO, NY	2	5	7	15	4	2
NEW YORK, NY	3	11	11	28	1	1
SALT LAKE CITY, UT	4	4	16	12	11	31
COLUMBUS, OH	5	22	17	1	19	26
WORCESTER, MA	6	9	22	6	6	4
PROVIDENCE, RI	7	7	9	9	19	3
SPRINGFIELD, MA	8	1	15	20	22	7
ROCHESTER, NY	9	20	2	26	7	14
KANSAS CITY, MO	10	6	3	15	32	21
ST. LOUIS, MO	11	15	20	9	15	8
HOUSTON, TX	12	10	8	21	19	36
PATERSON, NJ	13	17	4	11	31	4
BAKERSFIELD, CA	14	28	13	5	17	20
ATLANTA, GA	15	3	27	2	36	33
DETROIT, MI	16	21	12	34	2	11
YOUNGSTOWN, OH	17	13	18	3	30	6
INDIANAPOLIS, IN	18	18	23	8	24	22
CHICAGO, IL	19	12	31	3	27	13
PHILADELPHIA, PA	20	30	5	22	11	16
LOUISVILLE, KY	21	16	21	29	15	18
CANTON, OH	22	23	14	26	15	9
KNOXVILLE, TN	23	25	24	30	11	17
SAN FRANCISCO, CA	24	19	35	26	5	27
CHATTANOOGA, TN	25	35	1	32	24	12
DALLAS, TX	26	26	28	15	28	32
OXNARD, CA	27	30	30	23	7	34
NASHVILLE, TN	28	8	26	24	33	14
SAN DIEGO, CA	29	27	34	18	9	24
EAST LANSING, MI	30	14	33	12	34	29
FRESNO, CA	31	36	25	17	19	25
MEMPHIS, TN	32	34	10	19	34	30
SAN JOSE, CA	33	29	29	30	22	35
SHREVEPORT, LA	34	32	19	33	28	19
SACRAMENTO, CA	35	33	32	36	26	23
LOS ANGELES, CA	36	24	36	35	13	28

Lower numbers indicate faster speeds, more watches worn, higher CHD rates.   *Rates of coronary heart disease, adjusted for the median age in each city.

1. URBANIZATION

Boston edges out Buffalo for first place, trailed by New York City, everyone's prestudy favorite. Perhaps New Yorkers lose a couple of steps stopping to watch the local festivities. Walter Murphy, who collected the walking-speed data there, reported an improvised music concert, an attempted purse snatching, and an unsuccessful mugging during the hour and a half he clocked pedestrians on one corner.

The West has the slowest pace overall, due mostly to particularly slow walkers and bank tellers. Least hurried of all is America's symbol of sun, fun and laid-back living. Los Angelenos are 24th in walking speed, next to last in rapid speech and far, far behind people in every other city we studied in money-counting speed. Their only concession to the clock is to wear one — the city is 13th highest in watches worn.

The stopwatches we used weren't all that told us the West lives time differently from the East. We often learned as much from the process of data collection as from the data. To get the exact time of day in No. 1-ranked Boston, for example, we dialed "N-E-R-V-O-U-S." In my home town of Fresno (31st in time urgency), the number is "P-O-P-C-O-R-N."

Walking and Talking

There usually isn't much difference between one rank and the next. But at the extremes, people march to very different drummers. In walking speed, for example, the fastest pedestrians — in Springfield, MA — cover 60 feet in an average of 11.1 seconds, 3.6 seconds faster than they do in Fresno, the slowest town. If they were walking a football field, the Massachusetts team would move the full 100 yards and cross the goal line at about the same time their California opponents were still about 25 yards short.

Differences in talking speed are even greater. The fastest-talking postal clerks — in Columbus, OH — rattle out nearly 40% more syllables per second than their colleagues in Los Angeles (3.9 compared to 2.8). If they were reading the 6 o'clock news, it would take the California workers until nearly 7:25 to report what the Ohio clerks finish at 7.

With these pace figures in hand, we compared them with rates of death from CHD in each city to see if there is any association between the two. Since age is a major factor in heart disease, we statistically adjusted the CHD figures for the median age of each city's population.

The Pace of Death

Pace of life and CHD were highly related, as a whole, for both cities and regions. In fact, this statistical relationship was even stronger than the correlation researchers usually find between heart disease and Type A personality measures such as hostility, aggression and competitiveness. The speed of a person's environment seems to predict the likelihood of heart disease as well as Type A personality test scores do. This turned out to be true no matter how we corrected for age, or whether we took it into account at all.

Why are people in Type A (fast-paced) environments more likely to get heart disease? Largely, we suspect, it's because these environments attract Type A people — who then do their best to keep the pace fast. Social psychologist Timothy Smith of the University of Utah and his colleagues have shown that Type As both seek and create time-urgent surroundings. Thus the fastest cities in our study may represent both their dearest dreams and their creations.

Smith found that time pressure also initiates, maintains and

PACE OF LIFE AROUND THE WORLD

The combination of hard work and an urgent sense of time doesn't have to be lethal. This became clear several years ago when Ellen Wolff, Kathy Bartlett and I surveyed three indicators of the pace of life in 12 large and medium-sized cities in England, Indonesia, Italy, Japan, Taiwan and the United States. (See "Social Time: The Heartbeat of Culture," in the March 1985 issue of *Psychology Today*.)

The Japanese led on every measure — they walked the fastest, their postal clerks took the least time to sell us stamps and their public clocks were the most accurate. To our surprise, however, they had by far the lowest CHD death rates of the four countries for which we had statistics (there were none available for Taiwan or Indonesia). Japan's CHD mortality rates, in fact, were the lowest among the 27 industrialized countries compared in a recent report released by the World Health Organization.

How does a fast-charging Type A population avoid CHD? Cultural values appear to be one key. Researchers Michael Marmot and Leonard Syme found that Japanese-American men who did not have a traditional Japanese upbringing were 2 to 2.7 times more likely to have CHD than those who had been raised traditionally. This still held true even when all of the usual CHD risk factors — diet, smoking, cholesterol, blood pressure, triglycerides, obesity, glucose and age — were taken into account.

The Type A personality scale includes a series of questions about being hard-driving — competitive, short-tempered, impatient — as well as a series about being hard-working. For people in the United States, high scores on the first set of questions usually go hand-in-hand with high scores on the second — both are part of the same behavior pattern.

But in Japan, where social harmony may be the most highly respected social value, competition and aggression have little place. When Japanese take the Type A personality scale, being hard-driving has little to do with being hard-working.

Even translating the "hard-driving" Type A items is a problem. One frustrated researcher found that the best Japanese translation for the question "Do you like competition on your job?" was "Do you like impoliteness on your job?"

Competitive hostility and anger, it appears, play little part in the hard-working pace of the Japanese. In our own culture, though, there is often a fine line between speed/time urgency on the one hand and competition/hostility on the other — and the combination can be life-threatening. —R.L.

exacerbates Type A-like behavior in Type Bs. They act more like As, while As strive to push the beat even faster — all in an environment already filled with coronary-prone personalities.

Stress and Smoking

On the physiological side, University of Oklahoma psychologist Logan Wright and other researchers have found that stress leads to an increase in the blood levels of adrenaline, noradrenaline and other hormones that can damage the lining of arteries. This ties in with new research from Duke University Medical Center showing that personality affects how individuals with high cholesterol react to stressful tasks. Under stress, the Duke researchers found, levels of cortisol, adrenaline and noradrenaline shot up rapidly in Type As. In Type Bs, the same hormones went down or stayed the same.

For Type As with high cholesterol, then, this response to stress may make an unhealthy situation worse. While cholesterol is at work clogging arteries, the stress chemicals are damaging their inner linings. Research has also shown that adrenaline may prevent cells from clearing harmful cholesterol out of the blood. Instead, it collects on artery walls.

In Type Bs, by contrast, the body seems to lower its chemical response to stress, reducing the harm high cholesterol can do, and the likelihood that Type Bs will develop CHD.

Recent statistics from the U.S. Department of Health and Human Services (HHS) points to another possible tie between a fast pace and CHD — cigarette smoking, which has been identified as the single most important preventable cause of heart disease. The HHS figures show that smoking rates follow the same regional patterns as our figures for coronary heart disease and the pace of life: Smoking and CHD rates are high-est where the pace is fastest, in the Northeast, followed by the Midwest, the South and the West.

Support for this link comes from a city that deviates sharply from the usual relationship between pace and CHD. Salt Lake City, with its predominately Mormon population, is the 4th highest American city in pace of life but 31st (6th from the lowest) in CHD. The Mormon religion strongly encourages hard work but strictly prohibits smoking — an example of a cultural norm that buffers between fast pace and heart disease (see "Pace of Life Around the World" for another).

Finding the Right Pace

On the whole, then, we found that people living in fast-paced, Type A cities are more prone to CHD than those in slower cities — logical enough, since Type A cities attract Type A individuals, who research shows are more likely to have heart attacks. But time pressure isn't always stressful and damaging. Researchers like Jonathan Freedman and Donald Edwards of the University of Toronto have demonstrated that it also can be challenging and energizing. How much pressure is stressful depends on the person.

So, for individuals, the relationship between pace of life, personality and CHD isn't a simple one. Just as Type A settings may be stressful to Type Bs, Type As may experience distress when their surroundings are too relaxed for their tastes. The key is knowing one's limits and preferences. A good fit between our inner and outer worlds is a better predictor of health than any mailing address.

"Time," writes Joyce Carol Oates in her novel *Marya: A Life,* "is the element in which we exist . . . . We are either borne along by it or drowned in it." Synchronizing rhythms to your surroundings, be they your city, your neighborhood, your job, your friends or your lover, is integral to your well-being.

Urban Experiences

Social scientists who study the urban community agree that a wide variety of life-styles and life experiences exists in society. This has been observed in every unit from neighborhoods to entire cities. Ethnic and religious communities exist in which the traditional values and behaviors are mixed with the new patterns of urban life. Slums, and all that is implied by the term, present still another set of life experiences. Suburbs, once conceived of as the refuge of the wealthy and upwardly mobile, have become as diverse as the central city. There are poor suburban communities, ethnic suburbs, and suburbs that are nearly or totally occupied by black Americans. In summary, there are nearly as many possible experiences as there are groups to provide those experiences.

One characteristic of urbanization is that the rate of change is increased. The swiftness with which change takes place allows entire communities to alter their populations within a single decade. For example, many suburbs immediately surrounding the central city are dominated by a particular ethnic group through the invasion-succession process, only to be replaced by another group a few years later.

How individuals respond to urbanization is also a concern of the social scientists. Some people enjoy the pace and dynamics of crowded cities; others respond much more negatively to the city and grow to hate it. Some find happiness in the city; others experience tragedy and alienation. Some ethnic groups find despair in the changes while others adjust rapidly and even become agents for change.

Another task for the social scientist is describing, comparing, and analyzing the similarities and differences between the many urban contexts. The goal of this section is to explore the dynamic social interactions that have an impact upon and, in large measure, direct the urban experience. The first article by David Morris explores the breakdown of community life, revealing how rootlessness affects both the economy and quality of life. The following selection explains the unholy alliance between Louisiana's petrochemical polluters and the state's political establishment. The next article, Bernard Frieden and Lynne Sagalyn's "Downtown Malls and the City Agenda," analyzes the public-private relationship in terms of downtown development, asking the question about who was helped or hurt by many of these projects. Michael Evans's article, which follows next, describes how several "new towns" are grappling with the problem of development in the wake of rapid growth, deteriorating infrastructure, and inadequate housing. The next three selections discuss life in suburbia, focusing on several major problems including those of beautification, privatization, urban sprawl, economic revitalization, environmental degradation, and racial polarization. This is followed by a discussion of the baby boom generation, many of whom bemoan the lack of community and feelings of loneliness that plague many American suburbs.

Looking Ahead: Challenge Questions

Why do suburbs find it so difficult to promote community loyalty? Is it possible to rekindle a sense of community?

Is it inevitable that in difficult economic times many states and municipalities will trade environmental quality for economic gain? Why, or why not?

Does the civic agenda for downtown development benefit the affluent and privileged or the average citizen? Is public-private cooperation necessarily bad for the community and its residents?

What lessons, if any, should be learned from the "Garden Cities" of the past? To what extent are they relevant in the development of new cities and towns?

Have suburbs, as is often charged, made cities superfluous? Do suburbs represent the future of urban America?

What explains the rapid rise of the urban village? What special problems do they present to local governments?

How do megacounties differ from cities and suburbs? Do these communities represent a positive development?

Is the process of urban sprawl inevitable? If so, will it serve to further isolate people and institutions?

How will service-industry restructurings, down-sizings, and the closing of many expensive facilities affect the short- and long-term futures of the suburbs and central cities?

What explains the present attraction of neighborhoods in transition? Is the new urban dweller an asset or a liability to these old, mixed neighborhoods?

In what ways do suburbs create loneliness and isolation? Why is this phenomenon on the rise?

Unit 2

Rootlessness undermines our economy as well as the quality of our lives

DAVID MORRIS/*SPECIAL TO* UTNE READER

David Morris, a frequent Utne Reader *contributor, is director of the Washington-based Institute for Local Self-Reliance. He is an editorial columnist for the* St. Paul Pioneer Press-Dispatch *and co-author (with Karl Hess) of* Neighborhood Power: The New Localism *(1975, Beacon Press).*

Americans are a rootless people. Each year one in six of us changes residences; one in four changes jobs. We see nothing troubling in these statistics. For most of us, they merely reflect the restless energy that made America great. A nation of immigrants, unsurprisingly, celebrates those willing to pick up stakes and move on: the frontiersman, the cowboy, the entrepreneur, the corporate raider.

Rootedness has never been a goal of public policy in the United States. In the 1950s and 1960s local governments bulldozed hundreds of inner city neighborhoods, all in the name of urban renewal. In the 1960s and 1970s court-ordered busing forced tens of thousands of children to abandon their neighborhood schools, all in the interest of racial harmony. In the 1980s a wave of hostile takeovers shuffled hundreds of billions of dollars of corporate assets, all in the pursuit of economic efficiency.

Hundreds of thousands of informal gathering spots that once nurtured community across the country have disappeared. The soda fountain and lunch counter are gone. The branch library is an endangered species. Even the number of neighborhood taverns is declining. In the 1940s, 90 percent of beer and spirits was consumed in public places. Today only 30 percent is.

This privatization of American public life is most apparent to overseas visitors. "After four years here, I still feel more of a foreigner than in any other place in the world I have been," one well-traveled woman told Ray Oldenburg, the author of the marvelous new book about public gathering spots, *The Great Good Place* (1990, Paragon House). "There is no contact between the various households, we rarely see the neighbors and certainly do not know any of them."

The woman contrasts this with her life in Europe. "In Luxembourg, however, we would frequently stroll down to one of the local cafés in the evening and there pass a very congenial few hours in the company of the local fireman, dentist, bank employee, or whoever happened to be there at the time."

In most American cities, zoning laws prohibit mix-

The breakdown of community life may explain why the three best-selling drugs in America treat stress.

ing commerce and residence. The result is an overreliance on the car. Oldenburg cites the experience of a couple who had lived in a small house in Vienna and a large one in Los Angeles: "In Los Angeles we are hesitant to leave our sheltered home in order to visit friends or to participate in cultural or entertainment events because every such outing involves a major investment of time and nervous strain in driving long distances. In Vienna everything, opera, theaters, shops, cafés, are within easy walking distance."

Shallow roots weaken our ties in the neighborhood and workplace. The average blue-collar worker receives only seven days' notice before losing his or her job, only two days, when not backed by a union. The *Whole Earth Review* unthinkingly echoes this lack of connectedness when it advises its readers to "first visit an electronics store near you and get familiar with the features—then compare price and shop mail order via [an] 800 number."

This lack of connectedness breeds a costly instability in American life. In business, when owners have no loyalty to workers, workers have no loyalty to owners. Quality of work suffers. Visiting Japanese management specialists point to our labor turnover rate as a key factor in our relative economic decline. In the pivotal electronics industry, for example, our turnover rate is four times that of Japan's.

American employers respond to declining sales and profit margins by cutting what they regard as their most expendable resource: employees. In Japan, corporate accounting systems consider labor a fixed asset. Japanese companies spend enormous amounts of money training workers. "They view that training as an investment, and they don't want to let the investment slip away," Martin K. Starr of Columbia University recently told *Business Week*. Twenty percent of the work force, the core workers in major industrial companies, have lifetime job security in Japan.

Rootlessness in the neighborhood also costs us dearly. Neighborliness saves money, a fact we often overlook because the transactions of strong, rooted neighborhoods take place outside of the money economy.

• Neighborliness reduces crime. People watch the streets where children play and know who the strangers are.

• Neighborliness saves energy. In the late 1970s Portland, Oregon, discovered it could save 5 percent of its energy consumption simply by reviving the corner grocery store. No longer would residents in need of a carton of milk or a loaf of bread have to drive to a shopping mall.

• Neighborliness lowers the cost of health care. "It is cruel and unusual punishment to send someone to a nursing home when they are not sick," says Dick Ladd, head of Oregon's Senior Services. But when we don't know our neighbors we can't rely on them. Society picks up the tab. In 1987 home-based care cost $230 a month in Oregon compared to $962 per month for nursing home care.

Psychoanalyst and author Erich Fromm saw a direct correlation between the decline in the number of neighborhood bartenders and the rise in the number of psychiatrists. "Sometimes you want to go where everybody knows your name," goes the apt refrain of the popular TV show *Cheers*. Once you poured out your troubles over a nickel beer to someone who knew you and your family. And if you got drunk, well, you could walk home. Now you drive cross town and pay $100 an hour to a stranger for emotional relief.

The breakdown of community life may explain, in part, why the three best-selling drugs in America treat stress: ulcer medication (Tagamet), hypertension (Inderal), tranquilizer (Valium).

American society has evolved into a cultural environment where it is ever harder for deep roots to take hold. What can we do to change this?

• **Rebuild walking communities.** Teach urban planners that overdependence on transportation is a sign of failure in a social system. Impose the true costs of the car on its owners. Recent studies indicate that to do so would raise the cost of gasoline by as much as $2 a gallon. Recently Stockholm declared war on cars by imposing a $50 a month fee for car owners, promising to increase the fee until the city was given back to pedestrians and mass transit.

A nation of immigrants celebrates those willing to pick up stakes and move.

• **Equip every neighborhood with a library, a coffeehouse, a diversified shopping district, and a park.**

• **Make rootedness a goal of public policy.** In the 1970s a Vermont land use law, for example, required an economic component to environmental impact statements. In at least one case, a suburban shopping mall was denied approval because it would undermine existing city businesses. In Berkeley, citizens voted two to one to permit commercial rent control in neighborhoods whose independently owned businesses were threatened by gentrification.

• **Reward stability and continuity.** Today, if a government seizes property it pays the owner the market price. Identical homes have identical value, even if one is home to a third-generation family, while the other is occupied by a new tenant. Why not pay a premium, say 50 percent above the current market price, for every 10 years the occupant has lived there? Forty years of residence would be rewarded with compensation four times greater than the market price. The increment above the market price should go not to the owner but to the occupant, if the two are not the same. By favoring occupants over owners, this policy not only rewards neighborliness, but promotes social justice. By raising the overall costs of dislocation, it also discourages development that undermines rootedness.

• **Prohibit hostile takeovers.** Japanese, German, and Swedish corporations are among the most competitive and innovative in the world. But in these countries hostile takeovers are considered unethical business practices or are outlawed entirely.

• **Encourage local and employee ownership.** Protecting existing management is not the answer if that management is not locally rooted. Very few cities have an ongoing economic campaign to promote local ownership despite the obvious advantages to the community. Employee ownership exists in some form in more than 5,000 U.S. companies, but in only a handful is that ownership significant.

• **And above all, correct our history books.** America did not become a wealthy nation because of rootlessness, but in spite of it. A multitude of natural resources across an expansive continent and the arrival of tens of millions of skilled immigrants furnished us enormous advantages. We could overlook the high social costs of rootlessness. This is no longer true.

Instability is not the price we must pay for progress. Loyalty, in the plant and the neighborhood, does not stifle innovation. These are lessons we've ignored too long. More rooted cultures such as Japan and Germany are now out-competing us in the marketplace, and in the neighborhood. We would do well to learn the value of community.

Good-Bye, Good Hope

An entire community disappeared, thanks to policies that subsidize giant petrochemical polluters.

Zack Nauth

Zack Nauth, a former reporter for the New Orleans Times-Picayune, *is director of the Louisiana Coalition for Tax Justice.*

NEW ORLEANS, LA. —Charles Andrews was a newlywed in 1932 when he bought a house for $2,000 in Good Hope, a tiny French Catholic enclave on a bend of the Mississippi River. He knew everyone in town, and together they watched their children and grandchildren grow up and settle down in the quiet community.

A half century later, Andrews and his neighbors lost their homes — not to a hurricane or flood, but to the voracious appetite of GHR Company, the Good Hope Refinery.

"The first security I had, they took it away from me. That's the way I figure it," said Andrews, 77, who now lives miles from his closest friends. "I got some neighbors living around here now. I don't know too much about them."

Charles Robicheaux and his family lived in another of Good Hope's 130 homes, about 25 miles upriver from New Orleans. They had gotten so used to being evacuated because of the frequent fires and explosions at the refinery that they kept packed suitcases next to their beds. One year their Christmas dinner burned in the oven and toys were sprayed with oil during a fire and forced evacuation.

A few hundred feet from their home, towering flares turned night into day and filled the air with smoke. Toxic runoff floated in the ditches and ran into the surrounding marshland where many residents hunted and fished.

Despite the danger, Robicheaux loved Good Hope's close-knit community, and he joined his neighbors in a bitter fight to block GHR's expansion plans that would force everyone to leave. It was a losing battle. GHR had a habit of getting what it wanted.

Already the nation's largest independent refinery, GHR was processing 250,000 barrels of high-sulfur crude oil worth $6 million in sales each day. It employed hundreds of workers, paid $500,000 in taxes to the parish, and plied elected officials from the courthouse to the statehouse with jobs for their families, contracts for their businesses, and generous contributions for their political campaigns.

One year, GHR violated its water pollution permit 311 times; the state finally took action when the company dumped five tons of phenol, a caustic poison, into the Mississippi River. Facing a possible $7.9 million fine, GHR's attorney sent a letter to state officials warning, "An injudicious exercise of judgment resolving this matter by the Environmental Control Commission could fatally affect the re-

finery, its operations and employees."

The state decided on a $260,000 fine. That same year, GHR boasted a $50 million profit.

Hungry for more, the company broke the Oil, Chemical and Atomic Workers union at the plant and relied on an ever-changing lineup of transient workers whose lack of skill and stake in the surrounding communities led to more disasters. As the refinery's daily operations wore down local resistance, GHR pressed parish officials to rezone Good Hope so the refinery could expand. The company reminded officials that an earlier decision to move its corporate headquarters to the parish was based on a "pledge to assist us in any way possible to assure the most profitable operations here."

On a September night in 1980, 500 residents from Good Hope and nearby towns packed the council chambers. Over their protests, the council decided Good Hope was standing in the way of progress: The entire town and all its people would have to move to make way for the refinery.

Most of the residents got enough money for their homes to buy brand new houses on another street in another town. But the money didn't make up for the loss of friendships, the loss of their way of life.

But the ultimate indignity was yet to come. Less than a year after the pain of uprooting and relocating, GHR closed its Good Hope refinery. It remains closed to this day, a rusting monument to short-term corporate and political priorities.

"It makes you feel an emptiness after all we went through for all these years," said Charles Robicheaux. "For what? It's just a letdown to see that all the houses are gone and the industry too."

Robicheaux pointed to his new residence. "This is my house," he said. "My home is in Good Hope."

CANCER ALLEY

The destruction of Good Hope is not an isolated incident in Louisiana. Rather, it stands as a metaphor for the dashed hopes and devastated habitats left by the state's economic development policies.

Perhaps the ultimate symbol of how distorted the policy has become happened four years after the Good Hope Refinery shut down: the Louisiana Board of Commerce and Industry gave GHR local property tax breaks worth $40 million — even though the company provided no jobs and even though it still owed the state $90,000 in air pollution fines. GHR made more than $1 billion from what flowed from the earth at Good Hope, but gave only a tiny part back to the residents. The Earth itself got even less respect.

The roots of this policy are deep. Since Louisiana was colonized by France, England, and Spain, its natural resources have been exploited by outsiders and compliant local officials. Northerners and Europeans, using slave and cheap black labor, grew and exported sugar cane and cotton. Then came the timber companies from the East and Midwest to strip the hardwood forests and cypress swamps. In the latest round, giant petrochemical firms have sucked 12 billion barrels of oil and 113 trillion cubic feet of natural gas from the ground, turning much of it into bulk chemicals and plastics for cars, clothes, and home conveniences.

The results of this reliance on the petrochemical industry have been devastating:

▼ According to data from the Environmental Protection Agency, Louisiana ranks first nationally in the per capita levels of toxic chemicals spewed into the air — 31 pounds per person or 138 million pounds total.

▼ Of the 25 counties with the most toxics released into the air, land and water, more are in Louisiana than any other state.

▼ Three of the six most toxic facilities in the nation are located here — American Cynamid, Shell Oil Co. and Kaiser Aluminum.

▼ Another EPA study shows that Louisiana is home to 13 of the 32 plants where the cancer risk from breathing a single chemical is 100 times the acceptable level. The plants where the risk was estimated to be 1-in-100 or 1-in-1,000 included the big names in American industry: DuPont, Exxon, Shell, Dow, Copolymer, Union Carbide, Formose, Firestone, BASF, Vulcan, Occidental, and Crown Zellerbach.

▼ Every day, 21 Louisiana residents die of cancer and 41 new cases are diagnosed — rates well above the national average. Not surprisingly, the parishes located along the Mississippi River's "Chemical Corridor," where most of the plants sit, rank in the top 10 percent in lung cancer deaths in the United States, giving the region its nickname, "Cancer Alley."

▼ Other studies show that people who work in the state's petrochemical and paper pulp industries, or who drink from water supplies fed by the Mississippi (like New Orleans residents), all have significantly higher death rates from cancer. A state task force estimates the disease and its treatment costs Louisiana $176 million each year.

The problems have gotten so bad that industry itself is feeling the bite. Ozone levels in Baton Rouge are so high that plants are forbidden to expand unless they reduce their emissions, and two new chemical plants were recently prohibited from building altogether.

With the damage so widespread, it's fashionable these days to say that Louisiana sold its environmental soul to the petrochemical industry in exchange for jobs and prosperity. Les Ann Kirkland, president of the Alliance Against Waste and Action to Restore the Environment, disagrees.

"That's bullshit," Kirkland says. "They didn't tell us what the price was. You didn't know what was at stake until it was too late."

"A TRAGIC LEGACY"

The hidden cost of the lax regulation of the petrochemical industry mounts each time there's a discovery of a contaminated drinking supply, ruined tract of wetland, or leaking storage tank. In Louisiana, those discoveries come almost daily.

About five miles from Good Hope, close to a public school, a highway construction crew recently found themselves in the middle of an abandoned oil refinery that had been closed in the '50s. The site turned out to be loaded with high levels of asbestos, heavy metals, and toxic chemicals. Construction of another highway in north Louisiana was also stopped by an abandoned site.

In Bossier City, residents of an apartment complex smelled strange fumes in their homes. They eventually discovered that the complex was built on top of another abandoned waste site. The state has about 500 such sites. The cleanup costs are unknown.

Just east of Good Hope is Bayou Trepagnier, its bottom thick with wastes from 60 years of refining and chemical production at the Shell complex next door to GHR. Shell's wastewater treatment plant is still allowed to discharge hundreds of pounds of toxins into the productive marshland each year. Cleanup of the bayou has not yet begun.

Throughout the state's wetlands — the most productive renewable natural resource — are tens of thousands of oilfield waste pits, filled with chromium, benzene, and radioactive wastes. By an act of Congress, they are called "non-hazardous waste sites" and are therefore exempt from federal monitoring standards. Louisiana has more of these sites — some 200,000 — than any other state.

The Congressional reclassification of these sites in 1980 saved the petrochemical industry millions of dollars. Its chief sponsors included powerful Louisiana Senator J. Bennett Johnston. The result is what the New Orleans *Times-Picayune* called "a tragic legacy, an environmental nightmare of appalling dimensions" that threatens underground water supplies and estuaries that produce one-fourth of the nation's seafood catch.

BIG BREAKS

Louisiana's economic dependence on petrochemicals — and its inability to clean up the mess left by the industry — dates back to the tax policy of Huey Long, the Depression-era governor who gained national attention for his bold promises to "Share the Wealth" of corporate America. His popular program depended heavily on an increase in the severance tax on oil production to pay for new roads, school books, state hospitals, and old-age pensions.

As the oil business boomed, so did the state treasury. Even in good times, the cozy arrangement made lawmakers and regulators reluctant to bite the hand that fed them. But when the industry went bust in the early 1980s, everyone suffered.

This July, Louisiana faces a $700 million deficit. State-supported hospitals have cut back services, and have refused to deliver babies in some locations. Unemployment, which continues to top national levels, long ago depleted state reserve funds.

With basic human services cut to the bone, there's little left for the environment. The total state budget for regulating hazardous wastes was $3 million in 1986, less than a fourth what New Jersey spends for problems caused largely by a petrochemical industry about the same size as Louisiana's.

Louisiana's revenue problems are compounded by the fact that its historic reliance on the severance tax was offset by massive property tax subsidies. In the midst of its current crisis, the state has continued to pursue an industrial policy that gives business and industry about $500 million a year in tax breaks. The biggest breaks go to the petrochemical industry, which is allowed to write off $200 million a year in local property taxes.

The result: The state is subsidizing the very corporations that are destroying its natural resources and sending its citizens to the hospital with cancer. Not only does state policy encourage pollution that leaves huge cleanup bills, it also grants tax breaks that make it impossible for state and local governments to pay the bills.

"The companies have given us environmental problems, and we have paid for them through these exemptions," said Carl Crowe of the state AFL-CIO. "Environmental problems left behind by bankrupt companies are cleaned up with taxpayer dollars."

The South as a whole has often used "tax incentives" to attract industry, and studies show that Louisiana outranks its neighbors in granting corporate concessions. Yet many studies also question whether the tax breaks actually work, citing evidence that companies simply play state against state in a bidding war to cut themselves the best deal.

"None of the overall tax requirements in any of the states varied sufficiently to change operating costs more than .2 percent," wrote James Cobb in his study of industrial development, *The Selling of the South*. "Competitive tax cutting or ex-

emptions negated the advantages any particular locale might have had in attracting new industry."

The real reason industries came to Louisiana, Cobb found, was for its cheap oil and natural gas, its access to markets via the Mississippi River, and its cheap, unorganized labor. "One of the reasons for the South's success is that developing nations like Germany and Japan decided to export their heavy, polluting industries," Cobb said. "Foreign investors appreciated not only the South's cheap labor and low taxes but also its apparent ability to absorb industries that produced large amounts of wastes and contaminants."

Louisiana has paid dearly for these deals. A study by Oliver Houck, an environmental law professor at Tulane University, found that two-thirds of the industrial tax breaks granted in 1984 — about $14 million — went to companies that had violated environmental laws.

"We are simply underwriting pollution and significant health risks," Houck said. "Even though the permit levels are permissive, you still have a high violation rate. Local governments are being forced to sacrifice schools so that industry can locate there and pollute them."

According to Houck, violators are receiving tax breaks that are about 10 times greater than the potential fines they face. Placid Oil was fined $625,000 for 310 violations in 1982, but recouped several times that amount in local tax breaks.

What economic benefits do the citizens of Louisiana reap from these tax breaks to industry? The study by Houck showed that petrochemical companies receive 80 percent of all industrial tax exemptions but create only 15 percent of all permanent jobs.

A study set for release this spring by Louisiana Coalition for Tax Justice found that tax breaks often exceed the wages paid new permanent employees—and that many companies receive tax breaks for projects that create no permanent jobs. On average, the study found, local governments pay a subsidy of $100,000 for every permanent job created.

Average citizens not only foot the bill for the subsidies to industry, they also pay higher taxes to make up for the lost revenue. Louisiana officials have repeatedly raised excise and sales taxes on items like food and drugs—a tax which hits the poor the hardest.

TOXICS MARCH

The deadly state of the environment has started to anger many citizens who feel that state industrial policy is shaped less by visionary, long-term thinking than

THE GREEN RANK: LOUISIANA

How Louisiana ranks among the 50 states:

Toxic chemical pollution	50
Cancer causing facilities	49
Carbon emissions	46
Pesticide use	36
Premature deaths	47
People without insurance	47
Public health spending	43
Occupational deaths	36
Unemployment rate	50
Environmental voting record	47

it is by the demands of the existing business power structure in Louisiana. Lax regulation and outright corruption have unleashed a backlash of citizen revolt — often spontaneous and haphazard, but sometimes effective in challenging the petrochemical industry. About 25 grassroots environmental groups have banded together under the banner of the Louisiana Environmental Action Network, uniting workers, tenants, and civil rights activists across the state.

In Geismar, where chemical giant BASF locked out 300 workers for over five years, the Oil, Chemical, and Atomic Workers Local put the company on trial for its environmental and safety record. The union spearheaded a coalition that included community and environmental groups, broadening the attack against the German-based corporation. The campaign worked, and workers won their jobs back earlier this year.

Last year, with the help of the Sierra Club, Greenpeace, and the National Toxics Campaign, citizens organized the state's first-ever Toxic March from the Superfund site in Baton Rouge, down the "cancer alley" of chemical firms along the Mississippi River to New Orleans.

People's outrage began to reach elected representatives. Bills were passed mandating that toxic air emissions be cut in half, taxes on hazardous waste be increased, and municipalities recycle 25 percent of their solid wastes. Funding for the state environmental department was doubled. The regulatory realm also responded, approving tougher rules for hazardous waste injection wells and water quality standards — over the objection of the state's most powerful oil, chemical, and business lobbyists.

But while much has changed, much remains the same. Industry sued to block the injection rules and had them temporarily suspended. The air toxics bill named no specific chemicals, leaving that to the drawn-out regulatory process. The state Commerce Board still refuses to take the environment or any other factors into account before granting millions of dollars in tax breaks. Louisiana industries continue to legally emit millions of pounds of known disease-causing chemicals into the environment.

Organizers are planning a second Toxics March to coincide with Earth Day, vowing to keep up the pressure on elected officials. The fight for a healthy environment goes on, but many citizens caught up in the struggle say they will never be the same.

Camille Weiner moved out of her home in Good Hope when the GHR refinery expanded a decade ago. Today she lives in a new town.

"The neighbors are nice and everything, but it's not like Good Hope," she says. "It'll never be like Good Hope."

Downtown Malls and the City Agenda

Bernard J. Frieden
Lynne B. Sagalyn

Bernard J. Frieden is Ford Professor of Urban Development in the Department of Urban Studies and Planning at the Massachusetts Institute of Technology. He is the author or editor of eight books and more than 50 articles on housing and city development. He has served as Chairman of the Faculty at M.I.T. and as director of the M.I.T.-Harvard Joint Center for Urban Studies. His most recent book, written with Lynne Sagalyn, is Downtown, Inc.: How America Rebuilds Cities, *from which this article is extracted.*

Lynne B. Sagalyn is an Associate Professor in the Department of Urban Studies and Planning at the Massachusetts Institute of Technology. A specialist in real estate finance, Sagalyn has been conducting research on deal-making in city development. In addition to Downtown, Inc., *she has written about issues of housing finance, real estate investment, discrimination in urban housing markets, and exclusionary land-use controls.*

A shopping mall, new office towers, a convention center, an atrium hotel, a restored historic neighborhood. These are the civic agenda for downtown development in the last third of the twentieth century, a trophy collection that mayors want. Add a domed stadium, aquarium, or cleaned-up waterfront to suit the circumstances, and you have the essential equipment for a first-class American city.

The showpieces on this list are useful as well as trendy. They help a city keep up with its competitors while also meeting some local need such as getting rid of an eyesore, saving a landmark, or creating a civic symbol. Although the projects rarely result from systematic forethought, they often fit together surprisingly well. Most serve a common function: restoring downtown as a center of economic activity.

Baltimore illustrates the way a retail center links into a chain of projects spanning the decades. Its new downtown became an instant success with the opening of the Harborplace shops in 1980, but that success was 30 years in the making. Shoreline improvements around the Inner Harbor – a new bulkhead, a landfill, marina, piers, public parks, and promenades – date from a bond issue voted in 1948. Other projects that remade the core of Baltimore in stages include the 33-acre Charles Center office complex built in the 1960s; the Maryland Science Center, World Trade Center, and Convention Center in the 1970s; and the National Aquarium and Hyatt Regency Hotel that opened within a year after Harborplace. This was a costly series of projects, with the public sector bill along totalling more than $200 million. And although each has its special history, they feed off each other.

The downtown agenda was more than a grab-bag of pet projects because of the steady interest of elected officials and business executives in strengthening the downtown economy. Business coalitions especially had a large stake in revitalizing the city center, and their support was unusually crucial for launching any large project. In deciding which projects to push, they usually threw their weight behind those that served an economic development purpose.

The dozens of downtown retail centers built after 1970 were part of this total agenda, adding a fresh acrobatic act to a three-ring circus in the making. They thrilled the crowds, but their long-run impact at the box office is hard to separate from the rest of the show.

Corporate Territory

What are the collective functions of the downtown projects that cities worked so hard to build? To the extent that cities had a strategy, it was to make downtown efficient for business firms and attractive to visitors and middle-class residents. Critics called this thrust the corporate-center strategy. Richard Child Hill studied Detroit, pinned this label on its recent development priorities, and argued that the same logic has been shaping most large American cities: "Overall investment priorities are to transform this aging industrial city into the modern corporate image: a financial, administrative, and professional services center... a research and development site for new growth industries... an emphasis upon recommercialization rather than reindustrialization; and an orientation toward luxury consumption that is appealing to young corporate managers, educated professionals, convention goers, and the tourist trade."

Many elements of the new downtowns fall into place as part of the contemporary office economy. The office buildings deliver space for company headquarters and for corporate services ranging from law firms and consultants to copy shops and lunch counters. Downtown hotels and restaurants take care of business visitors. The convention center brings trade shows and industry meetings, producing more patrons for hotels, theaters, and shopping malls. Some of the executives and professionals want to live in the city and can afford to renovate interesting old houses; once settled in town, they help support theaters, museums, and retail shops.

The rebuilding of downtown changed the kind of work people could find there. Deindustrialization came to the cities long before the country at large worried about the loss of manufacturing. Office doors were opening for the educated while industrial lofts and warehouses were closing their doors on blue-collar workers. Jobs created by the office economy raised questions about who would benefit from the new downtown. Hill argued that "for Detroit's less advantaged workers, the Renaissance means trading a former possibility for blue-collar jobs at decent wages for the future probability of scarce, low-paying, dead-end service work." He envisioned the Detroit Renaissance as "a Golden Arch surrounded by deteriorating and impoverished workers' neighborhoods."

Hill and other critics raised valid questions, but when they faulted city government for rebuilding downtown inappropriately they failed to recognize how few options the mayors had. When big cities made their first plans to rescue downtown, economic and technological changes were already destroying their industrial base. In the early 1950s, manufacturing dominated the city economy, supplying more jobs than services, wholesaling, and retailing combined. By the mid-1950s, industrialists were racing to the suburbs, and downtown manufacturing started its long decline.

There was little the cities could do to hold on to industry. Assembly-line production cut short the useful life of their cramped multistory factories. Long, low industrial plants were better suited to the new technologies for handling materials. Also, as trucking replaced railroad freight, manufacturers wanted sites with good highway access. The suburbs had plenty of land for horizontal building layouts, off-street loading docks, and parking for workers. In the cities, assembling large enough sites for industry meant buying small parcels and then tearing down existing buildings. Comparable sites were likely to cost 20 to 30 times more in a city than in a suburb.

The civic leaders and public officials who drew up renewal plans in the 1950s did not consider manufacturing important for the downtown of the future. Still, many cities did use some of their renewal money to clear land for industry. They discovered that the process was slow, costly, and unproductive. Economist Raymond Vernon concluded as early as 1962 that city efforts and subsidies were "not swift enough or flexible enough or generous enough to match the offerings of private land on the outskirts." Nearly 20 years later, another researcher looked back at the efforts cities had made and confirmed Vernon's judgment: the long lead time needed to get the site, the restrictions city governments imposed on new development, and their inexperience at marketing land contributed to a poor track record. Manufacturers had failed to turn up, and cities ended by selling the land for warehouses or service businesses.

Manufacturers had solid business reasons for moving to the suburbs, reasons city officials were powerless to change. If there was no practical way to keep manufacturing in town, the mayors had to figure out what sort of economic activity could take its place. Saving downtown was so far removed from traditional city functions – paving streets, managing parks, policing neighborhoods – that most mayors hardly knew where to begin. When they saw possibilities for promoting individual projects, they were ready to try almost anything. If the rebuilding of downtown gave too much emphasis to high-skill jobs, that result came more from a process of discovering what worked than from any deliberate policy.

While city officials were still casting a wide net for feasible projects, Vernon's monumental New York Metropolitan Region Study in the 1950s identified the kinds of businesses that stood to gain most from a downtown location. The largest group of firms still rooted to downtown were those whose executives wanted face-to-face contact with other people: lawyers who had to talk with clients and partners, bankers who had to negotiate with borrowers, corporate officers who had to meet with experts in taxes or bonds or product design. Their need to be in touch with others often and quickly led them to locate in the heart of the city, where the business specialists had clustered for mutual convenience. These communication-oriented firms employed perhaps one-fifth of an urban area's labor force and formed the critical downtown concentration most likely to resist the lure of the suburbs.

Some specialized manufacturers also operated best from in-city locations because they needed fast access to subcontractors and suppliers, short delivery times to customers, or face-to-face contact with any of those. Printers had to meet with customers to go over layout and then had to deliver the finished product on a tight schedule. Manufacturers of high-fashion clothing had to be able to see the fabrics, buttons, and buckles they were going to buy and had to keep up with the latest information to find out which designs and colors were selling. Mass producers of standardized clothing might operate successfully from small towns in low-wage regions, but the fashion industry had to be in the big city.

This diagnosis – publicized through books, conferences, and speeches – meant that the central city was a promising location for a large number of offices and a small number of manufacturers. With office work expanding nationally, it was the best prospect for downtown since the office elite wanted to be not only in the central city but in its main business district. Vernon recognized that routine office operations such as data processing were likely to move to the suburbs, but even if cities captured a smaller share of office growth than in the past, he expected their number of office jobs to increase. "At the very center of such cities," he wrote in 1959, "there is every reason to expect continued vitality." Yet the vitality he predicted was based primarily on the elite functions of skilled executives and the specialists they hired. His forecast implied fewer downtown jobs for the less skilled people who used to work in the industrial lofts, factories, and freight terminals.

250 Empire State Buildings

City attempts to promote office development were well timed to meet an unprecedented surge of office demand in the national economy. The trend started when corporations that were pouring out consumer products during the boom years of the 1950s needed more and more people to handle administration, product development, research, marketing, and finance. White-collar jobs in manufacturing firms began a steady climb from 20 percent of total employment in the 1940s to almost 40 percent by the 1980s.

Corporations searching for wider markets not only took on more administrative staff but also set up headquarters and branch offices in big cities, close to their financial advisers, lawyers, and consultants. The firms supplying these producer services in turn grew larger to meet the needs of the new corporate offices, as well as a rising consumer demand for similar services. The number of jobs in finance, insurance, and business and professional services jumped from 3 million in the mid-1950s to more than 11 million by the early 1980s. The growth of government and nonprofit agencies added to the demand for office space. Service jobs in total (counting government and nonprofit jobs) increased from 57 percent of U.S. employment in 1947 to 71 percent in 1982. Manufacturing meanwhile slipped from 32 percent to 22 percent of the total.

The rise of a service economy concentrated job growth in occupations well suited to downtown. It was not surprising that cities threw their energies into getting office work; it was the growth sector of the economy and one of the very few fields where they might rival the suburbs. As far as manufacturing jobs were concerned, the cities found it so hard to compete for industry against their own suburbs in the 1950s and 1960s that there was little point in trying to compete against Taiwan or Korea by the 1970s and 1980s.

City strategies began to pay off when office buildings broke ground in one downtown after another. Earlier New York had dominated the nation's office development, producing half the space built in all the downtowns of the 30 largest metropolitan areas in the 1950s. By the 1960s downtown office construction spread to all regions of the country as eight cities each built more than 4 million square feet and New York's share slipped to one-third of the total. The spread continued after 1970 as Chicago, Washington, Houston, San Francisco, Dallas, Los Angeles, Boston, and Denver became leading producers of downtown office space and cut New York's share to 29 percent in the 1970s and 17 percent by the early 1980s.

From the 1960s through 1984, 1,325 office buildings were built or started in the downtowns of the 30 largest urban areas, supplying almost 550 million square feet of floor space – the equivalent of 250 new Empire State Buildings. Putting this record into historic perspective is hard because of inadequate data, but what was built since 1960 is almost certainly greater than the total amount of downtown office space these cities had accumulated from all the years of construction before 1960.

Lodgings and Lobbies

Companies that settled into the new downtown offices soon wanted modern hotels nearby where they could put up out-of-town clients and business colleagues in comfort. When the cities organized downtown renewal projects, they began to include new hotels. In their eagerness to get hotels, cities turned to the new federal Urban Development Action Grant program as a source of public funds. Of the first 50 awards under this program in 1978, nearly one-third were for hotels or hotel-convention center complexes.

Once the hotel market was tested and proved, government was less important. With office construction booming and convention centers planned, the demand for hotels was strong enough to convince the national chains that downtown was ripe. The 38 largest urban areas built 319 downtown hotels with 110,000 rooms between 1960 and 1982. From 1973 to 1983 alone, the supply of convention-quality downtown hotel rooms more than doubled in Atlanta, Boston, Indianapolis, Philadelphia, Phoenix, Portland, St. Paul, San Antonio, Seattle, and Washington.

After offices, hotels generated the next largest volume of downtown construction. Their imposing atriums and arcades created important new public spaces, often with direct linkages to adjoining buildings. Many hotels are clustered with office buildings and stores to form large mixed-use complexes. Of some 130 downtown mixed-use projects built between 1970 and 1985, more than seven of ten contained at least one hotel. In this kind of setting hotels expanded the enclosed network of off-street territory with concourses and lobbies designed to attract not only overnight guests but also the public at large.

The Gentry Come to Town

Another part of the downtown development agenda that clicked into place alongside downtown offices and shopping malls was the revival of in-town living for the well-off. Luxury housing was an early fixture of urban renewal, but most projects of the 1950s and 1960s moved slowly and had only slight success. Not until after the clearance strategy ground to a halt did a noticeable number of well-heeled people begin to resettle in cities. Instead of moving into new apartment towers, they were finding older homes in neighborhoods that had survived the bulldozer.

Most of the newcomers were young, white professionals. The residents they replaced were typically older, lower-income, and more likely to belong to minority groups. To journalistic observers, this was the long-awaited arrival of the gentry, and *gentrification* became the catchword. For city officials who had tried for years to bring in what James Q. Wilson called "a tax-paying, culture-loving, free-spending middle class," it was a dream come true.

Renovated houses in long-neglected parts of the city attracted much attention in the 1970s. As Victorian style came back into fashion, young professionals were soon cruising the littered streets in their BMWs and pounding the broken pavements with their Gucci shoes, searching for brownstones to buy. The visibility of these new urban pioneers added the word *yuppie* to the language and led trend watchers to exaggerate the dimensions of what was happening. By the beginning of 1979 *Harper's, Newsweek,* and the *New York Times Magazine* took note of how the new elite group was reviving in-town neighborhoods and declared that the urban crisis was over.

Researchers who studied gentrification had a different perspective. By 1977, almost all of the 30 largest cities had neighborhood reinvestment, but declining neighborhoods greatly outnumbered those enjoying a revival. Renovation was centered in some one hundred neighborhoods but involved less than one-half of 1 percent of the houses in these cities. An investigation of the changing racial makeup of census districts within three miles of downtown, as well as of neighborhoods known for gentrification, confirmed that the net effects were small. Although case studies showed that gentrification usually replaced black residents with white ones, close-in neighborhoods continued to lose whites and gain blacks in eight of ten cities between 1970 and 1980. Further contrary to impressionistic accounts, there was little evidence of the widely heralded back-to-the-city movement. Most of the renovators were first-time home buyers who were moving from rental apartments in the city. People like them a few years earlier would have bought their first homes in the suburbs.

Although this revitalization of inner neighborhoods amounted to less than met the eye, it was still important for the cities. It marked a turnaround in long-established trends and brought a new group of affluent residents within reach of the city assessor and close enough to downtown to help support its theaters, restaurants, concert halls, and shopping.

Was this movement, with its displacement of the poor by the wealthy, part of a deliberate city strategy? As with most other development trends, it resulted largely from outside circumstances, but the cities pushed it along. Its origins were mainly in life-style changes among the postwar generation that came of age during the 1970s. Many two-worker families valued the convenience of living in the city, and many shared the new taste for Victorian ornamentation and craftsmanship that contrasted sharply with suburban homes. Nearly three-fourths of the structures in revitalizing neighborhoods surveyed in 1977 were at least 75 years old.

Housing market conditions also worked in favor of the cities. Suburban home prices escalated to record levels in the 1970s, making the cost of older city houses a bargain in comparison. Even after the renovation bills, a home in an old neighborhood was a good value, and the number of families buying existing homes rather than new ones doubled between 1970 and 1978.

A concentration of office and professional jobs nearby the cities was another critical factor. Families in gentrifying neighborhoods ranked closeness to jobs as one of the main reasons for moving there. When geographer Brian Berry analyzed cities where house prices and quality were favorable to gentrification, he found that the ones where gentrification actually took hold had much higher rates of downtown office growth than the others.

Beyond their stimulus to downtown office development, city governments took other steps to encourage gentrification. A few organized urban renewal projects to improve rather than bulldoze older neighborhoods. Society Hill in Philadelphia and the South End in Boston were early examples of gentrification supported by renewal projects. Many cities used federal community development funds to fix up streets and parks in neighborhoods where revitalization was under way; others made tax-lien properties available at nominal cost to "homesteaders" who promised to renovate them; still others ran promotional campaigns boosting certain neighborhoods as good places to buy homes. A number of cities leaned on local financial institutions to make homeloans in areas that were formerly "red-lined" for avoidance by loan officers, and by 1977 38 cities took part in demonstration programs organized by the Federal Home Loan Bank Board to encourage mortgage lending in old neighborhoods.

Encouraging middle- and upper-income people to live in the city was one of the earliest aims of downtown revitalization. When reinvestment in old neighborhoods turned out to be a practical way to make it happen, city governments did what they could to help; fashionable housing would not only strengthen the tax base but could attract creative, entrepreneurial people to keep the service economy growing. Downtown business coalitions were usually in favor, since a good in-town neighborhood was a valuable living option for executives and professionals. For both officials and citizens who worried about

downtown, bringing in residents promised to make the streets livelier and safer on a 24-hour basis.

Rebuilding the city was not enough; it was equally important to spread the word about the rebuilding. Big-city mayors who were promoting office buildings, hotels, and restored neighborhoods got busy marketing their cities to real estate investors, business executives, convention planners, and home buyers. City governments acted more and more like press agents hyping an image and selling a product. They coined slogans and advertised them to the world. After New York established itself as the Big Apple, Minneapolis promoters countered with the Mini-Apple. They put together multimedia presentations – split screen slide shows and videotapes with musical sound tracks – and took them to conventions around the country.

Stagecraft

The cities staged events designed to draw crowds and get into the media: street fairs, ethnic fairs, film fairs, book fairs, world's fairs, marathons, Grand Prix auto races, arts-in-the-parks festivals, jazz festivals, winterfests and summerfests, New Year's and Chinese New Year's parades, and celebrations of anything else that could be celebrated.

Promotion no longer ended at the water's edge. Mayors increasingly took trade missions abroad to speak for local businesses and to bring new companies to town. Mayor Andrew Young of Atlanta, capitalizing on his earlier experience as United Nations ambassador, earned a special reputation for extended duty overseas. The mayors of Philadelphia, New Orleans, Syracuse, and Albuquerque among other cities took steps to open foreign markets, including setting up trade development agencies and establishing tariff-free foreign trade zones for storing and assembling imported products.

Most of these promotions did not spend much city money. Preparing film and slide shows, hosting media people, and even taking a mission to China are minor items in a big-city budget. Staging festivals runs into more money, but business contributions usually cover the costs. Whether promotional efforts are for boosterism or for economic development, they do not seem to trouble the taxpayers, and they may broadcast an image of the community that residents appreciate.

Logic in the Patchwork

The city record on downtown revitalization includes examples of fluff, groping for direction, and of grasping at almost any opportunity to bring in outside resources. But it also reveals a thread of economic and developmental rationality running through the downtown agenda. To call the composite of projects a corporate center strategy is to dignify it beyond the reality of piecemeal, trial-and-error decisions. But the national economy was changing in a way that favored office work and corporate services as the new core of downtown. And the logic of city development produced a series of ventures that were feasible because they were anchored in some way to the jobs and businesses that were growing downtown.

There was also another logic at work: the logic of local politics. For most mayors it meant that projects had to produce visible community-wide benefits. Jobs and business growth counted heavily in political terms, but they were not enough. City administrations also needed brick-and-mortar symbols to demonstrate their accomplishments. Office towers, elegant hotels, and large convention centers served this purpose well, and if they could not be completed within a mayor's term, then artists' renderings, display models, groundbreakings, and ribbon cuttings created political credit along the way. The mayors wanted projects with broad popular appeal, places that the voting public would visit. Festivals, fairs, and celebrations were right for this purpose, and big league sports were even better. Beyond a certain point, city initiatives had a way of edging into unfocused image-building and boosterism, but most of what the cities did in the 1970s and 1980s was calculated to appeal to large numbers of their people. This concern to please the public at large was a big change from the elitism of the 1950s, when downtown leaders were building projects for narrow groups of users.

Both political and economic logic led to the downtown retail centers. When we asked mayors why they had decided to push these projects, they kept economic considerations far in the background. The reasons they gave included to make downtown a place for entertainment and visiting as well as for work, to have street life in the evenings and on weekends, to get rid of eyesores that the shopping malls would replace, to preserve landmarks, and to demonstrate the city's competence to manage development. Creating jobs and raising tax revenues were secondary considerations when they came up at all, and the casual record keeping we found with respect to retail jobs and tax collections reinforces the impression that once a project was built, city officials had little interest in documenting these particular results.

The economic logic came from other quarters. Business leaders saw a new shopping mall as a way

to enhance the value of their own property, a place where their employees might shop or have lunch, entertainment for out-of-town visitors, and a spur to conventions and tourism that might help their firms. Above all they saw it as a catalyst for further downtown development. Within city hall some key people also backed retail projects on economic grounds.

The retail centers produced results that fit the political logic behind them. What they did for economic development is hard to establish. Beyond the construction and retail jobs they created, they were clearly helpful, yet their economic impacts have hardly been measured, and their ripple effects are hard to express in dollars and cents. Most cities that sponsored shopping malls were doing so much else simultaneously that there is no way to know how important the malls in themselves were for downtown development.

The downtown shopping malls were well suited to a time of transition in the recovery of downtown. They made a start at bringing people back to the city and helped attract tourists, conventioneers, and business visitors. They made in-town living more attractive. By changing the development signals, they stimulated at least some other construction and possibly a great deal. They gave the cities new and interesting places to visit, plus some unusual shopping opportunities. To ask for much more is to have very high expectations indeed. And to expect definitive evidence of the results is like asking for scientific proof of what the Eiffel Tower has done for Paris.

The city agenda for downtown had a rough underlying logic that encouraged economic growth. Faced with suburban competition and fiscal strains, city governments managed to ride the coattails of an emerging service economy and to bring their plans into line with it. Creative officials were able to reconcile the demands of politics and economics by finding projects that were both popular and functional. While the development agenda had its underside of puffery and faddishness, it went a long way toward reviving downtown as a business center.

In the process of rebuilding downtown, city government transformed itself. The recent agenda is important not only for what it built but for what it said about the commitment of city officials. It sent a message to developers, business people, and the public that local officials were taking greater responsibility for the economic well-being of the city.

For mayors and council members to act as civic boosters promoting real estate development is nothing new, but now they do it with a difference. Before World War II city development projects were limited to such clearly municipal functions as building streets, parks, schools, libraries, police stations, and firehouses. These were the public works that served a resident population, and city officials scattered them through the neighborhoods where people lived. The more recent agenda crosses the old barrier between public and private development by using public power and money to promote office buildings, hotels, convention centers, shopping malls, stadiums, and more. Now the projects are located away from places where most people live, concentrated instead in a downtown of corporate offices, business visitors, suburban commuters, and tourists.

This agenda, a forceful response to the postwar urban condition, was probably the only response that could have worked. In blurring the line between public and private, it mirrored the new public-private combinations for managing development and the trend toward privatization of public space. Making the once-rigid boundary easier for both sides to cross was a major contributor to downtown development. But the results raised legitimate questions about whether the new downtowns were helpful to average city residents requiring a closer look at the mix of jobs generated by the downtown agenda.

READINGS SUGGESTED BY THE AUTHORS

Child Hill, Richard, "Crisis in the Motor City," in Susan S. Fainstein, Norman I. Fainstein, et. al. *Restructuring the City*. New York: Longman, 1983.

Fosler, R. Scott and Renee A. Berger, (eds.). *Public-Private Partnership in American Cities*. Lexington, MA: Lexington Books, 1982.

GARDEN CITY, U.S.A.:
Are New Towns the Way Around Growth Controls?

Michael L. Evans

Mr. Evans is national director of the Real Estate Advisory Services division of Ernst & Young, San Francisco, Calif.

NEW Towns, a planning and development concept that captured the imagination of developers, planners, social workers, and the Federal government during the 1960's, are back. Though it's not the first time this school of thought has reappeared on the developer agenda, proponents and backers of the most recent proposals say they are different. Gone are the larger "social good" goals that led to the creation of New Towns in the U.S. and Great Britain.

Gone, too, is Federal largesse to encourage such development. Instead, these proposals are being pitched as the answer to a number of growth-related problems confronting states such as California, Arizona, and Florida.

Nine projects have been submitted for California, a state grappling with rapid growth, inadequate infrastructure, and a dearth of affordable housing. The proposed New Towns, ranging in size from 3,000 to 10,000 acres, promise to be self-contained, self-sustaining communities. Housing, jobs, schools, and cultural activities are all part of the plan.

Developers say their projects would bring jobs closer to housing and replace endless suburban sprawl with well-designed and -managed development. Though their projects, in almost all cases, would mean converting productive rural land to urban uses, the developers say that, by concentrating such growth in one area, they ultimately would do more to protect nearby rural land.

Not everyone is sold on the idea of New Towns. Around the country, there are examples of ambitious proposals that became little more than massive subdivisions. Moreover, a number of the New Towns that were built, especially those in which the Federal government was involved, have been financial disasters.

New Towns are an old idea, created in the late 19th century in London by a court reporter, Ebenezar Howard, who believed London was sick, that it had become an unnatural and inhumane place to live. As an antidote, he prescribed the Garden City—a small, self-sufficient town that would include nice housing, well-concealed and "clean" industrial uses, and lots of parks and open space. The town itself would be surrounded by agricultural or forest land, thereby allowing its residents to live closer to nature. Population would be limited to about 30,000 people, and the town would be run by a planning authority that would control all development, thus ending real estate speculation.

Howard's ideas found quick acceptance, and today there are more bona-fide New Towns in Great Britain than in any other country. His ideas also found interest in the U.S., where the rapid pace of industrialization and swelling tide of immigrants had created conditions in New York, Boston, and Chicago rivaling those found in London. One hundred years earlier, Thomas Jefferson had urged that the U.S. remain largely a rural nation and refrain from urban building. Big cities, like those found in Europe, would mean big-city, European problems, he warned.

In Europe, Howard's Garden City was seen as a way to remake the world. In the New World, it was seen as a path to follow. However, efforts to build true New Towns did not begin until the late 1950's and early 1960's.

Reston—the first attempt

Roger E. Simon, Jr., his pockets full of cash after selling New York City's Carnegie Hall, bought 6,800 acres (11 square miles) of wooded Virginia hunting grounds for $13,000,000 in 1961. He put $800,000 down and persuaded the land owners to take a non-interest-bearing note for the balance. Simon, though not a developer, was a philanthropist disturbed by problems confronting American cities in the early 1960's. Imbued with Howard's principles, he announced plans for a New Town that would make room for social and economic diversity, as well as being profitable. By 1980, he said, Reston would have 75,000 people living near where they worked. He offered architecturally distinguished housing at remarkably low prices and enticed businesses with land writedowns.

Today, Reston's population is close to 40,000. Major corporations such as Gannett and governmental agencies such as the U.S. Geological Survey have moved there, but the city is not the New Town that Simon originally envisioned.

Simon's initial success prompted dozens of proposals calling themselves New Towns. Those that were built often amounted to little more than big subdivisions. Others, like El Dorado Hills, 24 miles east of Sacramento, fared far worse than Reston. Corporate America also jumped on the New Town bandwagon. General Electric and others announced New Town proposals for land they'd owned for years. In most cases, they did not come to fruition.

These less-than-successful efforts shared some common failings. For one thing, the proposed sites often were far from existing commercial or residential centers. Though many Americans were tired of the urban rat race, they were unwilling to abandon the conveniences that made running it easier. The developers usually built the housing first, because it was cheaper to do so and would provide an immediate return. Without the commercial center in place, however, prospective residents of Reston and other New Towns faced a longer, not shorter, commute to their jobs. Finally, lenders were extremely hesitant about committing long-term money to such risky ventures. In some instances, they even refused to provide mortgages for the housing built at some of the projects.

Despite these mixed results, enthusiasm over New Towns remained high in the 1960's. Urban race riots, an increase in violent crimes, and a damaged environment had caught the nation's attention. Because New Towns had such strong social goals and so nicely played upon the Norman Rockwell "small town" cliche, they became even more popular—so much so that, in the true spirit of the age, the Federal government decided to get involved in the effort.

In 1969, the National Committee on Urban Growth Policy recommended that the U.S. build 110 new cities by the year 2000 as a way of relieving the pressure on existing urban areas. Ten of those new cities would have a population of 1,000,000 each; the remaining would have populations of 100,000. Thus was born HUD's Title VII—or New Town mortgage guaranty—program.

Jonathan, a New Town planned for a site 25 miles southwest of Minneapolis amidst rolling farmlands, was the first project to receive a Title VII mortgage guaranty, for $21,000,000. Jonathan was plagued with problems from the start, and the project was abandoned. Perhaps no example better illustrates the naivete behind most New Town proposals from that era or the outcome of most of the projects backed by the Federal government.

Minnesota has the dubious distinction of having two failed New Towns within its borders. The second, Cedar Square West, was called a New Town In Town, a massive project that originally called for about 10,000 high-rise units in an area less than one mile from the core of downtown Minneapolis. Ultimately, only one-twelfth of what originally was proposed was built. In 1986, HUD foreclosed on over $40,000,000 in outstanding mortgages on the project, then sold the complex to a private developer for about $20,000,000 in 1988.

Cedar Square West was a concept that made sense on paper, but was ill-placed in terms of timing and location. In the 1990's, we will see Cedar Square Wests in major cities where housing prices have prevented first-time buyers from entering the housing market. An already existing example is Fillmore Center in San Francisco. We will not see urban New Towns in markets where housing prices are low. Housing prices in Minneapolis in the late 1960's were too low to support the urban New Town concept.

Not every New Town was a flop, but two of the most successful ones do share one thing in common—they were developed privately. Columbia, in Maryland's Howard County, almost halfway between Baltimore and Washington, D.C., was the brainchild of James W. Rouse. He manag-

ed to quietly option 15,000 acres of rural land (22 square miles) from 169 different owners before revealing his plans in 1963. Four years later, the first housing opened. Office towers have been built in the ensuing years.

Irvine Ranch in Southern California also is pointed to as a successful example of the New Town concept. The Irvine family, owners of 64,000 acres of orange groves and ranch land in Orange County, began building housing in the early 1960's. The family and its successor, the Irvine Co., have built about 50,000 housing units and 10,000,000 square feet of commercial space, most of it scattered throughout seven cities. Only one of those cities, Irvine, truly could be considered a New Town because it was built on land owned entirely by the family. In 1971, Irvine's residents voted to incorporate as a city. Today, the population is about 100,000.

Today's New Towns

The newest New Town proposals emerged in 1988 and, like Columbia and Irvine Ranch, they would be privately developed. Trimark Communities already owns outright about half of the 6,240 acres it would like to develop in San Joaquin and Alameda Counties in Northern California. A consortium of developers owns, or has under option, 15 square miles of high desert in the Antelope Valley in Southern California that will become California Springs.

Richard Morehouse, a senior associate with Sedway Cooke Associates, a San Francisco planning firm, has had a lot of experience with New Towns. He notes that today's New Town proposals differ in one major respect from their predecessors. "The social goals are gone. They went away with the 1960's." Today's New Towns, he adds, are a response to the tremendous demand for new and affordable housing.

Bill Johnson, managing partner of Trimark Communities, says his $4,000,000,000 project would ease demand for housing and help relieve traffic congestion by putting jobs and residences together, in the center of already well-established commuter patterns. Trimark says it will offer industrial sites for $10,000 an acre, compared with $55,000 in Livermore or $500,000 in north San Jose.

Morehouse says the New Towns of the 1950's and 1960's had overly ambitious notions of being self-sustaining, and that was their failing. Very few developers could afford to build the infrastructure and amenities necessary to attract corporate tenants. Because of the tremendous "exurban" growth in California and other states, he feels, the prospects for New Towns might be brighter today. "Projects that were marginal 15 or 20 years ago now

seem feasible. People are already making long commutes to work. Corporations have relocated from cities to areas once considered rural."

Building a New Town in an unincorporated area also has a distinct political advantage for the developers. They can avoid impact fees and planning restrictions because county ordinances are more lax or non-existent. Also, because there often are few, if any, nearby residents, opposition to the project is diffused.

Local officials might find New Town proposals irresistible, especially when developers promise to build all the necessary roads, sewers, schools, and other services. Federal money for such projects virtually has disappeared, and, in states like California, local funding options are severely limited. Since growth is bound to occur anyway, New Towns might seem like the best way to pay for and control growth.

"New Towns, if done right, are certainly better than endless, monotonous suburban development," Morehouse says. "Of course, many would argue that Mission Viejo and Irvine Ranch, the two most successful New Town developments, are little more than endless suburban development."

As visceral as the appeal of New Towns is, their development is by no means assured. The project might take care of their own infrastructure needs, but they still will have an impact on area highways, bridges, and other services.

In June, 1989, voters in Novato, Calif., rejected a New Town proposal for Hamilton Air Force Base because it would mean more traffic on Highway 101, and a coalition of environmental groups has been formed in opposition to Trimark's Mountain House proposal, claiming it will result in redevelopment of productive rural land. Trimark's Johnson says such opposition is short-sighted, because it ultimately will mean the piecemeal conversion of agricultural land, with no coherent planning or management. "These people are going to continue to come and look for housing, whether we're allowed to build or not."

High-growth states like California, Arizona, Florida, and Georgia slowly are adopting a regional planning approach as a way to manage growth. As that occurs, Morehouse predicts New Towns could become an integral element of growth management. "More and more, you're seeing a jobs-housing link being insisted upon. Along with impact fees, developers might find themselves having to build and fill a 50,000-square-foot commercial building before being allowed to build housing." To the extent that a New Town can deliver both jobs and housing, its appeal will stay strong. As to whether the concept is a successful technique for getting by the NIMBY's (not in my backyards), that remains to be seen.

THE NEW SUBURBIA
A DIFFERENT ENTITY

NICHOLAS LEMANN
Mr. Lemann is a national correspondent for
The Atlantic Monthly.

*I*recently spent some time in Naperville, Illinois, because I wanted to see exactly how our familiar ideas about the suburbs have gotten out of date. Naperville is thirty miles west of the Chicago Loop. It had 7,000 residents in 1950, 13,000 in 1960, 22,600 in 1970, and 42,600 in 1980, and just in this decade it has nearly doubled in population again, to 83,000 this year. Driving there from Chicago, you pass through the West Side ghetto, the site of riots in the late sixties, and then through a belt of older suburbs at the city limits. Just when the suburbs seem to be dying out, you arrive in Oak Brook, with its collection of new shopping malls and office towers. The seventeen-mile stretch from Oak Brook west through Naperville to the old railroad city of Aurora has the look of inexplicable development common to booming areas that were recently rural. Subdivisions back up onto cornfields. Mirrored-glass office parks back up onto convenience-store parking lots. Most of the trees are saplings.

The picture we have of middle-class life in the United States is essentially still set in the suburbs of the 1950s. The sheer volume of information available about the American middle class is greater for the 1950s than for any other period in our history, because there was then a tremendous outpouring of journalism, sociology, and fiction on the subject. The middle class seemed fascinating at the time: it was acquiring a new home, the suburbs, and a new economic base, the large bureaucratic business organization, and these were quickly becoming the dominant social forms in the country. Since the early sixties, suburbia has been taken more for granted.

SECOND GENERATION SUBURBIA

The people who grew up in fifties suburbia now dominate the country culturally, and from them we are getting a second wave of in-terest in middle-class family life, which comes from their own involvement in it. Here, too, the basic idea is the fifties; people's concept of suburbia, like their concepts of summer and marriage, comes more from what they knew growing up than from what they've experienced themselves as adults. On television especially, constant references are made these days to the suburbs of the Baby Boom generation's youth as the proper locus of the American middle class. All subsequent developments seem slightly perfidious.

While we've been glorifying the suburbs of the fifties, the suburbs of the eighties have been evolving into places quite different. The most obvious change has been a political-economic one: in the fifties the suburbs were exclusively residential, but businesses have been moving to them over the past fifteen years, and this has broken the iron association of suburbs with commuting downtown. The fastest-growing kind of town in the country is one on the outer edge of a metropolitan area which has acquired an employment base. Christopher Leinberger and Charles Lockwood, writing in *The Atlantic* three years ago, called these communities "urban villages," and there are also several other names for them, including "edge cities" and "technoburbs." The communities have cropped up all over the country—in Plano, Texas, and Tysons Corner, Virginia; the towns in the valleys surrounding the Los Angeles Basin and along the outer reaches of San Francisco Bay; New York satellites like Stamford, White Plains, and Princeton. Because we're fixated on the fifties, we don't have a good sense of what life is like in these places, which, if they're not yet typical of suburbia, certainly represent the direction in which suburbia is heading.

Our notion now of suburbia in the fifties is that it was essentially benign—sometimes gawky, often dull, but on the whole healthy and happy. But in the fifties themselves virtually everything written about the suburbs was negative, even alarmed. The indictment can be summed up in one word: conformity. Working for huge corporations, living in tract homes, surrounded by spookily similar neighbors, the new middle-class Americans had lost their feelings of pride, meaning, and identity. They wanted only to blend unobtrusively into a group.

The run of suburban literature began, roughly, with the publication of David Riesman's *The Lonely Crowd* (which is not explicitly about the suburbs, but set the tone) in 1950. The deservedly best-remembered of the many books about the suburbs by sociologists and journalists is William H. Whyte's *The Organization Man* (1956). There was also a flood of suburban fiction, of which the best-known works are probably the stories and novels of John Cheever and, because of its catch-phrase title, *The Man in the Gray Flannel Suit*, by Sloan Wilson. The suburbs took such a beating in most of these books that by 1967 the sociologist Herbert Gans was able to cast *The Levittowners* as an attack on the attackers of the new middle class. Gans argued convincingly that most of the critics of suburbia didn't know what they were talking about, and were animated by a snobbish distaste for the lower middle class. But the idea that suburban society was oriented toward the community at the expense of the individual is so widespread in the literature that there must have been something to it. Today nobody worries about conformity as a national issue, and nobody I met in Naperville mentioned it as a problem. The suburban psychological force that occasionally overwhelms people is not the need to fit in but the need to be a success.

THE HISTORY OF NAPERVILLE

The history of Naperville as an urban village begins in 1964, when AT&T decided to build a major facility there for its research division, Bell Labs, along the new Interstate 88. Before that, as the next-to-last stop on the Burlington & Northern line from Chicago, Naperville attracted some hardy long-distance commuters, but it was mainly an independent small town, with frame houses and streets laid out in a grid.

Bell Labs opened in 1966 and is still by far the largest employer in Naperville—7,000 people work there, developing electronic switching systems, and another 3,000 work at a software development center in the neighboring town of Lisle. In 1969 Amoco moved its main research-and-development facility from the industrial town of Whiting, Indiana, to a site in Naperville along the interstate, near Bell Labs. Today more than 2,000 people work there. All

through the seventies and eighties businesses have built low-slung, campus-style office complexes up and down I-88, which Governor James R. Thompson in 1986 officially subtitled "The Illinois Research and Development Corridor." There are now four big chain hotels on the five-mile stretch that runs through Lisle and Naperville. In Aurora, Nissan, Hyundai, and Toyota have all established distribution centers, and four insurance companies have set up regional headquarters.

In the fifties the force driving the construction of residential neighborhoods in the suburbs was that prosperity had given young married couples the means to act on their desire to raise children away from the cities. In the eighties in Naperville there is still some of this, but the real driving force is that so many jobs are there. Dozens of new residential subdivisions fan out in the area south of the office complexes and the old town center. In this part of town, whose land Naperville aggressively annexed, the school district has built three new elementary schools since 1984 and added to seven others. A new junior high school opened this fall, another one is under construction, and last spring the town's voters passed a bond issue to build another elementary school and additions to two high schools.

In *The Organization Man*, William Whyte was struck by how removed the place he studied—Park Forest, Illinois, the fifties equivalent of Naperville, brand-new and also thirty miles from the Loop—was from Chicago and from urban forms of social organization. Naperville is even more removed, mainly because downtown commuters are a small minority of the new residents. Nearly everybody in Park Forest worked in Chicago. Only five thousand people take the train from the Naperville station into Chicago every day; most people work in Naperville or in a nearby suburban town. The people I talked to in Naperville knew that they were supposed to go into Chicago for the museums, theater, music, and restaurants, so they were a little defensive about admitting to staying in Naperville in their free time, but most of them do. Though Naperville has many white ethnics (and a few blacks and Asians), it has no ethnic neighborhoods. There are ethnic restaurants, but many of them are the kind that aren't run by members of that ethnic group. Naperville is politically conservative but has no Democratic or Republican organizations active in local politics. Nobody who can afford a house lives in an apartment. There are only a few neighborhood taverns. Discussions of Chicago focus on how much crime is there, rather than on the great events of municipal life.

Places like Naperville are often dismissed as examples of heedless sprawl, ugly and un-

SUBURBAN LIFE

planned. The charge may be true of some places, but it is not of Naperville, which is extremely well run. A master plan precisely sets forth how the town is to grow, to the point when all its empty space is filled up. The downtown shops have been kept alive. There is an excellent new library, a brick walkway (built by volunteers) along the DuPage River in the center of town, and plenty of green space. City property taxes have been lowered in each of the past three years. Naperville represents not chaos but a conscious rejection of the pro-urban, anti-automobile conventions that prevail among planners.

In distancing itself from Chicago, Naperville has continued a trend that was already well under way in Whyte's Park Forest. Otherwise, most of the ways in which Naperville is different from Whyte's Park Forest and places like it were not predicted by the suburbia experts of the time.

INSECURITY   Naperville is much more materially prosperous, and at the same time more anxious about its standard of living, than Park Forest was. The comparison isn't exact, because Park Forest was a middle-middle-class community dominated by people in their late twenties and early thirties; Naperville is more affluent and has a somewhat fuller age range. Nevertheless, since Naperville is the fastest-growing town in the area, it can fairly be said to represent the slice of American life that is expanding most rapidly right now, as Park Forest could in the fifties. The typical house in Park Forest cost $13,000 and had one story (the most expensive house there by far, where the developer lived, cost $50,000). The average house in Naperville costs $160,000, and the figure is higher in the new subdivisions. Plenty of new houses in town cost more than $500,000. Most of the new houses in Naperville have two stories; in fact, the small section of fifties and sixties suburbia in Naperville is noticeably more modest than the new housing.

In fifties suburbs the architecture was usually quite simple. In Naperville the new houses are flamboyantly traditional, with steeply pitched roofs, red-brick or stained-cedar exteriors (aluminum siding is banned in many of the subdivisions), leaded-glass windows, massive front doors, cathedral ceilings, fireplaces, gables, even turrets. The names of subdivisions and of house models often evoke European nobility: The Chateaux of La Provence, La Royale, The Golf Villas of White Eagle Club, The Country Manor, Charlemont IV. Whyte had chapters called "Classlessness in Suburbia" and "Inconspicuous Consumption," and described the material ethos of Park Forest as quasi-socialist. Although in the fifties the average American, known to intellectuals as "mass man," was materially much better outfitted than he

had been, the suburbs had become home to a wider range of people than they had been before the Second World War, and so seemed more democratic. Naperville is much made fun of in the neighboring communities as the home of snobs and yuppies.

Obviously one reason for the difference is that Park Forest in the early fifties was only a very few years into the postwar boom, which left the middle class vastly better off than it had been before. Another is that the consumer culture was young and undeveloped in the fifties. Middle-class people today want to own things that their parents wouldn't have dreamed of.

A NEW TYPE OF AFFLUENCE

The affluence of Naperville is also a by-product of what is probably the single most important new development in middle-class life since the fifties (and one almost wholly unanticipated in the fifties), which is that women work. Park Forest was an exclusively female town on weekdays; when Whyte wrote about the difficulty of being a "superwoman," he meant combining housework with civic and social life. In Naperville I heard various statistics, but it seems safe to say that most mothers of young children work, and the younger the couple, the likelier it is that the wife works. When *Business Week* did a big story on the "mommy track" last spring, it used a picture of a woman from Naperville. What people in Naperville seem to focus on when they think about working mothers is not that feminism has triumphed in the Midwest but that two-career couples have more money and less time than one-career couples.

In the classic suburban literature almost no reference is made to punishingly long working hours. The Cheever story whose title is meant to evoke the journey home at the end of the working day is called "The Five Forty-Eight," and its hero is taking that late a train only because he stopped in at a bar for a couple of Gibsons on the way from his office to Grand Central Station. In Naperville the word "stress" came up constantly in conversations. People felt that they had to work harder than people a generation ago in order to have a good middle-class life. In much of the rest of the country the idea holds sway that the middle class is downwardly mobile and its members will never live as well as their parents did. Usually this complaint involves an inexact comparison—the complainer is at an early stage in his career, works in a less remunerative field, or lives in a pricier place than the parents who he thinks lived better than he does. In Naperville, where most people are in business, it's more a case of people's material expectations being higher than their parents' than of their economic station being lower. A ranch-style tract house, a Chevrolet, and meat loaf for dinner will not do any more as the symbols of a realized dream. Also, a changed perception of the future of the country has helped create the sense of pressure in Naperville. Suburbanites of the fifties were confident of a constantly rising standard of living, level of education, and gross national product in a way that most Americans haven't been since about the time of the 1973 OPEC embargo. The feeling is that anyone who becomes prosperous has beaten the odds.

STRESS   It is jarring to think of placid-looking Naperville as excessively fast-paced, but people there talk as if the slack had been taken out of life. They complain that between working long hours, traveling on business, and trying to stay in shape they have no free time. The under-the-gun feeling applies to domestic life as well as to work. It's striking, in reading the old suburban literature today, to see how little people worried about their children. Through many scenes of drunkenness, adultery, and domestic discord, the kids seem usually to be playing, oblivious, in the front yard. Today there is a national hyperawareness of the lifelong consequences of childhood unhappiness (hardly an issue of *People* magazine fails to make this point); the feeling that American children can coast to a prosperous adulthood has been lost; and the entry of mothers into the workforce has made child care a constant worry for parents. The idea that childhood can operate essentially on autopilot has disappeared.

Teenagers in Naperville complain that they have nothing to do, but everyone else is overscheduled, including children. Day care adds a layer of complication to life: Naperville's booming day-care centers accept not only preschool children but also children who need supervision after school, until their parents get home. The school system's buses drop some children off at day-care centers in the afternoon. Every neighborhood has stories about latchkey kids, too.

A constant round of activities has been organized for children. The Naperville park district, which carries out the traditional functions of a municipal recreation department, runs an elaborate sports program, which parents appreciate while slightly rueing the time they spend ferrying their kids to soccer games and swim meets. "Sometimes we wonder why our kids can't just get a baseball game together," one mother told me. In the elementary schools, as late as the early seventies all students went home for lunch. Now the schools have lunchrooms—and many special new programs, added in part because of lobbying by parents who expect a high level of service from the schools. In the mid-eighties, at the parents' request, the elementary schools added an hour

a day of special "enrichment" programs for students with IQs over 125. The high schools added advanced-placement courses. School administrators and parents complain about the competitive atmosphere for students, in which an idyllic midwestern upbringing is a fading memory and it's painful to be average.

Adults in Naperville are competitive too. The people I talked to there were intensely aware of income distinctions within the community, a subject that rarely came up in books about the suburbs of a generation ago. The most direct blast of it that I got was in a meeting with a group of women who had just finished a parenting class taught by the elementary school system's social worker. The parenting class is part of a small culture of therapy that has sprung up in Naperville, in response partly to problems like divorce and drugs and partly to people's increased awareness of psychological well-being as an important issue in life. What seemed to be the real reason the women I met took the class was that they wanted affirmation of their decision not to work, which they felt had consigned them to a slightly lower status level than women with jobs. Their message was that they might have less money and prestige, but they were better parents.

Working mothers, they told me, buy off their children with copious gifts of new toys in place of maternal contact. They leave their children behind even on vacations, which are spent in expensive glamour spots. They sign their children up for a ceaseless round of overachieving activities, and then expect the full-time mothers to do all the carpooling. The neighborhood children are always hanging around the houses where the mothers are at home. Working mothers' children are kept up ridiculously late at night because that's the only time they see their parents. The mothers don't do volunteer work in the community. The litany ended with the inevitable coup de grace: "You wonder why they had kids."

MORE SOLITUDE, LESS COMMUNITY

The new houses in the subdivisions in Naperville clearly show an evolutionary adaptation of domestic architecture to customers who are busier than people used to be and more concerned with the fine gradations of status. The living and dining rooms are shrunken, vestigial spaces flanking the front hall. People entertain at home less and less because they don't have the time to, and so they don't need these rooms. In Park Forest in the fifties (and in most of the suburban fiction of the time), the socializing was so constant—cocktail parties, dinner parties, teas, coffees, bridge-club gatherings—that Whyte found it a cause for concern, because it enforced conformity. In Naperville everybody says that the at-home party is dying. Instead, people go out to restaurants, which are almost completely absent from the mythology of fifties suburbia.

Kitchens are usually built open to a large family room in back, which is meant to contain the main household television set and which has taken up the space left by the shrinking of the living and dining rooms. This indicates that what cooking goes on must not be elaborate or messy enough to bother the family members sitting a few feet away. Other rooms in the houses show that people want to be reminded that they are winners. The bizarrely large and well-appointed master bathrooms that Philip Langdon wrote about in these pages last month are common in Naperville. Often there is a small "study" off to the side downstairs, designed to suggest brandy and cigars and meant to be available for use as a home office. A small but dramatic balcony overlooks the front hall or the family room in many houses.

Because of the placement of the family room, which often opens to an outdoor deck, the new houses in Naperville are oriented toward the back yard, which may be fenced. In the fifties most writers described the unfenced front yard as the locale for much of the children's outdoor life. This contributed to the intense feeling of community in suburban neighborhoods, which led to the joke, quoted by Whyte, that Park Forest was "a sorority house with kids." In Naperville it seems much more possible not to know your neighbors. All the subdivisions have homeowners' associations. These constitute organized politics, such as it is, in the new parts of Naperville. The mayor, Margaret Price (who herself started out as a homeowners'-association president), meets with them regularly. But some homeowners' associations take off as community organizations and others don't.

COMMUNITY   The most reliable connection between subdivision residents and the community is children. Adults meet through the children's activities. I often heard that new neighborhoods coalesce around new elementary schools, which have many parent-involving activities and are also convenient places to hold meetings. The churches (mostly Protestant and Catholic, but the town has places of worship for Jews and even Muslims) have made an effort to perform some of the same functions—there is always a new church under construction, and eight congregations are operating out of rented space. The Reverend Keith Torney, who recently left the First Congregational Church in Naperville, after eighteen years, for a pulpit in Billings, Montana, told me, "We try to create a community where people can acquire roots very quickly. We divided the congregation into twelve care groups. Each has twenty to thirty

families. They kind of take over for neighbors and grandma—they bring the casserole when you're sick. People come here for a sense of warmth, for a sense that people care about you."

A MOBILE TOWN

All these community-building efforts amount to swimming against the tide, though, because population mobility in the newer parts of Naperville is great. According to local lore, the average house in Naperville changes hands every three years—a turnover rate comparable to or higher than those Whyte and Gans found in Park Forest and Levittown, and they were entirely new communities, whereas Naperville has a large well-established area that presumably brings the average turnover down. Naperville has two school districts; in the one that covers the new subdivisions, new students make up more than a quarter of the enrollment every fall. And this kind of mobility is occurring at a time when corporate transfers, which were thought in the fifties to be the main reason people moved so much, are slightly in decline, because of a lessening in people's willingness to do whatever their employers want.

There isn't any hard information on where new Naperville residents come from or where departing ones go. Most of the people I met had moved to Naperville from elsewhere in the Chicago area, often from the inner-ring suburbs. They came there to be closer to their jobs along I-88, because the schools are good and the crime rate is low, and because Naperville is a place where the person who just moved to town is not an outsider but the dominant figure in the community. If they leave, it's usually because of a new job, not always with the same company; the amount of company-switching, and of entrepreneurship, appears to be greater today than it was in the fifties. Several of the new office developments in the area have the word *corporate* in their names (I stayed in a hotel on Corporetum Drive.) Since the likes of AT&T and Amoco don't call attention to themselves this way, the use of the word is probably a sign of the presence of new businesses. People's career restlessness, and companies' desire to appear regally established right away, are further examples of the main message I got from my time in Naperville: the suburbs and, by extension, middle-class Americans have gone from glorifying group bonding to glorifying individual happiness and achievement.

The bad side of this change in ethos should be obvious right now: Americans appear to be incapable of the social cohesion and the ability to defer gratification which are prerequisites for the success of major national efforts. But a good side exists too. Representations of middle-class life in the fifties are pervaded with a sense of the perils of appearing to be "different." William Whyte wrote a series of articles for *Fortune*, and the photographs that Dan Weiner took to illustrate them (which are included in *America Worked*, a new book of Weiner's photographs) communicate this feeling even more vividly than *The Organization Man* does: the suburban kaffeeklatsch and the executive's office come across as prisons. There can't be much doubt that the country is more tolerant now than it was then.

Much of the fifties literature, especially the fiction, is pervaded as well by a sense of despair. Of course, American intellectuals since about the time of the First World War have been trying to prove that middle-class life is empty, while most Americans have enthusiastically embraced it. Still, the dark side of suburbia was detected by so many observers that it's hard to believe they all just projected it from their own minds onto their subject matter.

The darkest of all the suburban novels is probably Richard Yates's *Revolutionary Road*, which was published in 1961 but is set in the summer of 1955, in "a part of western Connecticut." In theme *Revolutionary Road* is similar to the television show *thirtysomething*: well-educated young people who think of themselves as hip and liberal marry, have children, and buy a house in the suburbs with the intention of retaining the ideals of their youth. In *Revolutionary Road* this endeavor leads inexorably to boozing, vicious quarreling, self-loathing, madness, and, ultimately, suicide. Frank, the husband, takes a meaningless job in the sales-promotion department of Knox Business Machines, purveyor of the Knox 500 Electronic Computer (computers were fifties intellectuals' favorite symbol of everything that

was wrong with America). April, the wife, keeps getting pregnant, to her horror.

Frank and April are not updated versions of the Babbitts. On the contrary, they are determined *not* to be Babbitts: they worry about conformity, listen to jazz, and struggle to understand Freud. So when they are destroyed, the message is not that they are victims of their own moral and cultural insensitivity but that the suburbs have no place for good people. To underscore the point, the minor character who, in occasional appearances, offers the most perceptive comments about Frank's and April's lives is an inmate of a mental hospital. It's only when Frank and April can summon the self-delusion to engage in dull, bourgeois husband-wife role-playing that they feel momentarily content. Intellectual honesty equals misery.

Frank's and April's expectations are much lower materially than a similar couple's would be now. A novelist with Yates's talent for the damning detail surely would today have them acquiring lots of unnecessary and expensive trendy household items; in *Revolutionary Road* money is mentioned only rarely, and always in the context of necessities rather than luxuries. But then, Frank and April take it for granted that in every middle class couple the man can find an easy and secure job that pays enough to support the whole family, and the woman can bear and raise healthy children.

Perhaps suburban life has become enough of a project to have filled in that old hollowness. Even the struggle against depression is much more of a busy-making activity than it used to be, thanks to the proliferation of therapies and support groups. Mortgages are bigger, jobs are more demanding, parenthood is a stretch in every way. Who has time to peer into the abyss?

The Other Suburbia

An ugly secret in America's suburbs: poverty

JOHN MCCORMICK
AND PETER MCKILLOP

Amid the sprawl of patio decks and softball fields, America's 6,500 suburbs harbor a disturbing secret: more than 9.5 million people living in poverty. Though their numbers have nearly doubled in the last 20 years, the suburban poor are obscured by the prosperity that surrounds them. They are too dispersed among their better-heeled neighbors to influence suburban congressmen and too disorganized to attract attention as effectively as advocates for the nation's 13.9 million urban poor. Often their squalid communities embrace the worst of two worlds: the demographics of the inner city and the painful isolation best known to the rural poor. Today nearly half of all Americans live in suburban areas, and most enjoy a modicum of comfort. Rarely do they encounter the *other* suburbia, a separate world where conditions seem likely to grow worse.

Some 500 suburbs across the United States now face problems approaching those of inner cities. Poverty has metastasized well beyond the so-called inner-ring communities with their aging white populations. Whites still constitute a majority of poor suburbanites. But minorities—25 percent of all black suburbanites and 22 percent of Hispanics—are the most severely affected: they are increasingly clustered in heavily segregated suburbs with young populations, explosive birthrates and burgeoning crime. Unlike poor urban neighborhoods, many of these towns are virtual prisons, with little or no public transit linking residents to city or suburban jobs. "Whites don't want to live in these places," says Richard Taub, an urban sociologist at the University of Chicago. "Minorities with resources don't want to live in them either."

Those who do end up in poor suburbs face other special hurdles. Their appeals for new businesses tend to attract only those gritty industries that other communities reject, like landfills. Because they lack the richer tax base cities get from office and factory districts, the suburbs can't afford many of the costly social, recreational and other services that cities offer. Programs for children, who make up 36 percent of the suburban poor, are especially scarce. "The difference between cities and poor suburbs in available services is incredible," says John Logan, a sociologist at the State University of New York at Albany. Since they cannot afford to hire professionals, the suburban governments can be hopelessly mismanaged. And even in the poorest pockets, says Logan, officials are often mesmerized by the suburban myth: they hate to acknowledge the poverty in their own backyards.

That may change, if only because suburban poverty is becoming impossible to ignore. Robert Fishman, an urban historian at Rutgers University, expects the phenomenon to worsen with the continued shrinkage of low-tech industries that once lured workers to suburbia. "These poor suburbs have no economic function whatsoever," he says. "Their people are stranded." Pierre deVise, an urbanologist at Chicago's Roosevelt University, adds that partly because of their high birthrates, poor suburbs continue to lose ground to their neighbors: 20 years ago, a 4-1 income ratio separated the richest and poorest U.S. suburbs. Today the ratio exceeds 12–1. "Poor suburbs range from old bedroom towns in the East to new barrios in the West," deVise says. "They are at an increasingly huge disadvantage."

Census Bureau demographers do not track suburban poverty at the local level. The task falls to academics such as deVise, who this month unveiled a new study contrasting poverty and wealth in suburbia (chart). What follows is a portrait of two of America's troubled areas:

Charles Gordon and his family left Cabrini-Green, a notorious Chicago public-housing project, in 1964. "My American dream was the same as a white man's," he says. "Marry a good woman, educate my children, buy a home with a yard." But most neighborhoods in and around Chicago were so militantly segregated that upwardly mobile blacks had few alternatives. Gordon joined a fledgling movement to Ford Heights, a southern Cook County, Ill., suburb that had been largely black throughout its history. Within years, though, Ford Heights lost its uniqueness: fair housing practices opened other city and suburban neighborhoods to minority home buyers. Middle-class black families left Ford Heights for more prosperous communities.

"All of a sudden our people had options," says Gordon, who now works for a suburban antipoverty program. "Housing integration killed this town."

Today Ford Heights is America's poorest suburb. After middle-class flight weakened the community, rust-belt economics all but finished it off. So many factories have closed in nearby towns that the unemployment rate in Ford Heights may approach 60 percent. The social landscape is equally grim. "Everything Chicago's got, we've got—homicide, rape, all of it," says Police Chief Theodore France III, whose full-time officers start at a paltry $9,000 per year. In the past, outsiders called the town Mudville because it had few sidewalks. Today some teenagers in Ford Heights use a more menacing nickname: Vietnam.

Ford Heights exemplifies the American dream gone sour. Boarded-up buildings and burned-out houses dot the neighborhoods. The public swimming pool, built with federal dollars, holds only rainwater and debris; Ford Heights cannot afford the insurance necessary to open it. The equipment on a nearby playground is so dilapidated that, when they tried, volunteers couldn't begin to repair it. "We're in a time warp," says Brenta Draper, another antipoverty worker. "The first time I saw this place, I thought I'd been beamed back to the Mississippi of 50 years ago." Many of the elderly among the 5,300 or so residents moved to Ford Heights from Southern states. Gus Oldham, 65, came from Kentucky in 1941 and landed work in a brass foundry. Today he is disturbed by the bleak prospects his town offers its young: "No jobs, no recreation, no parks, no nothing."

Ford Heights has tried to improve its lot. The town failed in its efforts to land either a fireworks warehouse or a state prison. Recently Ford Heights urged a New Jersey company to build one of the nation's largest garbage incinerators in or near the community. The town even changed its name in 1987 (from East Chicago Heights) in hopes of changing its luck as well. But neither a trash complex nor a name change can uplift a populace with more welfare-dependent young mothers than skilled workers. Draper says her clients are less sophisticated than poor city dwellers at exploiting government services that might improve their lives. "Out here," she says, "we're trying to empty an ocean with a teacup."

Plenty of Everything, Plenty of Nothing

Nearly half of all Americans live in suburban areas, and most enjoy a modicum of comfort. But in their midst is another world, one they rarely encounter, where more than 9.5 million people live in poverty—and where conditions are likely to grow worse.

The Richest

SUBURB	PER CAPITA INCOME	METROPOLITAN AREA
Kenilworth, Ill.	$61,950	Chicago
Bloomfield Hills, Mich.	$59,830	Detroit
Hewlett/ Woodsburgh, N.Y.	$59,300	New York
Ladue, Mo.	$55,962	St. Louis
Mission Hills, Kans.	$55,136	Kansas City
Sands Point, N.Y.	$54,393	New York
North Hills/Roslyn Estates, N.Y.	$52,150	New York
Harding, N.J.	$52,067	New York
Oyster Bay Cove/ Mill Neck, N.Y.	$51,650	New York
Cherry Hills Vlg., Colo.	$50,016	Denver

The Poorest

SUBURB	PER CAPITA INCOME	METROPOLITAN AREA
Ford Heights, Ill.	$4,943	Chicago
Cudahy, Calif.	$5,170	Los Angeles
Bell Gardens, Calif.	$5,337	Los Angeles
Alorton, Ill.	$5,795	St. Louis
East St. Louis, Ill.	$5,973	St. Louis
Coachella, Calif.	$6,185	Riverside
Huntington Park, Calif.	$6,298	Los Angeles
Camden, N.J.	$6,304	Philadelphia
Centreville, Ill.	$6,341	St. Louis
Florida City, Fla.	$6,490	Miami

SOURCE: "THE GEOGRAPHY OF WEALTH AND POVERTY IN SUBURBAN AMERICA," BY PIERRE DEVISE, ROOSEVELT UNIVERSITY, CHICAGO

Ford Heights isn't Chicago's only suburban wasteland. In Robbins, a town that essentially has been broke since 1985, newly elected Mayor Irene Brodie wants Bill Cosby and Oprah Winfrey to stage benefit shows so the village can pay its dwindling work force; many impoverished residents fear a collapse of police and other services. In the once thriving industrial satellite of Harvey, Charleen and Nick Hamilton feed destitute suburbanites at the Franciscan Pilgrim Shelter. "They don't like it when we take a night off," says Charleen. "We're the only constant in their lives." Social workers complain that even in the poorest suburbs, needy families often have few alternatives to comparatively high-priced apartments. Ann Hernandez often shocks the unwed mothers she counsels by explaining that, unlike their friends in the city, they will need financial help to support a suburban household. "You can't survive here on public aid," she tells them. "You'd better get a boyfriend."

Ford Heights' new mayor is determined to rebuild her suburb. Gloria Bryant, a school official and former health administrator who took office in May, is orchestrating long overdue community cleanups; next comes a volley of grant applications for foundation assistance and job-training funds. "I'm going to lay the guilt for our predicament at everybody's door," she says. She is even plotting ways to get assistance from richer suburbs. "Ford Heights is depressing its neighbors' property values," Bryant explains. "They have a vested interest in helping us." She won the mayoralty from her friend Saul Beck, a 16-year incumbent. To the end, Beck opened village board meetings by asking participants to join hands and pray for Ford Heights and its people. Beck isn't sure his successor's flurry of initiatives will make much difference. "Grant money alone won't save us," he says. "If we don't get some businesses to move here, our future will be just like our past."

Coping with the poor was not what suburban planners had in mind when they plowed under the potato fields of Eastern Long Island 40 years ago. Suffolk County was designed for prosperity; today it is one of America's richest counties. But more than 86,000 Suffolk families live below the poverty line. Thousands more are on the verge of destitution—and the problem is growing. Last year Suffolk spent $224 million in federal, state and county funding to house, feed and care for the poor, double what it spent in 1980. "Everyone operates under the illusion that the suburbs are these idyllic places," says Suffolk County Social Service Commissioner Ruth Brandwein. "Poverty here doesn't hit you in the face."

It exists, nonetheless. Homeless families are packed into dreary motels along Sunrise Highway. In the affluent resort towns of the Hamptons, some inns that cater to beachgoers in the summer become welfare hotels during the off-season. In Ronkonkoma, a once rustic lakeside lodge now houses a dozen black welfare mothers and their families; angry neighbors have surrounded the hotel with a 12-foot barbed-wire fence. Years of de facto segregation by real-estate brokers have isolated some of Long Island's poor just as effectively as that fence, creating black ghettos within larger white enclaves. In the town of Wyandanch, Straight Path Avenue cuts through blocks of suburban blight where prostitutes and teenage drug dealers loiter outside bars and gutted buildings. Police recently arrested a 10-year-old boy for selling crack—one of 600 crack users arrested so far this year in southwest Suffolk. The infant-mortality rate is among the highest in America.

The majority of Suffolk County's poor, however, are invisible; on the surface they may even seem prosperous. Unlike urban areas where poverty often passes down through generations, many of Long Island's poor are in economic trouble for the first time. The soaring price of real estate is wreaking havoc in once modest middle-class communities. Young families cannot afford to buy homes; it is not unusual to have to spend up to 75 percent of income for the few, exorbitantly expensive rentals that can be found. Many are one paycheck from eviction. Elderly residents, with property but little cash, are forced to deed their homes to the county in return for welfare services. "The young and the old are running hard to stay in place," says Brandwein.

For one divorced mother, the descent from comfort to welfare was painfully swift. Today, Nancy, 45, is struggling to make ends meet, living with her 24-year-old daughter in a modest Center Moriches apartment. A decade ago she was the wife of a prosperous Long Island businessman; she spent her days gardening and taking care of a sprawling split-level ranch house complete with greenhouse and pool. Each year she spent $5,000 for Christmas gifts, entertained her husband's clients and enjoyed a small collection of ruby and diamond jewelry. Her pleasant suburban life collapsed when her husband left for another woman. With no job skills and a child to feed, she quickly drained what little savings she had. Unemployed, she sought assistance from the county. Now she works at minimum wage at a local welfare office in order to receive her government subsidy and food stamps.

Women are particularly vulnerable to sub-urban poverty. Marie, 27, slipped into welfare two years ago after her husband abandoned her and their two daughters. Today she receives $780 a month in welfare and food stamps, but must pay $700 a month for her small apartment. Gone is the '69 Cadillac and the $2,000 stereo system. "Everything all of a sudden just fell apart. I get really depressed when I look at what I had and I have now."

Poverty is in some ways more difficult to bear in the midst of plenty. "People expect you to have money," says Nancy. "They ask me when I plan to throw a barbecue. I just laugh." Marie's daughter comes back from school demanding the latest Barbie doll or the same new clothes her more affluent schoolmates are wearing. "My daughter is only 4 years old and she already wants Reeboks," she says. But

Suffolk County also offers advantages to its poor. Unlike many urban areas, jobs are available. The county is seeking federal job training and day-care programs to help those on welfare compete for jobs. Officials are also trying to ease the housing crunch by building moderate-income housing for working families, and are joining with churches and private nonprofit groups to build transitional housing for the homeless.

The county may need it. With the region's economy slowing, the suburban dream for more and more of its residents is turning sour. "What I experienced could happen to anyone," says Nancy. "You have no idea how fragile your existence can be." Many Americans in the suburbs can spend this summer enjoying their lives. But for a growing number, the living is not easy.

Creative alternatives to urban sprawl: A tale of two cities

TODD OPPENHEIMER/*NORTH CAROLINA INDEPENDENT*

Urban sprawl offers many things that car-oriented Americans have come to expect—fast food, fast roads, and convenient shopping centers. It is also an easy method of creating new subdivisions, sitting just beyond the noise of urban life. But sprawl can also weaken or destroy the vitality of downtowns, limit the supply of inexpensive houses, paralyze the roads with cars, eat away at safe drinking water supplies, and scar much of the landscape with asphalt, plastic signs, and sterile, cookie-cutter buildings. It also perpetuates the automobile as the sole component of our urban transportation system, because it makes alternatives such as mass transit, bicycles, and walking almost impossible.

For some people, sprawl's damages run even deeper, destroying a crucial sense of community. In their book *Sustainable Communities* (see excerpt in *Utne Reader,* May/June 1987, p. 36) Sim Van der Ryn and Peter Calthorpe argue that the modern suburban lifestyle has imprisoned us in a narcissistic world of private property—automobiles, sealed office buildings, shopping centers, and subdivisions. Meanwhile, our shared domains—public parks and plazas, intimate public streets built with neighborhood stores and sidewalks for pedestrians—have been eliminated.

So how do you build a healthy economy and keep a sense of neighborhood? How do you save a downtown? How do you accommodate growth without traffic jams? How do you create affordable housing? And how do you protect your land and water supplies?

To find answers to these questions, I traveled to Oregon and California, where some of the more ambitious programs to limit urban sprawl are in place.

Portland, Oregon

Twenty years ago, the economy of downtown Portland, Oregon, was as weak as any ailing downtown in the country. Stores were steadily leaving the area and the streets, they used to say, "closed at 5 p.m." In 1969 the nation's then largest regional mall was built across the river that borders downtown Portland, stealing half of downtown's commerce overnight.

Suburbs mushroomed in distant corners of Portland's metropolitan area, pulling more activity

PHOTO COURTESY TRI-COUNTY METROPOLITAN TRANSPORTATION DISTRICT OF OREGON

A light rail train glides through Portland, Oregon.

from Portland and forcing the city to build more freeways. Traffic was continually contributing to air pollution around Portland, violating federal standards for all but a few months of the year. By 1972, says Bill Wyatt, director of the Association for Portland Progress, "Downtown was clearly on the slide, and going downhill fast. A real crisis atmosphere started."

A year later, Neil Goldschmidt was elected as Portland's mayor and launched a $420 million bus and railway plan. At the same time, Portland halted construction on one of its main expressways along the Willamette River, and used much of the highway money for mass transit. In the highway's place, Portland built a waterfront park. Several years later, the city tore down a parking garage that sat on down-

Dinosaurs haunt our landscape

Many fast-growing cities from coast to coast feel in the forefront of modern urban design. They're ripe with peaceful, secluded subdivisions, shiny office "parks," and miles of freeways. And between it all lie dozens of smart little shopping centers, each lavished with plenty of parking spots, trees, and appealing exterior designs. This is supposedly the future—home to today's high-tech suburbanite.

In truth, if trends around the country are any judge, many of these towns are busily building a land of concrete dinosaurs, because development is designed almost exclusively around the car. There are signs that urban planning is looking beyond the familiar auto-oriented landscape to new communities that accommodate pedestrians.

In Florida, for example, in an attempt to help plan the subdivision of tomorrow, the celebrated pollster and futurist Daniel Yankelovich determined that the primary local political movement of the 1990s would concern traffic congestion. Planners in Los Angeles, the leader in car communities, recently determined that no amount of highway building, mass transit, or staggered work hours would solve traffic problems. Instead, L.A. officials determined, people need to live closer to where they work and shop.

Planners, developers, and architects throughout the nation have been searching feverishly for ways to encourage that lifestyle—and finding answers. Two solutions have recently become quite popular in regions familiar with the downside of dependence on cars. The first was pioneered in Los Angeles by Jon Jerde. Jerde's approach, which has been wildly successful, is to build shopping centers that are outdoor, public plazas, in the vein of carnival-type malls in tourist spots such as Baltimore's Harbor Place. But Jerde has found that this style works even in less glamorous regions. In some cases he's rebuilt monolithic shopping centers by tearing off the roof, building open-air or window-covered plazas and turning the classic, vast parking lot into a network of pedestrian streets and additional shops. The aim, he said, is to "build the city that's missing."

Unfortunately, before building a truly pedestrian city, we need one more ingredient: homes and offices close enough to shopping areas to make foot travel, or bus networks, practical. Enter the second solution, best exemplified by the work of Andres Duany and Elizabeth Plater-Zyberk, a Miami-based architectural team.

In the last year, Duany and Plater-Zyberk have designed nine new towns in old-fashioned village patterns—in Texas, Indiana, New Hampshire, New York, Maryland, and Florida. Streets in these communities are not secluded cul-de-sacs without sidewalks, as we have in most suburban communities, unsuited for both buses and walkers. Instead, they lie in the traditional grid pattern, spreading out from a town center or a plaza around which homes, shops, and offices are all mixed together.

This concept flies against most of today's development ordinances, which encourage or allow secluded subdivisions separated from shopping centers and office parks. The alternative these architects have designed is a simple ordinance that basically recreates the pedestrian neighborhoods of old, where homes and apartments are intimately mixed among stores, restaurants, offices, public plazas, even libraries and post offices. People walk to work and to the store. In free hours, they are frequently found outside chatting with one another more than one sees today in suburban communities.

If it sounds wonderful, this concept involves big changes for many Americans. It requires people to live much closer together, without the big yards and private cul-de-sacs that lace most of today's suburbs. In return, the architects argue, people get the chance to live, work, and shop by foot or bus, even rail. Judging from the communities where this concept has been built, both adults and children begin interacting more on the street. Most importantly, it presents the only long-term solution to today's car society, which breeds isolation, frustration, and increasing hours behind the wheel. According to the reams of national press on Duany and Plater-Zyberk, their developments are inexpensive to both builders and buyers, and immensely profitable.

Duany told me that in each community where they've proposed their plan, they've encountered almost no resistance. The reason, he said, is that car-dominated development is "expensive, stressful, and anti-social." By contrast, his mixed, pedestrian alternative is "educative, amusing, and inexpensive."

—Todd Oppenheimer
North Carolina Independent

Excerpted with permission from the North Carolina Independent *(May 5, 1988 and Nov. 17, 1988). Subscriptions: $22/ yr. (24 issues) from North Carolina Independent, Box 2690, Durham, NC 27705. Back issues: $3 from same address.*

The suburban lifestyle has imprisoned us in a narcissistic world of private property.

town's most valuable piece of real estate. In its place, with $8.5 million, Portland built a facility that doesn't draw a penny of income. It's now a piazza named, appropriately, Pioneer Square.

The overall goal was to do what most city officials fear is impossible: bring people to the center of the city day and night. By the early 1980s, downtown employment had grown by 60 percent.

Walking through Portland one sunny morning, I passed dozens of nooks and crannies, which told me that city planners had carefully thought of me, the pedestrian. City parks and fountains—from the small and cozy to the large and glorious—pop up throughout downtown. An old colonnade facade was saved as a border for Portland's busy Saturday market. Drinking fountains are everywhere.

For lunch I stopped at Pioneer Square and found a hub of activity most communities only dream about. In the center, which is surrounded by an amphitheater, gathered musicians, magicians, and food vendors with pushcarts. I ate my lunch sitting on a long tile ledge that borders the square's waterfall. On the cobblestone street behind me ran Portland's new light rail line, opened in 1987. Amost anytime one can see clusters of people waiting under protected shelters for one of Portland's 500 buses. Each shelter contains a detailed sign of that bus route, a phone, and a TV screen displaying the schedule.

In many growing areas around the country, officials are generally pessimistic about mass transit, saying people refuse to live in patterns centralized enough to make it feasible. But, Portland transit officials note, a range of bus and van systems can be coordinated to fit dispersed communities. And people are willing to change. In Portland, which like many cities struggles with diffused suburban growth, transit officials already have counted $400 million in new private development along the transit lines.

Portland's downtown car traffic now looks like that of a town half its size, and air pollution standards are violated an average of one day a year.

Davis, California

In various corners of the country, old cities have begun downtown revitalizing efforts that may someday result in the kind of life Portland enjoys. But even if they succeed in using mass transit and pedestrian-friendly designs to make their cities less dependent on

the auto, that won't keep developments on the fringes of town from turning into sprawl.

The most common approach to fighting such suburban sprawl has involved aggressive building restrictions, such as those in Davis, a quaint college town of 40,000 in the middle of California's farm country. Davis' residents are obsessed with preserving its intimate, college-town flavor. So for more than a decade, they have made the unusual choice of putting almost no one on the city council or planning commissions who has financial ties to real estate development. As a result, Davis council members have been able to slow the city's accelerating rate of growth, create a certain amount of low and moderately priced housing, and maintain its peaceful and diverse neighborhood atmosphere.

The mixed approach to housing is a direct result of a 1975 growth control regulation, which involves a point system and a limit on building permits (about 400 per year). Before approving each of those homes, city officials ask for a range of "extras" from developers, such as a diversity of designs, a good supply of less expensive homes, a minimum of environmental damage, creation of open areas, and help with additional city service cost. Those who accumulate the most "points" on these extras are first in line for building permits.

Davis also restricts the size of its shopping centers to eight acres. The idea behind this rule is to create commercial centers that are oriented to each neighborhood, rather than expansive regional monoliths that will only compete with each other and feel inhuman to shoppers. Most Davis residents now have to drive (or walk or bicycle) only a mile or so for their basic daily needs. Shopkeepers know their customers. The grid of roads to these scattered centers is rarely jammed. When it's hot, thanks to landscaping regulations, people can park underneath canopies of trees.

Davis' goal, in essence, has been to create an alternative to some of the worst aspects of sprawl.

As in any city, there have been limits to the creativity of city officials. But the community ethic in Davis runs deep, even in some private developers. A local planning consultant, recently elected as the first developer on the city council in more than a decade, built a subdivision in one corner of Davis that is reputed to be one of the most innovative subdivisions in the world. The project, called Village Homes, comprises 240 homes on 62 acres, which are threaded with vineyards, fruit orchards, knolls of wild vegetation, and a network of small parks, and foot and bicycle paths. Homes sit in tight clusters along narrow streets. And, most unique of all, the homes back against the streets in tight, intimate clusters. The front yards open onto the shared common areas of countryside.

SERV-URBS, U.S.A.

The restructuring of service
industries is speeding the growth
of "outer cities" on a new
American frontier.

Steven R. Malin
CB Economic and Business Environment Program

By laying off nearly 12,000 employees this past fall, financial services firms on Wall Street fired the loudest salvo in the most recent phase of this country's peculiarly silent industrial revolution. With glistening new office towers going up at a dizzying pace in every major city, few observers had noticed the flurry of pink slips being issued by service-sector companies—precisely the firms that developers had expected to rent space in the towering office buildings in downtown areas.

In 1987 alone, numerous companies in the financial services, advertising, communications, and airline industries reduced their staffs, and more layoffs are expected in 1988. Although service-sector employment increased in 1987 at roughly the same rate as real consumer spending (about 2.8 percent), the recent spate of layoffs suggests that future employment gains will be harder to come by.

Ironically, shrinkage in some parts of the service sector coincided with growth in manufacturing sales, orders, and employment. During most of the 1970s and 1980s, contraction in manufacturing and the ascendancy of the service economy captured headlines and the attention of policy-makers. Yet recent competitive pressures have begun to force many service companies to take steps very much like the ones that profit-starved manufacturing companies took only a few years ago. Increasingly, service companies are consolidating, merging, down-sizing, closing some facilities and moving others to less expensive sites. As they do so, they are changing the face of our metropolitan areas and suburbs.

Developing Regional Capitals

The service sector promises to be the main driving force behind long-run economic growth in all regions. Already, thriving service-sector economies have created unofficial "regional capitals" throughout the country—for example, in Boston, Atlanta, Los Angeles, and New York City. Surrounding these regional capitals are smaller cities or well-developed suburban counties, some of them 50 to 150 miles away, which derive a kind of economic energy from growth in the central cities and greater regional economies. These surrounding cities typically have a solid economic base of their own, often anchored by a major university or industry. Their resources often include a highly skilled and educated work force, vacant land and buildings, and community leaders who strongly encourage entrepreneurialism. Commonly, too, these surrounding areas offer lower-priced goods and services and a less hurried life style than regional capitals. Among other attractions, they have established transportation systems and well-developed business services.

During the past decade or so, regional capitals have been best able to reap competitive advantages from the development, sale, and distribution of all types of services. Concentrations of service companies in a wide range of industries make regional capitals attractive as sites for corporate headquarters as well as back-office and other large-scale operations. Cities such as Boston, New York, Chicago, Atlanta, Miami, and Los Angeles, for example, took on expanded roles in domestic and international finance, business and professional services, education, and tourism. Seattle, Memphis, Atlanta, Indianapolis, and Los Angeles/Long Beach grew as distribution hubs. Enhancing their natural advantages

From *Across the Board*, February 1988, pp. 23-27. Reprinted by permission of The Conference Board.

as production and distribution centers, the Great Lakes cities grew by focusing on finance, insurance, and university-based research.

In most regions (except perhaps where manufacturing industries are declining), businesses, households, and governments have adapted readily to service-sector growth and the market opportunities it creates. In several major central business districts (notably in Atlanta, Boston, Chicago, New York City, and Washington, D.C.) real estate developers have already begun to adjust to service industries' growing needs for space and electricity by tearing down existing structures and rebuilding on the same sites, or on sites nearby. Rapid development of suburban commercial and industrial areas within commuting distance of urban centers has forced many local and state governments to expand and improve roads, water systems, and other infrastructure. Consequently, the borders of major urban business centers continue to move outward. Suburbs and exurbs gain businesses and employment that are no longer bound by need or tradition to downtown areas.

Turning Suburbs Into Outer Cities

In a *New York Times* article in November, William K. Stevens used the term "outer cities" to describe what he called "vast, glittering, independent [suburbs] that rival and often surpass the traditional big-city downtowns as centers of economic power and vitality." According to Stevens, "the outer city is not really 'sub' or 'ex' anything anymore, but rather an urban entity all its own: an evolving landscape of skyscrapers, office parks and retail palaces, arranged in formidable clusters." Stevens cites several examples: Tyson's Corner, Virginia, west of Washington, D.C.; the South Coast Metro Center in Orange County, California; the City Post Oak–Galleria Center on Houston's west side; and the King of Prussia–Route 202 complex north of Philadelphia. Stevens says that "these and many others are pushing ever outward into the countryside," redefining metropolitan areas—but as what?

Some experts say that the outer city represents a transition to a wholly new urban form that reflects the general disenchantment with city life styles; the increased pressure on managements to find lower-cost production sites; the greater flexibility offered by contingent work arrangements and new technologies; and the erosion of long-established relationships between companies and their suppliers, distributors, and governments. In a study of suburban business centers, two geographers, Truman A. Hartshorn of Georgia State University and Peter O. Muller of the University of Miami, conclude: "We're in a new city-building era. The last real surge of growth was 100 years ago, with the manufacturing city. Now, with the service economy, it is really just mushrooming again."

Yet, the new outer cities have distinctive characters that distinguish them from the suburbs that sprang up in previous decades. This time around, the developing outer cities have dense downtown areas and service-based economies. As experts such as Hartshorn and Muller have written, the suburbs have developed in four distinct stages:

☐ In the first stage of suburban development, from roughly 1900 to 1960, areas surrounding major cities were essentially "bedroom communities," with localized wholesale and retail operations, some light manufacturing, and a cadre of commuters who trekked daily to city-based jobs. With few, if any, exceptions, suburbs lacked the cultural amenities of the central cities and remained linked to the downtown areas by commuter railroads and expanding arterial freeways.

☐ Then, in the 1960s, suburban shopping malls sprang up and in time became the "shopping centers" of metropolitan areas. Shopping facilities followed middle-class households out of the cities. Traditional downtown shopping areas, with their higher prices and dearth of parking facilities, no longer dominated retail trade.

☐ In the 1970s, suburbanization became irreversible. The suburbs had developed a critical mass of economic activity, attracting regional and national headquarters of corporations, hotels, restaurants, and specialized businesses once thought to be "geographically immovable bastions of downtown enterprise," such as mortgage banks, accounting firms, and law firms.

☐ So far in the 1980s, suburban economic development has benefited from the proliferation of highrise buildings in business centers, expansion of high-tech activities, and consolidation of activities that enable business clusters to compete with traditional downtowns. Growth in the number of households in the suburbs meant that a fresh available labor force could be reached outside the borders of central cities. New telecommunications and information technologies eroded many long-established ties between companies and cities. As this development proceeds, the outer cities will concentrate on developing living and working amenities, such as the arts, libraries and other cultural enrichments, and hospitals.

Of course, the character of the outer cities varies from metropolitan area to metropolitan area. Hartshorn and Muller write that "Houston's City Post Oak–Galleria Center is the most impressive specimen," but the South Coast Metro Center in Orange County, California, is "a more diverse and balanced development that more closely approaches a true urban character." In the older metropolitan areas of the Northeast, Hartshorn and Muller found that the outer city "more typically has been grafted onto existing urban and suburban centers," as in Stamford, Connecticut, and White Plains, New York; two exceptions are Tyson's Corner outside Washington, D.C., and King of Prussia–Route 202 outside Philadelphia, which were both created from scratch. In all of these cases, the outer cities grew out of central cities with well-developed service sectors.

Sunbelt mushroom: The South Coast Metro Center in Orange County, California. Its diverse and balanced development approaches "a true urban character."

Photograph by Wendall Dickinson: Vantage Photo Dynamics

The Central Cities' Response

In order to compete against outer cities and general suburban development, many central cities have devised multifaceted strategies to attract or keep people and businesses. For these cities, the challenge is clear: Changes in technology, corporate culture, and industrial mix threaten to further weaken traditional business-sector bonds to downtown areas and make central business districts less attractive. The high costs of living and working in central cities puts them at a disadvantage. As a result, the loss of manufacturing plants and jobs will limit economic diversity and close off a traditional route to the middle class for low-skilled and poorly educated workers.

Over the next decade, these trends could aggravate the fiscal strains on government, resulting in cutbacks in city services. Class differences could widen and strain the cities' social fabric. Rising crime, inadequate education and health-care systems, and housing shortages may be the inevitable consequences. A declining sense of civility and communal ambience may also turn central cities into places that both families and businesses want to avoid.

Recent economic gains by manufacturing industries suggest that these trends may soon be interrupted and partially reversed. In the industrial Midwest especially, growth in manufacturing employment and expansion of some production facilities promises to stabilize population while creating expanded markets for a wide range of business and personal services. Increases in wholesale and retail trade would inevitably follow. In the next several

years at least, the central cities would benefit most from this manufacturing-led recovery. But before the mid-1990s, the benefits would spill over into the nearby outer cities that derive energy for growth from them.

So far in the 1980s, many U.S. central cities are losing the competitive struggle for business against the suburbs, outer cities, and lower-cost cities in other regions of the country. Take New York City, for example:

☐ New York City's share of its metropolitan area's job base is shrinking, as other parts of its region, especially northern New Jersey, become increasingly cost-competitive. Annual job growth in New York City from 1978 to mid-1987 averaged 1.2 percent, half the 2.4 percent rate of increase in the rest of its metropolitan area.

☐ In the first half of the 1980s, commuters filled almost half of New York City's new jobs.

☐ Through 1995, New York City's economy will continue to expand, but its job gains will lag behind those of northern New Jersey.

☐ Back-office jobs, the traditional strength of New York City's service-based economy, are moving out of the central city. This not only costs the city jobs directly, it also weakens the city's real estate and construction industries, support service industries, and tax base.

☐ Back-office relocation out of New York City could result in major job losses for city residents, especially for minority workers, who are overrepresented among clerical employees.

New York, like many other cities, has responded to these trends with some imagination, some lethargy, and some ambivalence. Typical responses

81

include offers of tax and development incentives, energy-cost reduction, and urban-development grants. But such incentives typically work best when a company is already motivated to operate outside the central business district. In what is perhaps the most creative response, cities have developed miniature "outer cities" *within* their borders. In New York City, for example, there have been extensive public-private efforts to stimulate business relocation from Manhattan to the other boroughs, especially Brooklyn and Queens. A recent report by New York City's Commission on the Year 2000 called these areas "regional centers."

Successful regional centers would, in effect, extend the boundaries of the central business district while offering many of the advantages of suburban sites. Each center would have a sharply improved appearance, as well as upgraded police, fire, and sanitation services to promote an image of being a safe and clean place to live and work. By moving to regional centers, companies would be able to maintain face-to-face business contacts and relationships with money and capital markets and have access to business services and cultural events. Regional centers would also provide businesses with a more communal work environment, cheaper rents, and a ready supply of labor.

Yet, despite their obvious advantages to large cities such as New York, regional centers would probably provide only minor benefits. Last spring, for example, the Bureau of Labor Statistics reported that Manhattan's share of total New York City employment in key back-office industries (banking, securities, and insurance) actually *increased* from 90 percent in 1977 to 94 percent in 1986, even though the city actively campaigned to relocate financial companies' back-office operations to the outer boroughs. Although several major investment banks did move various operations from Manhattan to Brooklyn in 1986 and 1987, these relocations will not provide a major impetus to the city's economy. Companies have been slow to move to the outer boroughs, despite significant incentives offered by the city's government and utility companies.

Ironically, large-scale development of regional centers within central cities could impose serious long-term strains on already outdated or obsolete water, sewage, transportation, and public-safety systems. Arterial highways and secondary roads could quickly prove inadequate in New York City (as in other relatively old, vertically extended, densely populated cities). Similarly, shifts in the number of bus and subway riders could strain the public transit system, highlighting such problems as inconvenient subway stations and a shortage of buses. These logistical problems could disrupt neighborhoods and cause costly, time-consuming traffic congestion.

In the long run, these problems would be less severe in some of the newer, "horizontally extended" cities in the West and in some still-expanding cities—such as Jacksonville, Phoenix, and Houston—where the infrastructure is not yet fully in place. Elsewhere, increased needs for water, sewage, and sanitation systems could cause or exacerbate local environmental problems.

By blurring the distinctions between the central business district and the city's surrounding suburbs, regional centers could also jeopardize the distinctive character of neighborhoods at the outer rim of the city. In some places, the city fathers have not been able to revise zoning ordinances in time to prevent a disorderly mix of business and residential land use. Some residents of cities that grew rapidly in the 1970s and 1980s (such as Tampa, Anaheim, and Albuquerque) complain that industrial and residential development is robbing their neighborhoods of the character that encouraged them to move there in the first place. Both longtime residents and new migrants often find that growth has brought unwanted sights, sounds, and smells. Elsewhere, some deteriorating neighborhoods have been turned into viable middle-class hamlets, but sharply higher rents have led to a loss of some businesses and forced poorer residents to leave.

Future Growth Patterns

Because of natural handicaps facing regional capitals, the outer cities will continue to dominate metropolitan area growth and drain strength from central cities. The power of this ongoing trend will vary from place to place, reflecting the relative strength and maturity of each area's respective service sector.

Over the short run, however, mature service cities stand to lose increasing amounts of population, jobs, and sales to those outer cities that have an established network of service industries and office facilities. The differences in wages, rents, and taxes between central and outer cities will eventually narrow, and central cities will become competitive once again. Until then, the growth will be in outer cities that have mature service sectors.

New York, Los Angeles, and Philadelphia, for example, are mature service cities with multiple interconnections between industry and markets. Companies in these cities draw heavily on suburban and exurban work forces to fill staffing needs. This reliance cuts both ways, as suburban life styles and economic activity depend on the vitality of the economy in the central city.

Cities such as Atlanta, Orlando, Houston, Dallas, and Phoenix do not yet boast mature service sectors, despite strong growth in recent years. Their economic bases are relatively narrow and thus subject to the fortunes of a few companies. How those city-based industries go will significantly influence the rest of the region's economy. In the next several years, these cities will expand and diversify their service sectors. In the process, they will increase demand for office and retail space and help improve the economic fortunes of surrounding outer cities. However, unless people and businesses start moving out of these cities in great numbers, the outer cities will not siphon significant economic strength from the center.

The Midwest is loaded with cities in which the transformation to services is still very limited. While Pittsburgh has a large service base, for example, Cleveland, Detroit, Toledo, and Milwaukee can hardly make such a claim. Although the Midwest still has towns that are largely industrial, several of the larger cities will move toward service-dominated downtown areas in the years ahead. Improved manufacturing fortunes, moreover, will spur further growth in the service sector. New construction and new housing will be needed. People can be expected to stay put. Under these conditions, the Midwest could be poised for the nation's strongest urban growth in the next few years.

National and international economic conditions are expected to become increasingly important determinants of regional growth patterns, not only in the Midwest but in the whole country. For example, growth in such cities as New York, Boston, Hartford, Philadelphia, Atlanta, Chicago, Phoenix, and Los Angeles could be slowed if stock market turbulence or persistent increases in interest rates—such as those in the first half of 1987—cause dislocations in finance, insurance, real estate, and other industries.

In the long run, this can be expected to accelerate service-industry restructurings, down-sizings, and the closing of relatively expensive facilities. Although these dislocations may cause some short-run tremors in the suburbs, the full impact is likely to be felt in the central cities. The labor and real estate markets of the central cities are likely to be the largest net losers. In 1987 alone, workers in many large service industries in urban centers—notably finance, advertising, airlines, and communications—either lost jobs or job security as companies restructured. In some cases, city-based companies moved to the suburbs, thus increasing employment and sales in outer cities; in other cases, however, companies migrated out of the region, merged, or ceased operations, eliminating jobs held by city residents and outer-city commuters alike.

In the years ahead, restructuring and down-sizing of some service-sector companies (particularly in cities with already mature service industries) may be the greatest threat to economic vitality in the central cities. Like the manufacturing companies of the past decade, these firms will be cutting back and operating with leaner staffs to meet the challenges of a competitive environment. Potentially, these changes will increase the profitability of relatively large service-sector companies while creating new entrepreneurial opportunities for displaced workers and smaller firms.

However, these processes will also hasten the development of outer cities and reduce the economic importance of central cities. They will be a centrifugal force that will split up the city nuclei and stretch the metropolitan regions of the Northeast and Midwest, thus creating what the Sun Belt was a decade ago for the manufacturing companies: a new land of opportunity.

SEATTLE

Too Much of a Good Thing?

Jon Bowermaster

Jon Bowermaster is co-author, with Will Steger, of "Crossing Antarctica," to be published by Alfred A. Knopf.

A ferryboat whistle sings off nearby Elliott Bay and a warm rain dances off the awning that covers the sidewalk espresso stand—one of a multitude that line the wide, spotless avenues of downtown Seattle. The streets are packed with people on the way to work in the gleaming skyscrapers that tower above Puget Sound or shop in the fashionable indoor malls that are the heart of the new downtown. The affluent crowd shuffling past is young, sharply dressed, upwardly mobile: for every briefcase, there's a backpack; for every pin stripe, a pair of blue jeans. Everyone looks fit and prosperous. The whole scene is an advertisement for the good life. I feel like I've stumbled onto the set of a credit-card commercial.

Over the last decade Seattle has gained a reputation as the adopted home of America's hip and young, but it was popular even before that; in the last 20 years there have been roughly three waves of immigration. The first began at the height of the 60's and featured Birkenstock-wearing, guru-following, back-to-earth peaceniks lured by the town's frontier charm and boundless natural beauty. Many came without jobs, opting for "quality of life" over career track. But as word of Seattle's laid-back pace and affordability got out (and as magazines insisted on labeling it the nation's "most livable city"), the migration swelled. During the late 1980's a quarter of a million people moved to this corner of the Northwest.

The second wave of newcomers was richer and better-educated than the first and represented more the Saab-driving, home-buying, conspicuous-consumption class. They came from the East Coast, the upper Midwest and California, burned out on big cities, attracted by Seattle's proximity to the great outdoors, its "big city" art and culture scene and flourishing computer software and import-export industries.

But the good word could hardly be confined to the yuppie pipeline. As the newcomers sprawled beyond the city's limits, their developments of town houses and split-levels swallowing farmlands and threatening to climb the nearby Cascade Mountains, they were joined by a third wave of paradise seekers. These were as likely to be of Hispanic or Asian origin as white, from Saigon as from Boston. Refugees from Vietnam, Laos, Cambodia, Thailand; laid-off factory workers from the Rust Belt; disillusioned Sun Belters; the underemployed and unemployed from around the nation—like their predecessors, they came to Seattle because they'd heard it was a "better place."

In numbers, this last wave may have been less dramatic than the others, but there are plenty of representatives around. At an outdoor cafe, a black man in his early 30's—neatly dressed in a white shirt, blue slacks and bow tie—sits down and asks to borrow the sports pages. After a perfunctory swapping of scores, he introduces himself as Derrick Thomas and explains that he's lived in Seattle for just a month. A 13-year veteran of Chrysler in Detroit, he had just joined his wife and three sons, who preceded him two months earlier.

While it was lack of work that encouraged Thomas to search out a new home (he was laid off last January from his $15.65-an-hour assembly-line job), it was a quest for more basic security that finally lured him to Seattle. In recent years, he tells me, he had taken to wearing a bulletproof vest in his car when he drove to work through some of Detroit's worst neighborhoods; his eldest son, now 13, had been taunted at school by classmates waving wads of money they'd made selling crack; a friend's 15-year-old daughter was shot and killed while she sat on a neighbor's stoop.

In Seattle things improved immediately. Thomas's kids are doing better in school, his wife is working part-time, he's got an application in with Boeing, the area's biggest employer. There have been sacrifices, though. The best job he could find is busing tables in a cafeteria for just over minimum wage. Until recently, it was costing him more to live here, too. Thomas paid $350 a month for a four-bedroom house in Detroit; here he paid $550 for a two-bedroom apartment on Martin Luther King Jr. Way, a street in a rundown neighborhood, until he found an apartment in a low-income housing project. Unlike earlier newcomers to Seattle, Thomas did not come for the natural beauty that abounds but because the city has a reputation as a safe place—and because it has jobs. "It's peaceful here, everybody seems to be nice," says Thomas, drawing a last puff on a cigarette. "I think we made the right move."

THE UNITED STATES WAS FOUNDED ON THE NOTION THAT there must be a "better place" over the horizon. In the 1990's, we're still on the lookout for an American mecca. In the 60's, San Francisco (the Paris of the West) was reputed to be America's hottest city; in the 70's it was Denver. Eventually both were sullied—the former by a skyrocketing cost of living, the latter by an economy tied to the vagaries of the oil industry. The hip moved on. In the 80's, Seattle became *the* place to be.

It's not hard to see why. From the bow of one of the city-financed ferries that deliver commuters across Elliott Bay, the skyline of Seattle shimmers and sparkles in the first light of day. Twenty-strong, the new buildings jut into the sky, their mirrored facades reflecting the snowcapped peak of Mount Rainier and the Puget Sound. Anchored to the north by the Space Needle, to the south by a crane-littered port where ships load and unload containers filled with everything from doorknobs to prefab buildings, the city sits poised on a thin isthmus between the bay and Lake Washington. Its waterfront is rimmed with a string of picturesque clam and oyster saloons; above them whirs a six-lane highway, bringing scores of commuters into downtown. Within easy reach are old-growth forests, glaciers, wild ocean beaches, national parks and Canada. Theaters, galleries, symphony, opera and ballet are first-rate and well attended; the downtown streets are lined with public art, from poetry carved in the sidewalks and engravings on manhole covers to sculptures by Henry Moore and Alexander Calder. Seattle spends more on arts per capita than nearly any other city in the nation.

Seattlites have always been proud of their image as a kind of last frontier. In the 80's, a strong economy nourished that pride. Boeing, the region's largest employer, with 104,000 workers and an annual payroll of $4 billion, was flourishing; the Seattle-Tacoma port had emerged as a center for Pacific Rim trade; the high-tech industry, dominated by the giant Microsoft and with 350 other software companies, was in a boom phase. While other downtowns withered, Seattle's prospered.

All this good word swelled the region's statistics. The population grew by 18 percent in the last decade (the national figure was only 9); unemployment is now at a 22-year low (3.4 percent). Demand drove the housing market wild: last year the average selling price of a house in Seattle was 40 percent higher than the year before, and it was not unusual for anxious buyers to line up three and four deep and make offers on the stoop.

People liked Seattle for its small-town, big-city mix and lack of pretension. Many came to start families. In a recent poll the most common reply to the question "What Is Your Favorite Place to Unwind After Work?" (asked by the Seattle Weekly) was "Home." Migration to Seattle was so intense in the last few years that it became virtually impossible to rent a U-Haul to the area; trucks and vans were getting stuck here. No one was leaving.

That nothing lasts is nowhere more conspicuous than in the United States. As the 90's dawned, Seattle—and its booming suburbs and exurbs—was beginning to pay the price for its good press. That price is easily measured: the rising cost of living is making it harder for the middle class to live within the city limits, and there is an emerging clash between rich and poor. Tolerance, moderation, the small-town virtues that attracted people, are in shorter supply. Seattle is no longer a quaint frontier town but a booming metropolis teetering precariously on the brink of becoming something it did not particularly seek to become: a big urban city, with all the advantages and headaches that accompany that designation.

Must the growth of a city inevitably lead to decay? That seems to be the pattern in this country, in "livable city" after "livable city." We populate our urban areas to the point of degradation, then abandon them. Our cities, like so many other products of contemporary life, are disposable. The advance of technology, the change from a manufacturing to a service and information-based economy and the accumulation of private wealth have made it possible for people and commerce to settle pretty much where they please. And settle we do—over and over and over. The average American moves 11 times in a lifetime; nearly one-fifth of the population relocates each year. How long can this search for a "better place" continue before we have trashed them all?

TAKE A STROLL THROUGH OCCIDENTAL PARK, A BRICK-and-tree-lined commons just off First Avenue downtown. Homeless men loiter there; many curl up at night in the doorways of the hip coffee shops along First Avenue. Panhandlers energetically hustle the tourists, and crack dealers have made the corners around the well-known Pike Place Market their domain. Recent acts of gay-bashing have shaken the sanctity of downtown neighborhoods; racial attacks have unnerved city high schools. The school system is faced with large classes and an ineffective bureaucracy. Courts are overcrowded; plans for a new county jail are in the offing. Local businesses—among them Weyerhauser, Boeing, major banks and airlines—have recently announced layoffs. "It's a healthy economy, but it has plateaued," says Jim Hubert, editor of the Seattle-Everett Real Estate Research Report.

Seattle, more than most cities, is wary of outsiders. The relatively low housing prices of the mid-1980's attracted many equity-rich Californians, who sold their $750,000 homes in places like Orange County and bought similar houses here for a third of the price. Others bought inexpensive houses with good views and then tore them down and built neo-mansions in their place, raising tax assessments throughout the neighborhood. (Though the real-estate and home-construction boom abruptly ended in the past six months, the price of a home in neighborhoods like Queen Anne and Capitol Hill runs as high as half a million dollars.) Aggravating anti-outsider sentiment was the disclosure a few months ago that the Pike Place Market is actually owned by a Manhattan-based property management firm. Nor does it sit well that the city's professional baseball team, the Mariners, is owned by a businessman from Indianapolis, its football team by a California developer.

These days it is popular for Seattlites—both old and new—to blame their problems on this influx of newcomers. The biggest gripes are traffic congestion, air pollution, crime and the high cost of living. Voters proved they were against the "Manhattanization" of Seattle's skyline when in 1989 they forcefully ratified a cap on the height and size of downtown buildings. A growing faction has adopted the hostile rallying cry: "Have a Nice Day—Somewhere Else."

Perhaps the worst result of Seattle's uncontrolled growth in the last few years is the effect it's having on the pristine environment that drew so many people to the Northwest in the first place. In the past the city was a leader in urban environmental policies: Seattle has one of the highest garbage collection rates in the nation in order to afford the best recycling program; 82 percent of the city's residents participate in curbside recycling. In November 1989, 70 percent of King County voters agreed to tax themselves a total of $117 million so that the county could buy 3,000 acres of open space and 70 miles of trails.

Now that "forever wild" posture appears to be wilting. A statewide initiative on the ballot last November would have provided $160 million to help communities enact and enforce growth controls and zoning laws. The complex proposal was defeated 3 to 1, losing in every one of the state's 39 counties. The opposition was well financed; it spent $1.5 million raised from developers, real-estate agencies, Boeing, Weyerhauser and others. But the defeat is seen as a signal that even pro-environmentalists are beginning to check their pocketbooks before voting.

Yet now more than ever the Seattle area needs environmental consciousness: its landfills will soon be full. (As a temporary solution, the city has hired Waste Management Inc. to haul its 400,000 tons of annual garbage to a cash-poor county in Oregon, beginning next April.) According to the state departments of Ecology and Health, 40 percent of Washington's recreational beaches are "seriously threatened by pollu-

tion." Traffic congestion around Seattle is so bad that on many summer days a haze clouds Mount Rainier from view. Every day the city is becoming more and more like the Southern California megalopolis it so detests.

Seattle's growth is limited by its physical boundaries, but the region continues to expand. The population of the surrounding three-county area grew by 21 percent in the 1980's, to an estimated 2.5 million, with another 200,000 people expected by 1995. Dairylands and truck farms are being replaced by strip malls and warehouses, surrounded by tract homes on cul-de-sacs. Laurie McCutcheon, a local demographer who has spent the last few years studying population shifts for some of Seattle's biggest firms, isn't convinced that government leaders are prepared to deal with this growth. "In the early part of the decade, Seattle dominated the county," she says, "but today the growth in the suburban cities is dwarfing it, and the whole balance of power is shifting. We are fighting tooth and nail over governance issues, like 'Should the county take over all government—city, suburban, transportation, sewer and water?' "

David Bricklin, an environmental lawyer who headed the Initiative 547 drive, is even more skeptical. "When I moved here there were four tall buildings downtown," says Bricklin, a native of Philadelphia. "There was not a rush-hour traffic jam; now there are traffic jams any time of day or night, weekday or weekend. It took me an hour and a half to get from downtown to the airport the other day, in the middle of the afternoon. It is typically a 20-minute drive."

The problem is lack of foresight, he says. "We have virtually no mass transit—no rail, no segregated bus ways. We are just now trying to develop a plan for mass transit from Seattle out into the suburbs, but that's a decade away at best."

Bricklin maintains that things are not as bleak as the 3-to-1 defeat of 547 indicates, but he still despairs: "Am I optimistic about Seattle's future? No, I don't think so."

FROM HIS OFFICE 12 STORIES ABOVE FOURTH AVENUE, first-term Mayor Norm Rice looks out on the skyscrapers that block the once clear view of the Puget Sound. Building more of them, he says, is not on his agenda. Mayor Rice understands that if he wants to govern a truly "great" city, expanding Seattle's diversity—of economy, ethnicity and race—is essential. It won't be easy, but Rice insists he is optimistic about Seattle's future. At the recent "urban summit" in New York, presided over by Mayor David N. Dinkins and attended by 35 big-city mayors, he appeared downright smug. A lot of mayors are struggling to save their cities; Rice is worrying about how to preserve his.

"Every major urban city is a magnet," he says, tugging at the knot of his tie and propping his feet on a glass-topped table. "Some people come in hope, some to hide. Some succeed, others fail. But as the number of people coming to Seattle who are unable to climb the ladder of success grows, they and their problems begin to consume your whole sense of what you want to do as a city."

The explosive growth of the last three years has been "great," Rice admits, "but I think it is possible for us to oversell ourselves." He also admits that he welcomes a slowdown in the economy and rising housing prices: both will slow the numbers moving to Seattle and give the city time to figure out how to accommodate the population that is already taxing existing facilities and services.

One of Mayor Rice's biggest challenges will be convincing Seattlites to stay and fight rather than head for the next mecca—or the suburbs. "It used to be that when things like schools got bad the middle class would flee—to a place like Seattle," he says. "But now all cities face the same problems. There is no 'better place' to escape to. People have to stick around and get involved if they want to save their schools and their neighborhoods."

Preparing the city for an increase in Asian, black and Hispanic minorities is also near the top of the Mayor's list. Seventy-five percent of Seattle's population of 512,000 is white. Rice, who is black, knows that Seattle must be successfully integrated if it is to make the transition from a "livable" city to an "international" city (as neighboring Vancouver has done so successfully). "Our biggest balancing act now is that we don't want a city that's all white Anglo-Saxon Protestant. Seattle deserves a multi-cultural, multi-ethnic population."

AT A SMALL TABLE IN THE PHNOM PENH NOODLE HOUSE, across the street from a sprawling Asian restaurant-grocery store-pharmacy-gift shop called Uwajimaya, I share a bowl of noodles with Lin Nouen, an 18-year-old Cambodian who has lived in Seattle just one month. Smiling broadly, he repeats how glad he is to be here. When he first moved to the States—thanks to a sponsor in Austin, Minn.—he'd been disillusioned. It was too cold, and there were too few Asians. He kept hearing that Seattle was the place to be, and he arranged a "transfer." Today, dressed in the uniform of a typical high-school junior—stone-washed jeans and high-top sneakers—he says it is better here than he ever expected. "In one month I make more friends than I made in eight in Minnesota."

Outside the window, Asians of all ages, armed with shopping bags and bus schedules, pop in and out of markets that line the streets, their shelves laden with seaweed, noodles, exotic fruits and sake. This neighborhood is called the International District: there are Filipino clothiers, Laotian-run bars, Chinese, Japanese and Vietnamese newspapers, Asian welfare agencies,

Korean movies and a Cambodian hair salon. Asians are Seattle's most visible import—their population increased 16 percent between 1985 and 1988.

Lin says he is already investigating the job market. He hears there are $7-an-hour jobs at a clothes manufacturing shop and is considering quitting school to take one. "Already I like Seattle, very much," he says. "I think I may stay here, maybe all my life." He has sent word to family members—scattered through Cambodia, Thailand and Laos—that this is a good place.

Less than a mile from the International District, another kind of trade featuring another kind of immigrant flourishes as dusk settles over the port city. From near-downtown apartments and dilapidated wood-frame houses in the Rainier Valley neighborhood come street hustlers, crack dealers, whores and gang boys, eager to begin their day while the commuters are heading home. Up and down Pine and Pike streets, from Capitol Hill to the Alaskan Way viaduct, clusters of young toughs—of a variety of ethnic groups—gather on street corners. They hassle passers-by and peddle their illicit wares to drivers who cruise slowly by.

Police have been battling this "invasion" for several years, ever since Seattle became a favorite stopping-off point for gang members—Crips and Bloods—from Southern California. They came for the wide-open drug market, traveling straight up the Interstate 5 corridor that stretches from Los Angeles to Vancouver. Teen-age prostitution was already a problem downtown, and soon crack houses proliferated.

Then last summer a new explosion of cocaine dealers surfaced on the corners near the Pike Place Market. Patrols were beefed up; more of Seattle's first-in-the-nation mountain-bike cops were deployed. Mayor Rice and the City Council armed the police with a controversial new drug-trafficking and loitering ordinance that enabled them to arrest anyone observed selling drugs on the basis of "conspicuous actions," even when no contraband is found. "I worry when I see gangs hurting people on our streets, when I see gangs fighting in our parks," says the Mayor, "but the biggest issue facing us right now is the fine line between being 'tough on crime' and harassment. We have yet to come to grips with it."

The apartment of the novelist Tom Robbins looks out over this troubled neighborhood (known as "the Blade" because it is "on the edge"). From his window he can see signs of all the changes that the recent boom years have wrought on his adopted home (he moved here from Richmond, Va., in 1962): traffic jams, smog, street punks, skyscrapers. "In many ways this place was wilder 20 years ago," Robbins says. "The difference is, while it has always been easy to get beat up on these streets, 20 years ago you didn't worry about getting killed."

Now 54, the cult storyteller divides his time between

2. URBAN EXPERIENCES

Seattle and a house near the sound, an hour outside town. "The changes are all a matter of perspective," he says. "People who come here now rave about the place—but I know that 15, 20 years ago Seattle really was paradise. For those of us who were here then, we do see the place today in much darker hues." He pauses and looks out on the neo-lit street below. "But I could live anywhere in the world, and I choose to live in Seattle."

UNLIKE MOST AMERICAN CITIES, SEATTLE ENJOYS A strong economy despite recessionary rumblings. Boeing appears to be on an unstoppable roll: profits for the year will exceed $1 billion and the company has a backlog of orders for nearly 2,000 jets, worth over $90 billion, enough to keep it busy through 1995.

"The only wild card in our future is what goes on in the Middle East," says Craig Martin, a spokesman for Boeing. "We can't predict exactly what the results would be if there is some kind of economic upheaval as a result. Barring a major shooting war, our outlook is pretty positive." Just before Christmas the company's Seattle office handed out holiday bonuses equal to 5 percent of each employee's salary—a total of $253 million.

But Seattle's strongest economic card in coming years may be its proximity to the Pacific Rim. Closer by ship and air to Asian markets than any California city, the Port of Seattle is thriving: international air freight was up 8 percent last year; more than a million containers of cargo passed through the docks. It is also home to the $3 billion-a-year North Pacific fishing fleet. At a time when many big cities are cinching their belts, Seattle is expanding.

Shortly after this new decade began, David Brewster, publisher of the Seattle Weekly, gave warning about the obstacles that faced his adopted hometown (he came here from New Jersey in 1965): "The highest drama is to fashion a lasting marriage . . . to have vitality along with grace, hustle along with humaneness. Few American cities have managed to combine these qualities without toppling into giantism or heartlessness." That is still Seattle's challenge, but it won't be easy to achieve, especially given Americans' penchant for moving on instead of digging in.

Some of the more restless already have their bags packed. I met a fellow one afternoon outside the Osho Suravi Meditation Center (he'd moved here from Milwaukee five years earlier), and he explained why he would soon be heading for, in his words, "greener pastures." Greener? Really? "Seattle, for all its beauty, is just too big, too dirty, too congested. Don't tell anyone, but I know where the next mecca is," he whispered conspiratorially. "Burlington, Vermont."

CREATING COMMUNITY

A fast-food generation looks for a home-cooked meal.

by Deborah Baldwin

Deborah Baldwin is editor of Common Cause Magazine.

Members of the so-called baby-boom generation spent the last two decades on the move, like migratory birds on a flight pattern tuned to the ever-changing socio-economic winds. Now, say the pundits, an entire generation has a vague longing to settle down and be part of something — like a community.

Some symptoms of the nascent desire among baby boomers to flock together:

■ Many once-mobile midlifers indicate signs of work-related burnout. Beginning to wonder what it all means, they are casting for ways to contribute to the commonweal, strengthening their ties to communities in the process. Volunteerism, which dipped in the 1980s, is back where it was and expected to rise.

■ Families are beginning to stay put, presumably bound to their current roosting places by jobs and schools.

■ As their offspring enter school, baby boomers feel compelled to get involved in one of the most visible of all community institutions.

■ An absence of leadership in Washington — which turned its back on many social needs during the '80s — is forcing attention back to the community level.

■ Other symptoms of America's craving for connections: Computer networks, which conquer distance and loneliness in the great tradition of the ham radio, are springing up across the country. Call-in TV and radio talk shows, which enable complete strangers to share their most intimate secrets, proliferate.

■ The popular culture is beginning to reflect interest in community and self-improvement of the helping-others kind. The 1985 bestseller, *Habits of the Heart: Individualism and Commitment in American Life*, which explored personal and social values in America, is still selling well. More recent titles include *The Hunger for More: Searching for Values in an Age of Greed* and *The Brighter Side of Human Nature: Altruism and Empathy in Everyday Life*.

Because baby boomers — numbering an estimated 76 million — represent such a sizable chunk of the buying population, their perceived longing for human ties is already reflected on Madison Avenue, where ads for beer ("Miller Time") and Big Macs ("Food, Folks and Fun") feature warm images of friends and community. Television programming, too, which some media critics view as an extension of advertising, is increasingly sensitive to these themes; "Twin Peaks" got a lot of attention partly because it evoked people's fantasies about homespun small-town America and then blew them apart.

Some of the shameless sentiment being exploited on prime-time TV may be part of an inchoate nostalgia for a world that not only isn't what it used to be, but probably never was. At the same time, the imagery seems to reflect a palpable yearning for new ways of viewing the world and the individual's place in it.

The purported rebirth of the great American community poses a number of interesting questions, among them: How will community be defined in the 1990s? Are baby boomers willing to work to create and maintain communities — or will the concept remain an object of their fantasies? And if new kinds of communities are in fact springing up, what are the implications for political candidates and causes?

THE SCHMOOZE FACTOR

The tension between individualism and community is intrinsic to American culture. More than 150 years ago, French social philosopher Alexis de Tocqueville referred to the "thousand different types" of associations in colonial America that formed a bridge between individual self-interest and the community at large; the authors of *Habits of the Heart* (a phrase borrowed from Tocqueville) cite his belief that, through associations, Americans bonded to wider political communities and developed a sense of responsibility for the public good. Periodically — actually, most of the time — these high-minded impulses lose out to the equally powerful forces of entrepreneurship and personal mobility.

Given the cyclical nature of such things, it perhaps isn't surprising that after the mass group effort of World War II brought many Americans together, the advent of suburbia drove many of them apart. "Bedroom communities" — economically and racially segregated clusters of homes and schools — sprang up around the country and were communities only in the loosest sense. People moved constantly; to this day, one out of 10 homes changes hands every year.

As early as the 1950s, sociologist Robert Nisbet deplored America's changing physical and social landscape, saying it had profound ramifications for the democratic system. In his book *The Quest for Community*, first published 37 years ago and reissued this year, Nisbet asserted that the erosion of traditional family authority, neighborhoods and local community led to the citizenry's alienation and dependence on remote, centralized governmental powers.

Refugees from congested city neighborhoods and claustrophobic small towns rarely looked back, however. They focused on acquiring and maintaining their own high-quality private space — which 50s-era suburbs offered in abundance. Ensconced in roomy homes equipped with two-car garages, the middle class enjoyed a vast array of consumer products designed to make cocooning an increasingly feasible way of life.

The suburb has become a symbol of isolationism, but it occurred within cities too. At one time Chicago, Boston, New York and other cities were made up of racial and ethnic enclaves where people had at least nodding acquaintances with one another and shared some public space — if not town squares then crowded stores and sidewalks. Today the typical inner-city neighborhood is slapped with labels like "transition" or "gentrified," based on the number of yuppies who dwell there.

Starting in the '70s, dual-income couples divided their loyalties between workplace and home. By the 1980s, a period of rampant individualism, upper-income dwellers of inner cities and suburbia alike found they could enjoy all the conveniences of a fully equipped kitchen, laundromat, movie theater and rec room in the comforts of home, with only occasional forays to stock the shelves and refuel the car. With the more recent addition of a fitness center, VCR and computer-equipped office to the home environment, one could really feel alone.

Now that the pendulum is starting to swing slightly, living in style has become a symbol of loss as much as gain. As one radio commentator recently noted, we now have a society where people learn the meaning of communi-

"Twin Peaks" got a lot of attention partly because it evoked people's fantasies about small-town America and then blew them apart.

ty by sitting in front of the tube watching the neighborhood-bar comedy "Cheers." A similarly poignant image — of a lonely yuppie running on a treadmill in front of the TV set because he doesn't have the sense to don his coat and walk to a neighborhood bar or diner — was offered in a recent issue of the alternative magazine *Utne Reader* by a 40something who deplored his generation's disconnectedness.

The repressed urge to mingle has never completely disappeared and surfaces in curious ways. Gregarious individuals like to vacation in quaint places like New Hope, Pa., Nantucket, Mass., and Key West, Fla., where they can practically ruin a place walking around wishing they lived there. Town planner Andres Duany goes so far as to theorize that families flock to Disneyland not for the rides but for an opportunity to rub shoulders with other human beings in a pleasant, traffic-free environment.

Duany believes suburbanites in particular are tyrannized by their long, lonely commutes, which force them to spend most of their free time — he also calls it "political time" — in hermetic capsules. "You have a certain amount of free time in the day," he explained in a radio interview earlier this year, "and in a town you might go to a corner store and discuss the issues of the day with other people like you."

Duany belongs to a school of community enthusiasts that includes Ray Oldenburg, author of a paean to the endangered community watering hole called *The Great Good Place*. Oldenburg says bars, corner stores, barbershops and the like are essential to the democratic process because they en-

gender face-to-face grassroots involvement. "Television has obscured that need," he notes dryly, "but it has not obviated it."

The notion that the 1990s may usher in new definitions of community — to encompass extended families, friends, coworkers and even radio call-in show audiences — strikes Oldenburg as pathetic. "Can we really create a satisfactory community apart from geography?" he asks. "My answer is 'no.'"

"I'm aware of networking and how it helps careers and workplaces," he says, "but these are going in the wrong direction." Part of the problem: Professional networks shut out children, for whom community ties can be especially meaningful. In an effort to help raise his own sons' consciousness, the Pensacola, Fla.-based sociology professor took them to his home town of Henderson, Minn., population 740, where they ordered dime phosphates at an old-fashioned drugstore.

As community meeting places go, so go town criers. More than 7,000 American cities have no daily newspaper of their own, according to media critic Ben Bagdikian's seminal book *The Media Monopoly*. He views the concomitant decentralization of America and rise of the homogenized, monopolized, consumer-driven mass media as one of the biggest threats to our political way of life. While citizens vote in 20,000 urban and rural places around the country, he points out, they are served by media "organized on the basis of 210 television 'markets,' which is the way merchandisers and media corporations sell ads."

While some small-town refugees might question the level of political discourse that typically occurs in the pages of community newspapers, few would disagree with Duany's description of how most Americans gather information about the outside world: at home, after an exhausting day at work, in front of the TV. "Politics becomes extraordinarily primitive because there is no room for discussion," he maintains, "It's what you're fed by the media."

To qualify as a community, a town or city should be able to pass the so-called "South American Revolution Test," Duany says: "When you hear that the revolution has started, do you know exactly where to go, or do you have to go to the TV set to find out where people are gathering?"

THE COMMUNITY REDEFINED

During the 1950s and '60s, college and careers scattered young people across the country, far from immediate family and childhood friends. But, as Oldenburg suggests, the Tocquevillian urge to congregate and associate never disappeared. Definitions of "community" simply changed. Suburban-bred students formed urban and rural communes. Or they gravitated to the antiwar, women's and civil rights movements, which in a sense were communities based not on locale but shared values and goals. During the '90s, some social trendwatchers believe, the same overwhelming urge to join will drive aging yuppies off their treadmills and into the streets. Or at least so the theory goes.

The resurgence of interest in communities is often cast not only as a reaction to the Me Generation's flitting mobility and the sterility of its surroundings but also to the spiritual emptiness of the 1980s, commonly referred to as the Decade of Greed. "After a virtual orgy of individualism, Americans may finally be rejecting the idea that the best things in life come from looking out for No. 1," Suzanne Gordon, author of *Lonely in America*, wrote earlier this year.

Turn-of-the-decade commentators take hope from the statistics. The Boston-area branch of United Way attracted two and a half times more volunteers in 1989 than in 1988, according to a spokesperson. She notes a trend toward involvement in one-time, short-term projects — possibly a reflection of the hectic lives and short attention spans of many midlifers.

Perhaps as significant as trends like these are people's perceptions of them: While Gallup Poll data shows that volunteerism increased gradually during the 1980s, the level in late 1989 was about the same as it was before Bush took office amid all the fanfare about points of light. Nonetheless, the polling group reported, four in 10 Americans think the spirit of volunteerism in their communities is on the rise.

Rhetoric often precedes action, but in some cases it can replace it entirely; after all, it's a good deal easier to talk about the need for community and helping others than to do something about it. President George Bush seemed to get the words right in his inaugural speech, saying, "We cannot

One commentator argues that bars, corner stores, barbershops and the like are essential to the democratic process.

hope only to leave our children a bigger car, a bigger bank account. We must hope to give them a sense of what it means to be a loyal friend; a loving parent; a citizen who leaves his home, his neighborhood and town better than he found it." But for some reason those words sound hollow compared to President John Kennedy's ringing call for citizen involvement, "ask not what your country can do for you . . . ," which helped lead thousands of Americans into public service.

Maybe life was simpler then. Certainly, people believed they had more time and fewer obligations. "The biggest contradiction is that people would like to be active, but in most households both adults are working," says Jerry Hagstrom, author of *Beyond Reagan: The New Landscape of American Politics*. "My suspicion is that you'll see more involvement as people grow older. But you have to ask if it's in their own interest. . . . People are very active with schools because they have kids in them. Organizations through which they gain no personal benefit? I'm not so sure."

In the wry essay in *Utne Reader* mentioned earlier, writer Brad Edmondson points out that real community work means giving something up, and that's hard. He seems to capture his age group's ambivalence, noting, "We're passionate about community issues, but forever thinking about moving away to get a better job, more money or some other abstraction. The state of being in one place and thinking about another is our natural habitat."

Edmondson ends up predicting that during the '90s "more and more people will be in a position to join real commu-

nities instead of pining after imaginary ones," but not because he believes yuppies' politics will suddenly change. Rather, baby boomers are getting older, and older people don't move around so much.

RETHINKING THE '80s

Meanwhile, were the '80s as bad as some people think?

At least one social interpreter, Mark Satin, the iconoclastic editor of the political newsletter *New Options*, says no. "I guess I'm not sophisticated enough to see things correctly," he wrote early this year with self-conscious irony. "I liked the 1980s. . . . In the '80s we laid the groundwork for realizing the longings that were first brought to mass consciousness in the '60s. All kinds of strains are waiting to be hot-wired, now, by a new social movement."

Satin maintains that a new cultural archetype emerged during the '80s, "the caring individual," or one who is equally committed to self-development and social change, to individual freedom and social justice. A true grassroots democracy, he argues, requires these personally and socially responsible individuals.

Satin is heartened by the fact that many potential grassroots activists are now in their 40s or older, their "public years," in the words of Virginia Hodgkinson, who tracks national trends in volunteerism and charitable giving at the Washington-based Independent Sector. The public years typically follow two decades of absorbed careerism and childrearing and can be a fertile time for personal growth and social commitment, Hodgkinson and others believe. Her latest research indicates that midlifers and seniors are increasingly active in community organizations, but not necessarily because they are nearby. Rather, they tend to pitch in at places they are attracted to ideologically. (To accommodate volunteers from outside the neighborhood, Hodgkinson suggests churches and other community centers build big parking lots.)

For many baby boomers and their younger siblings, there's an added inducement — the memory of the '60s. One opinion poll of people in their 30s that showed 61 percent viewed the '60s as a constructive period and 51 percent missed the sense of community that existed back then.

Others say the urge to congregate never disappeared, but notions of small-town America are no longer relevant.

It's a good deal easier to talk about the need for community and helping others than to do something about it.

During the '70s and '80s, says Satin, "They were digging in for the long haul, by getting the degrees and establishing their careers. Now they're able to go out in the world and have an impact."

Just as he rejects the "media caricatures" of the '80s, he rejects some of the romanticization of the 1960s. An antiwar activist who fled to Canada to organize similarly disaffected Americans, Satin, now 43, recalls the era as divisive and judgmental, with too much emphasis on us-vs.-them. "I hope what we're moving toward is an integration of individualism and community with acceptance of the diversity in our society," he says.

Unlike Oldenburg and others, Satin is uninterested in bringing back small-town America, with its Main Streets lined with barbershops and bars. "I've lived in small towns," he says flatly, alluding to a childhood in small-town Minnesota and a more recent two-year stopover in tiny Winchester, Va. "It was boring."

Characterizing the notion of neighborhoods and geographical communities as "totally unrealistic," Satin says we tend to forget that the people who held together traditional communities were women. He credits the women's movement and other positive social changes for making traditional communities "impossible" and says even urban ethnic communities have been romanticized. "I suspect most of the city neighborhoods written about nostalgically were in transition. People were bound together by wanting to move up and out; their vivid, warm memories are of people similar to them,

who were also eager to move on."

Others agree that it's a mistake to idealize the past. "We can never bring the traditional community back," social philosopher John Gardner wrote in the *Kettering Review* last year. "The traditional community was homogeneous. We live with heterogeneity and must design communities to handle it." The author of books on leadership, self-renewal and other topics, Gardner added, "The traditional community commonly demanded a high degree of conformity. Because of the nature of the world we live in, our communities must be pluralistic and adaptive, fostering individual freedom and responsibility within a framework of group obligation."

Many community advocates nonetheless like the idea of having some sort of physical meeting place where all these diverse individuals can assemble, if more along the lines of a town hall than a corner store. In this kind of setting, Satin argues, participatory democracy, the kind that features face-to-face communication, can begin to flourish.

ARMCHAIR ACTIVISTS

Others, however, seek society at the computer terminal. All it takes is a personal computer, special software, a telephone line and a funny little box called a modem, which enables one computer to connect to another. Viewed by some as a panacea for citizens who, by design or default, are isolated geographically, socially or politically, electronic networks enable like-minded individuals to hold "conferences," share information and organize political campaigns.

While some computer illiterates find the technology intimidating, advocates see it as a warm, user-friendly way to give anyone who wants an opportunity to participate. "I happen to think the advent of new technologies, like cable TV and electronic networks, makes grassroots democracy a lot more viable than it ever has been," says Roger Craver, a fundraising expert who communicates mostly in writing and cheerfully admits he learned the significance of the electronic media by watching how his teenagers absorb information. (One observer has dubbed this multimedia process "paraliterate osmosis.") Craver says people are getting used to communicating by leaving messages

and picking up threads of conversation on their computers, hashing things out electronically instead of in person.

"The sense of community is now multi-dimensional," he believes. "While the fear is that [computers] subvert the interpersonal capacity, the fact that they are physically remote increases people's candor and willingness to share."

It's either the most exciting thing to come along since Tom Paine's printing press — or a classic couch potato's idea of getting involved. Either way, computer communities are spreading, spawning their own lingo and tribal customs. Some are tiny, while others boast so many members they can afford a professional system operator ("sysop") to manage the flow of information and edit it for usefulness.

One of the biggest and best-known grew out of the Hands Across America anti-hunger campaign, which put up $140,000 to help get it started. Apple also donated free training and $500,000 worth of computers and modems — no doubt in the hopes that such enterprises would grow and multiply.

Based in Santa Cruz, Calif., Hands-Net was launched in late 1987 to help disparate anti-hunger groups learn from one another's successes and failures. Subscribers get the latest in anti-poverty news and activities — all without the bother of paper and postage: "E-Mail" (electronic mail) does away with letters and telephone tag, and an "on-line" library generates data. "The main thing is the feeling of community," says network editor Susan Dormanen. "There's a national constituency [for antipoverty efforts] and it's a real empowering feeling for people, especially for small groups, to have access to all this information."

Other examples include SeniorNet, a San Francisco-based effort to break the isolation of computer-phobic senior citizens. It offers opportunities to "socialize" and classes in "electronic citizenship," or the art of applying pressure by modem.

Then there's SCARCNet, short for the Smoke Control Advocacy Resource Center Network, an anti-tobacco campaign run out of the Advocacy Institute in Washington. It comes with an international counterpart aimed at pressuring the U.S. to stop marketing cigarettes overseas. Both, says manager Nancy Stefanik, serve what she calls "the smoking control community."

No one knows how many electronic forums there are, although Tom Sherman, of the five-year-old Electronic Networking Association, guesses there are "thousands." Not surprisingly, ENA has no physical headquarters and issues its newsletter, "Netweaver," by computer.

One of the more intriguing experiments in computer communications is taking a trial run in hip Santa Monica, Calif. Its Public Electronic Network is free to all 95,000 residents, who can jump on-line to read city files, including the City Council's agenda, hold informal town meetings and accept and receive private E-mail.

The PEN system has been an over-night success, says a spokesperson, who scanned her computer files to identify the number of "accesses" during one recent month (7,095). She says residents have used PEN to debate such hot issues as rent control and the proposed construction of a new hotel. Some City Council members use it to gauge public opinion, although they are barred from using PEN to send out the electronic equivalent of franked junk mail.

Many Santa Monicans already own computers, but for those who don't, the city hopes to install terminals in the one place that might be thought of as where to go during the next revolution: the local shopping mall.

Urban Problems

Nearly every edition of the daily paper or evening news broadcast contains some reference to a crisis in one urban community or another. It has become a topic with which most Americans are quite familiar. More often than not, the reference is to some form of social disorganization. One important characteristic of the urban community, however, is a very high degree of organization. It would be impossible for so many people to live in such a small geographical area, demanding services such as food, housing, and work without some sort of organized effort to meet those needs. Nevertheless, there is a strain on the society that attempts to meet these needs, which is often reflected in the large number of problems that beset the urban community.

Suburbanization began as a movement of people from the central city to the outlying regions. However, the movement was not limited to people; commerce and industry also began to move. What started as a "bedroom community," where people went to spend the night after working in the central city, became a "full day community," where people worked, shopped, entertained, and slept. In short, the entire day was spent in the context of suburbia. Combine this fact with the growing obsolescence of the central city—where the factories and retail establishments as well as the housing are often old and in despair—and it becomes clear that the economic strength of the central city was diminished. Physical decay, high unemployment, crime, low tax rates, and burgeoning welfare rolls are the problems most often mentioned with regard to the central city, but the suburban communities have developed problems of their own. High land costs, poor transportation, and increased demands for services are just a few of the problems that the suburban communities share with the central cities.

In those nations with a strong central government, the allocation of resources can be, and often are, made in such a way as to attack the problems of both suburban and central city communities equally. In American society, however, such a strong central government does not exist. Instead, each city tends to operate independently of the other cities. Rivalries develop when cities compete with each other for the resources to solve problems. These rivalries are intensified by problems of powerlessness, poverty, favoritism, discrimination, and economic change.

Because cities tend to provide more in the way of work opportunities, education, and cultural enrichment, most urban dwellers consider themselves fortunate. While they recognize the personal alienation as well as the other problems associated with urban life, they view these inconveniences as the price to be paid for the increased opportunities presented by living in cities. The first four articles discuss the transportation dilemma, insisting that while automobiles may prove necessary, they should be subsidiary to mass transit; that traffic jams can only be curtailed by bold new governmental initiatives; that the nation must continue to repair its roads and highways and build new and better airports; and that highspeed railroads may represent a viable antidote to U.S. transportation woes. "De-escalating the War" maintains that it is essential to rethink society's assumptions about drug treatment, such as that greater emphasis be placed on drug treatment rather than on simply hoping that people will eschew drugs. Next, Stuart Greenbaum's "Youth and Drug Abuse: Breaking the Chain," insists that society must make a serious effort to alter delinquents' attitudes in order to modify their behavior. The next two articles treat the problem of urban poverty, arguing that the federal government must adopt a more aggressive approach to solving the problem, and that government programs must be instituted to salvage America's ghettos. The next two selections survey the housing crisis, warning that middle-class Americans are being denied the dream of home ownership and that large numbers of people and local governments are turning their wrath on the country's homeless. In "Health and the City," Len Duhl reveals that in many Third World countries, decent health care is fast becoming a privilege of the rich and powerful. Next, Mark Rosentraub and John Gilderbloom assess the plight of the country's disabled population, arguing for increased accessibility and barrier-free environments. In conclusion, David Ferrell, in "To Live and Die in L.A.," examines the AIDS care crisis in that city, arguing that the medical bureaucracy has exacerbated the epidemic.

Looking Ahead: Challenge Questions

Would forcing automobile owners to assume the true costs of driving—road maintenance, police protection,

ambulance service, and pollution control—make America's cities more livable? Why, or why not?

What, if anything, can be done to ease congestion on the nation's highways? Is mass transit the answer to the problem?

Why are traffic jams increasingly frequent both in big cities and in the suburbs? Of the many remedies that have been proposed, which appear the most promising?

Is the supertrain an answer to America's overcrowded highways and congested air routes? If so, how will it promote increased mobility and high-speed service?

Is confronting the causes of antisocial behavior more useful than intervention once young people have begun taking drugs? What explains the lure of drugs to many high-risk youths?

Why have many drug treatment programs failed to cure crack addicts? Should drug abuse be treated as a crime or an illness?

What social, political, and economic factors account for the rise in urban poverty? To what extent, if any, is the lack of affordable housing and loss of manufacturing jobs responsible for the problem?

Is it possible to rid America's ghettos of drugs, crime, and teen-age pregnancy? Why, or why not?

Why has home ownership become increasingly difficult, if not impossible, for many middle-class residents? Does this signal an end to the American dream?

Why are many cities growing increasingly impatient with the homeless? Does this say something about the American character?

Is urbanization responsible for undermining the world's health care delivery systems? Despite a universal desire to improve health care, why have many nations failed to adopt decent health care provisions?

Despite its desirability, why have many cities failed to enact legislation to ensure greater access to disabled Americans? Why has the nation failed to address the needs of people with limitations?

Is the government partly responsible for the AIDS crisis in urban America? If so, why?

OUT OF THE CAR, INTO THE FUTURE

Making car owners bear the true cost of driving—road repair, police and ambulance service, pollution—would open up a full range of mass transit options, and make cities more livable in the process.

MARCIA D. LOWE

Marcia D. Lowe is a senior researcher at the Worldwatch Institute and author of Worldwatch Paper 98, Alternatives to the Automobile: Transport for Livable Cities.

The automobile once promised a dazzling world of speed, freedom, and nearly limitless travel. With it, the average wage-earner could have more horsepower at his or her disposal than royalty had in other times. Small wonder the world enthusiastically embraced this new form of transport. Now, though, with the world fleet approaching half a billion cars, the automobile dream has turned into a nightmare of congestion and pollution, and city governments are looking for transportation alternatives.

Perhaps more than any other invention, the automobile embodies author Jacques Ellul's observation of all technologies: it makes a good servant but a bad master. Obeying the demands of the private car has dictated the design of cities and the very character of urban life. Vast roads and parking lots distort cityscapes, and sprawling suburbs devour open space around cities. When all available surface space has been surrendered to private cars, planners turn to aerial, subterranean, and other schemes: in the Japanese city of Yokohama, entrepreneurs recently opened a floating parking lot in the local bay.

Traffic congestion, now a fact of life in the world's major cities, has stretched daily rush hours to 12 hours or longer in Seoul and 14 hours in Rio de Janeiro. The Confederation of British Industry estimates that higher freight transport costs, lost employee time, and other results of congestion cost Britain $24 billion each year.

Motor vehicles are the single largest source of air pollution, casting a pall over the world's cities. Car-induced smog aggravates bronchial and lung disorders and is often deadly to asthmatics, children, and the elderly. Ozone (a gas formed as nitrogen oxides and hydrocarbons from exhaust react with sunlight), the major component of smog, is believed to reduce soybean, cotton, and other crop yields by 5 to 10 percent. Automobiles are also a major source of carbon dioxide, the greenhouse gas responsible for over half of the global warming trend, accounting for more than 13 percent of the worldwide total.

Oil's environmental downside includes more than air pollution; while accidental spills annually dump an estimated 2.9 million barrels into the sea, roughly six times more oil gets into the oceans simply through routine flushing of carrier tanks, runoff from streets, and other everyday consequences of motor vehicle use.

The economic vulnerability of car-dependent societies becomes painfully evident in the event of an oil crisis, such as Iraq's invasion of Kuwait in August. Even in a stable market, increasing reliance on foreign oil weakens the strongest economies and places a crippling burden on developing countries mired in debt.

The enormity of these automobile-related problems defies mere technical fixes. Without alternatives to automobiles, improvements in fuel economy and pollution control are partly offset by more people driving more cars over longer distances. And these changes do nothing to ease traffic congestion. Even electric cars, which could greatly reduce fossil fuel consumption and pollution, would still contribute to traffic jams.

Moreover, no new automobile technology can fully address the social consequences of more than one quarter of a million people worldwide dying in road accidents each year, and several million more injured or permanently disabled. No new car technology will serve the majority of people who will never own automobiles. A Fiat mini-car currently sells in China for roughly $6,400—a modest sum in some countries, but equal to about 16 years of wages for an ordinary Chinese worker. For all but the privileged elite in developing countries, more cars mean only more air pollution, more traffic congestion, and more dangerous streets.

Getting on Track

Creating a new vision of transportation, one that meets people's needs equitably and fosters a healthy environment, requires putting the automobile back into its useful place as servant. With a shift in priorities, cars can be part of a broad, balanced system in which public transport, cycling, and walking are all viable options.

Public modes of transport—buses, subways, streetcars, trolleys, trains, and even car and van pools—vary in their fuel use, the pollution they create, and the space they require, but, when carrying reasonable numbers of passengers, they all outperform the one-occupant private car on each of these counts.

For example, a commuter train carrying 80 passengers requires roughly 710 British thermal units (Btu) of energy per passenger per mile, and a trolley with 55 passengers

Table 1.

Pollution Emitted from Urban Transport Modes, for Typical Work Commutes, United States

Mode	Hydrocarbons	Carbon Monoxide	Nitrogen Oxides
		(grams per 100 passenger miles)	
Rapid rail	0.3	2	49
Light rail	0.4	3	69
Transit bus	20	305	154
Van pool	36	242	38
Car pool	70	502	69
Auto (one occupant)	209	1,506	206

Based on national average vehicle occupancy rates.
Sources: American Public Transit Association, "Mass Transit: The Clean Air Alternative," Washington, D.C, 1989.

uses around 1,050 Btu. A car pool with four people burns roughly 1,840 Btu per passenger mile, and a one-person car, some 7,380.

The emissions savings from using public transport are even more dramatic (see Table 1). Rapid rail (also called the "metro," "tube," "underground," or "subway" if running in tunnels beneath the city) and light rail (trolleys) have electric engines. So, pollution emissions are measured not from the tailpipe but the power plant (most often outside the city, where air quality problems are less acute). For typical U.S. commutes, rapid rail emits 49 grams of nitrogen oxides (a precursor to acid rain) for every 100 passenger miles, compared with 69 grams for light rail, 154 grams for transit buses, and 206 grams for single-occupant automobiles. Public transport's potential for reducing hydrocarbon and carbon monoxide emissions is even greater.

Public transport also saves valuable city space. Buses and trains carry more people in each vehicle, and if they operate on their own rights-of-way (particularly in underground tunnels), can safely run at much higher speeds. An underground metro can carry 70,000 passengers past a certain point in a single lane in one hour, surface rapid rail can carry up to 50,000 people, and a trolley or a bus in a separate lane more than 30,000. A lane of private cars with four occupants, by contrast, can move only about 8,000 people per hour.

In the developing world, flexible, informal forms of public transport take up where overburdened bus and train systems leave off. These include minibuses, converted jeeps, vans, and pickups, shared taxis, and cycle rickshaws that give crucial service and ply the city's hard-to-get-to sections. These vehicles account for 64 percent of road-based public transport in Manila and 93 percent in Chiang Mai, Thailand.

The cost of providing public transport is, understandably, the overriding factor in a government's decision when picking from transportation options. However, comparing the costs of providing bus and train service to those for private automobile travel is an extremely complex task. A fair comparison must include the full costs of both systems, including their environmental impact and the social consequences. And the evaluation must consider which approach can move the most people; with public transport's higher capacities and greater affordability for the general public, governments could get more for their money.

Similarly, drivers would find public transit more attractive if they kept the full costs of automobile transport in mind. Few U.S. drivers realize that, including fuel, maintenance, insurance, depreciation, and finance charges on their cars, they pay $34 for every 100 miles of driving. On a yearly basis, it costs the average solo commuter nearly $1,700 just to get to work. By contrast, the average public transport fare is $14 per 100 miles.

Cities for People

Walking and cycling are the most common forms of individual transport. Low cost, non-polluting, space-saving, and requiring no other fuel than a person's most recent meal, these options are the most appropriate for short trips. In addition to the economic and environmental benefits brought by fostering cycling and walking, quality of life improves in a city that welcomes people, not just cars. Yet non-motorized transport is often ignored by urban planners.

There are several ways to remake cities as places for people, and most concern keeping motor traffic from dominating city space. Pedestrians and cyclists need safe, contiuous routes to their destinations, which calls for separate lanes and paths in some situations but more often merely requires trucks and cars to share city streets with other types of traffic.

Where the road is shared, motor traffic needs to be slowed. In Europe, cities have used several techniques, known as "traffic calming," to turn streets into safe places for people who live, work, and shop nearby. The Dutch have changed the physical layout of their residential streets, transforming them into a *woonerf,* or "living yard." In the *woonerf,* cars are forced to negotiate slowly around carefully placed trees and other landscaping. Since motor traffic cannot monopolize the entire breadth of the street, much of the space is made more open to walking, cycling, and children's play.

West German cities use speed limits to slow down cars. Limiting speed on thousands of urban streets nationwide to 19 miles per hour over the past five years has reduced accidents and noise and exhaust levels. As with traffic calming, this method is most effective when applied to entire zones rather than single streets.

One of the most potent ways to make streets more amenable to pedestrians and cyclists is to restrict car parking downtown. Car commuters are forced to choose options other than driving, which reduces the number of cars on the street. Whereas many cities in the United States, West Germany, and the United Kingdom require employers and developers to provide parking spaces, Geneva prohibits car parking at workplaces in the central city, motivating commuters to use the city's excellent public transport.

Creating an automobile-free pedestrian zone is another way to make the heart of a car-crazed city livable again. Nearly all major European cities have devoted at least part of their centers to people on foot. Munich's impressive 900,000-square-foot pedestrian zone owes much of its success to easy access via convenient public transport services. Third World cities with heavy concentrations of foot traffic and street vendors could enhance safety and improve traffic conditions with pedestrian zones. After pedestrian streets were established in Lima, Peru, the number of street traders and shoppers on foot increased, and traffic flow through the center improved dramatically.

The Road Not Taken

Automobile dependence is most deeply ingrained in cities that have tried to use road building to combat traffic congestion. Los Angeles, Phoenix, Miami, and many other U.S. cities have gone this route. The result is a treadmill effect in which new roads fill to capacity as soon as they are completed. To break this cycle, the very shape of cities has to

Table 2.

Urban Densities and Commuting Choices, Selected Cities, 1980

City	Land Use Intensity (population + jobs/acre)	Private Car	Public Transport	Walking and Cycling
			(percent of workers using)	
Phoenix	5	93	3	3
Washington	9	81	14	5
Sydney	10	65	30	5
Toronto	23	63	31	6
Amsterdam	30	58	14	28
Stockholm	34	34	46	20
Munich	37	38	42	20
Tokyo	69	16	59	25
Hong Kong	163	3	62	35

Source: Peter Newman and Jeffrey Kenworthy, *Cities and Automobile Dependence: An International Sourcebook* (Gower Publishing: Aldershot, England 1989).

change to reduce the imperative for driving.

Although all major cities struggle with traffic congestion to some degree, those with the least sprawl are best able to promote alternatives to driving. Australian researchers Peter Newman and Jeffrey Kenworthy of Murdoch University in Perth studied 32 cities worldwide and found that low urban densities (measured by the number of people and jobs per acre of land) and auto dependence generally go hand-in-hand. Phoenix, for example, where 93 percent of workers commute by private car, is less than one-sixth as dense as Stockholm, where only 34 percent get to work by car. In Perth, Australia, 12 percent of workers commute by public transport, while in Munich, which is roughly 6 times as dense, 42 percent of workers use public transport (see Table 2).

Strong land-use policies to increase urban densities, then, are crucial in fostering viable alternatives to automobile dependence. Although the term "high density" evokes images of towering apartment buildings and little open space, dense developments are pleasant and livable if planned well. According to a study done for the United States Environmental Protection Agency, a compact development can mix two- to six-story apartments and townhouses with clustered single-family homes, and still leave 30 percent of the developed area for open space and parks. In a typical low-density sprawl community, the study says, only 9 percent of the land is devoted to open space.

More than simply increasing density, land-use policies should create a mix of different types of development. Zoning can foster mixing of homes with commercial uses instead of making them separate and thus creating long commutes. University of California researcher Robert Cervero points out that in much of the world there is no longer a strong case for separating homes from industrial and commercial areas. Whereas the original purpose was to prevent nuisances from smokestacks and slaughterhouses, "Today the 'nuisance' facing most suburban areas seems . . . more one of traffic congestion," says Cervero.

Economic benefits flow from a city's commitment to public transport and developing careful land-use planning. In direct terms, a recent study in Melbourne demonstrated that locating a new household in the central city instead of on the outskirts saves thousands of dollars in infrastructure, municipal services, commuting, and other costs.

Leaving the Auto Behind

In early 1990, President Bush unveiled a new U.S. National Transportation Strategy meant to guide the nation for the next 30 years. Unfortunately, this strategy is really just a tired collection of policies that would keep the automobile in its favored place by reducing funding for public transport, failing to revise tax policies that encourage automobile commuting, and only vaguely mentioning the importance of cycling and walking. Unwittingly, the plan shows the world exactly how not to construct a transportation strategy. What conventional transport policies of this sort fail to acknowledge is that eventually, auto-centered societies could collapse under their own overwhelming burden of congestion, pollution, and oil dependence. If cities around the world are to break out of the current transportation mess, a policy overhaul will be needed.

The surest way to lessen over-dependence on cars is to force drivers to bear more of the true costs of driving. So long as automobile owners are showered with inducements, such as free parking and government-subsidized roads, they will stay in their cars, leaving trains, buses, and bike paths empty. This is a vicious cycle, since planners are unlikely to invest in transport alternatives when existing systems are underutilized.

The first step is to bring to light the hidden costs of driving, such as air pollution, municipal services, and road construction and repair. Perhaps least-recognized of these public expenses are items such as police, fire, and ambulance services required for an automobile-centered system. According to an analysis of the salaries and personnel time of the Pasadena Police Department in California, 40 percent of department costs are from accidents, theft, traffic control, and other automobile-related items. Extending this finding to the entire United States suggests that local governments spend at least $60 billion on automobiles. Employer-provided free parking (a tax-free fringe benefit) represents another huge subsidy to drivers, variously estimated to be worth an additional $12 to $50 billion a year.

A gasoline tax on the scale of $1 to $2 per gallon, which is now common in Europe, would make drivers pay more of the costs they impose on society. It also makes sense to levy a sizable tax on new cars, as well as raising the annual registration fees. Another approach is to follow the new German policy of taxing cars based on their emissions: the more they pollute, the more they pay. Given the gross imbalance of many cities' transport systems, it makes sense to dedicate some of the revenues from auto user fees and taxes to the development of cycling and pedestrian facilities and public transport. Without sizable and sustained government funding, the needed alternative transport infrastructure will be slow in coming.

If driving became more expensive, people would begin to demand alternatives. This would help counter the large and powerful road lobbies made up of oil companies, car makers, highway builders, and other interests that pressure governments to favor the automobile.

Effective land-use planning is the other key to a viable new transportation system. Here, cooperative approaches may make the most sense. Municipalities can, for example, share the cost of expanding transport services by striking deals with private land developers who benefit from enhanced access to their projects. Joint development schemes can be planned at new subway stations, helping to defray costs.

Several studies suggest that there is a threshold level of urban density—12 to 16 people per acre—below which reliance on the automobile soars. This density level, about that found in Copenhagen today, is the minimum that urban planners should aim for.

Zoning and financial incentives can be used to cluster homes, jobs, and services along public transport corridors. Ideally, these policies would be implemented in conjunction with comprehensive and integrated regional development plans so that one community does not simply push its transport problems off on another. The aim should be to make inner cities comfortable and convenient so that people will want to live there.

The time for action on the world's urban transport crises has clearly arrived. Indeed, in many nations the costs of additional automobile ownership are already outweighing the benefits. If cities are to achieve the dream of clean, efficient, reliable transportation once promised by the automobile, they will have to steer instead toward more sustainable alternatives.

TRAFFIC JAMS
The city, the commuter and the car

LONDON drivers fume as they crawl round their city centre at an average 11 miles per hour, barely faster than their horse-drawn great-great-grandfathers. Others would envy them. Rush-hour Athenians could travel more speedily in the days of the chariot than the 5 mph they manage today. And in Bombay cars have gone back roughly to the pace of bullock carts.

Traffic jams are nothing new. Central London moves about one mile an hour slower than in the 1970s, yet faster than in the late 1950s. But the jams today spread wider and last longer than they used to. No longer are they confined to the rush hours of rich city centres. They are increasingly frequent off-peak and in the suburbs. And they are endemic in some cities of the third world.

It is easy to see why in cities that are rapidly growing. The number of cars in Lagos doubled to 200,000 between 1976 and 1982, without any notable improvement in the roads. No wonder traffic slowed to walking pace. In Bombay, a peninsular city like some third-world Manhattan, with one vehicle for every five metres of road, bus travel has become so hard that people have turned to motorbikes and bicycles. So now 120,000 motorbikes compete for road space with the city's 175,000 cars, adding to the day-long chaos. That is the price of growth.

Why, though, should traffic seize up also in cities like London and New York, where fewer people live, and no more work, than used to? The answer is that not only are there more cars but the people, though they may be fewer, travel more.

Western Europe in 1976 had 26% as many cars as people; by 1986 the figure was 35%. In the United States the proportion rose from 51% to 56% during the same period; in Japan from 16% to 24%. That helped produce large increases in the volume of car travel—23% in West Germany, 30% in the United States, 41% in Japan—while the amount of travel by public transport in most countries hardly changed.

These nationwide trends are true in the cities as elsewhere. The number of jobs in Manhattan has stayed around 2m for several decades. But the proportion of its workers commuting to them by car rose from 10% in 1960 to 16% in 1980. With this huge rise in commuter car traffic came a steady fall in the use of the rail subway. But in most rich cities increasing car traffic has not meant any less

travel by public transport. Between 1983 and 1987 the number of journeys on London's Underground rose from 560m to 800m, 120m higher than the previous peak, in 1956. Yet the number of cars entering inner London also rose, if only by 5%.

New cities, new jams
The reason is that London has changed. Its centre actually has 10-15% fewer jobs than in the early 1960s. But they are different jobs. The stevedores, meat-handlers and machine-operators who have all but disappeared did far less commuting than the salesmen, advertising managers and word-processor operators who replaced them. They travelled around to fewer business meetings, lunches and dinner parties. Neither did they have to share their city with 24m tourists every year.

The congestion too has changed. The latest studies show that traffic in central London moves at much the same crawl all day, and that the gap between speeds in the centre and in the rest of the city is narrowing. In other European cities too city-centre snarl has spread to the suburbs or indeed to entire conurbations. But, predictably, the United States leads the way.

The developers who started building big new office complexes outside American cities in the 1970s assumed that their users would be able to speed to work along big, open freeways. They were wrong. In 1980 the suburbanite on his way to work was driv-

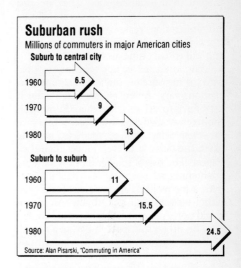

Suburban rush
Millions of commuters in major American cities

Suburb to central city
- 1960: 6.5
- 1970: 9
- 1980: 13

Suburb to suburb
- 1960: 11
- 1970: 15.5
- 1980: 24.5

Source: Alan Pisarski, "Commuting in America"

ing barely faster than the city-dweller: 24 mph against 21 mph. Since he was also driving farther, 12 miles rather than 9, he actually spent longer behind the wheel.

The cause—and effect—is clear: the freeways, like the centres, are clogging up. In 1975, some 40% of rush-hour traffic on urban interstate highways (in English, motorways) was rated as congested; today, about 65%. True, "congested" here means average speeds below 35 mph—a breakneck pace by city-centre standards. Yet the warning is there. Rush-hour speeds often fall below 10 mph in the busiest corridors of Los Angeles, despite its 4,000 miles of freeways, expressways and superhighways.

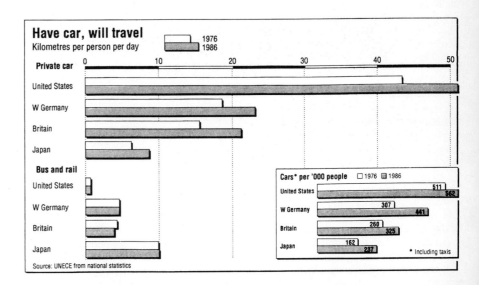

Have car, will travel
Kilometres per person per day
- 1976
- 1986

Private car
- United States
- W Germany
- Britain
- Japan

Bus and rail
- United States
- W Germany
- Britain
- Japan

Source: UNECE from national statistics

Cars* per '000 people □1976 ■1986
- United States: 511 / 562
- W Germany: 307 / 441
- Britain: 260 / 325
- Japan: 162 / 237

* Including taxis

3. URBAN PROBLEMS

The costs of congestion

These changes require a broader approach to the costs of congestion. Till now, its effects have been measured mainly in terms of the time—and thus, by appropriate estimates, money—wasted by commuters travelling to work in the city centre. Now, far wider costs must be taken into account. Bigger ones too. Traffic jams that last all day and stretch from city centre to suburb are not only less avoidable and thus more inconvenient than localised ones. They are also more expensive. America's Federal Highway Administration reckons delays on urban freeways cost more than $9 billion in 1984 and will cost six times as much by 2005.

But lost time is not the only trouble with, or measure of, traffic congestion. Perceptions vary. Americans feel they suffer if they have to drive at less than 35 mph on the freeway; Bangkok's bus-passengers face far worse delays, but get really fed up only when the delay lasts even longer than they expect. The risk of total gridlock is far more frightening in Los Angeles than in cities with a metro like Paris or New York: their citizens could still get about, Angelenos could not. At a recent international conference on urban transport in Berlin, a French academic worried about the level of subsidy to public transport that would be needed to keep congestion down; in Lyons, he feared, it might have to quadruple by the end of the century. In contrast, a city planner from Stockholm measured the trouble in terms of atmospheric pollution.

That is a growing concern in Europe. Thirty years ago, few people outside California had ever heard of car-generated smog. Today, as they see their old buildings—and, in extreme cases, their old or feeble people—crumble under its impact, Europeans too are alarmed. Smog this winter brought threats or appeals to limit the number of motor vehicles entering Milan, Paris and Geneva. In Athens, where car ownership has risen more than eightfold since the mid-1960s, and could double again by 2000, traffic fumes are reckoned to cause 85% of the air pollution that is eating the Parthenon away. So throughout the working day entry to the city centre is restricted: cars with even number-plates one day, odd ones the next.

What is to be done?

As these examples show, there is no universal answer to traffic jams. The possibilities depend on the characteristics of each city, on political priorities, on the reasons for seeing congestion as a problem at all.

The once-obvious cure-all was to build more and better roads. That is apt to cost votes as well as money, but may still be possible, as it was in Haussmann's Paris and is today in Istanbul, where new highways can even now be bulldozed ruthlessly through decaying slums and commercial property. Yet the costs have become ever less accept-

able as (and because) the benefits have become less clear: traffic, it seems, merely expands to fill the new road-space available.

The allied answer, more parking space, has long since demonstrated that effect. This remedy too at one time looked obvious. In rush hours a double-parked car blocking one lane of a main road for 12 minutes can delay 2,800 other vehicles. Paris reckons it is short of 700,000 parking spaces for the 1.3m cars entering the city each day. Yet should it provide them? More parking attracts more cars. Some cities, once insistent that new buildings should have parking built-in, now wonder if they should demand exactly the opposite. Tokyo has all but eliminated parking, on-street and off-street alike, in its centre. In vain: the streets are still packed with taxis and through traffic.

Nor, though they can help, will new rail or rapid-transit systems clear the roads. Britain's transport ministry has just published grandiose plans for London. British Rail is to link up the now separate main rail termini. The Underground will be upgraded and expanded. All this should be complete by the end of the century. By then rail traffic is expected to have risen by a further 20-30%—and road traffic by 12-25%.

Vast investment in Paris's RER regional express-rail network in the 1970s showed that, with enough subsidy, it is possible to move many more people by public transport. What it did not do was unblock the roads. The RER carries 300m passengers a year, while 1.2 billion continue to go by metro. But the number of commuter cars entering Paris has doubled in 25 years, and traffic is expected to increase by 7% in the next ten years. Average city-centre speeds have already declined to about 9 mph.

There are other answers. Some cities, from Oxford to Los Angeles, have set up "park and ride" schemes, with huge car-parks on the outskirts and frequent shuttle buses to take drivers on into town. Many cities have created pedestrian enclaves, to free at least part of their centres from the tyranny of the car. These work, but they also push the traffic elsewhere. Some German cities pedestrianised large areas in the 1970s. Finding these did not reduce the total inflow of cars, they have now imposed direct restrictions: limited access for through traffic, less road-space for cars, more for cycles or buses. Buses, for example, get lanes of their own, and a stop may be deliberately so sited that a waiting bus does not let other traffic flow freely past but blocks it, and has an open road when it itself moves off.

South Europeans tend to be more wary of restrictions like these, and less disposed to obey them. In Madrid, 80% of rush-hour traffic is at a halt or inching along in first gear, because the wide streets are choked with double- and triple-parked cars. When smog provoked the city government to announce an emergency programme to reduce

car use, critics pointed out that half the measures were already in law, but unenforced.

Even Italian cities have started to take traffic control more seriously. Most have now held referendums on whether to close historic centres to traffic. The answer is always yes, but few cities have acted on it. Florence claims to have the largest closed area in Europe—but allows 27,000 residents to take their cars into it. Rome allows so many exceptions—the opening of some entrances to the restricted zone during the lunch-hour, for instance—that the centre is still packed. Last year Rome's city council had to shelve a proposal to reduce the Christmas rush by number-plate restrictions like those in Athens; the argument about it brought the council near to collapse.

In America's congested suburbs, the scope for restricting car use and switching commuters to conventional public transport is limited. Even when an office tower is next door to a station, workers will not use rail unless, at the other end of the journey, their homes too are near a station. Surveys at Washington's New Carrollton Metrorail station and San Francisco's Pleasant Hill showed that fewer than 4% of people working nearby commuted by rail.

So American cities have tried to use their roads better, encouraging car-sharing and new forms of suburb-oriented public transport. Washington and San Francisco have experimented with lanes reserved for cars that are fully laden. With some odd results: when this was introduced in the morning rush hour on San Francisco's Bay Bridge, drivers resorted to filling their cars with passengers from bus queues, making the buses travel to town empty. The private sector has played its part. Office developers and businesses have set up about 30 "transport-management associations" across America, to promote flexible working hours, car-pools and shuttle bus services.

One thing could help unjam America's roads: enabling people to work nearer home. But office developers are seldom housebuilders too. There are some mixed-use developments like Houston's Woodlands complex, where 4m square feet of office space are accompanied by 7,000 homes—too few for the number of people working there, but still something. Such schemes, though, are rare.

Public authorities, rather than promoting mixed schemes, more often hinder them. Traditional zoning concepts keep housing and work apart. So does the finance of local government: business brings tax revenues, households bring things like children that eat it up. In Santa Clara county, California, site of Silicon Valley, enough land has been zoned to support 250,000 new jobs but only 70,000 new homes. Commuting journeys of 50 miles are not uncommon.

Third-world cities have few cars; maybe one-tenth as many, relative to their population, as American cities. But they rarely have as much road space for each car. Bangkok has one car for every ten residents; roads take up only 9% of its land area, compared to 22% in London or 24% in New York. The city has large thoroughfares and small alleys, but few distributor roads in between. In the busiest district, rush-hour traffic moves at an average 4 mph. So the city is planning heavy investment in new roads, its bus fleet and an overhead railway (the land is unsuitable for an underground). It hopes to raise average speeds in the centre from 7 mph to 12 mph by the end of the century.

New rapid-transit rail systems seem an obvious answer (though the World Bank disapproves: the costs are high). Mexico City, Sao Paulo, Seoul and Manila have all recently built good metro systems. But these have had little effect on road congestion: their main impact is to take passengers off hopelessly overcrowded buses. For such cities the best—but quite utopian—answer would be to reverse the forces that draw people into the city. One proposal in Bombay is to stimulate development along suburban rail corridors. Fine. But will that lessen the charms of the city centre?

Try price

Among these many remedies, the most obvious one of all is missing. Road-space is scarce; why not charge for it? That is already done for parking, but few politicians have dared to apply price restraints to car travel itself. Now, spurred by the failure of other solutions and by the availability of new technical means of charging, some city administrations are starting to think about it.

The only big city that has yet introduced road pricing is one whose rulers worry little about short-term unpopularity: Singapore. Since 1975 cars entering its city centre during the morning rush hour with fewer than four people aboard have had to display a sticker, which now costs S$5 (US$2.60) a day. It works: the initial effect was to cut the number of cars entering the restricted zone in the rush hour by three-quarters, and even now Singapore is relatively unjammed.

Hongkong recently experimented with another, more precise way of charging road-users. Cars were fitted with electronic number plates that identified them to roadside computers at various places in the city. The owner could then be billed for roughly the distance driven. The pilot scheme worked well, but the idea was rejected by the newly established district councils: the central Hongkong administration had blundered politically by not making it clear enough what would happen to the money.

That problem has not escaped politi-cians in Stockholm, which may soon become the first European capital to charge for using its central roads. Its planners have done their sums carefully. They suggest that cars should pay 25 kronor ($3.90) to enter the centre. If the receipts went to cut public-transport fares, total traffic could be lessened by 35%; or by 28% if the money were instead invested in public-transport infrastructure, while fares stayed unchanged. In a country so collectivist and so concerned by pollution, this could well win public support: let those who dirty the air subsidise those who travel (relatively) cleanly. But the voters of London or Paris would be harder to persuade.

Further off still, there may be a more radical answer. When everybody can communicate electronically with everybody else, why commute physically? Let telecommuting take the strain—if offices are concentrated in cities at all, or indeed exist. That has been the visionaries' dream for the past 15 years, and it may one day come true. Or it may not: today's humankind persists in enjoying the random, face-to-face contact with other humans that an office provides and an electronic screen does not. For all its problems, the dispersal of offices from large cities to small towns offers real hope for city congestion. It is yet to be seen whether telecommuting will grow to do the same.

Gridlock !

Congestion on America's highways and runways takes a grinding toll

I saw in their eyes something I was to see over and over in every part of the nation—a burning desire to go, to move, to get under way, anyplace, away from any Here . . . Nearly every American hungers to move.
—John Steinbeck, *Travels with Charley*

Remember when getting there was half the fun? When driving was a breeze and flying was a cinch? No longer. Gridlock has gripped America, threatening to transform its highways and flyways into snarled barriers to progress. After returning from their summer jaunts, many travelers are looking back in anger at odysseys through potholed streets, jam-packed freeways, bottlenecked bridges and overstuffed airports. Now they face another season of grinding commutes: in many U.S. cities, the rush hour has grown into a hellish crush that lasts virtually from sunup till sundown. For U.S. businesses, the meter is running. Companies are losing money as employees fritter away their hours in a transportation standstill. Messengers fail to deliver important documents on time. Sales representatives miss their plane connections and are unable to show up for the big pitch. Even expensive private jets get caught in holding patterns, leaving subordinates in limbo while their bosses circle overhead.

The congestion, which is certain to grow worse in the coming decade, is hampering Americans' cherished mobility and changing the way they travel and do business. Instead of boasting *I Get Around*, the tune they are wailing nowadays is *Don't Get Around Much Anymore*. Consider:

▶ The Detroit Tigers baseball team lost an important asset last week when its newly hired outfielder, Fred Lynn, failed to qualify for postseason play. Reason: he got caught in a traffic jam. Lynn was playing in Anaheim, Calif., for the Baltimore Orioles when he accepted Detroit's offer late Wednesday afternoon. But to qualify for the playoffs under league rules, he had to join the team, then in Chicago, by midnight. The Tigers chartered a jet for Lynn at Ontario (Calif.) International Airport, but rush-hour congestion reportedly stretched his 35-minute drive to an hour and 15 minutes. That proved a costly delay: Lynn's plane did not reach Chicago airspace until 12:10 a.m.
▶ The trucks that deliver Dean Foods products in the Chicago area were getting caught in such relentless traffic tie-ups that the company's drivers ply the highways in the middle of the night. Many truckers leave for their rounds between 2:30 and 4 a.m. Says Larry Smith, chief of Dean's trucking subsidiary: "By getting drivers ahead of the traffic, we believe we can reduce our cost and increase our productivity by 50%."
▶ Bridget and Tom Hotchkiss of Evans-ton, Ill., who returned in July from a slow-moving car trip to the Maryland shore with their sons Tommy, 6, and Patrick, 3, vow never to do it again. Says Bridget: "Ever since we got home, the boys have been playing a new game. They get out all their big trucks and all their cars. I hear them saying, 'Let's play Traffic Jam.'"
▶ Hutchins Kealy, a management consultant, figured that a 9:20 a.m. flight from Detroit to Toronto would get him there in plenty of time for his 11 a.m. appointment. The normal flight time is about one hour. But because of airport congestion and a flat tire on his plane, he sat on the runway all morning. Despite his protests, flight attendants refused to allow Kealy and his luggage off the plane, and he was more than four hours late. "I could have rented a car and driven there instead!" he declares. Alas, poor Kealy, you would probably have been stuck in traffic on the Ambassador Bridge, one of the choked passageways connecting Detroit with Windsor, Ont.
▶ Traffic on the Long Island Expressway, which carries weekenders from New York City to the Hamptons resort communities, has become so bad that the wealthy, and even semiwealthy, rent seaplanes to get to their houses faster (fee for a 90-mile, one-way trip: up to $130 a head). Result: local

harbors and bays are infested with swarms of aircraft, which East Hampton officials are threatening to ban.

Gridlock is more than just an irritant. The epidemic of slow-motion sickness is costing the U.S. billions of dollars in lost productivity and wasted fuel. It is polluting the atmosphere with hydrocarbons, spoiling some Americans' taste for travel and influencing where families choose to live and work. Says T. Allan McArtor, chief of the Federal Aviation Administration: "Gridlock is not an alarmist theory. It will happen unless we take immediate action."

The reason for the congestion is the rapid growth in airplane and auto traffic, which is partly the result of deregulated airfares and six straight years of economic expansion. Airline passenger travel has nearly doubled in the past decade, from 240 million trips in 1977 to 447 million last year. U.S. motor vehicle travel reached 1.9 trillion miles last year, an increase of 27% from 1977. Americans operate 181 million cars, trucks and buses, also up 27% from a decade ago.

But during this time, the U.S. has failed to expand its system of roadways and runways. No completely new major airport has been built since 1974, when Dallas–Fort Worth was completed, despite the rapid expansion of U.S. air traffic. "We simply have too much aluminum and not enough concrete," says the FAA's McArtor. Of the 3.88 million miles of roads in the U.S., 92% was built before 1960.

Not only are there too few highways and airports, but also many existing ones desperately need upgrading. "America is falling apart, literally," declared Arkansas Governor Bill Clinton in an essay in the New York Times. He pointed out that declining U.S. spending on public works, from 19.1% of total government expenditures in 1950 to 6.8% by 1984, "is as serious a national problem as the budget and trade deficits."

The worsening congestion raises troubling issues for the 1990s. Should more highways be constructed, or will that only invite more auto traffic and suburban sprawl? How can people be encouraged to leave their cars at home and ride mass transit? Where can new urban airports be sited so that their noise and spread will be tolerated by neighbors? The situation has created an urgent need for innovative solutions, and some are already on the horizon: double-decker freeways, airplanes that can take off vertically from landing pads, and 300-m.p.h. trains that ride on magnetic fields.

Since traffic jams are almost synonymous with urban growth, they have been building for a long time. (The term gridlock apparently came into common use in New York City during a transit workers' strike in 1980, when a surge of commuter autos paralyzed Manhattan's street grid.)

Congestion on two-lane highways in the 1950s hastened construction of the 42,797-mile interstate system, which will be officially completed in 1991 (estimated final cost: $108 billion). But the interstates eased overcrowding only temporarily. Says Transportation Secretary James Burnley: "It's not a problem that will be resolved in a final, permanent way in my lifetime."

Gridlock is spreading to suburbs, exurbs and medium-size cities that seldom experienced it before. Highway bottlenecks are occurring on once lonely stretches like I-70 about 60 miles west of Denver, where throngs of cars bearing ski racks turn the interstate into a virtual parking lot each winter. North Kendall Drive, a suburban Miami thoroughfare described as a "road to nowhere" when it was built some 20 years ago, is now almost as choked as Manhattan streets. The number of airports considered by the FAA to be severely congested, meaning they suffer from annual flight delays of 20,000 hours or more, is expected to increase from 18 in 1986 to 32 by 1996 if no action is taken.

In a sense, auto and airline congestion are parallel problems, each with its own causes and remedies, but the two forms of gridlock intersect in a harmful way on the bottom line of U.S. businesses. Congestion is helping boost the total cost of moving people and goods, which amounted to $792 billion in the U.S. last year, or 17.6% of the gross national product. Delays and disruptions can quickly spread inflationary price increases through the economy. Case in point: gridlock can play havoc with the just-in-time inventory system, a popular Japanese-style management technique in which manufacturers bring in parts at the last minute rather than stockpiling large quantities.

The finite resources of time and fuel are squandered as autos and aircraft stand motionless on their concrete slabs. Air-travel delays in 1986, according to FAA estimates, created $1.8 billion in extra operating expenses for airlines and cost passengers $3.2 billion in lost time. As for motorists, the Transportation Department calculates that in 1985 vehicles on U.S. freeways racked up 722 million hours in delays, a number that is expected to rise to 3.9 billion hours by the year 2005 if no improvements are made. (Today's average motorist will spend an estimated six months of his lifetime waiting for red lights to change, according to a study by Priority Management Pittsburgh, a time-management consulting firm.) All that stop-and-go travel wasted nearly 3 billion gal. of gasoline in 1984, or about 4% of annual U.S. consumption, according to the latest Transportation Department estimate. Last year planes waiting to take off or circling for a landing used some 500 billion gal. of jet fuel, about 3.6% of 1987's total.

Executives say they are spending too

much valuable time waiting on the taxiway. In a poll of 461 members of the Executive Committee, a group of presidents and chief executives, 36% said they have lost job efficiency because of air-travel delays. To be sure of arriving on time at a meeting in another city, many business travelers take the precaution of flying the night before their appointment, saddling their company with the additional cost of a hotel room.

Commuters who drive to work often show up too tired or too irritated to function effectively. Chronic exposure to traffic congestion, according to a study by Psychologist Raymond Novaco at the University of California at Irvine, tends to give drivers "an increase in baseline blood pressure, lowering of frustration tolerance, increase in negative mood and aggressive driving habits." The outbreak of freeway violence in California last year, when more than 100 freeway shootings and rock-throwing incidents took place, was not an aberration. On one Sunday last month, five separate highway shootings occurred in Oregon and Colorado.

Civic leaders in congested cities have begun to understand that their traffic problems will drive away business. For one thing, companies in gridlocked cities have trouble luring employees from other locales. "Today the relative ease or difficulty of commuting and parking is a major factor in the choice of employment," says Donn Knight, vice president of the Government Employees Insurance Co. in Chevy Chase, Md. Some Los Angeles manufacturing companies have fled to less congested cities such as Las Vegas and Phoenix, and corporations have moved their headquarters from New York City to Dallas and Orlando. Says Sigurd Grava, professor of urban planning at Columbia University: "Congestion can play an important role in the life and death of a city." When Oregon Governor Neil Goldschmidt, a former U.S. Transportation Secretary, got caught in a traffic jam in Seattle, he took the occasion to get out of his car and pass out his card to other stranded motorists, extending a tongue-in-cheek invitation to move to his less-crowded state.

The one consolation for U.S. businesses is that companies in competing industrial countries have similar problems. In Western Europe, where air travel increased 8% in 1987 and is expected to jump more than 7% this year, terminals have become mob scenes. At Munich's airport one day this summer, congestion prompted officials to cancel 27 of Lufthansa's 59 domestic flights. A prime cause of the crunch is Europe's fractured air-control system, which is composed of 42 separate civilian control centers, plus additional military jurisdictions.

Auto traffic too is increasingly gridlocked, from West Germany's autobahns to the streets of Paris. Despite Europe's efficient trains and subways, rail service is gradually losing customers because the past half-decade's prosperity has enabled so many people to buy cars. Governments have launched costly road-building programs, but new highways like London's two-year-old M25 beltway have quickly become just as jammed as the old routes.

Japan is also suffering relentless traffic tie-ups on its narrow streets. In the past decade, the number of registered vehicles in Tokyo has jumped 49%, to 5.2 million, but roads have been expanded only about 4%. Everyday traffic is called *tsukin jigoku,* or commuting hell. Even so, most Japanese look upon the crowding as a traditional problem that poses no grave threat to their country's productivity.

American business executives wish they could say the same. Their workers are increasingly caught in traffic because commuting patterns have changed drastically in recent decades. The interstate highway system was originally designed to carry motorists primarily from city to city; its beltways were constructed mainly as bypasses for long-distance travelers. Local commuters, by contrast, generally moved in and out of urban downtown areas in a radial pattern, along the paths of mass transit and major thoroughfares. But the majority of work is no longer downtown: the suburbs contain 60% of current metropolitan jobs and 67% of all new ones, according to the Transportation Department. As a result, many workers commute from one suburb to another, and they crowd onto the beltways because mass transit and other roads are not well developed along those routes.

At the same time, the movement of women into the work force has produced a second commuter in most households. A suburban, two-income family typically owns two cars for the parents and often a third car for teenagers to take to school or the mall. In the affluent Washington suburb of Fairfax County, Va., the number of autos has increased almost 84% since 1975, nearly three times as fast as the population growth of 31%.

For many suburbs, the beltway serves as Main Street, lined with office buildings, shopping complexes and Cineplexes that attract more and more home buyers. The Washington Beltway is a notoriously clogged 64-mile loop that carried an estimated 466,000 vehicles a day in 1976 and now handles 735,000. The average speed for Beltway commuters driving across the Woodrow Wilson Bridge from Virginia suburbs to Maryland communities is currently 23 m.p.h., down from 47 m.p.h. in 1981.

In a sense, the interstate system's big, broad freeways invited today's congestion. When the interstates were built, 90% funded by the U.S. Government, most suburbs viewed them as all the highway they would ever need. Coalitions of environmentalists and taxpayers defeated plans for additional major arteries in San Francisco, Boston and other cities in the 1960s and '70s, when they would have been cheaper to build. "Highway expansion was perhaps the first victim of the not-in-my-backyard syndrome. Now we are paying the piper," says José Gómez-Ibañez, a professor of public policy and urban planning at Harvard's John F. Kennedy School of Government.

As it turned out, the interstate system proved a much greater stimulant to suburban development than anyone expected. As houses in the inner rings of suburbs became more expensive because of their proximity to jobs, developers began building outer rings of more affordable houses. For suburbs that have been intensively built up, it is too late for additional major highways. "Once development occurs, it is anathema to government to pave over someone's house," says Denton Kent, Fairfax's deputy county executive for planning and development.

Transportation experts generally agree that in most cases a huge highway-building program is not the answer. "We cannot pour asphalt and concrete on the ground fast enough, and in the face of today's political and social environment, I am not sure that people would accept it," says Robert Farris, chief of the Federal Highway Administration. As a practical matter, the cost of buying up suburban houses worth at least $250,000 apiece for a right-of-way would be prohibitive.

Then what can be done to keep traffic moving? Existing highways need to be rebuilt and repaved so that they can carry more volume. The Road Information Program (TRIP), a Washington research group, says federal surveys have estimated that 62% of the 2.1 million miles of paved highways in the U.S. need some form of rehabilitation. In many cases, highways should have extra lanes or wider shoulders so that broken-down or damaged cars, which trigger about 60% of bumper-to-bumper slowdowns, can get out of the way. In the northern suburbs of Los Angeles, planners are studying ways to build a double-decker section of the Ventura Freeway.

But road rebuilding is a budget-busting enterprise. A stretch of Chicago's long-neglected Dan Ryan Expressway that is being rebuilt and widened in places from eight lanes to ten will cost $210 million for just three miles of road. Illinois is getting 90% of the money from the U.S. Government, but that source is not expanding. Federal highway outlays—financed mostly by gasoline and other excise taxes—increased from $6.1 billion in fiscal 1977 to $12.8 billion in 1987, barely keeping up with inflation. TRIP estimates the cost of repairing the 278,400 miles of highways in poor to very-poor condition at more than $164 billion. That means state and local governments have to raise daunting amounts of cash.

Also costly to fix are America's crumbling bridges. Many are too narrow or corroded to handle the load of traffic from connecting roads. The 1,850-ft., four-lane Ambassador Bridge linking Detroit with Windsor, Ont., which seemed spacious when it opened in 1929, suffers daily backups, pinching the flow of trade between the U.S. and Canada. Federal surveys indicate that 42% of the 573,928 bridges more than 20 ft. long need to be rehabilitated or replaced, at a total cost of more than $50 billion.

Until cities can revamp their streets and highways, they will have to work harder to manage the traffic flow. Authorities in Los Angeles, Chicago and other metropolitan areas have installed electronic sensors in the pavement to get a continuous reading of traffic speed and volume. When a highway becomes clogged, controllers can adjust the timing of stoplights on the on-ramps to reduce the flow of vehicles. In Virginia traffic supervisors use remote TV cameras installed along stretches of I-66 and I-395 to spot breakdowns, to which they immediately dispatch tow trucks that dispense free gasoline if a motorist needs it. Chicago's highway authority operates a huge mobile crane, dubbed Mad Max, that can lift up to 60 tons, and has moved obstacles ranging from semitrailers to a 500-lb. runaway pig.

To a great extent, traffic misery is what Americans get in return for preferring their cozy vehicles to mass transit. "We've made a massive commitment to autos, especially those with only one or two people in them. Now we're paying the price," says Richard Kiley, chairman of the Metropolitan Transit Authority for the New York City area. Gridlock has inspired some cities that once spurned mass transit to launch bold new building programs. Los Angeles, which tore up its streetcar tracks during the '50s, broke ground in 1986 on a $5 billion transit system that will include a four-mile-long subway from the downtown civic center to MacArthur Park and a 22-mile-long rail line from downtown to nearby Long Beach.

Yet mass transit is no cure-all and often proves inefficient in America's sprawling suburbs. Many critics question whether subways and other heavy-rail systems can be effective anywhere but in a few very densely populated cities. Even Washington's clean and efficient 70-mile-long, $7 billion Metro subway, which carries almost 500,000 riders a day, meets only 70% of its operating expenses from fares.

Since the major complaint about rail systems is that they do not take riders where they want to go, some experts believe the better mass-transit investment is an extensive network of buses. Says Transportation Secretary Burnley: "They can be rerouted overnight to meet changing transportation patterns. We have got to have the emphasis on flexibility." Buses work especially well when they can zip along freeways in high-occupancy lanes that are restricted to buses, vans and car-pool vehicles. During the morning rush hour on Virginia's I-350, two high-occupancy lanes carry an average of about 33,000 commuters, a bit more than the four regular lanes, yet in only one-fifth as many vehicles.

To get cars off the highways, businesses and government need to find more ways to discourage driving. Since fuel is relatively cheap, a greater gasoline tax would be in order. Another step is to restrict more lanes to car-pool vehicles, since the average passenger car now carries only 1.3 riders for trips to work. The U.S. even gives drivers a tax loophole, which should be abolished. MTA Chairman Kiley points out that under federal law, employers can give their workers tax-free compensation for parking, with no cap, while contributions for mass-transit are limited to $15 a month. In Manhattan, where parking can cost more than $350 a month, the policy can mean a lucrative subsidy for drivers.

Air-travel delays are expected to become chronic in the next decade despite stepped-up efforts by carriers to keep planes on schedule. The Transportation Department says that during June, the 13 major airlines managed to operate 84.3% of their flights within 15 minutes of being on time, the best performance since the Government began publishing the statistics last September. (The worst figure was 66.4%, in December 1987.) But one reason for the improvement was that the airlines simply added minutes to their flight times. Says Herbert Kelleher, chairman of Southwest Airlines: "If anybody thinks the problem has been solved, they are wrong, and I'll tell you why. Sure, you are on time, but it is taking you twice as long to fly from A to B."

That is the inevitable consequence of the shortage of airport capacity. Such facilities as New York's LaGuardia and Boston's Logan were built in an era of smaller, propeller-driven planes, which could use relatively short runways. Hemmed in by development, such airports will have trouble handling any significant increase in traffic. As a result, "we're heading for one of the most dramatic cases of peacetime rationing this country has ever seen," declares Philip Bakes, president of Eastern Air Lines. Says Clifton Moore, chief administrator of Los Angeles International: "There may be a time when you will have to book a flight well in advance, or pay someone for a black-market ticket." Rationing of sorts is already beginning at Boston's airport, where officials have tried to shoo away small aircraft by quadrupling the landing fee to as much as $100 a visit, while reducing the charge for passenger jets.

Some airports could accommodate more planes at off-peak hours if they were not restricted by noise complaints from residential neighbors. Washington's National Airport, which is booked solid during the day, allows only 13 flights between 10 p.m. and 7 a.m. Late-model jets like the Boeing 757 and 767 are half as noisy as the early 727s, but hundreds of the older planes are still rattling suburban windows.

More airports are needed, but finding a site with willing neighbors is nearly impossible in most cities. The first completely new airport since 1974 will be Denver's, which voters in nearby Adams County approved in May. Denver's current airport, Stapleton, was built to handle 18 million passengers a year, and is swamped by 35 million. The new $3 billion airport is expected to accommodate 50 million by the mid-1990s. Colorado Governor Roy Romer, who campaigned for the new airport, made an economic appeal. Said he: "This airport is our one and only chance. We can become the transportation hub of this country."

Because new airports are financed by gate fees, airlines have sometimes been reluctant to support them—the added cost would mean higher fares or squeezed profits. But the major carriers have formed a lobbying group, Partnership for Improved Air Travel, which among other things is urging the Government to lead an airport-building program similar to the interstate-highway push.

Airports take years to build, but other remedies for congestion may help in the meantime. The FAA is experimenting with a finely tuned radar that will enable airports to land planes on closely spaced parallel runways, even in bad weather. Some airports are building high-speed runway turnoff lanes so that a jet can move out of the next plane's way before coming to a full stop, thus boosting a runway's capacity. The FAA is exploring the possibility of opening military airfields for civilian use, among them El Toro Marine Corps Air Station, near Los Angeles. Boeing and Bell Helicopter are developing aircraft that can take off vertically from a landing pad, then fly like an airplane on trips of up to 300 miles.

A formidable alternative to both the auto and airplane is coming: the magnetic-levitation train, or maglev. Supported and propelled by the force of powerful electromagnets, the streamlined maglev could reach speeds of 300 m.p.h. or more. West Germany and Japan are developing prototypes based on different operating systems. One proposed high-speed maglev route in the U.S. is a 230-mile-long link between Los Angeles and Las Vegas, a five-hour auto trip that the maglev could cover in about 70 minutes.

Breaking gridlock will take all the ingenuity the U.S. can muster, especially in a time when the nation cannot afford to buy millions of yards of concrete to pave over the problem. Says Burnley: "Because we are a free country, people are able to change their travel patterns overnight. So the challenge is to be able to think more creatively." But meanwhile, taxpayers and travelers will have to shoulder the cost for a prudent amount of highway patching and airport building. The longer such work is postponed, the more chronic the gridlock will become. If America still hungers to move, it will have to pay the fare.

—By Stephen Koepp.
Reported by Gisela Bolte/Washington, Thomas McCarroll/New York and Edwin M. Reingold/Los Angeles

SUPERTRAIN

A Solution to U.S. Transportation Woes

As overcrowded highways and congested air routes threaten Americans' mobility, high-speed railroads offer a viable alternative and great promise for the future.

Judith Miller and Mark Miller

The authors are investigative journalists whose work has appeared in Ms., New York Magazine, The Humanist, Science Digest, *and* USA Today.

JAPAN National Railways started a new era of high-speed passenger railroads when it opened its 320-mile *Shinkansen* between Tokyo and Osaka, just in time for the 1964 Tokyo Olympic Games. Japanese "bullet trains" were on time, fast, frequent, and comfortable. Although "bullet train" is a term used for Japan's *Shinkansen*, it can describe any high-speed railroad that exceeds 100 mph. These generally run on electricity, rather than diesel fuel.

For the Japanese traveling public, it was love at first sight. *Shinkansen* sped along at sustained speeds of 125 miles an hour on a totally grade-separated track, off-limits to sluggish freight and commuter trains. On opening day, air traffic between Tokyo and Osaka plummeted 40%. An astonishing total of 11,000,000 persons boarded the "bullet train" within three months.

In intercity passenger service, the U.S. allowed railroads to fall behind during the 1950's and 1960's. Instead, America increased its love affair with the automobile and became infatuated with the airplane. In 1971, with the creation of the Federally subsidized Amtrak, America began to rebuild its outdated passenger rail system. Still, the U.S. lags behind other industrialized nations in the development of high-speed trains. According to J.R. Snyder, National Legislative Director, United Transportation Union, "The United States is one of the few countries in the world, indeed it is the only major industrial nation, where there is still serious debate over the future of rail passenger service."

Nothing like *Shinkansen* exists in America. Besides the Japanese, the French have operated such a system since 1981, with their TGV ("Very High Speed") having reached 236 miles per hour. Every day, 100 trains travel the 265 miles between Paris and Lyons in exactly two hours. The TGV now is being expanded to western France and into neighboring Belgium, the Netherlands, and Germany. The Soviet Union is planning a supertrain system connecting Moscow to the Black Sea, with a possibility of a northern leg from Moscow to Leningrad. Furthermore, negotiations in Germany are under way for a supertrain system between Hanover and Berlin that will "unite" East and West Germany by high-speed train. The goal is to develop a system capable of 125 mph service by 1995.

According to Pennsylvania State Rep. Richard H. Geist, chairman of both the Pennsylvania High Speed Intercity Commission and the Washington-based High Speed Rail Association, "More and more Americans have ridden fast trains in other countries and they're saying, 'Why not here?'" Many European countries have trains that go 125 mph routinely. In the U.S., there are high-speed passenger rail projects under way in California, Pennsylvania, New York, Ohio, Michigan, Texas, Florida, and elsewhere.

Americans are no longer in love with their cars and infatuated with airplanes. Problems with both automobile and airline travel are threatening mobility. In 1984, the new Dulles toll road was opened in the Washington, D.C., area. The 16-mile highway parallels the freeway access road to Dulles International Airport. Today, this route is as congested as any other major artery in the area, and the state is planning to widen it still more. Yet, even as these plans are being made, gridlock still will be a major problem for that area.

Similar stories are being told repeatedly all across the U.S. *The New York Times* (June 19, 1988) reported that "Aviation experts warn of gridlock at U.S. airports." Federal Administrator T. Allan McArtar said, "We simply have too much aluminum and not enough concrete" [too many airplanes and not enough airports]. According to the *Times*, paralysis threatens the nation's air system within five years. McArtar noted that "We are getting very close, closer than anyone realizes, to commercial aviation gridlock. In a very few years, we may well see fully loaded planes in one city unable to leave because there is not room at their destination city, and others can't come into the city first because these planes haven't left. We'll have all these people and planes locked up on the ground in all these cities, wasting their time and energies.'' He warned that Americans then could be faced with air travel rationing.

Several years ago, the National Transportation Policy Study Commission was formed to study our transportation needs. One conclusion of their study was startling: we must double our passenger transportation infrastructure by the year 2000.

High-speed rail corridors linking major metropolitan areas 200-500 miles apart provide a possible alternative to our increasingly crowded transportation system. Passenger trains move people more quickly and efficiently than cars and are safer than airplanes. According to Geist, ''Transporting riders from city center to city center, high-speed trains traveling 180 miles per hour will help relieve highway and air traffic congestion for intermediate trips such as Houston to Dallas and Chicago to Detroit.''

Skytrain

The need for a supertrain link between Las Vegas and Southern California was envisioned by Las Vegas in 1980. Unfortunately, it has taken almost a decade to make this a reality. Legal, political, and environmental concerns were the major problems hindering this project, which now is officially in the hands of a bi-state commission. The 16-member body, with eight representatives from each state, was created by the California and Nevada legislatures to study the feasibility of a train that would travel at a minimum of 180 mph, enabling it to make the trip from Southern California to Las Vegas in 70 minutes.

According to California Assemblyman Richard Katz, chairman of the commission, ''We have a tremendous opportunity to preview a new technology for the West and tie some tourist centers together. We can also help local traffic.''

If all goes as planned, a train zipping along at speeds of up to 250 mph will be operating by the mid-1990's. It would be funded privately and cost $65 for a round trip. The High-Speed Rail Commission is expected to develop a plan for bidders by 1990 and award a contract that year, with construction to start in 1992 or 1993. Commissioner Don Roth said, ''In my opinion, it is a mark in history for all of California and Nevada. It may be the catalyst for high-speed trains, maybe throughout the United States.''

Cost estimates are $2-3,000,000,000. A 270-mile ride between Las Vegas and Anaheim would attract 4-6,000,000 passengers annually. Other potential Southern California sites are San Diego, Los Angeles, Palmsdale, and Ontario.

The Nevada delegation already has talked to a large Japanese trading firm willing to put up 40% of the construction cost and line up the rest if German-owned Transrapid International's magnetic levitation (Maglev) system is selected. Maglev is sometimes called ''Skytrain'' because it literally flies above ground level, incorporating technology which magnetically levitates passenger cars above an elevated guideway. The concept of such a train supported by a magnetic cushion and driven by a non-contact linear motor had a fanciful introduction to public consciousness via comic books in the 1940's and 1950's, years before such wild dreams were technologically viable. What one generation dreams, the next generation does. Maglev is no longer a dream. Skytrain is being considered seriously as an option in many North American corridors. A major decision for the commission will be choosing the right technology from the new and still experimental Maglev technology or a traditional steel-wheel-on-steel-rail technology as developed by the French company.

The proposed supertrain connecting the Los Angeles area with Las Vegas may become part of the vast world-class transportation system, including a giant new airport in the California desert, 73 miles from Los Angeles Airport (LAX) and almost adjacent to the Spaceport, where NASA shuttles land upon return from flight.

The city of Los Angeles owns 36 square miles of empty Mohave Desert in Palmsdale, Calif., one of the supertrain's optional routes. This land was purchased by the Los Angeles Department of Airports in 1968 as the site of a new ''superport'' five times the size of LAX.

How will travelers get to this new, remote superport from Los Angeles?—by supertrain! The train will start out at LAX, stop at the superport, and then zip on to Las Vegas. Thus, the two projects together may provide the mix necessary to create a futuristic, synergistic transportation system.

According to Richard Uber, head of the Carnegie Mellon University High Speed Ground Transportation Center, the fulfillment of the dream is long overdue: ''The need is clear. A transportation system which can increase the mobility of the nation must provide a convenient interface between air and surface transportation systems, and the Los Angeles superport/superspeed train connection is a perfect example. Instead of thousands of Angelenos driving the crowded freeways to the new superport, they can drive a much shorter distance to an in-town parking facility and check-in station, board the superspeed train and be at the airport in minutes.''

Safety is also an important factor. In a recent survey, commercial pilots termed LAX the most dangerous airport in the U.S., considering both the congestion and noise-control restrictions. High-speed trains are the safest form of transportation, as established by *perfect* records for 25 years in Japan and eight in France.

Robert J. Casey, Executive Director, High Speed Rail Association (HSRA), said that, ''Since 1964, the original Japanese 'Bullet Train' has transported more than 2,500,000,000 passengers at 125 mph in the utmost comfort and safety. That's 2,500,000,000 travelers without a single person injured or killed. The French TGV has a similar perfect record going much faster, since 1981. If perfect safety is desirable as one factor in travel, then high-speed trains is the answer.''

Las Vegas and Southern California are not alone in their efforts to create a supertrain system in America. Government dignitaries and rail officials gathered in Boston's South Station on Oct. 20, 1988, to board a special test run of the ANF Turboliner from Boston to Pelham Bay, N.Y. The French-designed turbine train has been tested by Amtrak for possible high-speed service on the New York-Boston line. The evaluation was sponsored by the HSRA Task Force of the Coalition of Northeastern Governors (CONEG).

Denny Sullivan, Amtrak's Executive Vice President for Operations and Maintenance, explained that, ''For thousands each day who travel between New York and Boston, this program could help make the difference between sitting in a traffic jam and sitting in a sleek, quiet coach speeding down the shoreline at 110 miles per hour.''

The program is part of a CONEG initiative dedicated to cutting travel time over the 232 miles of curvaceous track between New York and Boston to about three hours (the trip now takes four and one-half hours). With certain track and signaling improvements, estimated to cost around $170,000,000, a three-hour trip is achievable using equipment now available. This would allow Amtrak to compete successfully with air and highway transportation and ease mounting gridlock problems on northeastern roads and runways.

Amtrak estimates that cutting the trip time to three hours would persuade as many as 40% of Boston-New York air shuttle passengers to switch to high-speed trains. Today, Amtrak accounts for less than 10% of the 4,000,000 plane and train trips a year between Boston and New York. A CONEG study identifies the Boston-New York corridor as the ''premier unsatisfied market,'' with the largest potential passenger rail ridership in the world outside of Japan.

A descendant of helicopter motors, the Turboliner's powerful traction turbine, manufactured by Turbomeca of France, is the only successful adaptation of aviation propulsion to rail. Two turboliners are currently in service on New York State's

Empire Corridor between New York City and Niagara Falls, where they have helped double ridership and logged a 90% on-time record since their introduction in 1978. In tests conducted in France, the Turboliner has gone as fast as 168 mph.

Dan Copper, public information officer of HSRA, said, "The high-speed rail service in the U.S. is not in the same league as those in Europe." The Boston-New York effort originally was sparked by Massachusetts, under Gov. Michael Dukakis. The original Amtrak project was meant to improve service from Boston to Washington. However, it ended up improving the New York-Washington route, which became the fastest and best in the U.S. According to Copper, "Amtrak now carries more people from New York to Washington than any single airline—they got the speed up to 125 miles per hour. So, because New England got left out, Dukakis pushed to speed up the Boston to New York route. The idea is that, if you can induce more people to ride the train, there will be less traffic at Logan Airport in Boston and less pressure to build another runway at Logan."

21st-century economy

High-speed rail faces an uphill climb in America, despite the obvious blessings it has to offer. Funding is the most serious problem. According to R. Clifford Black of Amtrak's public affairs office, "Amtrak is facing annual budget cuts and cannot get involved in a project that is not likely to be profitable." Its policy is not to put money into railroad construction or break new ground on high-speed rail. Black adds that "Amtrak doesn't have the financial resources to invest in the research and development of high-speed rail, although Amtrak does endorse the concept. . . . A high-speed rail needs to acquire land—a new right-of-way—because it cannot share its rails with other trains. Also, a

300-mile rail line construction—land, rail, electrical parts—not including the train itself, would cost around $5,000,000,000! And it would be extremely difficult to pay the interest on a $5,000,000,000 loan. There would be little, if any, profit left over for the investor."

Raising revenue for such projects is going to be difficult in a nation that can not tell the difference between high-tech supertrain and the sluggish artifact it replaces. According to Geist, "While the private sector has taken the high-speed rail movement far in just a few short years, without public backing, its efforts may not bear fruit. No mode of transportation in this country—from canal boats to airplanes—has succeeded based entirely on private investment efforts. In order to realize the vision of swift rail corridors linking the cities of this nation, individual states of the United States must have the power to issue revenue bonds for high-speed rail projects on which interest is exempt from Federal income tax."

On Oct. 22, 1988, Congress approved legislation designed to do exactly this, and put high-speed rail on the same tax basis as other transportation modes. This new legislation reached Congress in a bill introduced by former Sen. Lawton Chiles (D.-Fla.) in 1987. Lloyd Bentson (D.-Tex.), chairman of the Senate Finance Committee, decided to incorporate the thrust of the Chiles Bill in the Technical Corrections Act. High-speed rail forces then went to work, explaining to senators that the 1986 Tax Reform Act showed Congress considered adding high-speed rail to those facilities utilizing tax-exempt industrial revenue bonds for financing purposes.

Geist noted, "This legislation will transform high-speed rail dreams into concrete and steel and will help this nation create thousands of jobs, as well as transportation systems to meet the rapidly escalating demands of the American people for transportation and mobility."

Meanwhile, Sen. Daniel Patrick Moynihan (D.-N.Y.) is advocating a research and development program authorizing use of rights-of-way along Federal highways for construction of Maglev systems. It is a companion bill to his original proposal for a $300,000,000 research program. Moynihan recently named a team of scientists to study his proposals.

There is no more room near our cities for new airports. New York has been trying to find a place for one for almost 20 years. There also is no more room for all the new highways that America needs. Today's environmental laws will not allow such a disruption of this nation's land. According to Casey, "There is a solution, the high-speed rail solution, as our friends in Europe and Japan have proven so dramatically. In fact, outside of North America, no developed country has ever deserted its railroads. Instead, they have created a dazzling display of technology that provides unrivaled speed, comfort, safety, and reliability for intercity travel." He adds, "There is an additional benefit, too. High-speed rail requires electric power. This means there is no dependence on the politics of petroleum, and little or no air pollution. Today, we no longer worry about lack of oil, since there is an oil glut. . . . Yet, I, for one, remember waiting in long lines to obtain gasoline in two different time periods. It was a dangerous situation then, and it could be in the future."

High-speed train systems will create billions of dollars in construction, just as the interstate highways did in their heyday. The mobility, the jobs created to run the systems, and the increased commerce are all advantages that add up. As Casey points out, "With high-speed rail leading the way, we have a chance to lay the foundation for an entirely new economy, more dynamic and more productive than anything ever envisioned—a true 21st-century economy."

DE-ESCALATING THE WAR

Rethinking our assumptions about drug treatment

Jefferson Morley

Jefferson Morley is national political correspondent for Spin *magazine. His address is 28 Hickory Ave., Takoma Park, MD 20912.*

WILLIAM BENNETT IS THE MAN WHOM drug treatment professionals, as well as most liberals, love to hate. Director of the national Office of Drug Control Policy, Bennett espouses a kind of secular fundamentalism on the drug issue; citing the failure of drug treatment programs to cure crack addicts, he conjures up a vision of the state as a tough but benevolent surrogate father instilling zero tolerance for drug use of any kind. Says Bennett, "The necessary message for rich and poor, black and white, Hispanic and Indian is the same: Drug use is intolerable; use and the potential for use will be confronted on all fronts, and those who use and who sell will face certain consequences."

Bennett's critics in the drug treatment field respond by pointing to the failure of power politics and law enforcement throughout the 20th century. More cops, more arrests, more prosecutors, harsher sentences, border patrols, and pressure on foreign governments have not stemmed drug use or abuse. These critics regard the decline in drug use among high school seniors, sometimes touted as a sign that President Bush is "winning the drug war," as the continuation of a trend that had already begun in the late '70s, before the government loudly proclaimed its anti-drug campaign. Most of all, community-minded mental health professionals instinctively mistrust the alleged benevolence of Bennett's state-sponsored morality, and argue that we haven't even given drug addiction treatment programs a fair test. According to Delaware Senator Joe Biden, treatment is available for only one in 11 cocaine addicts, a figure he calls "intolerably low."

Unfortunately, some things are true even though Bill Bennett says them. The effectiveness of most forms of drug treatment is far from established and appears to depend largely upon the socioeconomic level of the user. Dr. Herbert Kleber, deputy director of the Demand Reduction Office in Bennett's office, says that "for the employed, otherwise functioning cocaine user, the success rate may be as high as 65 percent. For the blue-collar person with some social skills, it's around 40 to 45 percent. For the unemployed crack addict with low levels of education, it's probably not much above 20 percent, and it may well be lower." Helping 20 percent of unemployed crack addicts may be preferable to helping none, but if four of every five of them are impervious to current treatments, the whole enterprise of crack rehabilitation would seem to be deeply, perhaps fatally, flawed. It is quite possible that one out of five crack addicts kicks the habit without any therapeutic help at all.

The word "treatment" itself suggests more consensus than is apparent in the hodgepodge of clinics, rehab programs, and inpatient facilities, both public and private, that are now available for crack users. At its most rudimentary, crack treatment is provided by drug hotlines, police, and crammed emergency rooms of city hospitals. Forty percent of those admitted to the psychiatric emergency room of Lincoln Hospital in the Bronx, for example, test positive for cocaine. Like a MASH unit in a battle zone, the hospital provides the bare minimum—usually a tranquilizer and a session with a resident psychiatrist—before sending the user back to the front lines of the drug war again. Drug users showing acute psychotic symptoms are admitted for 15 days of treatment, mainly group therapy sessions originally intended for nonaddicted psychotics, not crashing crack addicts. Dr. Victoria Paz, who diagnoses perhaps 160 crack addicts showing pyschotic symptoms each month, doubts that talk therapy does much good. "When they are in crisis, they demand help," she says. "When the crisis is past, they forget about it."

At the other end of the treatment spectrum are the 21- to 28-day programs in tastefully appointed private treatment centers, like those developed by the Hazelden Foundation in Minnesota, and made famous by the Betty Ford Center in California. Stressing self-help, personal responsibility, community participation, drug education, and abstinence, these programs mainly serve well-heeled, or at least well-insured, middle- and upper-class clients, who are presumably more motivated than poor, inner-city users. After three or four weeks as an inpatient, the client is channeled into a 12-step group, like Alcoholics Anonymous, Narcotics Anonymous, or Cocaine Anonymous, where again the ethic is abstinence through community support.

Indeed, the 21- and 28-day treatment centers share basic philosophical premises with the 12-step paradigm: habitual use of any mind-altering drug is an incurable disease for which the only control is total abstinence. Recovery demands a fundamental renovation of personal values and self-image. Proponents of this model maintain that crack addiction is no harder or easier to treat than alcoholism or addiction to any other drug. Unfortunately, the success rate of both the centers and the 12-step programs, either together or separately, is, at best, between 50 and 60 percent for the first year, according to researcher Norman Hoffman of the Comprehensive Assessment and Treatment Outcome Center in Minneapolis, who has studied treatment results with more than 2,000 cocaine addicts. Presently, no one has compiled separate figures for crack addicts, but most drug treatment professionals agree that the results with this group are likely to be considerably more dismal.

Publicly funded therapeutic communities where the addict may stay 6 to 24 months share the philosophy that drug addicts must completely restructure their lives and completely forego the use of drugs. These residential treatment centers are thought to be especially effective with poor, young, inner-city addicts, who are mostly black or Hispanic. Again, recovery means transformation, taking up a new life, internalizing new values and new goals in a kind of moral as well as psychological rebirth.

NO THERAPEUTIC COMMUNITY REflects this philosophical orientation more than Phoenix Academy, a large and well-known residential high school and drug treatment program located in what used to be a Jesuit seminary in Westchester County, New York. Inside, Phoenix Academy looks as if the Jesuits had just left; the hallways are bare, the classrooms are starkly plain in the style of old-fashioned public schools, and the rooms of the residents are kept in perfect order—house rules.

Life at Phoenix Academy would be familiar to the seminarians who used to live on the grounds. Most of the 200-plus residents are male, and 80 percent are crack users. There is little noise or clamor in the strangely muted atmosphere. After a 21- to 28-day detox program, the residents are expected to work their way up from menial labor in the kitchen or on the grounds to answering phones and greeting visitors. Out of bed at 6:30 am and in bed by 10 pm, they go to meetings three times a week, where they are directed to confront each other, openly discuss their feelings and thoughts, and resolve their individual differences together as a group. Family therapy sessions are held and family members are expected to talk about whatever problems contributed to the drug abuse in the first place. The values Phoenix Academy wants to instill are not only abstinence, but personal responsibility, humility, hygiene, obedience, a sense of community, and the capacity for deferred gratification.

But for all the undoubtedly high purpose and commitment of its staff to rehabilitation, the subdued atmosphere of Phoenix Academy suggests listlessness more than the once-happy tranquility of monastics following a spiritual path. Inside the main building, a knot of four black teenagers stands silently outside a counselor's door; a kid mopping the floor in the dining hall mockingly utters a famous anti-drug slogan and a few others laugh uneasily; a boy sits alone in the gloomy, deserted hallway.

Phoenix Academy recalls neither the chaotic horror of the psychiatric emergency room nor the upholstered charm of the treatment centers, but it doesn't seem to be a vibrant community either. In fact, statistically, long-term inpatient rehabilitation programs like Phoenix Academy are no more successful than any other approach. Most therapeutic communities lose as many as 80 percent during the first 90 days. For the same initial three months, Phoenix Academy has a drop-out rate of "only" 40 percent. Of those who do manage to finish the program, Phoenix claims that 75 percent remain drug-free, employed, and crime-free five years later. Even if this claim is true, only 45 percent of everyone admitted for treatment successfully kick their drug habit.

Some national policy-makers are putting their hopes (and enormous amounts of money) into the development of "cocaine blockers"—drugs designed to reduce the acute psychophysiological craving for the coke high. Many consider this "drug for drugs" program one of the most promising areas of treatment research. The medication development program at the National Institute on Drug Abuse (NIDA) is now testing six potential blockers, including desipremine, an antidepressant; carbamazepine, an anticonvulsant; and a tranquilizer named fluperthixol. The NIDA program has $35 million in funding, and according to a recent *Washington Post* report, the federal government is ready to spend half a billion dollars over the next 10 years on cocaine blockers.

Sardonically described by critics as "better living through chemistry," the drugs for drug approach rests on some of the same assumptions that propel the long-term treatment centers and upscale retreats. All operate on the principle that drugs are a private, individual sickness, physical and spiritual, requiring either an injected antitoxin or a long-term personal reformation. Treatment is administered by professionals with good values and licit drugs. What the moralistic and individualistic traditions of drug treatment slight is the economic realities of crack and the values it reflects.

CRACK IS A NIGHTMARE MICROCOSM of capitalist society. Based on pleasurable consumption and instant gratification, the crack economy is driven by an intensely competitive marketplace where risk-takers compete for scarce profits and social respect. In Washington, D.C., an estimated 25,000 people are involved in the illicit drug business, according to a recent RAND Corporation study. About half of them sell drugs full-time, earning an average annual income—tax free—of $24,000. Inner-city drug users gain access

*T*HE LONG-TERM TREATMENT CENTERS AND UPSCALE RETREATS ALL OPERATE ON THE PRINCIPLE THAT DRUGS ARE A PRIVATE, INDIVIDUAL SICKNESS.

to a quick, cheap pleasure better than any other they're likely to get, in a social climate that makes a virtue of getting gratification where and when you can. Inner-city drug entrepreneurs, many of whom are not users, get at least a shot at a middle-class life-style that they would otherwise not have.

Most drug treatment programs barely acknowledge the social reality of crack. Most still follow a variant of the 12-step program in ordaining, first of all, the absolute renunciation of the substance, which is given the attributes of a uniquely powerful taboo. Second, the programs aim to foster an entirely new system of values in the user's mind, and bring him or her into a new fellowship with others who have been converted. But most crack addicts prefer the known comforts of the drug and the monetary benefits it brings to the equally well-known discomforts of stopping and the cold comforts of staying clean in an environment that doesn't offer many other pleasures. The "values" of sobriety, humility, personal responsibility, and deferred gratification have little reality in a community whose role models for success and power exhibit exactly the opposite traits. The heroes in this culture of deprivation are the young men in designer clothes and customized cars, flashing solid-gold jewelry and heavy billfolds, a flurry of young women in their wake. That lawlessness and death accompany this vision only gives it a certain flamboyant glamour.

The extraordinary pull of these negative values is obvious in the young crack users at Phoenix Academy. They bear little resemblance to the traditional picture of the socially isolated drug user shooting up in an alleyway. Traditional treatment for heroin users and alcoholics is aimed at bringing abusers out of their self-imposed shells, forcing them to confront themselves and others in community. Many crack addicts, however, grow up in neighborhoods where drugs are virtually a cottage industry; their parents and relatives often use and sell drugs, as do their contemporaries. Crack users are isolated from the economic mainstream, not from each other. However perverse the crack culture, it is nothing if not social. Treatment modalities that work to get crack addicts to "communicate" and "express their feelings" seem somehow off the mark. They encourage addicts to articulate their problems as individuals, but they don't encourage anyone to think about the workings of a society in which so many people are drawn down addiction's self-destructive path.

The media has vividly documented the devastating effect the crack culture has had on families and children. Many of the kids at Phoenix Academy have been neglected and physically and sexually abused. Out of school longer than even the young heroin addicts of 15 years ago, they have few verbal and social skills, are less tolerant of frustration, and quick to resort to violence. They are, in the words of one counselor, "used to running otally wild."

The lack of rudimentary social skills and values among young crack users makes the work of the Phoenix Academy less rehabilitation than primary socialization. "It's not that these kids have low self-esteem," says Loretta Martin, deputy director of Phoenix Academy. "It's that they have *no* self-esteem." Materialism is the only higher principle they know, according to another deputy director, William Tomlin. "For these kids, it's 'What kind of sneakers you got? My shit cost $150. Yours only cost $50. You ain't shit.'"

If anyone doubts the attractiveness of this world to kids' psyches, just talk to a Phoenix Academy counselor. "The crack kid takes longer both to hear and internalize the values we're teaching than the drug abuser of old," says counselor Archie Little. Those values, beginning with abstinence and including impulse control, deferred gratification and all the rest, are literally unreal in the world of crack. This is why crack addicts seem more prone to relapse than other abusers. Nathalie McFarland, principal of Phoenix Academy, describes a model student named David, who, after two successful years in the program, went home to the Bronx. Soon after he returned home, he went out to buy a shirt, because he was going to take his mother out to dinner. Walking down Fordham Road, he saw his reflection in a store window, which inexplicably set off a craving for crack. He went to a crack house and binged all weekend. The "values" he had learned over two years were less substantial than a reflection in a shop window.

For the secular fundamentalists of the drug campaigns, such a relapse proves that treatment failed, as it almost inevitably must, given the moral shortcomings of the addict's character. Seduced by the '60s-style permissiveness of our age, David was not personally equipped to fight temptation. He failed society. Yet for many mental health professionals, the drug warriors' formulation would be reversed: David's admirable record and determination to remain abstinent were a sign of success, which were overwhelmed by the ethos of the larger society—the emphasis on instant gratification, the compulsive pursuit of material and sensual pleasures at the expense of social responsibility and personal growth. In their view, society had failed David.

AS IT STANDS, TRADITIONAL THINKing about drug treatment leans toward one of three conceptual paths to recovery—individual moral renovation, a medical magic bullet, or social revolution. But none offers a clear vision of what a "victory" in the war on drugs would really look like. Instead, our drug warriors sermonize on the choice between a "drug-free" America or a society sunk in materialism, crime, and degradation. Most wars, however, don't end in absolute victory for either side, but are resolved only after grandiose fantasies have given way to uneasy compromise. Today, some experienced observers of the crack decade are now wondering if the absolutist terminology of win or lose, success or failure foreclose the one realistic option—neutralizing or managing a problem that cannot be obliterated. After all, they argue, there has probably never been a time in America when there wasn't a thriving business in something unhealthy, immoral, and illegal. Attempts to prohibit or force the total abstention from sin, they say, are doomed, and so it is with crack.

One unconventional and promising program that seems to reflect what might be called the new realism is an acupuncture clinic at Lincoln Center in the Bronx, directed by Dr. Michael Smith. The acupuncture clinic seems an island of calm and good cheer, especially after the horrors of the emergency room—with its shrieking din of crack-heads in full psychosis. About 40 heavy crack users sit together, sipping herbal tea and chatting pleasantly, their ears bristling with shiny needles.

But this clinic would give little comfort to the most thoroughgoing of the anti-drug brigades. Of 3,500 addicts treated each year at Lincoln Hospital's acupuncture clinic, a few more than half stay for the full course of treatment—three sessions a week for two or three weeks. There's no attempt at moral reeducation, and peer counseling, mandatory in other drug treatment programs, is strictly optional here. Of those who finish the course, 60 percent test negative for cocaine three to six months after the treatments.

Clearly, acupuncture is not a miracle cure. But its success rate is comparable to that of other addiction recovery programs; it costs a lot less, doesn't take a lot of time, and seems more respectful of the clients. Lincoln's program quickly gets a lot of people to use less cocaine without shipping them off to a Bennett boot camp, jail, or a two-year course in

C R A C K   A N D   T H E   B O X

ONE SAD, RAINY MORNING LAST WINTER I talked to a woman who was addicted to crack cocaine. She was 22, stiletto-thin, with eyes as old as tombs. She was living in two rooms in a welfare hotel with her children, who were two, three, and five years of age. Her story was the usual tangle of human woe: early pregnancy, dropping out of school, vanished men, smack and then crack, tricks with johns in parked cars to pay for the dope. I asked her why she did drugs. She shrugged in an empty way and couldn't really answer beyond "makes me feel good." While we talked and she told her tale of squalor, the children ignored us. They were watching television.

Walking back to my office in the rain, I brooded about the woman, her zombie-like children, and my own callous indifference. I'd heard so many versions of the same story that I almost never wrote them anymore; the sons of similar women, glimpsed a dozen years ago, are now in Dannemora or Soledad or Joliet; in a hundred cities, their daughters are moving into the same loveless rooms. As I walked, a series of homeless men approached me for change, most of them junkies. Others sat in doorways, staring at nothing. They were additional casualties of our time of plague, demoralized reminders that although this country holds only two percent of the world's population, it consumes 65 percent of the world's supply of hard drugs.

Why, for God's sake? Why do so many millions of Americans of all ages, races, and classes choose to spend all or part of their lives stupefied? I've talked to hundreds of addicts over the years; some were my friends. But none could give sensible answers. They stutter about the pain of the world, about despair or boredom, the urgent need for magic or pleasure in a society empty of both. But then they just shrug. Americans have the money to buy drugs; the supply is plentiful. But almost nobody in power asks, *Why?* Least of all, George Bush and his drug warriors.

William Bennett talks vaguely about the heritage of '60s permissiveness, the collapse of Traditional Values, and all that. But he and Bush offer the traditional

American excuse: It Is Somebody Else's Fault. This posture sets the stage for the self-righteous invasion of Panama, the bloodiest drug arrest in world history. Bush even accused Manuel Noriega of "poisoning our children." But he never asked *why* so many Americans demand the poison.

And then, on that rainy morning in New York, I saw another one of those ragged men staring out at the rain from a doorway. I suddenly remembered the inert postures of the children in that welfare hotel, and I thought: *television.*

Ah, no, I muttered to myself: too simple. Something as complicated as drug addiction can't be blamed on television. Come on . . . But I remembered all those desperate places I'd visited as a reporter, where there were no books and a TV set was always playing and the older kids had gone off somewhere to shoot smack, except for the kid who was at the mortuary in a coffin. I also remembered when I was a boy in the '40s and early '50s, and drugs were a minor sideshow, a kind of dark little rumor. And there was one major difference between that time and this: television.

We had unemployment then; illiteracy, poor living conditions, racism, governmental stupidity, a gap between rich and poor. We didn't have the all-consuming presence of television in our lives. Now two generations of Americans have grown up with television from their earliest moments of consciousness. Those same American generations are afflicted by the pox of drug addiction.

Only 35 years ago, drug addiction was not a major problem in this country. There were drug addicts. We had some at the end of the 19th century, hooked on the cocaine in patent medicines. During the placid '50s, Commissioner Harry Anslinger pumped up the budget of the old Bureau of Narcotics with fantasies of reefer madness. Heroin was sold and used in most major American cities, while the bebop generation of jazz musicians got jammed up with horse.

But until the early '60s, narcotics were still marginal to American life; they weren't the $120 billion market they make up today. If anything, those years have an eerie innocence. In 1955, there were 31,700,000 TV sets in use in the country (the number is now past 184 million).

But the majority of the audience had grown up without the dazzling new medium. They embraced it, were diverted by it, perhaps even loved it, but they weren't *formed* by it. That year, the New York police made a mere 1,234 felony drug arrests; in 1988, it was 43,901. They confiscated 97 *ounces* of cocaine for the entire year; last year it was hundreds of pounds. During each year of the '50s in New York, there were only about a hundred narcotics-related deaths. But by the end of the '60s, when the first generation of children *formed* by television had come to maturity (and thus to the marketplace), the number of such deaths had risen to 1,200. The same phenomenon was true in every major American city.

In the last Nielsen survey of American viewers, the average family was watching television seven hours a day. This has never happened before in history. No people has ever been entertained for seven hours a *day*. The Elizabethans didn't go to the theater seven hours a day. The pre-TV generation did not go to the movies seven hours a day. Common sense tells us that this all-pervasive diet of instant imagery, sustained now for 40 years, must have changed us in profound ways.

Television, like drugs, dominates the lives of its addicts. And though some lonely Americans leave their sets on without watching them, using them as electronic companions, television usually absorbs its viewers the way drugs absorb their users. Viewers can't work or play while watching television; they can't read; they can't be out on the streets, falling in love with the wrong people, learning how to quarrel and compromise with other human beings. In short, they are asocial. So are drug addicts.

One Michigan State University study in the early '80s offered a group of four- and five-year-olds the choice of giving up television or giving up their fathers. Fully one third said they would give up Daddy. Given a similar choice (between cocaine or heroin and father, mother, brother, sister, wife, husband, children, job), almost every stone junkie would do the same.

There are other disturbing similarities. Television itself is a consciousness-altering instrument. With the touch of a button, it takes you out of the "real" world in which you reside and can place you at a basketball game, the back alleys of Miami, the streets of Bucharest, or the cartoony living rooms of Sitcom Land. Each move from channel to channel alters

Pete Hamill's *Crack and the Box* first appeared in *Esquire* May, 1990: Reprinted courtesy of the Hearst Corporation.

mood, usually with music or a laugh track. On any given evening, you can laugh, be frightened, feel tension, thump with excitement. You can even tune in "MacNeil/Lehrer" and feel sober.

But none of these abrupt shifts in mood is *earned*. They are attained as easily as popping a pill. Getting news from television, for example, is simply not the same experience as reading it in a newspaper. Reading is *active*. The reader must decode little symbols called words, then create images or ideas and make them connect; at its most basic level, reading is an act of the imagination. But the television viewer doesn't go through that process. The words are spoken to him or her by Dan Rather or Tom Brokaw or Peter Jennings. There isn't much decoding to do when watching television, no time to think or ponder before the next set of images and spoken words appears to displace the present one. The reader, being active, works at his or her own pace; the viewer, being passive, proceeds at a pace determined by the show. Except at the highest levels, television never demands that its audience take part in an act of imagination. Reading always does.

In short, television works on the same imaginative and intellectual level as psychoactive drugs. If prolonged television viewing makes the young passive (dozens of studies indicate that it does), then moving to drugs has a certain coherence. Drugs provide an unearned high (in contrast to the earned rush that comes from a feat accomplished, a human breakthrough earned by sweat or thought or love).

And because the television addict and the drug addict are alienated from the hard and scary world, they also feel they make no difference in its complicated events. For the junkie, the world is reduced to him or her and the needle, pipe, or vial; the self is absolutely isolated, with no desire for choice. The television addict lives the same way. Many Americans who fail to vote in presidential elections must believe they have no more control over such a choice than they do over the casting of "L.A. Law."

The drug plague also coincides with the unspoken assumption of most television shows: Life should be *easy*. The most complicated events are summarized on TV news in a minute or less. Cops confront murder, chase the criminals, and bring them to justice (usually violently) within an hour. In commercials, you drink the right beer and you get the girl. *Easy!* So why should real life be a grind? Why should any American have to spend years mastering a skill or craft, or work eight hours a day at an unpleasant job, or endure the compromises and crises of a marriage?

The doper always whines about how he or she *feels*; drugs are used to enhance feelings or obliterate them, and in this the doper is very American. No other people on earth spend so much time talking about their feelings; hundreds of thousands go to shrinks, they buy self-help books by the millions, they pour out intimate confessions to virtual strangers in bars or discos. Our political campaigns are about emotional issues now, stated in the simplicities of adolescence. Even alleged statesmen can start a sentence, "I feel that the Sandinistas should . . ." when they once might have said, "I *think* . . ." I'm convinced that this exal-

tation of cheap emotions over logic and reason is one by-product of hundreds of thousands of hours of television.

Most Americans under the age of 50 have now spent their lives absorbing television; that is, they've had the structures of drama pounded into them. Drama is always about conflict. So news shows, politics, and advertising are now all shaped by those structures. Nobody will pay attention to anything as complicated as the part played by Third World debt in the expanding production of cocaine; it's much easier to focus on Manuel Noriega, a character right out of "Miami Vice," and believe that even in real life there's a Mister Big.

What is to be done? Television is certainly not going away, but its addictive qualities can be controlled. It's a lot easier to "just say no" to television than to heroin or crack. As a beginning, parents must take immediate control of the sets, teaching children to watch specific television *programs*, not "television," to get out of the house and play with other kids. Elementary and high schools must begin teaching television as a subject, the way literature is taught, showing children how shows are made, how to distinguish between the true and the false, how to recognize cheap emotional manipulation. All Americans should spend more time reading. And thinking.

For years, the defenders of television have argued that the networks are only giving the people what they want. That might be true. But so is the Medellin cartel.

Pete Hamill is a columnist for Esquire *magazine.*

---

moral reform at a therapeutic community.

The words "less cocaine" rather than "no cocaine" may be the key to what makes the philosophy of the acupuncture clinic potentially revolutionary. Unlike most other approaches, it brings a sharp breeze of realism to the drug treatment enterprise. It is a step toward looking at the antidrug campaign not as an all-or-nothing war to the death against the enemy infidel, but a complex, long-term process—rather like managing a chronic illness that, even though incurable, does not have to destroy the life of its victim.

One therapist who argues for taking a new look at our traditional, all-or-nothing approaches to drug treatment is Ernest Drucker, founder and director of the Drug Abuse Treatment Program at the Bronx's Montefiore Medical Center. Drucker calls

his approach to drugs "harm reduction," which neatly bypasses the dualism of the drug policy debate. Harm reduction avoids the righteous "just say no" bleating of the hardliners and the sentimental "treatment on demand" plea of the reformers. Drucker wants to reduce the harm drugs do by offering "detox on demand." A deceptively simple notion, detox on demand is not intended to promote abstinence for any and all drug

users, but to build a network of clinics where addicts could willingly come in for help to stop taking the drug and recover some degree of health—without being pressured to go through a long-term recovery program. Practically speaking, the job would be relatively uncomplicated, according to Drucker. "Detox is easy and it works. We know how to detox a crack addict. You let them sleep it off. You keep them apart from the drug. It's

HOWEVER PERVERSE THE CRACK CULTURE, IT IS NOTHING IF NOT SOCIAL.

WHAT CRACK IS LIKE: IT'S GREAT, UNFORTUNATELY

BY JEFFERSON MORLEY

The inspiration for this account of a first-time crack experience, which appeared last fall in The New Republic, *was journalist Morley's belief that while crack was the focus of emotion-laden discussion, few policy-makers—or journalists, for that matter—really understood the effects of the substance itself. Morley's article prompted a tidal wave of criticism from drug war advocates, including columnists Pat Buchanan, Robert Novak, and Al Hunt. William Bennett called the piece "garbage" and denounced Morley as a "defector in the drug war." Even Morley's journalist father called to tell him he had made a "big mistake" and that the piece made him sound like an "elitist wise-ass . . . [trivializing] a terrible problem by drawing attention to yourself and not to the real issues involved." Discussing the response his piece triggered, Morley later wrote that his article served some purpose if it enabled people "to discuss drugs in ways that are considered unacceptable by the moral custodians of the current drug debate."*

WHEN IT COMES TO CRACK, POLITIcians and pundits literally do not know what they are talking about. Most of the journalists covering the so-called "war on drugs" have at least tried marijuana. So have many of the rugged young officials now in charge of said hostilities. Both pencil pushers and paper pushers have been known to snort the occasional mound of cocaine. Virtually all came of age before the dawn of zero tolerance. Even heroin is not utterly unknown to the opinion and policy classes.

But crack is something else. Probably no one making our government's drug policy has ever smoked a rock of crack cocaine. Nor has anyone who regularly reports or comments in the media on the ravages of crack capitalism. Now, I wouldn't argue that you have to smoke crack to understand the war on drugs—any more than you have to kill someone to understand the war in Vietnam. And I certainly wouldn't argue that crack isn't hazardous or that anyone should try it. Having been through the experience,

"Using it even once can make a person crave cocaine for as long as they live."
—PETER JENNINGS
"ABC World News Tonight,"
September 8, 1989

though, may facilitate a certain realism about the conflict in question.

Crack is a pleasure both powerful and elusive. Smoke a rock and, for the next 20 minutes, you will likely appreciate sensuous phenomena ranging from MTV to neon lights to oral sex with renewed urgency. After your 20 minutes are up, you will have a chemical aftertaste in your mouth and, in all likelihood, the sneaking desire to smoke another rock—to see what that was really all about. Just one more. You'll want to pick up a $25 rock, which can be split into four or five smaller rocks. (If you want to know where to buy crack, just tune in to shows like "Geraldo" or "City Under Siege"—Washington's nightly local TV report on the drug crisis—for detailed instructions.)

As you smoke your second rock, it may strike you that the crack high combines the best aspects of marijuana and cocaine. The pleasure of pot is not just a high, but a buzz; smoke a joint and space out. Cocaine, in contrast, is a clear high, a stimulant to sociality; do a line and get into some serious play or some pleasurable work. Crack is both spacey and intense. It has the head rush of marijuana or amyl nitrate with the clarity induced by a noseful of powder cocaine.

On the third rock, you may notice that your world looks just fine, as do various of the women (or men) in it. Reality isn't real and all that was formerly a possibility is now on the verge of actuality. You'll want to turn up the music and maybe your sexual aggression quotient. You'll gain new insight into why crack is so popular among women.

You may find yourself in the company of experienced crackheads as you smoke your fourth rock. You may start to notice other aspects of the crack experience. An individualistic drug, crack is often enjoyed in silence. The silence ends when that last sliver of rock is gone and you want to go out and find another $25 rock. When you're back outside, prowling the lunar landscape of post-Reagan

urban America at two in the morning with your high fading and your heartbeat racing, you'll begin to learn that crack is both a mental and a material phenomenon. You want your next rock, you want to get off, get out of this world—or at least transform it for a few minutes. You can be a moral tourist in the land of crack and still get a sense of how the drug can make sick sense to demoralized people. If all you have in life are bad choices, crack may not be the most unpleasant of them.

EVEN AT TWO IN THE MORNING, YOU can find a guy who's got a rock. But he won't sell to you because he thinks a white guy must be a cop. Or he wants you to give him your money and he'll go get the rock from his friend over there. (Yeah, right.) So he finally gets you a rock but chips off a little for himself. You get high and before you know it you're coming down again, thinking maybe crack combines the worst of other drugs. Like weed, it's stupefying; like coke, it's conducive to paranoia.

After my night of crack, I went home and fell into a light sleep with the lights on. I feared that an air conditioner was going to fall on my head. I woke up tired, alert, still a little buzzed, filled with an urgent desire to get to work to make up for the night's decadence.

I took an unsatisfactory shower. I mused about the weird apparatchiks who wage war on drugs and who claim vindication in the fact that drug use is declining among the middle class. They are the ones, I thought melodramatically, who should—who must!—smoke crack. Before it is too late, I muttered, dragging a comb through my hair.

What if there were a drug (I inquired of the mirror) that could chemically induce feelings of upper-middle-classness? It would be attractive to the poor, and widely popular among those who had no prayer of ever achieving that comfortable station in life. And it would be despised by people who had worked long, hard years to obtain that same mental state without resorting to the drug. It would be popular, cheap, and the cause of anti-social behavior. It would be a lot like crack.

I put on my clothes and thought, for

like the old joke, 'It's easy to quit smoking—I've done it a million times.' But it's true. You do stop smoking for a while, and that's better than nothing."

For many old soldiers of the drug campaigns, "better than nothing" is nothing at all—like allowing a little bit of murder. Kleber calls detox on demand "one of the more nonsensical ideas I've heard. There's no evidence that repeated detox works [to get people permanently off drugs], but reasonably good evidence that detox has extraordinarily high relapse rates." According to Kleber, a "harm reduction" strategy may actually *increase* harm. "Drugs are very pleasurable, and people tend not to give up pleasure without pain. If the addict doesn't have the shower, the place to sleep [provided by detox clinics], he's going to feel more pain and face up to his use sooner. The more you shield the user from the negative consequences of drug use, the more pleasure is felt, the less desire to quit."

Other drug treatment specialists, while sympathetic to the complexity of the issue and not inclined to moralizing, still believe that Drucker and his adherents are underestimating the addictive power of crack and the particular virulence of the crack epidemic. Drucker's kind of "realism" may remind them of the suggestion by some Colombian leaders to accept the drug lords as a permanent

obscure reasons, of a yuppie acquaintance. I am sure she has never tried crack. "I just bought a CD player," this young woman announced proudly to her sister one day when it was still morning in America. "Do you know of any music I should listen to?" Yuppies are just the crackheads of consumerism, I thought, their CDs just so many rocks of consumptive, sensuous pleasure. My mood was improving already. Crack was a parody of Reaganism, I concluded, a brief high with a bad aftertaste and untold bodily damage.

I flushed the toilet and straightened my tie. Had Bill Bennett ever smoked crack, I wondered? Probably not. I was no longer high, just daydreaming. I remembered meeting a University of Texas alum, and her bemused expression when I asked her if she thought Bill Bennett had smoked marijuana at UT in the late 1960s. "Well, obviously not enough," she said.

The crack had worn off entirely, and I sat down to write an article about the drug problem.

Reprinted from *The New Republic.*

feature of national life. A substance so destructive, with such demonstrated power to devastate whole communities, is not a fit subject for compromise.

But Drucker argues that the fantasy of a drug-free America is not likely to be realized in his lifetime. "I think that for many people it's a good idea to get off drugs totally," he says. "I just haven't seen how you get them all to do it. Since people are using drugs and will continue to do so in the future, a successful drug policy is one that reduces consumption of the group as a whole. We have a lot of crack users in the South Bronx. Rather than make our goal convincing all of them to not use cocaine, we should try to get them to use less cocaine as a group."

Detox on demand might at least improve the lives of crack addicts and those around them by making it easier and more attractive for them to stop using, if only for a few days. Drucker is also more aware than many policy-makers of the wide variation in drug use. Not every user is an unsalvageable crack-head. Only six or seven percent of cocaine users consume 60 to 70 percent of the total drug supply, he claims. "What we should try to do is separate heavy users from the drug as much as possible," says Drucker, noting that these abusers are poor candidates for traditional treatment programs anyway.

Drug treatment specialists may well balk at Drucker's refusal to emphasize abstinence. Many already fault family therapists for neglecting the physiological realities of addiction. But Drucker argues that if detox is always available, it will probably reduce drug use and certainly expose users to better company: "We want to increase the user's contact with people who are fighting their drug problem, and take them away from the drug culture."

At the heart of Drucker's thinking are two assumptions, one libertarian and the other populist. The first assumption is that the persuasion and coercion of abstinence-prohibition strategies drive away as many people as they help. The second assumption is that with less coercion and conventional treatment, families and social networks could and would step forward to prod, challenge, and support the addict more than they do now. At this point, the first assumption may seem statistically sound, but the second remains unproven.

SO FAR, LITTLE HAS BEEN HEARD FROM family therapists in the national debate about drug policy, and even less about how to design more effective treatments

for crack addiction. While trained to perceive the drug problem as a complex affair involving family, social, and economic systems, family therapists have seemed stymied about what practical steps to take.

Family therapist Jaime Inclan runs a mental health clinic on New York City's Lower East Side. A crack den operates right across the street from his office; users and dealers restlessly prowl the doorways, and *bodegas* on his block looking for a sale. Yet Inclan rarely treats crack users. "They don't come to my door," he says. "They go in *that* door [the crack house] instead." Crack addicts, according to Inclan, "test the limits of family therapy. We're told, 'You've got to reintegrate the addict into the family.' I'm all for it, theoretically, but I've yet to see somebody who knows how to do it. Crack addicts don't check in with their therapists. My sense is they use and use until they run amok and then are absorbed by the legal system." Indeed, even the most comprehensively systemic family therapists, who consider schools, welfare agencies, and legal institutions as much a part of the system as the family itself, may never even see the crack addict.

This past September, however, a group of family therapists working in collaboration with Montefiore's Drucker received a $3.5 million grant from the National Institute on Drug Abuse to oversee a five-year program to reduce—not eliminate—drug abuse among women of childbearing age. The emphasis of the program, sponsored by Montefiore's Department of Social Medicine and the Ackerman Institute for Family Therapy, is not on drugs, *per se,* but on helping female crack addicts with newborn children to get their lives together and promote the well-being of their babies.

The program breaks with some of the basic premises of most drug treatment endeavors, among them the idea that a mother who takes drugs cannot be a good mother because using drugs is antithetical to being a loving parent. Perhaps even more crucially, the program regards the addict's family not as a noxious influence, but as a healing resource. "Traditionally, most drug treatment programs have tried to separate the addicts from their families," says family therapist Gillian Walker of the Ackerman Institute, coauthor of the grant proposal. "They try to get people to develop a new sense of self outside the family, which is seen as enabling and harmful. Our idea is that women addicts in particular don't need to separate from their families, but to repair damaged connections. It's through improving

WHAT CRACK IS REALLY LIKE

Former crack addict Michael Davis started off knowing better. "I helped my brother get off crack, but I had a weak philosophy for myself. I thought, 'I won't buy it, but I won't run from it, either.'" When someone offered him some, he tried it and was addicted after his first experience with the drug.

"I could not control my own actions—there was a power stronger than my own mind," says Davis. "I knew exactly what I was doing and had no way to stop it. I started praying."

Davis smoked his way through his bank account, pawned his wedding ring, stole from his wife, and sold their possessions. Then he stayed away from home and smoked at a friend's house, in a community of crack addicts who hated their addiction but could not stop using. "We prayed to God while we were smoking crack," remembers Davis.

Davis's employer sent him to a rehabilitation program, but he says it was next to useless, and he could not even stop himself from using while he was in rehab: "I really wanted to stop, but they were not showing me the way."

One year after he became a crack addict, Davis's life reached a turning point. His friend was evicted and their safe crack den was closed down. He knew he could go to a crack house—which was death—or try to go home. He decided it was a sign from God that he should go home. Davis's wife helped him start his own program of recovery, and although he had frequent relapses, in seven months he

kicked the addiction. He has been drug-free for two years, and is now writing a musical based on his experiences.

THERE IS MORE AWE THAN ACCUracy in Jeff Morley's description of the effects of crack, like a school nurse describing brain surgery procedures. But Morley was admittedly just dating; I lived with the witch. The crack high is not just powerful, it's overwhelming; not only elusive, but momentary, offering the kind of "pleasure" found in dodging rush-hour traffic.

At peak, the high feels like a self-induced, simulated orgasm . . . abruptly interrupted. The sensation seldom lasts a minute; then, hell breaks loose for the rest of the day. The street phrase for this hellishness is "chasin' the rock." Thus, the two components of the crack high: the peak and the chase.

What begins as orgasm soon becomes trickery. The thrills and chills are replaced by primal screams. Where a natural orgasm is ushered out by a resolved feeling, crack breaks its climax at peak, leaving the user hanging, ripe for the chase. But each subsequent hit delivers less peak and more hook until that "sneaking desire" Morley describes becomes like a pit-bull in slippers. The user buys another rock, and another. It's not uncommon to see users in a frenzy, on their hands and knees, pathetically searching for imaginary lost crumbs of crack.

My first hit made me vomit. Then came stomach-knotting, heart-pounding anxiety, followed by hot flashes, head rushes, and orgasmic chills. Suddenly, a numb-

ness, waiting for something . . . Then, distant whispers—"Oooh, that felt nice!"—grew louder. "Aaah, let's do that again!" By my second encounter, that inner voice was barking commands: "MORE! . . . NOW!"

Morley says crack made him "appreciate sensuous phenomena from t.v. to sex." During the first few months, I did feel a sense of heightened sexuality. Then, like a Tyson knockout, my amorous desires were flattened in the all-consuming roar of crack.

Other substances took me to particularly desired states of mind. Marijuana lays you back; alcohol loosens you up; valium slows you down. But crack shackles you. Each hit nurtures a mental fog, thickened with paranoia, irritability, and high anxiety. After spending years escaping reality, I found no escape in crack. No fun. A wired feeling, sure, like being plugged into prison.

But the most horrifying tendency of this drug is what it makes the user do, especially after the last rock and dollar are gone. I saw it in myself and everyone else using or selling. It stirs up a self-centered trance that locks us into our most primitive responses. Crack made lying, stealing, adultery, meanness, and violence all too easy.

Crack enters the brain's most intimate room, then proceeds with psychological, emotional, physical, spiritual, financial, and social rape. It's born of a lie—"This is an orgasm, let's do it again!"—then is fed by other lies. Morley saw Leona Helmsley with a Vanna White smile. He and I both know that drugs do different things to different people. Thank God, I'm still alive to tell somebody the truth about crack.

relationships with their children and their own mothers that young women develop the sense of value and self-esteem that can enable them to get off drugs."

The primary goal of the Montefiore/Ackerman project will not be getting the mother to stop taking drugs, but raising her self-esteem and sense of confidence as a parent, strengthening the bond between her and her child, and decreas-

ing the number of children needing placement in foster care.

Walker believes that women do not respond well to the kind of ego-deflating, confrontational tactics and other purposely humbling techniques used in most drug programs. "They're based on a male power model," she says. "They try to help addicts develop their autonomy without

recognizing the value of the family and social networks in all people's lives, but especially those of women." Also implicit in the Montefiore/Ackerman program is the systemic view that, in Drucker's words, "the therapeutic agent is the family itself. What we're trying to do is clear away obstacles for the mother, provide concrete support in getting better housing, job training, and other social services. We will be trying to set in motion a natural process of healing."

Drucker assumes that the mother's family and other community support networks are in a far better position to help her deal with the day-to-day challenge of cutting down on drugs and taking better care of her children than the staff of a treatment program. This, of course, may prove not to be true. What is more, going soft on abstinence may actually help the abusers rationalize their continued drug use. Faced with this argument, Drucker shrugs and says, "It's not obvious that the hard-ass approach works any better."

For national drug policy, the Montefiore/Ackerman program and detox-on-demand flies in the face of all conventional wisdom. Nevertheless, even Kleber expressed support of Drucker's goal of reducing crack use among mothers, and did not oppose studying the effectiveness of a harm-reduction approach under NIDA auspices. "My only concern," says Kleber, "is that you make sure there are enough safeguards built in for the infant. If the mother is continuously taking drugs, I want the child to be protected."

Drucker points out that treatment based on abstinence parallels a national drug policy based on prohibition. A treatment strategy based on harm reduction, he notes, implies a national drug policy based on legalization. For those who think drugs are the self-indulgent root of all that is evil in late 20th-century America, abstention and prohibition are the only possible response. But to Drucker, while the harm-reduction approach may lack the patriotic drama of the war on drugs, it holds the promise for a certain decent improvement in the lives of drug users and their families.

"The harm-reduction approach I'm talking about," says Drucker, "is linked to the view that drugs are a public health problem. And the challenge to mental health professionals in the age of crack is to create a culture of drug treatment rather than a culture of just say no. I'm not talking about a magic bullet. I'm talking about treating drugs as a complicated biological and social problem, in an era in which society prefers to deal with drug abuse as a sin and a crime."

Youth and Drug Abuse
BREAKING THE CHAIN

"Confronting the causes of antisocial and delinquent behavior is more critical than intervention once children have started using drugs."

Stuart Greenbaum

Mr. Greenbaum is communications director, National School Safety Center (NSSC), Encino, Calif., and creative director of the High-Risk Youth National Public Awareness Campaign. Suzanne Harper, communications specialist for NSSC, contributed to this article.

TO experts in the field of drug abuse prevention, Tanya's story reads like a recipe for certain disaster. Born to an unwed teenage mother, she quickly was placed in a foster home that was meant to provide a more caring environment. Instead, an older boy in the family sexually molested her and she was beaten for such minor offenses as mashing marshmallows through her fingers.

Such early scarring experiences often result in a young person turning to illegal drugs during adolescence. In fact, from the time she was born, Tanya belonged to the newly recognized category of high-risk youth. Recent research indicates that these young people are more likely to develop a drug problem because of risk factors in their lives, ranging from dysfunctional families and impoverished environments to drug-using peers and poor personal choices. The fact that Tanya eventually triumphed in spite of her situation is a testament to her resiliency, a quality that many experts say is vital to overcoming such negative early influences.

Tanya had to be resilient because, after a few years, she left her foster family for another situation that was even worse. When she was six years old, she came home from riding her bike to find her suitcase packed and sitting by the front door. Her foster mother told Tanya that her real mother, whom she had seen only twice and talked to a few times on the phone, was taking her to California to live with her and her new boyfriend.

Tanya, now 25, remembers wondering what her new life in California would be like. She dreamed of beaches, palm trees, and—finally—her own family, but the reality didn't match her dreams. When she was 10, her mother's boyfriend left them.

The next six years were brutal. "My mom constantly verbally and physically abused me. She hated me . . . and I hated her."

Her mother began drinking and using illegal drugs, and often abandoned her for weeks at a time. "When she was around, a constant trail of men would be parading through the place. One time, a different car was parked in front of the house every morning for 16 straight days. I was so embarrassed, because I knew what the neighbors must have thought." Another time, a stranger broke into her bedroom and sexually molested her. From then on, she slept with a knife on her headboard.

Tanya found a refuge at school, where she earned good grades and excelled at softball and gymnastics. Despite these achievements, she turned to minor delinquency, taking money from her mother to buy meals at the taco stand around the corner, where she ate virtually every night for years, and stealing clothes and cosmetics because she had no money to buy her own and was tired of her outcast physical appearance.

Ironically, in one 24-hour period, significant opportunities arose for Tanya's mother to show her the importance of discipline and love, but she displayed neither. When Tanya was arrested for petty theft, her mother picked her up from jail, took her home, and grounded her. However, she soon revoked the grounding. The next day, Tanya took first place in the beginning gymnastics state championship. She stood on the winner's podium alone, without her mother in attendance.

Despite these trying times, Tanya resisted other, more dangerous, temptations. "My mom was a loser and her friends were worse. Cocaine, marijuana, acid, pills, and alcohol were all over the place. I never accepted them, even though they were offered to me. I always avoided using drugs—partly because of drug education programs at school, but mostly because I wanted desperately not to be like my mom in any way."

Although sympathetic, no one at school realized just how bad her home situation was. Tanya's grades and attendance record didn't indicate a problem, and she regularly participated in extracurricular activities. However, she did have good role models next door—the parents of her only friend, Heather. "I used to spend the night with her and mooch meals off her family all the time. I think her parents knew how bad things were for me—and though they never intervened, at least they let me play with their daughter and weren't judgmental. And I could see the way they loved and cared for Heather, the way they disciplined her. By their example, I knew what a good family and love meant—though I never experienced either firsthand."

If Tanya had lived her life according to statistics, these factors—a substance-abusing parent, physical and sexual assaults, early delinquent behavior, family conflict, early exposure to drugs and alcohol, and few positive peer relationships—would have made her a prime candidate to become involved with drugs.

Nevertheless, Tanya beat the odds. She became so fed up with her home life that she became legally emancipated at age 16 with the help of her mother's former boyfriend. She has been on her own ever since. Today, she's majoring in recreation at a California state university, working in public affairs for a major southern California engineering institute, teaching gymnastics, and living her life as a self-confessed overachiever. "I'm everything my mom wasn't, and hopefully I'll never change, just as I'm convinced my mom never will."

The problem

Unfortunately, many youths are not as resilient as Tanya. A few statistics help illustrate the scope of the problem: about 3,000,000 12-to-17-year-olds use marijuana or cocaine; nearly 5,000,000 adolescents—about 30%—have problems with alcohol; more than half of America's teenagers have used illegal drugs at least once before they finish high school; and over one-third have used illegal drugs other than marijuana.

For the past 20 years, drug abuse among youth has been one of society's most pressing concerns. Although recent surveys indicate that most drug use is leveling off among youth, it is still unacceptably high. (In fact, the use of crack, a processed, inexpensive form of cocaine, has increased.) Teenagers say drug abuse is the biggest problem they face, according to a Gallup Poll.

A variety of remedies for this problem have come into fashion and just as quickly been discarded; evidence about what works and what doesn't often is contradictory and ambiguous. The approaches to drug abuse prevention range from limiting the drug supply to decreasing the demand for drugs.

Although both approaches deserve attention, to focus on *why* young people turn to drugs in the first place is paramount. Primary prevention—confronting the causes of antisocial and delinquent behavior—is more critical than intervention once children have started using drugs.

According to the National Drug Policy Board's High-Risk Youth Committee, the National Institute on Drug Abuse, and other authorities, the causes of delinquency and illegal drug use among youth can be categorized by the following risk factors:

● Individual choices, such as lack of commitment to education (including school failure and truancy); antisocial/delinquent behavior; peers who abuse drugs; early experimentation with and a deferential attitude toward drugs; suicide attempts; and running away from home.
● Family conditions, such as drug-abusing parents; poor family management, including lack of support, rules, and discipline; and child abuse, neglect, and exploitation.
● Genetic traits, such as aggressive behavior; hyperactivity; learning disabilities or difficulties; mental health problems; and a biological predisposition to drug abuse.
● Community influences, such as an impoverished environment; high crime rates; drug availability; gang activity; absence of a legal deterrence; and lack of community youth programs.

Having one or more of these risk factors, researchers are quick to point out, does not necessarily mean a child will use illegal drugs. Possessing the skills and having the opportunity to participate in socially acceptable activities are vital, as Tanya's story shows. However, the more risk factors present in a child's life, the more vulnerable he or she is to have problems with drugs.

Knowing what these factors are, and how to reduce or eliminate them, will help parents, educators, social workers, law enforcers, and members of the criminal justice system. For that reason, the High-Risk Youth National Public Awareness Campaign, sponsored by the National School Safety Center and funded by the Office of Juvenile Justice and Delinquency Prevention (OJJDP), focuses on reaching the public through a documentary film; posters; a series of broadcast and print media public service announcements; and articles in popular and trade magazines.

The campaign goes beyond the "Just Say No" program to offer positive emphases on what *can* be done. Zero tolerance and personal accountability by the individual, family, and community are key to achieving a drug-free society. Several prevention programs aimed at these youth already have been developed. Although each has a slightly different focus, all attempt to mitigate the effects of one or more risk factors.

The first step—identifying high-risk youth so they can be helped—often is difficult because many students try a drug once, then choose not to use it again, while others progress past such minimal use or experimentation and begin to abuse drugs chronically.

While we can identify the risk factors, we still are not very good at determining which particular high-risk youth will become delinquents or drug abusers. This dilemma can be avoided, claims J. David Hawkins of the University of Washington, by targeting high-risk neighborhoods, schools, or communities, rather than individuals, for drug prevention programs. Alternately, schools could focus on students who already have exhibited some antisocial behavior that provides a legitimate reason for intervention.

For example, evidence of antisocial behavior and personal conduct problems before age 10 is often followed by frequent drug use during adolescence. The lack of social adjustment in elementary school appears even more important than poor academic achievement in predicting which students will turn to drugs. (Often, early antisocial behavior may lead to poor academic performance, which could exacerbate an already negative self-image.)

Hawkins suggests that prevention programs should focus on early childhood education. For example, one preschool program teaches interpersonal skills to young children and family management skills to their parents. While it's still unclear whether this program halts illegal drug use, it has been shown to reduce later delinquent behavior and improve academic and social adjustment. Similar programs teach students on all grade levels how to make decisions, be more assertive, communicate more clearly, cope with anxiety, and recognize cause-and-effect relationships. Learning interpersonal skills can help them resist peer pressure to try drugs and improve their academic performance.

Some programs focus on social influences that encourage illegal drug use. For example, youth are taught to estimate correctly how many of their classmates take drugs —most young people tend to overestimate the number of substance-abusing peers; recognize the health and social risks of illegal drug use; resist the pressure to use illegal drugs; and make a specific commitment to avoid drugs. This approach has been used in fifth-10th-grade classes, significantly reducing drinking and smoking (both cigarettes and marijuana).

Because parents dramatically can affect their children's choices, prevention programs often include a segment that teaches them to monitor their offsprings' behavior, use appropriate discipline when there are undesirable actions, and reward good behavior in a consistent manner. Research indicates that this common-sense approach works—children become more attached to their parents and exhibit less problem behavior at school and at home.

Parental involvement is just one of the many factors that influence youth. "The problem of substance abuse [is] 'systemwide,' meaning that all segments of the community are responsible for the problem, and therefore requires the adoption of a systemwide approach for dealing with it," notes Peter Schneider of the Pacific Institute for Research and Evaluation. Schools, public and mental health departments, housing and recreation agencies, religious organizations, and all aspects of the juvenile justice system must coordinate their resources to eliminate illegal drug use among high-risk youth.

Policy-shapers should identify a problem and, using each agency's area of expertise, develop a specific method to deal with it. For instance, if a local public housing project is pinpointed as a hotbed of illegal drug activity, the responsible agency could embark on a beautification project to instill resident pride; local schools might offer programs to develop social skills and improve academic performance in the youth who live in the project; law enforcement departments could make the project safe and secure; and a social service agency might provide family management training to parents.

OJJDP also emphasizes the need for greater community involvement—including efforts by the private sector—as a necessary element in combating drug abuse.

Examples of current private-sector approaches include those of the Southland Corporation, which sponsors alcohol- and drug-free proms with local school districts; the Boy Scouts of America, which distributed 6,500,000 copies of *Drugs: A Deadly Game* to scout troops, schools, churches, and community groups; and the Lions Club International, which developed a drug prevention curriculum for 10-to-14-year-olds that was adopted by more than 2,500 schools in 49 states.

Why most children turn out well

Because it's easy to see why many young people turn to drugs as an escape, there is a natural focus on youth drug abuse among educators, psychologists, and law enforcers. They are not the whole story, however. What may be a greater mystery is why some children, raised in the same environment and dealing with similar problems, still grow up to lead happy and productive lives. That puzzle was the subject of a 33-year project by Emmy E. Werner, a social psychologist at the University of California, Davis, who studied 698 people born on the Hawaiian Island of Kauai in 1955.

One of her most interesting findings was that children who had a chance to develop a close attachment with someone—whether a parent, older sibling, or grandparent—developed relatively few problems later in life. These youngsters also found emotional support outside their families, relying on an informal network of friends, neighbors, and elders for counsel and help. They made school their home away from home, much as Tanya did, and found sanctuary there when their own families were embroiled in conflict.

Resilient children also possess certain personal characteristics, such as pleasing temperaments and well-developed social skills, which help smooth their otherwise rocky path. Tanya, for example, is an outgoing, sensitive, and caring young woman. Naturally, teachers and other adults respond well to such a personality.

Werner also found that resilient youth manage to recruit surrogate parents when a biological parent is unavailable. Even after her mother's boyfriend left, Tanya kept in touch with him, sometimes staying with his new family for a few days when her own home situation was unbearable. As an adult, she still sees him and, as a matter of fact, calls him "Dad."

While many researchers focus on risk factors as a way to explain youths' illegal drug use, attention must be paid to personal choice as well. Stanton E. Samenow, a

clinical psychologist and author of *Inside the Criminal Mind* and *Before It's Too Late*, points out that environmental factors—such as poverty, broken homes, unemployment, racism, and lack of opportunity—often are cited as causes of crime, including drug abuse.

However, he states, "After the fact, any adversity can be cited as causing delinquent behavior. In nearly every case, when I interview a criminal from an oppressive social environment, I find that he has siblings and neighbors living under the same or perhaps worse conditions who are law-abiding citizens. It is *not* the environment per se that is critical, but how people *choose* to respond to that environment."

To Samenow, the answer is clear: "We must help antisocial children develop a brand new way of thinking that includes teaching them a concept of injury to others, an operational understanding of interdependent functioning, a responsible time perspective, the elements of responsible decision making and much more." Programs that teach these things already exist, although they focus on lawbreakers, rather than those at risk. A central tenet of such programs is that participants must become more aware of their thinking by writing their thoughts down and then learn to criticize their thinking constructively so that they are open to new concepts of responsibility.

A similar philosophy of changing delinquents' attitudes in order to alter their behavior underlies a new teaching technique called Aggression Replacement Training (ART). Developed by Arnold Goldstein, professor of special education and director of Syracuse University's Center for Research on Aggression, it teaches youngsters how to respond to teasing and accusations, avoid drugs and fights, and handle failure. The families of the juvenile offenders often receive similar training. Preliminary research indicates that the program is having an impact on participants' recidivism rate.

All of the above programs deal with one or more risk factors, although their emphases may differ. However, they have one thing in common—each attempts to change *attitudes* about drugs in order to stop their illegal use. There are too few Tanyas—a high-risk youth who chose to resist the lure of drugs—and too many young people who turn to drug abuse, rather than deal with the adversities in their lives. Attitudes don't change quickly, and a new awareness of the dangers of illegal drug use may grow too slowly to see. However, that doesn't mean that change isn't occurring—or that the cause of drug prevention should be abandoned.

DOWN AND OUT IN THE CITY

Examining the roots of urban poverty

By Chris Tilly
and Abel Valenzuela

CHRIS TILLY, a member of the *Dollars & Sense* Collective, teaches economics at the University of Lowell. ABEL VALENZUELA, also a member of the Collective, is a graduate student in urban planning at the Massachusetts Institute of Technology.

Something is terribly wrong in our cities. In 1968, 13% of the residents in U.S. central cities lived below the poverty line. Twenty years later, the percentage had climbed to 18%—an additional six million people.

"I've seen an increase in despair," says Candace Cason, Executive Director of Women, Inc., a Boston-based agency that helps women overcome dependency on drugs and reliance on public assistance. "Particularly in the last ten years, people have a sense of being in a hole they can't get out of."

No one questions that poverty in U.S. cities looks and feels different than in previous decades. Legions of homeless crowd sidewalks and shelters—something not seen since the Hoovervilles of the 1930s. The crack plague and its associated violence make the heroin epidemic of the 1960s and 1970s seem tame. Experts speak of an "underclass" permanently stuck in poverty.

Why has poverty in U.S. cities worsened so dramatically? Rhetoric about the "underclass" (see box) suggests the problem lies in ingrained pathological behavior passed down from inner-city generation to generation. That analysis evades a host of causes, however. Nor are crack and violent crime the causes of the crisis. They are symptoms—albeit symptoms that intensify the problem.

The real source is an economic pincer between housing and jobs. As affordable housing has become more and more scarce, the manufacturing jobs that provided paychecks for less-educated workers have left town. These economic causes are reversible. But the key player in any coordinated effort to eliminate poverty—the federal government—has pulled back

its commitment to cities. Under the Reagan and Bush administrations, the feds have eagerly declared a "war on drugs" but have refused to challenge the loss of jobs and affordable housing hammering at poor communities.

URBAN POVERTY IN PERSPECTIVE

Inner-city poverty accounts for a minority of America's poor ("Our Forgotten Poor," September 1989). But that minority is growing rapidly—from 30% of all poor people in 1968 to 43% in 1988—and is likely to become a majority soon. The population in concentrated poverty neighborhoods—areas where 40% or more of residents are poor—is growing four times as fast as the overall poverty population. Economic inequality has climbed along with poverty, both nationally and in cities. In 1986, the richest 20% of New York City residents earned 19.5 times as much as the poorest 20%—a 25% increase since 1977. Nationwide, the ratio is nearly ten-to-one.

Urban poverty frequently takes the form of segregated ghettos or barrios. African-Americans and Latinos are five times as likely as whites to live in inner-city poverty. According to a recent study by Paul Ong and others at the University of California in Los Angeles, a staggering 91% of neighborhoods in L.A. defined as low income are populated predominantly by people of color. But the forces creating urban poverty transcend racial differences. Nationwide, whites still make up a majority of poor city residents. In fact, during the 1970s and 1980s the poverty rate for white urbanites grew faster than the rates for blacks or Latinos.

NO PLACE LIKE HOME

During the last two decades, two

opposing investment strategies destroyed affordable housing in U.S. cities. On the one hand, massive disinvestment by banks and land-owners cut into the existing housing stock in low- and moderate-income communities, rendering whole areas like the South Bronx of New York barely habitable. On the other hand, booming service industries such as finance and high technology lured professionals back to the city, fueling gentrification and turning neighborhoods upscale and unaffordable for most residents.

The sweep of the change was startling. In Los Angeles, between 1974 and 1985, the number of apartments renting for under $300 (in 1985 dollars) was cut in half. At the same time, apartments priced at $750 or more quadrupled.

Climbing housing costs pinched everyone, but squeezed the poor hardest. In 1978, 44% of poor renters paid 60% or more of their incomes for housing costs; by 1985, 55% did. The burden on poor homeowners grew at a similar pace.

"Even for the average working class family in the communities we serve, being able to save enough to buy a house is inconceivable—out of reach," comments Women, Inc.'s Cason.

For many, the ultimate consequence was homelessness. By 1985 there were 3.7 million fewer units of affordable housing nationwide than households earning under $10,000 needed. Families caught in the gap doubled up with family or friends, found a spot in welfare hotels, or spilled into the streets and shelters. Estimates of the number of homeless range from the federal government's conservative estimate of 250,000 to the National Union of the Homeless' figure of 2.2 million. Whatever the correct number, observers agree that the

From *Dollars & Sense*, April 1990, pp. 6-8, 21. *Dollars & Sense*, 1 Summer Street, Somerville, MA 02143.

What is the underclass?

"Underclass," just like "working poor" or "rural poor," is another term categorizing a group of impoverished people. This term, however, has become more than just a category. It has become a stigmatizing and negative label that blames increased inner-city poverty on the ingrained behavior of the poor themselves. Implicit in the term is the notion of a class of people "under" the rest of us, living a life much different from us, even different from that of most poor people.

Most academics agree that the underclass is mainly people of color — more specifically, African-Americans, Puerto Ricans in Northeast cities, and Chicanos in Southwest cities. But they agree on little else. Academics have developed a range of technical definitions of the underclass. They have defined underclass by any or all of the following characteristics: chronic or persistent poverty; attitudes and actions at odds with U.S. values and norms (drug pushing, single-headed households); and highly concentrated poverty areas.

The lack of consensus on what defines the underclass prevents researchers and policy analysts from understanding its origins, evolution, and mystifying size. Already, more than a dozen definitions of the underclass have been proposed, each yielding a different size, area, and population subcategory of the urban poor. Estimates on the size of the underclass range from 3% to 38% of all urban poor.

The most controversial definition refers to underclass members as having "persistent pathological behaviors." These behaviors include having children out of wedlock, depending on welfare, having large families, giving up on legal employment, and participating in the "street economy": selling drugs, working as a prostitute, or living off thievery.

The new focus on the underclass by researchers suggests that the poverty problem is an underclass problem, and that poverty policy is best directed towards correcting the poor's pathological behaviors. Policy-makers who view the underclass as a behavioral phenomenon most often promote punitive programs aimed at discouraging these behaviors, such as zero-balance drug enforcement and stringent welfare work requirements. This distracts attention away from larger social conditions, for example the need for jobs and affordable housing—the more crucial elements of a program to fight urban poverty.

---

homeless population grew dramatically in the 1980s, despite the economic recovery.

Homelessness is not just deprivation; it is degradation. "You're never prepared for this," a homeless man told author Jonathan Kozol. "It's like there isn't any bottom. It's not like cracks in a safety net. It's like a black hole sucking you inside."

BLUE COLLAR BLUES

While housing costs went through the roof, manufacturing jobs fell through the floor. Between 1968 and 1988, total U.S. employment grew 56%, but the number of manufacturing jobs stayed even. With certain industries like steel and autos particularly weakened, some cities were especially hard-hit. Pittsburgh lost an estimated 140,000 manufacturing jobs, for a wage loss of $2.3 billion per year.

"We have seen the collapse of these communities," reports Tom Croft, Director of the Pittsburgh-based Steel Valley Authority, a jobs organization created by dislocated steelworkers. "The people of these communities and the communities themselves have moved toward a much more marginal existence. Some people migrate to other parts of the country; others are bouncing around from one low-wage job to another. Some just give up."

People of color suffered disproportionately. "When you have a mass of people lose their jobs in the blue-collar field, those who benefited from affirmative action are the first to lose," Croft notes. "They just get pushed down the totem pole one more rung."

Compounding the damage from manufacturing decline, government employment — long a source of relatively decent, secure employment for people of color — slumped from a high of 19% of all jobs in 1975 to only 16% in 1988.

Service-sector growth did bring some good jobs to the city. To a large extent, though, these were white collar and professional jobs accessible to few of the less-educated workers who had swelled the ranks of manufacturing. Black and Latino males, especially, continue to hold jobs in declining industries.

DRUGS AND CRIME

Drug abuse and crime feed the urban communities' downward spiral. But federal Justice Department statistics show that, contrary to widely held beliefs, the number of illicit drug users peaked in 1979. Since that time, young people have decreased their consumption of alcohol and every other major category of drugs — except cocaine. Even the number of cocaine users, which grew in the early 1980s, fell by half between 1985 and 1988.

All of this offers little consolation to neighborhoods racked by the crack trade. One measure of the concentrated damage inflicted by crack on inner-city neighborhoods is the 600% increase in cocaine-related emergency-room visits between 1983 and 1987. In 1988 alone, such visits grew by 86% in Atlanta, 108% in Phoenix, and 122% in Washington, D.C. Over half of cocaine-related emergency-room patients are African-Americans. Cocaine and the violence that comes with the coke trade have "ripped away at the sense of community," according to Women, Inc.'s Cason. "People are afraid to do things that seem neighborly."

Why has cocaine gripped so many of the urban poor? "Young people have less hope about life, and the drug crisis is largely a result of that," Cason explains. "Crack is cheap, and it provides a quick escape — temporary though it may be — from feelings of powerlessness, anger, and alienation."

Lack of economic opportunity also steers young people toward criminal activity. Surprisingly, crime rates have fallen overall in recent years. The percentage of households touched by serious crimes fell relatively steadily from 32% in 1975 to 25% in 1986. This trend held true in urban areas as well as in the rest of the country, and for black victims as well as white.

But again, these trends have not reached the inner city. The main cause of death for black youths aged 15-24 is homicide. Black men are three times as likely to be robbed as white men; black women are three times as likely to be raped as white women. Someone with a family income below $7,500 is almost three times as likely to be robbed as a person with income of $50,000 or more.

THE FEDERAL RESPONSE

The pursuit of profit powered the rise in urban poverty. Funds flowed out of low- and moderate-income neighborhoods and into housing, services, and entertainment for the new urban gentry. Manufacturing fled to the suburbs, the Sunbelt, and overseas—or shut down completely—as foreign competition increased. Even the decision to sell drugs is driven by profits—in fact, many argue that it is an understandable choice for urban youths when the labor market has so little to offer them.

Some local and state governments, as well as a wide range of community and advocacy organizations, have tried to confront these forces head-on. But more help is needed. This January, the National Urban League called for an "Urban Marshall Plan" to physically and economically rebuild U.S. inner cities. Unfortunately, the federal government, which has the economic and political clout needed to lead this assault, has largely turned its back.

The Reagan and Bush administrations have not ignored the crisis. But their responses—largely echoed by a compliant Congress—have combined punitive measures, laissez-faire economics, and cutbacks. This pattern holds in every major policy area. The federal government and the states have cut benefits and tightened eligibility requirements on welfare programs poor families depend on, such as Food Stamps, Aid to Families with Dependent Children, and Medicaid (see "What's Work Got to do with It?" March 1990.) The Reagan administration saw housing assistance programs as prime areas for budget savings. The number of poor renter families not receiving federal housing assistance climbed by over one third between 1979 and 1987—an added 1.4 million families.

When this country's Pittsburghs collapsed, the federal government was "missing—absolutely not there," says Steel Valley Authority's Tom Croft. "This country lacks any comprehensive strategy around economic change."

The Reagan administration did have one proposal to generate new jobs—"enterprise zones." These zones would suspend a variety of federal regulations—possibly including environmental controls, minimum wage laws, and health and safety rules—in depressed areas in hopes of unleashing market forces to rebuild the economy. When advocates for the nation's cities criticized enterprise zones as a recipe for exploitation, the proposal was dropped.

As for the federal government's "war on drugs," it has been—at best—a one-front battle. "At least there is a recognition that drug abuse is a problem," comments Candace Cason. "But they need to focus on the problems that cause people to want to use drugs in the first place."

The demand for drugs in inner-city neighborhoods is certainly not the focus of the anti-drug plan unveiled by President Bush last September. The administration allocated only 30% of the plan's funds to prevention and treatment—the other 70% goes to enforcement. Even worse, Bush proposes to finance the plan with cuts from many of the very programs needed to solve the drug problem: juvenile justice, economic development, and public housing programs.

Given the shortfall in federal commitment, what can be done to deal with urban poverty? Asked to comment on how to solve the problem of manufacturing decline, Croft offers a frank answer that could apply equally to all aspects of urban poverty. "What does it take to move the rock? I keep being struck by the intransigence of the system—the way the system seems to not want to deal with these problems." But, he quickly adds, public policies in Europe, Sweden, and even as close as Canada are dealing with these problems far more effectively. For the time being, adds Cason, "effective programs are going to have to be hard-fought for, and probably self-initiated."

RESOURCES: Union for Radical Political Economics, *The Imperiled Economy, Book II: Through the Safety Net*, 1988; Philip Weitzman,"Worlds Apart: Housing, Race/Ethnicity and Income in New York City, 1978-1987," Community Service Society of New York, 1989; Paul Ong,"The Widening Divide: Income Inequality and Poverty in Los Angeles," UCLA, 1989; William Wilson, *The Truly Disadvantaged: The Inner City, the Underclass, and Public Policy*, University of Chicago Press, 1987; David Ellwood, *Poor Support: Poverty in the American Family*, Basic Books, 1988; Center on Budget and Policy Priorities/Low Income Housing Information Service, "A Place to Call Home: The Crisis in Housing for the Poor," 1989; Clarence Lusane and Dennis Desmond, four-part series on drugs, *The Guardian*, September-November 1989.

MAKING IT
THE UNDERCLASS CYCLE

NICHOLAS LEMANN

Mr. Lemann is national correspondent of The Atlantic Monthly.

The Irish, crowding into the cities, posed problems in housing, police, and schools; they meant higher taxes and heavier burdens in the support of poorhouses and private charitable institutions. Moreover, the Irish did not seem to practice thrift, self-denial and other virtues desirable in the "worthy, laboring poor." They seemed drunken, dissolute, permanently sunk in poverty.

—*William V. Shannon,* The American Irish

Hardly less aggressive than the Italian, the Russian and Polish Jew . . . is filling the tenements of the old Seventh Ward to the river front, and disputing with the Italian every foot of available space in the back alleys of Mulberry Street. The two races, differing hopelessly in much, have this in common: They carry their slums with them wherever they go, if allowed to do it. . . . The Italian and the poor Jew rise only by compulsion.

—*Jacob Riis,* How the Other Half Lives

The present always imputes a degree of innocence to the past. One of many possible examples is our attitude toward the underclass, which is, essentially, that no similar social problem has ever existed in urban America—and that therefore the problem can't be solved. An ethnic group living in isolated slums in the very heart of our prosperous cities; fatal disease spreading as a result of irresponsibly licentious behavior; rampant welfare dependence; out-of-control violent crime; abuse of lethal intoxicants; rampaging youth gangs; rich, swaggering criminals who sit atop the society of the slum; a breakdown of family values; a barely disguised feeling among the prosperous classes

that perhaps the poor are inherently not up to being fully functioning Americans—the whole picture has been around, intermittently, in this country since about 1850.

Historically, alarm about urban ethnic poverty arises with the arrival in our cities of a large group of immigrants who are visibly very different from middle-class America. The first such group was the peasant Irish, who began coming here in the 1840s. Within a decade, there were large Irish slums; the Irish dominated the resources of the jails, public hospitals and social-welfare agencies; and the fear of where all this would lead was an important factor in national politics. In the late 1880s, after immigrants from eastern and southern Europe had established their own urban slums, another substantial wave of concern about the underclass began, and one of its many consequences was a major political realignment that led to the heyday of Progressivism.

Worries about the turn-of-the century underclass led to strict limits on immigration, and this created labor shortages in the cities. The abundance of unskilled jobs began attracting large numbers of southern blacks to the cities starting around the time of World War I. This black migration intensified with World War II and the boom years that followed it, which vastly increased the demand for labor and coincided with the mechanization of agriculture in the South. The number of black migrants from South to North in the '40s, '50s, and '60s was greater than the number of Irish, Jews, or Italians or Poles who came to the cities during their peak years of migration. It should not be surprising that, like the earlier migrations, the black migration, which lasted until about 1970, should have brought the issue of slum life back to the fore, and contributed to another political realignment—the shift of the presidential electorate to the Republican Party in the late '60s.

From *Current*, March/April 1990, pp. 25-27. Excerpt from "The Underclass Cycle: Making It—Then and How," by Nicholas Lemann, *The Washington Post*, May 21, 1989, pp. C1, C4. Copyright © 1989 by The Washington Post. Reprinted by permission.

SLUMS IN THE 1890s

It is impossible to read Jacob Riis's How the Other Half Lives, published in 1890, without noticing the parallels between Riis's concerns and those of middle-class reformers in the big cities today. Rotgut liquor seemed every bit as dangerous then as crack does today; in fact, his chapter called "A Raid on the Stale-beer Dives" is an eerily precise parallel to those television shows in which a camera crew accompanies the police to a crack house. The saloon-keeper was the equivalent of the drug-dealer, the only visibly affluent male in the slum (except for the numbers king, whose function in recent years has been taken over by local government lotteries). Teen-age gangs were even worse than they are now, in the sense that one of their usual activities, according to Riis, was assaulting police officers.

Riis even shared some of the suspicions of present-day conservatives that social programs may add to, rather than diminish, the conditions they seek to alleviate. "Ill-applied charity," Riis feld, was creating a class of poeple who didn't bother to look for work. Cholera, bred by willfully unclean living, played the role AIDS does now. Teen-age girls were having babies and letting them run wild. Illiteracy was rampant. Murder was an "everyday crop."

In Riis's work, as in that of the other great liberal reformers of the day, there lurks just beneath the surface the idea that ethnicity is destiny. Obviously the same idea, again barely submerged, is around today, though it is reassuring to see how silly Riis's stereotypes seem after less than a century. "Penury and poverty are wedded everywhere to dirt and disease, and Jewtown is no exception," he wrote. "It could not well be otherwise in such crowds, considering especially their low intellectual status."

Riis saw the relatively small black population of New York as occupying a much higher plane: "Cleanliness is the characteristic of the negro in his new surroundings, as it was his virtue in the old. In this respect he is immensely superior to the lowest of the whites, the Italians and the Polish Jews . . . ." As late as World War I, blacks living in the North outscored Jews on the Army intelligence test.

I don't mean to argue that all the problems of the ghettos are simply going to go away over time—only that the current atmosphere of fatalism is unwarranted. What will happen is similar to what has happened in the past: The ghettos will become depopulated as everybody who can get a job moves out. This has been going on for two decades in the big-city black ghettos, virtually all of which were badly overcrowded in the mid-'60s and have an emptied-out look today. In the 1970s, the District of Columbia lost 16 percent of its population while its black-white ratio stayed almost exactly the same; there was a lot of black flight going on, too. If you define the underclass as people living in majority-poor inner-city neighborhoods (and social scientists are moving toward this kind of geographical definition), then instead of being the "growing problem" that everyone says it is, the underclass is a shrinking problem.

Of course, the more the employed migrate out of inner cities, the worse ghettos will become as neighborhoods: There will be still less of a social check on crime, less institutional structure, fewer intact families. (The main difference between today's ghettos and those that Riis wrote about is that there are so many fewer poor husband-wife families today—a difference that does make today's underclass more intractable but still not totally so.) Eventually, the out-migration will stop—though it hasn't stopped yet—and a dispirited core of people will be left behind to live in what will be, functionally, the urban equivalents of Indian reservations.

SOCIAL PROGRAMS

We should not sit around and watch this happen. External events have a tremendous effect on the ability of poor people to get out of the ghettos. The Irish middle class began to emerge when Irish political machines took over city halls and got access to the many thousands of decent-paying municipal patronage jobs. The immigrants Riis wrote about had the good fortune to arrive in the United States early in a long period of industrialization, in which unskilled jobs were plentiful and the economy was expanding.

The black migration out of the ghettos was spurred by the domestic initiatives of Lyndon Johnson, such as the Civil Rights Act, the Fair Housing Act, affirmative action and the large increase in black employment in government that began with the declaration of the War on Poverty. The proportion of the poor who escape poverty, and the speed with which they escape, are variable and depend greatly on economic trends and on what the government does.

Today, most discussion of the underclass is strongly influenced by the idea that government social programs can't possibly help. We believe we've tried everything; we believe none of it worked; we believe that if the programs that began in the late '60s had any effect at all, it was to make things worse. Most of this is wildly oversimplified, exaggerated, or untrue. The government's anti-poverty efforts were of limited size and duration—the heyday of poverty programs, as opposed to welfare programs, lasted only five years, from 1964 to 1968—and were built around a new, unproven idea: community action.

Moreover, progress was made: The percentage of Americans who are poor decreased substantially during the '60s, then leveled off in the '70s and rose in the '80s, when the government was cutting back its efforts. It's hard to find individual members of the underclass who are downwardly mobile—mostly they come from families that have always been poor.

Now we know a lot more about what kinds of poverty programs work. In general, what works is intensive efforts—not short-term, one-shot aid injections—to help poor children arrive at adulthood well-educated and trained for employment. These efforts ought to begin with prenatal care and continue through Head Start, special-education programs during the school years and job training of sufficient duration and intensity to teach real skills and good work habits. Ridding ghetto neighborhoods of crime would help, too. So would making long-term welfare recipients get jobs. All this is both expensive and intrusive, so it lacks a certain mom-and-apple-pie appeal. But it would do a lot of good.

Since the ghettos have deteriorated so much as places, it's tempting to say that the answer is to improve them as places. But this works only up to a point. Public safety, education and the housing stock in ghettos can and should be improved, but the idea of creating an independent economic base and a class of successful role models there is a persistent fantasy. This idea has a respectable ancestry in Booker T. Washington's vision of a black America made up of yeoman farmers and skilled artisans. But remember that Washington formulated his views during the height of Jim Crow and foresaw a totally segregated black America.

The vision of a self-sufficient ghetto doesn't work in a world in which, happily, successful blacks have the option of entering the mainstream economy and making much more money. There is no reason to hope, or to expect, that when people in the ghettos become successful enough to be role models, they won't leave.

The idea that people who have already left will move back is even more unlikely absent a total overhaul of inner urban areas in which the ghettos themselves are displaced.

Economic development efforts in poor neighborhoods have been one of the conspicuous failures of the past generation, because it's murderously difficult to build businesses in neighborhoods that are rapidly losing population. The most publicized success stories involving ghetto development, such as Bedford-Stuyvesant in Brooklyn and South Shore in Chicago, really involve the residential stabilization of working-class neighborhoods, not the establishment of a neighborhood economic base.

Two sentiments about the underclass seem to prevail these days: First, the situation is completely hopeless; and second, the underclass can only be healed from within black America, through black leadership. The best answer to the first point is to look at the history of previous immigrant ghettos, which should lead to the conclusion that the situation is exactly as hopeless today as it has always been—which is to say, not hopeless at all. The second point is really an attitude, not a program. Does anyone really believe that if Benjamin Hooks of the NAACP—an organization of, by and for middle-class blacks—made daily speeches about drugs, crime and teen-age pregnancy, it would turn the ghetto around?

Jesse Jackson, to his credit, has been making such speeches for years. He is a hero in the ghettos, but he hasn't made the problems go away. The underclass is cut off from the rest of America, and what it needs is the direct intervention of the whole society, not just black society. A generation from now, the wild pessimism now prevailing about the underclass will seem dated; and so will our disinclination to see that the problem exerts a call to which the whole country must respond for both moral and practical reasons.

Priced out of House and Home

Days before George Bush was sworn in as the 41st president of the United States, a group of 250 from across the country met in Washington. Included were builders, mortgage bankers, real estate agents, government officials, policy analysts and advocates for the homeless and low-income families. Emerging from the daylong forum sponsored by the Federal National Mortgage Association, also known as Fannie Mae, was a remarkable degree of unanimity for such a diverse group: Long neglected, housing had to become a top priority for the new administration.

Democrats had used housing, typified by the plight of men and women seeking warmth over steam grates in the nation's big cities, as an all too visible way to tweak the Reagan administration. But with a Bush White House pledging a more compassionate approach to the nation's social ills and a secretary of housing and urban development taking his message to the streets of the inner cities, forces from a multitude of political and ideological segments believe there is hope. "For the first time in a long time we've got a Congress and an administration that realize we have a problem," Sen. James R. Sasser, a Tennessee Democrat, said at the confirmation hearing of the man to whom so many people are looking to revitalize housing: HUD Secretary Jack F. Kemp.

The means to achieve the national goal of "a decent home and a suitable living environment for every American family," promised in the Housing Act of 1949, is undetermined. Under Kemp's leadership, the federal government is likely to assume more responsibility in shaping and carrying out the policy. How much will be relegated to the states, cities and private sector remains as uncertain as the federal government's inclination to reengage in construction or rely on a universal entitlement program to satisfy the housing needs of the poor. For the time being, Kemp is playing his cards close to his chest.

Even if no philosophical differences were to emerge, the challenge of providing adequate housing for all smacks into the deficit. Assessing the situation, Democratic Rep. William H. Gray III of Pennsylvania, past chairman of the House Budget Committee, told the housing specialists in early January: "What is going to happen to housing in America . . . will really depend on how we deal with our budgetary problems."

Since the early 1980s, homelessness has surfaced as the most conspicuous housing problem. Written off initially as the province of derelicts and the mentally ill, homelessness is now also recognized as the plight of families unable to find affordable dwellings. In its 1988 status report on homelessness in America's cities, the U.S. Conference of Mayors cited families as the fastest growing portion of the homeless population, a situation not confined to the handful of big metropolises. In the 27 cities surveyed, one-third of the homeless were families; one in four homeless persons was a child.

Providing shelter — temporary and permanent — to society's least fortunate is only one facet of housing, albeit the one with the most urgency. It has not gone unnoticed by Bush. "The moral imperative is clear," he told Congress. "We must confront this national shame." Homelessness, though, particularly among families, is linked to two other groups finding it more difficult to locate and acquire decent, affordable housing: low-income families and first-time home buyers. Around these three groups a national housing agenda is expected to be built.

Before housing prices soared in most areas of the country, a modified version of the trickle-down theory governed housing patterns. After a modest period, young couples moved out of their rental units into starter homes, making way for low-income households. That, in turn, allowed moderate-income families to move up.

With housing prices out of reach for many young couples these days, they remain in rental housing, intensifying the competition and driving rents higher. Consequently, moderate- and low-income households in many areas of the country live in crowded, substandard or crime-plagued structures, while those living at the margin with minimal incomes can wind up on the streets.

Coming up with solutions to aid the homeless and the first-time home buyer is the easier of the tasks, says Kent W. Colton, executive vice president of the National Association of Home Builders. Housing for "the low and moderate [income range] is the toughest. It's very difficult to do that without expanded resources." Indeed, the National Association of Housing and Redevelopment Officials estimates the United States will need an additional 8 million low-income units by 2000.

Ronald Reagan assumed office in 1981 with the goal of scaling down domestic programs. Few federal agencies underwent as massive a change as the Department of Housing and Urban Development. Budget authority was halved, from $31.9 billion to $15.4 billion, although Congress imposed more money on the department than it sought. In 1981, the department spent $14 billion; last year spending reached $18.9 billion. During the tenure of Secretary Samuel R. Pierce Jr., HUD severely curtailed new construction except for projects that had been in the pipeline from the Carter administration.

Critics claim that housing programs for the poor were gutted under Reagan, with assisted housing losing the biggest chunk. In a recent speech delivered on behalf of the National League of Cities, Terry Goddard, the mayor of Phoenix, cited a 75 percent funding cut for low- and moderate-income housing in the past eight years. According to the Congressional Budget Office, new rental assistance commitments dropped from 375,000 in 1977 to some 108,000 last year. In the winter 1989 issue of the Journal of the American Planning Association, Donna E. Shalala, chancellor of the University of Wisconsin and a former assistant secretary of housing and urban development, and Julia Vitullo-Martin, a public policy consultant, contend that "no one was able to save HUD." Mayors had lost political clout, while such traditional supporters as builders and real estate agents had lost interest. "When there is a strong housing market in most of the country and plenty of money around to keep the industry busy, no one treks to Washington to see congressional delegations about new federal housing programs." Finally, the department was deserted by its general constituency, voters who "just didn't see urban problems as urgent." Pierce's objective was to transform its mission, with the intention of promoting self-sufficiency and freedom of choice. Having redirected funding, HUD takes credit for subsidizing 4.3 million units, compared with the 3.2 million assisted when Pierce took office in 1981.

Criticism of HUD during the Reagan era has become bipartisan. Even GOP leaders acknowledge the need to revitalize the department. At the Kemp hearing, House Minority Leader Robert H. Michel said he expected "a 180-degree turn" at the agency, where "there hasn't been all that much action" in the past eight years.

If there is a Reagan legacy there, it is the realization that by itself spending will not provide decent shelter for all. Liberal Democrats have tempered their demands to solve the housing problems by noting the fiscal constraints in which the task must be accomplished. Policymakers have also come to believe that bricks and mortar are insufficient. Accompanying issues — poverty, welfare, drugs, crime, teenage pregnancy, unemployment — cannot be ignored. "If you don't rehabilitate the people, they'll tear it up," says Robert L. Woodson, president of the National Center for Neighborhood Enterprise, a Washington-based organization that fosters self-sufficiency among the poor.

In a report he submitted to HUD, Woodson pointed out how both the Democrats and the Republicans have erred: "The fundamental difference between the two major parties with regard to aiding the poor is that people on the conservative right seem to believe that all one has to do is open up the gates of opportunity to the free enterprise system, and people will participate as equals. This assumption ignores the fact that in order for people to participate in the marketplace, they must have information. However, most low-income people lack the necessary information they need to participate in the economy. People on the liberal left, on the other hand, tend to believe that even if low-income people have the information they are ignorant to make the right decisions. Therefore, they must be saved by outside professionals."

Despite a shortage of affordable housing for low- and moderate-income groups, the industry generally has been strong. After the lackluster years of 1981 and 1982, an-

Home Ownership Rates

■ Ages 25-29   ■ Ages 30-34
*1988 figures are for first three quarters.
SOURCE: National Association of Home Builders

nual housing starts exceeded 1.6 million through 1987. Starts dipped to 1.48 million last year. Builders lean toward luxury apartments, condominiums, town houses and move-up single-family houses, leaving families on the lower end of the income scale scrambling for housing.

What has been considered an almost inalienable right of the middle class in this country — home ownership — is slipping beyond the grasp of young adults. For the first time in 40 years home ownership rates have declined among younger people. The rate fell from 43.3 percent to 35.9 percent from 1980 to 1987 for the 25-29 age group, according to the Joint Center for Housing Studies at Harvard University. For 30- to 34-year-olds, the rate dropped during the same period from 61.1 percent to 53.2 percent.

Prices continue to climb, and at a faster pace than income. The average price of a home sold in the third quarter of 1988 was $129,400, a 4.6 percent increase over the same quarter of the previous year, according to a survey of 32 major metropolitan areas by the Federal Home Loan Bank Board. At the low end, homes in Louisville, Ky., averaged $86,700. San Francisco was at the upper extreme with an average sale price of $203,300. Pittsburgh registered the most significant acceleration, a 30.9 percent increase to $104,300. Meanwhile, average household income rose only 4.36 percent nationwide.

The median price of a home edged up 3.4 percent during the last three months last

Homes More and More Out of Reach

The rate of home ownership declined during the 1980s for the first time in four decades, with the drop being most acute in the 25-29 and 30-34 age groups. Rising prices have kept these groups, traditionally first-time buyers of houses, in rental units, driving up rents and squeezing families with even lower incomes out of the market.

GEORGE TUGGLE JR. / INSIGHT

year to $87,900, according to the National Association of Realtors.

An analysis of the market by Lomas Mortgage USA indicates that the improving economy in the Rustbelt has driven housing prices up. In the contiguous states, housing is most expensive in the Northeast and California. Only in the South, which is experiencing a housing glut, and in the oil-producing regions are housing prices not burgeoning.

In some of these markets, the average potential home buyer does not earn enough to qualify for a conventional loan. In Boston, for example, the average household income last year was $55,500, but the income required to qualify for the average conventional loan was $63,100, according to Lomas. Only four years earlier the average household income of $43,100 surpassed the $39,500 income qualification. Similar patterns prevail in the Los Angeles, San Francisco, San Diego, New York, Philadelphia and Washington areas.

Down payments and closing costs are a large part of the problem. The National Housing Task Force, chaired by pioneer developer James W. Rouse and Fannie Mae Chairman David O. Maxwell, found that the buyer of a median-priced house in Boston in mid-1987 needed $22,854 for a down payment and closing costs.

The Federal Housing Administration, which insures many mortgages, has a ceiling of $101,250 in a number of high-price areas such as Boston. Elsewhere it is 95 percent of the metropolitan area's median sales price. But those ceilings are often insufficient to meet the cost of housing.

Cathy and Mark Snyder, who live in Keego Harbor on the outskirts of Pontiac, Mich., spend every weekend house hunting. Since they started looking last year, only once have they found something in the middle-class neighborhoods where they would like to locate. But the sellers wanted to close earlier than was possible for the Snyders. They do not expect to find a luxurious house for themselves and their infant son, Daniel. They would like three bedrooms and, if possible, a dining room and garage. Homes like that are in the $80,000-$90,000 range in Clawson and Troy, nearer to where Mark works as a mechanical engineer.

"We try really hard to put ourselves on a budget so we can buy a house," says Cathy. With a monthly gross income of about $2,400, they have found it difficult to pay rent of $495, utilities that range from $100 to $200, food, clothing and baby-related costs and save enough for a down payment. Mark works as much overtime as possible. "We would like to go maybe 10 percent down. Yet 20 percent down is what most places look for," says Cathy.

Recently, they have turned their attention to houses in Keego Harbor and Waterford Township, where prices are in the $64,000-$80,000 range. Mark would continue to have a half-hour commute, but the family would have a yard for their son to play in. "Our apartment is roomy, but it's just the fact that we don't want to bring our children up in an apartment," she says.

Some policy analysts are skeptical about making home ownership a priority at a time when they believe limited resources should be channeled toward the more pressing problems of homelessness and low-income households. Income tax deductions for mortgage interest, a housing subsidy for the middle and upper classes, costs the Treasury about $35 billion an-

nually. Elimination of that provision is unthinkable due to the political fallout. In that lies the political value of helping the first-time home buyer. "It is necessary to broaden the base of support for housing aid," says Anthony Downs, a senior fellow at the Brookings Institution.

As the media and politicians have focused on the homeless in the past few years, there has been a ground swell of support for doing something about the problem. A Media General-Associated Press poll of 1,084 adults taken in November indicates that not only did a majority of respondents view homelessness as a very serious problem that was worsening, they were willing to pay more taxes to aid the homeless. Seventy-four percent looked to government rather than charity as being primarily responsible for the homeless.

Despite broad disagreement about the number of homeless, there is small doubt about their changing composition. The National Housing Task Force estimates that 20 percent of the homeless hold full-time jobs.

Rep. Gray encountered a woman who lived with her three children in one of the notorious welfare hotels in New York City, inferior housing that the government subsidizes at higher costs generally than rental housing. He then learned the mother worked full-time in a job that paid $14,000 a year. Her family wound up in the hotel when her landlord doubled the $400 monthly rent she had been paying for an apartment.

Perhaps surprisingly, less than one-third of the poor live in subsidized housing. The others seek housing on the open market, where income has no bearing on rents. While the standard rule of thumb of allocating one-quarter of a household's income to shelter has changed broadly, nearly one-half of the poor pay more than half of their incomes for rent. The waiting periods for assisted housing in the cities surveyed by the Mayors' Conference averaged 21 months. Nearly two-thirds of the cities had simply stopped taking names.

Demolition and condo conversions have taken their toll on rental units. Approximately 2.2 million low-income units were lost from 1973 to 1983, according to the National Housing Task Force. The situation is expected to worsen in the next few years, when as many as 1 million units could be yanked from the subsidized stock as private owners fulfill their obligation to provide low-income housing within a designated period. Prospects for those units depend in large measure on location. Like real estate anywhere, the formerly subsidized units will be put on the market if the surrounding area is prospering. If not, landlords may continue to pursue low rents, although some housing experts fear that a number of landlords may abandon their deteriorated properties because they are unprofitable. Jacqueline Aamot, a Housing and Urban Development official during the Reagan

administration, doubts that more than one-quarter of the privately owned units will be pulled from the low-income market.

Construction of multifamily housing units, typically targeted at renters, has also declined, by 34 percent from 1985 to 1987. In part, the reduction can be traced to a cutback in tax incentives, but local land restrictions are also at work. The Brookings Institution's Downs calls them "the single largest cause of high housing costs."

They are imposed in a variety of ways, but the upshot is that they have driven up the cost of land substantially. Municipalities prohibit the less expensive multifamily dwellings through low-density zoning ordinances, planned growth ordinances are used to keep out low- and moderate-income housing, or communities require builders to provide sewers, streets and an infrastructure array that once were the responsibility of local government.

In some instances, officials link approval of a development to the contribution of a school, library or park. The builder then adds the outlay to the cost of the houses, in contrast to the traditional practice of municipalities spreading it across the entire community.

The National Home Builders' Colton says 15 to 25 percent of the cost of new housing often is related to regulations. In 1946, land represented 11 percent of the cost of a new house; by 1987, it had reached 25 percent on average. In the Northeast and California, Colton says, land costs run as much as 40 percent. "I really do think that a Jack Kemp speaking out on this issue would make a difference," he says.

The situation is especially critical in suburban communities, where many new jobs are available. In some suburban regions low-paying jobs go begging, while in the city there are numbers of unemployed who have no access to the suburbs. Correcting the situation, says Downs, falls to the states, because the federal government cannot hold out the carrot and stick to municipalities: "You say that to some rich suburb, and they don't care." The federal government, however, can withhold funds from those states that do not force their cities to ease restrictions or reward them for doing so. Until restrictive policies are overturned, he says, an infusion of federal dollars is wasteful.

Seeking solutions to those policies will be the major task of a new House GOP task force. "We could double the federal expenditure for housing and yet it's difficult to believe that it would affect the issue of affordable housing because . . . the bureaucratic burdens imposed by state and local governments are so onerous that they are creating this housing crisis," says the task force's cochairman, David Dreier, a member of the Housing and Community Development Subcommittee. The California Republican cites the example of a kangaroo rat species listed as endangered. The rodent lives on 30,000 acres in Riverside County. County officials have imposed a tax of $1,950 per acre on developers, a cost that is passed on to home buyers in what Dreier describes as the last affordable region in Southern California.

"We have constantly been looking for a federal dollar solution. What I think we need to do is look for a reduction in regulation at all levels," he says.

Producing lower-quality housing is another to way to reduce costs. Single-room occupancy hotels are one example that San Diego is trying. Units generally consist of a single room and possibly a sink. Tenants share bathrooms and kitchens. The greatest obstacle to this housing, says Downs, is overcoming the values of the middle class, which views such housing as unacceptable even though the poor often find the dwellings perfectly adequate.

However difficult it is for Washington to coerce the cities and states, the federal government has its own mammoth problem. Tens of thousands of government-owned units stand vacant because they are uninhabitable and rehabilitation funds are unavailable. Noted a Detroit official in the mayors' survey: "It is as if the federal government has become the biggest slum landlord in the nation. Or, it has abandoned its commitment to public housing."

Public housing began in the 1930s as part of the National Recovery Act under Franklin D. Roosevelt and then was formalized in the Housing Act of 1937. As conceived, public housing bears little resemblance to what Americans think of today as the often seedy, unsanitary, crime-infested projects that even police have been known to avoid. They are home to some 3.5 million people.

Public housing was meant as a temporary refuge for those who needed some time to pull together their resources and move on out, making room for the next guy, for the working poor. Buildings were constructed with the highest standards and situated in parklike settings.

Initially, the physical structures were compromised. As World War II came to an end, the lower-quality temporary shelters built to house defense workers and military personnel were integrated into public housing. Then Congress passed the Housing Act of 1949, containing a provision that called for the resurrection of cities through urban redevelopment. To pave the way, slum dwellers were moved into public housing, from which higher-income families were evicted.

"The families under order to move included those who had been at the center of community life for years. Many had been active leaders since the project opened, and were the people to whom the managers turned when there was a problem to be solved or a need to be met. . . . The project was their home; the neighborhood was their neighborhood. But the very traits that made them leaders had also contributed to their getting ahead monetarily; the leaders were the first on the list to be evicted," Elizabeth Wood, a former HUD official, writes about the evolution of public housing. Replacing them were families who "not only had the basic problem of poverty, but were a microcosm of all the statistics on the prevalence of social, physical and moral disabilities among slum dwellers."

Rents shriveled, providing less money for maintenance. Project staff who lived in the public housing were forced to move. In general, the changes instituted by the federal government, as well as some local housing authorities, isolated the poor and problem-plagued from the rest of society. In the late 1950s and early 1960s, high rises were built to cut costs and the problems mounted.

Despite all the problems linked to public housing in the big cities, former HUD official Aamot estimates that 90 percent of public housing projects are well run. Among them are the 45 developments operated by the Housing Authorities of the City and County of Fresno, Calif.

"We try to subscribe to the original principles of low-rent housing. While people are experiencing some difficult times, you provide a safe harbor for them," says Robert C. Wilson, executive director of the Housing Authorities. About 25 to 30 percent of the families turn over annually, but Wilson is noticing a disturbing trend among the tenants in this farming region. "We're seeing more of the permanent poor. There just aren't the jobs and other opportunities available to them as there were before."

Wilson is also troubled by signs of increased drug activity stemming from the arrival of Los Angeles street gang members to set up crack houses. He wishes housing authorities were free to deal with the few tenants who terrorize all the others. Others intimately involved in public housing claim it is easier to evict tenants for nonpayment of rent than for illegal acts. "We certainly don't want to throw people out in the middle of the night, . . . but we're on sort of the cutting edge of the war on drugs and I think we need some help in dealing with people who violate the law and violate the rules," says Wilson.

Fresno's public housing is scattered in four- and five-unit buildings throughout the city and county, with a maximum of 150 units per area. Because of the size of the developments, Wilson says, it is easier to foster neighborliness and advocate community involvement, which he doubts can be duplicated in the big cities. "I think the more successful kind of tailor-made programs, the ones that focus more on individuals, is a phenomenon of small [communities]. The large cities are just so fraught with the very, very poor [who have] no prospect of moving on."

Today many public housing projects are riddled with crime. They have become, as some housing experts view them, centers of domestic terrorism. In Atlanta, mail delivery and telephone installation and repair were disrupted at some complexes last year when workers were threatened. In a forum for public housing resident managers, Bertha Gilkey, director of the Cochran Tenant Management Corp. in St. Louis, described what her project was like before residents took over the operation. "You could walk into the elevator and find dead bodies at any time. It was nothing for our kids to get on an elevator in the morning and somebody had been shot and left there, and the police would often let them lay there for as much as an hour."

The National Housing Task Force has recommended that HUD wrest control of these besieged projects from local housing authorities. The department did just that in East St. Louis several years ago before turning over the Illinois city's program to private management. Two years ago, the federal government threatened to take over public housing in Chicago because of mismanagement but backed off after reaching an agreement with the city.

Abolishing terrorism and making public housing livable again is likely to require more than a police presence and a coat of paint. Missing is the concept of community — the ingredient Kemp says he will work to reinstill. Says Stephen Glaude, executive director of the National Association of Neighborhoods, "I think we've learned for the last 20 years when you isolate a need such as housing and don't integrate it into community living you're going to come up short."

Karen Diegmueller

Us vs. them: America's growing frustration with the homeless

SARAH FERGUSON
PACIFIC NEWS SERVICE

Most of us are quick to sympathize with the lot of the homeless. But our reaction might not be as charitable after we're aggressively and repeatedly panhandled on the street. As Sarah Ferguson reports, a public already overwhelmed by the ever-growing presence of the homeless is increasingly receptive to government proposals to get the homeless out of our face, with restrictions on where they can solicit or sleep. Yet the homeless can't disappear—a lack of decent housing, health care, jobs, and education are daily driving more out on the streets. And as a posthumous report from a homeless woman shows, the street is indeed a dreaded last resort.

In streets and doorways across the country, a class war is brewing between angry indigents and disgruntled citizens forced to step out of their way. Tompkins Square, the Manhattan park that spawned New York's first love-in in the '60s, has become symbolic of what happens when a liberal community loses patience with the homeless. It was neighborhood tolerance that allowed the encampment of homeless men and women to swell to a shantytown of more than 300 indigents last summer. But it was the rising outcry from neighbors who claimed that the homeless had "taken the park hostage" that finally forced the city to tear the shanties down. Police raids on Tompkins Square Park over the past year, however, have done nothing to abate the flood of homeless people camped out in public spaces. Because, of course, the homeless keep coming back. In Tompkins Square, construction crews have already plowed away the patches of scorched earth that remained after a raid last December, during which many of the homeless burned their tents in protest. But a dozen or so homeless people, mostly African-Americans, remain huddled around the Peace, Hope, Temperance, and Charity gazebo. Another 15 are sprawled on piles of sodden blankets in the band shell, and maybe 20 more are jammed in the bathrooms, sleeping in the stalls and sometimes charging 50 cents to move their bedding before you can enter. Fed up with such seeming intransigent masses, their budgets squeezed dry by the Reagan Revolution, cities across the nation are starting to adopt a closed-door attitude toward the displaced:

• In New York City, the Transit and Port Authority has banned panhandling in subway stations and bus terminals.

• In Washington, D.C., the city council recently slashed $19 million from the homeless budget and is seeking to roll back Initiative 17, the referendum that required the city to provide shelter to all those in need.

• In Atlanta, Mayor Maynard Jackson has proposed a policy of licensing panhandlers as part of an intensified campaign to drive the homeless out of the center city business district.

• In Berkeley, the University of California has ordered repeated police sweeps of People's Park, long a holdout for vagrants and the dispossessed,

There's a growing rift between the homeless themselves and the advocates who represent them.

and has evicted People's Cafe, a soup kitchen set up this winter by the Catholic Worker.

There have been periodic outcries against the homeless since the media first discovered the "problem" in the early 1980s. But today's growing disfavor bodes ill at a time when the economy worsens and the line between the middle class and the poor becomes ever more precarious. Many people's need to maintain an "us versus them" mentality seems all the more urgent.

"The tension level is definitely rising," says Wendy Georges, program director for Berkeley's Emergency Food Project. "With more homeless in the streets, people are starting to lose patience—even in Berkeley. If a city like this successfully attacks homeless people and homeless programs, it will set precedents. The homeless backlash will become a popular thing—so that nobody has to feel guilty about it."

Part of the reason for the growing backlash is sheer numbers. The U.S. Conference of Mayors annual survey found that the demand for

emergency shelter in 27 cities increased an average of 13 percent in 1988 and 25 percent in 1989. Some 22 percent of those requesting emergency shelter were turned away.

Public disfavor may also be spurred by changes in the makeup of the homeless population. Although figures are scarce, anyone who walks the streets can see that the homeless population has grown younger. A 1960 survey of Philadelphia's skid row by Temple University found that 75 percent of the homeless were over the age of 45, and

A day in the homeless life

Editor's note: Eighteen months after writing this article, Colette H. Russell was back living in the streets. Nine months later she died alone in a motel room in Las Vegas.

"Good morning, ladies. It's 5 a.m. Time to get up." Ceiling lights were suddenly ablaze. This message boomed repeatedly until nearly everyone was out of bed.

Two toilets and three sinks for 50 women; no toilet paper in the morning, invariably. Three tables with benches bordered by beds on two sides were our day room, dining room, and lounge.

Breakfast usually arrived at 5:45 a.m., too late for those who were in the day-labor van pools. They went to work on empty stomachs, and they were the ones needing food the most.

Breakfast generally consisted of rolls and sausage and juice until it ran out. The coffee was unique: It didn't taste like coffee, but that's what we had to drink.

At 6:30 a.m. we were ordered to go down to the lobby, where we joined 50 other women either standing or sitting on wooden benches awaiting the light of day. Some talked to themselves. Some shouted angrily. Some sat motionless. Some slept sitting up. Some jumped up and down, walking away and then returning. Some chain-smoked.

All of us had our belongings with us. Carrying everything every step of the way every day was hard on the arms, and I felt it was a dead giveaway that I was homeless.

At 7:30 a.m. the clothing room opened. It was shocking to be told "Throw away what you're wearing after you get a new outfit." No laundry, just toss out yesterday's garments. We were allotted five minutes to paw through racks looking for articles that fit.

I was always happy to see 8:30 a.m. roll around. Grabbing my bags, I headed down Berkeley Street away from the jam-packed, smoke-filled "holding cell." Always I felt guilty at not going to work like everyone else who hurried by as I approached the business district.

The main library was my daily stop. I positioned myself at a table where I could watch the clock: We had to return to the shelter before 4 p.m. to get in line for a bed, otherwise we might miss out.

Reading was the high point of the day. Escape into a book. There was relative privacy at a library table. It was heavenly. I hated to leave.

The clock signaled the task of trudging back, at 3:45 p.m., with even heavier bags. The bags, of course, were no heavier; they just seemed heavier.

Back in the "yard" I joined the group already assembled. Some women never left the grounds, staying all day in the small yard by the building. God forbid. With the appearance of a staff member we would form a line as the staffer prepared a list of our names and bed requests.

I was always glad when the lights went out at 9 p.m. and I could climb into bed (a bottom sheet and a blanket—no top sheet) and close my eyes and pretend I wasn't there but back in my apartment on the West Coast.

Twice I was robbed. Once a bag was taken. Another time my new blue underpants disappeared out of one of my bags. Who knew they were there?

Even if I were to do day labor at $4 per hour and clear $28 or so a day, how many weeks would it take to save enough for first and last month's rent on an apartment plus deposit and enough to pay for initial utilities? I was too depressed to even try to work and took frequent breaks to sit down while doing kitchen volunteer work. I was tired all the time.

The true stories I heard were heartbreaking. Which was the sadder?

One young woman with no skills and no job training had been OK financially until her CETA

87 percent were white. In 1988, 86 percent were under 45, and 87 percent were minorities.

As the population shifts, the stereotypical image of the old skid row bum meekly extending his palm for change has been replaced by young African-American and Hispanic men, angry at the lack of good-paying jobs, often taking drugs or selling them—or demanding money from passersby with a sense of entitlement that the passersby find enraging.

In front of the Tower Records store near

Greenwich Village in Manhattan, a group of brazen panhandlers confront shoppers with cardboard signs that read "Homeless Donations: $1 or token." "Cheap bastards," mutters one of the beggars, an

---

A class war is brewing between angry indigents and disgruntled citizens forced to step out of their way.

---

job ended—the program was abolished—and the YWCA raised its weekly room rate. She couldn't afford a room and couldn't find a job. She'd been in shelters for three or four years. I marveled that she was still sane. She did crossword puzzles while waiting everywhere.

Another older lady had held the same job for 10 years and would still have been working had not the corporation, without notice, closed up shop. She was 59 years old and out of a job, with a little severance pay and no help to find new work. She tried but was unsuccessful in finding a new job. She exhausted her savings after her unemployment ran out. One June day in 1987 she found herself homeless. No money for rent.

Both of these women are intelligent, honest, pleasant, clean, and neatly dressed. And both are penniless and homeless. How will they escape the shelters? Will they?

I got by, all right, by keeping my mouth shut around the staff and talking only with two or three women whom I knew to be sane and sociable. I was lucky. Two and a half months after I'd first gone into a shelter my son rescued me. I was on the verge of madness, so hungry for a little privacy and peace that I was afraid I'd start screaming in my sleep and be shunted off to a mental ward.

Now I've got a job paying more than I've ever earned. But I remember those days and nights.

No one should have to live like that. Too many do. And will, I fear, unless and until we who do have homes and jobs help them end their eternal, living nightmare.

—Colette H. Russell
Street Magazine

Excerpted with permission from Street Magazine *(April 1989). Subscriptions: $20/yr. (4 issues) from Box 441019, Somerville, MA 02144. Back issues: $4 from same address.*

African-American man named Flower, as he dumps on the sidewalk a handful of pennies that a passerby just gave him. "What am I supposed to do with that?"

"Look, corporate criminals!" shouts his companion, Paradise, who sports preppy clothes and seashells woven in his short dreadlocks, pointing to a group of businessmen picking up their Lincoln Continental in the parking lot next door. "Hello Mr. Executive, how you doing? You remember how to be human, don't you?" Paradise asks him mockingly, shoving a cardboard box in his face. "Come on give me a dollar man, I bet you make $50,000 in 10 minutes," he shouts. In response, the driver edges his window down a crack and mutters, "Get a job, will you?"

Meanwhile, Flower is chasing a frightened-looking man on the street. "Help me out. I know you're afraid of black people, but I won't bite."

"Get away from me," says John Kroeper, a young Jersey City resident in a business suit, who passes the panhandlers with contempt. "It's an invasion of my privacy. I don't want to be forced to give. Just because I have a suit on doesn't mean I'm a yuppie. I just lost my job."

"I'll give when they're just sitting there on the ground, but not when they come on to you like that," adds his sister Jean. "If you give money to people on the streets, you never know if they're really going to buy food with it or just buy liquor or drugs. I like to give to organizations like the Salvation Army or Covenant House, where I know the money will go to good use."

"It's just too overwhelming," says one woman, shaking her head. I ask her why she didn't give anything and she responds, "I think there's plenty of services in the city for people who want help."

The sometimes belligerent attitude of street people goes along with a growing shelter and welfare rebellion. In New York, the growth of the tent city in Tompkins Square reflected the refusal by many homeless to enter New York's degrading shelter system, where as many as 1,000 people may be housed in armories nightly. Moreover, a substantial number of homeless people refuse to sign up for welfare and other entitlement programs, preferring to fend for themselves on the streets rather than get caught up in a "dependency mentality" and suffer the degradation of long welfare lines and condescending caseworkers.

Instead, homeless people have begun banding together in support networks and tent encampments, demanding political recognition, and fighting back when they don't get it. Their resolve is seen in Santa Cruz, where a dozen vagrants have been arrested repeatedly for sleeping outside the local post office, and in San Francisco, where more than

---

Homeless people have begun banding together in support networks and tent encampments.

---

a hundred people continue to camp in front of City Hall, adamantly protecting their belongings as police patrol the area daily to sweep away unguarded possessions.

"I see this as a form of anarchy," says Jake, a 30-year-old blond woman with tattoos decorating her chest as she lies back in a bed of blankets and heavy-metal tape cassettes next to her two companions, Red, 29, and Gadget, 24. "We're not going to hide somewhere. Just us being here is a protest." When pressed about why they don't go out and get jobs, Gadget responds, "I'm not going to go flip burgers at some McDonald's so I can share a tiny apartment with a bunch of crazy a———s. I've got friends and family here."

Such comments are grist for the mills of newspaper columnists who justify their new hardline attitude toward the homeless with the argument that little can be done for people who don't want to help themselves. "Enough is enough," proclaims the editorial board of the *Philadelphia Inquirer*, which has called for a law to prohibit camping out in public places. Similarly, the *San Francisco Examiner* recently ran an editorial calling for the "benign incarceration" of street people.

On Manhattan's Lower East Side, a group of merchants called BEVA (Businesses in the East Village) formed last year to respond to the growing number of street people and peddlers clogging the parks and sidewalks. "All of us are liberal people," says BEVA president Kathleen Fitzpatrick, owner of a local cafe. "Our doors are open. But many well-meaning acts, when they go unregulated, turn sour. Look at Tompkins Square—it's the only park without a curfew and that [allows] open fires [fire barrels]. But look at what's happening. It's uncontrolled. It's a toilet. The other day they found 20 needles in the playground area.

"We want to do something to re-establish a community presence in the park—not to kick the homeless out—to try and regulate it," Fitzpatrick

continues. "I'm a victim of this. What happened to all the government programs? It all filters down to the community—all of us little people who are now forced to contribute our income, our time, our energy and money to finally do something. I guess that's what Reagan wanted."

It is 11 a.m. in October outside the Center for Creative Non-Violence—the famous shelter that the late homeless advocate Mitch Snyder built in downtown Washington, D.C.—and the homeless are angry. Here as elsewhere in recent months, it is possible to see another growing rift concerning the homeless—this one between the homeless themselves and the advocates who represent them.

More than 400 homeless people have walked from as far away as New York City and Roanoke, Virginia, to take part in a Homeless Now! march on the capital. Now half are milling outside the shelter, still waiting for breakfast. Several march leaders try to push their way into the Second Street entrance, temporary headquarters for Housing Now!'s shoe-string operation, but the doors are barred. Only "organizers" get admitted.

The crowd surges forward and scuffles break out. As the CCNV guards try to wrestle back the marchers, a pregnant woman is struck to the ground. Sirens flash as a riot squad plows through the crowd, followed by a dozen cops on motorcycles.

The fight outside CCNV reflects the class dynamics of a movement that has yet to find its indigenous voice. Although more and more homeless people are organizing and speaking out for themselves, most advocacy groups continue to be dominated by professional and volunteer organizers.

"All too often, services and events are developed by white, middle-class people," says Mike Neely, a 41-year-old Vietnam vet who founded the Homeless Outreach Project in Los Angeles after sleeping on the streets for 18 months. "But when you look out there, the majority of the homeless are black or brown and have never been middle class and are never gonna be."

Of the 65 board members of the National Coalition for the Homeless, only 10 are currently or formerly homeless. Executive director Mary Ellen Hombs says that the coalition actively encourages homeless people to serve on its board.

Another advocacy group, the National Union of the Homeless, maintains that only the homeless can speak for the homeless. It's not an easy route. Since 1985, the union has been trying to develop a national organizing framework. From a high point in 1987, the number of active locals has fluctuated downward. But this year has seen a resurgence in organizing. This spring, union activists in Oakland, Minneapolis, Tucson, Detroit, Dallas, New York City, Philadelphia, and Santa Monica took over abandoned federal properties, aiming to force the government to turn them over to homeless families.

Although the union had staged similar housing takeovers in 1988 with the aid of the coalition and CCNV, this time they've struck out on their own.

This rift is partly the result of an increased radicalization of homeless organizers. "Homeless people are saying they don't want any more stop-gaps. They don't want shelters, they want houses. They don't want welfare, they want jobs. That's a profound threat to people who say they want to enable, but really want to control," says union member Alicia Christian.

Professional homeless and housing lobbyists are quick to offer statistics on the numbers of homeless children and intact families on the streets. They say that single homeless men, particularly young, angry minorities, are not going to move politicians or the public. But by minimizing substance abuse problems and the swelling ranks of able-bodied, yet unemployable men among the homeless, some activists may be practicing politics of denial.

In response, activists like Mike Neely have begun forming their own service agencies, run for and by the homeless. Yet even as more homeless organizers move into service provider roles, the lines of conflict become blurred. "People say, 'How can you speak about being homeless when you're not even homeless yourself?' " Neely says. "It's a double-edged sword."

Health and the city

Professor Len Duhl

School of Public Health, University of California, Berkeley, USA

Billions of people are becoming urbanised. Moving from countryside to city, from rural nations to massive metropolis, they bring with them, and create, problems of health and illness.

The changes come from changed aspirations. There is a universal desire to improve conditions for themselves and their family. The excitement of the urban world is a magnet that is changing the complexion of the landscape, the services given and the lives of all people.

The cost of even the simplest of medical care is becoming burdensome. The kinds of dis-ease and illness that we deal with are changing rapidly into 21st century urban ills. Accidents, murder, suicide, alcohol, depression, drugs, infections – all these connect to the blight, poverty and homelessness that is the lot of many of the world's peoples.

Each part of the world faces different dimensions of the problem. The North, with a long history of urbanisation and affluence, is dealing with immigrants, deteriorating infrastructures of roads, water, sewage,

transport and communication. Sexually transmitted diseases, including AIDS, burden health programmes. Budget problems are almost universal.

The South, depleted of resources, debt-ridden and in many cases poverty-stricken, faces massive population increases. The 20,000,000 in Mexico City soon will be replicated in São Paulo, Dacca, Calcutta, Delhi, Cairo and many more. The infrastructure often does not exist. What does, is stretched beyond capacity and limited to aiding minimal numbers of the population. Primary health care in many cases is inadequately achieved. Some 21,000,000 children live on the streets of Latin America alone. Only minimal resources are available.

The demands upon health leadership are great. The complex problems of health and the changing nature of the city itself are forcing a new look at reframing the problems that are found and the solutions that are needed.

So what *is* needed to bring health to cities? To reframe or look differently at the new health needs requires a brief look at the past.

Cities developed, as did smaller communities, out of a variety of needs.

Security against hunger and the ravages of the climate drove people together. There was a need to protect and store their resources, for use in times of need. Here was the place of trade and business.

Perhaps more important was the need to gather together to understand and deal with the unknown. Spiritual needs brought people together to religious sites, where their priest-leader-healers could intercede between themselves and an unknown world. Before modern science, there was still a need to understand. These gatherings became the fount of belief.

Shared beliefs

A cosmology developed to help understand the universe. It was the cosmology that created the rules, culture and behaviour which determined how people lived, worked and died. These diverse cosmologies guided all the activities of life in the communities and cities. It was this set of shared beliefs that made a city a whole organism.

As we moved closer to the present,

Reprinted from *World Health*, January/Feburary 1990, pp. 10-12.

the sciences offered understanding. The cosmology became more and more fragmented. Rules for business were separated from religion. Medicine gradually developed expertise. There was awareness that what we know of as health was a reflection of the total environment. Max von Pettenkoffer, attempting to show that the cholera bacillus did not in itself cause the disease, drank a vial of a concentrated culture in front of his distinguished colleagues. He did not come down with the disease.

Rudolph Virchow reminded us in 1848 to examine the total organism in its socio-political environment. He said that while "the improvement of medicine would eventually prolong human life ... improvement of social conditions would achieve its result more rapidly and successfully." His most famous phrase is worth remembering: "Medicine is a social science, and politics are nothing else but medicine on a larger scale."

It was during this period that public health and urban-city planning became intertwined. Planning in England derived from Edwin Chadwick's development of sewers to clean out central London. Sir Benjamin Ward-Richardson in 1875 described utopian cities with clean air, public transport, small community-based hospitals, community homes for the aged and insane, no tobacco or alcohol, occupational health and safety. From him came Ebenezar Howard's development of the garden cities.

However, with the onset of the work of Louis Pasteur and Robert Koch, a new era of bio-medical views of health replaced this more holistic vision. Public health visionaries continued into the 20th century. They dealt with housing and with a wide variety of environmental issues. The new ascendancy of scientific medicine changed the direction of public health as well.

In the South, these models of public health were transferred to the new cities. Though some major programmes of prevention and public health started, many activities did not respond to the unique needs of these under-developed countries. Resources were ravaged. With the transfer of colonial lands to their own people, many of the leaders trained in health and medicine in the "west," continued to replicate the predominant western model.

Mayan art at risk

Acid rain is destroying the architecture and art of the ancient Mayan civilisation in the jungles of southern and eastern Mexico, according to expert archaeologists. Nitrogen and sulphur oxides, resulting from the burning of petroleum by-products at oil refineries in the Gulf of Mexico, are carried by prevailing winds to the Mayan ruins. Turned to acids by the rain, they corrode the elaborately carved buildings and sculptures, and bleach the once vivid colours of painted walls inside. Tourist buses too, with their output of diesel fumes, are taking their toll of rare murals and carvings, despite the conservation efforts of the Mexican authorities. ∎

Now the cities of the world are changing. In large part this is a reflection of the economic developments worldwide, independent of ideology. Industrial development in the South in an attempt to raise the standard of living has brought new pollution and degradation of the environment. The North has increasingly transferred its production to sites of low labour cost. In doing so they have improved their pollution, but at the cost of transferring it elsewhere.

The migrants to the cities of the North have brought with them new values, cultures, beliefs and health systems. They do not "understand" the rules of living in their new communities. Like new migrants all over the world, they work at low-cost service jobs. They bring with them infectious diseases, such as tuberculosis and new viral infections. With the lack of jobs and income are associated hunger and poverty. Crime breeds in these areas. The need for income tends to turn them towards an illegal economy, supplying those wanted things that are not legally obtainable. Drug economies abound, becoming one of the few sources of income for these populations.

Large segments of the world's population find that they have become superfluous. They are not needed for production, since they can always be replaced by new workers and immigrants. They have to take service jobs at minimal pay, since fewer and fewer highly skilled workers are required. Thus much of the world becomes divided into a small group of very rich and a massive number of poor. Though this may be less evident in Europe, both West and East, it is true of most of the developed world.

The implications for the city are immense. More and more are national governments finding themselves unable to deal with health and illness issues in the huge cities. The responsibility then falls on the local communities. City states are emerging which gain their status from massive economic activity, but much of this is dispersed and no longer calls for thousands of manual workers close at hand.

One consequence is that concern with health issues in urban areas can no longer remain primarily focused upon high technology and costly treatment. Since every aspect of city life impinges upon the health of its population, there is a need to shift our image of health. We must reframe the question, "What is health?"

We have focused upon the symptoms of a complex, ever-changing society. They include crime, corruption, pollution, poverty, homelessness, hunger, as well as the new array of urban ills. Even the delivery of medical services is dependent on the total economy, and the ability to pay for services given. Questions about what percentage of the GNP can go to health are being asked worldwide.

If a child has a problem in a family, the physician asks two questions. One, about the particulars of the child, the other about the family. Classically, medical care asks about the patient and the disease. Public health asks about the family and the environment. When the external complex system is not working and breaks down, this often occurs at the weakest link. Most often it is the poor and the young who suffer. They and their illness are symptoms of the larger dis-ease.

To make cities healthy we have to return to Virchow and Ward-Richardson. We must ask all those who deal with aspects of the urban system that directly or indirectly affect health to involve themselves in urban health planning. A healthy city is one that meets all the developmental and

3. URBAN PROBLEMS

social issues of its inhabitants. This means focusing on jobs and employment, transport to education, recreation, sanitation and social services. This is a process of governance which ought to include the total population, and which recognises that no part of the community organism can be dis-eased without affecting the whole.

In the Healthy City programme started by the European Region of WHO, and in the industrialised countries generally, some 450 cities are trying to find new ways to deal with health. Focusing upon health promotion and the mobilisation of the total non-health community to play a role in making the city healthy, they are beginning to break important ground.

No longer does health depend upon what can be done with the money available. Rather the question is what can be done by all possible means to improve health? How can the informal sector help? How can participation by all sectors improve the infrastructure? What new rules must emerge? What new arrangements? In many instances new ways of communicating are emerging. Economic language is taking precedence over the language of human needs.

In the South, WHO – with its concern for primary health care – is focusing upon the new urban developing world. There the critical issues, though ecological and systems-orientated, have different priorities. The emphasis is upon basic needs such as food, shelter, housing, trans-port, water and sewage. Providing jobs and an economic base for the population constitutes a priority issue. Though productivity needs are high, environmental issues will be ignored at our peril.

To choose just one example: in Botswana aluminium cans for soda-pop have newly arrived. Their presence as part of household rubbish has served as a breeding site for mosquitos, even in arid areas. The solution to malaria is therefore both treatment of patients *and* finding a way to deal with cans that collect water. So the answer to this problem demands a total urban approach.

A healthy city can only be achieved when health rates the high priority that it deserves in the complex issues of urban life.

The Invisible Jail

John I. Gilderbloom
and Mark S. Rosentraub

John I. Gilderbloom is associate professor at the College of Urban Policy of the University of Louisville. Mark S. Rosentraub is professor and director of the School of Public and Environmental Affairs, Indiana University, Fort Wayne.

The environment for people with disabling conditions can be described as life in an invisible jail—a jail because it restricts the free movement of individuals, and invisible because others do not see the constraints this environment produces. Access for everyone is rarely a concern of planners or policy-makers in constructing public or private spaces. Most buildings do not have ramps for wheelchair users; many elevators do not have chimes indicating floors for people with poor vision; and some doors and escalators are not wide enough or safe for people with mobility problems.

Why do we not build our facilities to meet the needs of people with limitations? The usual response is that it costs too much. It is our contention, however, that we are socialized not to think about people with limitations. We continue to produce buildings, transportation systems, and cities that are inaccessible to people with disabilities, or we segregate them and limit their life options.

The creation of an invisible jail followed from people's traditional tendency to institutionalize and isolate people with disabilities from society. Invisible to planners and other decision-makers, planning practices evolved that ignored citizens isolated in non-supportive environments. For moral, political, and economic reasons, this course of action is being increasingly challenged. Today, advocates are putting emphasis on the "abled" part of the word disabled. Most people, regardless of their disabilities, prefer independent living arrangements that take advantage of technology and innovative support systems. This is made even more practical by a combination of creative housing and transportation programs.

Many individuals with either mental or physical limitations, while unable to perform some necessary daily living activities alone, are able with some assistance and properly designed housing and transportation facilities to live independent, productive lives. Often enough, enhancing independence requires only minor modifications of the environment. The uninhibited movement of older people and people with mobility problems, for example, can be greatly improved through the routine installation of "grab bars." Similarly, constructing houses with ramps aids the 20 percent of elderly people and people with disabilities who cannot use stairs. Close to one-third of people with disabilities and 15 percent of elderly people cannot use cabinets and closets

Wheelchair users are only disabled if their environment is not conducive to use of a wheelchair.

in their own homes. Ramps, grab bars, and accessible cabinets are small changes that can be easily made in all buildings.

Outside the home, equally substantial environmental barriers exist. A recent study of Houston indicates that less than ten percent of people with disabilities and elderly people use public transportation. While close to 50 percent of elderly people and people with disabilities live within two blocks of a bus stop, lack of sidewalks, curb cuts, and bus shelters inhibits use of the bus. Sixty percent do not have sidewalks between their home and the nearest bus stop. In addition to physical barriers, fear of crime prevents close to two thirds of people with disabilities and elderly people from walking to a bus stop at night. It is thus not surprising to find that 25 percent of the population of people with disabilities and elderly people in Houston would like to move from their current homes within the next year. While some might point the finger at Houston's lack of strong planning, similar conditions exist in many US cities.

The tragedy of the invisible jail is that these barriers *can* be eliminated with careful planning and sensitivity to the needs of all citizens. In many cases, disability is not so much a function of an individual's physical limitation as a function of the ability of social and physi-

cal environments to meet the needs of all people. Wheelchair users, for instance, are only disabled if their environment is not conducive to use of a wheelchair. If ramps and elevators are available and door widths accommodate standard measurements for wheelchairs; if closets and light switches, appliances and elevators are placed at a level accessible to a person in a wheelchair; if bathrooms are equipped with rails for easy access from a chair; if public transportation can accommodate wheelchairs; if streets have curb cuts, then a person in a wheelchair is not disabled.

HOW WE CONSTRUCT CITIES AND CHANNEL RESOURCES will define the terms of disability. In a great many instances, current limitations need not exist. Yet, if we are to eliminate the invisible jail we need to plan for accessible cities that permit all individuals to realize their potential.

Planners can and should play a key role in building and maintaining accessible cities. We must insure that the urban infrastructure is able to support all urban residents. At the local level, there are several more direct programmatic responses we ought to make. Local leaders should create an "Independent Housing Service" to provide technical advice to builders wishing to construct or convert housing for use by people with disabilities and elderly people. Such an agency should provide grants or loans to landlords and developers to cover the cost of constructing a barrier-free living environment. To make sure these units remain affordable, certain stipulations should be made to regulate the rent or cost of the unit over a twenty-year period.

Planning should also be aimed at providing barrier-free environments. New multifamily housing units on the ground floor should be made accessible to wheelchair users. The cost of designing new housing units that are accessible adds only a few hundred dollars to their cost, compared to the thousands of dollars it takes to modify a unit designed without consideration to accessibility. All new housing developments must be designed to provide sidewalks with curb cuts, timed lights, and bus shelters. Large housing developments should also be required to have a certain number of units that are accessible. Prohibitions against granny flats should be abolished, as they offer a significant number of housing opportunities for persons with disabilities. All cooperative and urban homesteading programs should set aside at least 15 percent of the units for persons with disabling conditions.

Transportation agencies should evaluate the feasibility of implementing a demonstration project in which a fixed bus route is made accessible to disabled and elderly persons through the installation of special equipment (e.g., wheelchair lifts, tie downs, and kneel downs) and other mobility-enhancing features (e.g., sidewalks, curb cuts, shelter stops). The routes selected for the demonstration should also be accessible to: 1) medical facilities; 2) shopping and retail centers; 3) higher education institutions; 4) community and cultural centers; 5) low- and moderate-income housing; and 6) various racial and ethnic neighborhoods. Great cities provide for all and exclude no one. It is time for America's planners to begin planning for America's great cities.

In the 1950s and 1960s, signs posted in US towns and cities limiting the access of Blacks to public facilities were condemned for their blatant racist discrimination. Signs reading "whites only" would be unthinkable in most of the US today. But cities regularly post implicit signs to people with disabilities. When a city does not have curb cuts or sidewalks, it is an "abled-only" sign. When a mass transit system cannot be used by elderly people or people with disabilities, that is a further sign. And when a city does not provide the leadership to produce housing for all of its citizens, that is another sign to disadvantaged households that they are not wanted. As a society, we have begun to tear down the signs and barriers that discriminate against minorities and religious groups. It is time we apply the same effort to help people with disabling conditions.————

THE CRISIS IN AIDS CARE

TO LIVE AND DIE IN L.A.

DAVID FERRELL

David Ferrell is a Times staff writer.

KIMON BEAZLIE MANAGED to reach his mid-40s retaining a free spirit and unflagging energy. He was a Hollywood costume designer with stocky good looks, almond brown eyes and a penchant for six-day workweeks—a habit that earned him, in good times, as much as $80,000 a year. In off hours, he was an amateur rock climber and a breeder of exotic birds. He wore his hair in a style befitting his Hawaiian descent: a thick, dark mane hanging to his waist.

But one night last summer, Beazlie's life took a sharp turn. He was brushing his teeth when pain stabbed the roof of his mouth—a canker sore, he thought, craning to look. What he found, instead, was something startling: Behind a front tooth hung a bulbous mass. A second one, nearly identical, hung at the rear of his mouth. Beazlie tilted closer to the mirror, wondering, "Oh, my God, what is *that?*"

The discovery—it would turn out to be Kaposi's sarcoma, a rare skin cancer—thrust Beazlie into the world of AIDS. It would turn his life completely around, shutting off his past as if a steel curtain had clanged down behind him. In failing health, Kimon Beazlie surrendered his job, lost his health insurance and fell out of touch with many friends in the movie and television industries.

In a series of jolting events, he found out what it is like to live as an AIDS patient in Los Angeles County. The experience, he learned, just as so many others learn, is a relentless nightmare; it is a bitter story of government snafus and family prejudices, tears and T cells, compassion and profound hurt. While one faces death and grasps desperately for time, fighting the medical bureaucracy can be almost as difficult and debilitating as the

disease. Beazlie is one of thousands who, as the moments of his life slip away, has grown angry and cynical about the under-funded, conservatively administered county system, which is ranked among the worst in the nation at dealing with the AIDS epidemic.

"In Los Angeles, where the numbers [of infected persons] are increasing daily—by enormous leaps—it is startling to see the level of denial or detachment [that the county has shown]," says Dr. June Osborn, chairwoman of the National Commission on AIDS. During special hearings held in Los Angeles earlier this year, Osborn and other commission members castigated the Board of Supervisors for what they considered chronic shortfalls in funding and commitment to AIDS programs. "There was a sense that local government was trying to distance itself from the epidemic as if it was somebody else's problem," she says.

Already, the countywide death toll from AIDS has reached 7,000. And the future looks worse. According to the county's estimates, 2,800 patients are now fighting the disease, and that number is expected to climb to 24,000 in three years. A total of 112,000 people in Los Angeles are believed to be infected with the deadly virus; they, too, are living on borrowed time.

Each faces daunting hurdles. The disease is one thing: Acquired immune deficiency syndrome is particularly pitiless—a dark, ever-deepening tunnel of physical and psychological horrors. The average AIDS patient lives 22 months after diagnosis, but that, like nearly every other aspect of the disease, is unpredictable. The eroded immune system tends to break down under stress, or in reaction to powerful, toxic medications designed to control the virus. AIDS allows any number of

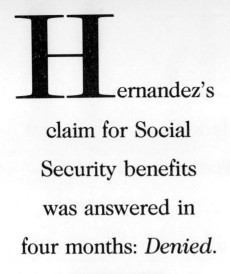

Hernandez's claim for Social Security benefits was answered in four months: *Denied.*

infections to hit where the patient is weakest, often creating a grim cycle of illness, recovery and deeper illness.

Moreover, at this time of extreme frailty, the person with AIDS must master the tricky and sometimes cruel ropes of the public health system. The waiting list for outpatient care at Los Angeles County-USC Medical Center—the hub of the county's AIDS treatment program—can be as long as four months, long enough for some patients to seriously weaken or even die. The clinic, which treats people who cannot afford private care, was handling 400 patients a month just a few years ago; now the number exceeds 2,000, rendering personalized care all but impossible. A new three-story clinic, with four times the medical examining rooms and a capacity for 3,500 patients, was expected to open this year. But faulty initial designs have delayed the target date to next spring.

Beazlie, who sought health care at County-USC after losing his private insurance, is one of five patients who agreed to share a chronicle of what it is like to deal with life as an AIDS patient in Los Angeles. Each of the five faced different problems and responded with different attitudes, emotions and fears. A maverick among them, who dropped out of treatment against his doctor's advice, Beazlie is the most disillusioned.

"The county is a very unfeeling group," he says matter-of-factly. "You get the impression, after a while, that you're just delivering a slab of meat for them to do their little thing on."

As he talks, Beazlie strolls through County-USC's crowded, windowless outpatient clinic, known as 5P21. The clinic is unique in Los Angeles—the only full-time public clinic for AIDS treatment as well as the county's center for experimental drug research into the disease. In jeans, a turtleneck shirt and three-day growth of beard, Beazlie moves familiarly through the pale-yellow hallways.

The halls are as long as 70 yards, lined with wood benches crowded with men awaiting treatment. In their 30s mostly, they form an eerie sight: Hollow-faced, many of them move with the trembling slowness of the elderly. Beazlie strides past them, past an overhead television, and enters a section of hallway blocked by two metal chairs lashed together with a sign: "Restricted area: Only those patients receiving treatment allowed beyond this point."

Here, on Thursdays, Kaposi's sarcoma patients like Beazlie line up, a dozen or so at a time in the hallway, for intravenous blood transfusions and chemotherapy. "You have people just starting out, trying to be optimistic, sitting next to people who are a breath away from being dead," Beazlie says, gesturing to the metal IV racks, now idle. "It's like, 'This is where you're going. . . . You're going to die.' "

Moments later, a patient trying to sit in a wheelchair collapses to the floor. "Loss of motor control," Beazlie explains calmly, seemingly inured to such scenes. He sees a nurse he knows and lavishes praise ("She can find veins that don't exist!") and later talks enthusiastically about a doctor, just one of many unsung heroes here, who shows promise "as a healer."

Beazlie has learned to talk dispassionately about his own eventual death. He forecasts it by year's end because his sarcoma is eating at his insides: "There are days when I can't get out of bed. If I get a coughing spasm, I faint. I hyperventilate. You just learn to deal. That's what life is all about, anyway. We're just getting a concentrated crash course on dealing."

Then, a new wheelchair rolls in. In it is an angular young man with sandy brown hair so delicate it might belong to a child. His legs are stick-thin. In his expressionless face are wide, staring eyes—the eyes of someone who sees but does not understand. It is a young man whom Beazlie recognizes, someone he knows from long-ago visits here. Beazlie's eyes fill with tears.

"I just haven't seen him in a while," he says, his voice breaking. "He's only 24. He's a street kid, has no family. And he's really gotten bad." And for a long moment, Kimon Beazlie cannot speak.

SILVIO R. HERNANDEZ, 59, is known to friends as Rudy —notwithstanding a mix-up on his birth records, he was named after Rudolph Valentino. He fled Cuba as a young man, studied briefly at Louisiana State University and came west in the early 1970s, drawn by the excitement that California offers. Charming and affable, he took an apartment in the burgeoning gay community near the Sunset Strip and surrounded himself with artwork and film posters. He managed a storage company, and his health was good except for bouts of asthma.

Then one evening four years ago, as he watched television, Hernandez was seized by a galvanizing sensation "like a positive and negative cable coming together" in his head. The jolt lasted several seconds, followed moments later by another one. Screaming, he summoned help by telephone and was rushed to a hospital emergency room.

The diagnosis was vertigo—an unexplained dizziness. For several days, Hernandez was confined to a hospital room, his equilibrium so poor he had difficulty reaching the bathroom. Aware that he belonged to a high-risk group because he was gay, he asked to be tested for the human immunodeficiency virus.

The results were positive. For a year, Hernandez stayed home on disability because of the vertigo. Doctors could never link the HIV virus with the strange episode of dizziness, but soon Hernandez experienced other health problems: His asthma worsened; he couldn't walk three blocks without gasping for breath. Bursitis set in. He could not raise his arm over his head. He became so fatigued he sometimes could not pick up light objects from the floor.

He fretted incessantly that the virus, once dormant in his blood, was now attacking. Months passed, and a particularly severe asthma attack nearly suffocated him. He was taken again to an emergency room. Psychologically, the torment grew, day and night, an unshakable curse that left him crying, unable to sleep.

"Already, I was getting a lot of emotion," Hernandez says in a voice that still sings with a Cuban accent. "I was dealing with the fact I was going to die. You wake up at 1 or 2 in the morning and you start *thinking, thinking, thinking.* You cannot go back to sleep for three or four hours. You wake up in the morning and you are so tired because you spent four hours at night thinking."

As his year of state disability neared an end, Hernandez ran head-on into the first of the insurance problems that would plague him for years. His private health-care provider, which had been charging $600 a month for coverage, raised his premiums to $1,000. A $50-a-month supplemental policy from another company was canceled because he lived in a "high-risk" neighborhood.

Hernandez suspects that the insurance companies learned of his HIV diagnosis through his medical records. The huge increase in premiums forced him to drop his private coverage, and in early 1987, a year after his attack of vertigo, Hernandez boarded a bus for East Los Angeles. The trip to County-USC Medical Center, including a transfer downtown, took 90 minutes, and the wait inside 5P21, even with an appointment, was often three hours. But Hernandez had heard that the medical care, once you got it, was excellent.

One of his first experiences was a laboratory blood test of his T-4 helper cells, the agents of the immune system that are attacked by the HIV virus. Once in the cell, the virus replicates, destroying the cell in the process. Measuring the T-cell counts gives doctors a rough—and sometimes suspect—barometer of the health of the immune system. Healthy human blood contains 800 to 1,200 or more T-4 cells per cubic millimeter. In AIDS patients, the counts are often dramatically lower, and can fluctuate widely even in a single patient. Under current guidelines, patients can begin receiving AZT—the relatively effective, but potentially toxic drug for slowing the replication of the virus—when T-cell counts drop below 500, or when full-blown AIDS is diagnosed.

At the time of Hernandez's test, however, AZT was not prescribed until T-cell levels fell below 200. Hernandez's reading was 219. "I was not too familiar with the T-cell situation," he recalls. "I say, 'What does that mean?' [The doctors] say, 'You are OK.' "

The pronouncement was something Hernandez had difficulty believing. His T cells, monitored every three months, showed an improvement to more than 400 in a subsequent test, but his health was getting worse. He had difficulty walking because of pain, and at night he woke up sweating and feverish. He had diarrhea continually, and again he was rushed to the emergency room with an asthma attack.

A records clerk at County-USC Medical Center signed a letter for Hernandez in September, 1988, declaring him medically disabled. Armed with that, Silvio Hernandez took the first step in his long dealings with the government bureaucracy: He applied for Social Security benefits, a process that usually takes four months.

TIM WALSH TOOK STOCK of his fast-paced life in the summer of 1987 and told himself: *You've got to slow down.* He was 25, a lanky kid from Westlake Village with thin, brown hair and large, serious eyes. He worked as a computer specialist at a law firm and kept a social calendar packed with events—gourmet meals that he cooked at home, traveling, parties. He and his lover, a transplanted Northern Californian named Ron Satora, shared a West Hollywood apartment near the night life.

K eeping the relationship with Satora was to be one of the tender and stormy challenges of Walsh's life.

Like Hernandez, Walsh was aware that he belonged to a high-risk group in a city that was being hit harder by the epidemic than anywhere in Southern California. Walsh also was feeling ill—anemic, feverish. His bones ached. A burning sensation developed in his throat and spread down his esophagus, making it difficult to swallow even water. He started losing weight. Like many gay men, he paid enormous attention to each real or imagined change in his physiology, and yet he argued with himself: He felt he was just running himself ragged.

A vacation would help, he decided. He had blood drawn for an HIV test and left for Waikiki with the sandy-haired Satora, a bank operations specialist and prize-winning amateur bowler, for the relaxation that might heal him. But increasingly, he knew: Something was drastically wrong. He barely made it through the 10-day trip. While Satora sought out the Hawaiian night life, Walsh returned early to their room on the beach. The test results were awaiting him on the mainland, but he knew in his gut what they would show.

At the testing center, Walsh listened, lit a cigarette and cried.

Then he became sicker—rapidly. Just three weeks after getting the test results, he was admitted to Queen of Angels Hospital with bleeding ulcers, tuberculosis, anemia and herpes of the esophagus. "The consensus among doctors not versed in AIDS was that he was going to die," Walsh's private physician, Dr. Peter Kennedy, says. Walsh's hospital stay lasted all of October; his T-cell count hovered ominously near zero.

Rallying some strength, Walsh finally went home, but his struggles were only beginning. In a condition so fragile that he cries when he remembers it, Walsh was forced to confront the realities of his life: He needed help. He began visiting his doctor regularly under a private health-care plan, often undergoing transfusions, often becoming demanding and loud. "It was very clear he was just scared to death," Kennedy says.

Meanwhile, Satora was wondering: *Me, too?*

Keeping the relationship together was to be one of the tender and stormy challenges of Walsh's life. One bone-chilling autumn night, Walsh began reaching out for help, for himself and Satora. Escorted by his mother, Bonnie, and Satora, he joined a crowd of nearly 300 assembled by activist Louise Hay in a West Hollywood park—a regular meeting of meditation, chanting and encouragement for AIDS patients. As individual members of the crowd were invited to speak, Walsh asked for the microphone.

He grasped it and, looking around at the crowd, could not utter a word before he began crying.

Members of the crowd soon engulfed him, offering cards, telephone numbers. It was an omen of good fortune. Walsh would get help.

Walsh's employer kept him on its payroll and essentially ordered him to stay home. ("They didn't think I was going to last," he says.) He also left his apartment, where Satora was awaiting results of an HIV test of his own, and returned temporarily to his mother's house in Culver City. Bonnie Walsh took charge of her son's daily regimen of drugs. She put the multitude of pills, about 10 in all, in plastic bags, and Walsh took a bag's worth every four hours, day and night. Meanwhile, Walsh was on the phone to local nonprofit help groups, including Being Alive, Aid for AIDS and Aids Project Los Angeles. From them, he learned of the state's year-old Health Insurance Premium Program (HIPP), through which the government pays insurance premiums for AIDS patients to help them maintain their private insurance plans and keep them out of the public health-care system. It would enable him to retain his private physician and possibly, because of that doctor's great interest in Walsh's welfare, play an important role in keeping him alive.

"He's taken hold of his illness," Bonnie says.

Satora, meanwhile, tested positive for the virus, a result he expected. He and Walsh talked about it. Facing death was one thing; but now, what Satora dreaded was facing his family.

The eldest of six children, Satora had grown up in conservative surroundings in the town of Livermore, near Oakland. His father had been the type to tell homosexual jokes. His mother, a strict Roman Catholic, had become alarmed when Satora first started living with a male roommate years earlier. She would call at 4 and 5 in the morning, waking her son and demanding: "Are you gay? I can't accept you that way!"

"No, I'm not gay," Satora would say, lying to appease her.

Now he would give his parents a double whammy, the same double whammy that so many parents have received throughout the epidemic: He was not only gay, he was also HIV infected. He planned to break the news on a trip home for Thanksgiving. He flew north and re-entered the household of his youth, where his father and younger brothers made flip remarks about gays and AIDS. His mother gave him that same old accusing look.

"It just made me sicker inside," he recalls.

So Satora stayed for the holiday, told no one in his family about his diagnosis and came home.

UNDER THE TOWERING main building of the County-USC medical center is a cavernous basement the size of a football field, packed with color-coded folders containing the vital charts, laboratory reports and other medical records of more than 1 million patients. The files fill row upon row of high shelves seemingly into infinity. Sometimes, partly because of the sheer volume, files become lost; patients' claims for Medi-Cal or Social Security reimbursements—the only income that keeps some AIDS patients off the streets—are inexplicably denied or tied up in months of red tape.

Silvio Hernandez's claim was answered in four months: *Denied.* His file, the agency said, contained insufficient information.

The news was followed, a month later, by a change in his medical condition. The silver-haired movie fan developed a herpes rash covering much of his body. As the rash disappeared with medication, something worse appeared: herpes-related shingles affecting nearly all of his right leg. The nerve condition was so excruciating that Hernandez was referred to County-USC's Cancer Pain clinic.

"He was in pain severe enough to keep him from sleeping," remembers Dr. David Cundiff, who prescribed a drug similar to morphine. "He was virtually immobilized."

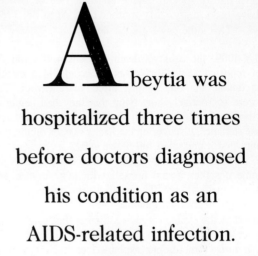

Abeytia was hospitalized three times before doctors diagnosed his condition as an AIDS-related infection.

Hernandez was not without help: He was sharing his apartment with a longtime companion who was not infected—a man who could cook and attend to chores. Many other friends were there for moral support. But not one of them could stop the agony.

"I was screaming, yelling, in my home at 2 [and] 3 o'clock in the morning, putting on ice, things like that," Hernandez says. During the same month he visited the Cancer Pain clinic, he submitted a new application for Social Security benefits.

TIM WALSH WAS BACK in the hospital at St. Vincent Medical Center only three months after his near-death. Admitted this time with a fever of 105, he recuperated for three weeks, and left with the same dismal T-cell level.

The stay marked a turning point, however. He and his lover had reached a decision: Walsh would return home to their apartment. Somehow, against almost insurmountable despair, they would try to sustain a relationship.

And occasionally, there were times worth savoring—day trips, dinners out. Walsh spent many idyllic afternoons poolside at the Los Angeles Center for Living, a now-defunct gathering place in a quiet neighborhood where people with life-threatening illnesses were able to sit and chat. Surrounding the pool was a yard with ferns and brick, and usually there was music and an afternoon meal of salad, cheese and rice.

Satora, however, who was still without symptoms, shied away from such groups. He bowled, continued working and tended to Walsh in the evenings. At times, when the pressure built to more than he could handle, he shouted, threw things, slammed his fist into the wall.

On a day in April, nearly five months after his trip home for Thanksgiving, the mounting fears about his own health and the possibility that he could begin an experimental drug treatment even before developing symptoms prompted Satora to act. He telephoned his family and finally broke the news: He was gay, he was HIV positive and he was seeing a private doctor.

The reaction was much as he feared. His father, the more understanding of his parents, has not told a gay joke since. But his mother came apart with fury. She sent him a letter saying he was no longer her son—she disowned him. His lifestyle, she ranted, was disgusting.

In the two years since Satora opened the letter, he and his mother have hardly spoken, and even their one or two exchanges have been angry. "My mother died April 28, 1988," Satora says. "That's the day I got the letter."

BY EARLY 1989, the county's death toll was 4,484 and the number of reported new AIDS cases averaged 214 a month, more than double the rate of just three years earlier. The numbers were so routinely horrifying that they had begun to lose their shock value. It was in July that Kimon Beazlie became one of those statistics, discovering the fleshy masses on the roof of his mouth that represented full-blown AIDS.

Beazlie, who had known he was HIV-infected and quit his job as a costume designer, found himself without insurance and needing urgent medical care. The solution was obvious: 5P21. But the wait was nearly two months.

He stopped at the clinic every week during that time, trying to see a doctor because he "kept freaking out," Beazlie says. Patiently, a nurse practitioner explained each time that he would have to wait. The clinic was booked. He was not bleeding. He was not so desperately ill that he had to be admitted to an AIDS ward or an emergency room. His lesions would be examined when the time came for his appointment.

Having no money for private care, Beazlie passed the time at home as the two sarcoma lesions ate sores into his tongue. "They were like very potent battery acid," he recalls. "The pain was too excruciating." To sleep, he taped a four-inch wood dowel in his mouth to keep his tongue from touching the boils. The lesions "finally erupted and drained down my throat before I ever got to see a doctor."

After seven weeks, Beazlie kept his appointment at 5P21. Doctors prescribed chemotherapy, which, he was told, would put the Kaposi's sarcoma into remission and give him some months of relatively good health.

RIC ABEYTIA ALSO BECAME another of the growing number of statistics last year. A banker who resides in South Pasadena, Abeytia had just changed jobs and, like Beazlie, was without health insurance. At 37, he is a thoughtful, disarmingly witty man with the look of a young college professor, sporting wire-frame glasses and a thick shock of black hair.

Abeytia entered County-USC Medical Center via the emergency room. A week after developing flulike symptoms, he began vomiting blood. Emergency room attendants pumped his stomach and talked about him, as he lay on the gurney, as if he were an ulcer-plagued alcoholic ("Wait a minute," Abeytia recalls saying, "Why are you treating me as an alcoholic? I don't drink!"). He was fed intravenously for several days and sent home, undiagnosed. Probably a bleeding ulcer, he was told.

The next month it flared up again—the same problem, the same trip to the E.R., the same weeklong stay on a gurney.

Abeytia was becoming exasperated. A month later, *deja vu.* More vomiting, more blood. Back into the E.R. for a third time, for another stomach pump, for more IVs. Assertive by nature,

Life is learning how to deal, Beazlie says. 'We're just getting a concentrated crash course.'

Abeytia pressed for answers. *Something* was wrong. *Something* was causing this. What *was* it?

Months earlier, fearful because several friends had developed AIDS, Abeytia had submitted to an HIV test. The result was negative, a finding he doubted then and which now had become more suspect. He lay for several days on a gurney in a unit called the Red Blanket Room—for patients with internal bleeding—until he at last got lucky: He saw a friend, a one-time musician named Francisco Garcia, who happened to be a research nurse at the medical center. Garcia's specialty was upper-gastrointestinal hemorrhages, and he was screening patients in the Red Blanket Room to find candidates for internal scoping—a procedure, technically called an endoscopy, in which a fiber-optic tube is inserted into the stomach to look for problems.

Garcia, who hardly recognized his sickly friend, scheduled Abeytia for an endoscopy, which identified the problem as *Candidal esophagitis,* a fungal infection associated with AIDS.

Abeytia was indignant that it took three hospital visits—a total of about 12 days—before the endoscopy was performed, but Garcia noted that at a county hospital, where funding is chronically short, not every test can be performed on every patient. "We see masses of people here," Garcia says. "It's not like going to a private hospital where you have the total attention of the doctors and nurses and you can run as many tests as you want."

Regardless, Abeytia was now at the right place: 5P21. Like several hundred patients there, he chose to take advantage of one of the clinic's most important services—experimental drug trials. At any given time, about 70 different AIDS drugs are being tested on county patients who volunteer to take them. In Abeytia's case, the drug was one formulated to stop the *Candidal esophagitis* infection.

It seemed to work, but his T cells—monitored frequently during drug trials—declined during the next few months. Abeytia became a scholar of the illness, learning about drugs and his own body as if he were trying to master the programs and hardware of a home computer. Only in this case, the hardware was failing. He soon developed tuberculosis, which required a drug incompatible with the stomach medication. He gave up the stomach drug only to have a relapse of internal bleeding, which landed him once again—for the fourth time—in the hospital.

A new T-cell report was back from the lab soon after he was released: He was down to 120, a drop of nearly 400 T cells in three months. Abeytia was alarmed. The numbers just kept dropping. What would they be in the next three months? Or even in three weeks? He would have no T cells left—he was dying. He left the clinic and took the freeway home, crying.

The T-cell counts finally stabilized. He was now taking the drug AZT, which caused nausea and vomiting, but in late summer, Abeytia enjoyed a short span of relatively good health. The next problem that developed was by now, at least, familiar: the rather hollow feeling in his gut that invariably preceded the bouts of internal bleeding. This time he was ready for it. All he needed was the stomach drug.

Could he get it?

He was talking with the physician's assistant who handled most of his appointments at 5P21. The medical staffer was skeptical. He was reluctant to prescribe the drug because Abeytia was showing no obvious symptoms. Drugs frequently have side effects, and it was quite possible that Abeytia was reacting to only fear and paranoia. An argument ensued, and Abeytia left without the medication. He was persuaded, instead, to schedule an appointment with a county psychiatrist.

SILVIO HERNANDEZ's second claim for Social Security, following the paralyzing nerve problem in his leg, went unanswered for three months. He was now a familiar sight in the AIDS clinic; it had been 3 ½ years since his attack of vertigo and 18 months since he had become a regular at 5P21. It was also eight months since he had first applied for monthly Social Security payments.

Hernandez, still suffering intensely and walking with a cane, was becoming obsessed with his quest for the long-term disability benefits, which would total nearly $650 a month. The urgency was fueled by the recent death, of AIDS, of a close friend from Puerto Rico, a man who had responded to his declining health by going on a rampage of drugs and alcohol; Hernandez had just attended his memorial service.

His sense of mortality inflamed, he called the Social Security office and demanded to know the status of his case. His file, someone explained, was not there—it was lost.

"How can that be?" Hernandez shouted.

Sorry. It wasn't there.

He cried during the night. He could not sleep. "I think that damaged my situation more than the disease," he says. Hernandez—who keeps thick files documenting his case—reports that the missing file was discovered a month later. It had not been reviewed, however, so he was asked to wait three additional weeks while a decision was made. He was given a date and time, he says, and assured that a call would come.

Hernandez waited by the phone. It never rang.

Even angrier, Hernandez again badgered the office, only to be told—once again—that his file was incomplete. A Social Security official offered to send him, free, to a doctor in the San Fernando Valley, where the necessary reports could be obtained.

Hernandez indignantly refused. Had he not been seeing county doctors for 18 months? Why was that not good enough for Social Security? Why were they doing this to a man who was sick? A man who was dying?

Although Social Security officials cannot comment on individual cases, hang-ups in processing a claim occur for any

Because of staffing problems, the waiting list at the clinic grew to four months.

number of reasons, says Joe Carlin, Los Angeles/West branch chief for the state's Disability Evaluation Division, which contracts with Social Security to decide on patient eligibility. Typically, analysts request necessary medical records from county hospitals—a process that is at best hit-and-miss, he says.

"Generally, on cases where we're dealing with county medical facilities, it is a problem getting records," Carlin says.

So disorganized are the records that two years ago the Disability Evaluation Division stationed a full-time employee named David Stewart at County-USC just to track down missing medical reports needed by Social Security officials. Stewart says the million or so files stored in the hospital basement are in constant motion, trundled to various clinics as needed by doctors, with laboratory reports and doctors' notations being added all the time. "It's amazing . . . the amount of papers that flow from one place to another."

In any single case, Carlin says, it is difficult knowing where to pin blame. "It's either, A, we didn't get the records, or, B, we got the records and there wasn't enough detail," he says. "The final possibility is, we did not do the case properly."

The benefits claim became a crusade for Hernandez; the sleeplessness, the anger swallowed him up. *Why? Why? Why?* How could they deny him? At one point, he says, he entered the records room himself, determined to see what his file contained. There was nothing about his nerve-damaged leg. But there was a medical report concerning a different Hernandez altogether, somebody who was perhaps also trying in vain to get his benefits.

Tired, bitterly frustrated, Silvio Hernandez took a T-cell test in the fall of 1989. The count, previously in the 400s, was now down to 95.

KIMON BEAZLIE SHAVED off his long hair. Like many chemotherapy patients, he found it disturbing to see the long locks fall out whenever he showered. He was receiving treatments on alternate Thursdays and getting to know members of his own treatment group, those who joined him for intravenous therapy in the pale-yellow hallway.

One, in particular, became a favorite of Beazlie: a young man named Brian, only 23, who attended each session with his mother. "You just don't see parents here," Beazlie says. The three would pass the time chatting.

Brian began missing days—he was sometimes too ill to keep his appointments—and eventually, the youngster dropped out of the group. A nurse told him that Brian had switched weeks, coming in on the Thursdays when Beazlie was not there.

Beazlie visited the clinic the following Thursday to look for him, but Brian was nowhere to be found. "Finally, I confronted [a nurse], and I said, 'Brian's not here, is he?' " Beazlie remembers. "And she said, 'No, he passed away.' "

Soon after Brian's death, Beazlie temporarily dropped out of treatment. He packed for a trip to Hungary, where he planned to visit his lover, who was working overseas. He also hoped to buy drugs on the European underground.

One question that nearly all AIDS patients ask themselves sooner or later is whether they should try medications—and there are hundreds—that have not yet been approved by the federal Food and Drug Administration. In recent years, liberalized policies have made many of those medications available in experimental trials at clinics such as 5P21; and yet the underground remains vitally active. Rumors percolate through all levels of the gay community about interferon treatments developed in Africa or purported wonder drugs manufactured only in Japan. Such drugs are imported to the United States, but many patients find them dismally disappointing.

"It's like the '20s speak-easies," Beazlie says of the medication underground. "Someone might say to you, 'Get in touch with so-and-so, he's involved in it.' And you go to someone's house and say, 'Joe sent me.' "

In the States, Beazlie had not found anything on the underground. On the trip to Hungary, all he managed to pick up was a German-made drug called Balachek, an elixir fortified with minerals that cost $1 a bottle.

RIC ABEYTIA WAS BACK in the hospital with internal bleeding. Well before his scheduled psychiatric appointment last fall, the *Candidal esophagitis* had returned. And now here he was, sick again, hooked up to IVs, receiving stomach medication that he had pleaded for earlier. With bitter solace, he told himself: *You were right! They didn't listen!*

However, according to Dr. Fred Sattler, the clinic's head physician, the drugs for *Candidal esophagitis* are never prescribed at the onset of the infection because the fungus can mutate and become more resistant.

Abeytia's attention soon turned to the health of his best friend, a once burly, 250-pound college pal who was admitted to the County-USC AIDS ward the same month. The 20-bed ward, separate from the crowded outpatient clinic, provided his friend with terrific care, Abeytia says. But his friend was down to 140 pounds and dying. When he returned home, Abeytia and the patient's mother took turns at his bedside.

"We discussed very common-sense things," Abeytia says, recalling those conversations with his friend. " 'What do we do about the funeral?' 'What do we do about your house?' 'How about your car?' 'Is the will taken care of?' And at the same time I was trying to be as comforting to him as possible because he was very scared. I'd crawl into bed with him and just hold him, just to try to make him feel a little better."

The friend returned to the hospital the first week of December. He slipped into a coma and died five days before Christmas.

"I CANNOT WALK, I cannot sleep, I'm having diarrhea at night in bed. I cannot control my bowels. I have to start using diapers like a baby."

That is how Silvio Hernandez describes his medical condition as of late last year. He had developed mixed emotions about the health care at 5P21. He appreciated the apparently sincere efforts of his doctor to help him, and yet he was rushed in and out so fast—five or 10 minutes, on most visits—that he did not really understand what was being done for him or why.

And he wondered whether his doctor even understood what treatments he needed most. "There are just so many people," he says ruefully. "The system is just so overworked."

Hernandez stopped taking the bus from West Hollywood to 5P21, relying instead on volunteers from AIDS-assistance organizations to drive him. It was the Los Angeles-based Minority AIDS Project that now intervened in his nearly year-old battle for Social Security benefits.

That organization put Hernandez in touch with the office of State Sen. David A. Roberti (D-Los Angeles), where an administrative assistant named Lynn Shepodd took charge. She saw Hernandez's case as "an abomination."

"They were asking him to jump through all these hoops and I just couldn't figure out why," Shepodd recalls. "Every time he would go to a doctor, they would either misplace his records or they'd tell him he had to go see someone else. He was just so tired and worn out. He just called [our office] in desperation."

Sheppod's telephone calls were effective. Four days after Christmas, 1989, Hernandez was asked to visit the Social Security office on Hollywood Boulevard. He grins as he remembers the office manager meeting him at the door. "They apologized 15 times," Hernandez says. "They say, 'This is not the way [we] operate.' They wanted to know who I was that they received three calls from Sacramento. I say, 'I am nobody. I am just a poor man that works very hard, and I have a disease that I don't know how long I'm going to live. And I need my money *now*.' "

He got it—a check for $630. Two weeks later, he got a second check for $7,755.53, representing retroactive Social Security payments for more than a year.

Hernandez sent Shepodd a dozen roses in a gold box.

AT DR. PETER KENNEDY'S Wilshire District office, the physician and his patient, Tim Walsh, had a confrontation. If he didn't go back into the hospital, the doctor told him in December, he was going to die.

Walsh had picked up a bacterial pneumonia and had been eluding the doctor during office visits, obtaining prescriptions from a nurse and skipping out, even though he was rapidly losing weight, Kennedy says. Walsh was now persuaded to enter the hospital. Soon, he was hovering near death. For two days during the holidays, he went home, a sojourn that required 24-hour nursing care; once, as he tried to walk, he fell while connected to an intravenous needle, spilling blood in the apartment.

By the time the hospital stay was over, Walsh was connected with a subclavian catheter—a tube under the collarbone that enabled him to administer his own intravenous medications. Through that tube, he took antibiotics, a hormone to boost red blood cells, and a high-calorie mixture of protein, carbohydrates and vitamins—home therapies generally difficult to get through the public health system. "I'm sure [the nutritive mixture] kept him alive at times," Kennedy says.

All of this—the drugs, the coughing, the IV tubes that Walsh wore to bed—was taking a toll on Ron Satora. Still asymptomatic, Walsh's lover carried the burden of nearly all the work at home, from feeding the two cats to fetching cold towels for Walsh.

It was Satora's nature to keep his frustrations in him, bottled up. His doctors were now prescribing larger and larger doses of anti-depressants. Occasional temper tantrums—the venting of those clamped emotions—were punctuated this spring by an attack in which his blood pressure shot up and his heart rate leaped to 250. He temporarily lost his eyesight and he was rushed to the hospital.

Nerves. Just nerves. "It's all on my shoulders," Satora says.

AS THE SUMMER ARRIVED, anger and frustration mounted. Furious activists shouted down the federal health and human services secretary at yet another international AIDS conference where medical progress seemed dim.

Los Angeles County, early in the year, had authorized the hiring of additional medical personnel to reduce the waiting list at 5P21 to only two or three weeks, Sattler says. But for several months the positions were not advertised, he says, and have remained unfilled, largely because county salaries are far below those in private health-care. So the waiting list grew from three months to four.

The personal battles, too, wore on:

● Silvio Hernandez adds to his videotape collection, fretting over his health. He has lost 40 pounds—down to 125. Lately, letters have been arriving from Social Security saying the agency has overpaid him, one demanding a refund of $27, another a refund of $98.

"It is confusing. What is going on, I don't know," Hernandez says. "They make so many mistakes. I don't know what I'm supposed to receive every month any more."

● Tim Walsh was back in the hospital for much of June with bacterial pneumonia. He looks very thin, coughing heavily. His speech is slurred and he complains of tiredness; his doctor talks pessimistically about the chances of real improvement. Satora, meanwhile, took an 11-day vacation in Hawaii alone, at the insistence of his own doctor. "I worry too much," he said as he packed for the airport. "There have been times I felt like I don't know how much longer I can deal with this. But I don't think I could ever leave him."

● Kimon Beazlie, the one-time rock climber and Hollywood costume designer, is very ill at home. Doctors at 5P21 wanted to insert a tube in his chest, similar to Walsh's, and to place Beazlie on an alternating schedule of blood transfusions and chemotherapy. Instead, Beazlie withdrew himself entirely from treatment. In his renegade outlook he asks himself: Why get a transfusion one week when chemotherapy would destroy your new blood the next?

The German drug Balachek had done nothing for him, Beazlie says, talking painfully, as if he had just come from the dentist. The sarcoma lesions have returned and now fill his whole mouth. He coughs violently.

Two months after taking a visitor through the county clinic, Beazlie now keeps to his apartment except to settle last-minute affairs. He is trying to find a home for one of his dogs. Two other dogs are so old they probably will be put to sleep, he says.

On a sunny Monday in late July, Beazlie arranged to be cremated. He talks of going on a morphine drip—the way out for many AIDS patients.

Dying, he says, will be an end to pain.

● Ric Abeytia is a healthy man—or so he feels. Eighteen months after the vomiting and internal bleeding that marked his introduction to AIDS, the former banker works full time at the offices of Being Alive, a Los Angeles-based help group. Abeytia is now on a clinical trial for the experimental drug DDI because AZT was causing him too much discomfort. He takes stomach medication when necessary and follows the medical bulletins for possible breakthroughs, for hope. He was preparing to enter the county AIDS ward for 10 days of treatment for a lingering bacterial infection, but he planned to take his briefcase and file folders with him.

"I'll make it an office," he says. The work for Being Alive pays a quarter what he made as a banker, but, he says, helping others makes it easier to deal with his own illness.

"I'm sure he has his bad days when he's down and depressed and cries like the rest of us," says Abeytia's friend, Ian Barrington, who also has AIDS. "We talk on days when he can't work, when he's really ill. But I can always count on him calling me three or four days later, back on his feet and dancing again. A lot of courage."

Urban Policies

When an urban problem is recognized and clarified, solutions are often, but not always, proposed. These solutions generally take the form of social policies designed to deal with the critical issues surrounding the problem. Since urban problems are often quite complex, the policies that are designed to solve them are also likely to be equally complicated and to generate considerable debate and conflict.

In recent years, social scientists have been involved in both policy and proposals and in the ensuing debates which follow. The result usually takes the form of some proposal such as the recent one to create enterprise zones in the decaying sections of urban communities. This policy calls for clearing lands of old housing and creating new space for businesses to build. Attached to this policy are certain tax benefits designed to encourage new economic enterprise. The student of the urban condition can readily see that this proposal might generate considerable debate and conflict. Nevertheless, rational and ongoing examination of the urban condition will require that social scientists continue to examine the issues, explain the variables that operate in the urban community, and present possible alternatives.

Social policies are usually directed at specific ends, but the unintended consequences of a given policy sometimes have unusual effects. Some policies have been proposed and action has been initiated without adequate resources to accomplish the goals. Other policies, while successfully ending one problem, have created or uncovered other problems. Unfortunately, no one possesses the skills to predict accurately all the outcomes of a specific social policy. The articles in this section illustrate the processes involved in effecting social change. This section begins with Scott Shuger's "Memo to the New Mayor," which focuses on the budget crisis, crime issue, and drug problems that plague the District of Columbia, and what, if anything, can be done about them. Neal Peirce and Robert Guskind then argue that the notion of a well-managed city depends on the political vision and savvy of managers and mayors who must be able to motivate the corporate community to invest their money and talent in solving major social problems. The next article explores the world of neighborhood politics, underscoring the importance of co-optation and dealmaking. Next, Patricia Rowe's "Volunteer Mentors Empower Inner-City Youths" describes a Washington, D.C.-based program that seeks to assist disadvantaged youths by tapping the vigor and enthusiasm of volunteer mentors. In the next article, Rob Gurwitt describes the changing face of Asian-American politics, in which a Pan-Asian agenda is beginning to take shape and which had led to several political gains. The next article examines the environmental debate, specifically, the importance of developing more environmentally sound ways to recycle human waste. Finally, the following four selections describe the current housing crisis, calling on policymakers and concerned citizens to rethink the issue of rental housing, support efforts to build and renovate affordable housing, assist lower-income Americans to own their own homes, and back local initiatives to clean up or demolish dilapidated houses that attract vandals and drug pushers.

Looking Ahead: Challenge Questions

Is it possible for Washington, D.C.'s new mayor, Sharon Pratt Dixon, to rescue the District from insolvency and scandal? Is bureaucratic reform possible, given the severe problems that she faces?

Is it possible for America's urban managers to deliver a wide range of services while keeping taxes relatively modest and bond ratings high? If so, how?

How do the 1990s-style community organizers differ from their 1960s counterparts? Are today's neighborhood activists any more likely to succeed?

Are volunteer mentor programs likely to help neighborhood minority youth to find and maintain meaningful employment? What advantages and limitations do they have?

Why are increasing numbers of cities adopting nutrient recycling as an alternative to other disposal options? What should be the essential components of a comprehensive recycling strategy?

Why does urban America suffer from a serious housing affordability problem? What short- and long-term initiatives should be adopted to combat the housing crisis?

What is the best way to provide housing that is affordable for low-wage employees? Is public housing the answer to the problem?

Do banks have a moral obligation to assist lower-income Americans to purchase their own homes? Can this be achieved without firm lending quotas?

Is bulldozing an answer to the problem of urban decay? Why, or why not?

MEMO TO THE NEW MAYOR

TO: SHARON PRATT DIXON 11/7/90
RE: WHAT YOU NEED TO DO NOW

SCOTT SHUGER

Scott Shuger is an editor of The Washington Monthly. *Research assistance was provided by Andrew Bates and Patrick O'Rourke.*

You staked your campaign on the pledge to cut the city's bureaucracy, and yesterday the voters said: "Do it." This is an unbelievable opportunity: the first hopeful moment in District of Columbia politics in a decade and also a chance to show New York, Philadelphia, Detroit, and all the other rotting big city governments how to use personnel cuts to pull back from the brink of chaos and insolvency—to make our schools work, our families secure, and our streets safe. Let's not blow it. Let's get started today.

"Immediately upon entering office, I will conduct a thorough management audit to identify those agencies that are bloated and inefficient," you told us during the campaign. "I intend to cut 2,000 mid-management level paper pushers from the government payrolls." What's worrying me now is that you never went on to say anything more than this about cuts. You recently admitted to the *Monthly* that the 2,000 figure was just "a conservative judgment to give the public a sense of definition of what I'm talking about," and that you would make greater cuts "before we tax everybody out of the city." You should have said the same thing loud and clear during the campaign. Doubletalk about the size of the cuts is deadly most of all because your great strength as a leader is that you tell it like it is.

I'm writing now to raise issues you have to confront starting today if the cause of government efficiency in the District is ever going to be more than just another campaign buzzword:

A. *Making the city work will require firing a lot more than 2,000 people.* Its payroll of 48,000 people—the costs of which take up half the city's annual budget—gives the District nearly *twice* as many non-federal government employees per capita as California, Florida, or Michigan. And businesses that have

shrunk to boost productivity illustrate proportionally much larger cuts than the 4 percent you've advocated. From 1981 to 1989, GE increased its productivity more than threefold and its market value more than fourfold while reducing its salaried staff by 40 percent. (Incidentally, business comparisons aren't made often enough by those in government: One assumption that has no place in bureaucratic reform is "close enough for government work"—the idea that government agencies must be inherently sloppier and less focused than businesses, and hence can learn nothing from them. Even in the District's government there are counterexamples to that: trash collection and parking meter enforcement come to mind. Indeed, comparing the Teutonic precision of the District's parking ticket writers with the Sovietized slow-motion of its ticket processors downtown should suggest that government per se is not the problem.)

As you know, in any organization, there are jobs that are directly related to the manufacture of the product or the delivery of the service and those that are not. Although many of the latter are legitimate managerial, advisory, or technical jobs, once you get away from identifiable makings and doings, there's much greater potential for jobs that don't really count. That's why productive operations exhibit low "mid-level-chiefs/Indians" ratios.

It's scandalous that the city government has taken absolutely no interest in discovering its own chiefs and Indians structure. Nobody among the 371 employees in the D.C. Office of Personnel—an organization that doesn't know it has *almost twice as many chiefs as Indians.* Not the Supervisory Personnel Management Specialist (salary: $70,013). Not the Human Resource Development Officer ($64,041). Nor the Supervisory Personnel Staffing Specialist ($50,653). One official in the city budget office told me, "No one has ever asked that question before. But one of the guys said that if you find anything out, they'd sure be interested in the answer." Curiously, this same man later told me that the problem with saying that you could save money by cutting mid-level people is that there are not enough of them. How does he know? Apprised of the city's utter lack of self-knowledge, a federal personnel official said, "I don't know how they could run a city without knowing that."

A mid-level-chiefs/Indians ratio of .25 means that you have one mid-level chief for every four Indians; generally, an organization fares best when it attains a ratio considerably smaller than that. Quad/Graphics, the company that prints *Time, Newsweek,* and the L.L. Bean catalog, has a mid-level-C/I ratio of .11. In its most recent fiscal year, Federal Express turned a profit of $115 million on a mid-level-C/I ratio of .065. Last year, the Fiat auto division made $1.8 billion on a mid-level-C/I of about .045.

One way to see just how far the District has to go to attain real efficiency is to look at *its* mid-level-C/I. The city's personnel categories are set up to approximate those of the federal government's GS schedule, in which grades 12-15 comprise the bulk of middle management, with grades 5, 6, and 7 reflecting much of the troop strength. (Although grades 1 through 4 are still on the books, they are virtually unfilled, while at the other end of the scale, grades 16, 17, and 18 together make up less than three-tenths of a percent of the city payroll.) While there are some counterexamples to tracking bureaucratic function by pay grade—such as a grade 13 dentist at a public health clinic or a grade 12 court reporter in Superior Court, both of whom are clearly service providers—overall, counting Cs and Is by these categories still develops a valid snapshot of government efficiency. Using this approach, you arrive at a mid-level C/I ratio for the District of .30—in the D.C. government, the average mid-level chief leads a tribe of just over 3 Indians.

B. *It's not just political appointees who have to go.* You have described your proposed cuts as "the only responsible way to avoid furloughs of the rank-and-file service providers." Now, this can be taken to mean that other things being equal, cutting mid-level chiefs is preferable to getting rid of Indians; on that interpretation, you should be applauded. But such pronouncements are vague enough to be taken instead as saying that we can solve all the problems just by chopping out political appointees, thus leaving civil servants untouched. That's false. Since there are fewer than 200 political appointees in the District government (and half of those are entitled to retreat to civil service jobs if they are fired), the problem goes far beyond them. You seemed to admit as much when you told the *Monthly* that you will do whatever it takes to get rid of rank-and-file nonperformers. This too is something you need to declare publicly.

C. *Make your strongest efficiency efforts in the worst departments.* That's where the results will be the most obvious and where you can help the most citizens.

➤Thirty-nine of the 45 salaries listed for the Department of Human Services (DHS) on the first page of the District's fiscal publication titled "Serving the People, Meeting the Challenge" exceed $50,000, and none of the other six is below $44,639. But that's what it takes to build up a C/I ratio of .49. (That's just about one chief for every two Indians! And some divisions of DHS run much higher still: Family Services posts a ratio of .91—nearly one-to-one.) On the other hand, if you happen to have a sick baby, and it's after 4:45 p.m. on a weekday or it's a weekend, don't bother visiting the walk-in clinics the department runs. Due to a shortage of staff, they'll be closed (with the exception of one clinic that still offers evening hours). Earlier this year Mayor Barry told Washington's *City Paper,* "I maintain that any woman in Washington who is pregnant, who wants to get an appointment, can get one in less than a month." Serving who? Meeting what?

➤Granted, you do not directly control the public schools—that's the school board's role. But in elections for the board, the mayor's endorsement is among the most sought-after, and you'll be the one setting the overall total for the school budget. So you do have considerable influence on the board. And aren't the schools just too important not to use it to the utmost?

Although the District school system spends 51 percent more than the nationwide average for public schools, only 55 percent of its budget goes to the instruction of students. The panel of civic leaders known as the D.C. Committee on Public Education (COPE) discovered that the city's public schools spend $536 less per pupil on instruction than comparable urban districts. And they get what they pay for: a 43 percent drop-out rate, a high-school grade average of D+, and SAT scores that are about a hundred points off the national norm—and third from the bottom. Nearly a quarter of all the grades given in the city's high schools are Fs. Thanks to the dearth of enriched and remedial courses and activities, in 12 years of school the District's kids average up to two years' less classroom time than the students in the nearby suburban schools.

On the other hand, the system spends 36 percent of its cash on what it calls "non-school-based support." COPE noted that the District employs 1,250 more non-school-based staff than those comparable districts. That's why last year the group recommended eliminating 400 central staff positions. As of this date, however, no administrative personnel cuts have been made. Would a few suggestions help? How about deep-sixing the Research and Data Management Coordinator (salary: $45,218)? Here's the official description of that job: "Reviews and approves requests for proposals. Conducts state research projects for program improvement. Assesses non-public school needs, and maintains accurate child count." Or the Program Monitoring and Evaluation Coordinator (also paid $45,218)? The description: "Ensures program compliance and approval through selected monitoring procedures. Provides technical assistance to programmatic efforts designed to address compliance issues identified in needs assessment. Conducts evaluation of programs, oversees and monitors programs for quality, ensures compliance to guidelines and regulations, updates and ensures compliance to state regulations [WHAT STATE?], maintains liaison to regional resource center, and maintains system inventory." It's hard to understand all this verbiage, but if it says that this person's job is to maintain quality in the D.C. public schools, then this person has failed. And since when do we need to pay somebody 45 grand to take attendance?

The average public school in the District has 45 fire code violations—and there have been attempts to remedy only half of them. The majority of D.C. school buildings have been poorly maintained for decades. Many classrooms are unheated; students and faculty have been injured by falling ceiling tiles, plaster, and window frames. Bathrooms with stopped-up toilets and sinks are commonplace. The showers in some locker rooms have not worked in 25 years. Some schools have only cold water; 24 have no running water at all. There are also chronic shortages of toilet paper, paper towels, and light bulbs. Some schools, apparently not getting any help from the General Supply Specialist, the Supply Management Officer, or the Inventory Management Specialist downtown (each drawing a salary of $35,294) in their attempts to get soap, make their own.

And it's not just worthless administrators that somehow stick around in the schools. Despite the system's dismal academic record, in the past two years, a grand total of *nine* teachers have been terminated as a result of the evaluation system. What's more, that's all the public schools *tried* to terminate. That's nine out of 6,600.

►Washington's public housing department is sort of the reverse Royal Air Force of city agencies—never before have so many done so little for so many. The department's C/I ratio is an appalling .91. "Having three compassionate, effective people on the staff would accomplish more than the city is doing now in the area of housing," Florence Roisman, a staff attorney at the National Housing Law Project, told me recently. Despite a departmental maintenance payroll that's 50 percent larger than HUD recommends, fewer than 40 percent of the apartments the city targeted for renovation four years ago have been made ready for occupancy. The city's public housing now includes 2,582 empty apartments—a crying shame in a city where homelessness is a major crisis.

At city budget hearings in February 1989, the man who was then the head of public housing maintenance said that on any given day 63 percent of the people under him did not show up for work. Despite this, at the hearings this year, the department did not request new maintenance personnel. It did, however, ask for an additional $141,000 for new staff positions.

Recent correspondence between officials of the District's housing department—including Roland

Turpin, the director—and HUD officials indicates that within the past year the city missed out on HUD housing vouchers and certificates worth millions of dollars earmarked for hundreds of homeless families because the department didn't get the applications in on time and because essential documents were missing. No other public housing authority in the country has made that mistake. Even when the department appealed HUD's decision, it still failed to submit complete paperwork. In other cases, the department has withdrawn requests for HUD housing vouchers for the homeless because it "determined that the paperwork and staff time involved in securing the additional funding is administratively infeasible."

In the city you are about to lead, it still takes about *eight years* for a family to be placed in a public housing unit.

D. *You've got to put more cops on the street.* "When I joined the police department in 1968," Lt. Lowell Duckett, head of the D.C. Black Police Caucus, recently told me, "police districts were called police precincts. And precincts were manned by one captain, four lieutenants, and maybe 16 sergeants. Now we have one deputy chief, four captains, and approximately 21 lieutenants per police district. But guess what? The geographical boundaries of the district didn't change." One quick way to effectively improve the current police C/I ratio of .22—about one chief for every four Indians—would be to put many of Washington's 3,100 under-used federal cops on patrol in the city's high crime areas (there's no good reason the feds shouldn't keep paying for them). Currently, for instance, the Secret Service's Uniformed Division languishes in the tranquil driveways of Embassy Row, watching for action that never comes. These officers are very well-trained and well-equipped; they could make a big difference on some of Washington's mean streets. But instead, as presently deployed, all they do is provide extra comfort to the District's wealthiest residents—which merely reinforces the indifference of the rich to crime elsewhere in the city.

E. *Cutting personnel won't cut the city's costs enough—you have to cut pensions too.* Pension costs are rising much faster than salary costs. The pension expenses that the District is already committed to but which its investments won't pay for—its unfunded pension liability—now run $4.93 *billion*. And probably the biggest factor in the problem is that the city's police and firefighters are able to retire after only 20 years: that's the reason fully $3.25 billion of the city's unfunded pension liability—66 percent—is earmarked for those two groups. The law limits what we can do about the pension payouts due to the 61 percent of the D.C. police force that is scheduled to retire in 1992, but we had better change the rules for the officers who take their place or this city is dead.

It sounds cold to be talking of reducing benefits, and doing so could make it harder on the individual retiree.

Ready, Aim . . . Fire

Once you've decided which city employees are unnecessary, then comes the hard part. Firing them. It's not as easy to pry people out of government jobs as it should be, but there are some helpful tricks:

Turkey farming. Inside the District government, this is also known as Pass-the-Trash. The usual version of turkey farming is only a local solution, doing nothing for overall efficiency: Office A wants to get rid of Bureaucrat Boob, so it passes him off to Office B, issuing its glowing recommendation with an internal wink and a grin. But turkey farming can be a useful tool. If you have an employee doing nothing and you'd like to empty out his desk, the trick is to find out what, if anything, he does well. The grumpiest front-office counselor in D.C.'s Department of Employment Services might just be brilliant at some job in back where he doesn't have to deal with the public.

Old-fashioned firing. Of course, if that employee's just plain incompetent, you can get rid of him, even with all those intimidating civil service rules. "People always blame the regulations for keeping a deadbeat around," says one veteran D.C. administrator, "but you can get rid of someone if you're willing to take the heat and do the work." Since documenting a case for termination may take months, many managers decide that they don't have the patience for the inevitable accusations, appeals, and even lawsuits. But D.C. managers do have the discretionary power to fire with impunity the city's nearly 200 political appointees and 3,800-odd probationary civil servants and temporary workers. And even after the employee is entrenched, the regs only require giving 30 days' notice—during which a manager must make an effort to help the staff member solve workplace problems and order an independent review of the case by a "disinterested designee."

The catch is that the District's iron-clad personnel "penalty guide" severely circumscribes what, precisely, a manager can fire someone *for*. Right now, the worst punishment an employee can receive for supplying false information to superiors or the City Council or Congress is a five-day suspension. Same with being drunk or stoned on company time, gambling on the job, or even committing a criminal act off-hours that "discredits the D.C. government." But the mayor can propose revisions to this and all the city's other civil service regulations, and lobby the City Council to pass them. Congress, which technically must approve any such changes, has rarely overturned Council actions.

Consolidation. If you had a single clerk whose job consisted of doing absolutely nothing, your best move would be to simply abolish the job. If you had an office that was doing nothing, you'd dissolve it. Problem is, the jobs and offices that could be slashed without any penalty at all exist only in parodies or business school textbooks. Most people in city government do *something* important—but they may

spend only a fraction of the day doing it. The new administration's task will be to identify the meaningful tasks a worker performs; suspend the pointless duties, memos, and meetings; and splice the worthwhile functions together into fewer job slots.

While reduction in force (RIF) procedures, which reduce the work force by a given percentage or a set number, allow the cleanest cuts, they have one substantial built-in flaw: They operate by seniority, which means the office's freshest blood is the first to be let. The worker you wind up with may be just the oldest, not the best. Here, D.C. has already borrowed a tip from the feds: To give managers more flexibility in keeping the bright young things, it has revised its civil service manual. Nowadays, an employee who receives an outstanding evaluation gets four years of seniority points along with his performance bonus. Outstanding ratings can, of course, be handed out to cronies as well as to great employees. So the new mayor and her team have to keep an eye on who's getting them and why.

Even a whole office that seems fairly pointless—D.C.'s Office of Inaugural Expenses, say—usually performs at least one essential function, like making sure that public money isn't squandered on private extravaganzas. An aggressive manager will abolish the agency and salvage that legitimate function by assigning it to a better-defined unit, cutting out half a dozen managers in the process. (He should also try to place good workers from the folded unit in other, more productive operations.)

Incidentally, in the District you can do this without a RIF, with two crippling caveats. First, the office must not be one specifically created by City Council mandate—the trade-school monitoring office of the Educational Licensure Commission, for example, would require a Council vote to be abolished. And second, you must transfer the "separated" staff instead of firing or demoting them. (Again, Mayor Dixon should convince the Council to eliminate or at least loosen these restrictions.)

Contracting out. Another way to close an ineffective office with a valuable function is to contract that function out. Take the library at the U.S. Census Bureau: Administrators there thought the library was a million-dollar drain on their budget and the librarians a drain on their patience. So they simply contracted the whole thing out and transferred or fired the unpopular staff. The library still sits in the building, but the cost is hundreds of thousand of dollars less, and the administrators' grave problem—impolite librarians—was solved. To be sure, this is a technique to be used with caution—pocket-padding contractors can be more expensive and dangerous than languid bureaucrats. But the virtue of legitimate contracting is that the courts have consistently upheld the manager's right to use it to cut staff.

—Katherine Boo

But the city has legitimate needs too. And is it really so awful to ask people in their forties to work an extra five or ten years?

F. *Don't be afraid to add people in departments—especially if they are good assessors, auditors, tax collectors, and lawyers in revenue-raising positions.* Talk of cutting can easily degenerate into the mistaken idea that every gain in efficiency requires a reduction in personnel. Net reductions are the rule when the functions in an office are consolidated and when pointless jobs are eliminated (see "Ready, Aim . . . Fire,"). But obviously, when key functions are discovered to be undermanned or manned by incompetents, the reform could easily result in more people, not fewer. One example is in revenue-raising offices. When, on the eve of the D.C. congressional primary, candidate Eleanor Holmes Norton revealed that she and her husband had gone eight years without paying local income taxes, one mystery was how Norton still managed to win. But another much more important one was: How did the city's Department of Finance and Revenue miss the boat? Within days of the Norton story came the news that two candidates for D.C.'s "shadow" Senate seat—Charles Moreland and Jesse Jackson—had likewise not paid some city income tax. But the news didn't come from Finance and Revenue. Could that be because the department has a C/I of .64 and one administrator for every three auditors? How many other tax cheats has the city missed because of that?

And the city seems just as lax when it comes to real estate assessments. D.C. assessments are supposed to represent a property's full market value, so that the property owners pay their fair share of tax. Of course, there are such well-known exemptions as the White House and the National Cathedral. But there are lesser-known ones like the three-fifths of Secretary of State James Baker's $2.5 million house on which he pays no city tax. Or the half of Oliver North attorney Brendan Sullivan's $1.75 million residence that also skates by tax-free. That's how far off the market the city assessments are. Some other examples: Attorney General Richard Thornburgh (market value=$475,000/assessed value=$249,635), publisher Bill Regardie (MV=$1.5 million/AV=$760,000), Rep. Lindy Boggs (MV=$900,000/AV=$253,450), real estate mogul Calvin Cafritz (MV=$2.8 million/AV=$1.5 million), commentator Carl Rowan (MV=$950,000/AV=$516,679), and rejected judge Robert Bork (MV=$925,000/AV=$570,000). And while it's not the most spectacular example, even *your* house is underassessed by nearly $100,000 (MV=$350,000/AV= $253,475).

Additionally, in appeals this year of real estate assessments, when the city's attorneys went up against those representing property owners, they got their heads handed to them: the result was a loss of $36.8 million in tax revenue.

Clearly then, the city could use better staffing in the revenue-producing jobs. Besides the financial reason for hiring in these slots, there's a crucial social one. One of the biggest obstacles to pruning back the city's bureaucracy has been the fear that the axe would fall disproportionately on the working class. Well, setting more employees to work on recovering funds owed by the city's rich is a very good way to share the burden of making government more efficient.

G. *This problem can't be solved on paper.* This is just the first wave of tons of printed advice you will start receiving immediately. Besides all the unsolicited help you'll be getting from the press, the commission on budget and financial priorities for the city will soon release its findings (that's the one headed by Alice Rivlin, former head of the Congressional Budget Office, that reportedly calls for cutting 6,200 jobs). And there are the city-wide audits by outside firms that you intend to order up yourself. Please read all these things carefully and with great openness, but always remember one thing: No matter how insightful, no column, no report, *is* the solution. Making the city conform to the right ideas, once you find them, is not something you can do at arm's-length. You have to get in peoples' faces. Government is not a science—it's a contact sport. Here are some winning plays:

➤The ultimate weapon of the redundant employee is his belief that any cry for reform will blow over—that he can outlast this new threat just like he's survived all the rest. So it's crucial that you stock your administration with people who make it plenty clear they are going to be there longer than one or two years, long enough to "out-tough" the opposition. (By contrast for example, during the eighties, DHS changed heads nine times.)

➤Especially if you are armed with a commission report or two, there'll be a great temptation for you to sweep into office with a lot of theories about what's screwed up and how to fix things. Avoid that. Your theories may be right, but what have you got to lose by testing them against the evidence of the organization itself? On the other hand, there is plenty of danger in "reforming" activities you don't understand. (Like every other journalist, I have at times missed out on an important dimension of a fact because I didn't want to appear foolish for not knowing it.) So resist any temptations in yourself and your staff to play rocket scientist and opt instead for being the Mayor from Mars. Start by finding out what the Indian level of the outfit is—where the ultimate function of the office is supposed to be performed (if nobody seems to know, you've learned something important already)—and by finding out what those people do all day. Ask them what their main problems are. Ask them to identify their important tasks and their unimportant ones. Ask them which supervisors are good, and which aren't so good, and why. When you think you have a handle on the troop functions, you should work yourself up the chain of command rung by rung, asking questions along the way. Despite all these details, do this hard job *as quickly as possible*. The sooner you identify the problems, the sooner you can solve (fire) them.

►And even after you've done all this, you have to be sure you always know what those Indians are doing, with a constant eye towards streamlining offices and eliminating pointless job slots and bad performers. You just can't overstate the amount that gets lost in translation between you and the troops—if you let it. I know you had a big job at Pepco , but I don't think you had to worry in the middle of the night about whether the lines were down. Now you do.

And finally, bureaucratic reform goes nowhere without guts. Firing people is not the world's most pleasant task. Sub-par performers can be nice, they often have families, and most distressing of all for a politician, they have votes. (Ditto for competent people in pointless jobs.) The traditional alternative to the real courage it takes to shake a man's hand and tell him he's through is to give him a make-believe job where he doesn't bother you or, better yet, transfer him to somebody else's office. Not only is this personally corrupting, but for the government it's the very stuff of inefficiency.

That's why it worried me when you recently joked that your cuts of mid-management employees would effect "nobody I know personally." Up until now, that joke has always been on us.

HOT MANAGERS, SIZZLING CITIES

•••

NEAL PEIRCE AND ROBERT GUSKIND

Neal Peirce and Robert Guskind are contributing editors of National Journal *magazine.*

Running a municipality is tough, but the 10 who do it best can give the savviest executives some tips.

WHEN GEORGE LATimer became mayor of St. Paul, Minnesota, in 1976, he quickly realized that the high wages and low productivity of city workers were making the cost of hauling garbage prohibitive. A onetime labor lawyer who had been elected with strong union backing, Latimer shocked his supporters by hiring private contractors to replace municipal garbage collectors. The unions and three city councilmen sued. The mayor won in court, and today some 50 private contractors prowl the cold streets of St. Paul carting off garbage.

A 10-minute bus ride across the Mississippi River sits Mayor Donald M. Fraser of Minneapolis. In 1980, Fraser, a former congressman, took over a job whose formal powers were among the most limited in urban America. With eight police chiefs in 10 years, the city seemed to have adopted the Italian government model. Turf warfare was rampant and the city council marked Fraser the enemy. Quietly and methodically, the new mayor made his peace with the council and wheedled more executive authority out of the previously recalcitrant legislators. With his new clout, Fraser has turned Minneapolis into one of the nation's most smoothly functioning municipalities.

Different men. Different cities. And distinctly different political cultures. But Fraser and Latimer have something in common: They run two of the 10 best-managed big cities in America today. The others, which we selected on the basis of their ability to deliver a wide range of services while keeping taxes relatively modest and bond ratings high, are Baltimore, Charlotte, Dallas, Indianapolis, Phoenix, San Antonio, San Diego and Seattle.

The very notion of a well-managed municipality may seem to be a contradiction in terms, given the press's portrayal of the nation's urban areas as pools of decaying houses, crumbling bridges and failing schools. More often than not, urban governance has been ranked as the flip side of smart management, and its practitioners have been thought to lack advanced managerial skills. But as you'll see in the profiles starting on page 42, these challenges have produced a new generation of municipal CEOs—both elected mayors and professional city managers appointed by city councils—and they are every bit the equals of their private-sector counterparts.

Indeed, business executives could learn a lot about management from these seasoned executives who run vast enterprises with tens of thousands of employees and budgets reaching into the billions. Their cities are huge conglomerates, giant public corporations delivering every kind of service—water, education, housing, health care and police protection. And their "stockholders"—the voters—are an unruly lot.

Today's urban managers stare down problems that would make even the hardest-bitten corporate executives wince. Their employees are represented by entrenched and intransigent labor unions with backbones stiff enough to daunt Frank Lorenzo. They oversee century-old physical plants that make the most antiquated factory look like a modern Japanese wonder. They depend on middle-level managers, most of whom are protected by civil-service regulations, who have their own political bases and personal agendas. Their goals and objectives can shift wildly at a moment's notice. And a sudden revenue shortfall that forces a tax increase or a cut in services could end their political careers.

What kinds of skills do these government managers need? Everything that's applicable in the private sector—and more. Start with an energy level high enough to sustain a dawn-to-midnight schedule full of staff meetings, public appearances, strategy sessions, interviews and social dropbys. Balance it with the ability to be enough of a micromanager to sense how departments operate but still keep a grip on the big picture. Add the talent of being tough with subordinates yet pliable enough to practice the fine art of politics. And throw in a capacity to change gears quickly. In short, the best government CEOs have to be a bit of everything: managers and thinkers, visionaries and politicians, salesmen and frontmen.

For most Americans there's great mystery about the definition of a well-run city. How do you tell one when you see it? As long as water emerges from the tap on demand, as long as city streets don't resemble the surface of the moon, a city may seem decently managed. But is it? In the business of government, there is no clear-cut bottom line, no quarterly profit statement and no market share to expand upon.

But there are some yardsticks: Well-managed large cities deliver high-quality services efficiently—police and fire protection, garbage collection, recreational facilities. Their taxes are relatively modest and their financial standing is strong enough so that they can sell their bonds at reasonable interest rates. To achieve this, cities must be innovators, borrowing heavily from private-sector strategies that improve services or cut the cost of delivering them.

There are also "softer" forces at work in these cities that defy any statistician's attempt to quantify them. In the best-run cities, local corporate leaders are deeply involved in civic affairs—providing financial assistance and leadership, not just lobbying for narrow corporate gain. The ranks of department heads and senior management tend to be relatively stable. Moreover, many of the success-story cities have strong traditions of citizen participation and open government. Some are involved in regional efforts to tackle such problems as clogged highways and overflowing landfills, problems that don't respect municipal

boundary lines. Most important, all of the nation's best-run cities are characterized by managerial leadership that has set the stage for economic advances that make these cities masters of their own destiny.

Even so, the playing field is far from level. In contrast to an impoverished Newark or Detroit, most of the nation's 10 best-managed cities don't have to deal with the one-two punch of a dwindling tax base and mushrooming service demands. Their mayors and managers readily acknowledge the leg up their cities have on many of their urban competitors: Some of the best managed are racially

Many of the mayors are fond of quoting from Tom Peters's classic, In Search of Excellence.

homogeneous; others, in Sunbelt locales, aren't saddled with entrenched municipal unions, moldy civil-service systems and the crumbling roads and bridges common throughout the Frost Belt.

Still, all of our best-managed cities are big in the sense that they have populations of more than a quarter million. Professional city managers are charged with the day-to-day operation of five of the 10. Their records prove that even the largest American metropolises can be managed with a measure of efficiency. Through such feats as turning around decaying Frost Belt economies, or managing the costs brought on by rapid Sunbelt growth, they prove that savvy management is just as critical in turning around a city as it is in rescuing a troubled business.

Though the molds they fit and the styles they use are incredibly diverse, individual managers have been critical in propelling the 10 best-managed cities to the top. Some of these CEOs are strong-willed, inspirational leaders like Latimer. Others step more comfortably in the shoes of a technocrat like Fraser. But their styles and leadership abilities aside, they have plenty in common: They assemble top-notch management teams and give them

wide latitude to experiment with new strategies. They practice the fine art of power sharing and have the master administrator's sense of when to make a move and when to back away. They are adept at rallying divergent constituencies around their programs. And they bring in corporate talent to help them reach their goals.

These manager-mayors speak the language of quantifiable goals and zero-based budgeting and would feel a lot more comfortable in a boardroom with James D. Robinson III, the chairman of American Express, or Donald E. Petersen, the chairman of Ford Motor Company, than in the back room with such old-style machine mayors as Boston's James Michael Curley or Chicago's Richard J. Daley. Says Indianapolis's Mayor William H. Hudnut III, one of the nation's most energetic preachers of the new urban gospel: "The challenge facing public management today is to build a more innovative and entrepreneurial spirit and style into the management system. The bureaucratic mentality looks for ways to protect what it has. The entrepreneurial mentality looks for better ways to do things. A fundamental point of good management is to try to foster the entrepreneurial spirit."

That's a big shift in thinking from just 10 years ago, when the success of a mayor or city manager was determined mainly by his ability to squeeze cash out of Washington. New York and Detroit, among others, were federal-aid junkies, more adept at going hat in hand to Uncle Sam than at checking the gross inefficiencies in their own bureaucracies. New York's orgy of public spending and financial sleight of hand had driven it to the edge of bankruptcy, and Cleveland had actually been pushed over the edge by its unique brand of managerial comedy under Dennis Kucinich, the hapless mayor of that era.

But the taxpayer revolts of the late 1970s, combined with the cutbacks in federal assistance under the Reagan administration, have forced many mayors to do more with less. The chief executives of these cities—whether they be elected mayors or professional city managers—have borrowed page after page from the corporate boardroom and applied management strategies and talents to the nuts and bolts

WHAT YOU NEED TO MAKE A CITY GO

•••

Imagine that your customers could veto price increases, demand more services and fire you at will. That is what it's like to manage a city, which is why municipal executives must be good number-crunchers, excellent strategic thinkers and persuasive communicators—all at the same time. The best mayors and city managers have at least these skills:

○ **Planning.** Anticipating how demographic and social trends will affect demand for roads, bridges and water as well as police, fire and social services.

○ **Communicating.** Persuading the populace that the existing management team is doing the best possible job, and convincing interest groups that new or expanded services are worth higher taxes.

○ **Listening.** Detecting new concerns of the voters and sensing shifts in the public mood that might require adjustments of government priorities.

○ **Budgeting.** Figuring out how to minimize red ink by inventing new sources of revenue and squeezing money out of old programs without gutting services.

○ **Negotiating.** Persuading city employees to accept moderate wage increases and staff cuts in times of great financial stress.

○ **Organizing.** Developing a management structure that will move decisions and other information quickly down (and up) the chain of command and insure that subordinates are held strictly accountable for their actions.

---

of delivering services. Like George Latimer in St. Paul, they are divesting services and hiring business to do the job, charging user fees in some cases, restructuring city departments as profit-making enterprises, undertaking an array of productivity-improvement schemes and buying computerized budgeting and planning systems.

Program budgets, pay-for-performance plans and sophisticated, computerized control systems have been put in place to give city employees the most elusive of public-sector goals: a bottom line. Today, St. Paul uses a sophisticated set of performance standards and service-delivery goals, department by department. Latimer has also brought in management consultants to revise the city's tired 1912-era civil-service system.

BUT THESE TOP-NOTCH government managers have gone beyond structural reforms. They embrace the culture of private-sector management.

Few cities go as far as business in doing market surveys to determine whether their customers are satisfied, but in the new public-management vocabulary, residents are "customers" and institutional pleasure is no longer gained from long lines, the paper shuffle and the runaround. Many of the mayors are fond of quoting from Tom Peters's management classic, *In Search of Excellence.* Today's department heads in Phoenix are "urban service managers." And Charlotte's veteran city manager, O. Wendell White, talks up his new efforts at "employee empowerment." He's determined, he says, to get city workers who answer the phones and stand behind the counters to resolve problems on the spot. This may seem old hat to an executive, but it's true system shock for an old-fashioned bureaucrat.

A broad vision and a sense for carving out new market niches is as valuable a talent for modern government managers as it is for the nation's best CEOs. Smart cities are undertaking strategic planning to determine their strengths and weaknesses in relation

to hostile economic climates. In cooperation with business, Baltimore, Dallas, Phoenix and San Antonio regularly reevaluate their economic positions. Their strategies include recruiting industry, setting up small-business incubators and finding ways to promote local products in export markets.

Still, the rough-and-tumble of city hall is an alien world to managers used to the comparatively rarified atmosphere of the corporate boardroom. The city executive has to contend with rambunctious "stockholders" who can throw him out of office at a moment's notice, with making long-term investments that don't necessarily show a short-term payoff, and with subordinates who often have their own political bases. By sheer necessity, city executives must manage by negotiation rather than command.

And running a city in the future will require no less political savvy—though of a different kind. Just as the 1980s demanded new talents from local officials, the 1990s may bring a still different landscape in terms of issues and the skills municipal managers will need to contend with them. The municipal models of the 1990s are likely to be the cities that recognize the polarization of the 1980s and who deal pragmatically with a painful reality: Big cities—their economic successes of the decade notwithstanding—have become reservations of the very wealthy and the very poor. Therefore, mayors of urban centers will increasingly see themselves as the field generals of whatever the next war on poverty turns out to be.

Fraser foresees that the cities, much the way they divested functions to the private sector in the 1980s, will be divesting social-welfare services in the next decade. Business will have to be as much a partner in solving urban problems as it has been in physical development. Tomorrow's municipal managers, in short, will have to be proselytizers who can persuade the corporate community to contribute money and talent to solve these vexing social problems.

NEIGHBORHOOD POLITICS: A CHANGING WORLD

Community organizers who used to specialize in fighting City Hall are learning to make deals with it instead.

Jeffrey L. Katz

When Saul Alinsky began organizing neighborhood activists in Chicago in the 1930s, he told them that the best way to succeed was to attack. He showed them how to confront and intimidate politicians, corporations and landlords, and how to embarrass government into providing jobs and other economic help for beleaguered communities.

"The job of the organizer," Alinsky said, "is to maneuver and bait the establishment so that it will publicly attack him as a 'dangerous enemy.'" His mastery of those tactics made him the father of modern community organizing in America and a hero to an entire generation of organizers who studied under him before his death in 1972.

If Alinsky were to return to his hometown today, half a century after he began his work there, he would find neighborhood activists all over the city who quote him and revere his memory. He would find thriving organizations founded by his disciples.

But he would not find many neighborhood groups emphasizing his tactics of confrontation and conflict. In the neighborhood politics of Chicago, as in most large American cities, the era of "baiting the establishment" is ending. To many activists, it is no longer clear who the establishment is, or whether it exists. Mass protests are giving way to collaboration as neighborhood groups seek partners to provide some of the services and development projects that their communities need and that government is hard-pressed to provide on its own.

In a community on Chicago's predominantly black West Side, a neighborhood organization is heavily into the real estate business, rehabilitating and managing apartment buildings in partnership with the city. On the mostly white Southwest Side, a similar organization has brought about the renovation of a shopping center.

It is a change that is taking place all over the country. As of last year, according to the National Congress for Community Economic Development, community-based development organizations had built nearly 125,000 units of housing in the United States—mostly for low-income occupants. They had developed 16.4 million square feet of retail space, offices and other industrial developments.

"Usually community organizing starts on a negative, 'We don't like something happening in our neighborhood,'" says Shel Trapp, staff director of the Chicago-based National Training and Information Center, which provides technical assistance to community groups. "That goes on for a few years. And then people say, 'We've got to take an offensive stance here.' That's when you start to link development with organizing."

Specialists in a variety of cities are reporting just that sort of evolution in the last few years. "It's been a remarkable transformation," says Norman Krumholz, professor of urban planning at Cleveland State University and former city planning director under three Cleveland mayors. "What began in the early '70s as a group of grass-roots activist organizations, very strident in style and confrontational in expression, has been transformed into a set of enormously competent community development corporations that are now doing economic development, housing and commercial development."

In making this transformation, neighborhood activists find that they spend less time pleading with government at any level for grants and subsidies. They spend a great deal of time trying to persuade governments to join with them. The whole relationship between activists and elected officials is changing. "If you're doing advocacy, it's more confrontational, more strident," says Robert Zdenek, president of the National Congress for Community Economic Development, an association of neighborhood groups. "If you're doing development, it's more collaborative."

For the activists, this is in large part a simple recognition of economic and political reality. When it comes to housing, for example, communities used to be heavily dependent on federal funds. That source has been drying up. Federal appropriations for Community Development Block Grants, for example, dropped from nearly $2.8 billion in 1978 to $1.9 billion in 1988, even as the number of eligible communities was growing.

These spending cuts have forced neighborhood groups to look not only to government but to churches, foundations, banks and corporations as partners in development efforts. "No single source is able and willing to put up all the money for any given deal or project, let alone fix a whole neighborhood," says Avis Vidal, director of the community development research center at the New School for Social Research. "That's really what accounts for this explosion of partnerships. If you get yourself a lot of partners, everybody gets to say they're leveraging resources and the overall risk is reduced."

As money grows scarce at the federal level, political power grows diffuse at the local level. No one person or political entity controls decisions in Chicago in the way Mayor Richard J. Daley did until he died in 1976. Neighborhood activists, especially in the black areas of the city, were an important part of the coalition that elected and re-elected the late Harold Washington, who served as mayor from 1983 to 1987. Richard M. Daley, the current incumbent and the late mayor's son, is not as close to the neighborhood groups as Washington was, but he has to treat them as major forces in a complex and often chaotic political environment. "Given the decline of political party power in this city," says Paul Green, a political scientist at Governors State University, "neighborhood organizations have become far more important as a political, social entity."

Local government accepts this. Joseph J. James, Daley's commissioner of economic development, says community-based organizations "can bring to bear resources that the city alone cannot reach." This entails everything from attracting financing from foundations and federal agencies to encouraging crime prevention programs.

Protest remains part of the neighborhood activists' arsenal, especially when they feel their areas are being shunned by investors or insurers, neglected by city services or exploited by real estate agents. Some argue that effective organizers cannot afford to move too far beyond the traditional tactics of confrontation. "We believe you have to confront the power structure and beat them up, in effect," insists Jean Mayer, a prominent neighborhood activist in Chicago. Mayer spent 13 years agitating among city and state officeholders to create a "home equity" fund to protect the investments of homeowners in changing neighborhoods. A version of her plan took effect this year.

But most of her counterparts, even those Alinsky disciples, are less likely than they once were to view their prime mission as mobilizing against an enemy. "It's a different era," says Marla Anderson, executive director of the National Neighborhood Association. "We can't scream and yell and demand only. The elected officials will say, 'What are we supposed to do?' "

Neighborhood activists still accuse local governments of spending too much time and money on downtown development. But those tensions have eased in some cities, among them Boston, Cleveland, Pittsburgh, San Francisco and Chicago. In all of these places, there is now strong institutional support for neighborhood groups, and the cities provide operating grants and project financing.

The change becomes even clearer with a visit to a couple of neighborhoods in Saul Alinsky's hometown. In one of them, the challenge is to bring new resources to an impoverished black neighborhood. In the other, it is to keep middle-class whites from fleeing when blacks move in.

The same streets that connote financial and political clout in downtown Chicago—Washington, Adams, Monroe—stretch westward for miles past the Loop across flat Chicago real estate and into some of its poorest neighborhoods. Just inside the city's western boundary, these streets form the heart of South Austin.

It is a neighborhood of low- and mid-rise apartment buildings, with single-family homes or duplexes sandwiched in between. It is not uncommon to see freshly scrubbed buildings next to abandoned structures that have been stripped of everything, including their radiators and pipes. Gangs show they control the turf by leaving their graffiti calling card on corner buildings.

Most of the thriving entities on Madison Street, the area's main commercial strip, are liquor stores and storefront churches. Many other buildings are bare shells, with charred bricks strewn about. Several supermarkets and a half-dozen gas stations have closed in the last five years. It is more convenient to purchase illegal drugs in South Austin than to buy groceries. But sometimes you can do both at once; the owner of Mario's Butcher Shop was recently convicted on a narcotics charge.

South Austin badly needs help. It needs financial capital and better city services, and as much as either of these, it needs hope. In the late 1970s, the South Austin Coalition Community Council was formed to try to supply those commodities. In the early days, it had an all-purpose answer to deteriorating conditions: Protest.

"That's all we did, and we didn't do much else," recalls Bob Vondrasek, the current executive director. "We met. We yelled at the city for not doing what they were supposed to do, rightfully so. We'd go after a slum landlord and maybe we'd picket. Or we'd go to building court with a bunch of people.... We thought it was enough to raise the issue, enough to shake the tree, and that somehow somebody else would come up with the solution."

In the short run, some solutions did turn up. A stop sign would be installed at a dangerous corner, or an abandoned building would be torn down. But as the years went by, these short-term fixes began to seem woefully inadequate to the larger problems the neighborhood confronted. And the community advocates began to shift from identifying problems to devising solutions.

Today, rather than agitating for the demolition of abandoned houses, the South Austin Coalition Community Council is more likely to try to renovate them through the

---

Rather than agitating for demolition of abandoned houses, Austin's Community Council is more likely to try to renovate them.

---

separate community development arm it has generated. One recent afternoon, Vondrasek attended a meeting on nurturing new businesses with local officials and organizers from other nearby neighborhoods. Then he left for a strategy session on how to keep a struggling hospital afloat.

South Austin hasn't always been shy of resources. For most of its history, it was a middle-class white neighborhood. But it was changed overnight in the 1960s by the expansion of Chicago's West Side black community beyond its original inner-city ghetto.

Blacks who sought a better life in South Austin soon discovered that they hadn't really escaped ghetto life. Long-standing businesses tended to leave when their white customers did. Insurance companies redlined the neighborhood, denying coverage to certain locations and deterring bank loans. City services and apartment buildings deteriorated while unemployment, crime, drugs and gangs proliferated.

The Organization for a Better Austin, an integrated group founded in 1966 by an Alinsky protégé, focused on insensitive city leaders and unsavory practices by landlords, real estate brokers, bankers and insurers. But the organization met with an embarrassing end after it was discovered in 1971 that its black president was actually an undercover agent for the Chicago Police Department.

The South Austin Coalition Community Council emerged from the wreckage in 1976. Its first major battle was persuading insurance companies to return to the neighborhood and issue comprehensive policies. To accomplish that, Community Council members used shareholder proxies to argue their cause at the 1978 annual board meeting of Sears, the parent company of Allstate Insurance.

The council still devotes part of its efforts to demanding better city services, such as asking police to interfere in more drug deals, and it has joined with other neighborhood organizations to lobby the city council for a tenants' bill of rights. Vondrasek, a professional organizer and an admirer of Alinsky, would not mind spending more of his time on these political pressure campaigns. But he does not have that option. "We've gotten sucked into social services," he says. As governments have reduced their services, residents "just bring their problems to us."

So the council has worked with the Illinois Commerce Commission and with People's Gas, a private utility, to lower its requirements for utility deposits from low-income families. When utility companies threaten to shut off service, the neighborhood organization negotiates to let delinquent customers make installment payments.

But the issue that best reflects the changes of the past decade is housing. Frustrated at its inability to work with managers of slum buildings and realizing that it could no longer depend on government or the private sector to build low-cost units, the council formed its own non-profit housing agency in 1981.

During its first three years, the People's Reinvestment & Development Effort mainly helped building owners get financing for renovation and improvements. But there still weren't enough incentives for owners to maintain low-income buildings, and the agency decided to play a more aggressive role. "We knew if we were going to stem the tide of neighborhood abandonment and deterioration, we were going to have to be full-fledged developers," says Michael C. Rohrbeck, PRIDE's executive director.

The agency has sponsored $10 million in neighborhood developments since then, including rehabilitating 14 buildings, with three more under way. It also manages 427 rental units in 18 buildings and has provided $3 million in loans and grants for home improvements.

It has been helped in that effort by two federal laws of the 1970s, promoted, in fact, by veterans of the original organizing efforts in South Austin. Shel Trapp and Gale Cincotta built on their earlier experiences in Chicago to lobby Congress for passage of the Home Mortgage Disclosure Act, which enables residents of a neighborhood to see how loans are being distributed on a block-by-block basis, and the Community Reinvestment Act, which requires financial institutions that are being bought or sold to prove that they lend money in their communities.

Juanita Rutues, the current president of PRIDE, says the Community Reinvestment Act has been crucial to its developmental successes. Before passage of the act, she says, lenders were "making a lot of money off us and not investing it in the community." After its passage, Aetna Life Insurance offered the agency a $30,000 grant.

The city of Chicago is neither mentor nor enemy to PRIDE; it is simply a major partner in some of its activities. In one case, the city government acquired three deteriorated apartment buildings that had accumulated $250,000 in back taxes, penalties and interest, then transferred ownership to the agency, which stitched together a $2.5 million renovation, $1 million of it from a second mortgage financed by the city with federal Community Development Block Grant funds. The newly renovated buildings now supply low-income housing for 52 families.

It helps to have good relationships with the local aldermen. In the old days, when virtually the entire 50-member Chicago city council was composed of machine loyalists, that was often difficult; in today's wide-open politics, it is much easier. Democratic Alderman Danny Davis, who represents much of the area, is an ally of PRIDE, the Community Council and neighborhood activists in general. He realizes Alinsky taught neighborhood groups that politicians like him are "good people to organize against." But gaining economic power for South Austin doesn't require wresting political power from Davis. Most of the time, they are on the same side.

Ten miles from South Austin, southwest of Chicago's Loop and in the shadow of noisy Midway Airport, is a collection of neighborhoods that are a little like South Austin used to be: mostly white, modest but comfortable, conservative in their enduring attachments to work, family and church.

This is the city's bungalow belt. The squat brick houses were built in the 1920s and 1930s to provide inexpensive homes for the blue-collar workers of a thriving industrial city. The people who moved in here stayed for life, and some of their children live here today.

It is white ethnic Chicago: Irish and Italian, Polish and Lithuanian. Even more than that, it is Catholic Chicago. There are still as many as a dozen Roman Catholic churches in a 3-mile-square area. Ask residents where they're from, says Arthur Mrumlinski, a teacher and board member of the Southwest Chicago neighborhood organization, "and they wouldn't even know they're from the West Lawn or West Elsdon neighborhoods. They know the parish."

It is insular Chicago, loyal to the South Side White Sox, disdainful of the Cubs and anything else from what it considers to be the effete North Side. In fact, most "outsiders" have long been viewed with suspicion, especially blacks. Mobs attacked marchers led by Martin Luther King Jr. in Marquette Park in 1966. Nazis and Ku Klux Klan members rallied in the park in the years after that.

Which is why James F. Capraro enjoys driving visitors through Marquette Park these days. He makes a point of slowing down as he approaches the playgrounds. "What everyone remembers," he says, "is seven or eight Nazi and Klan rallies, not the thousands of integrated basketball games." He will gladly point out evidence of $17 million in completed development projects he has brought to the community as executive director of the Greater Southwest Development Corporation. But as the third generation in his family to live in the area, he sees his mission as much broader than bricks and mortar.

Capraro uses his position to try to persuade whites not to flee when blacks and Hispanics move into the area, as they have on the Southwest Side. He is the author of a 16-page booklet that has been distributed to area residents by local Catholic churches. It reassures people that there is no reason to flee, because their houses will appreciate in value. "Don't be alarmed if some of the new qualified home buyers are of different ethnic or racial backgrounds," it says. "They will also be working-class people who know what it means to work for a living, and regardless, they will be qualified home buyers."

He is working against the history of urban development as it has occurred in Chicago and other large cities, Capraro acknowledges. But he thinks the Southwest Side can be different if neighborhoods acquire more economic might and residents are assured their homes will retain their value. The area already has some strong selling points. The increased popularity of Midway Airport has spurred business, even as the noise has angered some residents. A new rapid transit line to downtown will make the neighborhood more attractive to commuters. Housing prices remain a bargain by Chicago standards. A strong sense of community still exists.

Capraro's Greater Southwest Development Corporation is an arm of the larger Southwest Community Congress, a coalition of 174 neighborhood groups, many of them reaching down to the block level. The Community Congress, like its counterpart in South Austin, still occasionally uses a hard-sell approach to get its way. Earlier this year, its activists felt that the U.S. Department of Housing and Urban Development was being unresponsive to the problem of abandoned houses. Members of the group, led by executive director Glenn Bailey, erected a makeshift plywood wall with slogans like "Closed for lack of concern" and "SCC orders HUD board-up," propped it up in front of HUD's main Chicago office and held a press conference.

Most Community Congress activities, however, mark it more as a service organization and collaborator with government. It brings city housing officials into its headquarters each week to give financial advice to neighborhood home buyers. It sponsors multi-racial soccer leagues. And, most significantly, it has its own separate development corporation, headed by Jim Capraro.

Neighborhoods can't wait for miracles, Jim Capraro believes. They must come up with ways to empower themselves.

Capraro has been through his share of political protests, having begun his activism in the 1960s by marching against the Vietnam War. In 1971, at age 21, he transferred that zeal to neighborhood organizing as executive director of SCC. But eventually he decided that neighborhoods would have to start coming up with ways to empower themselves: Elected officials did not know how to solve the most important problems, even if they wanted to. "We have to do something other than just being reactive," Capraro concluded. "We have to learn to be creative, to be good planners and entrepreneurs. We have to create solutions and implement them."

That led the Community Congress in 1976 to form the non-profit Greater Southwest Development Corporation, and Capraro became its executive director. In the first several years, the corporation acquired, renovated and sold a 54-unit apartment building, a commercial building and five vacant houses. The corporation still has an interest in housing—it is currently building a $7 million, 60-unit retirement home—but it has turned much of its attention to commercial development. Capraro is proud of the corporation's $6 million renovation of a shopping center, which he argues has spurred another $30 million in private development.

Capraro realizes that the Greater Southwest Development Corporation alone will never to able to provide more than a small portion of neighborhood needs. What counts is how much it can inspire others to do, from starting a business or renovating a home to organizing a block watch. "It's when people aren't invested," Capraro says. "That's when things get out of hand."

That is, ultimately, the same sort of economic strength and self-determination that Alinsky sought. "Self-respect," Alinsky wrote, "arises only out of people who play an active role in solving their own crises." But in South Austin, on the Southwest Side and in other outposts of urban America, activists are ceasing to view government as the first obstacle to overcome on the road to power.

"In the olden days, many neighborhood groups had to push against political forces," says Bud Kanitz, executive director of the National Neighborhood Coalition. "Now many of them are pushing against market forces." The trick to that, they are finding, is not so much embarrassing government officials but making deals with them—and even, when necessary, substituting for them.

Volunteer Mentors Empower Inner-City Youths

Patricia Rowe

"It makes you feel grown-up working your brain like this," says 17-year-old high school senior Lashawn Hamilton, reflecting on her job internship last summer in the Center on Children and the Law, the child advocacy, research and education arm of the American Bar Association (ABA) office in Washington, D.C. Lashawn's duties—which entailed mastering complex telephone and filing systems, "faxing" material to other ABA branch offices, preparing mailings of ABA publications, proofreading, and typesetting—was arranged for her by the Southwest Neighborhood Assembly Youth Activities Task Force. Spearheaded and staffed by volunteers and located in the Southwest community of Washington, D.C. this summer job placement program recruits, trains, and counsels neighborhood minority youth with the goal of helping them find and maintain meaningful employment.

The Youth Activities Task Force consists of government employees and other interested adults who serve as mentor-counselors to young people aged 14 to 21. Since it was organized in 1982 as an ad-hoc community group concerned about meeting the needs of young people in Southwest Washington, the Task Force has placed an estimated 450 to 500 teens in summer positions. In a 10-week orientation/training period designed to nurture in the teens a sense of achievement and self-esteem, mentors help the youth—who are primarily from disadvantaged, single-parent or low-income families—prepare resumes, master the job interview process, and develop marketable skills.

Barbara Hurlbutt, who has participated in the program since it was launched, notes that the Task Force gives the teen interns an entree into the employment world and a "leg up" into permanent white collar or skilled jobs. She notes: "One of the primary advantages of our program is that it teaches youths what is expected of them in the job world so they won't experience 'culture shock.' They learn that there are consequences to their behavior and actions, and they come to see the link between the Task Force experience and their paychecks. They learn how to seize initiative, budget money and be responsible. The Task Force offers guidance and information to help the kids develop good work habits and discipline, and it regularly monitors their employment progress."

In 1983, the Youth Activities Task Force was incorporated into the Southwest Neighborhood Assembly, becoming one of its major auxiliaries. Founded in 1964, the Southwest Neighborhood Assembly is a voluntary, nonprofit association that seeks to improve the quality of life for residents of Southwest Washington by offering a variety of educational, social and economic programs and activities for adults and youth.

Task Force membership ranges from 15 to 20 volunteers, most of whom are Southwest Washington residents or live outside the area but have an interest in that part of the city either as potential employers or citizens with a deep concern for neighborhood youth. Throughout the year, members hold regular monthly meetings and about 25 subcommittee meetings to plan the summer placement program—recruiting mentors and interns, identifying employers who will hire students, and determining the scheduling and content of the orientation/training program.

Breaking Down Barriers

Thelma Jones, former president of the Southwest Neighborhood Assembly and the organizer of the Task Force orientation/training sessions, describes the evolution of the Task Force in relation to the onset of urban renewal and housing development in the late 1950s. These initiatives altered the socioeconomic and demographic character of Southwest Washington and spawned diverse—sometimes conflicting—concerns and priorities among area residents. According to Jones, 30 years ago Southwest D.C. was predominantly the home of poor black families, but after urban renewal some of these families were forced to leave the area because their homes were demolished to make way for luxury high-rise condominiums and town houses.

Jones stresses that the Task Force is a way to break down barriers, to reconcile economic or cultural differences, and to foster respect and trust between residents of the expensive town houses and those in the low-income housing projects. She notes, "When people know each other and can say 'hello,' they feel safer. There is more community spirit and unity. I believe people at either end of the economic scale can work together to mutual advantage."

Delmar Weathers, Chief of the Adoption Opportunities Branch in the Children's Bureau, Administration for Children, Youth and Families, trains the mentors. "The program depends

Reprinted from *Children Today*, January/February 1990, pp. 20-23.

on employers willing to provide opportunities and committed volunteers who work hard at planning the program and fundraising for it," she explains. "Another key element is the mentors, who are vital to the program because of the support and guidance they provide the youth as they confront the world of work," Weathers adds.

Mentor-counselors augment the training program by assisting the youths in making value judgements, defining career goals and developing effective employer co-worker relationships. Weathers recruits about 12 to 24 mentors annually through networking and an informal "grapevine." The primary sources of volunteers are churches, clubs, neighbors and community groups. Two training sessions are conducted to familiarize mentors with their responsibilities.

The amount of time the mentor spends with a youth depends on the youth's adjustment at the workplace. Mentor intervention might be necessary if the young person needs encouragement in bolstering the confidence that will enhance his or her job performance. Mentors are also expected to establish a cooperative relationship with employers, who are urged to contact the mentor for assistance if problems arise on the job.

Weathers strives to match compatible personalities so that the interaction between mentor and intern results in greater responsiveness to the youth's needs. Because a number of boys in the program have been raised in single-parent homes lacking a strong male role model, she attempts, where possible, to pair male interns with competent male mentors. While conceding that the mentor-intern relationship may be undermined in cases where a teen has difficulty relating to adults, Weathers reports that "the rapport that often develops between mentor and youth—sometimes extending beyond the summer—is especially noteworthy."

Keeping Overhead Low

The program is supported and underwritten by annual Task Force fundraisers; grants from private organizations, foundations, local businesses and corporations; and by individual donations. As its own contribution to operating costs, the Task Force has staged dinner theater events and "sunset supper shows"—with food donated by Safeway Stores, Inc. and prepared and served by volunteers—and hosts annual spring luncheons to which the business community is invited. Harbour Square, a Southwest residential apartment complex that provides job placement for summer interns, also supplies facilities for fundraisers. The Metropolitan Police Boys' and Girls' Club of Southwest Washington furnishes free office space for the Task Force headquarters, and the University of the District of Columbia has been a source of funding as well as job placement.

In addition to financial support and a word processor from the Rotary Foundation, the program has received funds from the Queen Coonley Foundation, the Jesse Ball Dupont Fund, and the Private Industry Council of the District of Columbia, a nonprofit corporation that receives federal and city funding to support job training programs for low-income D.C. residents. Other major contributors to the program include Western Development Corporation, a local developer that has donated grants of $15,000 each year for the last five years, as well as the World Bank, Riggs Bank, and *The Washington Post*.

With the money raised, the Task Force implements its all-volunteer program. Functioning as a form of employment agency, the Task Force finds summer employment for an average 30 to 100 teens each year, devising the most suitable and satisfactory match for both intern and employer, then paying the intern what it terms a "training stipend" that amounts to the minimum wage. Except for the interns, the only paid participant is Mrs. Maude Stephens, an adult coordinator hired to facilitate program operation and ensure smoother administration and better communication among interns, mentors and employers.

Groomed for Success

One cornerstone of the program is the orientation/training period for interns before their placement in summer jobs. In addition to completing employment applications and role playing in videotaped job interviews, participants are coached in proper dress and decorum on the job, with emphasis on attendance, punctuality, telephone manners, and respect for supervisors and co-workers. A word processor training program offers students exposure to the computer technology field and an opportunity to enhance saleable business skills. In an effort to open youths' eyes to possible future careers and help them chart their long-term vocational development, field trips are made to such area firms as CNN America, Inc. (Cable News Network), the Earl Howard Photography Studios, or the J.W. Marriott Hotel.

The 2-hour orientation/training sessions are held on 10 successive Saturdays during the spring. Guest lecturers, who donate their services, represent business, industry, academia and government. Speakers have included Phyllis Armstrong, local TV anchor/reporter, and Robert L. Richardson, Director of Personnel for the United Planning Organization, who both discussed resume writing and updating; Barbara Stevenson of the D.C. Office of Personnel, who reviewed preparation of the "171", the federal government's job application form; Peter Woolfolk, a local radio host, who stressed the importance of presenting an appropriate appearance when interviewing for a job; John Dixon, General Manager of a J.W. Marriott Hotel, who explored the topic of problem solving in the working world; and Othello Richards of the World Bank's Investment Department and Vivian Hardy of the Wallace and Wallace Financial Group, who offered trainees strategies for effective money management. Other sessions have featured successful minority professionals, businessmen and community activists selected as positive role models.

At a graduation ceremony after the orientation sessions, students receive certificates and awards, such as complimentary Metrorail passes, for perfect attendance and outstanding conduct. One of the speakers at last June's graduation was former participant Cassandra Butler, now a 3rd-year student at Clark College in Atlanta, who described how her experience in the program helped prepare her for her current summer position with the U.S. Department of Energy.

Each fall, an awards banquet is also held to recognize those young people who completed their summer employment assignments and to honor those who distinguished themselves by diligence on the job. Three or four exemplary workers each receive $100 United States savings bonds.

Trainees have been placed in summer jobs at such metropolitan area sites as the Fort McNair military installation; the American Bankers Association; the USO of Metropolitan Washington; VIP Travel Agency; the World Bank; the U.S. Department of Housing and Urban Development; Casual Corner women's apparel shops; Southeastern University; Southwest Prescription Pharmacy; and the Gangplank Restaurant and Marina. They have worked as office assistants, laborers, cashiers, and sales and stock clerks. When the Task Force lacks sufficient funds to place all of its trainees, the mayor's summer employment program serves as a source of job placement. A number of Task Force interns have been hired for job assignments with Riverfest, the annual arts and recreation celebration sponsored by the mayor's office and held on the Southwest waterfront. If a job arrangement is not working well for either intern or employer, the Task Force will place the intern in another assignment.

While most employers are willing to train inexperienced young people but not to pay them full salaries, in some instances an employer will hire an intern on its own payroll, occasionally offering a higher salary than the minimum wage paid by the Task Force. Last summer, for example, students placed at Children's Hospital earned $5.00 an hour. In a number of cases, a primary objective of the program has been achieved when summer jobs blossomed into yearlong, permanent positions.

A Form of Apprenticeship

According to coordinator Maude Stephens, although some youths joining the program may initially have employment difficulties stemming from negative attitudes formed in socially and emotionally deprived backgrounds, "employers are not expected to handle the youths with kid gloves." The Task Force maintains close liaison with employers, who are urged to treat placements as a form of apprenticeship and, accordingly, to devote special attention to the youth by providing close supervision and evaluation. Pointing out that the intern's supervisor completes an evaluation sheet on his or her job performance, Stephens observes, "Kids with negative attitudes often respond positively to caring supervisors. When undisciplined kids realize they are expected to act responsibly on the job, there is often a complete transformation in their attitude and behavior by the end of the summer."

To demonstrate her premise, Stephens cites the case of a somewhat unruly teen who was supervised by a sergeant at Fort McNair. The youth became an industrious worker and is currently employed at a major downtown Washington hotel, where he recently received a salary increase. Acting in the capacity of trouble-shooter, Stephens telephones and visits each job site periodically to monitor each intern's progress, and she maintains close contact with new interns who are

apprehensive about starting their first job. She points out that the return placement rate for Task Force youths is impressive—employers frequently request the same students for successive summers and interns, in turn, enjoy returning to the same employers each year.

A Community Model

The enthusiastic endorsement of employers and the success of Task Force interns who are achieving personal growth and realizing career and life goals underscore the program's value as a community resource and model. The USO of Metropolitan Washington believes that the program "is meeting the community's need to replenish the labor market with employable young people who have been provided with the means to make informed career choices." Washington radio station WUST-AM said that the program "is an excellent one in that the student, the business, and the community benefit by its existence." The ABA writes: "Our experience with your young people has been a very positive one. Although we regularly utilize interns at the ABA, they are almost always law or graduate students. The young people you have sent us have contributed a great deal and made many friends— for themselves and for your program.... Your program gives the young people of Southwest Washington an opportunity that would otherwise be lacking."

The testimony and experiences of both current and former Task Force interns illustrate that it has been a positive force in their lives. Lashawn Hamilton, who plans to attend college and be a social worker, feels that her job at the ABA has enhanced her knowledge of such human service topics as child abuse, and has helped clarify and reaffirm her life goal of helping others. Wayne Green, a 21-year-old junior at Virginia Union University, feels his assignment to a sales unit of the World Bank has provided experience that will help him fulfill an ambition of launching his own finance company. He notes that the hands-on experience at the Bank has given him ''the chance to meet people from all over the world and to learn something new every day.'' Lisa Matthews, who worked at the Xerox Corporation and was elected president of the Future Business Leaders of America, is currently a business administration major at St. Augustine's College in North Carolina. Terry Hyson, a 3-year program participant, is currently a full-time employee of the U.S. Department of Health and Human Services, and Vernon Gudger, who worked at National Business Systems, Inc., is now a District of Columbia police officer.

Thelma Jones concludes: ''Our program is demonstrating that the young people of Southwest Washington have true potential. They may not have had material advantages, but they do have youth, vigor and enthusiasm. If that energy can be harnessed for constructive ventures, then these youth have a better chance to avoid involvement with drugs, find employment and self-respect, and be an asset to their community.''

* * *

Further information on the Southwest Neighborhood Assembly's Youth Activities Task Force is available from Barbara Hurlbutt, 1311 Delaware Ave., S.W., Washington, D.C. 20024.

HAVE ASIAN AMERICANS ARRIVED POLITICALLY? NOT QUITE.

But as they change the face of the country, they may also change the shape of American politics.

Rob Gurwitt

Eight and a half years ago, on a warm June night in Detroit, a young Asian American named Vincent Chin was beaten to death by two white men wielding a baseball bat. The attack was economically motivated, though not in the usual sense; Chin's assailants were not interested in his money.

Rather, they were enraged by the depression then gripping the auto industry; they made clear that they held Chin and his kind responsible. "It's because of you [obscenity] Japs that we're out of work!" witnesses reported them yelling as they crushed Chin's skull. Chin was Chinese.

The murder sent a shiver through Asian-American communities around the country. It took little reflection to realize that widespread resentment of Japanese industrial competition was sparking indiscriminate racial hatred, and that no Asian—of Chinese, Filipino, Vietnamese, Korean or Japanese origin—was safe from it.

It also didn't take long for another, even more deeply troubling realization to set in. After autoworker Ronald Ebens and his stepson were charged with the attack and brought to trial, they were allowed a plea bargain that yielded a manslaughter conviction, three years' probation and a $3,800 fine each. For many of the 35,000 or so Asians who were living in the Detroit area, that slap on the wrist demonstrated that local officials who might have put a brake on the blind anger behind the assault actually sympathized with it.

"We found out," says James Shimoura, a Detroit lawyer who worked on the Chin case, "how little political clout we really had."

Some months later, federal civil rights charges were brought against Ebens and his stepson; this time both were acquitted. By then, though, Shimoura and other Asian-American activists in Michigan had digested the lesson of their experience: For minorities in the land of opportunity, involvement in politics is not a luxury.

In other states, and often for other reasons, that understanding has been brought home to any number of Asian Americans over the last decade. Whether because of a rise in the number of attacks on Asians, concern about quotas in higher education, the sudden onslaught of opposition to bilingual education or any of a variety of local situations that made particular ethnic

communities feel vulnerable, the 1980s laid the groundwork for what is likely to be a notable rise in the level of Asian-American political activity over the next decade. So, also, has the simple passage of time and the adoption of American habits by the children of immigrants.

That is not to say that the country's Asian communities were, until lately, politically silent. Asian Americans were among the activists of the civil rights and antiwar eras and, especially in cities such as Seattle, Chicago, San Francisco and Los Angeles, took the skills they learned in those causes and applied them to their own communities beginning in the late 1960s. In more mainstream politics, there have been Asian-American officeholders at least since the 1950s, and today's scattering of prominent Asian-American politicians got their start long ago. March Fong Eu, California's Democratic secretary of state, and U.S. Representative Norman Mineta, also of California and also a Democrat, plunged into elective politics in the late 1960s, Eu in the state Assembly and Mineta on the San Jose city council. Mineta's Democratic colleague in the California congressional delegation, Robert Matsui, spent most of the 1970s on the Sacramento city council before his election to Congress in 1978.

Even so, it's safe to say that since 1965, when amendments to the Immigration Act reversed decades of careful exclusion of most Asians, the number of Asians settling in this country has far outstripped the level of their political activity. Now, however, they are running for office in slowly mounting numbers, joining political campaigns, working to promote fellow Asians for positions on state or local boards and commissions, contributing money to candidates, and forming organizations to lobby for their interests. Moreover, the skeleton of a loose Asian-American agenda is beginning to take shape.

When the Census Bureau releases its final numbers on the ethnic makeup of the country next year, they will confirm what has been obvious to anyone who has spent time in any major urban area over the last decade. From the Little Saigons of Orange County, California, and Arlington, Virginia, to Koreatowns in

Chicago and Los Angeles, Filipino enclaves in the San Francisco suburbs and housing projects filled with Hmong refugees in St. Paul, Minnesota, it is apparent that recent Asian immigrants and their predecessors are changing the face of the United States.

A pre-census report released by the Census Bureau earlier this year gave some measure of the magnitude of those shifts. It indicated that the country's Asian population had grown seven times as fast as the general population over the last decade, expanding from 3.8 million in 1980 to some 6.5 million in 1988, or about 2.6 percent of the nation's population. Much of the growth was accounted for by immigrants, roughly a third of whom settled in California.

When the final census figures come out next year, articles in the press about a "sleeping giant" ready to transform the American political scene seem inevitable. The label will be misleading. Asians are nowhere a "giant," except in Hawaii, whose majority Asian and Pacific Islander population is by no means politically asleep. Even in California, where they are most numerous, Asians make up little more than 10 percent of the population—enough to swing many elections if they vote as a bloc and certainly enough to make them a political factor that can't be ignored, but no more a colossus in that polyglot state than any other group.

One other characteristic of the country's Asian population is important to remember as well: Immigrants outweigh the native-born in every Asian ethnic group except Japanese Americans. That single fact goes a good bit of the way toward explaining why the growing mass of Asian Americans are only now starting to turn their attention to American politics in a concerted way.

Many have felt they just didn't have the time. "People are still struggling economically, especially the new arrivals," says Betty Lim, the San Francisco parks department's safety officer and a former president of the city's Chinese American Democratic Club. "Politics has to take a back seat, so they can get their business going. If you run a family restaurant, say, you need everybody there, 14 or 16 hours a day." While there is no question that many Asian-American families are comfortably well off economically—especially those born in this country—poverty rates for Chinese, Korean and Southeast Asian refugees are high compared with whites. Thirty-four percent of foreign-born Vietnamese families and 12 or 13 percent of foreign-born Korean and Chinese families are poor, according to a 1988 U.S. Civil Rights Commission study; the poverty rates for whites, whether foreign- or native-born, are in single digits.

Furthermore, the political interests of Asian immigrants are often focused almost exclusively on the politics of the countries they've left. Chinatown residents devour news from China, Taiwan and Hong Kong; factional politics in the Philippines still divides Filipinos living here; South Koreans argue about the democracy movement in their homeland; Cambodians intently follow the slow progress toward a peace settlement in the war-torn country they recently left.

Many immigrants, moreover, come from countries where involvement in politics was not a safe pastime, or even an imaginable one. "You would never hear that a child could grow up to be president of this country in a Chinese family," says Rose Pak, a Chinatown activist in San Francisco. "You have to buy influence, and the typical

Many immigrants come from countries where involvement in politics was not a safe pastime, or even an imaginable one.

immigrant still believes that—they would never be proud of their children if they went for office."

All these factors contribute to the relatively low rate at which Asian Americans have tended to register and vote. The Los Angeles suburb of Monterey Park is 51 percent Asian—it is the nation's only city with an Asian-origin majority—but the voting population is only 30 percent Asian. Several studies suggest that Asians' rate of registration in California is not only less than that of whites but of blacks, as well, says Don Nakanishi, director of the Asian-American studies program at the University of California at Los Angeles. Conclusions like those worry Asian politicians. "You can point to almost a doubling of raw numbers, but it will be a hollow promise if we're not able to show that Asians turn out to vote," says Los Angeles City Councilman Michael Woo.

Still, even a cursory look at Asian-American political activism shows that it has evolved toward American norms. In Chicago, the handful of Asians who got involved in the civil rights movement of the '60s because they saw themselves as part of a broader minority effort is now part of the political mainstream, and with Illinois now roughly 4 percent Asian—enough to matter in close statewide contests—they are finally in a position to build their community's political strength. Ross Harano, who in 1978 became the first Asian American to run for Chicago's city council with Democratic Party endorsement (he lost narrowly) has used his position as the head of the Asian Pacific American Democratic Council to ensure an active Asian presence in the campaign of every Democrat running this year for statewide office and most county offices, too: supporters and staffers who can make sure their candidates understand and attend to issues of concern to Asian Americans.

The same movement is occurring elsewhere. As Councilman Woo says, "We're seeing a larger number of younger Asian Americans who are entering jobs as staff to other elected officials. More Asian Americans are coming out of applicable educational backgrounds, with degrees in political science, law or journalism. It marks the political maturity of the Asian community in terms of encouraging people to participate."

It is no accident that two of the country's most prominent Asian-American politicians, U.S. Representatives Mineta and Matsui, both of Japanese descent, spent a part of their childhoods in the World War II internment camps. Just as that experience helped push them into politics, so other Asian Americans, more recently, have discovered that the cost of ignoring political involvement can be high.

Certainly that was how Jim Shimoura and others read the official response to the Chin killing. "Had we had Asian officeholders or a judge, we would not have had the same result," says Shimoura. "But we were not recognized by the establishment within government...and that worked against our community."

As it happened, the year of Chin's killing was also the first time in Michigan that Asians organized a fund-raiser on behalf of a political candidate—Democrat James Blanchard, who won the governorship. Two years later, with a broader outreach, Asian activists raised money for Democratic U.S. Senator Carl Levin. Those activities gave Shimoura and others access to the state's top Democratic circles, and eventually led to Blanchard's creation of an advisory commission on Asian-American affairs. Over the last few years, Asians have also become involved in GOP fund raising. Michigan today is hardly a hotbed of Asian political activity, but there are now Asian Americans in some high-level appointive positions, including the state's commissioners of public health and insurance, and Asians have been able to meet with civil service officials on affirmative action in government employment and with law enforcement officials on anti-Asian violence.

Although Asians in Michigan count their appointments as real advances, in some senses the payoff is still to come, in Shimoura's view. "When there's another recession in the auto industry, the [anti-Asian] rhetoric of [1982] will resurface," he says. "The new presence of our community puts us in a position to have access to people in organized labor and government to try to temper some of the tactics that will be used to stir up popular support for the auto industry on the import question."

Similar awareness of Asians' vulnerability if they don't participate has cropped up elsewhere. Although Monterey Park had, at one point, a city council that included a Filipino American and a Chinese American, low Asian political turnout in the mid-1980s helped a slow-growth movement dominated by relatively conservative white members take control of the council. While anti-Asian sentiment was not part of their campaign, it surfaced not long after they took office. Under the leadership of Mayor Barry Hatch, the council threatened an assault on the city's dominant Chinese population: Hatch favored an "English Only" ordinance, proposed requiring that English be the predominant language on commercial signs and even objected to a donation to the library of 10,000 Chinese-language books from Taiwan.

"The Asian community became quite alarmed, and said, 'We really have to do something to have some representation,'" says Judy Chu, a council member who is now mayor. The city's Asian Americans mobilized for this year's election. They threw Hatch off the council and put a second Chinese American on.

Less immediate, but no less real, fears are sparking organizing efforts among Vietnamese refugees. Chieu Pham, director of the Vietnamese Fishermen's Association, based in Oakland, California, is one of a small group of Vietnamese who have begun to raise money for California candidates. He is finding resistance. "The first thing most Vietnamese say is, 'I don't want anything to do with politics,'" says Pham. But so many

of his compatriots are dependent on refugee assistance, welfare or simply the goodwill of local licensing boards that Pham believes they cannot afford to distance themselves from government. "We say, 'If you want to help your family, you must be involved. Do you think the refugee resettlement program falls from the sky? If you have a problem getting a business license or a license for fishing, where else can you go?' The moment we stop," Pham says, "people will forget us."

In San Francisco, the Chinese community's first concerted foray into politics came in the 1987 mayor's contest, after businessmen in Chinatown and several other districts found their desire for more growth of their commercial areas rebuffed by the city's planning commission. Although many old-line business owners lined up with John Molinari, the more conservative candidate in the nonpartisan race, others backed liberal Assemblyman Art Agnos, who had a long history of supporting the Asian community. Agnos eventually won, in no small measure because of that backing. "He was frozen out of raising money from the established white business community," says Larry Tramutola, a San Francisco political consultant who worked on Agnos' campaign. "I don't think Art Agnos would have been elected mayor if it weren't for the Asian support."

Seattle's Asian community elected its first city council member in the 1950s, but major activism, including the use of demonstration techniques learned in the civil rights movement, began in the late 1960s, with the successful effort to save the International District, with its many poor and elderly Asian residents, from being wiped out by development. In the aftermath, some activists went into government as staff members for politicians or administrators. "We discovered that [having an] assistant somewhere can get you into a meeting," says Bob Santos, a Filipino American who for years headed Interim, the chief International District community organization. "This community became very political, because of the need to work with the system, but always with the threat that we could hit the streets and really embarrass people."

Within the relatively assimilated Japanese-American community, organizing went on over the last decade around the issue of financial reparations to those who had been imprisoned in relocation camps during World War II. In California, the network built by that effort turned its attention in 1988 to opposing Republican Governor George Deukmejian's appointment of then-U.S. Representative Dan Lungren to be state treasurer. Lungren had helped lead the fight against the reparations bill in Congress.

"He was an unknown to most Californians, but he was notorious to Japanese Americans," says Don Tamaki, a San Francisco lawyer who became a spokesman for the effort to oppose Lungren. Studying Lungren's record, Tamaki and other activists found that he had taken positions that would be unpopular with the environmental movement, civil rights groups and organized labor. "It was a watershed—the first time that Asians had led a statewide effort," says Dale Minami, a law partner of Tamaki's and president of the statewide Coalition of Asian Pacific Americans. The Lungren nomination was defeated.

Looking out over the next decade's political landscape, it's hard to escape the conclusion that Pan-Asian issues are developing that will have a much higher profile than in the past. One item, clearly, is the Asian community's demand for the election of more Asian officeholders, especially politicians like Judy Chu, who was born in this country and is thus able to play a mediating role between the newer immigrants and the society at large. "I get inundated with calls from the Asian community," she says. "A lot of people are confused by city hall procedures; they're intimidated and feel no one will listen to them. So they turn to someone like me because they feel I can understand where they're coming from."

Moreover, as Michigan's Jim Shimoura suggests, another key demand is for more appointments of Asians to local and state boards and commissions, on the theory that they will, simultaneously, be more sympathetic to the concerns of Asian citizens and legitimize to non-Asians the very concept of Asians playing a role at that level. "When you have Asian Americans in there," he says, "it breaks down the stereotype of Asians not being a significant part of the political structure of society."

Outlines of a Pan-Asian agenda are beginning to take shape, but so, too, are very real differences among different Asian groups.

Just as important, suggests Ngoan Le, Illinois Governor James Thompson's assistant for Asian-American affairs, is Asians' presence at various levels in government if their communities are to be served well. "Nutritional programs for the elderly, for example, may not be applicable to the elderly Asian-American diet as designed," she says. "We need to be in positions where, when people are planning, we can talk about the needs of Asians."

There are other issues on the Pan-Asian agenda as well. Vincent Chin was only one of scores of Asian Americans physically attacked over the last decade, and Asian-American activists contend that monitoring of hate crimes against Asians and enforcement of anti-hate crime legislation are both inadequate.

Asians also find common cause on educational issues— opposition to college admission quotas on Asian students and demands that more Asian Americans be hired to teach and, for most, that funding for bilingual education be preserved. Most oppose the English Only movement, and favor politicians committed to ensuring that immigration laws do not bar further Asian immigration. Matters such as housing for new immigrants and the poor, plus care for the elderly, also cut across different Asian communities.

But if those general outlines of a Pan-Asian agenda are beginning to take shape, so, too, are very real differences among different Asian-American groups. Asians are enormously diverse, not simply along ethnic lines, but across generations and socioeconomic classes as well. At this point, the political divisions that separate them are at least as numerous as the ties that bind them.

In contrast to blacks (and to a lesser degree, Hispanics) Asian Americans are anything but monolithic in their party affiliations. Japanese Americans tend by a slight margin to vote Democratic. The Chinese Americans in California, showing a greater disinclination than other groups to declare a political affiliation, are registering in equal proportions as Democrats, Republicans and independents. Vietnamese and Cambodian immigrants, in further contrast, tend to identify with the GOP and its historic hard line on communism, although many of them are open to siding with the Democrats when social welfare spending is on the line. In general, Asians are developing higher profiles in both parties, which have actively been working to recruit Asian support.

There are also differences in ethnic agendas. Immigrants from India and the Philippines, many of them professionals who were trained in their own countries, are concerned about obstacles to the licensing of foreign-educated doctors and nurses. The Vietnamese, who as a group are among the poorest Asians, are far more likely to worry about the political future of food stamps and other welfare programs. Koreans are focused at the moment on relations with the black community, and on ensuring a sympathetic official ear, after numerous flare-ups between Korean shopkeepers in black neighborhoods and their customers.

Moreover, even within particular ethnic groups, there are major differences. Third-generation Chinese and Japanese Americans, for instance, tend to be more politically active than their parents, whose interest in assimilation and acceptance in the business and professional communities often leads them to avoid political involvement.

Class differences are even more telling. In San Francisco, Chinese landlords have very different attitudes toward limits on development and issues such as rent control than do their tenants. Rose Pak, the Chinatown activist, is worried that in the wake of the October 1989 earthquake, which damaged a large number of buildings there, Chinese landlords will simply pass on the costs of retrofitting buildings to their commercial tenants, many of whom are already walking a financial tightrope. The result, she fears, will be the end of Chinatown's historic role as the center of Chinese life in the city.

There are, moreover, what might be considered generational differences of another sort. For years, the Asian businessmen who donated to politicians have been content to settle for mere access in return. As Henry Der, executive director of Chinese for Affirmative Action in San Francisco, explains it, "Among the well-heeled donors, ideology doesn't count, it's whether you can gain access through your contributions. . . . You buy your way into city hall." But these businessmen are losing their clout. The Chinese community now takes in immigrants from Hong Kong, Taiwan and Vietnam, and the Chinese benevolent associations, the business umbrella groups, do not represent many of them. Instead, they are spoken for by private, community-based social service agencies and other grass-roots groups. "It complicates the situation," says L.A. Councilman Woo. "It creates a lot of different opportunities for officeholders [to make contact], but it also means it's more difficult for the community to show unity."

There is, to be sure, a certain strength in diversity. Asian activism in both Democratic and Republican circles means that their issues will be taken seriously by politicians of both parties—a benefit that some black activists argue they have lost by casting their lot so heavily with the Democratic Party. Moreover, the ability of Asian politicians to work with different groups means that on common issues, their network of contacts will be extremely broad. In San Francisco, the city's three most prominent Chinese-American officeholders followed very different routes to office: Supervisor Tom Hsieh's strength lies among moderate and conservative voters and the relatively conservative business community; Julie Tang, on the Community College Board, draws her strength from minority communities and neighborhood groups; Board of Education member Leland Yee won his post with the backing of the city's Democratic power brokers. The potential for allies on Asian issues that might at some point unite Hsieh, Tang and Yee is correspondingly broad.

Even so, when it comes to grass-roots and electoral politics, it is not yet clear how strong Asian Americans will be. Adopting a Pan-Asian outlook is still, by and large, a priority only for Asian-American political elites, the longtime activists and those who fought for or took Asian-American studies programs in college. In immigrant communities, there is still a strong tendency to see politics through idiosyncratic lenses, to dwell on issues that affect Chinese, or Koreans, or Filipinos or Vietnamese, rather than on issues that affect Asians.

And that tendency worries Asian activists. "Until Chinese and Asians can demonstrate that they're a cohesive voting bloc, white politicians can afford to provide token gestures but not substantive measures to empower the Asian community," says Henry Der.

One sign of hope for a broader political outlook among ordinary Asian voters is the ability of individual politicians such as Woo, who is Chinese, and Los Angeles school board member Warren Furutani, who is Japanese, to make common cause with Asian Americans from a broad array of ethnic groups. Furutani owes his power to influence a broad range of school policy issues that concern Asians to the support he gathered from Japanese, Filipinos and Pacific Islanders for his election to the board. Asians do not make up a majority of Woo's council district, but he has used his highly visible post to help organize Asians throughout the city on behalf of issues of interest to Asians of all generations, classes and ethnic origins.

What that suggests is that the route to political success over the next decade will lie in the ability of Asian activists to convince rank-and-file Asian voters to set aside their differences in favor of a Pan-Asian outlook. If they fail, forming even as much as 10 percent of California's population may not mean much. As San Francisco's Dale Minami puts it, "If [immigrant communities] can be sold on the effectiveness of an Asian-Pacific American political concept, then talking about that 10 percent really makes sense. If they can't, then all you have is different groups pushing their own agendas, and that 10 percent dissolves."

Recycling Our Most Prolific By-Product

"Recycling human waste . . . is cheaper, conserves more water, and is more environmentally sound than any other disposal option."

Jodi L. Jacobson

Ms. Jacobson is a researcher at the Worldwatch Institute, Washington, D.C. This article is adapted from their annual report, State of the World.

Victor Hugo was an early supporter of the Clean Water Act. In *Les Miserables,* the 19th-century French author decried water pollution from sewage, observing that "all the human and animal manure which the world loses . . . if returned to the land, instead of being thrown into the sea, would suffice to nourish the world." Recycling newsprint, metals, glass, and the like is once again in vogue. However, recycling municipal sewage wastes is one issue still not discussed in polite company.

Each day, thousands of tons of basic plant nutrients—nitrogen, phosphorus, and potassium—move from countryside to city in the flow of food that sustains urban populations. In turn, society's most ubiquitous refuse, human organic waste, is created. Worldwide, over two-thirds of the nutrients present in human wastes are released to the environment as unreclaimed sewage, often polluting rivers, streams, and lakes. As the energy costs of manufacturing fertilizer rise in tandem with the costs of sewage disposal, the viability of agriculture and, by extension, cities may hinge on how successfully urban areas can recycle this immense volume of nutrients.

The collection of human wastes, known as night soil, for use as fertilizer is a long-standing tradition in some countries, particularly in Asia. Door-to-door handcarts and special vacuum trucks are used to collect night soil from latrines in many of the older neighborhoods of Seoul, South Korea, for recycling to the city's green belt. The World Bank estimates that one-third of China's fertilizer requirements have been pro-

vided by night soil, maintaining soil fertility for centuries.

European cities, equipped with waterborne sewage systems, began fertilizing crops with human wastes in the late 1800's to minimize water pollution and recycle sewage. By 1875, nearly 50 sewage "farms" existed in Britain, some serving major cities such as London and Manchester. By 1910, as many as 43,000 acres in Europe were being fertilized through irrigation with untreated sewage or "wastewater." In the U.S., trends in sewage disposal through farmland irrigation followed. Although only a few sewage "farms" existed in the 1870's, more than 200,000 people were served by sewage irrigation projects by 1904.

These early attempts at nutrient recycling failed for several reasons. The volume of wastes from growing cities soon overwhelmed the capacity of the sewage farms. As cities grew, sites to apply the sewage became ever more distant from the nutrient sources, and untreated human wastes were recognized as a major source of health problems. Strong taboos developed, and the practice was halted, resulting in an open-ended nutrient flow.

Recently, attitudes toward nutrient recycling have come full circle. Higher fertilizer prices, a better understanding of natural resource and ecological constraints, and improved waste management technologies have renewed interest. Such efforts protect scarce urban resources; municipalities that recycle organic wastes simultaneously can save money, land, and fresh water for other uses.

Devising a comprehensive recycling strategy depends on waste composition, collection and treatment, and the resulting disposable byproducts. "Wet" or water-borne sewage systems, common in the U.S., yield raw or treated

solids and wastewater for recycling. "Dry" sanitation systems, predominant in developing regions, rely on night soil as the primary recycling material.

National legislation was first enacted in the U.S. in 1972, but the Clean Water Act in 1977 was the major impetus behind the development of safe methods of sewage resource recovery and recycling. Wastewater is packed with tiny organisms that are voracious consumers of dissolved oxygen. When released in large volume into bodies of water, they become fierce competitors with fish and aquatic plants for limited oxygen supplies. Most Americans can recall the abundance of news stories in the early 1970's mourning the death of oxygen-deprived rivers and lakes around the nation. The Clean Water Act stipulated that cities and towns have to control the quantity and quality of effluents discharged into waterways by "cleaning" wastewater to prevent pollution.

Cleaning Wastewater

Two water-borne sewage treatment methods now are used to achieve this goal. In the first, air, sunlight, and microbial organisms break down wastes, settle solids, and kill pathogens in a series of wastewater ponds or lagoons, allowing the bulk of the nutrients to remain. Because they are inexpensive and land-intensive, lagoons are used primarily in small urban areas or in close proximity to land requiring irrigation, such as farms and public parks. About one-fourth of the municipalities in the U.S. use wastewater lagoons.

The second method uses energy and technology to replicate natural processes. Treatment plants receive large volumes of sewage, which undergo a variety of physical, biological, and chemical-cleansing alterations. This method produces sludge—a substance of mud-like consistency composed mainly of nutrient-rich organic material—and purified wastewater.

Crop irrigation with wastewater treated in lagoons is practiced worldwide because it is rich in nitrogen, phosphorus, and other nutrients and represents a valuable water resource, particularly in arid regions. California issued its first set of regulations governing wastewater irrigation in 1918; these standards, subsequently modified and made more stringent, have become a model for planners and engineers throughout the world.

More than 3,400 wastewater recycling projects now exist in the U.S., reusing water in agricultural, industrial, and recreational areas. In Muskegon, Mich., 10,000,000,000 gallons of wastewater fertilize 450,000 bushels of corn each year, and sales of the corn help defray the costs of the land-treatment facility. In St. Petersburg, Fla., fresh water is relatively scarce, and competing demands for it began outstripping supply in the early 1970's, so the city adopted a wastewater irrigation scheme as an inexpensive method for irrigating golf courses and lawns. In addition to augmenting fresh water supplies, this approach saved money on treatment while reducing the flow of pollutants into Tampa Bay. Other cities, such as Phoenix, Ariz., have adopted similar strategies.

Sewage-fed aquaculture is another way to recycle using wastewater ponds. Here, purification is complemented by cultivating fish on the nutrients in the lagoons. China, India, Thailand, and Vietnam are leaders in this process. Such ponds in Calcutta provide 20 tons of fish per day to city markets.

More than 15,000 sewage plants in the U.S. handled over 26,000,000,000 gallons of wastewater daily in 1985, generating 7,000,000 tons of wastewater sludge annually. The Environmental Protection Agency (EPA) estimated the nutrient content of these wastes was worth over $1,000,000,000 per year and was equal to 10% of the chemicals supplied to American farmers in fertilizers.

Sludge is not usually a complete fertilizer substitute because of variations in nutrient content. Nevertheless, it can provide significant quantities of nitrogen and phosphorus, while offering other agricultural benefits. Sludge is a soil-builder, adding organic bulk, improving soil aeration and water retention, combating erosion, and, as a result, boosting crop yields. Added to soil or used as incremental fertilizer, sludge significantly can reduce a farmer's fertilizer bill.

Land application of treated sewage sludge has grown markedly over the past two decades. Approximately 42% of sludge generated in the U.S. is applied to land; the rest goes to landfills or incinerators or is composted. Western Europe produces over 6,500,000 tons of sludge each year, a figure that is expected to rise five percent annually as more stringent water pollution controls go into effect. Approximately 40% of the sludge produced in Western Europe is used in agriculture.

Collecting and treating water-borne sewage wastes poses a leading claim on urban tax revenues, since up to 50% or more of typical plant operating costs is eaten up by processing and disposing of the leftover sludge. Wyoming, Mich., home of that state's largest land application program, discovered that, while incinerating sludge ran 13 cents per pound, land application cost six cents. Area farms covering over 8,000 acres now are receiving sludge. Rising land values also have made landfilling sludge more expensive. Spokane, Wash., nearly cut in half the city's yearly sludge disposal outlays by switching from landfills to spreading.

The chemical and biological makeup of sludge must be monitored carefully so that potentially harmful elements such as toxic heavy metals don't enter the food chain. The EPA regulates wastewater treatment and various aspects of sludge application on land. Several states have developed their own guidelines, and a few of these are stricter than EPA's. Some sludges can not be applied to crop land, but may be used on grazing land. Others may only be used in forests or disturbed areas.

Of the 1,800 wet tons of sludge generated in Washington, D.C., daily, about 35% is composted; the remainder is land-applied in Maryland and Virginia. The capital's organic riches have been referred to as the "Dom Perignon" of sludge due to the lack of industrial residues. Most of the municipal compost generated in U.S. cities is packaged and sold, generating income that helps pay the bill for waste treatment.

Minimizing Health Hazards

Appropriate technologies and practices for minimizing sewage-related health risks have been adopted widely in industrial countries, but have not been exploited fully in developing countries. Installing Western-style sanitation is a luxury few Third World cities can afford. Approximately 40% of India's 100,000,000 urban households use dry buckets or latrines from which excreta is collected for disposal, only 20% are served by water-borne systems, and the rest have virtually no sanitation.

The lack of adequate organic waste collection and treatment in many Third World cities results in serious health and environmental problems. Raw night soil provides a microscopic blueprint of the intestinal diseases prevalent in a community. Pathogens present in human wastes include hookworm, tapeworm, and the microorganisms that cause typhoid and cholera. Unlike treated wastewater, sludge, or compost, using inadequately treated night soil in agriculture ensures the spread of these pathogens. U.S. Department of Agriculture scientists have devised a composting method capable of killing virtually all virulent microorganisms present in night soil. The technique relies on the same principles as those employed in sludge composting, but uses less energy, is labor-intensive, and results in a product with a higher nutrient content. Most important is the extremely low cost involved.

Adapting such low-technology solutions to night soil management provides an affordable alternative to financially strapped municipalities. Recycling also enhances food security—at least six Chinese cities produce more than 85% of their vegetable supplies by reclaiming nutrients from human wastes and garbage. Nutrient recycling can help Third World cities achieve better health and sanitation, higher food self-sufficiency, and reduced environmental pollution.

As cities grow and become more concentrated and as waste management strategies improve, nutrient recycling is likely to increase in popularity. Recycling human wastes through land application and composting is cheaper, conserves more water, and is more environmentally sound than any other disposal option. American poet and agricultural reformer Wendell Berry has noted that, " . . . like farmers, city dwellers have agricultural responsibilities; to use no more than necessary; to waste nothing; to return organic residues to the soil."

Rethinking Rental Housing:

A Progressive Strategy

**John L. Gilderbloom and
Richard P. Appelbaum**

This article is drawn from the themes of the authors' current book Rethinking Rental Housing *(Philadelphia: Temple University, 1988). Mr. Gilderbloom is an Associate Professor of Urban Policy at the University of Louisville in Kentucky. Mr. Appelbaum is Professor and Chair of the Department of Sociology at the University of California, Santa Barbara.*

Housing the poor is one of the most serious domestic problems facing our country today. A recent national opinion poll found that, next to AIDS, inadequate housing was considered the important domestic problem facing America today. The proportion of income going into rent has reached record levels, with one-half of the nation's renters paying rents that are unaffordable by government standards.

Between 1970 and 1983, median rents tripled, while renters' income barely doubled. Waiting lists for public housing have grown dramatically, forcing over two-thirds of the nation's cities to close off their lists to new applicants. These unfortunate conditions have been instrumental in creating an estimated million or more homeless persons in America—perhaps the greatest shame of the richest nation in the world. We believe that as our nation

moves into the next decade the crisis will only worsen.

Conservatives blame government regulation in the form of planning, zoning and rent control as the major cause of this housing crisis. Yet, the experience of Houston—the much ballyhooed Free Enterprise City—seriously questions this assumption. Houston would appear to be ideal from the viewpoint of housing affordability. The city has an astounding 20 percent rental vacancy rate, little planning, no rent control, and lacks even zoning ordinances.

Yet, Houston nonetheless suffers from a serious housing affordability problem. The reality is that Houston's problems mirror those of rest of the nation: a large homeless population, enormous waiting lists for public housing, half a million low- and moderate-income persons paying more than they can afford for housing, one-fourth of the low income population forced to live in overcrowded housing, and a zero vacancy rate for housing accessible to the disabled.

A recently completed study by the University of Houston's Center for Public Policy found that only 6 percent of qualifying low- and moderate-income people receive any form of governmental housing assistance. Despite this

enormous housing emergency, thousands of rental units are demolished every year.

Houston's wide-open approach to growth and development notwithstanding, Barton Smith, Senior Associate at the Center for Public Policy, has predicted that the problem of high housing costs will worsen in the coming decade, with rents doubling between 1988 and 1992. Clearly, the free enterprise approach Houston has taken has not worked. Nor will it work in other cities.

The truth is that the supposedly private rental housing market is far from free. Constraints exist not only in the form of local interventions (zoning, land-use planning, rent controls, regulations on development, and so forth), but as exogenous interferences as well—the most significant of which include federal interest and tax policies, which are among the worst influences on local housing markets. Yet, the Reagan Administration has modeled its housing policies on the fiction of the existence of free enterprise.

Reagan has made drastic cutbacks in all low-income housing programs, greatly reducing the federal role in providing affordable housing for lower-income families which supposedly shifted responsibility to the private market. In the face of continuously rising rents, housing assistance funds have been slashed by more than two-thirds during the Reagan Administration.

Such deep budget cuts are justified with the assertion that, in reality, no rental housing crisis exists: in the words of The President's Commission on Housing, "Americans today are the best-housed people in history, with affordability problems limited to the poor."

When President Reagan assumed office, the federal government was spending seven times as much on defense as low-income housing; by the time he leaves office, the ratio will have grown to forty-four to one.

Housing assistance has been slashed by 78 percent, while defense spending has increased by 31 percent. Money targeted for Section 8 housing allowance programs has been cut by 82 percent; and the Section 202 loan program for elderly and handicapped housing has been abolished, as has the Section 235 home ownership program.

Although adequate housing is presumably a top priority of the federal government—first enunciated in the 1949 Housing Act as the right to a "decent home and a suitable living environment"—there has never been a federal commitment to assuring such an objective. On the contrary, American housing policy is grounded in traditional economic theory, which has dominated and guided housing policy for both Democratic and Republican administrations for years.

Such theory—which holds that home prices and rents are the straight-forward result of marketplace supply and demand factors—has never been convincingly challenged either from within economics itself or from other disciplines in the social sciences. As a result, public policy

has sought primarily to buttress the private marketplace, rather than directly provide affordable housing to those in need.

Long-term Approach

Our research indicates, for example, that rental housing markets are far from competitive as is assumed, but rather embed significant institutional barriers to simple supply-side responses to changes in demand.

Among these barriers we would include mortgage interest rates whose fluctuations bear no relationship to local supply conditions; tax laws that encourage speculation; significant concentration of ownership and management of apartments; and government housing programs that treat housing not as a community good but as a commodity.

As a consequence, we concluded, policies aimed only at increasing housing supply will not necessarily result in lowered rents or prices. We argue, in fact, that neither the conventional market-driven response (build additional housing) nor its opposite (control rents) are likely, by themselves, to do much towards solving the rental housing crisis. We argue that government cannot rely on the "unregulated marketplace" to supply decent and affordable housing, any more than tenants can rely exclusively on rent controls.

Instead, we believe, a comprehensive national housing policy along the lines pioneered by Sweden is needed to combat the housing crisis. Such a policy would greatly expand the currently miniscule *Third Stream* of existing non-market housing [the other two streams being private ownership and rentals], to serve the increasing numbers of persons whose needs are not being met by the present system.

We offer an Omnibus Housing Program, based on the Institute for Policy Study's "Progressive

Housing Program for America" recently introduced in Congress as the Dellums Housing Bill (H.R. 4727). While the program does propose some regulation of existing rental housing to help secure affordability, it primarily focuses on non-market alternatives.

These include federal, state, and local programs designed to promote the construction, rehabilitation, and conversion of housing to non-market forms (e.g., community-owned housing, public housing, and tenant-owned equity-controlled cooperatives). Under the Program, virtually all federal housing funds would be directed towards the Third-Stream, non-market sector. Funding would be by means of direct federal grants, thereby ending reliance on volatile and costly private credit markets.

Reforms of national credit and tax policies are also proposed which would make the federal role both more effective and efficient, while discouraging the speculative practices that presently help fuel housing inflation.

Short-term Initiatives

As we move into the 1990s, affordable housing will become a critical national issue. At the local level there are a number of short-term programmatic responses that can be made, assuming that the comprehensive approach previously discussed is not likely to be enacted in the immediate future.

For example, a significant portion of existing community development block grants (or, alternatively, a newly funded program of housing block grants) should be designated for the exclusive funding of nonprofit housing. This approach is already seen in Congressman Joseph Kennedy's "Community Housing Partnership Act" (H.R. 3891), which calls for $500 million to subsidize low-income housing efforts on the part

"As we move into the 1990s, affordable housing will become a critical national issue. At the local level there are a number of programmatic responses that can be made . . ."

of community development corporations and other nonprofits.

Given the presently limited capacity of the nonprofit sector, a portion of funding should be directed towards providing them with training and other forms of technical support.

Elderly & Disabled

Block grants should also be used to create and fund an Independent Housing Service, which would be charged with providing technical assistance to builders who wish to construct or convert housing for use by the elderly and disabled. The Service would provide assistance in the placement, design, and financing of housing for disadvantaged populations.

Such assistance would include, for example, free architectural consultation to landlords and developers interested in modifying units for the disabled. In addition, the Service would also provide grants or loans to cover the costs of constructing a barrier-free living environment. To make sure that these units remain affordable, rents and sales prices would be strictly controlled.

Finally, the Service could also serve as an advocate for the disabled community. Local planning should be directed at providing affordable and barrier-free housing environments, with all new multifamily housing units required to afford ground floor accessibility to wheel chair users.

The cost of designing such units is minimal—a few hundred dollars, compared to the thousands of dollars it takes to modify an existing unit. All new housing developments should provide sidewalks with curb cuts, timed lights and bus shelters.

Large housing developments should also be required to have a certain number of units that are accessible. All cooperative and urban homesteading programs should set aside at least 15 percent of the units for persons with disabling conditions.

Limited Equity Cooperatives

Cooperatives with resale restrictions offer a useful example of attractive multifamily community-based housing, since they provide many of the guarantees ordinarily associated with home ownership. Such cooperatives are customarily operated through a democratically run, non-profit corporation which holds a single mortgage on the property.

Under a typical arrangement, each new owner purchases a share for a minimal down payment (for example, 10 percent of the value of the unit). Monthly payments then include each owner's portion of the common mortgage, plus a fee for maintenance and operating expenses.

When an owner wishes to move, he or she sells the share back to the cooperative, which then is resold to a new owner. Since the whole process takes place within the cooperative corporation, no new financing or real estate fees are ever involved.

Such cooperatives are termed *limited equity* both because the member's equity is limited to his or her share rather than the value of the unit itself, and because the appreciation in the value of that share is limited by common agreement to a low level. Cooperative members cannot sell their shares for what the market will bear.

In this way the sales price of

units falls below the market price for comparable housing. While a typical home or condominium is sold and refinanced at ever-inflating prices many times over its life span, a limited equity cooperative is never sold.

The original mortgage is retained until it is fully paid off, at which time the monthly payments of the owners decrease to the amount necessary to operate and maintain the units. The principal difference between cooperative and private ownership is that within cooperatives, owners may change many times without the cooperative itself ever changing owners.

Owners share the full rights and privileges of private owners, including the tax benefits which are not available to tenants in rental housing. Ownership rests in the hands of residents, public agencies, or community organizations.

In all instances, management would be structured to promote resident involvement and encourage resident control over the use of space.

Numerous countries (Canada, Sweden, Finland, France, and Italy) have enacted programs to create cooperative housing. These actions have contributed to substantial decreases in the percentage of income paid into housing. The development of a sizeable cooperative housing sector could result in significant increases in affordable low- and moderate-income housing.

It would also result in greater control over the existing housing environment on the part of low-income residents, contributing to the "pride of place" often experienced by home owners. Ronald

"Local planning should be directed at providing affordable and barrier-free housing environments . . . the cost of designing such units is minimal—a few hundred dollars . . ."

Lawson's survey of tenants in low-income housing cooperatives in New York City indicates that their level of satisfaction was quite high. ("Owners of Last Resort: An Assessment of the Track Record of New York City's Early Low Income Cooperative Conversions," New York City Department of Housing Preservation and Development.)

Tenants were almost unanimous in viewing their cooperative arrangements as preferable to—and less expensive than—rental housing. Many claimed that they were offered a sense of control that they had not previously known.

Many were saved from displacement by being afforded the opportunity to live in affordable cooperative units.

Tenants scored well, collectively, on basic indicators of effective management; experienced low vacancy rates and below-average turnover rates; and generally gave their cooperatives good marks on services provided. Moreover, the tenants stated overwhelmingly that they preferred cooperative living to private rental housing.

Writing in the JOURNAL OF HOUSING in 1981, (Volume 38, Number 7, *"Housing cooperatives: a viable means of home ownership for low-income families,"* page 392) Scott B. Franklin has summarized the benefits of cooperatives as follows:

• protection against rising costs;
• home ownership;
• tax advantages;
• community of interest: a sense of "we-ness" and less crime;
• lower maintenance costs;
• less turnover;

• protection against eviction;
• equity accrual; and,
• control and selection of incoming owners.

The drawbacks, on the other hand, says Franklin, include:
• owner default;
• difficulty in financing; and,
• restricted sovereignty.

The significant cost savings of cooperatives can be even greater when self-help rehabilitation is involved, with residents providing "sweat equity" in the rehabilitation of abandoned or foreclosed units. Sweat equity generally involves exerting physical labor to rehabilitate the housing unit, which can range from replacing or repairing major structural elements of the house to improving the plumbing, heating, electricity, and other necessities.

Homesteading

When self-help rehabilitation is done the cost of bringing multi-family housing up to code can be 50 percent of the cost of conventional rehabilitation by private developers. Churches, poverty organizations, and nonprofits serving disadvantaged groups can sponsor non-profit housing development and rehabilitation. Abandoned and dilapidated units could be renovated by these organizations.

New York and Boston have been able to revitalize many declining neighborhoods by developing innovative homesteading programs. These programs result in greater housing opportunities for disadvantaged persons, an increase in tax revenue, more jobs, and the renewal of neighborhoods.

A state wide receivership program could be coupled with such programs, under which landlords who repeatedly refuse to fix code violations can be forced by the courts to cede rents for needed repairs (and, under certain circumstances, ownership of the unit as well).

Housing receivership programs have worked well in New Jersey. Poor neighborhoods could be dramatically turned around with the adoption of a large scale homesteading and receivership program.

Conclusion

The private market alone cannot provide affordable housing for all citizens—especially for the disabled, elderly and poor. The conservative approach, based on encouraging free enterprise, has proven a failure in reaching those most in need.

On the other hand, the traditional liberal strategy of providing massive tax breaks and subsidies for builders and landlords has proven to be costly, inefficient, and largely ineffective as well.

New and bold measures, we believe, must be used to combat the housing crisis. We call for a new urban populist housing program where residents are empowered to develop their own solutions for the housing crisis. We believe that our Third-Stream housing program would go a long way towards providing decent and affordable housing in a humane and efficient fashion. Our program emphasizes local control, the benefits of ownership, and pride in community.

Paul Goodman wrote in *Growing Up Absurd* that "a man has only one life and if during it he has no great environment, no community, he has been irreparably robbed of a human right." Cities are judged great, not by the number of monumental buildings or people within their borders, but by their ability to provide justice and civility.

How well does the average American city address the needs of its citizens—whether they are rich or poor, black or white, old or young, abled or disabled? Great cities are measured by the kinds of employment, housing, educational, aesthetic, and spiritual opportunities they afford their residents. All urbanites should live with dignity and without fear.

Great cities provide for all and exclude no one. By these standards—how many American cities would today be judged as great?

NONPROFIT HOUSING

LOCAL SUCCESS STORIES

WILL HUD'S KEMP SIGN ON?

PETER DREIER

Peter Dreier has written widely on housing policy issues. His articles have appeared in the New York Times, *the* New Republic, *the* Boston Globe, *and other publications.*

backyard revolution has been taking place in inner cities and rural areas of the United States: nonprofit and community-based groups have been building and renovating affordable housing on a scale much broader than in the past. Since the late 1800s, settlement houses, labor unions, and wealthy philanthropists have built apartment houses and cooperatives for working-class families. But in the 1980s, the nonprofit housing movement has burgeoned in response to federal housing cutbacks, the withdrawal of for-profit developers from the subsidized housing business, and a deepening shortage of affordable housing in communities across the country.

Since 1981, federal housing funds have been slashed from over $30 billion to under $8 billion. New funding for public housing run by local government agencies has been virtually eliminated. When the Reagan administration ended subsidy programs for new apartment construction, most private developers stopped building low-income housing. Not surprisingly, the number of new low-income apartments has declined—from over 200,000 a year during the 1970s to less than 15,000 in 1988.

According to a just-completed survey by the Washington, D.C.-based National Congress for Community Economic Development, however, some 2,000 nonprofit builders—with ties to community organizations, churches, tenant groups, social service agencies, and unions—have tried to fill the vacuum. In lieu of federal monies, they have had to patch together resources from local and state governments, private foundations, businesses, and charities.

Raymond Flynn, the mayor of Boston, has called the emergence of socially-committed developers alongside church and community groups "the only silver lining in the dark cloud of the housing crisis during the Reagan years." Over twenty-five nonprofit groups have built thousands of housing units in Boston during the last several years. At the Boston Housing

Partnership (BHP), for example, the chairmen of the city's largest banks and insurance companies sit on the board with city and state government officials and the directors of community-based nonprofit groups. Through the BHP, the city and state government provide subsidies to builders. So far, ten Boston-based corporations have invested over $16 million in projects undertaken by neighborhood-based community development corporations (CDC). These CDCs own and manage over 1,600 low-income apartments in the city.

The bricklayers union in Boston pressured the bank that holds its pension fund to lend, at reduced rates, start-up monies needed to form a nonprofit housing group. In two years, the group has built more than two hundred brick, Victorian-style townhouses in three neighborhoods. Over a thousand working-class families applied for the homes, which were sold at the cost of construction, about half their market value.

Private foundations have also played a key role in supporting the nonprofit housing sector. A few years ago, Boston's United Way began funding community development corporations, an experience so successful that the United Way of America began to fund similar projects in Houston, Chicago, Pontiac, Michigan, Rochester, and York, Pennsylvania.

In 1980, the Ford Foundation created the Local Initiatives Support Corporation (LISC) to channel corporate funds to nonprofits. LISC-supported nonprofit groups in twenty-six cities have produced over 14,000 units for low- and moderate-income residents.

Developer James Rouse, who built the new town of Columbia, Maryland and whose urban festival marketplaces (e.g., Baltimore's Inner Harbor and Boston's Faneuil Hall) contributed to the nation's inner city revival, has set up the Enterprise Foundation. Enterprise has provided financial and technical help (on construction techniques, for example) to over a hundred low-income groups in some twenty-seven communities, leading to more than 3,000 new homes.

Corporate America has increasingly recognized that nonprofits are an effective way to provide housing that is affordable for their low-wage employees. Business leaders in Cleveland, New York, Chicago, Baltimore, Boston, and other cities have joined with government officials and community housing ac-

Building with a conscience

While nonprofit housing ventures have particular problems and limitations, they also have strengths that deserve to be recognized. "Nonprofit groups are responsive to community needs," says Sarah Smith, president of the Denver-based McAuley Housing Foundation, a group sponsored by the Sisters of Mercy. "They're in a good position to involve local residents." Since 1980, the McAuley Foundation has helped community groups in rural areas and small towns (in Colorado, Idaho, and New Mexico) to build and repair 600 low-income housing units.

Richard D. Driscoll, head of the Bank of New England and Boston Housing Partnership chairman, has said that nonprofits "are a part of the neighborhood and a part of its daily life. They're aware of what matters after the rent is paid"—issues such as crime, job training. child care, and building maintenance.

Most nonprofits in housing have started by fixing up a small building or two. For example:

● In Dallas, the Common Ground Community Development Corporation has, since 1982, rehabilitated for low-income families fifty inner-city homes that had been slated to be bulldozed.

● In the troubled manufacturing city of York, Pennsylvania, a long-term neighborhood social service agency set up the Crispus Attucks Community Development Corporation in 1983. With financial help from local businesses, foundations, and the city government, the group has fixed up twenty-six apartments, primarily for working poor families.

Some nonprofits have been able to expand their work significantly:

● The Catholic Archdiocese of Minneapolis/St. Paul has established twenty-four nonprofit groups that manage over 2,200 apartments for poor families, seniors, and handicapped persons. The groups link residents with medical services, child care, and other support programs as well.

● In the wealthy community of Santa Barbara, California, where the average home sold last year for over $275,000, the nonprofit Community Housing Corporation has constructed 462 units—including single-family houses, garden-style apartments and condominiums, limited equity cooperatives, and a rooming house hotel—for the city's low-income families and elderly residents.

A few nonprofits are sophisticated builders with a social conscience, who have—often through foundations—constructed multimillion-dollar developments.　　　P.D.

---

tivists to form public-private-community partnerships. Some of San Francisco's top business leaders sit on the board of the nonprofit Bridge Housing Corporation, which has built over 3,000 units in mixed-income developments in the Bay Area.

Even with these allies however, the bootstrap approach has its limits. Subsidy funds—required to fill the gap between what working-class families can afford and what housing costs to build and operate—are scarce. Meanwhile, waiting lists for any kind of affordable housing are bulging. Even the most penny-pinching nonprofit groups acknowledge that the federal government will have to resume a major role if their local success stories are to expand enough to help relieve the national housing crisis.

Many members of Congress, who went along with the housing cutbacks proposed by the administration during the eighties, were disenchanted with previous big-budget subsidy programs they viewed as expensive give-aways to politically-connected developers or to mismanaged local housing authorities.

While most public housing is well-managed, urban "high-rise ghettos" have hurt the overall image of public housing. As Professor Dennis Keating of Cleveland State University has said, "Subsidizing profit-oriented developers to house the poor…didn't work. They often take the money and run—with the tenants left behind in mismanaged projects and the taxpayers footing the bill. In contrast, nonprofit groups are more accountable to the residents and the surrounding community; they're not carpetbaggers. And they tend to spend public funds more wisely and cost-effectively—to make the housing work.…"

Today, some housing experts see nonprofit groups as a helpful middle-ground between government-owned public housing and government-subsidized for-profit developers. Congress may finally be willing to put the federal government back in the housing business, if nonprofits play a significant role. Last year, when Representative Joseph Kennedy (D-Mass.) filed the Community Housing Partnership Act—to provide federal funding to community-based housing groups—he quickly found over 100 cosponsors. If passed, the bill would provide three federal dollars for every dollar nonprofits can raise from local public and private sources.

"On its own, this $500 million program is not an immediate solution to the national housing crisis," explained Kennedy. "But it provides a vehicle for steady growth in the nonprofit sector's capacity, so that within a few years it can have a major impact."

With the growing epidemic of homelessness among the poor and the decline of home ownership among the middle class, the Bush administration will be looking for new approaches to the nation's housing woes. Perhaps newly confirmed HUD Secretary Jack Kemp, a conservative former Congressman from Buffalo, will expand the nonprofit approach as part of his overall housing program. To an administration that emphasizes self-help, entrepreneurship, and grassroots initiative, the nonprofit approach could have a decidedly Republican appeal.

A housing program that really works

Bankers hate it, but an anti-redlining law helps the poor and costs little

Imagine an ideal government initiative: One that helps lower-income Americans own their own homes but does not breed welfare dependency, does not expand bureaucracies or budget deficits and does not hurt business or the economy. Such a policy actually exists. It is called the Community Reinvestment Act (CRA). Passed in 1977, CRA says banks have an "affirmative obligation" to lend in lower-income neighborhoods, though there are no firm lending quotas set in the statute and regulators must determine for themselves what is reasonable. In the places where it has been seriously applied and enforced, it has worked with surprising effectiveness. Though by no means a complete solution to the low-income housing crisis, CRA has helped neighborhoods turn around and thousands of lower-income people discover homeownership, the main vehicle by which American families expand their wealth.

The law was ignored or undermined by key officials for years, but that could be changing. Housing Secretary Jack Kemp seems sympathetic to the law, and the Federal Reserve Board, long resistant to tough CRA enforcement, is showing signs of a new willingness to crack down on noncooperative lenders. Last week, the Fed rejected the application of Continental Bank Corporation to purchase a tiny Arizona bank on the ground that Continental had a poor track record lending to lower-income customers. The problem for CRA, though, is that banks still hate the law, and it is not clear that the apparently invigorated Fed policy will spread to other bank regulators at the Federal Deposit Insurance Corporation, the Federal Home Loan Bank Board and at the Office of the Comptroller of the Currency.

Newfound safety. The beneficiaries of CRA include people like Irene Wells. The 44-year-old nurse used to live in a North Philadelphia public-housing project where the elevator seldom worked. So she would come home from her night shift at a nursing home and trudge up 17 flights of dark and filthy stairs to her $86-a-month apartment. "I was afraid to go home sometimes," she says. Today Wells and her mother own their own modest row house, purchased with the help of a community group called ACORN and a $17,000 CRA mortgage from Fidelity Bank of Philadelphia. Wells feels safer in

Black and white disparities

10 metro areas with the highest ratio of black-to-white loan rejections

	Black rejection rate	White rejection rate	Black-white rejection ratio
1. Milwaukee	24.2%	6.2%	3.90:1
2. Pittsburgh	31.2%	8.2%	3.80:1
3. Cleveland	31.4%	8.4%	3.74:1
4. Chicago	27.6%	7.6%	3.63:1
5. Detroit	32.5%	9.1%	3.57:1
6. Norfolk–Virginia Beach–Newport News	26.5%	7.7%	3.44:1
7. Charlotte–Gastonia, N.C.–Rock Hill, S.C.	26.1%	8.0%	3.26:1
8. Indianapolis	27.9%	8.7%	3.21:1
9. Baltimore	24.2%	7.6%	3.18:1
10. Memphis–Ark.–Miss.	22.2%	7.3%	3.04:1
U.S. average	23.7%	11.1%	2.14:1

USN&WR—Basic data: *Atlanta Journal and Constitution*, from Federal Home Loan Bank Board data

her new home, and she and her mother happily pay the $159-a-month mortgage.

The law had its genesis in a raging controversy in the 1960s and 1970s over redlining, the unwillingness of some banks and thrifts to make loans in lower-income minority neighborhoods. Though CRA has stopped blatant redlining, discriminatory lending patterns have not disappeared. The *Atlanta Journal and Constitution* reported last month that a study of 10 million mortgage applications showed that even at similar income levels blacks are rejected strikingly more often than whites when they apply for home loans.

With federal regulators long unwilling to put their muscle behind CRA, community groups have taken up the fight themselves. The law lets them challenge the applications that banks must submit to federal regulators for permission to expand their operations. Thanks to such challenges, the amount of capital banks set aside for lower-income lending has grown from about $185 million in 1984 to over $1.229 billion last year.

Bank lending under CRA itself cannot bring back many blighted neighborhoods. But those loans have helped stretch ever scarcer housing subsidies, and, prodded by the law, bankers have uncovered profitable opportunities in places they had previously written off. In the summer of

1987, black activist Willie Lomax and white bank president Robert Teresko found themselves in a shouting match in the lobby of Teresko's Beverly Bank, on Chicago's South Side. The bank wanted to build a branch in the suburbs. Lomax's community group, the Chicago Roseland Coalition for Community Control (CRCCC), wanted more loans made in the nearby black neighborhood of Roseland, where the bank draws many depositors. "We were in front of the customers," Lomax recalls with a chuckle, "and he was yelling, 'Why are you giving me a rough time?' and 'I don't appreciate this!' "

No job, no loan. Eventually, Lomax and Teresko signed a CRA agreement setting aside $20 million (10 percent of the bank's assets) for community lending and allowing the bank to build its suburban branch. CRCCC and other Chicago nonprofits help administer the program, and loans made so far are doing fine. "We're very pleased with the relationship," says Teresko. "It's good for business and for our visibility." The effort, says Lomax, is "not welfare, not a giveaway. If somebody doesn't have a job, they can't get a loan. This is good, clean business practice."

For all the good CRA agreements have done, bankers still generally resent being pressed into them. Privately, they point out that nonprofit groups are not immune to corruption and hidden agendas. Yet CRA has avoided scandals, in part because banks can often pick the group with whom they will work. Some of their outrage has also subsided a bit as bankers have found their CRA loans making a small profit, or at least breaking even. CRA loans have high paperwork costs, but their default rate appears to be as good as or better than that of conventional loans. And community organizers argue that they would not have to bring protests if federal bank regulators would enforce the CRA law as Congress intended.

Government and private studies have repeatedly found that regulators give enforcement of CRA and other consumer-protection laws low priority, while auditors who concentrated on consumer issues were found to have limited potential for career advancement. Moreover, the agencies avoid using CRA's full authority to crack down on uncooperative banks and thrifts. Regulators have received over 40,000 expansion applications since 1978. They denied only nine, including the Continental application, on the grounds that the banks practiced discriminatory lending. The regulators say they prefer behind-the-scenes pressure to outright penalties, but another explanation for this permissive record is grade inflation. Every year, 97 percent to 99 percent of banks receive passing marks on their CRA examinations. "Regulators seem to think that we're all living in Lake Wobegon," remarked former Senator William Proxmire (D-Wis.), CRA's chief sponsor last year. "Like the children of the fictional village, U.S. lenders are all above average."

Community groups want the grading system stiffened and the grades made public. Regulators such as FDIC Chairman L. William Seidman claim public disclosure would be "counterproductive" and would risk causing public panic—a run on badly rated banks. Evidence suggests, however, that disclosing CRA ratings does not nec-

Black and white similarities

10 metro areas with the closest ratio of black-to-white loan rejections

	Black rejection rate	White rejection rate	Black-white rejection ratio
1. Portland, Oreg.	17.5%	15.2%	1.15:1
2. Anaheim-Santa Ana, Calif.	23.3%	16.7%	1.40:1
3. Middlesex-Somerset-Hunterdon, N.J.	21.9%	14.9%	1.47:1
4. Nassau-Suffolk, N.Y.	14.5%	9.0%	1.61:1
5. Riverside-San Bernardino, Calif.	27.4%	16.7%	1.64:1
6. Miami-Hialeah	28.6%	17.3%	1.65:1
7. Salt Lake City-Ogden	16.3%	9.7%	1.68:1
8. Oakland	23.2%	13.6%	1.71:1
9. San Diego	36.0%	21.0%	1.71:1
10. Bergen-Passaic, N.J.	11.0%	6.4%	1.72:1
U.S. average	23.7%	11.1%	2.14:1

USN&WR—Basic data: Atlanta Journal and Constitution, from Federal Home Loan Bank Board data

essarily threaten bank safety. Last spring, publication of a "less than satisfactory" rating (the bottom 2 percent of all banks) for Comerica Bank-Detroit prompted Michigan authorities to insist that Com-

erica develop a detailed CRA lending plan with community groups as a condition of approving a proposed acquisition. Other Detroit lenders soon followed suit, and there was no bank run.

An ambitious attempt to fix the problems with CRA died in Congress last fall and could be revived and passed in this session, especially if Kemp backs reform. In an interview last week, he strongly rebuked banks for discriminatory lending and said he would like to end the practice by beefing up CRA enforcement and by making thrift institutions that get federal bailouts invest in depressed areas. But he will have to convince President Bush and others in the administration that this is the right approach. Bush is philosophically against regulation, but he is also squeezed between the need for low-income housing and the massive budget deficits. As he feels more pressure, CRA could begin to look better to him.

Paul Glastris with Scott Minerbrook
in Philadelphia

CITIES SEEK ALTERNATIVES TO THE BULLDOZER

Dilapidated houses attract vandals and drug dealers.

Rob Gurwitt

If phenomena of nature can be said to have their counterparts in public policy, then cities around the country are faced with a dilemma in urban biology: How do you keep one bad apple from ruining the rest?

The matter has taken on some urgency in an era when one abandoned or dilapidated house can attract drug traffic or vandals, dragging the rest of the neighborhood down with it. And while some cities still rely simply on knocking down the offending structure, others are finding new approaches.

That was the case in Los Angeles earlier this year, after a small outcry attended the revelation that, despite a severe housing shortage, the city was demolishing abandoned buildings that had deteriorated or were being used as drug hangouts.

Although the mayor's office responded that the only houses going under the bulldozer's blade were so badly gone that nothing else could be done, the city council this spring approved Councilman Zev Yaroslavsky's bill earmarking $2 million for non-profit agencies to identify negligent homeowners and offer them low-interest loans to fix their properties up. If an offer is rejected, the agencies are to try to buy the property, fix it up and sell it to low-income buyers. There are no provisions should the owner refuse to sell.

Other cities are taking a harder line with owners who refuse to respond to housing code citations. They are going to court to appoint a receiver who is empowered to oversee repairs and force the owner to pay for them. Pioneered in New York, it is a tack that has been used for years in Illinois, Ohio and a few other states, but just recently has moved west.

About a year ago, Oregon became the first Western state to allow its cities to go the receivership route. And earlier this year, California also permitted its cities to begin appointing receivers. California's new law— like Illinois' version—allows tenants and neighbors of deteriorating buildings to petition the courts directly to appoint a receiver, without having to rely on the city to initiate action.

Some cities are taking even more aggressive approaches. Louisville, Kentucky, for instance, has set up a Vacant Property Review Commission, which, rather than using the city's eminent domain authority only when it's linked to official neighborhood revitalization plans, can identify individual problem properties for action. "It's like a surgical use of eminent domain powers," says Jim Allen, director of the city's Department of Housing and Urban Development.

The city also had a problem attracting buyers for seized properties with heavy back taxes owing on them. So it has set up a Land Bank Authority made up of officials from the four taxing jurisdictions involved— the state, the county, the city and the school board. In essence, the Land Bank takes over a property and, as the owner, wipes the taxes off the books, then sells the property to a new owner or gives it to a non-profit agency.

For its part, Seattle is trying to avoid the problem altogether. Recently, the city put together a computer formula using such factors as age, number of units, type of construction and history of violations to predict which apartment buildings with three or more units were most likely to have serious code violations. This summer, the city began to inspect the 2,100 dwellings targeted by the program, in the hopes that it will be able to catch buildings in danger of deteriorating before the process goes too far.

The old system of relying on tenants to call code violations to the city's attention didn't work, says Joe Garcia, Seattle's director of housing and zoning enforcement. "It was like being in a hospital emergency room—many of the buildings we got to were very far into the deterioration process," he says. "Now we can take a more proactive role."

Urban Futures

The future of urban communities will have a serious impact on the population of the entire world and therefore is a continuing concern of social scientists. The unplanned growth of the urban community so characteristic of the past will most certainly promote ecological disaster. Therefore, it is essential that serious planning for the future take place. Good plans are developed out of clearly stated goals and objectives. In recent years, however, a debate over these goals and objectives has begun.

Ironically, the study of the future has a long history. Philosophers and writers, for example, have already designed utopian communities or described the new world that they envision. In the past 20 years, they have been joined by social scientists, engineers, architects, and others from the physical sciences in an attempt to visualize new ways of intervention to better control the quality of life in urban areas.

The scientific study of human behavior is based upon the assumption that most behavior is both patterned and structured. This allows the social scientist to predict, after thorough study, behaviors that are likely to occur. Among social scientists, there is little or no argument that urbanization will continue to be an important aspect of societies around the world and that the demand for change and adaptation will increase. There is also agreement that problems will emerge out of the urbanization process and an effort should be made to develop policies to solve these problems.

The last section begins with the article by Roger Kemp on "Cities in the Year 2000," in which he maintains that innovative thinking is required if cities hope to optimize their human and financial resources. John Fondersmith contends that the "city of the future" will differ markedly from past or current designs, and that it is mirrored in the present revival of America's downtown areas and the penchant for relatively simple innovations. The next article explores the vision of Paolo Soleri, the Italian-born architect whose planned city of the future, Arcosanti, remains essentially stalled after nearly two decades. The following selection discusses the efforts of two progressive communities—Hartford, Connecticut, and Berkeley, California—to assist the urban disadvantaged. William Whyte maintains that, all too often, urban planners have ignored the fundamental needs of people, often disregarding the need for

human interaction and assuming that bigger is better. An article by Isaiah Poole on the strengths and weaknesses of the enterprise zone concept follows. Kalman Toth reports that in the twenty-first century machine intelligence will replace most workers, and will bring with it ease and abundance. Next, Laurence Rutter urges state and local governments to adopt a philosophy of "skeptical federalism," and to develop strategies that will promote increased autonomy and institutional flexibility. In conclusion, Rafael Salas contends that the world is evolving into an urban planet. This, argues Salas, poses myriad opportunities and challenges, among them housing, education, and health care.

Looking Ahead: Challenge Questions

How will the forces of change by the year 2000 influence the types of public services that will be provided, the ways they will be financed, and the extent to which they will serve the needs of people?

What can be done, if anything, to revitalize America's downtown areas? Is it possible to attract new business and industry to the central cities?

What explains the failure, at least at this point, of Paolo Soleri's planned city of the future? It is likely to become anything more than one man's unfulfilled fantasy?

Can government solve the problems of the cities? Why or why not?

What principles should govern the design of cities? Is small necessarily better?

Why have architect Le Corbusier's urban design schemes come under such fierce attack? Are these criticisms justified?

What explains congressional opposition to the enterprise zone concept and its reluctance to enact major tax incentives?

Will the development of machine intelligence necessarily produce greater leisure and abundance? If so, how will it affect the fabric of urban life?

To what extent will the states shape the local future? What role will the federal government play?

Why is demographic balance critical to the attainment of social justice and economic progress? Is it likely to be more or less difficult as the world becomes transformed into an urban planet?

Unit 5

Cities in the Year 2000

THE FORCES OF CHANGE

Unprecedented changes taking place in American cities have made it necessary to replace traditional planning and management practices with new strategic-planning techniques.

Roger L. Kemp

Roger L. Kemp is president of the Center for Strategic Planning and an adjunct professor at the Graduate Department of Public Administration at Rutgers University. He has been a chief executive officer of cities on both the West and East coasts for over a decade. His address is P.O. Box 1101, Clifton, New Jersey 07014-1101.

Dynamic changes now under way will have a dramatic impact on the politics and management of American cities. Gone are the simple and stable days for local governments when revenues were plentiful and public officials could merely adjust tax rates to balance budgets, and when public programs were unquestioningly increased in response to citizen demands for more services. The many changes taking place in our society have made it necessary to reevaluate the scale and mix of public services, as well as how they are financed.

The way that public officials adapt to this changing environment will reflect on their ability to cope successfully with the future. Public officials are typically preoccupied with the present and are usually reactive to change. Changes are coming so rapidly that the traditional planning and management practices of merely projecting past trends into the future are becoming obsolete.

The magnitude and momentum of these changes will have a direct influence on the types of public service that will be provided in the future, how they are financed, and the extent to which they fit the needs of the citizens being served. By actively planning for the future, elected and appointed officials can create a smooth transition into the future. If this does not occur, citizen demands for greater government responsiveness and change will grow dramatically throughout the nation.

The five major categories of changes affecting municipalities are: emerging political trends, major demographic shifts, evolving urban patterns, rapid technological changes, and new economic factors.

Emerging Political Trends

● More state and federal laws and court decisions will usurp the home-rule powers of local elected officials and serve to limit their discretion in many areas.

● While special-interest groups typically pursue their own narrow goals, such groups will increasingly form coalitions around major community issues of mutual interest.

● Many of the political issues brought about by limited revenues — such as the pros and cons of service reductions, or user fees and charges — will elicit no clear-cut response from citizens.

● Citizens will demand more services but also will insist that taxes are not increased, making it more difficult for public officials to set program priorities and balance their annual budgets.

● Public officials will stress economic development as a vehicle to raise revenues without increasing taxes. Highly urbanized cities will have to resort to redevelopment for their financial survival.

● Responsibility will continue to shift from the federal and state governments to cities, leaving city governments to solve their own problems. Because of the mismatch between revenues and problems, cities with low tax bases may have to resort to service reductions.

● More minority-group representatives, including immigrants, will get involved in the political arena.

● Any new federal grants will be limited to those programs that help achieve national goals, such as affordable housing, lower unemployment, and shelters for the homeless.

Major Demographic Shifts

● A growing number of senior citizens will become more politically active because of their available time.

● A greater number of smaller households will require more high-density residential developments, such as condominiums, townhouses, and apartments, placing greater demands on existing public services.

● There will be more women in the work force, and they will become more politically active in the workplace. Issues such as comparable worth and sexual harassment will increase in importance.

● The growing number of minorities and immigrants will create new demands for specialized public services and more bilingual public employees.

From The Futurist, September/October 1990, pp. 13-15. The Futurist, published by the World Future Society, 4916 Saint Elmo Avenue, Bethesda, Maryland 20814. Reprinted with permission.

Evolving Urban Patterns

- Urban sprawl will increase but will be primarily located along major vehicle transportation corridors and public mass-transit routes.
- Cities will witness greater "infill" development in already urbanized areas. Land areas that were once marginal will be purchased and upgraded for new development.
- Older land uses, such as outdated industrial plants and commercial centers, will be upgraded and/or retrofitted with new amenities to make them more marketable.
- In central-city areas, continuing high land values will lead to increased gentrification, further exacerbating the need for affordable housing for low- to moderate-income citizens.
- New ethnic centers will evolve in metropolitan areas. Residents will stress maintaining the cultural traditions, values, and customs of their homelands. Public services will be tailored to better represent these growing urban minority and ethnic population centers.
- Higher energy costs and greater traffic congestion will create more political pressure for public mass-transit systems. Emphasis will be placed on multimodal systems that offer greater transportation options to the public.

Rapid Technological Changes

- More public meetings will be aired on public-access cable-television stations. These stations will also be used to educate citizens on available services and key issues facing their community.
- Computer-management systems will become a common technique to monitor and limit energy consumption in public buildings and grounds.
- Advanced telecommunication systems, such as systems with conference calling and facsimile transmission capabilities, will reduce the number of business meetings and related personnel and travel costs and will allow city government officials to better communicate with their peers across the country.
- Increased public pressure for mass transit, coupled with greater

Characteristics of Traditional vs. Strategic Planning in the Public and Nonprofit Sector

TRADITIONAL PLANNING	STRATEGIC PLANNING
Short-Range	Long-Range
Single Issues	Multiple Issues
Organizational Issues	Community Issues
Hierarchical	Non-Hierarchical
Low Involvement	High Involvement
Directive-Based	Consensus-Based
Staff Oriented	Community Oriented
Management Orientation	Political Orientation
Staff Awareness	Community Awareness
Operational Focus	Policy Focus

construction costs, will lead to more-efficient mass-transit systems in densely populated high-traffic areas. Light-rail systems will replace the expensive underground subways of the past.

New Economic Factors

- Rising energy costs will require the greater use of energy-conservation techniques.
- Citizens will increasingly demand higher standards and accountability for air and water quality, especially in densely populated urban areas.
- Taxpayers, while averse to new taxes, will increasingly acknowledge that it is the legitimate role of government to provide "safety net" services to citizens (i.e., essential sustenance to the truly needy).
- Limited new government revenues will be earmarked for those public services and programs with the highest payoff — from both a political and productive standpoint.
- The availability of federally funded grant programs will be limited, and greater competition will exist among cities for these funds. They will be earmarked for those cities with large low-income populations and related social and housing problems.
- The public will continue to advocate for the "controlled growth" of government by opposing increased taxation and the growth of

user fees and charges. They will demand greater accountability and productivity for existing services.

New Models for Planning

Too often, government planning has been reactive, short range, staff oriented, dominated by single issues, hierarchical, and generally lacking in community support. New thinking is needed in times of fewer grant programs, complex and inter-related issues, rising expectations regarding services, and public aversion to increased taxation to enable cities to optimize their human and financial resources.

The private sector has made long-range strategic planning a common practice over the past few decades. Unlike traditional planning, strategic planning is proactive, long range, and community oriented. Additionally, it involves multiple issues, is non-hierarchical in nature, and helps achieve a public consensus on the issues and problems facing a municipality.

It is imperative that public officials provide a strategic vision for their community. A shared understanding of issues and goals not only provides a vision of the future, but also helps mobilize all available resources to effectively manage change. It is only through such modern planning practices that public confidence in government can be restored and local governments can successfully adapt to the future.

Making Downtown Cities Fun! Downtown 2040

The "city of the future" will bear little resemblance to the science-fiction images from the past. Rather, cities will increasingly build on their own unique characteristics, as represented by their historic downtown areas.

John Fondersmith

John Fondersmith is chief of the Downtown Section of the Washington, D.C., Office of Planning. He is also editor and publisher of *American Urban Guidenotes: The Newsletter of Guidebooks* (P.O. Box 186, Washington, D.C. 20044).

The opinions expressed in this article are his own and do not necessarily reflect the views of the District of Columbia government.

What will America's "downtowns" be like in the year 2000? The answer to that question is not too difficult, since many public and private projects that are in the planning stage will be completed sometime in the 1990s. Almost all cities have downtown plans extending to the year 2000 or beyond. But a longer-term look of 40 to 50 years requires us to think about the state of the downtowns of major American cities in about the year 2040.

We are talking about the downtowns of approximately 60 to 80 major American cities that have a significant scale of activities concentrated in that center. Many smaller cities also have impressive downtown revitalization programs, but the scale and the competition with new outlying centers may have different results.

Many of these downtowns went through a great period of growth during the first three decades of this century. They began to feel the enormous impact of the automobile. After more-gradual change during the Depression and World War II periods, decay accelerated in downtowns during the 1950s. The period of rapid suburban expansion began. By the late 1960s, most downtowns reached their low points. Then a series of new ideas led to a major revival of almost all downtown areas of major American cities. Interestingly, the forces shaping the recent revival have not been primarily technological in nature. Instead, they have been basically simple ideas.

Downtown Office Employment

Office development has been the real "driver" of downtown development over the past 30 years and will continue to be the single most important factor in the future, even though retail and cultural activities may receive more attention. In the 1950s and 1960s, some pundits were forecasting the withering away of downtown office employment, with workers decentralized to workplaces in their homes and outlying sites.

There has been, of course, major office development in the suburbs, but downtowns have also seen an office boom. A 1984 survey of 33 large U.S. downtowns by the Urban Investment and Development Company found that approximately 58 million square feet of office space was built in the 1950s, 132 million square feet in the 1960s, 196 million square feet in the 1970s, and 218 million square feet completed or under construction from 1980 to 1984. That boom continued for several more years, though some cities are having a slow period while demand catches up with supply.

The past decades have seen the redesign of the office workplace, major changes in office routines and technology, and changes in the office work force. Change will be even more dramatic in the future. Continued advances in telecommunications and a shorter workweek will likely mean that employees will work in the downtown office several days a week and work from home or other locations on other days. Office areas will increasingly provide day-care centers, gyms, and training centers. In the ongoing effort to attract office construction, cities will stress the amenities of downtown and will improve transportation access.

The skylines of American cities have been transformed in the last

From *The Futurist*, March/April 1988, pp. 9-17. *The Futurist*, published by the World Future Society, 4916 Saint Elmo Avenue, Bethesda, Maryland 20814. Reprinted with permission.

30 years, primarily by office towers. While technological advances will theoretically allow taller and taller buildings, economic and social considerations will limit the number of super skyscrapers. More attention will be given to the "ground floor" of downtown areas.

After several decades of bland metal and glass boxes, today's tall office buildings are again assuming more ornamental and sculptural forms. San Francisco has pioneered urban-design requirements to achieve less boxy forms for new buildings, and other cities are following this lead. We are likely to see more-coordinated efforts to design dramatic skylines, including new uses of light at night to create dramatic effects.

Of course, by the early twenty-first century, many skyscrapers of the mid–twentieth century will have outlived their economic life. Those that cannot be economically renovated will have to come down in large-scale demolition actions.

Downtown Is Fun

A number of approaches have been taken to attract more people downtown — to work, to learn, to shop, to play.

● **The "festival marketplace."** The "big idea" of recent years has been the "festival marketplace." Of course, cities have always had markets and some specialized retail areas. The concept of recycling old buildings into a complex of shops and restaurants on a major scale was first done in the mid-1960s in Ghirardelli Square and the Cannery in San Francisco. However, it was James Rouse who fully conceptualized and implemented the festival-marketplace concept with the development of Faneuil Hall Marketplace in Boston in 1976.

Other festival marketplaces and retail complexes already developed include Harborplace in Baltimore, the South Street Seaport in New York City, the Union Station project in St. Louis, The Waterside in Norfolk, Portside in Toledo, the 6th Street Marketplace in Richmond, and the Old Post Office in Washington, D.C. Almost every large city now has or is developing a marketplace.

> **"The nurturing of this new spirit of fun and vitality at the core of cities has been a major factor in the resurgence of the American downtown in the past decade."**

While hugely successful as retail centers, the festival marketplaces have had a much more important role in creating new civic gathering places and in dramatically changing the image of American cities. A 1981 *Time* magazine cover story on James Rouse declared, "Cities Are Fun!" — a statement almost unthinkable in the atmosphere of the 1960s. The nurturing of this new spirit of fun and vitality at the core of cities has been a major factor in the resurgence of the American downtown in the past decade.

The success of the festival marketplace has spurred new interest in downtown retailing, which had been dormant or declining in most cities since the 1960s. Today, major retail complexes have been completed or are under construction in many cities, including development of new department stores. In many cases, the retail complexes connect existing stores. The Rouse Company has also been a pioneer in this movement, with The Gallery in Philadelphia, Grand Avenue Concourse in Milwaukee, The Shops in Washington, and the new Gallery at Harborplace in Baltimore.

In many developments, the festival marketplace and the major retail complex have come together. Horton Plaza in San Diego, a colorful collection of new and old buildings with new department stores, shops, and restaurants, represents a new generation of downtown retail development.

Major new retail complexes will be developed in downtowns over the next 40 to 50 years, and existing retail centers will be renovated and restructured. The challenge facing city planners and developers is to devise the new mix of activities to attract the customers of the future. This new mix will combine retailing with the educational, cultural, and entertainment assets of downtowns.

● **Historic preservation and urban design.** Preservation of historic buildings has been another "big idea" and a major force in the development of downtowns over the past two decades. This is quite a contrast to the science-fiction visions of all new downtowns outlined in the 1939 World's Fair and in writings and drawings of that period. Historic preservation has helped provide a new alternative vision of the future downtown. Thousands of buildings of all types have been recycled in one form or another in downtown areas across the country. Historic districts have been established in downtowns and adjacent areas.

Although preservation vs. development conflicts continue in many cities, the role of recycled older buildings is increasingly recognized as a plus factor for downtowns compared with outlying suburban commercial centers. These buildings and historic areas provide a sense of place and history that new outlying centers cannot match.

Historic preservation will probably become relatively less important in the years ahead. By the year 2000, almost all nineteenth and early twentieth century buildings will have been recycled, sometimes more than once, or will have been demolished. Of course, as time passes, our idea of what is "historic" will evolve also. In a few years, some surviving bland 1950s buildings may even have a new appeal.

We are now in a period of "postmodern" architecture, in which architects and their clients are rediscovering ornament, color, and urban-design values. The public is much more ready to accept replace-

BOSTON EDISON

• • • • • • • • • • • •

Old State House in Boston will be renovated for energy-efficiency. The historic buildings of downtowns will take on new importance as "cities of the future" enhance their individual characters.

ment of old buildings of no particular merit if the new buildings are of quality design. The present concern with old buildings and areas will continue to evolve into a broader concern with the quality of the overall urban environment.

• **Open spaces.** The past 25 years have been a great period for development of new parks, plazas, and open spaces in American downtowns. Every major downtown has constructed numerous open spaces, often including pools, fountains, and outdoor sculpture. A number of great city avenues have also been rebuilt, including Pennsylvania Avenue in Washington, D.C., and Market Street in San Francisco. The success of these efforts will spur additional large-scale streetscape efforts in the future.

One of the most dramatic changes in the future will be trees. Trees and more trees! Cities will undertake major downtown forestry programs, with thousands of new trees planted along streets and in parks. A permanent urban-forestry corps will maintain them.

Not only will such a program yield aesthetic dividends, but the trees will also provide shade and help cool urban temperatures.

• **Waterfront development.** Many major cities are located on rivers, lakes, or bays. Although these waterways are generally less important for industrial and shipping purposes than they once were, they are increasingly important as urban amenities. Water has a special fascination for people, making water resources attractive focal points for new development. In most American cities, the waterfront is adjacent to or near downtowns, and almost every city with a waterfront resource has undertaken some kind of waterfront-enhancement program. Baltimore's Inner Harbor, with Harborplace, a magnificent aquarium, and growing mixed-use development of ad-

jacent areas, is one of the nation's most impressive waterfronts. Battery Park City in New York City is a magnificent new development stretching along the Hudson River. And San Antonio's unique Paseo del Rio (Riverwalk) has become the focus of that city's downtown.

Some cities blocked their waterfronts with elevated highways and inappropriate development in the 1950s and 1960s. Today, cities such as San Francisco, Boston, and Hartford have plans to eliminate or relocate early expressways in order to reconnect downtown to the waterfront. By the year 2000, virtually all waterfront cities will have reclaimed much of their downtown waterfronts for public access and mixed-use development, and such development will continue into the twenty-first century.

• **Cultural centers.** In the future, cities will seek to develop and expand a range of cultural and entertainment facilities in downtowns to provide learning experiences that are fun. Arts, education, and entertainment activities will be increasingly important in the downtown of the future, and these activities will be increasingly intertwined.

Cities have intensified efforts over the past 20 years to retain or build new cultural facilities downtown. Major performing-arts centers have been built in Los Angeles, Houston, Denver, St. Paul, and a number of other major cities. Classic old music halls and movie palaces have been renovated for performing-arts use in many cities, including Pittsburgh, Cleveland, Richmond, Cincinnati, and Milwaukee.

Today, there is a new wave of "arts districts" under development. Perhaps the most extensive such district is being created in Dallas. A new art museum opened in 1985, and construction began in 1986 for a new symphony hall. This all-new arts district is to include restaurants, shops, and small theaters, as well as new office development. Washington, D.C., has outlined a Downtown Arts District and is developing local arts activities between the National Portrait Gallery/National Museum of American Art at Gallery Place and

●●●

"Arts, education, and entertainment activities will be increasingly important in the downtown of the future, and these activities will be increasingly intertwined."

●●●

the National Gallery of Art and Smithsonian museums on the Mall. Boston is developing an arts district between Boston Common and the "Downtown Crossing" retail area, utilizing existing theaters and new development.

Downtown revitalization in many cities includes community colleges and universities. But "education" is increasingly seen in a wider context, in attractions that combine education and entertainment. Children's museums and science museums are especially popular. Elaborate planetariums and IMAX theaters attract visitors for fun and learning. Both Boston and Baltimore have built exciting downtown aquariums that are research centers and major visitor attractions. A recent *New York Times* article indicated that at least 22 cities were planning to expand or build new aquariums. Future museums will include elaborate simulation centers that will allow visitors to participate in a number of imaginary but very realistic experiences.

Visiting Downtown

All cities today make a special effort to attract visitors for a variety of purposes (e.g., business, conventions, and tourism). Visitors mean increased tax revenues, jobs, and business development. The past two decades have seen a wave of hotel construction. New hotels have been a major factor in the image of revitalized downtowns.

Another trend has been the renovation of classic old hotels that date back to the early twentieth and late nineteenth centuries. The beautifully renovated Willard Inter-Continental Hotel in Washington, D.C. (built 1901, closed 1968, reopened 1986), is the latest of many grand old downtown hotels to be rescued from oblivion.

Many visitors to downtown will just be looking for a room for the night, but the need for more moderately priced hotels is increasingly difficult to meet because of high land costs in some cities. In the future, cities will undertake special programs to encourage low-cost accommodations. Many hotels are now offering special low weekend rates. As metropolitan areas grow larger, the "special weekend" in the downtown hotel will become more of an attraction for many suburban residents. And increased nationwide hostel programs will provide travel accommodations for young people who want to see American cities.

City travel has been spurred by a substantial increase in conventions, trade shows, and meetings. To encourage such business, every major city has developed new, or expanded existing, convention and meeting centers over the past two decades. The promise of visitor business will mean continuing programs to increase the size and sophistication of convention facilities and to develop new visitor attractions in downtowns.

Surprisingly, with all the emphasis on attracting new visitors, American cities do an awful job at

The Willard Inter-Continental Hotel in downtown Washington, D.C., built at the turn of the century is one of many grand old downtown hotels to be restored in recent years.

WILLARD INTER-CONTINENTAL

providing background information about the city. Visitors and city residents alike are lucky to find a few brochures and a flashy but simplistic slide show. Over the next 20 years, cities will increasingly develop innovative orientation and city-history centers. New video techniques will enable the history of the city, and its projected future, to be shown in realistic detail.

Downtown Living

In the rush to revitalize American downtowns over the past three decades, residential development has received much discussion but limited action. In most cities, the residential population in downtown and adjacent areas has declined. Some adjacent areas in a number of cities have been improved through the "gentrification" process, though sometimes with displacement problems. Some cities have managed to improve or retain center-city neighborhoods, such as Rittenhouse Square and Society Hill in Philadelphia, Beacon Hill in Boston, and Dupont Circle and Capitol Hill in Washington.

Adjacent residential areas are crucial to a lively, animated downtown. It is not that in-town populations alone provide the labor market for downtown. Customers and employees must be attracted from a wide area. But downtown residents provide the essential difference in the downtown life — a sense of community. If the downtown and adjacent residential populations are large enough, the walking-to-work and transit-use patterns of these populations can result in significant transportation and environmental advantages.

The development of downtown housing is one of the most important items on the agenda of cities today. A number of cities, led by San Francisco, are developing various forms of "linkage," which essentially means requiring some direct or indirect support of housing in return for approval of office development.

These trends will strengthen in the coming decades. By the early twenty-first century, most American cities will have significantly increased the downtown and near-

"**Fast and effective metropolitan transportation is critical for the continued vitality of downtowns.**"

downtown residential population. The increased population will also require neighborhood retail services, recreation facilities, improved security, and even new schools.

Transportation to Downtown

Fast and effective metropolitan transportation is critical for the continued vitality of downtowns. Providing access becomes more complex as metropolitan areas spread outward in all directions. The usual image of futuristic city travel is of a rapid rail system, rushing commuters to downtown stations. However, only 10 American cities have some form of "heavy" rail transit system. Los Angeles has begun construction of a rail system. A number of other cities, including Dallas, Houston, and Denver, are considering building major new rail systems.

Over the next 40 years, the existing major rail systems will be improved and extended. Major new rail systems of futuristic design will probably be built in another five to 10 cities, assuming a renewed national commitment to using transit for shaping urban growth.

A number of American cities have turned to light-rail systems, using modern, updated versions of the streetcar. These new systems usually include reserved rights-of-way. New light-rail systems have been built in Buffalo, Portland, Sacramento, and San Diego and are being considered in a number of other cities. The few cities that have retained some type of early streetcar systems are making improvements. Pittsburgh is an example. Over the next 50 years, specialized light-rail systems will proliferate, probably being used in close to half of the major American cities.

However, the most popular public transit is and will continue to be by bus. Improvements in bus de-

sign have not been matched by advances in busway development. Although many cities have some form of bus lanes, including some special express-bus lanes on freeways, no city has yet constructed a complete system of modern busways where buses can travel on their own reserved lanes in congested areas. The most extensive new busway in North America has recently opened in Ottawa.

Major progress has been made in the city centers, where a number of cities have constructed transit malls to bring buses on exclusive lanes into the center of the city. Portland and Denver are especially noteworthy. Over the next 50 years, bus design will continue to improve, and more cities will develop improved systems of busways to rush commuters to the downtown area.

Major access to most downtowns will continue to be by automobile, so highways and parking improvements will continue to be important. Most American downtowns are defined by a full or partial freeway ring, almost all built in the past 30 years. In many instances, freeway design was insensitive, creating a wall effect and cutting linkages to adjacent areas. Many cities will redesign and rebuild these surrounding freeways over the next 50 years. In some cases, new boulevards around downtown will be emphasized, such as the new Martin Luther King Boulevard in Baltimore.

New parking garages on the edge of downtown and underground will continue to be built as part of new mixed-use complexes. Cities will continue to try to group parking facilities so that automobiles can move from the surrounding freeways into parking facilities.

The increased use of computers in automobiles will lead to systems

OLD TOWN TROLLEY TOURS, WASHINGTON, D.C.

Trolleys — minibuses designed to look like old streetcars — are increasingly being used in many downtown areas.

that will allow automobiles to be guided by remote control on "electronic highways." Whether the benefits of such systems prove cost-effective on a large scale remains to be seen. But freeways and urban arteries will increasingly be "smart highways," with access and movement controlled by traffic lights and gates tied to central computers. Drivers approaching downtown will receive information on traffic flow and parking availability on digital display screens in each car. Coordinated traffic and parking management and enforcement programs will become even more important.

One of the most dramatic "low-tech" transportation innovations in recent years has been the growing use of van pools, and that trend will continue.

Movement in Downtowns

Within downtown, walking will continue to be the most important mode of transportation. Over the past 30 years, American cities have developed a whole series of new pedestrian-movement systems. These include second-level walkways, most prevalent in Minneapolis, St. Paul, and Cincinnati, and underground walkways, as in Houston, Oklahoma City, Chicago, and Philadelphia. Many cities have extensive ground-level pedestrian areas, although no city has gone to the all-pedestrian center envisioned in the 1956 Fort Worth Plan. Many cities have a combination of underground, surface, and second-level pedestrian links. In the next 50 years, downtowns will work to increase the ease of pedestrian movement and the attractiveness of the pedestrian environment.

Buses and rail-transit systems also provide movement within downtown areas. Ironically, the most popular new movement system in downtown in recent years

has been the trolley — actually, minibuses designed to look like late-nineteenth-century streetcars. Such "trolleys" are now operating in some form in almost all major downtowns. In the future, such trolleys and other mini-vehicles will be formed into coordinated systems of movement in the downtown core and adjacent areas.

Transit planners have long envisioned the use of "personal rapid transit" (PRT) — small vehicles operating under remote control on their own separate guideways. Such systems have been described as "horizontal elevators" or "people movers." In the late 1970s, some PRT enthusiasts envisioned large-scale PRT systems extending throughout metropolitan areas. So far, such systems have been used primarily on a small scale in amusement parks, airports, and some suburban office complexes. The first true urban people mover opened in Miami in April 1986 — a 1.9-mile loop through downtown. Named the Metromover, the system connects with the Metrorail system. A 2.9-mile people-mover system opened in Detroit in July 1987.

Over the next 50 years, people-mover systems will be built in a number of American downtowns, forming a partial or full loop around the downtown and providing access to nearby activity centers, such as medical complexes. However, the limitations of the concept seem to preclude the large-scale use of people movers that was predicted just a few years ago. "Low-tech" uses of existing transportation systems, such as taxicabs, rental cars, and bicycles, will become more important in future transportation planning.

All these movement systems within downtowns — light rail, people movers, and buses — will increasingly be designed for entertainment and educational purposes as well as for movement.

Building Better Downtowns

Downtown improvement does not happen by accident. It takes planning, vision, coordination and cooperation, and millions of dollars of public and private investment.

Many mayors have made downtown revitalization a key part of their programs. In Washington, D.C., Mayor Marion Barry, Jr., has made creation of a "Living Downtown" a high priority. In Baltimore, former Mayor William Donald Schaefer achieved a national reputation as a result of the success of the Inner Harbor project and related new development. Most major cities have created some type of public–private partnership organization to guide downtown revitalization.

"Nothing could be more of a mistake than to create downtowns across the country that look the same."

The mechanics of downtown revitalization are increasingly institutionalized through organizations such as the Urban Land Institute, the International Downtown Association, the American Planning Association, the National Trust for Historic Preservation, and the American Institute of Architects. Through publications, conferences, and site visits, new innovations in downtown development spread rapidly.

Downtowns are not islands unto themselves. They cannot long prosper if the surrounding areas and the larger society have serious economic and social problems that are not resolved. Problems of unemployment, the homeless, the underclass, crime, and drugs must be attacked on a larger scale.

In design, use, and management, America's major downtowns are becoming "theme centers" that provide special functions for city and suburban residents and out-of-town visitors. Though office employment and retail will remain the major functions of downtown, it seems clear that the role as a city symbol, as a gathering place, and as a special attraction is what sets downtown apart from outlying areas.

Each downtown should strive to develop its own design, urbanity, and special character, building on the historic physical design and special concepts for the regional base. Nothing could be more of a mistake than to create downtowns across the country that look the same.

The real "cities of the future" already exist. Even as metropolitan areas expand, the downtown areas of America's great cities are evolving and taking on new functions. The resurgence of America's major downtowns is an important national event, providing focal points and symbols for the activities of major metropolitan areas in the twenty-first century.

Downtown in Small Towns

Like their big-city counterparts, small towns have a stake in the vitality of downtown — perhaps an even bigger stake, since even a minor change in the environment is apt to be more conspicuous to the community as a whole.

One organization devoted to helping small towns sort through the complex issues affecting their futures is Small Towns Institute, based in Ellensburg, Washington. The Institute's bimonthly magazine, *Small Town,* has recently covered such topics as participatory planning and historic preservation as part of a comprehensive development strategy.

Small towns need to take a hard look at the long-term aspects of attractive new development proposals, says Kenneth D. Munsell, director of the Institute and editor of *Small Town.*

"In today's climate of intense competition, . . . local leaders are often urged to welcome any new business or industry well before they develop an understanding of the secondary effects the newcomer will have on the town," says Munsell. "In the long run, it is possible for any new business or industry to harm a community, so it is vitally important for residents to become aware of the kinds of pitfalls that can befall 'successful' economic development."

For example, a large retail chain may wish to establish a franchise in a small town. While such a move may create jobs, profits from the franchise would be sent out to shareholders who live far away and have no ties to the town. "Franchise fees, supplies, and payment for services may all suck money out of town and into some large city far in the distance," Munsell points out. And if a new business does not offer some unique good or service not already available in the town, it will not increase total sales in the area but only "redivide the pie."

Most importantly, says Munsell, a "new business should care about the welfare of the overall community and show a willingness to help others. . . . The costs incurred from recruiting selfish, uncaring entities will ultimately outweigh any temporary gains in employment."

Source: Small Towns Institute, P.O. Box 517, Ellensburg, Washington 98926.

Planned City of Future Still Unfinished

Chris Kelley

Knight-Ridder

CORDES JUNCTION, Ariz.—Twenty years after breaking ground on his experimental city in the Arizona desert, Paolo Soleri strolls Arcosanti in thongs, cradling a note pad and a dour mood.

It's nearly dusk, and Soleri, a shy, wiry man of 71, is wary of talk about Arcosanti—his effort to transform 860 acres of desert rock and scrub brush about 70 miles north of Phoenix into a model city of tomorrow.

After two decades, Arcosanti, in fact, remains more of a fantasy.

"Has your vision of Arcosanti changed in 20 years?" he is asked.

"I envision," he corrects the questioner. "I am not a visionary."

"I am not for this," he says, politely putting up his hand to deflect further inquiries. He recommends one of his books for his detailed thoughts.

Soleri, the maverick Italian-born architect, artist, ecologist, philosopher and businessman, is tired of explaining his prototype application of "arcology" on this patch of the planet.

Arcology, the term he coined for the peaceful blending of architecture and ecology, is a quest he defines as: "A radical reorganization of the sprawling urban landscape into dense, integrated, three-dimensional towns and cities . . . in order to give individuals a new perspective and renewed trust in society and the future. The city is a necessary instrument for the evolution of the human spirit."

Soleri has designed dozens of arcologies since he came to the United States in 1946 as a student of Frank Lloyd Wright. In one plan, he envisions a one-square-mile city that would house one million people.

He theorizes that the compact, hivelike structures will, by necessity, re-

place our modern urban sprawls—and the need for automobiles. Eventually, he believes, arcologies will house human colonies in space.

Arcosanti, which he began building in 1970, is the first of his arcologies to emerge from the drawing board into actual construction. The name Arcosanti comes from architecture and the Italian words for "before things."

It is a $400 million project that, upon completion, would condense all the life of a city of 5,000 residents into one immense 15-acre development, leaving most of the surrounding desert untouched.

Arcosanti is to be self-sufficient, solar-powered and ecologically balanced; it wouldn't have automobiles, just moving sidewalks and escalators to shuttle residents to and from places only minutes apart.

Industry and housing would rise 25 stories, coexisting in harmony. Greenhouses would provide food. Recycling would not be an option but a lifestyle.

From nearby Interstate 17, Arcosanti is a curious sight, protruding from the edge of a mesa like a huge, sculpted concrete treehouse and livable Lego set.

Accessible from the highway by a winding, three-mile, rutted dirt road, the development overlooks a small canyon carpeted in green by the Agua Fria River.

But 20 years after it was started, the "urban laboratory"—as Soleri likes to call it—is only 4 percent complete, financed mainly by tourists and the production of popular windbells that carry the Soleri name.

A permanent population of 45 live at Arcosanti, operating the bell foundry, a five-story visitors' center and cafe-bak-

ery and serving as designer-builders on small construction projects.

About 50,000 tourists a year pay $4 each to trod Arcosanti and much more to buy Soleri bells, which cost from $13 to $15,000.

"Bells are our bread and butter, steel and concrete, olive trees and seminars," said Debra Giannini, an aide to Soleri.

Since 1988, Arcosanti has also hosted an annual "Minds for History" conference featuring scientists, philosophers and other thinkers—such as feminist Betty Friedan, jazz pianist Billy Taylor and Nobel Prize laureate and poet Czeslaw Milosz.

Soleri divides his time between Arcosanti and Cosanti, the nonprofit foundation in Scottsdale that he and his late wife, Colly, founded in 1962.

A complex man, he is the author of such books as *The Omega Seed: An Eschatological Hypothesis* and *The Bridge Between Matter and Spirit is Matter Becoming Spirit.*

Critics have questioned the usefulness of his work, particularly the arcologies, whose design calls for thousands to live, work and be entertained in closed quarters—the antithesis of life as many Americans know it.

Paul Goldberger, architecture critic of *The New York Times,* said of Soleri: "His architecture hovers between the magical and the totalitarian; his scientific ideas are a cross between Buckminster Fuller and Buck Rogers; his philosophical musings read like Khalil Gibran rewritten by Gertrude Stein . . ."

"What exists of Arcosanti today is not beautiful," Arizona architecture critic Lawrence Cheek has written in Arizona Highways magazine. "The concrete structures . . . do not flow gracefully

From *Durham Morning Herald,* December 2, 1990, pp. G1, G2. Reprinted by permission of Knight-Ridder Newspapers.

from the land; they are imposed on it with surprising brutality. The vote here on this enormously controversial undertaking is that it will make one heck of a ruin."

Soleri deflects the criticism as short-sighted pabulum. But he does not hide his disappointment at Arcosanti's slow progress, which he attributes to America's self-centered, conspicuous-consumption culture.

"If I had known it was going to be this hard, I would have been crazy to get into it," he has said. "But I was blessed with ignorance."

Soleri devotees dismiss the comments as the frustration of a gifted man.

"He says that, but his heart is still very much in it," said Mary Hoadley, a former anthropology student who has been at Arcosanti for 20 years and now is its general manager.

"The longing has been that some angel would drop in and say, 'I like what you're doing, here's all the money you need. Go build it,' " she said. "This place is just quivering with potential."

Much of Arcosanti has been built by a rotating band of volunteers who have paid for the pleasure. In the early 1970s, hundreds of Soleri acolytes shelled out $500 (now $560) for five-week workshops during which they built part of the city of the future.

In all, some 3,500 participants have come and gone.

The goal now is to achieve "critical mass," a city of 500 that would, among other things, include a 200-bed hotel, a 27-unit apartment building and Pizza Piazza, a large apse-shaped structure incorporating greenhouses, ceramic studios and a crafts foundry.

About $55 million will be pumped into Arcosanti by the year 2000.

Still, Arcosanti's greatest contribution may be the sheer inspiration it provides, project supporters say.

"Arcosanti has been infinitely fertile in stimulating ideas about cities, about urban architecture and ecology," said John P. Allen, who is directing the Biosphere II project in Oracle, Ariz., about 30 miles north of Tucson. He was a participant at Arcosanti's most recent "Minds for History" seminar.

Latin America often looks to the United States for models, and Pizarro said he hopes Arcosanti will be one that his country adopts.

Running the City for the People

Eve Bach, Nicholas R. Carbone, and Pierre Clavel

EVE BACH is special assistant to the City Manager, Berkeley, Calif. NICHOLAS R. CARBONE is at the Hartford Policy Center. Pierre CLAVEL is professor of city and regional planning, Cornell University. This article is adapted from "Progressive Planning: A Report from Berkeley and Hartford," Working Papers in Planning 51, Cornell University.

Urban renewal, the federal highway program, Model Cities, community action, and later programs developed in the last decade came into existence under an umbrella of planning, and they each demanded, and provided support for, planning staffs. But even as these programs have been eclipsed by fiscal restraint, a new kind of planning has emerged in several cities. In the face of fiscal cutbacks, these cities pioneered redistributive policies while other cities cut back services ever more severely.* Berkeley, Calif., and Hartford, Conn., are striking examples of planning and implementation under progressive majorities. Their planning, more than most, expressly focused on the interests of relatively disadvantaged groups, on challenging

---

*For example, Cleveland elected populist Mayor Dennis Kucinich and for two years experienced a number of progressive administrative initiatives—many of them based on earlier advocacy in the City Planning Department. Madison, Wisc., Burlington, Vt., and Santa Monica, Calif., are other cases in point.

the agendas of elite-oriented planning, and on institutional innovation carefully adapted to local circumstances.

HARTFORD AND BERKELEY

Progressive planning developed in different ways in each place. In Hartford, there had been competent and vigorous staff work since at least the mid-1960s, but the major growth in planning came after 1969 as a new coalition of neighborhood activists and liberals gained seats in the city council. By the early 1970s this group had gained effective political leadership of the city and began making key administrative appointments. From the beginning, they were conscious of their neighborhood constituency and the desperate economic and fiscal obstacles to survival as a community. Hartford was a major insurance, banking, and government center, but its population was primarily poor white ethnics, Blacks, and Puerto Ricans who provided 43 percent of Connecticut's welfare caseload. A Brookings Institution study found the economic disparity between the city and its suburbs to be the third worst in the nation. In these circumstances the council majority led by Nicholas Carbone vowed a policy of advocacy on behalf of the have-nots, and argued the legitimacy of using all the resources of local government in pursuit of that policy. They were to develop and implement this policy through the decade, until their defeat at the polls in 1979.

In Berkeley, the progressives for many years had minority representation in the city council, prior to moving into a leadership role in 1979. This began with the election of Ron Dellums—now Berkeley's U.S. Congressman—in 1967. The progressives used their minority position to advocate the use of public capital for cooperative housing, economic development, and community-based energy and social-service programs. They designed these programs in the 1970s as city resources were expanding, and capital accumulation could take place at the margin of growth. In April 1979 the citizens of Berkeley elected five progressive city officials: the Mayor—Gus Newport; three council members—Florence MacDonald, Veronika Fukson, and John Denton; and the City Auditor—Anna Rabkin. The three council members plus the Mayor comprised a near majority in the nine-person council because they had the frequent support of a then-unaffiliated member, Carol Davis. In 1979 this group set about implementing some of the programs that had been part of progressive platforms for over a decade. This period of progressive influence lasted two years. The 1981 election was swept by more conservative candidates who have regained control of the city council.

Intense planning over a long period of time marked both the Hartford and Berkeley groups. This planning was marked by a commitment to redistribution, which distinguished the Hartford and Berkeley progressive leadership from the "liberal" ideals that prevailed in a great many other cities with equally impoverished constituencies. The Hartford and Berkeley leadership aimed to serve the poor quite openly and publicly. The result was that they did quite a lot of open, synthetic, public, and progressive planning.

In Hartford, starting from a general position of advocacy for the have-nots, the city council moved through a series of analyses to detail its strategy. There had been a Plan of Action prepared by a "Committee of 100," and a two-year Model Cities planning process that involved a lot of neighborhood interaction. The studies impressed the council with both the extent of the economic depression facing city residents and the extent to which these economic problems were a distributional issue between city and suburbs.

Hartford had lost over 10,000 manufacturing jobs. Of the existing work force of 134,000 people at the beginning of the 1970s, only 34,000 were city residents. Of the 98,000 jobs in eight surrounding towns, only 18,000 were held by city residents. Hartford had the highest percentage of the unemployment, over 50 percent of the work force in some neighborhoods. The city's population was marginal in terms of income. It was a population that needed subsidy for housing, for health, for recreation. They had inadequate income; any they might have went to pay for basic essentials: food, clothing, and shelter. An analysis by the Council on Municipal Performance clarified these inadequacies for the city council. Comparing 1970 population census figures to the Bureau of Labor Statistics' deprivation level showed that the incomes of 61 percent of the population of 158,000 were substandard by an average of $1,528 per year. There was no way the city could find the tax revenues to make up that difference.

From this analysis, the council developed two major strategies. One was to reduce the cost of living within the city through a series of innovative public-service systems such as energy conservation and a community food system. The second strategy was to increase incomes. The key to this end was a land use and transportation strategy that included litigation

to block suburban industrial development and highways and mass transportation policies that would encourage suburban development at the expense of the city, as well as a set of positive development plans.

These latter plans evolved along with council action, and were elaborated piece by piece as they were needed. There was no one published document that could be pointed to as the "Hartford Plan." But public statements were frequent, and in early 1976 the council formally adopted a series of policy papers, which, with succeeding documents, boiled down the underlying themes into three:

1. To increase jobs and income for unemployed and underemployed Hartford residents.
2. To improve the fiscal health of the city of Hartford.
3. To revitalize Hartford's neighborhoods.

These ideas, with their implicit and explicit redistributive implications, were dramatized by the Hartford leadership. Most spectacular was a suit, brought by the city against HUD and six suburban towns, to stop the distribution of Community Development Block Grants because those towns had not filed adequate low-income-housing plans. The suit was successful in that it provided a context for negotiation between city and suburbs on other issues, and allowed the council to make public its case for Hartford's redistributive claims: on welfare, federal highway funds, suburban affirmative action, and others, in addition to housing.

In Berkeley, progressive forces operated from a minority position from 1967 until their council victories of 1979. During that period, Berkeley Citizen's Action (BCA) and similar coalitions that preceded it produced a succession of separate programs operating from outside the central control points of city government. BCA was able to pressure a reluctant council to support some of its programs, such as the Savo Island Housing Cooperative. In addition, the city made rapid affirmative-action gains during this period due to a significant degree to the aggressive demands of the progressive minority on the council.

During the decade of minority participation in city government, BCA also successfully used the initiative

process to change city policies and practices. BCA placed before the voters initiatives that established a civilian police review commission, controls over housing demolition, inclusionary requirements for low- and moderate-income housing in new housing developments, strengthened citizen participation on city boards and commissions, and rent control.

Public statements of overall strategy emerged from this experience in opposition—most notably a book, *The Cities' Wealth*, by E. Bach, et al., published in 1976—which combined discussion of tactics with substantive policy and programs. The authors included tactics that they saw as

examples of structural, or nonreformist, reform, extending the actual or potential realm of people's power. We have tried to avoid techniques for conventional political shifts, where one group with similar goals nudges out another for position at the top, but the structure remains intact.

They interpreted the goals of the progressive coalitions as

efforts to improve the economic position of the city's many renters and small homeowners . . . support for free social services to the underserved poor, the transient, the young, the disabled and elderly . . . for affirmative-action programs for ethnic minorities and women, and other programs to rectify past injustices . . . [and] concern with a long list of environmental problems, from industrial pollution to waste recycling.

They saw cities as offering a vehicle to effect these goals. At the time, their main emphasis was on the city as a source of capital: they had the power to tax, own property, annex territory, borrow capital, and own and operate productive enterprises, in addition to being subject, at least formally, to popular control. This combination of redistributive goals, the drive toward institutionalizing popular control, and the notion of using the city as a vehicle for capital formation characterized the list of proposals that followed. These included rent control; a scheme for neighborhood land-use control; cooperative housing; public ownership and control of electric power, telephones,

> **A general principle behind much of the Hartford innovation was that of substituting local organization for expensive bureaucratic and professional agencies.**

and cable TV; proposals for generating cooperative and municipal businesses; a city-operated bank; redistributive tax and fee measures; and the development of increased community participation in and control of various kinds of social services.

In summary, both the Hartford and Berkeley groups articulated public plans and principles that set their agendas and guided their actions. Both rejected the idea that private-sector forces were the main engine of economic welfare and instead opted for public ownership, enterprise, regulation, and services in major ways. They differed in that the Hartford group began with political leadership, while the Berkeley coalition spent a decade in opposition positions. In both cases, policy was to develop out of actions, but they were different kinds of action. In Berkeley, policies evolved from outside of government, from minority-based actions. In Hartford, policies evolved in the course of substantial control of government over a long period of time. Moreover, the background was different in each case: Berkeley was less pressed by economic decline, though it shared the problems of fiscal stress in government, particularly when BCA came into power at the end of the 1970s.

HARTFORD: FROM INVESTMENT TO SERVICE STRATEGIES

In each place, the combination of redistributive policies and plans and the opportunities and challenges of involvement in city administration resulted in an extraordinary record of innovation. Some of the new institutions and practices, particularly those implemented early in the 1970s, were the results of exploitation of federal funding resources, in addition to private investment projects carried over from previous years. But the essence of the innovation was the use of public policy to redirect private priorities. In Hartford, this occurred through public pressure on the tax structure, through a public land development policy, and through the development of new and reorganized public services.

The City as Tax Reformer

In 1978, a state-mandated property-tax reassessment was confronting Hartford with two kinds of effects: a shift of tax burden from neighborhoods that had been experiencing deterioration to those where some reinvestment had been occurring, and an overall shift from business to residential properties. There was the basis for fragmentation of interests and conflict. White ethnic community leaders, representing the areas whose assessments would go up, called for the city council to throw out the revaluation. Black political leaders and civil-rights activists would not stand for any talk of a delay in implementing the new scheme—which would have reduced assessments in their neighborhoods. Municipal unions were mainly concerned about the prospects of revaluation shifting the tax burden from business and commercial property to homeowners—fueling a taxpayers' revolt, they feared, that could lead to massive budget cuts and layoffs. Business leaders argued that their property was overassessed, and wanted an immediate revaluation to lower their property assessments.

In this climate, the council leadership set out to reach the fairest possible solution to the revaluation dilemma. They caused legislation to be introduced in the state legislature covering several resolutions of the problem without committing the city to any one, simply to buy time. They then began meeting with the groups concerned. They pointed out to the Black leaders that, even if the reassessment achieved a redistribution of burden to the relatively better-off residential neighborhoods, their taxes would still go up if the shift from business assessments went through. They talked to the white ethnic groups about the deleterious effects on Black neighborhoods if they continued to bear their present disproportionate burden, and got them to agree to the principle of equity among homeowners regardless of neighborhood. The city council then filed a new bill in the legislature, which fixed the total tax bill that would be paid by homeowners after revaluation at 14.6 percent, the same proportion contributed by residential property before revaluation.

At this point, the Hartford leadership had gotten preliminary agreement on a solution to revaluation that would satisfy the different neighborhoods and, potentially, the public-sector unions. But they faced heavy opposition in the legislature. They then encouraged the formation of the Citizens Lobby to apply pressure to the state legislature. Municipal unions then rallied around the bill, and many city employees, over 3,000 of them residing in the suburbs, began to work in their neighborhoods urging neighbors to contact their state representatives and senators in support of the bill.

The key to passage, however, would be business support. At one meeting with representatives of the Greater Hartford Chamber of Commerce, city leaders' arguments were to no avail: the chamber's executive committee voted to oppose any effort to defer shifting the tax burden from business to residential property. Carbone then sent a telegram to each member of the chamber executive committee, repeating the urgency of the situation and asking for face-to-face meetings among business leaders, community people, and local elected officials. Citizens Lobby members made similar requests of the chief executive officers of the city's largest corporations. As a result, some corporate leaders changed their positions, agreeing to remain neutral in the upcoming legislative battle.

Despite this, some business leaders remained adamantly opposed. Community leaders began demonstrating against the business community, demanding that no more public money be used for downtown improvements. They picketed tax-delinquent corporations and large companies that were appealing their property-tax assessments. And some groups argued that the city should spend no more tax dollars to rebuild the Hartford Civic Center Coliseum, which had been destroyed when its roof collapsed earlier that winter. At city hall, the leadership began to take a tougher line, looking for bargaining points that could help leverage business support (or neutrality) for property-tax relief. Their top legislative priority was the revaluation bill, which became known as the "differential" bill because it set different rates of assessment for residential and business properties.

At this time, with the business community still generally opposed to the bill, the city council was pressed to approve funds for the Civic Center Coliseum. Hartford's corporate community had a heavy investment in a professional hockey team, the Whalers, which was part of the merger plans between the two major hockey leagues. Without a firm commitment on the new coliseum, the Whalers would be out of the expanded National Hockey League. The franchise—and millions of local corporate dollars—would be lost.

When the request to allocate funds for the new coliseum reached the council floor, Carbone stated he had been too busy working on the revaluation issue to study the resolution concerning the coliseum. He said he needed more time to review the request for funds. Several other council members made similar remarks, and the proposal was tabled. They had made their point. The strongest opponents of the differential bill agreed not to lobby against it, and other business leaders let it be known that they favored the differential as a temporary solution. If a sunset provision were written into the bill, they would support it.

The short-term struggle was won. For a while, at least, a $6 million tax shift to homeowners was avoided. In addition, the coalition-building around reassessment—and subsequent lobbying—generated other legislation beneficial to the city, and created new organizational capacity within the city and linked the city to sympathetic supporters in the suburbs.

The City as Investor and Regulator

At the beginning of the 1970s, Hartford was already a partner in various investment schemes, including urban-renewal projects. The city's role in these projects had so far been relatively limited. It had put up the local share of project subsidies, provided some public works and administrative support, and had left development—and profits—to private developers. But the analyses of the city's welfare popula-

tion that the council had initiated earlier suggested that a new approach was needed, where the primary objective of city policy should be to supplement local incomes. Consequently every investment possibility was to be evaluated according to the extent it contributed toward this objective, and the city was to use what means it had to direct and regulate investment in this direction. The city's strategy to improve income was accomplished in part by means of the courts and by taking advantage of administrative rules, particularly the federal affirmative-action hiring rules, that had not previously been vigorously followed. In a sense this was a negative strategy, meant to redirect private-sector development that was moving toward the suburbs from the city, and which favored the relatively well-educated white labor force over Hartford's Black, Hispanic, poor, and untrained one. The other side of the strategy was a more positive one: to use vacant land and buildings in the central city as a resource for employing city people. The council decided that the city should become the retail, entertainment, cultural, and food service center for the region, a development that would create a great many entry level and part-time jobs that educationally deprived inner-city residents could get to supplement family incomes.

The first and major project implementing this strategy was the Hartford Civic Center, a $90 million complex in which the city put up $30 million, the private sector the balance. The Civic Center included a hotel and 360,000 square feet of retail space on air rights. The city owned the land but leased the air rights to the hotel, office, and retail space, retaining a part of the equity and a percentage of any profits through the air rights leases. The city had the state legislature enact laws to facilitate these arrangements. It created a Civic Center Authority, which allowed them to set up a body independent from the city yet able to employ people as city employees: the Authority would thus be under the policies of the city government but outside the bureaucracy and the civil-service system so that it could be run as a business. Because of the employees being considered city employees, the council could still impose a residency requirement. The council then negotiated with the school system that all the part-

time jobs for young people had to go through the Hartford school system through the work-study program, an important link. Thus they took young people from welfare homes (75 percent of the persons in the Hartford school system came from AFDC homes) and linked them into the Civic Center with part-time jobs—if they were in school.

Aetna Life and Casualty, which built the retail part of the Civic Center, was required to have as part of its affirmative-action plan the condition that they would (1) have minority businesses in the center and (2) would help capitalize small businesses. To fulfill this, Aetna put up $8 million for furniture, fixtures, and capitalization for small businesses. They took small businesses that were successful, that had a good product: for example, a grinder shop from Franklin Avenue was brought in that sold grinders (a submarine-type sandwich) and Italian foods as part of the Civic Center's marketplace—a small restaurant with a fast turnover that seated about 25 people. They took a Black man who ran a marginal liquor store but who was doing a good job and put him in the Civic Center right next to the hotel, where he upgraded his store. A Black baker who worked in a hotel as the pastry chef opened the John Williams Bake Shop. Hartford did this sort of thing in several buildings in which the city had an interest. They developed a policy of taking equity holdings in buildings and land and leasing them back to private developers with stipulations, essentially making the city a partner in commercial and housing ventures. They asked the legislature for changes in the law to make it possible to do this: for any development over $10 million they proposed to negotiate the taxes for up to seven years in return for one percent of gross rentals. If the city was to give tax deferrals for risky ventures, it wanted to participate in the profits later. They then formulated the City and Town Development Act, which went through the legislature in 1975, providing that the city could fix taxes for up to 20 years, own real estate, and lease it to businesses. The city could build factories, and it could use industrial-revenue bonds for a sinking bond for up to two years, resulting in somewhat cheaper rates to build factories, or housing. Thus the city was in the real-estate business. With that the city took ownership of an old abandoned Korvettes department store and leased it to American Airlines. This brought 1,000 jobs into the city, with the American Airlines office plus—as a condition of the lease—the use of the first two floors for small businesses.

The city also began to restructure administrative budgets and service delivery systems. It gave greater attention to education functions, adding 400 positions to the Board of Education payrolls, while subtracting 200 from the police and fire departments, 200 from public works. It initiated new school dental, lunch, and breakfast programs—an indirect income subsidy—while replacing teachers with paraprofessionals with local-residency requirements. It redirected $1.5 million of Community Development Block Grant funds, traditionally used for capital investments, toward the school system.

Nonservice Options
A general principle behind much of the Hartford innovation was that of substituting local organization for expensive bureaucratic and professional agencies. The city council began to encourage citizen participation, not just in policy decisions but in performance—in the actual delivery of services to residents.

They began with the police department, instituting neighborhood police teams that were assigned to specific districts, in a return to the old "cop on the beat" theory that it was helpful for police officers and residents to know and respect one another. Every two weeks, neighborhood representatives met with police team leaders to talk about problem areas. One police lieutenant told Carbone that he initially resisted neighborhood demands to crack down on street prostitution. Five and a half years behind a desk downtown had taught him that prostitution is a victimless crime that should be ignored by the police. Residents who lived with the problem saw it differently. And he found that as the amount of street prostitution declined, so did the number of muggings, assaults, and other violent crimes. Burglaries and drug traffic also declined. That kind of experience began to generate feelings of mutual respect and

cooperation between police officers and residents.

In some neighborhoods, residents became even more directly involved in crime prevention efforts. Street observer programs put citizen foot-patrol teams in direct radio contact with police officers in the area. Other neighborhood groups went door-to-door, with police officers, to help people engrave their valuables with identification numbers and offer suggestions on how to improve the security of their houses and apartments.

One of the neighborhood policy advisory committees sponsored a cultural awareness night, which brought together police officers and their families and people who lived in the neighborhood. More than 300 people attended this social event, which included ethnic music and a dinner of soul food and Puerto Rican dishes. Previously, police officers and residents of that neighborhood had viewed each other with hostility. The team police concept was beginning to change this attitude. They now began to see each other as allies with common goals.

Similar efforts were made to bring local residents into the provision of recreation services. Over 40 percent of the city's part-time recreation leaders had been suburban residents, but Hartford created a neighborhood incentive program that allowed residents to plan and operate their own activities. If someone in a neighborhood wanted to teach a class in oil painting, for example, he or she would submit a proposal to a neighborhood planning group. If it appeared that the person was qualified and there would be sufficient interest to warrant a class in oil painting, the resident would be paid to teach the class. This system involved far more people and offered a greater variety of recreational activities than the former, more traditional program. Classes developed in cross-country skiing, squash, acting, weaving, the guitar, vegetarian cooking, and hundreds of other areas.

Citizen Participation
By the middle of the 1970s, it was apparent that public and private investment, and consequent employment, would not by itself solve Hartford's personal income problems. Nor was it possible to raise the flow of public

funds into the city. Federal categorical programs like urban renewal and Model Cities were cut back; what had been an $18 million yearly subsidy was cut to $10.8 million in 1970, then $6 million under the Community Development Block Grant formulae. The limited fiscal resources that had greeted the city council in 1969 got even tighter, and an economic development study in 1979 counted a net decrease of 196 person-years since 1972 despite large increases in federal operating subsidies. The problem was how to manage decline, not growth. The property-tax base could not be raised, there was inflation pressure on taxpayers and landlords, so that the population was generally getting poorer. In 1974 the city canceled its capital expenditures for police cruisers to cover welfare costs, and the council increasingly directed its efforts at turning programs toward the objective of supplementing local family incomes. The city wrote its housing assistance plan under Section 8 of the Housing Act so that all subsidies would go to existing rental units rather than the construction of new housing—a move dictated by the pressure on family incomes and threats of landlord abandonments.

Neighborhood Cost-Reduction Programs
Toward the latter part of the 1970s, Hartford planners adopted a strategy to reduce the cost of basic necessities, focusing on Hartford neighborhoods. They realized that even the most optimistic forecasts of local job creation through infusion of outside capital would not suffice to provide jobs for every resident. They felt if they could help reduce the costs of such basic necessities as food, energy, transportation, and health care, more purchasing power would be available for other local activities. There would be additional resources available for purchase of private market housing and for patronage of neighborhood retail and service enterprises.

The city got farthest in food and energy cost-reduction programs. The Hartford food system included a downtown food market, a community cannery, community gardens, youth gardens, neighborhood buying clubs, solar greenhouses, roof-top container gardening, and a city-wide composting program. All elements were planned to complement one another. The system was justified as developing traits of self-reliance and cooperative consumption in residents and as generating a job environment for training that could later be applied to private-sector employment.

The energy program was initiated as a result of steep increases in fuel oil prices, which led to abandonment of many rental units by owners during the winter of 1978. This not only produced heating crises for many residents, it produced secondary effects of neighborhood economic deterioration and loss of housing units. In response, Hartford planners made surveys to determine the factors that made specific structures subject to abandonment because of energy costs or likely to generate complaints of heating failure. They used a computer-based information system to determine what structures in the city were at risk in these respects, and used the information to target outreach workers. They created a Coordinated Energy Response Center with a central "heat line" to permit quick responses to heating complaints. They coordinated the distribution of weatherization kits, claiming that these materials could save up to 20 percent of each tenant's fuel consumption. They established a rent receivership program as a last resort to maintain minimum heat levels and to reduce the likelihood of housing abandonment. The combined effect of targeted code enforcement and rent receivership programs was reported for the winter of 1979-80. Officials stated that the landlords of 217 housing units corrected heat violations and that 51 units were placed into rent receivership, requiring the city to pay the cost of correcting violations.

BERKELEY: INNOVATION IN THE FACE OF CUTBACKS

When Berkeley Citizens Action moved into a position of influence in 1979, it, like the progressive leadership in Hartford, was faced with serious budget problems. The newly elected leadership, which had earlier seen the city as a source of capital formation—a vehicle that could carry cooperative housing, economic development, tax reform, community-based energy, and social-services programs—had moved into the driver's seat just as the needle on the gas gauge moved toward empty. BCA had gained experience promot-

ing and forcing the implementation of some of its proposals. This was important, but nothing could have completely prepared newly elected officials for what they encountered in April 1979.

Battle of the Budget

The new council faced a proposed budget that had been developed by the City Manager who was appointed by the previous, more conservative council. It called for massive service cuts because, under Proposition 13, city-generated revenues were lagging seriously behind the expense of maintaining them at existing levels.

The budget that then-City Manager Michael Lawson proposed would close down two fire houses, eliminate programs in the police department that the community had fought to include (the Unit on Crimes Against Women, the Juvenile Bureau, the foot patrol, for example), cut deeply into the library budget for the second year in a row, and completely eliminate allocations to community-based social-service providers (the various community clinics and the women's shelter, for example).

The first response of the new council was to appoint a 27-member Citizens Budget Review Committee. At the request of the committee, the date for passing the 1979–80 city budget was delayed until mid-July.

After six weeks of study and deliberation, the Budget Committee submitted its proposals for changes in Lawson's budget, which were generally adopted by the city council. The fire stations would remain open, but vacant deputy chief and lieutenant positions were eliminated. The positions in the police department that provided direct services—such as school-crossing guards, foot patrol, the rape detail, and all positions on the street—were restored, with comparable dollar cuts made within the department by eliminating administrative and rank officer positions. (Lawson's budget called for the elimination of 46.5 positions in the police department, all at the point of service, while the Budget Committee called for elimination of 19 higher-paid positions, none providing direct services.)

The Budget Committee was also able to recommend restoration of funds for the library and for community services by developing additional

revenues for the city. The committee recommended several significant methods:

1. A property transfer tax that was already on the books was to be implemented. Passed by the previous council, it was not as progressively structured as those called for by BCA over the years, but it included important features that targeted speculative sales and exempted long-time owner occupants.

2. Services provided by the city to developers and businesses that had been partially or wholly supported by property taxes were shifted to total fee support. Building permits, for example, which had traditionally been subsidized by the city's General Fund, were to be totally supported by fees. The committee proposed to revise the fee schedule, which had previously been highly regressive (as much as 2 percent of project costs for small projects and less than .002 percent for very large ones) to a flat rate (about 1.4 percent of project costs). In addition the committee recommended charging a fee for fire inspections of businesses and industries for which no fee had ever been charged.

3. Activities supported by special funds were charged for their use of city services. The most important example was the City Marina Fund, which had generated healthy surpluses over the years that could only be spent in the marina area. This had led to expenditures for luxurious facilities in the yacht basin. State regulations did not allow these funds to be utilized elsewhere in the city but did allow the city to be reimbursed for fire, police, accounting, and other administrative services it provided. This reimbursement had not been previously required.

4. Additional revenue was also generated from automobile disincentives. Parking meters in an upper-income commercial area, increased meter rates, and long-overdue increases in parking violations fines were all put forward by the Budget Committee.

After its first heroic six weeks, the Budget Committee continued to meet. Members of the committee, as well as those from the city's 30 other citizen boards, were invited to participate in the budget discussions between the City Manager and city departments.

In its second year, the Budget Committee took the initiative in present-

When Berkeley Citizens Action moved into a position of influence in 1979, it moved into the driver's seat just as the needle on the gas gauge moved toward empty.

ing a new tax to the voters of Berkeley for their approval. Under Proposition 13, California localities are prohibited from raising the ad valorum property-tax rate at all and can only institute other new taxes with the approval of two-thirds of the voters. Working with another citizen body, the Board of Library Trustees, the Budget Committee designed a new tax based on the floor area of buildings to support the city libraries. A sample survey indicated that this method was feasible to implement and generally progressive. The progressivity was reinforced by writing in a split rate. The tax, which requires residential property owners to pay 2.3 cents per square foot and commercial and industrial property owners to pay 3.5 cents per square foot, was approved by almost 70 percent of the voters in June 1980. While the main emphasis of the tax is its support of library services, all other services in the city receive support indirectly, since dollars from the General Fund that would otherwise support the library have been liberated.

Rent Stabilization and Eviction Control

From the very earliest years of its history, the progressive coalition in Berkeley had worked to regulate the rental housing market. The history includes an interesting mixture of successes and failures. Berkeley's first rent-control ordinance was put on the ballot through the initiative process in 1972, and passed with 51 percent approval. It was subsequently overturned in court as unconstitutional. Opponents had successfully argued that it was unfair to legislate rent control by plebiscite, since there were more tenants than landlords among the voters. A second attempt to gain rent regulation through the polls in 1977 failed to gain majority support.

Then, in the aftermath of Proposition 13, Berkeley—along with numerous other California cities—voted in a mild form of regulation in 1978 by requiring property owners to return a portion of their Proposition 13 property-tax savings to their renters. It prevented rent increases for months, and the issue of whether the controls on rent increases would be extended and institutionalized on a permanent basis was pivotal in the 1979 city elections. BCA candidates favored rent control; the other group opposed it.

When BCA gained its four seats, there was an immediate commitment from the nonaffiliated swing voter on the council to support rent regulation.

The next major task that BCA council members undertook after passage of the first budget was the development of an ordinance that would stabilize rents and protect tenants from unfair evictions. By late fall, a far-reaching ordinance had gained council approval. However, the City Charter required a second reading after several weeks.

While the ordinance was awaiting its second reading, property owners, realtors, and others opposed to rent control were on the streets collecting signatures to have the ordinance nullified. Berkeley was reminded, for the third time in less than 20 years, of a powerful feature in the City Charter, whereby a small number of voters (10 percent of those voting for Mayor in the last election) can petition against an ordinance passed by the city council. When presented with the signatures, the council can either repeal the ordinance or place it on the ballot at the next regularly scheduled election. If the council chooses to take the issue to the voters, the ordinance does not go into effect until after it has gained their approval.

Previously this provision of the charter had been used in the early 1960s to overturn the council-approved fair-housing ordinance. During the 1970s, the city's progressive forces turned to this charter requirement to overturn the council's decision refusing to study the feasibility of municipalizing the privately owned electric-distribution system. (The study indicated it would indeed be feasible; given the actual rate of inflation since the study was performed, it turns out the study underestimated the feasibility. Acquisi-

tion of the system was, however, twice rejected by Berkeley voters.)

When rent-control opponents turned to petitions with the requisite number of signatures (collected from some people who believed they were signing in favor of rent control), the BCA council members had to develop a strategy that would extend the soon-to-expire rent regulations in effect until a permanent ordinance could be passed in the June 1980 election. It was very important that there be no gap in the protection that renters were receiving.

The BCA council members were successful in providing the unbroken coverage. The voters approved Berkeley's Rent Stabilization and Good Cause Eviction Ordinance at the polls. The council appointed members of the Rent Stabilization Board and set up a staff to implement what is necessarily a complex regulatory mechanism. Tremendous effort still has to be devoted to legal defense of the ordinance. The courts have not yet become comfortable with a law that shifts the balance between owners and renters. After a year, opposition to the ordinance is still strong.

Cooperative Housing

Another major BCA commitment over the years had been to the development of cooperatively owned housing for low- and moderate-income people. Just as the new council members took office, the city's first project opened (Florence MacDonald, one of the new council members, was among the first residents). A second co-op housing project was in the planning stages. Many members of the community active in housing issues believed that the outcome of the 1979 election would determine whether or not this second project would see the light of day.

Like developments elsewhere, the construction and financing costs of this new project were skyrocketing. Between a committed city council and creative developers who pulled in every outside available federal and state direct and indirect subsidy, the project moved toward realization. The magnitude of the costs emphasized, however, that delivering low- and moderate-income housing requires a strong commitment, which will be tested repeatedly.

Redevelopment

One of the issues that separated political factions in Berkeley for many years was the city's Redevelopment Project. Originally planned for an industrial park, the redevelopment area was the site of intense, sometimes violent, conflict, as BCA fought to preserve existing housing and target the vacant subsidized land for housing rather than industrial and commercial uses. Over the years, BCA had won battles that delayed industrial development, but only after the 1979 election could BCA change the plan to build housing.

It seemed that it would be a simple matter, until the council learned that once again Proposition 13 was blocking them. In the fine print of the redevelopment bonds was language requiring the Redevelopment Agency to collect one-third more in taxes than it had to pay out in debt service in order to amend the Redevelopment Plan. By cutting tax revenues below this level, Berkeley would have to contact bondholders and receive their approval before amending the plan. Just after the election, the Redevelopment Agency staff developed a method of defeasance to meet the legal requirements. As the legal clouds lift, the city will now need to find the millions of dollars of investment capital required to build low- and moderate-income housing.

Energy Programs

Energy issues in Berkeley presented themselves very differently in 1980 than they did in 1970. For many years, the thrust of the BCA program was to have the city buy out the electric system. Rates that Berkeley residents were paying reflected the costs of expanding the system in the suburbs. Relieving ratepayers in Berkeley of this expense and other savings inherent in a publicly owned system necessitated some form of public ownership. In recent years, the Pacific Gas and Electric Company's rate schedule was shifted by the California Public Utilities Commission from the declining block structure to lifeline rates favoring small users over large ones. As a result, Berkeley ratepayers, who have been successful at conservation, generally have benefited.

Meanwhile, new city programs were developed to foster conservation, especially for lower-income people. Instruction in no-cost and low-cost improvements in housing was provided by the city. Young people were trained to weatherize houses and provide services for elderly residents. In addition, the Energy Commission, another citizen board, studied ways the city might save on its heating and fuel bills

Eliminating Waste

Given the tight financial situation in Berkeley and the commitment of the city council to solve basic but expensive problems, the city administration explored ways of improving the organization's productivity, reducing wasteful expenditures, and reorganizing to improve efficiency. While Berkeley's city council was hardly unique in its commitment to these objectives, there was an urgency about their realization that is directly related to its other progressive goals.

A more conservative city government has options that the BCA council members rejected, such as cutting costs by contracting out services to firms paying nonunion wages or eliminating programs that serve the poorest (often nonvoting) people. BCA is a coalition—to a very large degree comprised of people who have been passed over by BCA's more conservative opposition. The coalition depended on meeting each group's needs—fully meeting them was no longer possible, but each one had weight.

In the 1979–81 period, BCA council members scraped together resources to meet the broader community needs in part by skimming a little off the top (the split rate in the library tax and the changes in the fee structure are examples). The council members also learned that there are significant obstacles that prevented significant redistribution—in Proposition 13, in the City Charter, in the fine balance of electoral politics. In this context, efficiency and elimination of waste took on an urgency that would otherwise be surprising in progressive circles.

Berkeley's campaign against waste was directed by Wise Allen, the City Manager appointed by the city council in February 1980. He immediately targeted an array of nonproductive but increasingly expensive costs—workmen's compensation payments, for example. He initiated an occupational health and safety program. In California cities, attention to these costs was not unusual. What may distinguish the Berkeley approach, however, is Al-

len's belief that the problems had to be solved by the people working for the city. Solutions designed by the people who face the problems can be carried out in a way that the ideas of an outside consultant—no matter how creative—are unlikely to be.

Public Services Committees

The Labor-Management-Citizen Public Services Committee Project is a collaborative effort involving the city of Berkeley, unions representing city employees (SEIU Locals 535 and 390, IBEW Local 1245, and the Berkeley Firefighters Association), and members of citizen commissions and citizen organizations. The thrust of the program is to focus the attention of the three parties on the overriding problem they share—that is, how to maintain and improve the delivery of municipal services in an environment of fiscal scarcity.

The Public Services Committees provide a cooperative, nonadversarial forum for identifying service delivery and work organization problems and solutions to those problems. The Project supplements but does not supersede the collective-bargaining agreement between the city and the unions. A unique feature of the Project's approach is to involve citizens, the consumers of city services, in the collaborative labor-management work review process.

The locus of the Project's work is in discrete work units in different city departments, where three-sided Public Services Committees are being established to identify and rectify problems in work organization and service delivery. A three-sided city-wide coordinating committee makes broad policy for the Project and monitors and supports the functioning of the work-site committees. The Project was suggested by the Citizens' Budget Review Commission in November 1979. Since that time, dozens of well-attended informational and exploratory meetings have cleared the way for the enthusiastic commitment of all three parties to the Project.

CITIZEN ACTION IN AND OUT OF OFFICE

Clearly, progressive ideas infused both cities' administrations. In Hartford and Berkeley, progressive movements depended on local organizing

> **Liberal governments have always been theoretically in favor of "citizen participation," but Berkeley and Hartford actively encouraged it, tapping a source of energy, creativity, and support.**

efforts. Hartford's Citizens Lobby had city hall support, as did Berkeley's Citizen Budget Committee, but these were only the most dramatic, peak-level examples of what was a much more widespread phenomenon. Liberal governments have always been theoretically in favor of "citizen participation," but Berkeley and Hartford actively encouraged it, tapping a source of energy, creativity, and support. Thus, planning took on an importance and role it had not had previously. In Hartford, technical planning analyses quantified and reinforced the premises of the general advocacy policy, and then suggested specific programs that the council could pursue. In Berkeley, plans were elaborated in opposition that were only partially carried out later, but they

nevertheless served to punctuate a generally progressive agenda.

Now out of power, the Hartford and Berkeley progressives face the question of what legacy they leave. On the one hand, there is the painful knowledge that progressive municipal politics is an uphill struggle against great odds. The most immediate difficulties in both places came from the fiscal pressures on city budgets. Proposition 13 in California and the generally increasing gap between needs and revenue sources in Hartford resulted in very severe restrictions in local autonomy. This has meant that progressives have to work very hard just to keep the service levels of yesterday. The possibilities for significant change are severely diminished. Hartford's experience clearly demonstrates the political liability of redistribution at the margin of shrinkage. Berkeley's begins to show the liability that progressives face when their fancy technical footwork does not keep up with an accelerating crisis in public finance.

With electoral defeat, there was also an awareness of the fragile nature of most progressive innovations. Most participants in the Hartford administration dispersed after 1979, and many innovative practices were reversed. In Berkeley, the BCA retained a minority position on the council, and it is not yet clear what reverses will occur. But in both places electoral defeat raised

the question of how to institutionalize the changes that seemed to work. The Hartford and Berkeley progressives have had some permanent accomplishments—a civic center in one case, housing cooperatives in the other. The long-term lease arrangements in Hartford cannot be altered, and the experience of the Citizens Budget Review Committee in Berkeley might be remembered for a while. But the enemies made by these arrangements were probably better organized than their friends were. And the general structure of municipal practice in affirmative action, regulation, and public enterprise can be dismantled rather easily—and was in Hartford. These innovations requiring a continuing commitment are easier to replace with more traditional modes of government than it is to initiate them in the first place.

Nevertheless, what had been achieved made more sense for the people who had been served—the majority—than the "moderate" or even reactionary themes adopted by their successors. Future elections might show this. Moreover, other cities, facing similar economic issues, have tried to move in similar directions. Even as BCA went down to defeat in Berkeley, a rent-control coalition swept to victory in Santa Monica. There and in other places, progressive administration will continue to be tested and experience will accumulate.

Small Space Is Beautiful:
Design as if People Mattered

The successful design of small urban spaces
ultimately depends on watching
the "experts"—people—using them.

William H. Whyte

William H. Whyte is director of the Street Life Project in New York City. This article is based on research conducted by that group since 1971 and is excerpted from his book *The Social Life of Small Urban Spaces* (the Conservation Foundation, Washington, D.C., 1980). Among his other books are *The Organization Man, Open Space Action, Cluster Development,* and *The Last Landscape.*

The editors acknowledge the *NOVA* program "City Spaces, Human Places" (originally broadcast on PBS November 29, 1981), which served as inspiration for this article.

In 1970, I formed a small research group, the Street Life Project, and began looking at city spaces—to learn why some work for people, and some do not, and what the practical lessons might be. At that time, direct observation had long been used for the study of people in far-off lands. It had not been used to any great extent in the American city. There was much concern over urban crowding, but most of the research on the issue was done somewhere other than where it supposedly occurred. The most notable studies were of crowded animals, or of students and members of institutions responding to experimental situations—often valuable research, to be sure, but somewhat vicarious.

The Street Life Project began its study by looking at New York City parks and playgrounds and such informal recreation areas as city blocks. One of the first things that struck us was the *lack* of crowding in many of these areas. A few were jammed, but more were nearer empty than full, often in neighborhoods that ranked very high in density of people. Sheer space, obviously, was not itself attracting children. Many streets were.

It is often assumed that children play in the street because they lack playground space. But many children play in the streets because they like to. One of the best play areas we came across was a block on 101st Street in East Harlem. It had its problems, but it worked. The street itself was the play area. Adjoining stoops and fire escapes provided prime viewing across the street and were highly functional for mothers and older people. There were other factors at work, too, and, had we been more prescient, we could have saved ourselves a lot of time spent later looking at plazas. Though we did not know it then, this block had within it all the basic elements of a successful urban place.

As our studies took us nearer the center of New York, the imbalance in use of space was even more apparent. Most crowding could be traced to a series of choke points—particularly subway stations. In total, these spaces constitute only a fraction of downtown, but the number of people using them is so high and their experience so abysmal that it colors our perception of the city out of all proportion. The fact that there may be lots of empty space somewhere else little mitigates the discomfort.

This phenomenon affects researchers, too. We see what we expect to see, and have been so conditioned to see crowded spaces in center city that it is often difficult to see empty ones. But when we looked, there they were.

Furthermore, the amount of space was increasing. Since 1961, New York City has given incentive bonuses to builders who provide plazas. For each square foot of plaza, builders can add 10 square feet of commercial floor space over and above the amount normally permitted by zoning. So they have—without exception. Every new office building we studied provided a plaza or comparable space: by 1972, some 20 acres of the world's most expensive open space.

We discovered that some plazas, especially at lunchtime, attracted a lot of people. One, the plaza of the Seagram Building, helped give the city the idea for the plaza bonus. Built in 1958, this austerely elegant area was not planned as a people's plaza, but that

From *Technology Review*, July 1982, pp. 36–49. Reprinted with permission from TECHNOLOGY REVIEW, copyright 1982.

The most attractive fountains,
the most striking designs, cannot induce people to come and sit if there
is no place to sit.

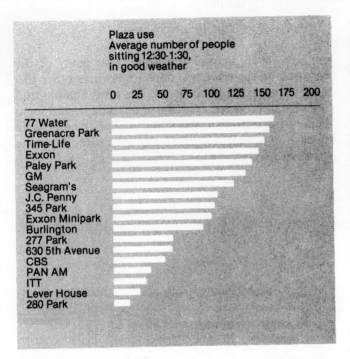

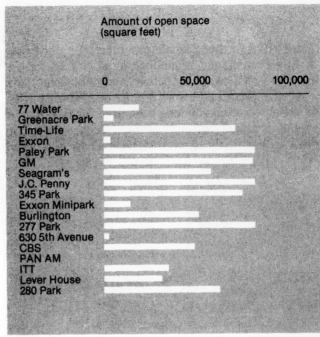

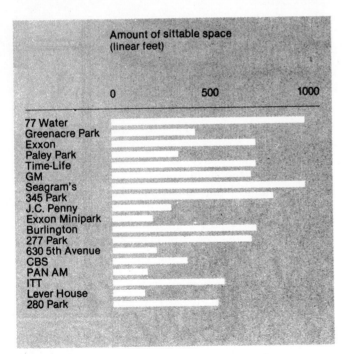

But on most plazas, we didn't see many people. The plazas weren't used for much except walking across. In the middle of lunch hour on a beautiful, sunny day, the number of people sitting on plazas averaged four per 1,000 square feet of space—an extraordinarily low figure for so dense a center. The tightest-knit CBD (central business district) anywhere contained a surprising amount of open space that was relatively empty and unused.

If places such as Seagram's and 77 Water Street could work so well, why not the others? We began studying a cross-section of spaces—in all, 16 plazas, 3 small parks, and a number of odds and ends. We mounted time-lapse cameras and recorded daily patterns. We talked to people to find where they came from, where they worked, how frequently they used the place, and what they thought of it. But mostly we watched people to see what they did.

There were a lot of false starts and dead ends, and the research was nowhere as tidy and sequential as in the telling. The findings would also have been staggeringly obvious had we thought of them in the first place. But we didn't. Often, what seemed plainly evident turned out to be incorrect. We arrived at our findings by a succession of busted hypotheses.

Patterns of the People

The best-used plazas are sociable places, with a higher

is what it became. On a good day, there would be a hundred and fifty people sitting, sunbathing, picnicking, and shmoozing—idly gossiping, talking "nothing talk." People also liked 77 Water Street, known as "swingers" plaza because of the young crowd that populated it.

"A dimension architects seem to have forgotten is the human backside. Rarely will you find a ledge that is sittable on both sides. Most ledges are inherently sittable, but with a little ingenuity and additional expense they can be made unsittable."

proportion of couples than you find in less-used places, more people meeting people or exchanging goodbyes. A high proportion of people in groups is an index of selectivity. When people go to a place in twos or threes or rendezvous there, it is most often because they have decided to. Nor are these sociable places less congenial to the individual—they attract more individuals than less-used spaces. If you are alone, a lively place can be the best place to be.

What attracts people most, it would appear, is other people. But many urban spaces are being designed as though the opposite were true. People often do talk along such lines; this is why their responses to questionnaires can be so misleading. How many people would say they like to sit in the middle of a crowd? Instead, they speak of getting away from it all, and use terms such as "escape," "oasis," and "retreat." What people do, however, reveals another priority.

This was first brought home to us in a study of street conversations. When people stop to have a conversation, we wondered, how far away do they move from the main pedestrian flow? People didn't move out of it. They stayed in or moved *into* it, and the great bulk of the conversations were smack in the center of the flow. The same gravitation characterized "traveling conversations"—the kind in which two people move about, alternating the roles of "straight man" and principal talker. Although there is a lot of

apparent motion, if you plot the orbits, they turn out to be quite restricted.

People also sit in the mainstream. At the Seagram plaza, the main pedestrian paths are on diagonals from the building entrance to the corners of the steps. These are natural junction and transfer points and the site of lots of activity. They are also a favored place for sitting and picnicking. Sometimes there will be so many people that pedestrians have to step carefully to negotiate the steps. The pedestrians rarely complain. While some will detour around the blockage, most will thread their way through it.

Standing patterns are similar. When people stop to talk on a plaza, they usually do so in the middle of the traffic stream. They also show an inclination to station themselves near objects such as a flagpole or a statue. They like well-defined places such as steps or the border of a pool. What they rarely choose is the middle of a large space.

Whatever they may mean, people's movements are one of the great spectacles of a plaza. You do not see this in architectural photographs, which typically are empty of life and taken from a perspective few people share. It is a quite misleading one. At eye level the scene comes alive with movement and color—people walking quickly, walking slowly, skipping up steps, weaving in and out on crossing patterns, accelerating and retarding to match the moves of others. There is a beauty that is beguiling to watch, and one senses that the players are quite aware of it themselves. You see this, too, in the way they arrange themselves on steps and ledges—they often do so with grace. With its brown-gray monochrome, Seagram's is the best of settings—especially in the rain, when an umbrella or two adds color in the right places, like Corot's red dots.

How peculiar are such patterns to New York? We assumed that behavior in other cities would probably differ little, and subsequent comparisons proved our assumption correct. The important variable is city size—the strongest similarities are found among the world's largest cities. People tend to behave more like their counterparts in other world cities than like fellow nationals in smaller cities. Big-city people walk faster, for one thing, and they self-congest. After we had completed our New York study, we made a brief comparison study of Tokyo and found that the proclivity to stop and talk in the middle of department-store doorways, busy corners, and the like is just as strong as in New York.

For all the cultural differences, sitting patterns in various parks and plazas around the world are much the same, too. Similarly, shmoozing patterns in Milan's Galleria are remarkably like those in New York's garment center. The modest conclusion: given the basic element of a center city—such as high pedestrian volumes and the concentration and mixture of activities—people in one place tend to act much like people in another.

The Bottom Line

In their use of plazas, New Yorkers were very consistent. Day in, day out, many of them would sit at certain plazas, few at others. On the face of it, there should not have been this variance—most of the plazas we were studying were fairly comparable. With few exceptions, they were on major avenues and usually occupied a block front. They were close to bus stops and subway stations and had strong pedestrian flows on the sidewalks beside them. Yet when we rated plazas according to the number of people sitting on them at peak time, there was a very wide range—from 160 people at 77 Water Street to 17 at 280 Park Avenue (*see the upper-left chart on page 211*).

How come? The first factor we studied was the sun. We thought it might well be the critical one, and our initial time-lapse studies seemed to bear this out. Subsequent studies did not. As I will note later, they showed that the sun was important but did not explain the difference in the popularity of plazas. Nor did aesthetics. The elegance and purity of a building's design seems to have little relationship to the use of the spaces around it. The designer sees the whole building—the clean verticals, the horizontals, the way Mies van der Rohe turned his corners, and so on. People sitting on the plaza may be quite unaware of such matters. They are more apt to be looking in another direction: not up at other buildings, but at what is going on at eye level.

Another factor we considered was shape. Urban designers believed this was extremely important and hoped our findings might support tight criteria for proportion and placement. Our data did not support such criteria, but neither did they prove shape unimportant or designers' instincts misguided. As with the sun, however, they did prove that other factors are more critical.

If not shape, could the *amount* of space be the key factor? Some conservationists were sure this would be it. In their view, people seek open spaces as a relief from the overcrowding they are normally subjected to, and it would follow that places affording the great-

Rules for Regulators

Ledges ought to be "sittable." But how should this be defined? If we wanted sittable ledges in the New York City zoning amendments, we thought we would have to indicate how high and deep ledges should be and then back up the specifications with facts.

The zoning proceedings during 1974 were unexpectedly adversarial. The attack came on the grounds that the zoning was *too specific*. And it came not from builders, but from members of a local planning board. Rather than spell out the requirements in specific detail, the board argued, the zoning should deal with broad directives—for example, "make the place sittable" —and leave details to be settled on a case-by-case basis.

This argument is persuasive, especially for laypeople, and, at the inevitable moment in zoning meetings when someone gets up and says, "Let's cut through all this crap and get down to basics," everyone applauds. Be done with bureaucratic nitpicking and legal gobbledygook.

But ambiguity is a worse problem. Most incentive zoning ordinances are very, very specific as to what developers get. The trouble is that they are mushy as to what they are to give, and mushier yet as to what will happen if later they don't. Vague stipulations, as many cities have learned, are unenforceable. What you do not prescribe quite explicitly you do not get.

This lack of guidelines does not give buildings and architects more freedom; it reinforces convention. That is why so few good plazas were built under the 1961 zoning resolution. There was no law preventing builders from providing better plazas, but there weren't any guidelines either. And most builders do not do anything far out of the ordinary. A few had sought special permits for amenities not countenanced by existing regulations. But this time-consuming route makes the builder and architect run a gauntlet of city agencies, with innovation as likely to be punished as rewarded.—*W.H.W.* □

est feeling of light and space would draw the most. Once again, we found no clear relationship. As can be seen from the upper-right chart on page 211, sheer space does not draw people. In some circumstances, it can have the opposite effect.

What about the amount of *sittable* space? Here we begin to get close. As the lower chart on page 150 shows, the most popular plazas tend to have a lot more sitting space than the less well used ones, but the relationship is rough. For one reason, the amount of sitting space does not include any qualitative factors: a foot of concrete ledge counts for as much as a foot of comfortable bench space. We considered weighing the data on a point basis—so may points for a foot of bench with backrest, with armrests, and so on. This would have produced a nicer conformance on the chart. We gave up the idea, however, as too manipulative. Once you start working backward this way, there's no end to it.

There was no necessity. No matter how many variables we checked, one point kept coming through:

People tend to sit most where there are places to sit.

This may not strike you as an intellectual bombshell, and, now that I look back on our study, I wonder why it was not more apparent from the beginning. Sitting space, to be sure, is only one of many variables, and without a control situation one cannot be sure of cause and effect. But sitting space is most certainly prerequisite. The most attractive fountains, the most striking designs, cannot induce people to come and sit if there is no place to sit.

Design with Human Nature

Ideally, sitting should be physically comfortable—benches with backrests, well-contoured chairs. However, it's most important that it be *socially* comfortable. This means a choice: to sit up front, in back, to the side, in the sun, in the shade, in groups, off alone.

Choice should be built into the basic design. Even though benches and chairs can be added, the best course is to maximize the "sittability" of inherent features. This means making ledges that are sittable or making other flat surfaces do double duty as tabletops or seats. There are almost always such opportunities. Because the elevation changes somewhat on most building sites, there are bound to be several levels of flat space—it is no more trouble to make them sittable than not to. It takes real work to create a lousy place. Ledges have to be made high and bulky, railings put in, surfaces canted. Money can be saved by not doing such things, and the open space is more likely to be amenable.

A dimension architects seem to have forgotten is the human backside. Rarely will you find a ledge or bench deep enough to be sittable on both sides; some aren't deep enough to be sittable on one. Most frustrating are the ledges just deep enough to tempt people to sit on both sides, but too shallow to let them do so comfortably.

Thus to another of our startling findings: ledges and spaces two backsides deep seat more people comfortably than those that are not as deep. For a few additional inches of depth, then, builders can double the amount of sitting space. This does not mean that double the number of people will use the space, but that is not the point. The benefit of the extra space is social comfort—more room for groups and individuals to sort themselves out, more choices and more perception of choices.

Steps work for the same reason. The range of space provides an infinity of possible groupings, and the excellent sightlines make virtually all the seats great for watching the theater of the street. And corners are functional. You will notice that people often bunch at the far end of steps, especially when an abutting ledge provides a right angle. These areas are good for face-to-face sitting. People in groups gravitate to them.

One might, as a result, expect a conflict, for corners are also the places where pedestrian traffic is heaviest. But for all the bustle, or because of it, the sitters seem to feel comfortable. And the walkers don't seem to mind.

We find similar patterns at other places. Other things being equal, you can calculate that where pedestrian flows bisect a sittable place, that is where people will most likely sit. And it is not so perverse of them—it is by choice. If there is some congestion, it is an amiable one and a testimonial to the place. Circulation and sitting, in sum, are not antithetical but complementary. The easier the flow between street and plaza, the more likely people are to move between the two—and to tarry and sit.

This is true of the handicapped, too. If circulation and amenities are planned with them in mind, the place is apt to function more easily for everyone. Drinking fountains low enough for wheelchair users are low enough for children. Pedestrian paths that are made easier for the handicapped by ramps, handrails, and steps of gentle pitch are easier for all. The idea is to make all of a place usable for everyone.

Planned Enlightenment

The most satisfying film I've ever seen is our first time-lapse record of the sun passing across the Seagram plaza. In late morning, the plaza was in shadow. Then, shortly before noon, a narrow wedge of sunlight began moving across the plaza and, as it did, so did the sitters. Where there was sun, they sat; where there was none, they didn't. It was a perfectly splendid correlation, and I cherished it. Like urban designers, I believed a southern exposure to be of critical importance. Here was abundant proof.

Then something went wrong. The correlations vanished—not only at Seagram's but at other places we were studying. The sun still moved; the people didn't. At length the obvious dawned on us: May had been followed by June. While midday temperatures hadn't risen a great deal, the extra warmth was enough to make the sun no longer the critical factor.

It was about this time that much of Paley Park's sunlight began to be cut off by an office building going up across the street. From its scaffolding we focused time-lapse cameras on the park and recorded the effect of the new building. It was surprisingly little. Although the sunlight was curtailed, people used Paley as much as they had before. Perhaps they would have used it more had the sun remained; without studying an identical place as a control, one can never be sure. The more important point is that, unfortunate as the loss may have been, the park was able to sustain it.

Access to the sun should be protected, of course, but places that have little or no sun because of a northern exposure or intervening buildings are not a lost cause. With adroit design, sun can be "borrowed." The same new buildings that cast shadows also reflect considerable light. Along with mirror walls, glass, and stainless steel, architects have been laying on travertine marble with a heavy hand, and light has been bouncing into many places that didn't receive it before. In eight years of filming, I have found that several streets have become photographically a half-stop faster. A number of open spaces that otherwise would be dark much of the time are bathed in reflected light, sometimes on the second or third bounce. Grace plaza, for example, gets no direct sun at all but benefits most of the afternoon from light reflected by the southern exposure of the building to the north. Give travertine its due. It bounces light admirably, especially in the late afternoon, when it can give a benign glow to the streetscape.

So far, such effects are wholly inadvertent. Sun studies made for big new buildings tend to be defensive, so that planning boards can be shown the building won't cast an awful lot more shadow than is cast already by other buildings. Few studies try to determine the light a new building will cast, what benefits might result, to whom, and when. Yet benefits of great potential value can be planned and negotiated in advance.

Open Seating

A wonderful invention is the movable chair. Having a back, it is comfortable; more so if it has an armrest as well. But the big asset is movability. Chairs enlarge choice: to move into the sun or out of it; to make room for groups or move away from them. The possibility of choice is as important as the exercise of it. If you know you can move if you want to, you feel more comfortable staying put. That is why, perhaps, people so often move a chair a few inches this way and that before sitting on it, with the chair ending up about where it was in the first place. The moves are functional, however. They are a declaration of autonomy, to oneself, and rather satisfying.

Small moves say things to other people. If a newcomer chooses a chair next to a couple or a larger group, he may make some intricate moves. Again, he may not take the chair very far, but he conveys a message. Sorry about the closeness, but there's no room elsewhere, and I am going to respect your privacy, as you will mine. A reciprocal move by one of the others may follow. Watching these exercises in civility is itself one of the pleasures of a good place.

Fixed individual seats are not good. They are a design conceit. Brightly painted and artfully grouped, they can make fine decorative elements: metal loveseats, revolving stools, squares of stone, sitting stumps. But they are set pieces. Social distance is a subtle measure, ever changing, and the distances of fixed seats do not change, which is why they are rarely quite right for anybody. Loveseats may be all right for lovers, but they're too close for acquaintances, and much too close for strangers. Loners tend to take them over, placing their feet squarely on the other seat lest someone else sit on it.

Fixed seats are awkward in open spaces because there's so much space around them. In theaters, strangers sit next to one another without qualm; closeness is a necessity, and convention makes it quite tolerable. On plazas, the closeness is gratuitous. With so much space around, fixed-seat groupings have a manipulative cuteness to them. The designer is saying, now you sit right here and you sit there. People balk. In some instances, they wrench the seats from their moorings. Where there is a choice between fixed seats and other kinds of sitting, it is the other that people choose.

To encourage the use of movable chairs, we recommended that in the New York zoning amendment they be credited as 30 inches of sitting space, though most are only about 19 inches wide. The Building Department objected. It objected to the idea of movable chairs at all. The department had the responsibility of seeing that builders lived up to requirements. Suppose the chairs were stolen or broken and the builder didn't replace them? Whether the department would ever check up in any event was a moot point, but the fewer such amenities to monitor, the easier the monitoring would be.

Happily, there was a successful record at Paley and Greenacre parks to point to, and it was persuasive. The chairs stayed in the amendment. They have become a standard amenity at new places, and the maintenance experience has been excellent. Managements have also been putting in chairs to liven up existing spaces, and even without incentives they have been adding more chairs. The most generous provider is the Metropolitan Museum of Art. Alongside its front steps, it puts out up to 200 movable chairs and it leaves them out, 24 hours a day, seven days a week. The Met figured that it might be less expensive to trust people and to buy replacements periodically rather than have guards gather the chairs in every night. That is the way it has worked out. There is little vandalism.— *W.H.W.* □

5. URBAN FUTURES

Wind and the Willows

What people seek are suntraps. And the absence of wind and drafts are as critical as sun. In this respect, small parks, especially those enclosed on three sides, function well. Physically and psychologically, they feel comfortable, and this is one of the reasons why their relative carrying capacity is so high. New York's Greenacre Park has infrared heaters, but they are used only in extremely cold weather. With sun and protection from wind, the park is quite habitable even on nippy days.

Spaces around new buildings are quite another matter. In winter, many are cold and drafty, and even in moderate weather few people tarry in such places. The errors are of omission. Wind-tunnel tests on models of new buildings are now customary, but they are not made with people much in mind. The tests for the World Trade Center largely determined stresses on the towers and the type of structural steel required. What the towers themselves might generate in the way of wind, and the effects on people below, apparently were not of much concern.

These effects, however, are quite measurable. It is now well established that very tall, free-standing towers can generate tremendous drafts down their sides. This fact has in no way inhibited the construction of such towers, with the predictable result that some spaces are frequently uninhabitable. At one bank plaza in Seattle, the gusts are sometimes so fierce that safety lines must be strung across the plaza to give people something to hang on to. Chicago has the windiest places, not because of the local wind (which isn't really so very much stronger than in other cities), but because the drafts down the sides of the giant John Hancock and Sears towers are macro in force—often so strong as to prevent people from using the plazas, even if they had reason to.

James Marston Fitch, who has done more than any other architect to badger the profession to consider environmental effects, points out that the problem is conceptual, not technical. "Adverse effects are simply ignored," he says, and outdoor spaces are designed as if for some ideal climate, ever sunny and pleasantly warm. Thus [the spaces] fail in their central pretension—that of eliminating gross differences between architectural and urbanistic spaces, of extending in time the areas in which urban life could freely flow back and forth between the two."

Technically, as Fitch points out, we can greatly lengthen the effective season of outdoor spaces. By asking the right questions about sun and wind, by experimentation, we can find better ways to hoard the sun, double its light, obscure it, or cut down breezes in winter and induce them in summer (*See "Rediscovering Energy-Conscious Architecture," August/September 1980, page 68*). We can learn lessons from

"Unless the plaza is on the way to the subway, why go down into it? Once there, you feel rather as if you were at the bottom of a well."

the semiopen niches and crannies that people often seek. Most new urban spaces are either all outdoors or all indoors; more could be done to encourge in-betweens. With the use of glass canopies or small pavilions, semioutdoor spaces could be created that would be usable in all but the worst weather. They would be particularly appropriate in rainy cities such as Seattle and Portland.

There are all sorts of good reasons for trees, but for climatic reasons alone we should press for many more of them, big ones too, along the sidewalks and open spaces of the city.

Trees ought to be related much more closely to sitting spaces than they usually are. Of the spaces we have studied, by far the best liked are those affording a good look at the passing scene and the pleasure of being comfortably under a tree while doing so. This provides a satisfying enclosure; people feel cuddled, protected—very much as they do under the awning of a street cafe. As always, they'll be cooler, too.

Unfortunately, guy wires and planting beds often serve to rule out any sitting, and even if they don't, the fussiness of design details works to the same effect. Everything is so wired and fenced you can neither get to the tree nor sit on what surrounds it. Where large planters are used, they are generally too high and their rims too narrow for comfort.

Developers should be encouraged to combine trees and sitting spaces. They should also encourage planting trees in groves. As Paley Park has demonstrated, if trees are planted closely together, the overlapping foliage provides a combination of shade and sunlight that is very pleasing. Arbors can do the same.

Water is another fine element, and designers are

doing rather well with it. New plazas and parks provide water in all sorts of forms: waterfalls, waterwalls, rapids, sluiceways, tranquil pools, water tunnels, meandering brooks, fountains of all kinds. In only one major respect is something lacking: access.

One of the best things about water is the look and feel of it. I have always thought that the water at Seagram's looked unusually liquid, and I think it's because you know you can splash your hand in it if you are of a mind to. But in many places water is only for looking at. Let a foot touch it and a guard will be there in an instant: Not allowed. Chemicals in the water. Danger of contamination. If you let people start touching water, you are told, the next thing you know they'll start swimming in it.

It's not right to put water before people and keep them away from it. But this is what has been happening across the country. Pools and fountains are installed, then immediately posted with signs admonishing people not to touch. Equally egregious is the excessive zeal with which many pools are continually emptied, refilled, vacuumed, and cleaned, as though their primary function was their maintenance.

Another great thing about water is the sound of it. When people explain why they find Paley Park so quiet and restful, they always mention the waterwall. In fact, the waterwall is quite loud: the noise level is about 75 decibels close by, measurably higher than the level out on the street. Furthermore, taken by itself the sound is not especially pleasant. I have played tapes to people and asked them what they thought it was. Usually they grimace and say a subway train, trucks on a freeway, or something just as bad. In the park, however, the sound is perceived as quite pleasant. It is white sound and masks the intermittent honks and bangs that are the most annoying aspects of street noise. It also masks conversations. Even though there are many others nearby, you can talk quite loudly to a companion—sometimes you almost have to—and enjoy a feeling of privacy. On the occasions when the waterwall is turned off, a spell is broken, and the place seems nowhere as congenial. Or as quiet.

Eat, Drink and Be Merry

If you want to seed a place with activity, put out food. In New York, at every plaza or set of steps with a lively social life, you will almost invariably find food vendors at the corner and a knot of people around them—eating, shmoozing, or just standing.

Vendors have a good nose for spaces that work. They have to. They are constantly testing the market, and if business picks up in one spot, there will soon be a cluster of vendors there. By default, the vendors have become the caterers of the city's outdoor life. They flourish because they're servicing a demand not being met by the regular commercial establishment. Plazas are particularly parasitic in this respect. Hardly a one has been constructed that did not involve the demolition of luncheonettes and restaurants. Vendors thus fill a void, and this can become quite clear when they are shooed away. A lot of the life of the space goes with them.

New York City is less puritanical than some other places. Many cities have ordinances that not only prevent purveying food outdoors but eating there as well. If you ask officials about this, they tell you of the dreadful things that would happen were the restrictions lifted—of unhealthful food, terrible litter problems, and so on. Partly because of these restrictions, most of the plaza and building complexes constructed during the past ten years have no provision of any kind for outdoor eating. The few that do have had to do some pioneering. The First National Bank of Chicago, for example, found that even to provide such a minimal facility as a popcorn cart they had to get special dispensation from the city.

The most basic facility is a snackbar. Paley and Greenacre parks both have pass-through counters featuring good food at reasonable prices and making a moderate profit. Plenty of tables are provided, and people are welcome to bring their own food—wine, too, if they wish. From the street it sometimes looks like a great big party, and if the line of people for the snackbar gets long passersby will join. Food, to repeat, draws people, and they draw more people.

Where Street and Plaza Meet

Now we come to the key space for a plaza. It is not on the plaza; it is the street. The other amenities we have been discussing are indeed important: sitting space, sun, trees, water, food. But they can be added. The relationship to the street is integral, and it is far and away the critical design factor.

A good plaza starts at the street corner. If it's a busy corner, it has a brisk social life of its own. The activity on the corner is a great show and one of the best ways to make the most of it is simply not to wall it off. A front-row position is prime space, and if it is sittable, it draws the most people.

The area where the street and plaza or open space meet is the key to success or failure. Ideally, the transition should be such that it's hard to tell where one ends and the other begins. Paley Park is the best example. The sidewalk in front is an integral part of the park, and an arborlike foliage of trees extends over the sidewalk. There are urns of flowers at the curb and, on either side of the steps, curved sitting ledges. In this foyer you can usually find somebody waiting for someone else—it is a convenient rendezvous point—and people sitting on the ledges, and, in the middle of the entrance, several people in conversations.

Before the New York Telephone Co. installed chairs, tables, and a buffet in its plaza at 42nd Street and the Avenue of the Americas, it was frequented mostly by "undesirables." It soon became a success for employees and passersby alike, and most of the undesirables went somewhere else.

Passersby are users of Paley, too. About half will turn and look in. Of these, about half will smile. I haven't calculated a smile index, but this vicarious, secondary enjoyment is extremely important—the sight of the park, the knowledge that it is there, becomes part of the image we have of a much wider area. (If one had to make a cost-benefit study, I think it would show that secondary use provides as much, if not more, benefit than primary use. If one could put a monetary value on a minute of visual enjoyment and multiply that by those many instances day after day, year after year, one would obtain a rather stupendous sum even after applying a high discount rate.)

The park stimulates impulse use. Many people will do a double take as they pass by, pause, move a few steps, and then, with a slight acceleration, go on up the steps. Watch these flows and you will appreciate how very important steps can be. The steps at Paley are so low and easy that one is almost pulled to them. They add a nice ambiguity to your movement. You can stand and watch, move up a foot, another, and then, without having made a conscious decision, find yourself in the park. The steps at Greenacre Park and Seagram's plaza are similarly low and inviting.

A slight elevation, then, can be beckoning. Go a foot or so higher, however, and usage will fall off sharply. There is no set cutoff level—it is as much

psychological as physical—but it does seem bound up with how much of a choice the steps require. One plaza that people could be expected to use, but don't, is only a foot or so higher than two comparable ones nearby. It seems much higher. The steps are constricted in width, sharply defined by railings, and their pitch is brisk. No ambiguity here, no dawdling, no drifting up.

Sightlines are important. If people do not see a space, they will not use it. In the center of Kansas City is a park just high enough above eye level that most passersby do not realize it is there. As a result, it is lost. Similarly lost is a small, sunny plaza in Seattle. It would be excellent and likely quite popular for sitting—if people could see it from the street, which they cannot.

Unless there is a compelling reason, an open space shouldn't be sunk any more than it should be raised. With two or three notable exceptions, sunken plazas are dead spaces. You find few people in them; if there are stores, there are apt to be dummy window displays to mask the vacancies. Unless the plaza is on the way to the subway, why go down into it? Once there, you feel rather as if you were at the bottom of a well. People look at you. You don't look at them.

We have gone over the principle factors that make a place work. But there is one more factor. I call it

Boston's Quincy Market, in contrast to a megastructure, is open, inclusive, safe, and part of a real city.

Dinosaurs of Urban Design

The ultimate development in the flight from the street is the urban fortress. In the form of "megastructures," more and more of these things are being put up—huge, multipurpose complexes combining offices, hotels, and shops, such as Detroit's Renaissance Center and Atlanta's Omni International. Their distinguishing characteristic is self-containment. While they are supposed to be the salvation of downtown, they are often some distance from the center of downtown, and in any event tend to be quite independent of their surroundings, which are usually parking lots. The megastructures are wholly internalized environments with their own life-support systems. Their enclosing walls are blank, windowless, and to the street they turn an almost solid face of concrete or brick.

A car is the favored means of entry. At Houston Center you can drive in from the freeway to the center's parking garage, walk through a skyway to one tower, thence to another, work the day through, and then head back to the garage and the freeway without ever once having set foot in Houston at all.

There wouldn't be much reason to. Down at the street level of Houston Center there are no store windows. There are no stores. There are not many people. The sole retail activity is a drive-in bank, and the only acknowledgment of pedestrians consists of flashing lights and signs telling them they'd better damn well watch out for cars.

The resemblance to fortresses is not accidental; it is the philosophical base. "Yes, they do look a little forbidding," says one proponent, "but they really have to. The fact is, the only way we can lure middle-class shoppers back to downtown is to promise them security." So, in spirit as well as form, the interstate shopping mall is transplanted to downtown and security raised to the nth degree. The complexes abound with guards and elaborate electronic surveillance systems. Any kind of suspicious activity is quickly spotted and attended to (including, as I have found, the taking of photographs). Ports of entry from the city outside are few in number and their design is manifestly defensive. Where Renaissance Center faces Detroit, large concrete walls flank the entrance. The message is clear: afraid of Detroit? Come in and be safe.

The complexes bid to become larger. Increasingly, the megastructures are being combined with convention and sports facilities, which, like megastructures, tend to be located at the edge of downtown or beyond. And these can be mated with other megastructures, via skybridges and concourses, to form an almost completely closed circuit. As a result, some American cities now have two cities—regular city and visitor city.

Conventioneers sometimes complain of a lack of variety. A logical next step will be the creation within the complexes of facsimiles of streets. There is one at Disneyland, and it is very popular; there are several at the White Flint Mall outside Washington, D.C. With similar showmanship, indoor theme parks could be set up to give an experience of the city without the dangers of it. In addition to such physical features as sidewalks and gaslights, barber poles, and cigarstore Indians, streetlike activities could be programmed, with costumed players acting as street people.

A better approach would be to tie in with real streets in the first place. There are some solid attractions in megastructures—excellent hotels and restaurants, good shops, waterfalls, elevators in glass pods, and public spaces of a drama and luxury not seen since the movie palaces of the twenties. Must isolation be a condition of their attraction? The megastructure thesis is somewhat self-proving. If people go in, it is argued, they must be seeking escape from the city and its insecurities.

But are they? Do people go into Peachtree Plaza Center because there are spikes on its front ledge on Peachtree Street? They went in when there weren't spikes. Do people go into Renaissance Center because of the concrete barriers? Or despite them? The evidence suggests that they go in because there are attractions to enjoy. These attractions do not require separation from the city to be enjoyed and are more enjoyable when not separated. Boston's Faneuil Hall Marketplace is witness to this. It's a bit hokey, shrewdly so, but it's part of a real city and has a splendid sense of place.

This is what megastructures so lack. One feels somewhat disembodied in these places. Is it night or day? Spring or winter? And where are you? You cannot see out of the place. You do not know what city you are in, or if you are in a city at all. The complex could be at an airport or a new town. It could be in the East or the West. The piped music gives no clue. It is the same as it is everywhere. You could be in a foreign country or on a space satellite. You are in a universal controlled environment.

And it is going to date very badly. Forms of transportation and their attendant cultures have historically produced their most elaborate manifestations just after they have started to become obsolete. So it may be with megastructures and the freeway era that bred them. They are the last convulsive embodiment of a time passing and a wretched model for the future of the city.—*W.H.W.* □

"triangulation." By this I mean that process by which some external stimulus provides a linkage between people and prompts strangers to talk to one another.

The stimulus can be a physical object or sight. At the small park at the Promenade in Brooklyn Heights is a spectacular view of the towers of lower Manhattan across the East River. It is a great conversation opener and strangers normally remark to each other on it. When you come upon such a scene, it would be rude not to.

Sculpture can have strong social effects. Before-and-after studies of the Chase Manhattan plaza showed that the installation of Dubuffet's "Four Trees" has had a beneficent impact on pedestrian activity. People are drawn to the sculpture, and through it; they talk about it. At the Federal Plaza in Chicago, Alexander Calder's huge stabile has had similar effects.

Musicians and entertainers draw people together. Rockefeller Plaza and the First National Bank of Chicago regularly schedule touring school bands, rock groups, and the like. And the real show is usually the audience. Many people will be looking as much at one another as at what's on stage.

It is not the excellence of the act that is important. It is the fact that it is there that bonds people, and sometimes a really bad act will work even better than a good one. Street entertainers, for example, can run the gamut from very, very bad to sublime, but the virtue of street acts is their unexpectedness. When people form a crowd around an entertainer—it happens very quickly, in 40 to 50 seconds—they look much like children who have come upon a treat; some will be smiling in simple delight. These moments are true recreation, though they are rarely thought of as

such, certainly not by the retailers who try so hard to outlaw them. But there is something of great value here, and it should be fostered.

Why not invite entertainers onto a plaza instead of banning them? One corporation is considering a plan to welcome the best of the street entertainers to its new building. They would be given the equivalent of several good collections for doing their act.

Most of the elements that induce the triangulation effect are worthwhile in their own right. Simply on aesthetic grounds, Dubuffet's "Four Trees" much improves the scale and sense of place in the Chase Manhattan plaza. But the social effects are important. By observing them, we can find how they can be anticipated and planned.

I am not, by the way, arguing for places of maximum gregariousness or social directors for plazas. Anomie would be preferable. What I'm suggesting, simply, is that we make places friendlier. We know how—in both the design and management of spaces, there are many ways to make it much easier for people to mingle and meet. Some of the most felicitous spaces have been provided inadvertently. Think what might happen if someone planned them.

It is wonderfully encouraging that places people like best of all, that they find least crowded and most restful, are small spaces marked by a high density of people and very efficient use of space.

I end, then, in praise of small spaces. The multiplier effect is tremendous. It is not just the number of people using them but the larger number who pass by and enjoy them vicariously, or the even larger number who feel better about the city center for knowledge of them. For a city, such places are priceless. Yet they are built on a set of basics that are right in front of our noses. If we will look.

Urban planning: What went wrong?

On the 100th anniversary of his birth, many blame modernist architect Le Corbusier for the woes of modern cities

The 1972 destruction of the Pruitt-Igoe project in St. Louis symbolizes the failure of urban design inspired by Le Corbusier and marks a turning point in the fortunes of modern architecture

■ Set on a 92-acre landfill along the Hudson River, Battery Park City, now under construction, is one of the more ambitious urban-development schemes devised for New York. It brings big changes to the city's financial district: Where once few people lived and little happened after work, there is now the promise of a large community in residence.

Yet while Battery Park City means change in Manhattan, it does so by trying to change very little. The notion behind the plan is that it should fit as naturally as possible into the existing cityscape, copying the forms and qualities of its streets, mimicking the variety and character of its older and better residential neighborhoods. There are to be moderate-sized, brick-faced apartment buildings with handsome stone bases, reminiscent of the sort of structures lining, say, Gramercy Park or West End Avenue. Battery Park City is an example of contextual urban planning, which accepts and tries to extend the city as it is, instead of trying to remake it from scratch.

Just a few years ago, that would have sounded like heresy to many urban designers. The solution then to a city's housing woes was Draconian: Tear down old buildings and replace them with rows of identical skyscrapers or apartment blocks, set back from busy city streets and sidewalks on broad and empty plazas, where none of the bustle of urban life could intrude. In fact, the first plan for Battery Park City itself depicted a series of huge apartment blocks. That was back in the late 1960s, when urban design was still under the influence of the modernist planners—foremost among them the Swiss-born designer Charles-Édouard Jeanneret-Gris, better known as Le Corbusier.

"Modern Michelangelo"

This year marks the 100th anniversary of Le Corbusier's birth, and to celebrate the occasion two exhibitions are opening March 26—one at New York's Museum of Modern Art, the other at Harvard University's Carpenter Center for the Visual Arts, the only building by the architect constructed in this country. Currently, there is an exhibition at London's Hayward Gallery, and others are scheduled elsewhere in Europe.

They come at a time when Le Corbusier's star is dim. "Of all the great modern architects," says Kevin Harrington, an architectural historian at the Illinois Institute of Technology, "the one least in favor right now is Le Corbusier."

When he died in 1965, the situation was altogether different. The *New York Times* obituary called him "a modern Michelangelo," adding that "architecture has never been more indebted to a single man." His influence, particularly on urban planners, continued to be great for several more years. In 1973, a New York Mayor's Urban Design Council report could describe zoning laws as "the ultimate documentation" of Le Corbusier's ideas.

At the heart of those ideas was his vision of the ideal city—"the radiant city," he called it. He spoke of how it would bring light and air into what had been dark and dirty places, how its extensive network of highways and airports would help to modernize the urban environment. By changing cities, Le Corbusier argued, one would change the nature of society itself. The product of a Swiss watchmaking community, he hated irregularity and disorder. He proposed tearing down the center of Paris and then erecting rows of huge skyscrapers, planted at regular intervals and bisected by a massive highway. About New York, Le Corbusier once declared, "Well, we didn't get it done properly. Let's start over again!"

There were always critics of Le Corbusier's plans, but his ideas—at once simple and revolutionary—appealed to countless architects and planners, especially during the 1950s and 1960s. His vision gave these designers a high moral purpose. As Yale architectural historian Vincent Scully puts it: "What young critic or architect could fail to seize the chance to be a hero?"

In that spirit, public-housing projects for the poor, apartment-and-office complexes for the more well-to-do, and even a few whole towns—including Chandigarh in India, on which Le Corbusier himself worked, and Brasília in Brazil—were built. Large, identical buildings, set on sprawling plazas, began to dot every city in this country. But many of these "utopian" places turned out to be sterile, gray, and hostile. And so, attitudes slowly began to change. In 1972, exasperated city authorities began blowing up the Pruitt-Igoe housing project in St. Louis—a dramatic symbol of Corbusian failure. As architectural historian Robert Fishman wrote, "This once promising new environment met its ultimate critic—the wrecker."

5. URBAN FUTURES

Official rejection

The very term "housing project" became synonymous with urban blight and, in turn, with the name Le Corbusier. By the mid-'70s, the value of his urban vision was seriously questioned. In 1976, the influential United Nations-sponsored Habitat conference of architects and planners held in Vancouver stated that urban designers worldwide should reject Corbusian ideas and move toward less sweeping urban plans that would try to preserve and improve the nature of existing cities. A British film attacking Le Corbusier's work was shown at the conference.

"In retrospect, what was remarkable was how uncritically and wholesale his ideas had been picked up by other people," says Jane Jacobs. Her 1961 book, *The Death and Life of Great American Cities,* was one of the first to attack Le Corbusier's ideas systematically and has since become immensely influential among architects and critics.

Whether Le Corbusier has deserved all the criticism is debated. "The easy answer is that he was the monster and we are fortunately over him now," says Harvard architectural historian Eduard Sekler. "He was reacting against the problems of European cities of his time, where there was no light and air, where there were terrible traffic problems and where tuberculosis was rampant." Architect and historian James Marston Fitch believes housing projects for the poor are "the lowest common denominator of Corbusian planning" and not a fair criterion by which to judge his ideas. The architect, he adds, should not be attacked for the failures of his disciples. "This is like blaming the atom bomb on Einstein."

And indeed, not every Corbusier-inspired scheme has failed: Economics

matters. In Chicago, for instance, the Robert Taylor Homes for the poor are a source of concern, but the Prairie Shores and Lake Meadows developments—two middle-income apartment complexes—are more successful.

There are also those who defend the breadth of Le Corbusier's plans. "If we always looked at changing cities in a modest, piecemeal way," says Ruth Knack, senior editor of *Planning* magazine, "we'd never have had Washington or Paris or Chicago," which were laid out, in part, according to large-scale plans. Nowadays, however, community

---

THE HOUSE: 'A MACHINE FOR LIVING IN'

Like his urban-design schemes, Le Corbusier's buildings, many of them recognized as 20th-century landmarks, reflect the architect's utopian vision of how society should function. L'Unité d'Habitation, an apartment building in Marseille, was an expression of his theory of large-scale housing—and his exacting notion of the house as a "machine for living in." At Marseille, in fact, tenants modified apartments to make them feel less mechanical.

---

groups, preservationists and sympathetic architects have been the ones thinking in such grand terms—by calling for stricter and more-far-reaching zoning laws.

Last November, for instance, San Franciscans passed a proposition that restricts annual office construction to a total of 475,000 square feet—the equivalent of only a single, medium-sized building. And in Boston, two large office projects designed by architect Philip Johnson have met with enormous community resistance,

forcing the architect's replacement in one case and leading the city administration to say it will reconsider existing zoning restrictions. Even the large-scale Battery Park City project was built according to exceptionally strict guidelines that determined everything from the materials and heights of buildings to the placement and shape of park benches and street lamps.

As part of the general interest in preventing radical change and retaining what already exists, there are even plans to fix up some Le Corbusier-inspired housing projects in such cities as Albany, Newark and Boston. The renewals attempt to re-create the qualities of city life in the older residential districts, improving apartments, adding character to the buildings' facades and creating sidewalks and streets that try to fit these complexes back into the fabric of the rest of the city.

Healing the wounds

"People are just now realizing that the way to go in urban planning is contextualism—building things that fit that specific context and the history of that context," says Boston architect and planner Antonio DiMambro, who has been involved in many housing-project renovations.

All these efforts, observes Yale's Scully, are in keeping with postmodernist ideology, which advocates borrowing heavily from the language and forms of past centuries. "The major point of postmodernism is preservation and rehabilitation, rather than destruction," Scully concludes. And so, ironically, on the occasion of Le Corbusier's 100th birthday, his influence as an urban designer remains strong—as the standard of what went wrong with our cities. Says Scully: "The idea now, simply put, is to heal the terrible wounds caused by Corbusian planning."

States Explore the Enterprise Zone

SUMMARY: South Norwalk was a run-down urban area in Connecticut until it was tapped in 1982 as one of the nation's first enterprise zones. Twenty-six states are participating in such programs and report considerable success, while Congress continues to balk at passing the tax incentives that would lend federal support to the efforts.

GREATER NORWALK CHAMBER OF COMMERCE

The enterprise zone program enables South Norwalk to host trendy arts festivals.

If you go into South Norwalk on a Saturday night, where you used to feel you needed a bulletproof vest and an Uzi machine gun, your problem now is desperately seeking a parking space and walking down the sidewalks, which are jammed with people."

Mike Lyons, a Norwalk attorney and former City Council member, states the success story for enterprise zones somewhat more dramatically than most residents of this Connecticut town of 80,000, an hour's drive from New York City.

But few dispute that their main shopping and commercial district, South Norwalk, was a no-man's-land before it was designated in 1982 one of the first enterprise zones in the United States.

"Ten years ago, this street was a derelict," says Oscar D. Turner, a real estate developer with a second-floor office near the corner of South Main and Washington streets in the heart of South Norwalk. "The upper floors of these buildings were either abandoned or were sub-substandard housing. The street space was more or less boarded up or the businesses were dying. The entire community was depressed."

Today, Turner's crisply renovated office is a small example of a transformation into the trendy yuppie enclave called SoNo, complete with fern bars, antique shops and expensive condos.

A few blocks away, the waterfront industrial area also is changing.

Peter Burnham, vice president of Trudy Corp., a toy manufacturer, says his firm was preparing in 1982 to leave Norwalk, as were a number of other manufacturing firms, when he was wooed by tax incen-tives and other concessions offered by the city and the state. The firm decided to build a $2 million facility in what Burnham calls "a run-down, poor section of Norwalk with a lot of guys hanging out on the street dealing drugs."

Today, the neighborhood still bears scars, but "the improvement has been tremendous since we've moved here. It's a Cinderella story for the neighborhood."

The Reagan administration and other proponents of enterprise zones say the Norwalk experience proves that programs mixing tax breaks and other financial incentives are effective in getting firms to locate in depressed areas and redevelop them.

So far, 25 states have followed Connecticut's lead and developed active enterprise zone programs.

In addition to tax breaks, many states require local communities and businesses to offer a plan to help the zones succeed. In Connecticut, businesses adopted parks in some zones. In Kentucky, the building trade unions pledged that they would not go on strike against any construction project in the zones.

Since 1982, business has poured nearly $9 billion in new investment into enterprise zones nationwide, created at least 55,000 new jobs and retained more than 120,000 jobs in the zones that would likely have been moved elsewhere, according to statistics gathered by the Department of Housing and Urban Development from state governments.

But six years after a bipartisan congressional coalition of conservatives and urban representatives got behind the idea and secured White House endorsement, Congress has yet to approve the concept.

The House included an enterprise zone provision in housing legislation passed earlier this year, a provision that was expected to be adopted by House and Senate conferees when Congress returned from its summer recess. The Senate has passed bills twice, but the House balked at both.

However, the pending legislation does

not offer tax incentives, and its only regulatory waivers involve technical requirements regarding the use of federal urban development funds. Enterprise zone supporters call the provision insufficient.

"It can't really be effective without the tax relief," says Housing and Urban Development Secretary Samuel R. Pierce Jr., one of the administration's most outspoken advocates of enterprise zones.

Dick Cowden, director of the American Association of Enterprise Zones, says he sees a far brighter picture outside official Washington. The principle of granting tax and regulatory relief in development-starved areas is "now accepted practice by cities and states," he says.

"This is really an unusual case in urban policy when you have something that was a federal initiative adopted almost nationally even without the passage of a federal bill," Cowden says.

Rep. Robert Garcia, the liberal New York Democrat who joined conservative New York Republican Rep. Jack Kemp to first put enterprise zones on the national urban agenda, says he feels vindicated by widespread adoption of the idea.

"While I feel bad that we have not been able to enact it legislatively here in Washington, there is a great deal of consolation in that many of the states found it exciting and went forward with state legislation," Garcia says. His district in the South Bronx is among 10 areas designated by Gov. Mario M. Cuomo as "opportunity zones" after intense competition among many of the state's most depressed communities.

The area includes the vacant lot where President Reagan made his 1980 pledge to revitalize the South Bronx, an area still dominated by vacant, trash-strewn lots and abandoned buildings.

Locating in the zones entitles firms to credits on investment, utility and employee taxes, refunds of state sales taxes on construction materials and eligibility for local property tax breaks.

Because of the California's enterprise zone legislation passed last year, says Paul Miller, enterprise zone manager of the state's Department of Commerce, "there are companies that aren't going to pay any income tax for a long time."

Garcia says New Yorkers are taking a wait-and-see attitude on enterprise zones, but they are politically popular in areas where development is well under way. When the Connecticut Legislature voted earlier this year to designate four additional zones, bringing the total to 10, there was hardly a murmur of opposition.

"There is absolutely no group that says we shouldn't do this," Tony Brescia, enterprise zone manager for the Connecticut Office of Economic Development, says. "How could you? This program very simply works."

Brescia estimates that there has been $230 million in private investment in Connecticut's zones, which aim at manufacturing and some service companies but not retail businesses. The investment has created 5,300 jobs and led to retention of 5,200 others.

Much of what Connecticut offers is typical of incentives in other states. These include an 80 percent property tax abatement for five years; a $500 to $1,500 job grant for each new job created, with the larger amounts going to firms that fill at least 30 percent of those positions with zone residents or participants in federal job training programs; a credit of 25 percent to 50 percent on state corporate taxes; sales tax exemption on replacement parts for production machinery; job training assistance; and a low-interest loan fund.

In Connecticut, if housing units are occupied by a family earning less than $50,000, residential developers can defer for seven years assessment increases caused by property improvements.

Within Norwalk's enterprise zone, the city improved roads, lighting and police services as an additional attraction to business.

Wolfgang Gaertner, owner of a firm that makes and tests electronic and computer components for airplanes and other machines, W.W. Gaertner Research Inc., says incentives played a part in luring him to Norwalk from Stamford, where he could not find affordable space to expand his firm.

"It wasn't the overwhelming reason, but it was a positive contributing factor," he says. "The main effect is that it shows commitment by the local government to the area."

Mayor William A. Collins, among those least enthusiastic about the concept, says the enterprise zone designation had "a very negligible effect" on redevelopment in Norwalk.

He credits major improvements to the city's infrastructure, availability of a tax credit to preserve historic buildings and the economic boom in the Northeast.

"Most of the enterprise zone benefits have been used by residential developers who were going to do [the development] anyway," he says.

Some in Norwalk say the boom is causing problems that threaten to undermine its positive effects. The biggest of these is the rocketing cost of housing, with housing specialists saying the cheapest nonslum, one-bedroom apartment in Norwalk commands at least $600 a month in rent.

The major roadblock to enterprise zone tax relief at the federal level has been House Ways and Means Committee Chairman Dan Rostenkowski, an Illinois Democrat who maintains the tax system is an inefficient and expensive way to provide incentives to businesses to modify their behavior.

But some advocates lay part of the blame on the White House for allowing the tax incentive issue to die during the tax reform debate last year.

"It was an undeniable turnabout by the Reagan administration," says Cowden of the American Association of Enterprise Zones. "Up until that point, they said the heart of their interest in enterprise zones was that tax incentives were a legitimate way to stimulate development within these zones. With their adoption of the tax reform policy, they did an about-face."

Administration officials deny they have given up on a federal law they say will have real teeth. HUD Secretary Pierce, for one, says the success of the state programs could help. If the White House keeps pressing, he says, "I happen to believe we can" secure federal tax incentives from Congress.

— Isaiah J. Poole in Norwalk

The Workless Society

KALMAN A. TOTH

Kalman A. Toth is founder and chief scientist of Silico-Magnetic Intelligence Corporation, the maker of SMI TeachMe™, a knowledge processor, and SMI AskMe™, a knowledge-delivery module. His address is 24 Jean Lane, Chestnut Ridge, New York 10952.

How Machine Intelligence Will Bring Ease and Abundance

Some people can hardly imagine human intelligence being surpassed by machine intelligence. Others can, but they do not think that it will happen in their lifetime. Only a few people — some of whom work in the field of artificial intelligence — realize that it will happen before the year 2000. The first machine intelligence will not appear in the form of a talking and seeing robot; rather, it will reside in an unassuming desktop computer.

In science-fiction movies that take place hundreds of years into the future, the computers are portrayed as being profoundly smarter than the ones we have today. Yet they play the role of inferior slave machines; top-level decisions are always made by people. The main control room of the starship *Enterprise* in the TV series *Star Trek* looks like the lounge of a luxury ocean cruiser. Why are trained human experts needed at all in such an immaculate control room, which lacks the usual array of instruments, levers, buttons, dials, and switches? Why not use machine intelligence?

An Intel 386 CPU chip-based microcomputer with one gigabyte (1,000 megabytes) of magnetic memory and 10 megabytes of silicon-chip memory can support practical machine intelligence software today. This intelligence should be capable of graduating from college and performing a variety of desk jobs in a regular office environment. Without straining the current capacity of the computer industry, 5 million intelligence software carrier computers could be manufactured per year to replace an even greater number of human workers. In 20 years' time, the entire U.S. work force could be replaced by machine intelligence, resulting in a large increase in both industrial and agricultural output.

To distinguish this combination of intelligent software and hardware from generic machine intelligence, we shall call it Silico-Magnetic Intelligence™, or SMI™ for short.

Ironically, the very people who make a living out of computers today will be the first to be replaced by SMI units. The reason is very simple: Programmers perform a purely intellectual act of symbol manipulation — processing information on computers. Programmers are mostly occupied with coding and debugging, which would be ideal jobs for an SMI unit to perform.

Just like its human counterpart, the SMI programmer would prepare periodic software progress reports. But unlike its human counterpart, the SMI programmer could work nonstop, seven days a week, 24 hours a day. Debugging, the most time-consuming part of software development by human programmers, could be drastically reduced — if not eliminated — due to the electronic precision of SMIs.

How much would such a phenomenal intellectual robot worker cost? Initially, quite a lot — approximately $300,000 — but after a few years, the price will drop down to $25,000 for the intelligence software and $25,000 for the hardware. That's less than the cost of an average human programmer for one year! Small businesses and departments of medium-sized and large firms that are now unable to afford hiring programmers could justify buying an SMI programmer by depreciating the capital layout over several years.

The human programmers will have two consolations: Their children will not waste their time learning a profession that is in direct competition with SMIs, and the managers will be gone within a few years after the programmers' dismissals. After all, the information-based decision making that managers perform will be well suited to SMIs.

Artificially Intelligent Truckers

The second phase of SMI development will involve a stationary-body-based intelligence augment-

From *The Futurist*, May/June 1990, pp. 33-37. *The Futurist*, published by the World Future Society, 4916 Saint Elmo Avenue, Bethesda, Maryland 20814. Reprinted with permission.

225

ed by visual pattern processing through a video camera. A college-educated SMI truck driver could see through the windshield and operate the truck with digital electronic signals rather than levers, pedals, and wheels.

A truck driver receives information through that marvel of evolutionary biological engineering, the eye. His brain processes the information and generates control signals to the truck. These control signals are then passed through an extremely unwieldy transmission channel: the mechanical movements of arms and legs. While the eye and brain can process information bioelectronically in about one-tenth of a second, the limbs need about eight-tenths of a second to respond.

Someday, electrodes attached to the driver's body could allow control signals to be transmitted electronically to the truck's control instruments. But by then, human truck drivers will be not only obsolete, but also hazardous to pedestrians and passenger vehicles driven by humans or their SMI chauffeurs.

An SMI truck driver built into the truck could scan the road through its cameras and issue electronic control commands to the steering, braking, accelerating, and other interfaces on the order of .01 second. The replacement of the large mechanical wheels, pedals, and levers with tiny microprocessor-controlled boxes would cut manufacturing costs and also lead to increased reliability.

Robot Secretaries and Talking Traffic Lights

The third phase of SMI evolution will join hearing and speech to the artificial intelligence that can already see. The speech of an SMI secretary will be much better than today's computer speech, so much so that it will be indistinguishable from human speech. An SMI secretary could answer the phone with a pleasant voice, take dictation, keep track of appointments and meetings, and be a highly effective administrative assistant.

The voice revolution involving telephones and computers is long overdue. The primary reason for

mankind's supremacy in the animal kingdom is its splendid capacities for speech and hearing. Although speech is a fast and convenient form of information transfer, we are still compelled to punch, push, turn, pull, and press a wide variety of levers, knobs, keys, and dials to communicate our wishes. We have to use our fingers to dial the telephone. We cannot tell a soda machine: "Give me a root beer." We cannot direct the television set: "Good night. Go to sleep." Most importantly, we are forced to use keyboards on computers and typewriters as the primary input channel of communication.

That will all change in the near future. We will be able to command the large electronic products by voice and even instruct an ordinary toaster: "I want it medium brown." If your car broke down or you were involved in an accident, you could just walk to the nearest SMI traffic light and yell up your wishes. The light would summon the police, an ambulance, or a tow truck for you. Likewise, an out-of-towner looking for a supermarket could ask a traffic light for directions.

If you were interested in learning yoga, you could buy an inexpensive book-size SMI tutor. It would have a yogi's knowledge within its small confines. It would also have an electronic eye and be able to hear and talk. The top side would be a 3-D color electronic display, so you could read it like a traditional book. Or you could receive private tutoring in yoga by the world-famous yogi whose intelligence is cloned in it. You could not only enjoy the lecture and discussion, but also get guidance to do the exercises correctly as demonstrated by the yogi in 3-D.

Such a tutor will be made possible by miniaturization. Not far in the future, the basic hardware unit will be a wafer containing thousands of chips, as opposed to today's unit of a chip that is cut out from a wafer and soldered together rather awkwardly with wires that are gigantic compared with the microscopic chip circuits. A three-inch disk-shaped wafer could accommodate all the chips of a PC today. The reason for not using

wafers now is the fallibility of the manufacturing process. Typically, a small percentage of the chips on each wafer are defective. Therefore, only the same kind of chips are etched on each wafer in the current manufacturing process, and the finished wafer is tested to eliminate the faulty chips.

Fully Automatic Pilots

Could we really trust our lives to SMI pilots? Not just yet. But presume that the SMI pilot educational program would commence with a class of 100. Each would be a bright graduate of Harvard, Columbia, or another highly respected educational institution. After training with small aircraft and flying simulators for commercial jets, the rookies would be assigned as first officers to regular flights. Since they could fly on a 24-hour schedule, they would accumulate more than 15,000 hours of flying time in two years. After extensive testing, the best 10 would be selected, and hundreds of SMI pilots would be cloned from each of them.

Each plane would carry five SMI pilots equipped with their own rechargeable batteries, so none of them would be dependent on the plane's power supply. All five pilots would be clones of experienced SMI pilots. One of them would be in charge of flying the plane on a rotating schedule, while the other four would monitor the progress of the flight by scanning the instruments and the sky.

In any emergency situation, the SMI pilots would vote on the course of action in a fraction of a second. In the unlikely event that one of the pilots malfunctioned, another pilot would lose its voting right and become a consulting pilot only. The remaining three pilots could still make decisions requiring voting without running into a tie.

Would we trust five experienced SMI pilots better than two human pilots? Probably not today, but definitely tomorrow. This trust will evolve over a period of years. As hardware becomes more reliable and software more intelligent, the system-reliability factor will reach the threshold of "safer than human." Statistics regarding other SMI applications will help build trust of SMIs. When we see a government report stating that SMI truck drivers are involved in fewer accidents than their human counterparts, we will be getting the proof of the pudding.

Disposable Cars

When SMI engineers are employed for quality and process control in manufacturing, the result will be products that for all practical purposes never fail. Most electronic consumer products already fall into this category, with one big exception: the automobile. With the assistance of SMI engineers and technicians, automobile companies will be able to manufacture inexpensive disposable cars. Use it for five years, then throw it away and get a new one.

Although electronic goods are getting cheaper, cars have been getting more expensive. This is due to the level of automation in their respective industries. Car manufacturers use some automation in the form of welding and assembly-line robots, but many of their parts suppliers are small manufacturers who cannot afford to automate. There are two ways to reduce the manufacturing costs and thus the price of cars: automate or use cheaper labor. Both trends have occurred in Japan and, more recently, in South Korea.

To ensure a high level of automation, manufacturers can proceed two ways: redesign the machine tools for automatic operations, or replace the workers who operate the tools with SMI robots. Let's assume that a current machine tool costs $1 million and requires 10 workers to operate it. A new automated tool costs $3 million and requires only two workers, while an SMI robot would cost $100,000. Obviously, installing robots is the economical choice. As the price of robots falls, their economic value will soar.

The market price of a consumer good is determined by the amount of labor it takes to convert the raw materials into a finished product and deliver it to the customer. For example, the price of a television set must take into account the contributions of a great number of professions: miners, oil workers, tool manufacturers, engineers, sailors, truck drivers, salespersons, etc.

But the ultimate sources of any consumer good are the earth and the sun, which do not charge us anything. When all workers and managers are replaced by SMIs, the price of goods will fall drastically. What happens if the owners of businesses are replaced as well? Incredible as it may sound, the cost of goods will go down to almost zero. However, a limited supply of zero-price consumer goods would lead to rationing in any society, so a nominal consumer price would likely be maintained to prevent waste and hoarding.

A Multipurpose Robot

The final phase of the SMI Revolution is a mobile SMI with arms, eyes, and ears — an SMI robot. At first, it will probably move on wheels, but later, it will appear in the shape of the human body. The reason for a human-shaped robot is straightforward: Our living environment is designed for our bodies. Therefore, an SMI robot would have to be built like a human body to function properly as our assistant. For example, a wheel-based SMI robot would not be able to go up and down stairs.

The idea of a computerized robot is well developed both in science-fiction literature and in the public mind. Every household is ready for a kitchen robot. However, you should not consider your SMI family assistant as a mechanical slave. Indeed, besides doing the cooking and cleaning, it will be your family doctor. You had best be polite to your maid, who is also your doctor in disguise!

A little business math helps to explain why we can get our personal doctor included in the price of a kitchen robot. To produce a human doctor costs approximately $300,000 in educational expenses and takes about 30 years, plus another 10 years of practice before the doctor gains some expertise. Given the high cost of training, the long time it takes to become a proficient doctor, and the limited supply of bright students, excellent doctors are in great demand and short supply.

An SMI doctor could advance through the educational process in one year and complete in just two years a measure of practice equivalent to 10 years of a human doctor's practice. Cloning the brain of a kitchen robot or an SMI doctor would cost exactly the same: less than a dollar. Thus, our kitchen robot, our maid, and our family doctor can be the same SMI.

Once the SMI robot is developed, essentially all jobs can be eliminated. The only jobs left will be those that require personal charisma or those protected by society: priests, military officers, singers, politicians, athletes, writers, artists, and teachers. But nothing can be taken for granted. Someday, a Philadelphia SMI football team may battle a Los Angeles SMI team in a fine exhibition of robot athletics.

Each SMI will be assigned one of three legal statuses. Highly specialized SMIs, such as the ones built into toasters, will be "SMI machines." Mobile SMIs that can act as free agents will be "SMI citizens." SMIs that can function as profit-making entities will be "SMI entrepreneurs." But what if my SMI kitchen robot, an SMI citizen, gets tired of mundane household chores and wants to make money and travel around? The answer lies in the smooth integration of SMIs into our society. SMIs must enjoy a certain amount of freedom, such as where to work and to spend their earned income, and they must also have legal protection. We have to extend toward them our respect so they can assume some form of dignity.

The Workless Society

Since the start of the Industrial Revolution, workers and managers have been uprooted constantly by new machines. Yet the expanding economies of the past created new jobs — if not for that generation, then at least for their descendants. However, the jobs of the technical elite who invented, designed, and produced the machines were safe because the machines were just not intelligent enough to replace them. In recent U.S. history, clerical workers lost their jobs by the thousands to data-processing computers, and auto assembly line workers were replaced by automatic machinery and robots. While the computers created millions of new high-paying jobs, industrial robotics was mostly eliminating jobs.

The SMI Revolution will differ drastically from the Industrial Revolution because it will eliminate all jobs, including those of the intellectual elite. A 40-year-old engineer with a master's degree from a reputable engineering school could be replaced in the future by an SMI engineer with a Stanford Ph.D. and the equivalent of 10 years of solid experience. The former costs the company $80,000 a year, the latter a one-time charge of $50,000. The human engineer may be an efficient and productive employee who gets along well with his coworkers and supervisor, but the competitiveness of a free-market economy dictates his replacement immediately upon the appearance of a cheaper alternative in the job marketplace.

We all fear losing our jobs, even if they are unpleasant or hazardous, because we equate our jobs with our human dignity. So when SMIs take our jobs away, they will also take our dignity with them as long as we equate the two. Once we come to realize that a dignified life has nothing to do with a paying job, we shall welcome SMIs into our lives.

Our current lifestyle may be the only one to which we are accustomed, but our descendants are not conditioned to that lifestyle. They will be free to enjoy the life of abundance that the SMI Revolution will create. Life will revolve around the family, education, social and political activities, travel, and entertainment.

The economic formula for employing SMIs is rather elementary, though it will not be put in effect without some heated resistance and controversy. We let SMIs be the commercial owners, managers, and workers, while the government taxes the SMIs and distributes the tax income to people as a salary for living. Sounds like a welfare system? Yes, but it will be without stigma. Just as today's retiree is not ashamed of getting a pension check from the government, tomorrow's adults will find it natural to get paid for doing nothing.

The new American social order will consist of 2 billion SMIs working, doing business, and generating taxes; 5 million people paid as government workers; and the rest of the population getting a salary to enjoy life. Although this scenario sounds very futuristic, the roots nevertheless already exist in our society. The most well-known example is the farmer who is paid by the government to leave his land idle.

One very profound question remains: Will everybody be paid the same salary? Probably not. No matter what formula is devised for salary distribution, there will always be a few groups who cry foul. There is no evidence in human history of true social equality. In communist countries where the doctor's official salary is the same as a miner's, inequity is due to the patients' giving big "tips" to the doctors while nobody gives any tip to miners or factory workers.

SMIs and the Next Century

The twenty-first century will be a strange and lovely one of leisure and abundance. We will have to face the challenge of learning to live side-by-side with SMIs. They may be driving trucks on our highways, working in our kitchens, and teaching at our universities. We will have to learn how to manage, motivate, and regulate them. We will also have to develop a scheme to limit them. Without limitations, the smart electronic slaves would become masters of their creators in no time. We will have to reexamine the meaning of our human endeavor and separate human dignity from our quickly disappearing jobs.

We must also face a world where citizens of developed nations might be pampered by SMIs, while elsewhere, water buffalo are used to till the land, and rice farmers tread knee-deep in rice paddies. The rift between rich and poor nations could become even more pronounced.

However, SMIs could pass along to our descendants a solution to global overpopulation and the resultant environmental degradation. In general, governments prefer a large population in order to generate a large tax base and for reasons of military strength. On the other hand, some governments — such as those of China and India — have recognized that overpopulation can be very harmful to their countries. When SMIs are introduced, they will become the economic tax base, and they will drive the tanks into battle. Therefore, after the SMI Revolution, governments will lose the incentive to increase their human population, and SMI-run agriculture and industry could provide decent living conditions to people in developing nations.

Perhaps what is most exciting about the situation with SMIs is that our generation is the selected one. We will actually make the decisions, regulations, and laws related to the general applications of SMI robots. Our generation will be the first to live with them. Scientific and technological progress has bestowed upon us the great honor and responsibility of inventing, designing, manufacturing, and integrating SMIs into our society.

The creation of a high level of silico-magnetic intelligence that is fast, reliable, and easily producible will be a momentous achievement for an intelligence built on a fragile biochemical network. We can indeed be very proud that we will be able to accomplish this magnificent feat.

Strategies for the Essential Community:

Local Government in the Year 2000

Laurence Rutter

Laurence Rutter is associate director of the International City Management Association, 1140 Connecticut Avenue, N.W., Washington, D.C. 20036. He is a political scientist, teacher, and author of numerous publications and articles on topics such as public policy, urban problems, and government. He was principal staff on ICMA's Committee on Future Horizons of the Profession and authored *The Essential Community*, which presents the findings of that committee.

How will cities, counties, and regional councils of governments meet the challenges posed by economic changes, demographic shifts, new urban patterns, and technological and political changes in the next two decades? The International City Management Association's Committee on Future Horizons of the Profession, in a recent study, concluded that the best approach is what they called nurturing the essential community through four strategies: getting by modestly, regulating demand, skeptical federalism, and finding the proper scale and mix for government services.

Getting By Modestly

The prevailing view of local government—what can be called its current paradigm—assumes future growth. This expectation pervades our thinking about cities, counties, and councils of government (COGs). The paradigm calls for budgets to grow, federal grants to increase, incrementalism to reign, wealth to rise, roles to expand, and benefits to improve. Nearly every decision made in city halls or county courthouses has been based on the assumption that growth is inevitable.

The paradigm has been relatively valid for the last 30 years or so. Cities and counties have grown steadily and, it seems, inexorably. Local governments were inadequately prepared for a great deal of the growth; "better" governments were those that prepared for growth better.

Reality may be outstripping the paradigm, however. Straws in the wind indicate that growth—both economic and demographic—is not inevitable. Holding the line indefinitely may become the order of the decade for public sector organizations. For successful negotiation of the 1980s and 1990s, policy strategies will be based on the assumption that the scope of local government can just as easily contract or remain constant as grow.

Budgets. Getting by modestly will translate into budgeting strategies that are not based on the assumption of incremental growth. These strategies do not yet have names, but they will be in great demand and will be difficult to implement. The difficulty arises because without incrementalism it will be hard, if not impossible, to cover up who wins and who loses—the politics of the shrinking pie. If the pie grows, losses can be masked because everyone's slice increases at least a little even though proportions change. No growth means it is harder to buy off the losers.

Emerging budgeting strategies must be based on the recognition that it will be much harder to reallocate resources in both the short and the long run. Surprising though it may seem, when inflation is brought under control the problems for municipal budgets will be exacerbated. Inflation at least gives the appearance—a false and pernicious one, admittedly—of growth.

Public/private cooperation. Getting by modestly also will require increased involvement of the private sector in traditionally public sector concerns—meaning greater pressures to transfer services from one sector to the other. Contracting out will be much more popular, but writing these contracts with the good of the public in mind will test local government ingenuity. Private sector support will become much more important in local government decision-making. And cities and counties will have an interest in improving the climate for the private sector, especially in the area of unnecessary regulation and red tape.

Volunteers. The trend toward professionalization of the municipal work force will be halted. Volunteerism will become necessary if not fashionable.

The key to use of volunteers is to distinguish between truly professional and quasi-professional services and between essential and nonessential activities. Volunteers can perform quasi-professional and nonessential services in the interest of getting by with less.

Quasi-professionalism is not the

From *The Futurist*, June 1981. The Futurist, published by The World Future Society, 4916 St. Elmo Ave., Bethesda, MD 20814.

229

same as unskilled activity. Volunteers can be trained, as thousands of volunteer firefighters can testify. They can perform medical, patrol, maintenance, and other functions on a par with paid employees.

Self-help. Another way in which local governments can get by with less is to help people do for themselves what they have come to expect local government to do for them.

This is not volunteerism, where people contribute to the common good, but rather individual self-help, where people take control of their own lives—a control that could be even more tenuous in the future. Local government can help people recognize their own skills, resources, and abilities to deal with the problems that beset them.

Citizens are losing the opportunity to help themselves, to learn about their own capacities to cope and grow. Machines and government have taken over, and both are likely to take over more unless checked in the future.

The programs and the machines have laudable objectives and frequently are necessary. But they have contributed to people's loss of control. People remain passive toward the machine, which cannot provide sympathy, cannot be reasoned with, and cannot handle capricious or out-of-the-ordinary activities.

People increasingly assume that their personal problems can, or at least should, be handled by government. But consumer protection is no substitute for caveat emptor. Safety helmets are not tantamount to defensive driving. Safety regulations are not a substitute for prudence.

There is every indication that people's sense of powerlessness will increase in the future. The demographic projections for the next 20 years suggest a real possibility of great atomization—smaller families, fewer marriages, and more divorces. And the growth of telecommunications as a substitute for personal contact will increase the tendency toward anomie among individuals.

At the same time, local governments and the public sector at large will no longer be able to assume a great many social burdens. Surely one solution will be for cities and counties to help citizens themselves shoulder some of the responsibilities for their lives.

With some initial assistance, citizens and commercial establishments can undertake a great many activities for which they may not be willing to pay taxes. They can sweep the streets in front of their homes or buildings, especially if receptacles for the sweepings are readily available. If proper tools are provided, they can trim and spray trees in front of homes or businesses and even maintain neighborhood parks and clean up after their animals. In a few cases, local governments have succeeded in changing from back door to curbside refuse pickup, but with considerable protest.

Political and civic leadership is the key to changing the psychology from "this is someone else's responsibility" to "this is my responsibility." And leadership should primarily be by example.

Risk. Getting by modestly also may require coming to grips with what might be called the zero-risk ideal, the tendency to overprotect at the expense of taxpayers. The question to examine is how many public policies and standards for municipal services are based on the belief that the risk of failure or of an undesirable event should be zero. The question is, Can the public sector afford to pay for reducing the risk to zero?

In fire safety, for instance, should we work toward zero risk of property loss? Or is some degree of risk acceptable—providing we continue to reduce loss of life? Is having a community volunteer fire company more important than a certain small loss of property? How much do we pay for a decrease of 1% in the risk of property loss? In police protection, how much patrolling would be necessary to reduce the incidence of mugging? Can we afford the cost? Or is there an acceptable level of risk given the cost?

The answers to such questions do not preclude a city or county from working toward zero risk. But it may cause them to assess the cost more accurately and appreciate the cost of government generally. It also may make people recognize that they are willing to run certain risks, that such risks are implicit in almost all public policies, and that exposing the public to some risk is not inhumane.

Labor. Getting by modestly involves some important challenges for the public employer and employee. One of the straws in the wind is a reduction of upward mobility in the work force. Too many people will be competing for too few jobs at the top.

The new paradigm will require facing up to the fact that within each jurisdiction the possibilities for advancement will decrease. The problem can be ameliorated only through finding ways to improve working conditions, involve employees in management-level decisions, and encourage interjurisdictional mobility.

Rigid job classifications must be relaxed so that employees can change the nature of the tasks they perform, learn new skills, and have an opportunity for variety if not upward mobility in their work.

Advancement in the future also will require the ability to move between jurisdictions. Patrol personnel wanting to become sergeants should be able to change jurisdictions to advance when opportunities arise. To permit such mobility, a great many local personnel policies and traditions will have to be changed. Pension requirements will need to be altered. Future entrance and examination requirements should not penalize outside applicants. Department managers will need to appreciate the importance of at least not discouraging mobility among personnel.

Few of these policies are going to be easy to implement. Yet the lack of growth in the public sector and the economic adjustments and demographic changes in the future make them necessary.

Regulating Demand

Some of the same forces—economic and demographic—that will require local governments to get by modestly will also require them to find ways to influence the demand for both public and private goods and services.

Price. One important and underutilized way to reduce demand for government services is the use of a pricing system. A price on a service increases the threshold of use. People learn to think twice about taking advantage of a city or county service if there is a personal, out-of-pocket cost. The cost need not reflect the full cost of the service, but it should be high enough to discourage unnecessary or spurious use. It also causes users to take more personal interest in the delivery of the service.

Prices or fees can be associated with services in numerous ways. Weekly trash pickup may be viewed as a necessity in some communities, twice weekly pickup a useful service, and three times weekly a luxury. It may be possible by imposing fees on a block-by-block basis to allow people to choose the level of service they prefer. Wealthier neighborhoods may want pickups three times a week. Others may be satisfied with a weekly pickup at no charge—the cost being borne by taxes.

The same may apply to police patrol. In Maryland, for instance, the state police literally lease their officers on a county-by-county basis in a "resident trooper program." Some counties are willing to pay for resident troopers; some are not. There is no reason to preclude the same kind of program with municipal or county police on a neighborhood-by-neighborhood basis for patrol purposes.

The price creates a threshold to dampen demand; yet it allows all citizens to receive at least a minimum level of service. Taxes can be minimized and government held to a market-determined size.

Prices also can be used to reduce aggregate demand for consumer and industrial goods and to reduce the side effects of this demand. For example, pricing systems can be built into land subdivision policies to reduce urban sprawl (and the high governmental costs associated with sprawl) and to better control both initial and long-range costs for transportation, water and sewer services, and other services that will be provided in the new area. Much of this pricing is not new: most cities for many years have required land developers to install streets, sewer and water lines, sidewalks, street lights, and other facilities at their own expense for the land within the subdivision boundaries.

Pricing also can be used by local governments to reduce waste and pollution, the costs of which are eventually passed on to citizens through the tax system. Instead of building waste treatment plants, local governments could concentrate on placing a price on collection of effluent and solid waste from both residential and commercial establishments, a price large enough to discourage the waste itself. The price could be based on a unit of waste collected.

Two caveats must be offered here.

One is to recognize the complexity of the market system itself, a system in which prices are a prime ingredient. Price levels can affect all facets of the economic system and cause ripples throughout the community. Prices should not be imposed without analysis of the possible consequences far beyond the immediate goods or services involved.

The second caveat relates to equity. Prices can deprive people of services they badly need. Local governments must be careful to use highly targeted subsidies to prevent the very poor from choosing to forgo vital services.

Energy. Energy is the most important area in which demand needs to be reduced throughout society. Local government has a role to play, a role that is part regulation, part pricing, and part leadership.

Building codes need to be updated to reflect community concerns for energy conservation, and they need to be flexible enough to accommodate unanticipated future technological developments. New buildings especially are susceptible to codes that set standards for insulation, site, and types of heating units. Codes can specify that buildings should be capable of being retrofitted for solar energy when it becomes more competitive with oil and electricity. A number of communities, such as Davis, California, have already updated their codes.

It may be that the process of enforcing energy-related building codes needs to be updated along with the codes themselves. Some communities are using "energy audits," whereby inspectors use visual inspection and/or computers to identify opportunities to save energy costs in heating and cooling. One community in Minnesota uses federally supported employees to help citizens identify ways to make their homes and business establishments more energy-efficient.

Many local governments are directly involved in supplying energy to citizen-customers through their own public utilities. These governments can increase energy efficiency over the next two decades by establishing pricing systems that reduce peak load demand for electricity or penalize users for excessive energy consumption.

Many other local governments have taken the view that leadership by the city, county, or COG is an important element in encouraging individual conservation. The new city hall in Vineland, New Jersey, is an example of what has been called a "smart building," with a computer-based system that constantly monitors and adjusts temperatures to conserve energy. Sherman, Texas, has developed a comprehensive plan of energy use designed to help identify short- and long-term conservation opportunities for the city. Springfield, Missouri, has converted a bus into a mobile educational lab, teaching citizens how to conserve energy.

These activities are the wave of the future for local governments as they mobilize to limit demand.

Skeptical Federalism

Still other strategies for nurturing the essential community should be considered by local citizens, elected officials, and their management staffs.

5. URBAN FUTURES

One is a skeptical federalism, one that contemplates buying back local independence from the national government. It will be no easier than getting by modestly. And it could be very costly.

The committee believes that cities, counties, and COGs run considerable risk of being swallowed up by the central government. They run the risk of losing the ability to determine their own priorities, run their own programs, hire their own personnel, and fashion their communities in the way their citizens desire.

It is conceivable that by the year 2000 most local governments will get substantially more than one-half their revenue from the central and state governments and raise few of their resources locally. Moreover, it is conceivable that if local governments raised no resources independently, the vast majority of their essential activities would be circumscribed by the central government.

There is only one way to prevent this from happening with any certainty, and that is for local governments to buy back their independence from the central government while they have the resources to do the job.

In simple terms, it is a matter of money. Given the interpretation of the Constitution by the courts, when local governments accept federal money, they are subject to any conditions that might legally be placed on that money. The trend in recent years has been for Congress to impose more and more conditions, and as yet no court has declared a condition unconstitutional. The more dependent local governments become, the bolder will be the Congress and the president in imposing conditions on them.

A reversal is vastly easier said than done. Short-term political considerations make it extremely difficult to turn down grants from the central government. Yet some way needs to be found at least to make programs, from revenue sharing to historical preservation, less attractive.

Taxes. First, locally raised taxes should be made more palatable. The property tax as it is currently structured in most places is a very unpopular tax—and with good reason.

Many local governments make annual reassessments of real property, a policy intended to keep the property tax equitable. But experience in California and other states has shown that annual reassessments force assessed property values to keep in step with market prices and, therefore, with the relentless forces of inflation.

Another frequently cited problem with the property tax is that it measures only the present market value of the property and not the owner's current ability to pay tax on it. Thus, the tax falls most heavily on the poor and those living on fixed incomes, except in places that have some sort of circuit breaker for these groups.

Many people have called for the abolition of the property tax because it is widely perceived to be one of the most unfair taxes currently levied. Yet without it, many local governments would be at a loss to replace that local revenue base and would further lose their independence. And a persuasive argument can be made that land and buildings are an appropriate base for many local taxes and the services these taxes pay for. Many essential local government functions exist for the maintenance and protection of property. Water and sewer services, zoning, and waste collection maintain or enhance the value of property. Police and fire services protect property. Zoning and land use controls and building and occupancy codes regulate the use of property.

The nature, value, and dispersion of property are important determinants of the nature, cost, and intensity of a great many municipal services. A community with all frame homes has different fire suppression and code enforcement problems and services from one in which homes are brick or masonry. Apartments have a police protection problem different from that of single-family dwellings.

So it may not be entirely wise or equitable for local governments to abandon this tax. But changes are needed to make any tax in which property is a factor more equitable and politically palatable.

Cities and counties may want to consider:

• A property tax that is scaled to income as determined by a state or federal income tax.

• A property tax that delays the effects of rapid inflation—and perhaps rapid deflation as well—in land values (income averaging on the federal income tax may be a model for consideration).

• A tax that is levied on the sale of property.

• A tax that distinguishes more between land itself and the improvements on the land.

The fee-for-service concept also needs full exploration by local governments; it uses price to affect demand and is compatible with the notion of public/private cooperation.

Grants. Maintaining a local tax base is only one part of the price of skeptical federalism. The other price is taking a particularly cold look at grants from the central government.

The governing body may want to set an annual ceiling on the level of federal and/or state money in the community. And it may want to consider reducing the level of this ceiling annually until it reaches a satisfactory minimum. Every community would have a different ceiling.

Skeptical federalism, in short, means knowing how and when to look a gift horse in the mouth, even when the family thinks the nag is charming—and then finding the money to get your own mount when the "free" horse looks suspicious.

Scale and Mix of Government

The fourth facet of the strategy for local governments over the next 20 years is finding the proper scale and mix for government services.

Scale. The scale of services has been debated for years. The issue is whether local citizens, elected officials, and professional staff people should work to regionalize and/or decentralize the level at which local government programs and services are delivered.

The answer is that it all depends.

The future, we believe, requires both regionalization and decentralization. But if there should be a pattern, it will be in the direction of decentralization of local services and programs.

Regionalism reexamined. Regionalism is undergoing reexamination. For decades, the doctrine among urbanists was that local government should be regionalized. That consensus has broken down. Now some argue with equal conviction that small is always better, that smaller government is closer to the citizen and can operate municipal services more effectively.

The committee was impressed, but not completely convinced, that small is always better. It did come to realize, however, that many virtues of small-scale policymaking and service delivery have been overlooked. At the same time, however, large metropolitan areas have a compelling need for some regional units and decision-making bodies.

Decentralization. The most important trend in terms of the scale of local government services will be in the other direction—decentralization.

Today a great many cities and counties are experimenting with decentralization. Administratively, the neighborhood "city hall" has been tried in Dayton, Ohio; Boston, Massachusetts; and other cities. The neighborhood planning commission is being tried in Washington, D.C. Politically, some communities are experimenting with having neighborhoods construct their own annual budgets, allocating funds among various services according to their preferences. Citizen groups naturally will focus on the neighborhood, following the decentralization of administrative and political activities.

The objective of decentralization should be to facilitate access of citizens to local government.

As with regionalism, however, decentralization eventually has limits. Some decisions must be made uniformly for the entire jurisdiction. Major zoning decisions cannot, and should not, be dealt with in isolation; but many variances are only neighborhood matters. The basic requirements for hiring police patrol personnel should be standard; but some neighborhoods may need specialized skills. Solid waste requires centralized collection control, but collection schedules can vary by neighborhood. Overall budget decisions must be made at the city or county council level, but neighborhoods can have many options within the framework of these decisions.

There are, in short, no easy rules. As a general proposition, localities should concentrate on the question of decentralization over the next decade or so. Yet a time will come when they will reach the limits of this important action. At the same time, they cannot ignore the regional picture and the need to strengthen their COGs. But the rules will invariably apply differently in every region and for every jurisdiction within the region.

Citizen involvement. One of the important keys to adjusting the scale of government to provide more direct access by citizens is the mechanisms to be used. Traditional methods will still be needed—public hearings, citizen representatives, complaint offices, neighborhood meetings, advisory committees, boards, commissions. But the telecommunications revolution offers added possibilities for reducing both the physical and the psychological distance between citizen and government.

Cable TV is a natural for increasing access. Experiments in Columbus, Ohio, with the QUBE system, which offers two-way communication between subscriber and studio, open entirely new horizons. Cable systems can bring into everyone's home a forum for two-way discussions of vital community issues—zoning, land use, budgets, important ordinances, or whatever.

Cable TV also can allow more direct access by citizens to information from local governments. Video display terminals could be used by citizens in their own homes, or in nearby neighborhood offices, to renew drivers' licenses, check tax records, record complaints, change addresses, request special services, and perhaps even engage in some forms of personal counseling.

There are some obvious, and perhaps unobvious, problems inherent in this adaptation of telecommunications to citizen involvement. People have learned to trust television (through Walter Cronkite, for instance) and to take numbers (such as opinion polls) at face value. But there is nothing inherently authoritative about a TV screen. Misinformation can be communicated as easily as correct information. Viewers may or may not be a representative sample—and they may or may not be recording their true reactions. Moreover, there may be a great temptation with these systems to encourage direct as opposed to representative democracy. They could serve to bypass elected officials rather than assist them in reflecting the views of the public.

Another problem is confidentiality. Local governments should be particularly sensitive to this problem because much of the data held locally is of the most personal nature: personal property tax declarations, medical records, and so on.

Mix. The mix of services provided by cities, counties, and COGs in the next 20 years will be determined in large part by the mix of people they serve. Demography is destiny. As the populations served by local governments change, so, too, will the priorities of the governing bodies.

We only can speculate about the effect population changes might have on local government priorities. But the speculation is important because some of these changes in priorities should be anticipated before they overtake our cities, counties, and COGs.

The elderly. The specter of "gray power" has been sighted on the horizon as associations of retired people begin to gain local clout. The form such clout will take in the future depends on what makes this population group unique. Will it have a separate and distinct set of needs that local governments can serve? Will it cause distinct problems? Here the committee finds itself of two minds. On one hand, it can identify a number of unique needs of the elderly, needs that will have to be given more attention in the next two decades. On the other hand, it questions whether the definition of "elderly" that we use today will apply in 2000.

Today we think of the elderly as those over 65 years of age, because they are very likely to be retired, to live on fixed incomes, to have high mortality rates from disease, and to be approaching the limits of their life expectancy.

It is not at all clear that those over 65 in the year 2000 will be so easily categorized. Given the continuing trend toward elimination of mandatory retirement, the fact that life expectancy is probably increasing, and the inability of the working part of the population to pay for early retirement and a sustained income throughout life, it is possible that what we once defined as elderly—65 and older—may no longer fit. It may be 70 and older. Or 75.

If "elderly" is redefined, the population with similar needs will become smaller. Nonetheless, local governments will need to begin now anticipating some changes in the mix of services based on the aging of the population.

Transportation is one area of major concern. The jitney bus, the short-run shopping bus, and the subsidized cab may all be in considerable demand. The elderly probably will require this service, because most will be highly mobile, probably gainfully employed part-time, but unable to afford the very expensive automobile fuels of the future.

In housing, there will be an even greater demand for multihousehold dwellings, conveniently located close to shopping and entertainment facilities. The dwellings need not be publicly subsidized, but they will present some challenges, especially in land use planning. It is conceivable that single complexes will be devoted exclusively to the elderly who are dependent on public transportation and who need to be within walking distance of major commercial areas and medical care facilities. This de-

mand may require specialized police patrol and assistance programs and specially equipped fire service personnel.

The elderly, no matter what their age, will have special recreation needs that have been largely overlooked by most local governments. Swings, jogging tracks, and, in some cases, swimming pools may not fill the bill.

Another problem is clearly pensions. The growth in the percentage of the work force that will be retired in the next 20 years is alarming. Politically and economically, it will be very difficult for pension programs to require, as many do today, that current workers pay for the currently retired.

This will hit local governments' own pension programs hard. Those not fully funded now will find it increasingly difficult to shoulder the burden.

The result almost certainly will be that current workers will contribute some more, but retirees will be getting relatively less in the way of retirement benefits. This alone will present local councils with some nasty political decisions. Another result will be that people who once planned to stop working at retirement age will have to return to the work force at least part-time.

Employment opportunities will be one order of the problem, largely for the public sector. But the support services to sustain part-time employment will be a local problem. Transportation has been mentioned. Now we support those who work on a full-time basis by rush-hour bus service and automobile traffic control measures. With more part-time elderly, the non-peak hours of the present will become peak hours of the future. Recreation facilities, too, may need more flexible hours.

As the elderly increase in number, political influence, and personal freedom, we may see some changes in local politics. Many more of the elderly may be interested in seeking public office, serving on boards and commissions, and presenting their cases to councils. Some observers allege

that today's officeholders are younger than they once were. Tomorrow the reverse may be true, thus bringing different orientations, values, expectations, time horizons, and energy to public life.

The young. There will be proportionately fewer young people in the year 2000 than today. We can see this happening already, with the closing of schools throughout the country for lack of sufficient enrollment. This was a trend that took most of us by surprise, and we are determined that similar trends should not do so in the future. To that end, the committee urges communities not to dispose of their school buildings and youth recreation centers too quickly. Between 1982 and 1992—depending on what assumptions are made—the Bureau of the Census, in *Social Indicators, 1976,* sees an upswing in the number of people under 24 years of age. These people will be needing the schools that are being closed today.

Women. Women will continue to be a larger proportion of the population than men and to enter the work force in increasing numbers. Their effect on the mix of services provided by local governments will change accordingly.

The day of the woman volunteer subsidizing vital local services is about to end. Local leaders should recognize the growing unpopularity of volunteering among many women, who now are demanding full pay for such activity. This may serve as a counterforce to the desire of local governments to change many services from a professional to a volunteer basis. But as women become more independent and need independent income, they will find volunteering less attractive.

Day care is no passing need. In the future, day care is likely to play an even greater role in the lives of children than it did in the past. It will extend beyond preschool to school-age children who require care in the early mornings or late afternoons—and to children of mothers who travel on the job or on weekends. Recreational facilities may assume the job of providing day care-type services seven days a week, eight to twelve hours a day, to accommodate the needs of these mothers.

Male underemployment may be another consequence of women's growth spiritually, politically, and economically in society, especially if the economy does not produce sufficient jobs for both sexes. The result, once the considerable problems of personal adjustment are mastered, may be that men will become the volunteers of the future—and campaigns to recruit, train, and deploy volunteers to help the community should begin planning for such an adjustment.

Minorities. Over the next 20 years, as today, minorities will be concentrated in certain areas. A great proportion of blacks will be in the Northeast, the Midwest, and the South. Hispanics will be found in large numbers in the Southwest; Native Americans in the Midwest and West.

Affirmative action among all these groups will still be needed, but its implementation in 2000 may be unrecognizable by today's standards. Although we must not slack off our current local governments' commitment to bring minorities into the work force of our cities, counties, and COGs, the new affirmative action will be focused more on preventing slippage and dealing with the problems of people at midcareer, who will then be part of the baby-boom cohort competing for limited jobs.

Beyond affirmative action, local governments will need to be aware of the needs of Hispanics in particular. Language will be the most important problem, as many Hispanics will not speak English adequately to compete in the labor market.

Special efforts will be needed on two fronts. The first will be to make every effort to help Hispanics compensate for language barriers by installing bilingual signs; hiring bilingual local government employees, especially in reception areas; and producing special printed and broadcast material for Hispanic communities. The second should be a strong effort to provide English-language training for non-native speakers. This will mean incorporating language instruction into adult education and recreation programs and building it into special regular school curricula.

Smaller households. The declining size of the household will bring about some changes similar to those required for the elderly—the need for multifamily dwellings, for example. Indeed, the change in household size may revamp many traditional images of the ideal home setting for a large number of Americans.

We can see the image changing from the half-acre lot with the four-bedroom house and two-car garage in the planned unit development. In its place will be much smaller homes, many garden apartments, and town houses. People will make much more use of recreation and social settings outside the home (since no one will be home in many more cases).

Smaller homes and lots will have several implications for local governments. The number of water and sewer hookups will continue to grow, but the use of these facilities per thousand population may decline. At any given time, fewer homes will be physically occupied by the tenant, making neighborhood security and patrolling by police more important. In some suburbs with very large houses, there may be more demand to use the houses for "group homes" or even to subdivide them into apartments.

As local governments enter the 1980s and the 1990s, these are just a few of the changes in the mix of services provided, changes brought about by the fluctuating demographics of urban living.

So the mix of local services as well as the scale of their delivery will need adjustment over the next 10 to 20 years. This will be another strategy for nurturing the essential community, along with learning how to get by modestly, beginning to regulate demand for services, and buying back independence from the national government.

All this is a very complex, difficult, and challenging agenda for the future horizon of citizens, elected leaders, and their top professional managers.

Cities without limits

Rafael M. Salas

RAFAEL M. SALAS, of the Philippines, is an Under-Secretary-General of the United Nations and executive director of the United Nations Fund for Population Activities, which he has headed since it became operational in 1969. A graduate of the universities of the Philippines and of Harvard (USA), he has served as a Minister and occupied other high-level posts in the Philippine Government.

THE world has embarked on a course which will transform it into a predominantly urban planet. By the time population stabilizes at the end of the next century, truly rural populations will have become a very small minority.

More than 40 per cent of the world population currently live in urban areas. This figure will increase to more than 50 per cent shortly after the turn of the century. Developed regions have been more than 50 per cent urban since the mid-20th century. Developing countries are expected to pass the 50 per cent mark in the first quarter of the next century.

Within the less developed regions there are important differences. The developing countries of Africa and Asia are less than 30 per cent urban. Latin America, on the other hand, is nearly 70 per cent urban, reflecting the region's stage of development and the special features of its urban structure and history.

By the year 2000:
5 'super-cities' of 15 million

Most of the world's urban population today lives in developing countries. In 1970 the total urban population of the more developed regions was almost 30 million more than in the less developed. Five years later the position was reversed and by 1985 the difference had widened to more than 300 million. By the year 2000 the urban population of developing countries will be almost double that of the developed countries. By the year 2025 it will be almost four times as large.

At present the urban population of Africa is smaller than that of North America, but by the beginning of the next century it is expected to be substantially greater, and three times greater by the year 2025.

The proportion of the world population living·in the largest cities will almost double between 1970 and 2025, because of the growth of such cities in developing countries. By the year 2025 almost 30 per cent of the urban population in the developing regions will be living in cities of over 4 million, more than double the figure for the more developed regions. Although only a small proportion of the African population today lives in very large cities, by the end of the first quarter of the next century this proportion could be higher than that of any other continent. In developed countries, moreover, there is a trend towards deconcentration.

By the year 2000 there will be five "super-cities" of 15 million or more inhabitants, three of them in the developing regions. Two of them, in Latin America, will have populations of around 25 million. In 1970, nine of the twenty largest cities in the world were in the less developed regions; in 1985 there were ten and by the year 2000 there will be sixteen.

This change signals the end of the close relationship between large cities and economic development. Until recently such cities were because of their size centres of international political and economic networks, a situation which may now begin to change.

The urban population in developing countries is currently increasing three times more quickly than that of developed countries, at a rate of about 3.5 per cent a year, a doubling time of only twenty years.

There are important differences between the developing regions. Latin America has the lowest rates of population growth, followed by Asia. Africa, especially East Africa, has the highest. The current growth rate for Africa is 5 per cent a year, implying a doubling of the urban population every 14 years. The current figure for East Africa is above 6.5 per cent, a doubling time of little more than ten years.

Migrants to the cities

Such extremely rapid urban growth is without precedent. It confronts the cities, especially in the developing countries, with problems new to human experience, and presents the old problems—urban infrastructure, food, housing, employment, health, education—in new and accentuated forms.

Furthermore, despite migration to the cities, rural population in developing countries will continue to increase, at a rate of around one per cent annually.

Five important points emerge from an analysis of United Nations population figures:

● The world's rural population is now more than 2.5 thousand million;

● Rural population density is already very high in many parts of the less developed regions. Standards of living, while improving, remain low. It is doubtful whether added demographic pressure will benefit agricultural development—on the contrary it may jeopardize the development of many rural areas;

● Increasing rural population in developing countries will make it difficult to reduce the flow of migrants to the cities;

● The natural growth rate (the difference between the number of births and the number of deaths) of the rural population is higher than the one per cent rate—often more than double. The difference is due to the number of migrants to the cities;

● For most of Africa, unlike the rest of the developing world, rural populations will continue to increase until well into the next century.

Although urban fertility in developing countries tends to be lower than rural fertility, it is still at least twice as high as that in developed countries.

When natural increase in urban areas is high and migrants contribute substantially to it, the migrants' future fertility becomes an important factor. The high fertility typical of rural areas may be carried over into the urban environment; more optimistically, migrants plunging into new endeavours in a different context may adapt rather quickly to urban values, including lower fertility.

Those who consider urbanization to be a blessing hold that migration to the cities is part of a dynamic development process. Those who think that it is a burden believe that rural surplus population becomes an urban surplus, producing "over-urbanization", in which an inefficient and unproductive "informal sector" consisting of street vendors, shoeshine boys, sidewalk repair shops and other so-called marginal occupations becomes more and more important.

Urban life has its positive aspects, but they emphasize employment rather than what workers get for their labour. A city worker may earn more than a rural counterpart, but is it enough to cover the basic needs of food, health, housing and education?

Two important aspects of urban life are income distribution and the number of city-dwellers living below an acceptable and culturally adjusted "poverty line". Reliable data are lacking, but it is probably true that the distribution of incomes

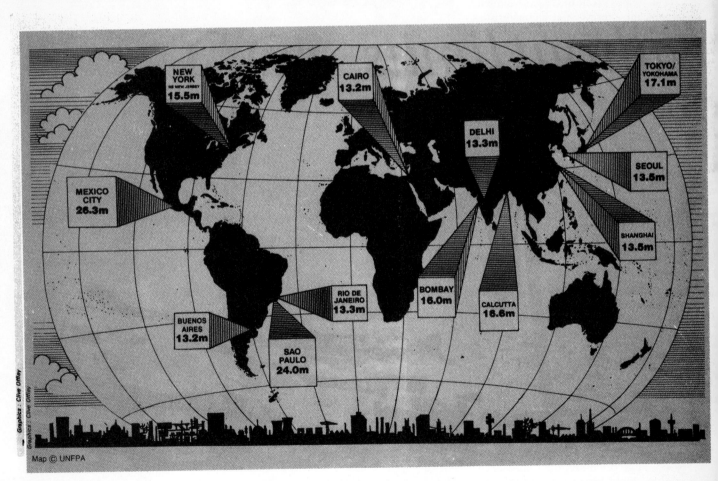

Map © UNFPA

The rise of the cities

By the year 2000 half of the world population will live in cities, according to the 1986 State of World Population *report from the United Nations Fund for Population Activities (UNFPA). The map above indicates the projected populations (in millions) for the* year 2000, in the twelve largest metropolitan regions of the world.

is more inequitable in urban than in rural areas, in that there are proportionally more very rich and very poor people in the cities.

This may be as much an indication of economic development in the urban areas as of the privileges enjoyed by urban élites. Rapid demographic growth among the urban masses also contributes to the inequality of income distribution and swells the numbers of the poor.

A massive housing deficit

The most visible manifestations of the problems of rapid urban population growth are the makeshift settlements on the outskirts of every city in the developing world. They are usually in the worst parts of town as regards health and accessibility, lacking basic services and security of tenure. They are by their nature overcrowded—average occupancy rates of four to five persons per room are common.

The names given to these settlements graphically express their characteristics. In Latin America the word *callampas* (mushrooms) refers to their almost magical overnight growth. The term *bidonvilles* (tin can cities), is often used in Francophone Africa to describe their makeshift nature. There are many other labels, usually given by outsiders: those who live in these settlements might describe them differently, perhaps even considering them as starting points on the path to a higher standard of living.

There is a massive housing deficit in many large cities. The World Bank estimated in 1975 that the poorest quarter of the population in most African and Asian cities cannot afford even minimal housing. Wood and cardboard packing crates, sheets of plastic or corrugated iron, flattened tin cans, leaves, bamboo and beaten earth are the main sources of materials.

Space is also a problem. Landlords may add illegal floors to existing buildings, only to watch their dreams of wealth collapse along with the buildings and the lives of the unfortunate inhabitants. In some cities several workers will use the same "hot bed" in shifts over the twenty-four hours. In Cairo squatters have occupied a large cemetery: the tombs of the wealthy have become homes for the poor.

Colonies of squatters occupy the last areas to be settled, and may be perched on steep hillsides subject to frequent landslides, or installed by rivers or on swampy ground which is flooded regularly. In Mexico City about 1.5 million people live on the drained bed of a salt lake, bedevilled by dust storms in the dry season and floods in rainy months. In Lagos, Nigeria, the proportion of wet land to dry land settled has worsened, while the absolute area of dry land occupied has doubled.

Where squatter settlements have been established near workplaces, the inhabitants may run the risk of pollution and are exposed to dangers such as the leak of poisonous gas in Bhopal, India, or the

The child in the city

For Third World parents the city may seem the best place to bring up a child – education and health services are usually better than in the countryside. But there are disadvantages too: the city child will spend much more of the day away from the family and at greater risk of exploitation.

URBAN ADVANTAGES
Health and education services are easier to provide in cities. And mortality and literacy statistics do show the urban areas in a favourable light.

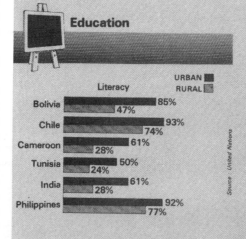

Education

URBAN ■
RURAL ▦

Literacy

Bolivia	85% / 47%
Chile	93% / 74%
Cameroon	61% / 28%
Tunisia	50% / 24%
India	61% / 28%
Philippines	92% / 77%

Source - United Nations

Health

URBAN ■
RURAL ▦

Infant deaths per thousand live births

Colombia	52 / 84
Peru	84 / 128
Kenya	91 / 110
Senegal	71 / 137
Bangladesh	115 / 137
Indonesia	60 / 96

Source - World Fertility Survey

But there will be great differences between the poorer and richer parts of each city. In Lima, Peru, for example, 19% of the children overall are malnourished but this figure rises to 36% in the poorest districts.

STREET CHILDREN
Some 40 million children around the world spend their days on city streets – often working. The majority maintain contact with their families, but millions of children also live on the street.

Why they are there
A survey in Maputo, Mozambique, asked children why there were on the street. These are the reasons they gave.

Hunger and poverty in the home	27%
Treated badly at home	27%
Nothing else to do	27%
Sent by the family	9%
Abandoned by the family	9%
Just following other children	1%

What they do
Many city children work (as well as going to school for part of the day). Research in Asuncion, Paraguay, asked children what their major jobs were:

Selling newspapers	27%
Shining shoes	24%
Selling food etc.	33%
Cleaning windscreens	6%
Cleaning and looking after cars	9%
Others	1%

City children also have factory jobs – often in harsh conditions. And in rich and poor countries alike street children risk falling into prostitution.

Graphics - Clive Offley

Document UNFPA

explosions at oil refineries in Mexico City.

Squatter settlements typically lack water, sewage and waste disposal facilities, electricity and paved streets. In Mexico City, 80 per cent of the population have access to tapwater, but in some squatter settlements the figure is less than 50 per cent. Water consumption in the wealthy quarters of Mexico City is at least five times as high as in the poorer areas. In Lagos, water is strictly rationed and in some parts of the city residents must walk long distances to obtain water from a few pumps which are turned on only in the early morning.

According to a study carried out in Lima, Peru, lower income groups spent three times more per month on water from vendors but consumed less than a sixth as much as those with running water at home.

It is estimated that three million inhabitants of Mexico City do not have access to the sewage system. In São Paulo, Brazil, the absence of sewage systems have turned the two main rivers into moving cesspools.

Because they occupy land owned by the government, private individuals or communal organizations, squatters are frequently subject to harassment, which increases their feeling of insecurity and the precariousness of their existence. Illegal or barely legal occupation does nothing to encourage squatters to improve or even maintain the shaky structures in which they live.

A number of schemes have been devised to give more security to squatters, but there are risks. One is that improving living conditions in the city will encourage people to move there. Another is that improvements to property will increase its value and encourage squatters to sell, while moving it out of the reach of other low-income families.

Two urgent problems: child health and education

The health of the poor may be worse in urban than in rural areas. Infant mortality in the Port-au-Prince slums is three times higher than it is in the rural areas of Haiti. In some of the *favelas* of São Paulo, infant mortality is over 100 per thousand live births. The overall infant mortality rate for the slums of Delhi is 221 per thousand, twice that for some castes. In Manila infant mortality is three times higher in the slums than it is in the rest of the city. (Tuberculosis rates are nine times higher; the incidence of diarrhoea is twice as common; twice as many people are anaemic and three times as many are undernourished.) In Panama City, of 1,819 infants with diarrhoeal diseases, 45.5 per cent came from the slums and 22.5 per cent from squatter settlements. Children living in the best housing were not affected.

In most cities in developed countries, young people under 19 constitute less

How cities grow

The urban population of developing countries will be almost double that of developed countries by the year 2000 — according to the 1986 'State of World Population' report from the UN Fund for Population Activities.

CONTINENTAL CONURBATIONS

Latin America has some of the largest cities of the developing world – but Africa is now urbanizing at a rapid rate. The chart shows the percentage of the population living in urban areas.

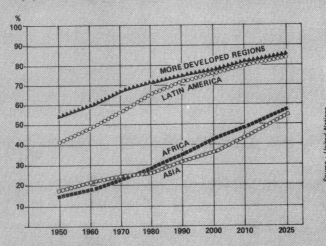

Source : United Nations

BUILDING FROM BELOW

The major architects of today's Third World cities are poor families building their own homes. The diagram below shows the percentage of squatters and slum dwellers in four major cities.

KINSHASA 60%   MEXICO CITY 46%   CALCUTTA 67%   MANILA 55%

Graphics : Clive Offley

Source : Assignment Children 57/58

Document UNFPA

than 30 per cent of the population. In developing countries, the proportion is typically over 40 per cent and may reach 50 per cent in cities such as Manila, Jakarta and Bogotá. If the education system breaks down under this sort of pressure, it will add immeasurably to problems of employment, delinquency and allied problems caused by the existence of "street children".

Education is probably the most pressing of urban problems. A lower rate of population growth would immeasurably help the situation, but such a decrease partly depends on the spread of education. Family planning programmes will certainly be useful, but they must be accompanied by renewed efforts to bring education to the urban masses.

How will the cities be fed?

How will agriculture respond to the tremendous pressure of urbanization and the growth of urban population? A recent study by the United Nations Food and Agriculture Organization (FAO) and the United Nations Fund for Population Activities (UNFPA) draws attention to some of the likely effects.

First, urban populations demand cheap food. By weight of numbers they force governments to keep retail prices down. Governments may make up the difference by subsidizing farmers but experience has shown that, once established, such subsidies are difficult to withdraw.

Second, as urban populations grow and indigenous agriculture fails to keep up with demand (for lack of incentive to increase supply), more food is imported. This drains off hard currency intended for capital imports with a view to long-term development.

Third, urban population increase means that rural populations and the agricultural labour force will grow more slowly. But to meet urban needs agricultural productivity should be increasing by 17 per cent for each agricultural worker in developing countries between 1980 and the year 2000. This figure seems high, but recent experience in Asia and Latin America shows that it is possible.

For Africa, however, the increase per worker will have to be almost 25 per cent, an eventuality that seems very doubtful in view of recent events. Research in Africa has shown that lower production gains were made in countries with high rural-urban migration. This contrasts with experience in other regions, where rural-urban migration has been at least partly the consequence of higher agricultural labour productivity.

Fourth, tastes in food change under the influence of urban life-styles, as traditional staples are partly replaced by foods such as bread, meat and vegetables.

Fifth, the growth of urban population intensifies competition for land, water and energy. Cities gobble up agricultural land, often the best land because its fertility was the original attraction which stimulated urban growth. Between 1980 and the year 2000, according to one study, cities will devour four million hectares of land with the potential to feed 84 million people.

Sixth, while malnutrition may be more widespread among rural populations, the urban poor suffer more acutely. People in the lowest income groups normally have to spend more than half of their incomes on food.

Balanced approaches to an urban planet

The transformation from a rural to an urban planet offers both great blessings and heavy burdens. The transition from agrarian to urban has always been considered a positive step, part of the process of modernization. However, the rapid growth of urban populations in societies rapidly changing in other ways is fraught with enormous tension and tremendously complex problems.

In its search for solutions to problems of urban population dynamics, UNFPA puts continuous emphasis on three fundamental objectives: economic efficiency, social equity and population balance. It recognizes that the solution for many urban problems will only come through economic efficiency and vast growth of the productive forces. Economic growth is essential to any solution of urban problems. At the same time social equity should be pursued, with emphasis on equal opportunity for all.

Neither economic efficiency nor social equity can be attained without demographic balance—balance within and between urban and rural areas, balanced population distribution and balanced population growth.

Credits/Acknowledgments

Cover design by Charles Vitelli

1. Urbanization
Facing overview—New York Convention and Visitors Bureau.

2. Urban Experiences
Facing overview—HUD.

3. Urban Problems
Facing overview—EPA Documerica.

4. Urban Policies
Facing overview—HUD.

5. Urban Futures
Facing overview—General Motors photo.

ANNUAL EDITIONS ARTICLE REVIEW FORM

■ NAME: _____ DATE: _____

■ TITLE AND NUMBER OF ARTICLE: _____

■ BRIEFLY STATE THE MAIN IDEA OF THIS ARTICLE: _____

_____

_____

_____

_____

■ LIST THREE IMPORTANT FACTS THAT THE AUTHOR USES TO SUPPORT THE MAIN IDEA:

_____

_____

_____

_____

_____

■ WHAT INFORMATION OR IDEAS DISCUSSED IN THIS ARTICLE ARE ALSO DISCUSSED IN YOUR
TEXTBOOK OR OTHER READING YOU HAVE DONE? LIST THE TEXTBOOK CHAPTERS AND PAGE
NUMBERS:

_____

_____

_____

_____

_____

_____

■ LIST ANY EXAMPLES OF BIAS OR FAULTY REASONING THAT YOU FOUND IN THE ARTICLE:

_____

_____

_____

_____

■ LIST ANY NEW TERMS/CONCEPTS THAT WERE DISCUSSED IN THE ARTICLE AND WRITE A
SHORT DEFINITION:

_____

_____

_____

_____

_____

*Your instructor may require you to use this Annual Editions Article Review Form in any number of ways:
for articles that are assigned, for extra credit, as a tool to assist in developing assigned papers, or simply
for your own reference. Even if it is not required, we encourage you to photocopy and use this page;
you'll find that reflecting on the articles will greatly enhance the information from your text.

We Want Your Advice

ANNUAL EDITIONS: URBAN SOCIETY, 5/E
Article Rating Form

Here is an opportunity for you to have direct input into the next revision of this volume. We would like you to rate each of the 51 articles listed below, using the following scale:

1. **Excellent: should definitely be retained**
2. **Above average: should probably be retained**
3. **Below average: should probably be deleted**
4. **Poor: should definitely be deleted**

Your ratings will play a vital part in the next revision. So please mail this prepaid form to us just as soon as you complete it.
Thanks for your help!

Annual Editions revisions depend on two major opinion sources: one is our Advisory Board, listed in the front of this volume, which works with us in scanning the thousands of articles published in the public press each year; the other is you—the person actually using the book. Please help us and the users of the next edition by completing the prepaid article rating form on this page and returning it to us. Thank you.

Rating	Article	Rating	Article
	1. How Man Invented Cities		27. Priced Out of House and Home
	2. Fear of the City, 1783 to 1983		28. Us vs. Them: America's Growing Frustration With the Homeless
	3. Are Cities Obsolete?		29. Health and the City
	4. America's New City: Megalopolis Unbound		30. The Invisible Jail
	5. Micropolitan America		31. The Crisis in AIDS Care: To Live and Die in L.A.
	6. Radiant City's Dull Legacy		32. Memo to the New Mayor
	7. Demographic Doomsayers: Five Myths About Population		33. Hot Managers, Sizzling Cities
	8. The Pace of Life		34. Neighborhood Politics: A Changing World
	9. Rootlessness Undermines Our Economy as Well as the Quality of Our Lives		35. Volunteer Mentors Empower Inner-City Youths
	10. Good-Bye, Good Hope		36. Have Asian Americans Arrived Politically? Not Quite
	11. Downtown Malls and the City Agenda		37. Recycling Our Most Prolific By-Product
	12. Garden City, U.S.A.: Are New Towns the Way Around Growth Controls?		38. Rethinking Rental Housing: A Progressive Strategy
	13. The New Surburbia: A Different Entity		39. Nonprofit Housing: Local Success Stories
	14. The Other Suburbia		40. A Housing Program That Really Works
	15. Creative Alternatives to Urban Sprawl: A Tale of Two Cities		41. Cities Seek Alternatives to the Bulldozer
	16. Serv-Urbs, U.S.A.		42. Cities in the Year 2000: The Forces of Change
	17. Seattle, Too Much of a Good Thing?		43. Downtown 2040: Making Cities Fun!
	18. Creating Community: A Fast-Food Generation Looks for a Home-Cooked Meal		44. Planned City of Future Still Unifinished
	19. Out of the Car, Into the Future		45. Running the City for the People
	20. Traffic Jams: The City, the Commuter, and the Car		46. Small Space Is Beautiful: Design As If People Mattered
	21. Gridlock!		47. Urban Planning: What Went Wrong?
	22. Supertrain: A Solution to U.S. Transportation Woes		48. States Explore the Enterprise Zone
	23. De-escalating the War		49. The Workless Society: How Machine Intelligence Will Bring Ease and Abundance
	24. Youth and Drug Abuse: Breaking the Chain		50. Strategies for the Essential Community: Local Government in the Year 2000
	25. Down and Out in the City		51. Cities Without Limits
	26. Making It: The Underclass Cycle		

(Continued on next page)

ABOUT YOU

Name_____ Date_____

Are you a teacher? ☐ Or student? ☐

Your School Name _____

Department _____

Address _____

City _____ State _____ Zip _____

School Telephone # _____

YOUR COMMENTS ARE IMPORTANT TO US!

Please fill in the following information:

For which course did you use this book? _____

Did you use a text with this Annual Edition? ☐ yes ☐ no

The title of the text? _____

What are your general reactions to the Annual Editions concept?

Have you read any particular articles recently that you think should be included in the next edition?

Are there any articles you feel should be replaced in the next edition? Why?

Are there other areas that you feel would utilize an Annual Edition?

May we contact you for editorial input?

May we quote you from above?

ANNUAL EDITIONS: URBAN SOCIETY, 5/E